Christmas 1994

Dear Mom,
    I hope you enjoy these writings. I read "Improving Your Serve" while training for Work Crew at Malibu. Much of it remains with me still.
                Love
                Eric.

The Inspirational Writings
CHARLES R. SWINDOLL

Improving Your Serve

Strengthening Your Grip

Dropping Your Guard

The Inspirational Writings

CHARLES R. SWINDOLL

Improving Your Serve

Strengthening Your Grip

Dropping Your Guard

THREE BESTSELLING WORKS IN ONE VOLUME

INSPIRATIONAL PRESS

Previously published in three volumes as

IMPROVING YOUR SERVE: THE ART OF UNSELFISH LIVING
Copyright © 1981 by Word, Inc.

STRENGTHENING YOUR GRIP: ESSENTIALS IN AN AIMLESS WORLD
Copyright © 1982 by Charles R. Swindoll

DROPPING YOUR GUARD: THE VALUE OF OPEN RELATIONSHIPS
Copyright © 1983 by Charles R. Swindoll

Published in 1994 by

Inspirational Press
A division of Budget Book Service, Inc.
386 Park Avenue South
New York, NY 10016

Inspirational Press is a registered trademark of Budget Book Service, Inc.

Published by arrangement with Word, Inc.

Library of Congress Catalog Card Number: 88-81310

ISBN: 0-88486-107-4

Printed in the United States of America.

CONTENTS

CONTENTS

The Inspirational Writings

CHARLES R. SWINDOLL

Improving Your Serve

Strengthening Your Grip

Dropping Your Guard

Improving Your Serve

With much appreciation this book is dedicated to

HELEN AND BEVERLY PETERS

A mother-daughter team whose serve could hardly be improved.

Because of their efficient and unselfish assistance behind
the scenes, my wife and I have laughed more and worried less.

Contents

Introduction

For over two years I have been intrigued with a verse of Scripture found in Mark's account of the life of Jesus. At times this verse has haunted and convicted me. On other occasions I have been encouraged by it. When I have used it as a basis for evaluating leadership, I have usually been both surprised and shocked. More often than not, the truth of the verse in daily living is conspicuous by its absence. And among those we would expect to see it best displayed—the Christian community—it is not uncommon to find it seldom demonstrated.

The verse? Mark 10:45:

For even the Son of Man did not come to be served, but to serve, and to give his life a ransom for many (NIV).

The truth? Authentic servanthood.

Read the verse again, this time aloud. When Jesus took the time to explain His reason for coming among us, He was simple and direct: to serve and to give. Not to *be* served. Not to grab the spotlight in the center ring. Not to make a name or attract attention or become successful or famous or powerful or idolized. No, quite frankly, that stuff turned Him off. The first-century world was full and running over with strong-willed dogmatists. Authority figures were a dime a dozen (they always are). There were Caesars and Herods and governors and other pompous hotshots in abundance. Some, like the Pharisees and Sadducees and scribes—people with whom Jesus locked horns from the earliest days of his ministry—even used religion as their lever to control others. But servants? I mean the authentic types who genuinely gave of themselves without concern over who got the glory? They were not to be found!

But before we cluck our tongues and wag our heads at those down the time tunnel, criticizing the Roman world for its conceit and arrogance, the fact is we've got some homework to catch up on in the 1980s. It was the startling realization of this over two years ago that forced me to stop in my tracks and do some serious thinking about servanthood. It's not that I'd never heard the word or tossed it around from time to time . . . but I honestly had not made a conscious effort to examine the concept of serving, either in Scripture or in its everyday outworking. I certainly had not been much of a model of it, I openly admit to my own embarrassment. Frankly, it is still a struggle. Serving and giving don't come naturally. Living an unselfish life is an art!

The result of my two-year pursuit has been more beneficial than words can describe. The finger of God's Spirit pointed me from one biblical passage to another. He then provided me perception in interpretation beyond my own ability and ultimately assisted me in appropriating and applying the principles that emerged from the pages of His Book. With remarkable regularity the Lord turned on the lights in areas that had been obscure or dark in my thinking throughout my Christian life. Big boulders that had blocked my vision and progress were shoved aside. Insight began to replace ignorance. Becoming a servant began to be something beautiful, yes, *essential*, rather than something fearful and weird. I not only desired it for myself (a process that is still going on), but I wanted to share with others what God was revealing to me.

I did just that. Sunday after Sunday I preached my heart out among the most teachable and responsive congregation a pastor could possibly enjoy. The series grew and multiplied from the pulpit at the First Evangelical Free Church of Fullerton, California, to our radio friends around the world who hear our broadcasts day after day on "Insight for Living." I have also spoken on the subject at Christian colleges, seminaries, banquets, and other gatherings in churches, radio rallies, and Christian conferences. Almost without exception those who have heard these messages have encouraged me to write a book that conveys this material in printed form.

While I was wrestling with this decision, Floyd Thatcher, vice president and editorial director of Word Books, expressed a keen interest in the subject and invited me to publish these chapters you are about to read. I freely express my gratitude to Floyd for both his vision and determination to make the dream become a reality. His contagious enthusiasm was like flint, continually prompting that spark I needed to stay at the task of putting my thoughts into print.

And to you, the reader, I will add just one final comment. This is a book to be applied. You don't have to be brilliant or gifted to pull off these truths in your life. *But you do have to be willing.* Before the ink on these pages can be permanently transferred to a change, first in your thinking and then in your living, there must be a willing spirit that says, "Lord, show me . . . teach me . . . help me . . . to serve and to give." If you will let that be your attitude, the process involved in your becoming more like Christ Himself will be much smoother, much faster, and much less painful.

CHARLES R. SWINDOLL
Fullerton, California

1

Who, Me
a Servant? You
Gotta Be Kidding!

The original idea of becoming a servant seemed either wrong or weird to me. I realize now I rejected it because my concept of a servant was somewhere between an African slave named Kunta Kinte straight out of *Roots* and those thousands of nameless migrant workers who, at harvest time, populate the farmlands and orchards across America. Both represented ignorance, objects of mistreatment, a gross absence of human dignity, and the epitome of many of the things Christianity opposes.

The mental image turned me off completely. Washing around in my head was a caricature of a pathetic creature virtually without will or purpose in life . . . bent over, crushed in spirit, lacking self-esteem, soiled, wrinkled, and weary. You know, sort of a human mule who, with a sigh, shuffles and trudges down the long rows of life. Don't ask me why, but that was my perception every time I heard the word *servant*. Candidly, the idea disgusted me.

And confusion was added to my disgust when I heard people (especially preachers) link the two terms *servant* and *leader*. They seemed as opposite as light and dark, a classic example of the proverbial round peg in a square hole. I distinctly remember thinking back then, "Who, *me* a servant! You gotta be kidding!"

Perhaps that's your initial reaction, too. If so, I understand. But you're in for a pleasant surprise. I have great news based on some very helpful information that will—if applied—change your mind and then your life. It excites me when I consider how God is going to use these words in this book to introduce to you (as He did to me) the truth concerning authentic servanthood. How desperately we need to improve our serve!

Several years ago I read of a fascinating experiment conducted by the National Institute of Mental Health. It took place in a nine-foot square cage designed to house, comfortably, 160 mice. For two and a half years, the colony of mice grew from 8 to 2200. Plenty of food, water, and other resources were continually provided. All mortality factors (except aging) were eliminated. Dr. John Calhoun, a research psychologist, began to witness a series of unusual phenomena among the mice as the population reached its peak. Within the cage, from which the mice could not escape, the colony began to disintegrate.

- Adults formed groups or cliques of about a dozen mice in each group.
- In these groups, different mice performed particular social functions.
- The males who normally protected their territory withdrew from leadership and became uncharacteristically passive.
- The females became unusually aggressive and forced out the young.
- The young found themselves without a place in the society, and they grew to be increasingly more self-indulgent. They ate, drank, slept, and groomed themselves, but showed no normal assertiveness.
- The whole "mouse society" ultimately became disrupted . . . and after five years *all the mice had died*, even though there was an abundance of food, water, resources, and an absence of disease.

What was the most interesting to the observers was the strong independence, the extreme isolation syndrome of the mice. This was greatly emphasized by the fact that courtship and mating—the most complex activities for mice—were the first activities to cease.

What result would similar conditions have on humanity? What would be the results of overcrowded conditions on an inescapable planet with all the accompanying stress factors? Dr. Calhoun suggested that we would first of all cease to reproduce our ideas, and along with ideas, our goals, ideals, and values would be lost.[1]

It's happening.

Our world has become a large, impersonal, busy institution. We are alienated from each other. Although crowded, we are lonely. Distant. Pushed together but uninvolved. No longer do most neighbors visit across the backyard fence. The well-manicured lawn is the modern moat that keeps barbarians at bay. Hoarding and flaunting have replaced sharing and caring. It's like we are occupying common space but have no common interests, as if we're on an elevator with rules like: "No talking, smiling, or eye contact allowed without written consent of the management."

Painful though it may be for us to admit it here in this great land of America, we're losing touch with one another. The motivation to help, to encourage, yes, to *serve* our fellow-man is waning. People have observed a crime in progress but refused to help so as not to be involved. Even our foundational values are getting lost in these confusing days. And yet, it is these things that form the essentials of a happy and fulfilled life.

Remember that grand declaration of biblical assurance etched in the rocklike truth of Romans 8? I'm referring to verses 28–29, which read:

And we know that God causes all things to work together for good to those who love God, to those who are called according to His purpose.

For whom He foreknew, He also predestined to become conformed to the image of His Son, that He might be the first-born among many brethren.

Maybe you've never before stopped to consider that God is committed to *one* major objective in the lives of all His people: to conform us to "the image of His Son." We need to blow the dust off that timeless goal now that our cage is overcrowded and our lives are growing increasingly more distant from each other.

Exactly what does our heavenly Father want to develop within us? What is that "image of His Son"? Well, rather than getting neck deep in tricky theological waters, I believe the simple answer is found in Christ's own words. Listen as He declares His primary reason for coming:

For even the Son of Man did not come to be served, but to serve, and to give His life a ransom for many (Mark 10:45).

No mumbo jumbo. Just a straight-from-the-shoulder admission. He came to serve and to give. It makes sense, then, to say that God desires the same for us. After bringing us into His family through faith in His Son, the Lord God sets His sights on building into us the same quality that made Jesus distinct from all others in His day. He is engaged in building into His people the same serving and giving qualities that characterized His Son.

Nothing is more refreshing than a servant's heart and a giving spirit, especially when we see them displayed in a person many would tag as a celebrity. A couple of years ago my wife and I attended the National Religious Broadcasters convention in Washington, D.C., where one of the main speakers was Colonel James B. Irwin, former astronaut who was a part of the crew that had made the successful moon walk. He spoke of the thrill connected with leaving this planet and seeing it shrink in size. He mentioned watching earthrise one day . . . and thinking how privileged he was to be a member of that unique crew. And then he began to realize en route back home that many would consider him a "superstar," for sure an international celebrity.

Humbled by the awesome goodness of God, Colonel Irwin shared his true feelings, which went something like this:

As I was returning to earth, I realized that I was a servant—not a celebrity. So I am here as God's servant on planet Earth to share what I have experienced that others might know the glory of God.

God allowed this man to break loose from the small cage we call "Earth," during which time He revealed to him a basic motto all of us would do well to learn: *a servant, not a celebrity*. Caught up in the fast-lane treadmill of Century Twenty—making mad dashes through airports, meeting deadlines, being responsible for big-time decisions, and coping with the stress of people's demands mixed with our own high expectations—it's easy to lose sight of our primary calling as Christians, isn't it? Even the busy mother of small children struggles with this. Mounds of ironing and the endless needs of her husband and kids block out the big picture.

If you're like me, you sometimes think, "I would give anything to be able to step back into the time when Jesus cast His shadow on earth. How great it must have been to sit back as one of the Twelve and soak up all those truths He taught. I mean, *they must have really learned how to serve, to give of themselves*." Right? Wrong!

Allow me to journey back with you to one of the many scenes that demonstrated just how typical those guys really were. I'm referring to an occasion when our Lord's popularity was on the rise . . . the knowledge of His kingdom was spreading . . . and the disciples began to be anxious about being recognized as members of His chosen band.

What makes this account a bit more interesting is the presence of a *mother* of two of the disciples. She's Mrs. Zebedee, wife of the Galilean fisherman and mother of James and John. Let's consider her request:

> Then the mother of the sons of Zebedee came to Him with her sons, bowing down, and making a request of Him.
> And He said to her, "What do you wish?" She said to Him, "Command that in Your kingdom these two sons of mine may sit, one on Your right and one on Your left" (Matt. 20:20–21).

Now don't be too tough on this dear Jewish mother. She's proud of her sons! She had thought about that request for quite some time. Her motive was probably pure and her idea was in proper perspective. She didn't ask that her sons occupy the center throne, of course not—that belonged to Jesus. But like any good mother who watches out for "breaks in life" that could lead to a nice promotion, she pushed for James and John as candidates for thrones number two and number three. She wanted to enhance their image before the public. She wanted people to think highly of her boys who had left their nets and entered this up-and-coming ministry. They were among "the Twelve."

And that needed recognition!

Just in case you're wondering how the other ten felt about this, check out verse 24. It says "the ten became indignant." Guess why. Hey, no way were they going to give up those top spots without a fight. They got downright ticked off that maybe James and John might get the glory they wanted. Sound familiar?

With biting conviction Jesus answers the mother with this penetrating comment: "You do not know what you are asking for . . ." (v. 22). That must have stung. She really thought she did. Enamored of her world of soldiers with medals, emperors with jeweled crowns, governors with slaves awaiting their every need, and even merchants with their employees . . . it seemed only fitting for those two sons of hers to have thrones, especially if they were charter members of the God movement, soon to be a "kingdom." Rulers need thrones!

No. This movement is different. Jesus pulls His disciples aside and spells out the sharp contrast between His philosophy and the world system in which they lived. Read His words slowly and carefully.

> But Jesus called them to Himself, and said, "You know that the rulers of the Gentiles lord it over them, and their great men exercise authority over them.
>
> "It is not so among you, but whoever wishes to become great among you shall be your servant, and whoever wishes to be first among you shall be your slave; just as the Son of Man did not come to be served, but to serve, and to give His life a ransom for many" (Matt. 20:25–28).

In the secular system there are distinct levels of authority. It's true today, for sure. In government there is our president, his cabinet, and a large body of personally selected men who have privileges the common citizen does not possess. In the military there are officers and enlisted men . . . and ranks within each. In sports there are coaches and players. In the business world there are corporation heads and lines of authority between managers and personnel, shop superintendents, foremen, and laborers. The person in the labor force is expected to punch a clock, show up on time, work hard, and not take advantage of his or her employer. There's a name for those who choose not to follow those directions. Unemployed! Why? Because the boss is in charge. That's the way the system works. As Jesus put it, "their great men exercise authority over them." But then he adds, "It is *not so* among you" (emphasis added). What isn't so? Simply this, in God's family there is to be one great body of people: servants. In fact, that's the way to the top in His kingdom.

> . . . whoever wishes to become great among you shall be your servant.

Forgotten words.

Yes, these seem to be forgotten words, even in many churches with their smooth pastors, high-powered executives, and superstar singers. Unfortunately, there doesn't seem to be much of the servant mentality in such settings. Even in our church life we tend to get so caught up in a success and size race that we lose sight of our primary calling as followers of Christ. The "celebrity syndrome" so present in our Christian thought and activities just doesn't square with the attitudes and messages of Jesus. We have skidded into a pattern whereby the celebrities and top dogs in our church life call the shots, and it is difficult to be a servant when you're used to telling others what to do.

Maybe I need to clarify what I mean. In the Body of Christ there is one Head. Christ Jesus is Lord of His body.

And He is the image of the invisible God, the first-born of all creation.

For in Him all things were created, both in the heavens and on earth, visible and invisible, whether thrones or dominions or rulers or authorities—all things have been created through Him and for Him.

And He is before all things, and in Him all things hold together.

He is also head of the body, the church; and He is the beginning, the first-born from the dead; so that He Himself might come to have first place in everything (Col. 1:15–18).

No human being dare take that position. A man named Diotrephes, mentioned in John's third letter, verses 9 and 10, attempted to do so and was openly rebuked by the apostle. Diotrephes becomes a warning to anyone who desires to become the "church boss." It may be a board member, a pastor, a teacher, a musician, a *former* officer or pastor in a church. No matter who, the Diotrephes mentality has no place in the Body. Only Christ is the Head. All the rest of us are in the class Jesus spoke of in Matthew 20 . . . *servants*.

You're probably saying, "But there must be leadership to get the job done." Yes, I agree. But it must be servant-hearted leadership among *all*. You see, I am not interested in which form of government you or your church may embrace, but only that every one involved in that ministry (whether leader or not) sees himself as one who serves, one who gives. It's the *attitude* that is most important.

Perhaps the finest model, except Christ Himself, was that young Jew from Tarsus who was radically transformed from a strong-willed official in Judaism to a bond servant of Jesus Christ—Paul. What a remarkable change, what a remarkable man!

It's possible you have the notion that the apostle Paul rammed his way through life like a fully loaded battleship at sea. Blasting and pounding toward objectives, he was just too important to worry about the little people or those who got in his way. After all, *he was Paul!* I must confess that is not too far removed from my original impression of the man in my earlier years as a Christian. He was, in my mind, the blend of a Christian John Wayne, Clint Eastwood, and the Hulk. I mean, he got things done.

But that false impression began to fade when I made an in-depth study of Paul—his style, his own self-description, even his comments to various churches and people as he wrote to each. I discovered that the man I had thought was the prima donna *par excellence* considered himself quite the contrary. Almost without exception he begins every piece of correspondence with words to this effect: "Paul, a servant . . ." or "Paul, a bond-slave . . ."

The more I pondered those words, the deeper they penetrated. This man, the one who certainly could have expected preferential treatment or demanded a high-and-mighty role of authority over others, referred to himself most often as a "servant" of God. Amazing. He was indeed an apostle, but he conducted himself, he carried himself, as a servant. I found this extremely appealing.

The longer I thought about this concept, the more evidence emerged from the Scripture to support it. In fact, most of the discoveries fell into one of three categories of characteristics related to this servant image—*transparent humanity, genuine humility, absolute honesty.*

TRANSPARENT HUMANITY

Listen to Paul's words to the Corinthians:

> And when I came to you, brethren, I did not come with superiority of speech or of wisdom, proclaiming to you the testimony of God. For I determined to know nothing among you except Jesus Christ, and Him crucified. And I was with you in weakness and in fear and in much trembling (1 Cor. 2:1–3).

"Aw, the guy is just being modest," you answer. No, not when you compare these words with the popular opinion of him:

> . . . "His letters are weighty and strong, but his personal presence is unimpressive, and his speech contemptible" (2 Cor. 10:10).

That's quite a shock. The man didn't have it all together—he wasn't perfect—and (best of all) he didn't attempt to hide it! He admitted to his friends in Corinth he was weak, fearful, and even trembling when he stood before them. I admire such transparency. Everybody does if it's the truth.

I forget where I found the following statement, but it's been in my possession for years. It vividly describes Paul as being ". . . a man of moderate stature with curly hair and scanty, crooked legs, protruding eyeballs, large knit eyebrows, a long nose, and thick lips."

Wow! Certainly doesn't sound like any one of the many smooth public idols of our day. And we know for a fact he suffered terribly from poor eyesight (Gal. 6:11), plus some are convinced the man had a hunchback.

Without hiding a bit of his humanity (see Romans 7 if you still struggle believing he was a cut above human), Paul openly declares his true condition. He had needs and admitted them. Servants do that. He didn't have everything in life wired perfectly . . . and he didn't hide it. Servants are like that. Immediately you can begin to see some of the comforting aspects of having a servant's heart. Paul admitted his humanity.

That brings us to the second characteristic of servants.

GENUINE HUMILITY

Going back for a moment to that first Corinthian letter. Paul also admits:

> And my message and my preaching were not in persuasive words of wisdom, but in demonstration of the Spirit and of power, that your faith should not rest on the wisdom of men, but on the power of God (1 Cor. 2:4–5).

Now for a preacher, that's quite a comment. The man comes up front and declares not only his lack of persuasiveness, but his reason why—that they might not be impressed with *his* ability, but rather with *God's* power. There's something very authentic in Paul's humility. Over and over we read similar words in his writings. I'm convinced that those who were instructed, face to face, by the man became increasingly more impressed with the living Christ and less impressed with him.

When people follow image-conscious leaders, the leader is exalted. He is placed on a pedestal and ultimately takes the place of the Head of the church.

When people follow leaders with servant hearts, the Lord God is exalted. Those people speak of God's person, God's power, God's work, God's name, God's Word . . . all for God's glory. Let me suggest a couple of revealing tests of humility:

1. *A nondefensive spirit when confronted.* This reveals a willingness to be accountable. Genuine humility operates on a rather simple philosophy:

> Nothing to prove
> Nothing to lose.

2. *An authentic desire to help others.* I'm referring to a sensitive, spontaneous awareness of needs. A true servant stays in touch with the struggles others experience. There is that humility of mind that continually looks for ways to serve and to give.

ABSOLUTE HONESTY

Finally, let's think about another mark of servanthood: integrity (absolute honesty).
Remember these words?

> Therefore since we have this ministry, as we received mercy, we do not lose heart, but we have renounced the things hidden because of shame, not walking in craftiness or adulterating the word of God, but by the manifestation of truth commending ourselves to every man's conscience in the sight of God (2 Cor. 4:1-2).

And how about these?

> For our exhortation does not come from error or impurity or by way of deceit; but just as we have been approved by God to be entrusted with the gospel, so we speak, not as pleasing men but God, who examines our hearts (1 Thess. 2:3-4).

There really isn't much to add. Honesty has a beautiful and refreshing simplicity about it . . . as do servants of God. No ulterior motives. No hidden meanings. An absence of hypocrisy, duplicity, political games, and verbal superficiality. As honesty and real integrity characterize our lives, there will be no need to manipulate others. We'll come to the place where all the substitutes will turn us off once we cultivate a taste for the genuine, the real.

I'm far from through, but this is enough for one sitting. We need to put it on the back burner and let it simmer for a while. Before going on into the next chapter, take time to give some thought to your own life. Think about becoming more of a servant . . . think of things like transparent humanity and genuine humility and absolute honesty. Being real, that's the major message of this chapter—being who you really are—and then allowing the Lord God to develop within you a style of serving that fits you.

Some time ago I stumbled across a book for children that contained a message for adults. The main character in the book is a little stuffed rabbit, all shiny and new, who goes through the process of becoming "real," that is, more than just a toy on a shelf. As he struggles with those initial feelings of uneasiness (as perhaps you are struggling with the concept of servanthood), he engages an old, worn-out, well-used, much-loved stuffed horse in conversation. Because the dialogue between the two says so clearly what I've been trying to say in this chapter, it is a conclusion that is both appropriate and needed.

> The Skin Horse had lived longer in the nursery than any of the others. He was so old that his brown coat was bald in patches and showed the seams underneath, and most of the hairs in his tail had been pulled out to string bead necklaces. He was wise, for he had seen a long succession of mechanical toys arrive to boast and swagger, and by-and-by break their mainsprings and pass away, and he knew that they were only toys, and would never turn into anything else. For nursery magic is very strange and wonderful, and only those playthings that are old and wise and experienced like the Skin Horse understand all about it.
>
> "What is REAL?" asked the Rabbit one day, when they were lying side by side near the nursery fender, before Nana came to tidy the room. "Does it mean having things that buzz inside you and a stick-out handle?"
>
> "Real isn't how you are made," said the Skin Horse. "It's a thing that happens to you. When a child loves you for a long, long time, not just to play with, but REALLY loves you, then you become real."
>
> "Does it hurt?" asked the Rabbit.
>
> "Sometimes," said the Skin Horse, for he was always truthful. "When you are Real you don't mind being hurt."
>
> "Does it happen all at once, like being wound up," he asked, "or bit by bit?"
>
> "It doesn't happen all at once," said the Skin Horse. "You become. It takes a long time. That's why it doesn't often happen to people who break easily, or have sharp edges, or who have to be carefully kept. Generally, by the time you are Real, most of your hair has been loved off, and your eyes drop out and you get loose in the joints and very shabby. But these things don't matter at all, because once you are real you can't be ugly, except to people who don't understand."[2]

2

A Case for Unselfishness

I
ME
MINE
MYSELF

Those four words stood out in bold print. They appeared as if they were forming an enormous monument, each letter seemingly chiseled out of granite. At the base of this strange "monument" were hundreds, perhaps thousands, of people with their arms held up high, as if worshiping at a shrine. And then in very small letters, this caption appeared at the bottom of the editorial cartoon: "Speaking of American cults . . ."

Surrounding the borders of this picture were four familiar lines from well-known commercials:

"Have it your way."

"Do yourself a favor."

"You owe it to yourself."

"You deserve a break today."[1]

Jab, jab. Twist, twist, That kind of stuff *really* hurts. Because it is so terribly true. Yet, we constantly applaud the I-me-mine-myself philosophy in subtle as well as overt ways. We make books on the subject of selfishness bestsellers by buying them by the millions. We put the gifted on a pedestal and secretly (if not publicly) worship at their shrine. And we make every effort to "look out for number one" at all cost. Let's admit it, ours is an age of gross selfishness. The "me" era. And we get mighty uncomfortable even when God begins to make demands on us. After all, this business of wholesale commitment to the cause of Christ needs to be kept in proper bounds!

20

Laced with similar tones of sarcasm are the words of Wilbur Rees:

> I would like to buy $3 worth of God, please, not enough to explode my soul or
> disturb my sleep, but just enough to equal a cup of warm milk or a snooze in the
> sunshine. I don't want enough of Him to make me love a black man or pick beets
> with a migrant. I want ecstasy, not transformation; I want the warmth of the
> womb, not a new birth. I want a pound of the Eternal in a paper sack. I would like
> to buy $3 worth of God, please.[2]

That's it. Our inner "self" doesn't want to dump God entirely, just keep Him
at a comfortable distance. Three dollars of Him is sufficient. A sack full,
nothing more. Just enough to keep my guilt level below the threshold of pain,
just enough to guarantee escape from eternal flames. But certainly not enough
to make me nervous . . . to start pushing around my prejudices or nit-picking at
my lifestyle. *Enough is enough!*

A PROPER PERSPECTIVE

Now before we get too carried away, a couple of statements need to be made to
clarify the issue. First, a good self-esteem is not the same as selfishness. Without a
strong belief in ourselves, we are easily crippled and wounded in life. A poor self-
image is not to be equated with humility or the mark of a servant. As a matter of
fact, without a healthy ego, without the confidence that God is in us, on our side,
pulling for us, we become fragile, easily bruised, counterproductive people.

I like what Mrs. Chuck Noll said about her husband, the coach of the
Pittsburgh Steelers: "He's got a very sturdy ego, but as for vanity—absolutely
none."[3]

Let's not confuse a strong, sturdy self-esteem with vain selfishness. They are
not twins, by any means.

Second, becoming a Christian does not automatically erase the presence of
selfishness. It helps, of course, but it isn't a cure-all. We Christians must still
fight the battle of pride. We evangelicals tend to be exclusive and snobbish
rather than broad-minded and accepting. We are proud that we have the
answers while others don't. We'd never come right out and call it pride, but
deep down inside we feel rather smug with our charts and diagrams of complex
theological issues. It's easy to look down our noses at those who aren't as
informed as we.

A BIBLICAL BASIS

It's been my experience that before I can fully conquer any problem, I need
to understand it as well as possible, especially its origin. To do that with "self"
we must go back, way back, to that ancient scene pictured for us in the second

and third chapters of Genesis, the garden of Eden. What a super spot! Beautiful beyond description, a perfect, pollution-free atmosphere, luxurious foliage, fragrant flowers, crystal-clear water—that garden would make Tahiti look like a pigsty by comparison. And on top of all the physical beauty, there was absolute innocence. No sin. Which means that Adam and Eve had a relationship that was free of hang-ups. The last verse in Genesis 2 verifies that: "And the man and his wife were both naked and were not ashamed."

Naked. Laid bare, open. Not just physically, but emotionally as well. That explains why they were not ashamed. The Hebrew construction suggests they were not ashamed "with one another." There was this remarkable openness, a lack of self-consciousness in each other's presence. Talk about the ideal marriage! Their discussions, their actions, their entire existence were nondefensive, unguarded, and absolutely unselfish.

How could it be? No sin. Therefore, no selfishness. Until . . .

You guessed it. Enter the devil with his alluring offer (read. Gen. 3:1–6) and exit innocence with its pleasurable benefits. And the result?

> Then the eyes of both of them were opened, and they knew that they were naked; and they sewed fig leaves together and made themselves loin coverings (3:7).

Don't miss what that says about their eyes. They were *opened*. There was a sudden, shocking realization they were naked. Seems amazing to us, doesn't it? You and I couldn't be more aware of those times when we are naked. Just a half-opened zipper makes us blush.

But remember the difference. Suddenly, those two became *self*-conscious. They'd never known those feelings before. You and I have never known anything else. What we read here in the Genesis account is the origin of self-awareness, self-concern, selfishness. If you read on you'll see that they immediately began to look out for number one.

> And they heard the sound of the Lord God walking in the garden in the cool of the day, and the man and his wife hid themselves from the presence of the Lord God among the trees of the garden (3:8).

Adam didn't assist Eve. She really wasn't concerned about him either. Both got busy and whipped up a self-made cover-up. And (can you believe it) they attempted to hide from the Lord God. Of course, you can believe it! To this day it's mankind's favorite game . . . even though we lose every time we play it.

> Then the Lord God called to the man, and said to him, "Where are you?"
> And he said, "I heard the sound of Thee in the garden, and I was afraid because I was naked; so I hid myself" (3:9–10).

J. Grant Howard does a splendid job of describing the inner turmoil of these two in the garden. Notice they've already started wearing masks.

Forced out of hiding. Adam stands shamefacedly before his Judge and mumbles his reply. These are the first recorded words of a sinner. Not how he communicates. He mixes truth—"I was afraid"—with half-truth—"because I was naked." The full truth was that he had disobeyed God and thus was aware of his nakedness. He did not level with God. He concealed his act of willful disobedience instead of openly and honestly confessing it. Adam can no longer function as a complete authentic person.[4]

As God probed deeper, Adam and Eve became increasingly more defensive. They hurled accusations at each other and then at God.

"The woman. . . !"

"The woman *you* gave me. . . !"

"The serpent. . . ."

The pattern hasn't changed, has it? Since the original scene down through the centuries, the history of humanity is smeared with ugly marks of selfishness. Unwilling to be authentic, we hide, we deny, we lie, we run, we escape. Anything but the whole truth!

And we hurl. We ridicule, we dominate, we criticize. We cut a person to ribbons with our words. And then we develop ways to keep from admitting it.

"I'm not dogmatic, I'm just sure of myself."

"I'm not judging, I'm discerning."

"I'm not argumentative, I'm simply trying to prove a point."

"I'm not stubborn, *just confident!*"

And all this comes pouring out of our mouths with hardly a second thought. And in case you live under the delusion that we are mild-mannered and gracious in getting our way, watch what happens in heavy traffic . . . or at the checkstand in the local grocery store. I mean, we go for the jugular!

A couple of summers ago my older son Curt and I took a few days off together and shot the rapids up at the Rogue River in Oregon. We went with several of the men from our church. It was great! While we were receiving instructions from the guide (there were about fifteen in the entire group) I began to study the canoes with my eyes. Some were old and worn, but a few were new. Being selfish, I wanted Curt and me to get the new ones . . . so I whispered in his ear,

"Curt, start moving over the left."

"Why?"

"Just do as I say, son. The two canoes on the end are new. Let's get 'em." He cooperated. And we got two of the new ones. I handled it so smoothly, nobody even knew it. The older ones were just as good . . . but they were old.

And there was a really salty old pro as a guide plus a couple of rookies. Guess which one we got. Right! I manipulated our way so efficiently, we wound up in his group.

Why? Because I'm selfish, plain and simple. And to make matters worse, I was *discipling my son to be selfish too*! In a couple of more years he will have it down pat.

By the way, on the way back to our campsite at the end of the day, all fifteen of us were packed like sardines in this old van. Everybody was dog tired. All of a sudden BOOM! A blowout on the right rear. All our gear had to come out to get to the spare tire. And then that beast of a van had to be jacked up. It was a hot, dirty job. Guess who directed traffic instead of helping to change the tire. As I recall not one car passed us on that country road during the entire episode.

Now, let me tell you the worst part of all, and it's really with embarrassment I do so. It was not until the next day that it dawned on me that I was being selfish in any of this. Talk about a blind spot! You see, I learned a lot about looking out for *self* in school; I perfected it in the Marine Corps, and I developed ways to pull it off with real finesse in seminary, learning to be a minister. Hey, this is the profession where a guy can get away with it and hardly ever be criticized for it . . . even though we should! But who in the world is going to point a finger at a man of the cloth? Who's willing to touch "God's anointed" (our favorite title) and risk an advanced case of leprosy?

But my selfishness didn't start at school or in the Corps or at seminary, for that matter. I, like you, caught the disease from Adam. It's a congenital illness in all of us. No person has ever lived on this earth completely free of this dreaded plague—except One. That's right, ever since Adam, only God's virgin-born Son has had immunity from contamination with sin. He did no sin, knew no sin, had no sin. Being sinless, He lived like no other man ever lived. He spoke as no other man ever spoke. And as that unique Teacher, He cut a new swath. He gave directions that had never been given before by *any* instructor.

. . . "You know that the rulers of the Gentiles lord it over them, and their great men exercise authority over them.

"It is not so among you, but whoever wishes to become great among you shall be your servant, and whoever wishes to be the first among you shall be your slave; just as the Son of Man did not come to be served, but to serve, and to give His life a ransom for many" (Matt. 20:25–28).

We who are infected with the Adam-Eve disease don't operate like that. Not on your life. This was emphasized afresh as I watched Leonard Bernstein, the famous orchestra conductor, perform one evening on television. During an informal time of discussion on the program, I recall one admirer asked: "Mr. Bernstein, what is the most difficult instrument to play?" He responded with quick wit:

Second fiddle, I can get plenty of first violinists, but to find one who plays *second* violin with as much enthusiasm or *second* French horn or *second* flute, now that's a problem. And yet if no one plays second, we have no harmony.

Wise words . . . and true!

That's one of the reasons Jesus Christ was so different. Not only did He encourage that sort of thing, He *modeled* it continually. On the basis of this, Paul could write:

Do nothing from selfishness or empty conceit, but with humility of mind let each of you regard one another as more important than himself; do not merely look out for your own personal interests but also for the interests of others.

Have this attitude in yourselves which was also in Christ Jesus (Phil. 2:3–5).

What different counsel we get from man! J. B. Phillips illustrates this when he alters the Beatitudes to read as follows:

Happy are the "pushers": for they get on in the world.

Happy are the hard-boiled: for they never let life hurt them.

Happy are they who complain: for they get their own way in the end.

Happy are the blasé: for they never worry over their sins.

Happy are the slavedrivers: for they get results.

Happy are the knowledgeable men of the world: for they know their way around.

Happy are the troublemakers: for they make people take notice of them.[5]

No, that is just the opposite of what our Lord originally said. In simplest terms, remember, He told us to serve and to give. In those words He built a case for unselfish living. Not being satisfied with just "three dollars worth of God." No, not for authentic servants . . . not on your life. But rather being willing to give it all up to Him, for His glory. This has been referred to as "buying the pearl of great price."

With a bit of sanctified imagination, one man offers this dialogue to illustrate just how much is involved in releasing our all to God so we are free to serve others:

"I want this pearl. How much is it?"

"Well," the seller says. "It's very expensive."

"But, how much?" we ask.

"Well, a very large amount."

"Do you think I could buy it?"

"Oh, of course, everyone can buy it."

"But, didn't you say it was very expensive?"

"Yes."

"Well, how much is it?"

"Everything you have," says the seller.

We make up our minds, "All right, I'll buy it," we say.

"Well, what do you have?" he wants to know. "Let's write it down."

"Well, I have ten thousand dollars in the bank."

"Good—ten thousand dollars. What else?"

"That's all. That's all I have."

"Nothing more?"

"Well, I have a few dollars here in my pocket."

"How much?"

We start digging. "Well, let's see—thirty, forty, sixty, eighty, a hundred, a hundred twenty dollars."

"That's fine. What else do you have?"

"Well, nothing. That's all."

"Where do you live?" He's still probing.

"In my house. Yes, I have a house."

"The house, too, then." He writes that down.

"You mean I have to live in my camper?"

"You have a camper? That, too. What else?"

"I'll have to sleep in my car!"

"You have a car?"

"Two of them."

"Both become mine, both cars. What else?"

"Well, you already have my money, my house, my camper, my cars. What more do you want?"

"Are you alone in this world?"

"No, I have a wife and two children. . . ."

"Oh, yes, your wife and children, too. What else?"

"I have nothing left: I am left alone now."

Suddenly the seller exclaims, "Oh, I almost forgot! You yourself, too! Everything becomes mine—wife, children, house, money, cars—and you too."

Then he goes on. "Now listen—I will allow you to use all these things for the time being. But don't forget that they are mine, just as you are. And whenever I need any of them you must give them up, because now I am the owner."[6]

That's what it means to come to terms with servanthood. Tough, tough concept, isn't it? Yes, tough . . . but now we know why.

Remember the monument?

I

ME

MINE

MYSELF

From now to the end of the book, we're going to assault that monument. We are going to give our full attention to what it means to be different.

Not a getter, but a giver.

Not one who holds a grudge, but a forgiver.

Not one who keeps score, but a forgetter.

Not a superstar, but a servant.

If you are ready to invest more than most . . . if you really desire more than three dollars worth of God, then read on. You're in for the time of your life.

3

The Servant
As a Giver

I like the tongue-in-cheek definition of philosophers one of my Greek teachers in seminary would occasionally use. It's classic:

Philosophers are people who talk about something they don't understand and make you think it's your fault![1]

Lots of philosophies are floating around, and most of them are more confusing than they are helpful. Interestingly, those that are clear enough to be understood usually end up focusing full attention on the individual. Consider a few of them:

Greece said, "Be wise, know yourself!"
Rome said, "Be strong, discipline yourself!"
Religion says, "Be good, conform yourself!"
Epicureanism says, "Be sensuous, enjoy yourself!"
Education says, "Be resourceful, expand yourself!"
Psychology says, "Be confident, assert yourself!"
Materialism says, "Be satisfied, please yourself!"
Pride says, "Be superior, promote yourself!"
Asceticism says, "Be lowly, suppress yourself!"
Humanism says, "Be capable, believe in yourself!"
Legalism says, "Be pious, limit yourself!"
Philanthropy says, "Be generous, release yourself!"

27

Isn't There a Better Way?

Yourself, yourself, yourself. We're up to here with self! Do something either *for* yourself or *with* yourself or *to* yourself. How very different from Jesus' model and message! No "philosophy" to turn our eyes inward, He offers rather a fresh and much-needed invitation to our "me-first" generation. There is a better way. Jesus says, "Be a servant, give to others!" Now that's a philosophy that anybody can understand. And, without question, it is attainable. Just listen:

> Do nothing from selfishness or empty conceit, but with humility of mind let each of you regard one another as more important than himself; do not merely look out for your own personal interests, but also for the interests of others (Phil. 2:3-4).

Know what all that means? Well, for starters, "nothing" means just that. Stop permitting two strong tendencies—selfishness and conceit—to control you! Let *nothing* either of them suggests win a hearing. Replace them with "humility of mind." But how? By regarding others as more important than yourself. Look for ways to support, encourage, build up, and stimulate the other person. And that requires an attitude that would rather give than receive.

"Humility of mind" is really an attitude, isn't it? It's a preset mentality that determines ahead of time thoughts like this:

- "I care about those around me."
- "Why do I always have to be first? I'm going to help someone else win for a change."
- "Today, it's my sincere desire to curb my own fierce competitive tendencies and turn that energy into encouraging at least one other person."
- "I willingly release *my* way this day. Lord, show me how You would respond to others, then make it happen in me."

Is All This Biblical?

Now before we get neck deep into this unselfish lifestyle, we need to determine if it is, in fact, promoted in Scripture. Does the Bible come right up front and encourage living like this? I'll let *you* determine the answer.

For the sake of space, let's limit our thoughts to just a few New Testament passages. Think as you read them slowly . . . and don't skip one line!

> Be devoted to one another in brotherly love; give preference to one another in honor; not lagging behind in diligence, fervent in spirit, serving the Lord; rejoicing in hope, persevering in tribulation, devoted to prayer; contributing to the needs of the saints, practicing hospitality (Rom 12:10–13).

For we do not preach ourselves but Christ Jesus as Lord, and ourselves as your bond-servants for Jesus' sake (2 Cor. 4:5).

For the love of Christ controls us, having concluded this, that one died for all, therefore all died; and He died for all, that they who live should no longer live for themselves, but for Him who died and rose again on their behalf (2 Cor. 5:14–15).

For you were called to freedom, brethren; only do not turn your freedom into an opportunity for the flesh, but through love serve one another (Gal. 5:13).

But we proved to be gentle among you, as a nursing mother tenderly cares for her own children.
Having thus a fond affection for you, we were well pleased to impart to you not only the gospel but also our own lives, because he had become very dear to us. . . .
Therefore encourage one another, and build up one another, just as you also are doing (1 Thess. 2:7–8; 5:11).

And let us consider how to stimulate one another to love and do good deeds (Heb. 10:24).

And you will remember the section we looked at in chapter 1:

And I was with you in weakness and in fear and in trembling.
And my message and my preaching were not in persuasive words of wisdom, but in demonstration of the Spirit and of power, that your faith should not rest on the wisdom of men, but on the power of God (1 Cor. 2:3–5).

Those words (there are many others) have a rare ring to them, don't them? In fact, some who read them might misunderstand and think I'm advocating inferiority. For your sake, a couple more biblical passages are needed:

For I consider myself not in the least inferior to the most eminent apostles. . . .
I have become foolish; you yourselves compelled me. Actually I should have been commended by you, for in no respect was I inferior to the most eminent apostles, even though I am a nobody (2 Cor. 11:5; 12:11).

There's the balance we're looking for. Authentic humility in no way should be confused with incompetence or lack of self-esteem. As a matter of fact, it is doubtful that anyone who wrestles with an unhealthy self-image can correctly and adequately give to others. Inferiority and unselfishness cannot coexist . . . not in the true sense, as Christ describes it.

WHAT ARE THE BASICS?

Now that we have laid a biblical foundation for servanthood, it is important to get some handles on what's involved in pulling it off. To get us started, let me suggest three basic ingredients: *giving, forgiving*, and *forgetting*. Once you and I make up our minds to implement the truth of Philippians 2:3–4 (taking a special interest in others) or Galatians 5:13 (serving others in love), these three basics will begin to emerge. Instead of always thinking about receiving, we'll start looking for ways to give. Instead of holding grudges against those who offended us, we'll be anxious to forgive. And instead of keeping a record of what we've done or who we've helped, we'll take delight in forgetting the deed(s) and being virtually unnoticed. Our hunger for public recognition will diminish in significance.

In the next couple of chapters we'll think deeply about those last two, but for the balance of this chapter, let's picture the servant as a *giver* . . . one who quickly, willingly, and generously gives so others might benefit and grow.

HOW SHOULD SERVANTS GIVE?

Rather than jumping from one biblical reference to another, let's fix our attention on 2 Corinthians, chapter 8. This grand chapter of Scripture has an interesting background. Paul, the writer, is involved in collecting money for a hurting congregation in Jerusalem. As he makes his way through Europe, specifically the region of ancient Macedonia, he announces the need of those fellow Christians in Jerusalem. What adds to the significance of the whole episode is that Macedonia was already an economically depressed area. Macedonia was to Paul a lot like India is to us. It would be like encouraging the people of Appalachia to respond to those who are hurting in the ghetto of Harlem. "You people on welfare . . . give to those people on welfare!" would be a strange appeal today.

But the most remarkable fact of all is this: *They did!* Those financially deprived Macedonian believers were so concerned over their brothers and sisters in Jerusalem who did not have sufficient money to make ends meet, they *really* gave. Let's look closer and see just how extensively they did it.

> Now, brethren, we wish to make known to you the grace of God which has been given in the churches of Macedonia, that in a great ordeal of affliction their abundance of joy and their deep poverty overflowed in the wealth of their liberality.
>
> For I testify that according to their ability and beyond their ability they gave of their own accord, begging us with much entreaty for the favor of participation in the support of the saints, and this, not as we had expected, but they first gave themselves to the Lord and to us by the will of God (2 Cor. 8:1-5).

What a tremendous section of Scripture! I find several ways those Christians demonstrated authentic servanthood in their giving. When we give as a servant gives, the same things are true in us.

Anonymously

Not one specific church is mentioned, simply "the churches of Macedonia." Not even one individual is highlighted. No statues of bronze were later erected in Jerusalem, no names of super saints chiseled in marble or recorded in some book for others to ooh and ahh over. A great proof of true servanthood is *anonymity*.

One of my favorite poets, Ruth Harms Calkin, puts it well, entitling her thoughts, "I Wonder":

> You know, Lord, how I serve You
> With great emotional fervor
> In the limelight.
> You know how eagerly I speak for You
> At a women's club.
> You know how I effervesce when I promote
> A fellowship group.
> You know my genuine enthusiasm
> At a Bible study.
>
> But how would I react, I wonder
> If You pointed to a basin of water
> And asked me to wash the calloused feet
> Of a bent and wrinkled old woman
> Day after day
> Month after month
> In a room where nobody saw
> And nobody knew.[2]

Let those final words sink in, "nobody saw . . . nobody knew." When we practice the art of unselfish living, we prefer to remain anonymous. In fact, most of the people I know who possess a servant's heart are greatly embarrassed when their names are put up in lights.

Generously

Did you catch something else Paul said about those Macedonian servant-saints? When they gave, they "overflowed" in the process, they liberally and sacrificially gave "beyond their ability." I love the way he says that. Their giving dripped with sacrificial generosity. There wasn't a tightwad among them. How refreshing!

Now, as we apply this passage to the way true servants give, let's understand that the giving involved is much broader than money. That's for sure. It includes giving ourselves . . . our time and energy, our care and compassion, even our belongings on occasion. And what a need there is for this trait within the ranks of humanity today. And yet, how rare. We clutch our possessions so tightly we live most of our adult lives with white knuckles. I often wonder why. We certainly can't take any of it with us. I've never seen a hearse pulling a U-Haul!

The name of Onesiphorus flashes into my head. He's a guy who once modeled generosity in his giving to such an extent that Paul remembered his help while he was awaiting death. Listen to the apostle's remarks:

> The Lord grant mercy to the house of Onesiphorus for he often refreshed me, and was not ashamed of my chains; but when he was in Rome, he eagerly searched for me, and found me—the Lord grant to him to find mercy from the Lord on that day—and you know very well what services he rendered at Ephesus (2 Tim. 1:16–18).

Did you miss a couple of choice, descriptive terms? Onesiphorus "often" refreshed the aging, imprisoned apostle, he "eagerly" stayed at the task of finding him. Those are words of great intensity, real determination, and eagerness. Paul's friend was a generous servant. He couldn't have cared less how much trouble it took to find him. He pursued!

Alexander Whyte, the insightful preacher of Edinburgh, Scotland, and writer of biographies, writes these moving words of Onesiphorus:

> Paul might be the greatest of the apostles to Onesiphorus, and he may be all that and far more than all that to you and to me, but he was only "Number so and so" to the soldier who was chained night and day to Paul's right hand. You would not have known Paul from any incognisable convict in our own penal settlements. Paul was simply "Number 5," or "Number 50," or "Number 500," or some such number. From one barrack-prison therefore to another Onesiphorus went about seeking for Paul day after day, week after week, often insulted, often threatened, often ill-used, often arrested and detained, till he was set free again only after great suffering and great expense. Till, at last, his arms were round Paul's neck, and the two old men were kissing one another and weeping to the amazement of all the prisoners who saw the scene. Noble-hearted Onesiphorus! We bow down before thee.[3]

Indeed, we do. Onesiphorus was the kind of servant we need more of: sacrificially generous. There is more.

Voluntarily

Back in 2 Corinthians 8, we're told that the Macedonians also gave voluntarily, not because somebody twisted their arms behind their backs. Paul writes:

. . . I can testify that they did it because they wanted to, and not because of nagging on my part. They begged us to take the money so they could share in the joy of helping . . . (2 Cor. 8:3–4, TLB).

A little later in that same letter, the apostle of grace encourages this spirit of voluntary spontaneity in our giving:

Let each one do just as he has purposed in his heart; not grudgingly or under compulsion; for God loves a cheerful giver (2 Cor. 9:7).

Sounds a lot like what Peter urges from pastors, elders, and other Christian leaders:

. . . shepherd the flock of God among you, not under compulsion, but voluntarily, according to the will of God; and not for sordid gain, but with eagerness; not yet as lording it over those allotted to your charge, but proving to be examples to the flock (1 Pet. 5:2–3).

Great counsel! If it is true that the best leaders are true servants (and I'm convinced that is correct), then one of the best ways to lead people into a willing spirit is to model it. That involves things like reaching out without being invited and sensing deep hurts without being told.

Marion Jacobsen, in a fine book entitled *Crowded Pews and Lonely People*, mentions a first-grader named Billy whose classmate Jim lost his father in a tractor accident. Billy prayed for Jim every day. One day as Billy was walking down the stairs at school, he saw Jim and decided to reach out to him.

"How are you getting along?"

"Oh, fine, jus' fine."

Bill continued, "Do you know, I've been praying for you ever since your daddy was killed."

The other little guy stopped and looked at Billy, grabbed his hand, and led him out back behind the school building. Then he opened up.

"You know, that was a lie when I said things were going fine; they aren't fine. We are having trouble with the cows and with the machines. My mother doesn't know what to do. But I didn't know you were praying for me."[4]

Just goes to show us, doesn't it, how many people are hurting, but don't feel free to say so until we voluntarily reach out to them.

Let's go back for a final glance at 2 Corinthians 8. There's one more characteristic we don't want to miss. The servants in Macedonia first gave *themselves* and then they gave their gifts.

Personally

This is a telltale sign of authentic servant-giving. It is impossible to give ourselves to others at arm's length or *in absentia*. Personal involvement is essential, not incidental, and it usually involves adapting our ways and schedules to fit into other's needs. Such personal involvement, however, certainly reveals the authenticity of our words.

Quite a while ago a young man I had known for several years expressed an interest in living in our home and being discipled in the context of our family. He assured me time and again, "I really want to help any way you or your wife may need me. My only reason for doing this is to serve. I just want to be a servant, Chuck."

Cynthia, the children, and I talked this over at length. We decided we'd give it a whirl . . . so in moved Mr. Servant and his family among our tribe of four kids, a dog, two hamsters, a rabbit, and a three-car garage full of stuff. It wasn't long before we realized those words, "I just want to be a servant" were mere words, little more. Time and again conflicts arose when our requests were met with his resistance. There was hardly an occasion when we would suggest that something be done a certain way without his out his offering an alternative suggestion. What began as an unselfish-sounding game plan (if I heard "I just want to be a servant" once I must have heard it fifty times) ultimately resulted in rather heated disagreements, much to our disappointment. Words come easy—but *being* a person who genuinely and personally gives to others calls for a plentiful supply of flexibility. There's much more to giving ourselves to the Lord and to others than making verbal statements.

According to these first five verses in 2 Corinthians 8, authentic servanthood calls for people with a passion for giving *whatever* without recognition, without reservation, without reluctance, and without restriction. And those types are rare indeed!

How Much Does Giving Cost Us?

Can you recall Jesus' radical philosophy I suggested at the beginning of this chapter? "Be a servant, give to others." The basis of that statement is tucked away in Luke 9:23:

> And He was saying to them all, "If anyone wishes to come after Me, let him deny himself, and take up his cross daily, and follow Me."

Following Christ as His disciple is a costly, unselfish decision. It calls for a radical examination of our self-centered lifestyles. Whew! That's another one of those easy things to say, but tough to carry out. Let's see if I can break this down into smaller bite-size chunks so we don't gag on it. When you look closely at Jesus' statement, a couple of things seem important. First, those who desire to follow Him closely must come to terms with *self-denial*. And second, this decision to give ourselves to others (taking up our cross) has to be a *daily* matter.

That's costly stuff. Terribly expensive.

If we read this back into the 2 Corinthians 8:1–5 guidelines regarding giving, and I really believe we should, then it isn't difficult to see some questions that we must ask and answer ourselves, like:

• Am I serious about being a close follower of Jesus Christ?

• Do I think of others to such an extent that self-denial is becoming the rule rather than the exception in my life?

• Is my walk with Him a *daily* thing?

Making a Thorough Self-Evaluation

This takes us back to 2 Corinthians 8. After Paul finishes describing the unselfishness of the Macedonian believers (vv. 1–5), he turns to the Corinthians and exhorts them:

> But just as you abound in everything, in faith and utterance and knowledge and in all earnestness and in the love we inspired in you, see that you abound in this gracious work also.
>
> I am not speaking this as a command, but as proving through the earnestness of others the sincerity of your love also (2 Cor. 8:7–8).

A thorough self-evaluation is one of the requisites for following closely. The Corinthians *abounded* in vision, spiritual gifts, knowledge, zeal, and even love. Paul then says to abound in generosity too. Be givers! Be people who excel in *unselfishness!* This is timely advice for our own generation . . . and worth our thorough investigation.

It reminds me of an actual situation I heard about recently over the radio. A woman in West Palm Beach, Florida, died alone at the age of 71. The coroner's report was tragic. "Cause of death: *Malnutrition.*" The dear old lady wasted away to 50 pounds. Investigators who found her said the place where she lived was a veritable pigpen, the biggest mess you can imagine. One seasoned inspector declared he'd never seen a residence in greater disarray.

The woman had begged food at her neighbors' back doors and gotten what clothes she had from the Salvation Army. From all outward appearances she was a penniless recluse, a pitiful and forgotten widow. But such was not the case.

Amid the jumble of her unclean, disheveled belongings, two keys were found which led the officials to safe-deposit boxes at two different local banks. What they found was absolutely unbelievable.

The first contained over 700 AT&T stock certificates, plus hundreds of other valuable certificates, bonds, and solid financial securities . . . not to mention a stack of cash amounting to nearly $200,000. The second box had no certificates, only more currency—lots of it—*$600,000 to be exact.* Adding the net worth of both boxes, they found that the woman had in her possession well over A MILLION DOLLARS. Charles Osgood, reporting on CBS radio, announced that the estate would probably fall into the hands of a distant niece and nephew, neither of whom dreamed she had a thin dime to her name. She was, however, a millionaire who died a stark victim of starvation in a humble hovel many miles away.

I conducted a funeral several years ago for a man who died without family or friends. All he had was a fox terrier . . . to whom he left his entire estate: around $76,000.

We need to make an investigation of our possessiveness, our tendency to hoard, to hold onto, rather than investing in the lives of others.

Sticking with a Commitment

There's another cost, equally exacting. As Paul continues with his instruction to the Corinthians, we see it clearly emerge:

> For you know the grace of our Lord Jesus Christ, that though He was rich, yet for your sake He became poor, that you through His poverty might become rich.
>
> And I give my opinion in this matter, for this is to your advantage, who were the first to begin a year ago not only to do this, but also to desire to do it.
>
> But now finish doing it also; that just as there was the readiness to desire it, so there may be also the completion of it by your ability (2 Cor. 8:9–11).

You see, a full year before he wrote them, they had begun that same project. No doubt they were filled with enthusiasm, the thrill of a fresh beginning. But in the passing of time, the newness had worn off. The spontaneous motivation to give had turned into a miserable marathon that dragged slowly on and on.

Paul says, "Get with it! You made a commitment to get involved, to give, and to help out—now stick with that commitment!"

Becoming a *giving* person sounds exciting. But it costs something. It will demand change, and no significant change ever got started without motivation and zeal.

Want a vivid illustration? Dieting. Oh, just the *word* brings up painful memories! Especially when I add exercising and jogging. Who hasn't had the experience? We finally get sick and tired of our flab. Zippers start ripping out, buttons pop off, the car leans dangerously to one side when we get in, the scales we step on punch out a little card that says, "Only one at a time, please."

We laugh understandingly at Erma Bombeck's continual battle with the bulge. You may remember she's the one who said something like, "I'm not telling you what I weigh, but when I measure my girth and then step on the scales, I oughta be a 90-foot redwood."

Okay, we're going to thin down. In the fresh enthusiasm of zeal, we buy $60 sneakers, a couple of $85 jogging outfits, we join a local spa (another $350), and we blow the dust off that miserable "Count Those Calories" booklet we bought back in the mid '70s. We are going to shave off 30 pounds!

The very first day we start with a flash. We hit the road, running like we're on fire. We drop our intake to 700 calories a day. We choke down dry toast, cottage cheese, sliced tomatoes, and boiled egg! We snack on stuff that tastes like canary mix and we sip on bitter herb tea until we think we're going to gag. By the third day we're so sore we can only trot a half a block . . . so we get up later. The Thanksgiving season brings too many temptations so we fudge . . . and finally gorge. In less than a month, our blimp is back in the hangar. And when the urge to exercise comes over us, we just lie down quietly until the urge goes away.

Sticking with any commitment is costly. And I can assure you, becoming a servant who gives and gives and gives to others is no exception. By comparison, it will make dieting look like a piece of cake (no pun intended).

IS IT WORTH IT, AFTER ALL?

Let me encourage you, however, in spite of the high cost of giving and the small number of servant-models you may see around you, to determine to be different. God tells us He "loves a cheerful giver" (2 Cor. 9:7), and He promises us that "he who is generous will be blessed" (Prov. 22:9). Let's believe Him! Deep down inside most Christians I know is a deep-seated desire to release instead of keep . . . to give instead of grab. It is worth *whatever* it takes to let that start happening. Moms, dads, singles, kids, teachers, preachers, businessmen, professionals, blue-collar workers, students—it is worth it! Become a giver . . . and watch God open the hearts of others to Himself. We are never more Godlike than when we give.

Shortly after World War II came to a close, Europe began picking up the pieces. Much of the Old Country had been ravaged by war and was in ruins. Perhaps the saddest sight of all was that of little orphaned children starving in the streets of those war-torn cities.

Early one chilly morning an American soldier was making his way back to the barracks in London. As he turned the corner in his jeep, he spotted a little lad with his nose pressed to the window of a pastry shop. Inside, the cook was kneading dough for a fresh batch of doughnuts. The hungry boy stared in silence, watching every move. The soldier pulled his jeep to the curb, stopped, got out, and walked quietly over to where the little fellow was standing. Through the steamed-up window he could see the mouth-watering morsels as they were being pulled from the oven, piping hot. The boy salivated and released a slight groan as he watched the cook place them onto the glass-enclosed counter ever so carefully.

The soldier's heart went out to the nameless orphan as he stood beside him. "Son . . . would you like some of those?"

The boy was startled.

"Oh, yeah . . . I would!"

The American stepped inside and bought a dozen, put them in a bag, and walked back to where the lad was standing in the foggy cold of the London morning. He smiled, held out the bag, and said simply:

"Here you are."

As he turned to walk away, he felt a tug on his coat. He looked back and heard the child ask quietly:

"Mister . . . *are you God?*"

We are never more like God than when we give.

"God so loved the world, that He gave. . . ."

4

The Servant
As a Forgiver

Forgiveness is not an elective in the curriculum of servanthood. It is a required course, and the exams are always tough to pass.

Several years ago I traveled to Trinity Evangelical Divinity School in search of a pastoral intern. In the process of interviewing a number of men, I met a seminarian I will never forget. As it turned out, I did not select him to come for the summer, but I was extremely impressed with his sensitivity to God. Although young and inexperienced, his spirit was tender and he spoke with gentleness. It was obvious that the Lord was deeply at work in his life. The marks of a servant's heart were clearly visible, so much so I probed to discover why. Among other things he related an incredible, true story that illustrated how God was molding him and shaping him through one of those tough "forgiveness exams." As best as I can remember, here's his story. I'll call him Aaron, not his real name.

Late one spring he was praying about having a significant ministry the following summer. He asked God for a position to open up on some church staff or Christian organization. Nothing happened. Summer arrived, still nothing. Days turned into weeks, and Aaron finally faced reality—he needed *any* job he could find. He checked the want ads and the only thing that seemed a possibility was driving a bus in southside Chicago . . . nothing to brag about, but it would help with tuition in the fall. After learning the route, he was on his own—a rookie driver in a dangerous section of the city. It wasn't long before Aaron realized just *how* dangerous his job really was.

A small gang of tough kids spotted the young driver, and began to take advantge of him. For several mornings in a row they got on, walked right past him without paying, ignored his warnings, and rode until they decided to get off . . . all the while making smart remarks to him and others on the bus. Finally, he decided that had gone on long enough.

The next morning, after the gang got on as usual, Aaron saw a policeman on the next corner, so he pulled over and reported the offense. The officer told them to pay or get off. They paid . . . but, unfortunately, the policeman got off. And *they* stayed on. When the bus turned another corner or two, the gang assaulted the young driver.

When he came to, blood was all over his shirt, two teeth were missing, both eyes were swollen, his money was gone, and the bus was empty. After returning to the terminal and being given the weekend off, our friend went to his little apartment, sank onto his bed and stared at the ceiling in disbelief. Resentful thoughts swarmed his mind. Confusion, anger, and disillusionment added fuel to the fire of his physical pain. He spent a fitful night wrestling with his Lord.

> How can this be? Where's God in all of this? I genuinely want to serve Him. I prayed for a ministry. I was willing to serve Him anywhere, doing anything . . . and *this* is the thanks I get!

On Monday morning Aaron decided to press charges. With the help of the officer who had encountered the gang and several who were willing to testify as witnesses against the thugs, most of them were rounded up and taken to the local county jail. Within a few days there was a hearing before the judge.

In walked Aaron and his attorney plus the angry gang members who glared across the room in his direction. Suddenly he was seized with a whole new series of thoughts. Not bitter ones, but compassionate ones! His heart went out to the guys who had attacked him. Under the Spirit's control he no longer hated them—he pitied them. They needed help, not more hate. What could he do? Or say?

Suddenly, after there had been a plea of guilty. Aaron (to the surprise of his attorney and everybody else in the courtroom) stood to his feet and requested permission to speak.

> Your honor, I would like you to total up all the days of punishment against these men—all the time sentenced against them—and I request that you allow me to go to jail in their place.

The judge didn't know whether to spit or wind his watch. Both attorneys were stunned. As Aaron looked over at the gang members (whose mouths and eyes looked like saucers), he smiled and said quietly, "It's because I forgive you."

The dumbfounded judge, when he reached a level of composure, said rather firmly: "Young man, you're out of order. This sort of thing has never been done before!" To which the young man replied with genius insight:

> Oh, yes, it has, your honor . . . yes, it has. It happened over nineteen centuries ago when a man from Galilee paid the penalty that all mankind deserved.

And then, for the next three or four minutes, without interruption, he explained how Jesus Christ died on our behalf, thereby proving God's love and forgiveness.

He was not granted his request, but the young man visited the gang members in jail, led most of them to faith in Christ, and began a significant ministry to many others in southside Chicago.

He passed a tough exam. And, as a result, a large door of ministry—the very thing he'd prayed for—opened up before him. Through the pain of abuse and assault, Aaron began to get a handle on serving others.

Forgiving (like giving) improves our serve!

GOD'S FORGIVENESS OF US

As we undertake a subject this broad, it's necessary that we limit our thoughts to horizontal forgiveness rather than vertical forgiveness. But instead of ignoring the vertical altogether, perhaps I should briefly explain its significance. Actually, it's God's forgiveness of us that makes possible our forgiving others.

When the penalty of our sin was paid in full by Jesus Christ on the cross, God's wrath was expressed against Him—the One who took our place. God was therefore satisfied in the epochal sacrifice . . . allowing all who would turn, in faith, to the Son of God to be totally, once-for-all, forgiven. Christ's blood washed away our sin. And from the moment we believe on Him, we stand forgiven, relieved of guilt, before a satisfied God, freeing Him to shower upon us His grace and love.

Remember the verse from that grand old song the church has sung for years?

> My sin—oh, the bliss of this glorious tho't—
> My sin—not in part, but the whole,
> Is nailed to the cross and I bear it no more,
> Praise the Lord, praise the lord, O my soul![1]

That says it well, but not as beautifully as the song from the oldest of all hymnals—The Psalms:

> Bless the Lord, O my soul;
> And all that is within me, bless His holy name.
> Bless the Lord, O my soul,
> And forget none of His benefits;
> Who pardons all your iniquities;
> Who heals all your diseases;
> Who redeems your life from the pit;
> Who crowns you with lovingkindness and compassion;
> Who satisfies your years with good things,

> So that your youth is renewed like the eagle. . . .
>> He has not dealt with us according to our sins,
> Nor rewarded us according to our iniquities.
>> For high as the heavens are above the earth,
> So great is His loving kindness toward those who fear Him.
>> As far as the east is from the west,
> So far has He removed our transgressions from us
> (Ps. 103:1–5, 10–12).

That's what Aaron helped the Chicago gang to understand. They ultimately had little difficulty realizing what Christ accomplished on the cross on their behalf. But what they did not understand at the time was that Aaron could never have done that for them, horizontally, if it had not been for what Christ had already done for Aaron, vertically. Not until we fully accept *and appropriate* God's infinite and complete forgiveness on our behalf can we carry out the things I mention in the rest of this chapter.

OUR FORGIVENESS OF ONE ANOTHER

It isn't long before anyone who gets serious about serving others must come to terms with forgiving others as well. Yes, *must*. As I said earlier, it's a required course in the servanthood curriculum. Since this is such a common occurrence, I find it helpful to break the subject down into manageable parts, with handles I can get hold of.

Only Two Possibilities

When wrong has been done against another person, there are only two possibilities. But whether we are responsible for the offense or are the recipients of it, the first move is always ours. The true servant doesn't keep score. The general principle is set forth in Ephesians 4:31–32, which says:

> Let all bitterness and wrath and anger and clamor and slander be put away from you, along with all malice.
> And be kind to one another, tender-hearted, forgiving each other, just as God in Christ also has forgiven you.

That's a beautiful summation of the whole subject of forgiveness. It describes how to live with a clear conscience and thus be free to serve. And observe the reminder—you forgive others ". . . as God in Christ also has forgiven you" (vertical). But we need to get more specific. Let's analyze both sides of the forgiveness coin.

When You Are the Offender

Matthew 5:23–24 describes, in a nutshell, the correct response and procedure to follow when we have been in the wrong and offended someone.

> If therefore you are presenting your offering at the altar, and there remember that your brother has something against you,
> leave your offering there before the altar, and go your way; first be reconciled to your brother, and then come and present your offering.

The scene is clear. A person in Jesus' day has come to worship. At that time, in keeping with the Jewish law and custom, worshipers brought sacrificial animals or birds with them. The sacrifice would be slain before God, providing cleansing of sin and a way of open access to prayer. Today it would simply be a Christian's coming to his Father in prayer. Either way, the worshiper is suddenly seized with the inescapable thought, the painful realization that he or she has offended another person. In the words of Jesus, you ". . . remember your brother has something against you." What do you do?

Stop! Don't ignore that realization. Don't just plunge on into prayer, even though that may be your first reaction. God wants us, rather, to be sensitive to His quiet prompting.

In verse 24, we are instructed to do four things:

1. Stop   "leave your offering there. . . ."
2. Go   "go your way. . . ."
3. Reconcile   ". . . first be reconciled. . . ."
4. Return   ". . . then come and present your offering. . . ."

The key term is *reconciled*. It's from a Greek root verb that means "to alter, to change" . . . with a prefix attached to the verb that means "through." In other words, we are commanded to go through a process that will result in a change. Clearly, the *offender* is to initiate the action.

One reliable authority defines this word rather vividly: "To change enmity for friendship . . . bringing about mutual concession for mutual hostility."[2] And another, "Seeing to it that the angry brother renounce his enmity. . . ."[3]

That needs little clarification. We are to go (ideally, personally—if not possible, at least by phone or letter) and confess both the wrong and our grief over the offense, seeking the forgiveness of the one we wounded. *Then*, we are free to return to God in worship and prayer.

"But what if he or she won't forgive?" Good question! The important thing for each of us to remember is that you are responsible for *you* and I am responsible for *me*. With the right motive, in the right spirit, at the right time, out of obedience to God, we are to humble ourselves (remember, it is servanthood we're developing) and attempt to make things right. God will honor our efforts. The one offended may need time—first to get over the shock and next, to have God bring about a change in his or her heart. Healing sometimes takes time. Occasionally, a lot of time.

"What if the situation only gets worse?" Another good question frequently asked. This can happen. You see, all the time the one offended has been blaming you . . . mentally sticking pins in your doll . . . thinking all kinds of bad things about you. When you go to make things right, you suddenly cause his internal scales to go out of balance. You take away the blame and all that's left is the person's guilt, which does a number on him, resulting in even worse feelings. But now it's no longer your fault. Illustration? King Saul and young David. In case you don't remember, young David became a threat to the paranoid monarch. No matter how hard he tried to win back the favor of Saul, things only got worse. It took *years* for the troubled king to realize that David was sincere in his efforts to make things right. Again, it may take awhile for God to get through.

"What if I decide to simply deal with it before God and not go through the hassle and embarrassment of talking with the other person?" We'll do *anything* to make things easier, won't we? Well, first off—that is a willful contradiction of the command. Jesus says, "Stop, go, reconcile, and return!" *Not* to go is direct disobedience. It also can result in things getting worse.

Let's say I am driving away from your church parking lot next Sunday morning. I back my car into the side of your beautiful, new *Mercedes 450 SEL.* CRUNCH! You are visiting with friends following the service and you hear the noise. Your stomach churns as you see me get out of the car, look at the damage . . . and then bow in prayer:

> Dear Lord, please forgive me for being so preoccupied and clumsy. And please give John grace as he sees the extensive damage I have caused out of sheer negligence. And provide his needs as he takes this car in to have it fixed. Thanks, Lord. Amen.

As I drive away, I wave and smile real big as I yell out the window, "It's all cleared up, John. I claimed the damage before God. *Isn't grace wonderful!*"

Tell me, how does that grab you? I have rather strong doubts that it would suddenly make things A-O.K., no matter how sincere my prayer might have been. You and I know that would do no good.

When I was a kid in church we used to sing a little chorus that sounded so pious, so right. In fact, we would often close our youth meetings by holding hands in a circle and sing this piece with our eyes closed:

> If I have wounded any soul today,
> If I have caused one foot to go astray,
> If I have walked in my own willful way
> Dear Lord, forgive![4]

I now question the message of that nice-sounding song. Wounded souls are offended people. And the Savior does not say, "Simply pray and I'll forgive you." In fact, He says, "Stop praying until you have made things right!" That is the part of the "forgiveness exam" that's tough to pass.

One final question before moving on to the other side of the coin: "What if it is impossible for me to reconcile because the offended person has died?" Obviously, you cannot contact the dead. It's impossible to get a hearing, but your conscience still badgers you. In such unique cases, I recommend that you share your burden of guilt with someone whom you can trust. A close friend, your mate, a counselor, or your pastor. Be specific and completely candid. Pray with that individual and confess openly the wrong and the guilt of your soul. In such cases—and only in such cases—prayer and the presence of an understanding, affirming individual will provide the relief you need so desperately.

After David had indirectly murdered Uriah, Bathsheba's husband, his guilt was enormous. Adultery and hypocrisy on top of murder just about did him in. If you want to know the depth of his misery, read Psalm 32:3-4:

> When I kept silent about my sin, my body wasted
>   away
> Through my groaning all day long.
> For day and night Thy hand was heavy upon me;
> My vitality was drained away as with the fever-heat of
>   summer.

Finally, when it all caved in on top of him, when he broke the hypocritical silence and sought God's forgiveness, Uriah was not there to hear his confession. He had been dead the better part of a year. But David was not alone. A prophet named Nathan was there, you may recall. And when the broken king poured out his soul, "I have sinned. . . ," Nathan followed quickly with these affirming words: "The Lord also has taken away your sin; you shall not die" (2 Sam. 12:13).

When you have been the cause of an offense, that is, when you are the offender, have the heart of a servant. Stop, go, reconcile, and then return.

When You Are the Offended

Turn now to Matthew 18:21-35 . . . same book, same teacher, similar subject, but a different style and setting entirely from the Matthew 5 passage where Jesus delivered a monologue communicating a large number of things to His disciples. He touched on each rather generally, all great truths . . . but many subjects. Here in chapter 18 He is engaged in more of a dialogue, dealing in depth with the right response toward someone who offends us. Rather than dump the whole truckload on you, let me present these verses in sections.

First, the disciple's question:

> Then Peter came and said to Him, "Lord, how often shall my brother sin against me and I forgive him? Up to seven times?" (Matt. 18:21).

Good, relevant question. What's the limit we should place on forgiveness? Peter was feeling magnanimous that day, for the going rate (according to the rabbis) was three times.[5] The Jews were instructed to forgive once, forgive twice . . . and a third time, but from then on, forget it. Peter doubled the limit then added a bonus for good measure.

Now, the Lord's response:

> . . . I do not say to you, up to seven times, but up to seventy times seven (Matt. 18:22).

Obviously, He is not saying literally, "Would you believe 490, Peter?" No, not that. He's suggesting an *infinite* number of times. *Limitless.* I would imagine that thought blew those disciples away! Which, no doubt, prompted Jesus to go into greater detail. Hence, a parable with a punch line. Read the story very carefully, preferably aloud and slowly.

> For this reason the kingdom of heaven may be compared to a certain king who wished to settle accounts with his slaves.
>
> And when he had begun to settle them, there was brought to him one who owed him ten thousand talents.
>
> But since he did not have the means to repay, his lord commanded him to be sold, along with his wife and children and all that he had, and repayment to be made.
>
> The slave therefore falling down, prostrated himself before him, saying, "Have patience with me, and I will repay you everything."
>
> And the lord of that slave felt compassion and released him and forgave him the debt.
>
> But that slave went out and found one of his fellow-slaves who owed him a hundred denarii; and he seized him and began to choke him, saying, "Pay back what you owe."
>
> So his fellow-slave fell down and began to entreat him, saying, "Have patience with me and I will repay you."
>
> He was unwilling however, but went and threw him in prison until he should pay back what was owed.
>
> So when his fellow-slaves saw what had happened, they were deeply grieved and came and reported to their lord all that had happened.
>
> Then summoning him, his lord said to him, "You wicked slave, I forgave you all that debt because you entreated me.
>
> "Should you not also have had mercy on your fellow-slave, even as I had mercy on you?"
>
> And his lord, moved with anger, handed him over to the torturers until he should repay all that was owed him (Matt. 18:23–34).

By now, you have probably begun to think in terms of vertical forgiveness and horizontal forgiveness. The vertical is clearly seen in verses 23 through 27.

This was an incredible debt (about $10,000,000!) requiring infinite forgiveness, which the king provided (read verse 27 again)—a beautiful reminder of God's forgiving the sinner.

The horizontal comes in view in verses 28 through 34. That same slave, having just been forgiven that incredible debt, turned against a fellow who owed him *less than twenty bucks* and assaulted the poor fellow. When the king got word of his violent reaction, he was furious. I mean, he was beside himself! And the confrontation that followed was understandably severe.

A couple of things emerge from the latter part of this story that provide us with reasons to forgive others.

1. To refuse to forgive is hypocritical. Note again verses 32 through 33.

> Then summoning him, his lord said to him, "You wicked slave, I forgave you all that debt because you entreated me.
> Should you not also have had mercy on your fellow-slave, even as I had mercy on you?"

Since we have been the recipients of maximum mercy, who are we to suddenly demand justice from others? The compassion God (illustrated in the parable as the king) demonstrates on our behalf calls for us to do the same toward others. Anything less is downright hypocritical.

2. To refuse to forgive inflicts inner torment upon us. Remember how the story ends? It is exceedingly significant. "And his lord, moved with anger, handed him over to the torturers until he should repay all that was owed him."

"Well," you say, "that was just a parable. We can't press every point and say each little detail applies to us." Granted, but in this case, it's not a *little* detail. It's the punch line, the climax of the whole story. How can I say that? Because verse 35 is not part of the parable. It is a statement Jesus makes *after* the story ends. It is His penetrating application of the whole parable on forgiving others.

He wrapped up His instruction with this grim warning: "So shall My Heavenly Father also do to you, if each of you does not forgive his brother from your heart."

Frankly, this is one of the most important truths God ever revealed to me on the consequences of an unforgiving spirit. When Jesus says, "So shall My heavenly Father also do to you . . . ," He is referring back to the closing words of the parable, which says:

> And his lord, moved with anger, handed him over to the torturers until he should repay all that was owed him.

This is no fictitious tale, like Bluebeard who tortured others behind a secret door. No, Jesus says God personally will allow those who refuse to forgive others to be tortured.

What in the world does that mean? The root Greek term from which "torturers" is translated is a verb meaning "to torment"—a frightening thought. When I first saw the thing begin to take shape in my mind, I resisted it. I thought, "No, that's too harsh!" But the further I probed, the clearer it became.

The same term is used to describe a person suffering "great pain" (Matt. 8:6). And it is used to describe the misery of a man being "in agony" in hell as he pleads for relief (Luke 16:23-24). When we read of a man named Lot, in 2 Peter 2:8, who was surrounded and oppressed by the conduct of unprincipled men, we read "his righteous soul was tormented day after day . . ." Again the same term is used. Pain, agony, and torment are all a part of this torturous experience.

But here in Matthew 18:34-35, Jesus refers to tormentors—a noun, not a verb. He is saying the one who refuses to forgive, the Christian who harbors grudges, bitter feelings toward another, will be turned over to torturous thoughts, feelings of misery, and agonizing unrest within. One fine expositor describes it like this:

> This is a marvelously expressive phrase to describe what happens to us when we do not forgive another. It is an accurate description of gnawing resentment and bitterness, the awful gall of hate or envy. It is a terrible feeling. We cannot get away from it. We feel strongly this separation from another and every time we think of them we feel within the acid of resentment and hate eating away at our peace and calmness. This is the torturing that our Lord says will take place.[6]

And who hasn't endured such feelings? It is one of the horrible consequences of *not* forgiving those who offend us. It makes no difference who it is—one of your parents or in-laws, your pastor or former pastor, a close friend who turned against you, some teacher who was unfair, or a business partner who ripped you off . . . even your former partner in marriage. I meet many divorcees who have been "handed over to the torturers" for this very reason. Believe me, it is not worth the misery. We are to forgive as we have been forgiven! Release the poison of all that bitterness . . . let it gush out before God, and declare the sincere desire to be free. It's one of the major steps each of us must take toward becoming God's model of a servant.

HOW TO MAKE IT HAPPEN

There is enough in this chapter to keep us thinking (and forgiving) for weeks. But there are a couple of specifics that need to be considered before we move ahead.

First, *focus fully on God's forgiveness of you.* Don't hurry through this. Think of how vast, how extensive His mercy has been extended toward you. Like Aaron, the young seminary student, must have done in the courtroom that day. Like David did when he wrote "Hymn 103." He got extremely specific. Remember?

> Bless the Lord, O my soul,
> And forget none of His benefits;
> Who pardons all your iniquities;
> Who heals all your diseases;
> Who redeems your life from the pit;
> Who crowns you with lovingkindness and compassion;
> Who satisfies your years with good things,
> So that your youth is renewed like the eagle
> He has not dealt with us according to our sins,
> Nor rewarded us according to our iniquities.
> For high as the heavens are above the earth,
> So great is His lovingkindness toward those who fear
> Him.
> As far as the east is from the west,
> So far has He removed our transgressions from us
> (Ps. 103:2–5, 10–12).

Meditate on that in your own life. Personalize these words by substituting *me* and *my* for *us* and *your*. Ponder the depth of God's mercy . . . the debts against you He graciously canceled. The extent to which you can envision God's forgiveness of you, to that same measure you will be given the capacity to forgive others.

Next, *deal directly and honestly with any resentment you currently hold against anyone.*

It's a tough exam. But think of the alternative—torturing, agonizing feelings, the churning within, the enormous emotional energy you burn up and waste every day.

Maybe you are willing to go just so far. You will bargain with God and agree to forgive *but* not *forget*. That is one of the most regrettable mistakes a servant-in-the-making can make. Because limited forgiveness is like conditional love—a poor substitute for the genuine item. It's no forgiveness at all.

Amy Carmichael said it best when she wrote these words:

> If I say, "Yes, I forgive, but I cannot forget," as though the God, who twice a day washes all the sands on all the shores of all the world, could not wash such memories from my mind, then I know nothing of Calvary love.[7]

So much for forgiving. We now need to think about forgetting. That's next. If forgiveness is the process God takes us through to heal inner wounds . . . then forgetting would be the removal of the ugly scar.

And God can even do that.

5

The Servant
As a Forgetter

I'll forgive . . . but I'll *never* forget." We say and hear that so much that it's easy to shrug it off as "only natural." That's the problem! It is the most natural reponse we can expect. Not *supernatural*. It also can result in tragic consequences.

Last week I read of two unmarried sisters who lived together, but because of an unresolved disagreement over an insignificant issue, they stopped speaking to each other (one of the inescapable results of refusing to forget). Since they were either unable or unwilling to move out of their small house, they continued to use the same rooms, eat at the same table, use the same appliances, and sleep in the same room . . . all separately . . . without one word. A chalk line divided the sleeping area into two halves, separating doorways as well as the fireplace. Each would come and go, cook and eat, sew and read without ever stepping over into her sister's territory. Through the black of the night, each could hear the deep breathing of the other, but because both were unwilling to take the first step toward forgiving and forgetting the silly offense, they coexisted *for years* in grinding silence.[1]

Refusing to forgive *and forget* leads to other tragedies, like monuments of spite. How many churches split (often over nitpicking issues) then spin off into another direction, fractured, splintered, and blindly opinionated?

After I spoke at a summer Bible conference meeting one evening, a lady told me she and her family had been camping across America. In their travels they drove through a town and passed a church with a name she said she would never forget—THE ORIGINAL CHURCH OF GOD, NUMBER TWO.

Whether a personal or public matter, we quickly reveal whether we possess a servant's heart in how we respond to those who have offended us. And it isn't enough simply to say, "Well, okay—you're forgiven, but don't expect me to forget it!" That means we have erected a monument of spite in our mind, and

49

that isn't really forgiveness at all. Servants must be big people. Big enough to *go on*, remembering the right and forgetting the wrong. Like the age-old saying. "Write injuries in dust, benefits in marble."[2] As we shall see, forgetting also includes other things besides forgetting offenses: doing helpful things for others without expecting something in return . . . being, in the true and noble sense of the term, self-forgetful.

CAN THE MIND EVER FORGET?

A question flashes through my head as I write these words: Can our minds actually *allow* us to forget? The way God has made us—with that internal filing system we call "memory"—it is doubtful we can fully forget even the things we *want* to forget.

Our minds are simply remarkable. Dr. Earl Radmacher aptly illustrates the truth of that statement:

> The human mind is a fabulous computer. As a matter of fact, no one has been able to design a computer as intricate and efficient as the human mind. Consider this: your brain is capable of recording 800 memories per second for seventy-five years without ever getting tired. . . .
>
> I have heard some persons complain that their brain is too tired to get involved in a program of Scripture memorization. I have news for them—the body can get tired, but the brain never does. A human being doesn't use more than 2 percent of his brain power, scientists tell us. And, of course, some demonstrate this fact more obviously than others. The point is, the brain is capable of an incredible amount of work and it retains everything it takes in. You never really forget anything; you just don't recall it. Everything is on permanent file in your brain.[3]

Because of facts like those, we need to understand that I'm not referring to forgetting in the technical or literal sense of the term. Rather, I'm thinking about forgetting the same way Paul does in 1 Corinthians 13:4–5 when he says:

> Love is patient, love is kind, and is not jealous; love does not brag and is not arrogant, does not act unbecomingly; it does not seek its own, is not provoked, does not take into account a wrong suffered.

That last statement is rendered this way in the J. B. Phillips translation:

> This love of which I speak is slow to lose patience—it looks for a way of being constructive. It is not possessive: it is neither anxious to impress nor does it cherish inflated ideas of its own importance.
>
> Love has good manners and does not pursue selfish advantage. It is not touchy. It does not keep account of evil or gloat over the wickedness of other people. On the contrary, it is glad with all good men when truth prevails.

True servants, when demonstrating genuine love, don't keep score. Webster defines *forget* as "to lose the remembrance of . . . to treat with inattention or disregard . . . to disregard intentionally: OVERLOOK: to cease remembering or noticing . . . to fail to become mindful at the proper time."[4] That's the thought.

A couple of scriptures illustrate and encourage this great-hearted virtue.

> Those who love Thy law have great peace,
> And nothing causes them to stumble (Ps. 119:165).

The psalmist openly declares that those who posses a deep love for God's Word will have great measures of His *shalom* . . . and, in addition, they will be big enough to resist stumbling over offenses.

Jesus hinted at that when He spoke out against a judgmental spirit. Read His words carefully.

> Do not judge lest you be judged yourselves.
> For in the way you judge, you will be judged; and by your standard of measure, it shall be measured to you.
> And why do you look at the speck in your brother's eye, but do not notice the log that is in your own eye?
> Or how can you say to your brother, "Let me take the speck out of your eye," and behold, the log is in your own eye?
> You hypocrite, first take the log out of your own eye; and then you will see clearly enough to take the speck out of your brother's eye (Matt. 7:1-5).

So then, as we talk about "forgetting" let's understand that we mean:

- Refusing to keep score (1 Cor. 13:5).
- Being bigger than any offense (Ps. 119:165).
- Harboring no judgmental attitude (Matt. 7:1-5).

Before proceeding, a positive thought is in order. We also have in mind the ability to go on beyond our own good deeds. Once they are done, they're done. No need to drop little hints on how thoughtful we were. Improving our serve includes forgetting our service.

A CLOSE LOOK AT FORGETTING

Tucked away in the New Testament is a chapter that illustrates this truth beautifully. It's Philippians, chapter 3. The writer, Paul, is listing a number of things in his past that could be food for pride.

... If anyone else has a mind to put confidence in the flesh, I far more: circumcised the eighth day, of the nation of Israel, of the tribe of Benjamin, a Hebrew of Hebrews; as to the Law, a Pharisee; as to zeal, a persecutor of the church, as to the righteousness which is in the Law, found blameless (vv. 4-6).

If you were looking for somebody to give a testimony next Sunday, Paul would be a winner. In fact, if he were not careful, he could turn it into a "braggimony." These are impressive facts . . . and they are absolutely true.

But Paul, servant that he was, kept it all in proper perspective.

But whatever things were gain to me, those things I have counted as loss for the sake of Christ.

More than that, I count all things to be loss in view of the surpassing value of knowing Christ Jesus my Lord, for whom I have suffered the loss of all things, and count them but rubbish in order that I may gain Christ (vv. 7-9).

In comparison to Jesus Christ and all the things He has made possible—His forgiveness, His love, His righteousness—everything else *we* may be or accomplish diminishes in significance. Paul's following words describe the healthy humility of a servant:

I don't mean to say I am perfect. I haven't learned all I should even yet, but I keep working toward that day when I will finally be all that Christ saved me for and wants me to be.

No, dear brothers, I am still not all I should be but I am bringing all my energies to bear on this one thing: Forgetting the past and looking forward to what lies ahead, I strain to reach the end of the race and receive the prize for which God is calling us up to heaven because of what Christ Jesus did for us (vv. 12-14, TLB).

Woven into those words are these three statements:
1. "I have not arrived."
2. "I forget what is behind."
3. "I move on to what is ahead."

Within each of these three statements, I find an important characteristic of servanthood: vulnerability, humility, and determination.

Vulnerability

"I have not arrived" is a concept that Paul mentions no less than three times in Philippians 3:12-13:
1. *"Not that I have already obtained it . . ."* (v. 12).
2. *". . . or have already become perfect . . ."* (v. 12).
3. *". . . I do not regard myself as having laid hold of it . . ."* (v. 13).

How refreshing!

Here is this brilliant, competent, gifted, strong leader who freely declares, "I don't have everything wired." Vulnerability includes more than this, however. It means being willing to express personal needs, admitting one's own limitations or failures, having a teachable spirit, and *especially* being reluctant to appear the expert, the answer man, the final voice of authority. Not only are these traits refreshing, they're rare!

If you're the type that always has to come out right . . . if you have the need to be "perfect" then you will always be in the position of having something to prove. And others around you must do the same.

Executive Howard Butt, a businessman in Corpus Christi, Texas, writes of this in a very honest and practical manner:

> If your leadership is Christian you can openly reveal your failures. Leaders who are fully human do not hide their sins. Within you operates the principle of the cross, the modus operandi of strength in weakness.
>
> This principle points up our problem—we who are religious. We want a Christian reputation more than we want Christ. And yet our Lord, becoming sin for us, "made himself of no reputation" . . .
>
> Am I willing to hide my strengths and reveal my weaknesses? Are you? Telling our triumphs, our successes, our achievements, we glorify ourselves . . .
>
> Bragging about my goodness, I build barriers up; when I confess my sins, those barriers come down. Pagan outsiders get driven away by our pious parade of religious achievements. Building our high walls of intimidation, we make their friendly corner bartender look good. Christians are not half-angels with high-beam halos, but real live forgiven sinners up close. . . .
>
> Christ's death frees you from hiding your sins. You can be vulnerable and open. When you are weak then you are strong. You shake the darkness with irresistible blows: the divine might of weakness. You hit your hardest when your guard is down.[5]

Being vulnerable is part of being a servant who forgets.

Humility

"I forget what is behind" is a statement that assures us Paul was not the type to live in the past. He says, in effect, "I disregard my own accomplishments as well as others' offenses against me. I refuse to dwell on that." This requires humility. Especially so when you examine Paul's past. Just listen:

> Five times I received from the Jews thirty-nine lashes.
>
> Three times I was beaten with rods, once I was stoned, three times I was shipwrecked, a night and a day I have spent in the deep.
>
> I have been on frequent journeys, in dangers from rivers, dangers from robbers, dangers from my countrymen, dangers from the Gentiles, dangers in the city,

dangers in the wilderness, dangers on the sea, dangers among false brethren; I have been in labor and hardship, through many sleepless nights, in hunger and thirst, often without food, in cold and exposure (2 Cor. 11:24–27).

Think of all the people Paul could have included on his "hate list." But he had no such list. With humility, he forgot what was behind him. He intentionally disregarded all those wrongs against him.

The very best example I can think of is a remarkable man named Joseph in the book of Genesis. Rejected and hated by his brothers, sold to a group of travelers in a caravan destined for Egypt, sold again as a common slave in the Egyptian market, falsely accused by Potiphar's wife, forgotten in a dungeon, and considered dead by his own father, this man was finally promoted to a position of high authority just beneath the Pharaoh. *If anybody ever had a reason to nurse his wounds and despise his past, Joseph was the man!*

But the amazing part of the story is this: He refused to remember the offenses. In fact, when he and his wife had their first child, he named the boy *Manasseh*, a Hebrew name that meant "forget." He explains the reason he chose the name:

And Joseph named the first-born Manasseh, "For," he said, "God has made me forget all my trouble and all my father's household" (Gen. 41:51).

His words include an extremely important point. In order for us to forget wrongs done against us, *God* must do the erasing.

Isaiah, the prophet of Judah, puts it in these terms:

Fear not, for you will not be put to shame;
Neither feel humiliated, for you will not be disgraced;
But you will forget the shame of your youth,
And the approach of your widowhood you will re-
member no more.
For your husband is your Maker,
Whose name is the Lord of hosts;
And your redeemer is the Holy One of Israel,
Who is called the God of all the earth (Isa. 54:4–5).

The Lord God promises us we can forget because He personally will take the place of those painful memories. To you who have had a shameful youth, to you who have lost your mate, the living Lord will replace those awful memories *with Himself*. Great promise! That makes the forgetting possible. Left to ourselves, no way! But with the promise that God will replace the pain with Himself—His presence, His power, His very life—we can "forget what lies behind."

There is yet another characteristic of good servants in addition to vulnerability and humility. It's implied in the words "I press on toward the goal . . ." (Phil. 3:14).

Determination

Those servants who refuse to get bogged down in and anchored to the past are those who pursue the objectives of the future. People who do this are seldom petty. They are too involved in getting a job done to be occupied with yesterday's hurts and concerns. Very near the end of his full and productive life, Paul wrote: "I have fought the good fight, I have finished the course, I have kept the faith" (2 Tim. 4:7). What a grand epitaph! He seized every day by the throat. He relentlessly pursued life.

I know human nature well enough to realize that some people excuse their bitterness over past hurts by thinking, "It's too late to change. I've been injured and the wrong done against me is too great for me ever to forget it. Maybe Paul could press on—not me!" A person with this mind-set is convinced that he or she is the exception to the truths of this chapter and is determined not to change because "life has dealt him or her a bad hand."

But when God holds out hope, when God makes promises, when God says, "It can be done," there are *no exceptions.* With each new dawn there is delivered to your door a fresh, new package called "today." God has designed us in such a way that we can handle only one package at a time . . . and all the grace we need will be supplied by Him as we live out that day.

I cannot recall reading a more moving illustration of this truth than the true story John Edmund Haggai tells regarding the tragic birth and life of his son. I share it with you in detail with the hope that at least one person will discover the all-important secret of pressing on one day at a time.

The Lord graciously blessed us with a precious son. He was paralyzed and able to sit in his wheelchair only with the assistance of full-length body braces. One of the nation's most respected gynecologists and obstetricians brought him into the world. Tragically, this man—overcome by grief—sought to find the answer in a bourbon bottle rather than in a blessed Bible. Due to the doctor's intoxication at the time of delivery, he inexcusably bungled his responsibility. Several of the baby's bones were broken. His leg was pulled out at the growing center. Needless abuse—resulting in hemorrhaging of the brain—was inflicted upon the little fellow. (Let me pause long enough to say that this is no indictment upon doctors. I thank God for doctors. This man was a tragic exception. He was banned from practice in some hospitals, and, as mentioned previously, he committed suicide.)

During the first year of the little lad's life, eight doctors said he could not possibly survive. For the first two years of his life my wife had to feed him every three hours with a Brecht feeder. It took a half hour to prepare for the feeding and it took another half hour to clean up and put him back to bed. Not once during that time did she ever get out of the house for any diversion whatsoever. Never did she get more than two hours sleep at one time.

My wife, formerly Christine Barker of Bristol, Virginia, had once been acclaimed by some of the nation's leading musicians as one of the outstanding contemporary female vocalists in America. From the time she was thirteen she had been popular as a singer—and constantly in the public eye. Hers was the experience of receiving and rejecting some fancy offers with even fancier incomes to marry an aspiring Baptist pastor with no church to pastor!

Then, after five years of marriage, tragedy struck! The whole episode was so unnecessary. Eight of the nation's leading doctors said that our son could not survive. From a life of public service she was now marooned within the walls of our home. Her beautiful voice no longer enraptured public audiences with the story of Jesus, but was now silenced, or at best, muted to the subdued humming of lullabies.

Had it not been from her spiritual maturity whereby she laid hold of the resources of God and lived one day at a time, this heart-rending experience would long since have caused an emotional breakdown.

John Edmund, Jr., our little son, lived more than twenty years. We rejoice that he committed his heart and life to Jesus Christ and gave evidence of a genuine concern for the things of the Lord. I attribute his commitment to Jesus Christ and his wonderful disposition to the sparkling radiance of an emotionally mature, Christ-centered mother who has mastered the discipline of living one day at a time. Never have I—nor has anyone else—heard a word of complaint from her. The people who know her concur that at thirty-five years of age and after having been subjected to more grief than many people twice her age, she possessed sparkle that would be the envy of any high school senior and the radiance and charm for which any debutante would gladly give a fortune.

Seize today. Live for today. Wring it dry of every opportunity.[6]

A CHALLENGE: TWO QUESTIONS

In these last three chapters we have considered the servant in three separate yet related roles: as a giver, as a forgiver, and as a forgetter. Of the three, I honestly believe the third is the most exacting. The other two bring with them benefits and blessings that encourage us almost immediately. But forgetting is something shared with no other person. It's a solo flight. And all the rewards are postponed until eternity . . . but how great they will be on that day! Forgetting requires the servant to think correctly—something we'll deal with in the next chapter—which means our full focus must be on the Lord and not on humanity. By God's great grace, it can happen.

Before reading on, let's pause long enough to ask ourselves two questions:

1. Is there someone or something I have refused to forget, which keeps me from being happy and productive?

If your answer is yes, stop and declare it openly to your Lord, asking Him to take way the pain and the bitterness.

2. Am I a victim of self-pity, living out my days emotionally paralyzed in anguish and despair?

If your answer is yes, stop and consider the consequences of living the rest of your life excusing your depression rather than turning it all over to the only One who can remove it.

And lest you are still convinced it's "too late" . . . you are "too old to change" . . . your situation is "too much to overcome," just listen to these immortal lines from Longfellow:

> "It is too late!" Ah, nothing is too late—
> Cato learned Greek at eighty; Sophocles
> Wrote his grand "Oedipus," and Simonides
> Bore off the prize of verse from his compeers
> When each had numbered more than fourscore years;
> And Theophrastus, at fourscore and ten,
> Had begun his "Characters of Men."
> Chaucer, at Woodstock, with his nightingales,
> At sixty wrote the "Canterbury Tales."
> Goethe, at Weimar, toiling to the last,
> Completed "Faust" when eighty years were past.
> What then? Shall we sit idly down and say,
> "The night has come; it is no longer day"?
> For age is opportunity no less
> Than youth itself, though in another dress.
> And as the evening twilight fades away,
> The sky is filled with stars, invisible by day.

It is never too late to start doing what is right. Never.

6

Thinking Like
a Servant Thinks

About now, some of you may be getting a little nervous.

All this talk about serving and giving and releasing rights and putting down self sounds okay for a while. It's part of the whole Christian package. It's expected, to an extent. But isn't it possible to go overboard on stuff like this? Aren't there some people who will take advantage of servants and turn them into slaves? You bet there are!

NOT MIND-CONTROL SLAVERY

In fact, that is the ace trump among cultic leaders. The secret of their success is mind control. They want your mind, and they are not satisfied until they have absolute control over it. The ultimate control is behavior modification, which is just another word for brainwashing. A perfect example? The People's Temple under the the twisted leadership of the late Jim Jones. May God help us *never* to forget that whole tragic episode!

Jack Sparks calls these cultic leaders "mindbenders," an appropriate title. In his book he describes the common method of mind control as a three-step program—not three steps in sequence, but three steps that occur simultaneously.

Step 1 is "deprogramming" . . . convincing you that your past is all wrong. What you always thought was right is wrong, wrong, wrong!

Step 2 calls for the complete subjugation of the will. This takes time. During the process a cult member learns the technique of putting the mind into neutral, sort of a "freewheeling" experience—perfect preparation for the third step.

Step 3 is the "reprogramming" phase. It is concentrated, intensive teaching (*indoctrination* is a better word) designed to replace old concepts with new ones.[1]

The result, of course, is a far cry from the role of a servant we've been considering. That form of cultic mind bending turns a human being into a puppet, a slave without personal dignity, without the privilege to think and to ask questions, and without the joy of serving others willingly under the control and authority of Jesus Christ. The thought of being enslaved to a guru and his or her demanding system of thought is something that ought to strike fear into all of us. If you question that, I suggest you read the incredible story of Christopher Edwards as he became a helpless pawn in the hands of one of the most insidious cults on the rise today. Not until the man was kidnapped was there any hope of recovery.

This bright, clear-thinking Yale graduate became virtually a glob of human putty in the hands of the "Moonies" in Northern California. Without realizing what was happening to him, the cultic system took him through the three-step process I just described. After his father and a group of trained professionals finally snatched him from the tight fist of that cult, it took a full year of intense therapy before Chris regained his equilibrium. He tells it all in his book *Crazy for God.*[2]

No, blind loyalty is not servanthood. Believe me, not only am I strongly opposed to the "mind bending" employed by cultic leaders, I see dangers in other ministries that take unfair advantage of people—ministries we'd certainly not think of as cults. *Any* ministry that requires blind loyalty and unquestioning obedience is suspect. Not all gurus are in the eastern religions, you know. Some discipleship ministries, quite frankly, come dangerously near this point. Now I am not discrediting all discipleship programs! To do so would be unfair. As a matter of fact, I personally benefited from an outstanding discipling ministry many years ago. Furthermore, we encourage a broad discipleship program in our own church here in Fullerton, California. My main concern is the abuse of power, overemphasis of loyalty to a human leader, an intense and unhealthy accountability that uses intimidation, fear, and guilt to promote authoritarianism. Weak and meek people can become the prey of such paranoid, self-appointed messiahs, resulting not in spiritual growth, but in exploitation and the loss of human dignity.

Ronald M. Enroth describes it rather well:

> For people who have lacked positive structure in their lives, who have difficulty making decisions or resolving conflicts or who are just plain uncertain about the future, these movements/churches/programs are a haven.
>
> The leaders of many of these groups consciously foster an unhealthy form of dependency, spiritually and otherwise, but focusing on themes of submission and obedience to those in authority. They create the impression that people just aren't going to find their way through life's maze without a lot of firm directives from those at the top.[3]

People in the pew and pastors alike need to beware of "bionic" leaders with an abundance of charisma. We need to watch out for the highly gifted, capable, winsome, and popular superstars who focus attention on themselves or their organization. Rather, the true leader must consciously turn people's devotion and worship to the Head of the body—Jesus Christ. The Savior is the Lord. He shares that preeminent place of authority and glory with none other.

> And He is before all things, and in Him all things hold together.
> He is also head of the body, the church; and He is the beginning, the first-born from the dead; so that He Himself might come to have first place in everything. . . .
> And we proclaim Him, admonishing every man and teaching every man with all wisdom, that we may present every man complete in Christ (Col. 1:17–18, 28).

A "Renewed Mind" Is Essential

With that cleared up we are now ready for some positive input on the correct mentality of a servant. Is it possible to think so much like Christ that our minds operate on a different plane than others around us? Not only is it possible—it's essential!

The familiar words of Paul in Romans 12:1–2 need to be reviewed.

> I urge you therefore, brethren, by the mercies of God, to present your bodies a living and holy sacrifice, acceptable to God, which is your spiritual service of worship.
> And do not be conformed to this world, but be transformed by the renewing of your mind, that you may prove that the will of God is, that which is good and acceptable and perfect.

At this point in his letter to the believers in Rome, Paul drops to his knees, as it were, and *pleads*. That means it's important, perhaps one of the most important truths he would ever write. After urging us to present ourselves to God as living sacrifices, he adds a warning:

> Don't let the world around you squeeze you into his own mold, but let God remold your minds from within, so that you may prove in practice that the plan of God for you is good, meets all his demands and moves toward the goal of true maturity (Rom. 12:2, PHILLIPS).

Stop being squeezed in! Quit aping the system of thought that surrounds you, its line of reasoning, its method of operation, its style and techniques! How? By a radical transformation within. By a renewed thought pattern that demonstrates authentic godlikeness. Living differently begins with thinking differently. A life that is characterized by serving others begins in a mind that is convinced of such a life. That explains why that great section of Scripture describing Christ's willingness to take upon Himself the form of a servant begins with the words: "Let this mind be in you, which was also in Christ Jesus . . ." (Phil. 2:5, KJV).

Jesus' life of serving was the outworking of His mind—"unsqueezed" by the world system in all its selfishness—and remains, forever, our example to follow. For *us* to be true servants, our minds must be renewed.

NATURAL THINKING IN TODAY'S WORLD

Instead of flashing from one scripture to another, let's settle in on a single passage and digest it carefully. One of the most helpful on the subject of the mind is 2 Corinthians 10:1–7. Take a few moments to read and meditate on these seven verses.

> Now I, Paul myself urge you by the meekness and gentleness of Christ,—I who am meek when face to face with you, but bold toward you when absent!—
>
> I ask that when I am present I may not be bold with the confidence with which I propose to be courageous against some, who regard us as if we walked according to the flesh.
>
> For though we walk in the flesh, we do not war according to the flesh, for the weapons of our warfare are not of the flesh, but divinely powerful for the destruction of fortresses.
>
> We are destroying speculations and every lofty thing raised up against the knowledge of God, and we are taking every thought captive to the obedience of Christ, and we are ready to punish all disobedience, whenever your obedience is complete.
>
> You are looking at things as they are outwardly. If any one is confident in himself that he is Christ's, let him consider this again within himself, that just as he is Christ's, so also are we.

The Corinthian Christians were an ornery lot! Although born again, they often operated in the realm of carnality because they had a secular mentality. To borrow from Romans 12, they were "in the mold" of the world system . . . their minds were "unrenewed." At times you would have sworn they weren't even in the family of God. For example, they fought with one another, they criticized Paul, they were competitive in the church, and they winked at gross immorality in their midst.

In this section of Paul's letter to them, he points out several of the ways they revealed natural thinking. I find five characteristics:
1. They were prejudiced instead of objective (v. 2).
2. They focused on the visible rather than the invisible (v. 3).
3. They relied on human strength, not divine power (v. 4).
4. They listened to men instead of God (v. 5).
5. They perceived things superficially rather than deeply (v. 7).

When our carnality is in gear, Paul's comments aptly describe our mind-set: surface judgment, shallow thinking, lack of depth, closed, independent, overly impressed with humanity, spiritually out of focus. When we get "squeezed into the mold," the world does a number on us, doesn't it?

Mental Barriers to God's Voice

Actually, God's message gets muffled. Our minds pick up on the strong secular signals so easily that we subconsciously tune Him out. It comes naturally. The passage in 2 Corinthians 10 sets forth a vivid description of the mental barriers that block out His directives and His counsel.

Look closely. Four terms are used by Paul which we need to understand. If you have a pencil handy, circle each in your Bible: *fortress . . . speculations . . . lofty thing . . . thought.*

A little historical background is needed. In ancient days a city, in order to prosper, needed a security system to protect it from enemy attack. Of primary importance was a wall which restrained enemy troops from invading and which also served as a major means of defense in battle. Guards needed to be on constant watch from their sentinel posts on the wall. There needed to be towers within the city high enough for those inside to see over the wall. And finally at the time of attack, men of military savvy and battle knowledge were needed to give orders and to direct the troops in the heat of combat from within the protection of those towers.

Paul drew a series of analogies from that familiar scene of his day . . . but remember, he's not dealing with a city, but rather with our minds.

Analogy No. 1: The Wall, Our Mental "Fortress"

As the Spirit of God attempts to communicate His truth to us (biblical information on servanthood, for example), He runs up against our "wall," our overall mental attitude, our natural mind-set. For some it's prejudice. With others, it's limited thinking or a negative mentality. Whatever, it is a huge mental barrier that resists divine input just as firmly as a massive stone wall once resisted the invading troops. We all have our *fortresses*. And occasionally we get downright obnoxious as we operate under the control of our "walled fortress."

A tramp discovered that one day when he was looking for a handout in a picturesque old English village. Hungry almost to the point of fainting, he stopped by a pub bearing the classic name, *Inn of St. George and the Dragon.*

"Please, ma'am, could you spare me a bite to eat?" he asked the lady who answered his knock at the kitchen door.

"A bite to eat?" she growled. "For a sorry, no-good bum—a foul-smelling beggar? No!" she snapped as she almost slammed the door on his hand.

Halfway down the lane the tramp stopped, turned around, and eyed the words, *St. George and the Dragon.* He went back and knocked again on the kitchen door.

"Now what do you want?" the woman asked angrily.

"Well, ma'am, if St. George is in, may I speak with *him* this time?"

Ouch.

Analogy No. 2: The Guards, Our Mental "Speculations"

Along with the wall-like fortresses, we have natural, humanistic reasonings that give the wall additional strength—defense mechanisms, rationalization, and other thinking patterns that are habitual to us. In Romans 2:15 we read of two such "guards"—*blaming* and *justifying*. One reliable authority states that the Greek term translated *speculation* suggests "the contemplation of actions as a result of the verdict of conscience."

As the Lord God pushes His truth to enter (and thus "renew") our minds, our habitual reflex "guards" the entrance of such alien thoughts! This explains why there is often such a battle that rages when biblical truth is introduced into a mind that has been walled and guarded by years of secularized thinking. We defend the old rather than consider and accept the new.

This could have happened in your own mind when you read chapter 4 on forgiveness. You read what the Bible teaches us to do when we have offended someone. More than likely, you found yourself resisting and defending. I certainly did when I first discovered those truths! We would much rather blame the other person than accept our responsibility. Our "speculations" work like that. They put up a guard against change, causing us to rationalize and justify our actions.

Analogy No. 3: The Towers, Our Mental "Lofty Things"

Accompanying the resistance of our internal wall and guards are "lofty things" that reinforce our defense system from within. It's the idea of a thing lifted up or exalted. What comes to your mind right now? How about *pride*? And those things pride prompts: argumentation, an unteachable spirit, stubbornness, and refusal to change. As the principles of the Scripture are declared, our natural, unrenewed minds not only resist them, they ask, "Who needs that?" or "I've gotten along pretty good up 'til now." Lofty things—things that are "raised up against the knowledge of God," as Paul put it (2 Cor. 10:5).

Analogy No. 4: The Strategic Men, Our Mental "Thoughts"

Along with the mental wall of habitual resistance, the humanistic reasonings that give it strength, and the proud, lofty reactions that keep the truths of Scripture at arm's length, there are actual thoughts, techniques, devices we employ that push away his Word and His promptings. For example, we have formed the habit of getting even rather than overlooking wrong done against us. So when we come across scriptural instruction that suggests an alternate plan, our inner reaction is "No way!" When God's counsel encourages us to be generous, to release rather than keep, we can think of half a dozen reasons it won't work. It's like having a "Murphy's Law" mentality that is immediately ready to spring into action. This keeps us from deciding favorably toward God.

A vital point I don't want you to miss is that we really have no reason whatsoever to keep serving our secular mentality. We have been freed. Gloriously freed! Before salvation we had no hope. We were victims of all those impulses and defenses within us. But at the cross, our Savior and Lord defeated the enemy. He said, "It is finished," *and it was!* No longer does sin reign as victor. But, you see, our old nature doesn't want us to believe that. It resists *all* messages that would give us freedom. "All *renewed mind* information is to be muffled," commands the old man within us. And with every effort, he puts up a wall, guards, towers, and thoughts to turn all such input away.

And do you realize what our old nature resists the most? It is revealed in verse 5 of 2 Corinthians 10: ". . . taking every thought captive to the obedience of Christ." When that happens, the "renewed mind" is in full operation . . . and it is marvelous! At that moment servanthood is neither irksome nor a thing to be feared. It flows freely.

Listen to a story—fictitious though it is—that Larry Christenson tells. It will help you understand the victory a "renewed mind" provides:

> Think of yourself as living in an apartment house. You live there under a landlord who has made your life miserable. He charges you exorbitant rent. When you can't pay, he loans you money at a fearful rate of interest, to get you even further into his debt. He barges into your apartment at all hours of the day and night, wrecks and dirties the place up, then charges you extra for not maintaining the premises. Your life is miserable.
>
> Then comes Someone who says, "I've taken over this apartment house. I've purchased it. You can live here as long as you like, free. The rent is paid up. I am going to be living here with you, in the manager's apartment."
>
> What a joy! You are saved! You are delivered out of the clutches of the old landlord!
>
> But what happens? You hardly have time to rejoice in your new-found freedom, when a knock comes at the door. And there he is—the old landlord! Mean, glowering, and demanding as ever. He has come for the rent, he says.
>
> What do you do? Do you pay him? Of course, you don't! Do you go out and pop him on the nose? No—he's bigger than you are!
>
> You confidently tell him. "You'll have to take that up with the new Landlord." He may bellow, threaten, wheedle, and cajole. You just quietly tell him. "Take it up with the new Landlord." If he comes back a dozen times, with all sorts of threats and arguments, waving legal-looking documents in your face, you simply tell him yet once again, "Take it up with the new Landlord." In the end he has to. He knows it, too. He just hopes that he can bluff and threaten and deceive you into doubting that the new Landlord will really take care of things.
>
> Now this is the situation of a Christian. Once Christ has delivered you from the power of sin and the devil, you can depend on it: that old landlord will soon come back knocking at your door. And what is your defense? How do you keep him from getting the whip hand over you again? You send him to the new Landlord. *You send him to Jesus.*[5]

When Jesus Christ truly takes charge of our minds, bringing our every thought captive to Him, we become spirtually invincible. We operate with supernatural power. We walk under God's complete control.

SUPERNATURAL ABILITY OF THE "RENEWED MIND"

As God's truth penetrates, displacing those mental barriers, we receive several very exciting benefits. In fact, I find two of them named by Paul right here in the 2 Corinthians 10 passage—divine power (v. 4) and authentic independence (vv. 11-12).

We get the distinct impression while reading these verses that nothing on this earth can intimidate us. The New International Version helps clarify this supernatural ability of the "renewed mind":

> For though we live in the world, we do not wage war as the world does. The weapons we fight with are not the weapons of the world. On the contrary, they have divine power to demolish strongholds. We demolish arguments and every pretension that sets itself up against the knowledge of God, and we take captive every thought to make it obedient to Christ (2 Cor. 10:3-5).

Divine Power

Did you catch the reality of divine power in verse 4? Servants with renewed minds have a perspective on life and a power to live life that is altogether unique—divinely empowered.

That explains how wrongs can be forgiven, and how offenses can be forgotten, and how objectives can be pursued day in and day out without our quitting. It's divine power. God promises that He will pour His power into us (Phil. 4:13) and supply all we need if we will simply operate under His full control. When we think correctly we instantly begin to respond correctly.

How can we "demolish" those things that once blew us away? With Christ living out His very life through ours, that's how. By His power we can give ourselves away again and again and again. And we won't fear the outcome. We won't even feel slighted when we don't get the same treatment in return. Servants, remember, don't "keep score." Dale Galloway tells a story in *Dream a New Dream* that beautifully illustrates this point.

Little Chad was a shy, quiet young fella. One day he came home and told his mother he'd like to make a valentine for everyone in his class. Her heart sank. She thought, "I wish he wouldn't do that!" because she had watched the children when they walked home from school. Her Chad was always behind them. They laughed and hung on to each other and talked to each other. But Chad was never included. Nevertheless, she decided she would go along with her son. So she purchased the paper and glue and crayons. For three whole weeks, night after night, Chad painstakingly made thirty-five valentines.

Valentine's Day dawned, and Chad was beside himself with excitement! He carefully stacked them up, put them in a bag, and bolted out the door. His mom decided to bake him his favorite cookies and serve them up warm and nice with a cool glass of milk when he came home from school. She just knew he would be disappointed . . . maybe that would ease the pain a little. It hurt her to think he wouldn't get many valentines—maybe none at all.

That afternoon she had the cookies and milk on the table. When she heard the children outside she looked out the window. Sure enough here they came, laughing and having the best time. And, as always, there was Chad in the rear. He walked a little faster than usual. She fully expected him to burst into tears as soon as he got inside. His arms were empty, she noticed, and when the door opened she choked back the tears.

"Mommy has some warm cookies and milk for you."

But he hardly heard her words. He just marched right on by, his face aglow, and all he could say was:

"Not a one . . . not a one."

Her heart sank.

And then he added, "I didn't forget a one, not a single one!"[6]

So it is when God is in control of the servant's mind. We realize as never before that life's greatest joy is to give His love away—a thought that brings to mind the saying:

> It isn't a song until it's sung.
> It isn't a bell until it's rung,
> It isn't love until it's given away!

Authentic Independence

Look at verses 11 and 12 in 2 Corinthians 10:

Let such a person consider this, that what we are in word by letters when absent, such persons we are also in deed when present.

For we are not bold to class or compare ourselves with some of those who commend themselves; but when they measure themselves by themselves, and compare themselves with themselves, they are without understanding.

Isn't that refreshing? No masks of hypocrisy. Not in competition with other believers—not even caught in the trap of comparing himself with others. It all comes to those with a "renewed mind" . . . those who determine they are going to allow the Spirit of God to invade all those walls and towers, capturing the guards that have kept Him at arm's length all these years.

I can't recall the precise date when these truths began to fall into place, but I distinctly remember how I began to change deep within. My fierce tendency to compete with others started to diminish. My insecure need to win—*always* win—also started to fade. Less and less was I interested in comparing myself with other speakers and pastors. This growing, healthy independence freed me to be *me*, not a mixture of what I thought others expected me to be. And now my heart really goes out to others when I see in them that misery-making "comparison syndrome" that held me in its grip for so many years. Not until I started thinking biblically did this independent identity begin to take shape.

SERVANTHOOD STARTS IN THE MIND

Wouldn't you love to live courageously in spite of the odds? Doesn't it sound exciting to be divinely powerful in day-to-day living? Aren't you anxious to become independently authentic in a day of copy-cat styles and horrendous peer pressure? Of course!

It all begins in *the mind*. Let me repeat it one more time: Thinking right always precedes acting right. That is why I have emphasized throughout this chapter the importance of the renewed mind. It is really impossible to grasp the concept of serving others—or to carry it out with joy, without fear—until our minds are freed from the world's mold and transformed by the Lord's power.

I began this chapter with a warning against falling under the spell of a mind-controlling guru. Hopefully, there is no misunderstanding with where I stand on that twisted concept of exploiting others yet calling it servanthood. I feel the need, however, to end with another warning. Not against becoming a victim of some strong personality . . . but against anyone who might "use" others to accomplish his purposes. How easy it is to encourage servanthood so others might serve us. That is not the way our Master walked and neither should we.

I admire the honesty of the man who wrote these words:

> I am like James and John.
> Lord, I size up other people
>   in terms of what they can do for me;
>   how they can further my program,
>   feed my ego,
>   satisfy my needs,
>   give me strategic advantage.
>
> I exploit people,
>   ostensibly for your sake,
>   but really for my own sake.
>
> Lord, I turn to you
>   to get the inside track
>   and obtain special favors,
>   your direction for my schemes,
>   your power for my projects,

> your sanction for my ambitions,
> your blank check for whatever I want.
> I am like James and John.
> Change me, Lord.
> Make me a man who asks of you and of
> others,
> what can I do for you?[7]

Servanthood starts in the mind. With a simple prayer of three words: "Change *me*, Lord."

7

Portrait
of a Servant,
Part One

What do you want to be when you grow up?

That's a favorite question we enjoy asking children. And the answers we get usually are "a policeman" or "a nurse" or maybe "a fireman." Some kids are visionary. They answer "a movie star" or "a singer" or "a doctor" or "a professional ball player." One recently told me he wanted to be either a car mechanic or a garbage collector. When I asked why, he gave the classic answer for a nine-year-old: *"So I can get dirty!"* I smiled as I had a flashback to my own childhood. And I understood.

Let's take that same question and ask it another way. Let's imagine asking Jesus Christ what He wants us to be when we grow up. Suddenly, it's a whole new question. I honestly believe He would give the same answer to every one of us: "I want you to be different . . . to be a servant." In all my life I cannot recall anybody ever saying that when he grew up he wanted to be a servant.

It sounds lowly . . . humiliating . . . lacking in dignity.

In his helpful book, *Honesty, Morality, & Conscience*, Jerry White talks about the concept of serving others.

> Christians are to be servants of both God and people. But most of us approach business and work—and life in general—with the attitude "What can I *get?*" rather than "What can I *give?*"

> We find it encouraging to think of ourselves as God's servants. Who would not want to be a servant of the King? But when it comes to serving other people, we begin to question the consequences. We feel noble when serving God; we feel

humble when serving people. Serving God receives a favorable response; serving people, especially those who cannot repay, has no visible benefit or glory from anyone—except from God! Christ gave us the example: "The Son of Man did not come to be served, but to serve, and to give His life as a ransom for many" (Matt. 20:28). To be a servant of God we must be a servant of people.

In business and work the concept of serving people must undergird all that we do. When we serve we think first of the one we are trying to serve. An employee who serves honestly in his work honors God and deepens his value to his employer. On the other hand, the self-serving employee will seldom be valued in any company.[1]

JESUS' COMMAND: "BE DIFFERENT!"

When Jesus walked the earth, He attracted a number of people to Himself. On one occasion, He sat down among them and taught them some bottom-line truths about how He wanted them to grow up. The scriptual account of His "Sermon on the Mount" is found in Matthew 5, 6, and 7. If I were asked to suggest an overall theme of this grand sermon, it would be— "Be different!" Time and again He states the way things were among the religious types of their day, and then He instructs them to be different. For example:

Matthew 5:21–22: "You have heard . . . but I say to you. . . ."
Matthew 5:27–28: "You have heard . . . but I say to you. . . ."
Matthew 5:33–34: "Again, you have heard . . . but I say to you. . . ."
Matthew 5:38–39: "You have heard . . . but I say to you. . . ."
Matthew 5:43–44: "You have heard . . . but I say to you. . . ."

In Matthew 6, He further explains how they were to be different when they gave to the needy (6:2), and when they prayed (6:5) and when they fasted (6:16). The key verse in the entire sermon is, *"Therefore, do not be like them . . ."* (6:8). You see, Jesus saw through all the pride and hypocrisy of others and was determined to instill in His disciples character traits of humility and authenticity. His unique teaching cut through the façade of religion like a sharp knife through warm butter. It remains to this day the most comprehensive delineation in all the New Testament of the Christian counterculture . . . offering a lifestyle totally at variance with the world system.

In the introduction of Jesus' sermon, doubtlessly the most familiar section is found in Matthew 5:1–12. Commonly called "The Beatitudes," this section is the most descriptive word-portrait of a servant ever recorded.

THE BEATITUDES: THREE OBSERVATIONS

Let's reread these immortal words slowly:

And when He saw the multitudes, He went up on the mountain; and after He sat down, His disciples came to Him.

And opening His mouth He began to teach them, saying, "Blessed are the poor in spirit, for theirs is the kingdom of heaven.

"Blessed are those who mourn, for they shall be comforted.

"Blessed are the gentle, for they shall inherit the earth.

"Blessed are those who hunger and thirst for righteousness, for they shall be satisfied.

"Blessed are the merciful, for they shall receive mercy.

"Blessed are the pure in heart, for they shall see God.

"Blessed are the peacemakers, for they shall be called sons of God.

"Blessed are those who have been persecuted for the sake of righteousness, for theirs is the kingdom of heaven.

"Blessed are you when men revile you, and persecute you, and say all kinds of evil against you falsely, on account of Me.

"Rejoice, and be glad, for your reward in heaven is great, for so they persecuted the prophets who were before you" (Matt. 5:1–12).

Let me suggest three general observations:

1. **These are eight character traits that identify true servanthood.** When all eight are mixed together in a life, balance emerges. It is helpful to realize this is not a "multiple choice" list where we are free to pick and choose our favorites. Our Savior has stated very clearly those qualities that lead to a different lifestyle which pleases Him. A close examination of each is therefore essential.

2. **These traits open the door to inner happiness.** Here are the fundamental attitudes which, when pursued and experienced, bring great satisfaction. Jesus offers fulfillment here like nothing else on earth. Study how each begins: "Blessed are. . . ." This is the only time our Lord repeated the same term eight times consecutively. J. B. Phillips' translation picks up the thought correctly as he renders it "How happy" and "Happy." Those who enter into these attitudes find lasting happiness.

3. **Attached to each character trait is a corresponding promise.** Did you notice this? "Blessed are . . . (the trait) for . . ." (the promise). Christ holds out a particular benefit for each particular quality. And what great promises they are! Small wonder when He finished the sermon we read:

The result was . . . the multitudes were amazed at His teaching; for He was teaching them as one having authority, and not as their scribes (Matt. 7:28–29).

Never before had His audience heard such marvelous truth presented in such an interesting and meaningful manner. They longed to have those promises incarnate in their lives. So do we.

An Analysis of Four Beatitudes

So much for the survey. Let's get specific. Rather than hurrying through all eight in a superficial manner, let's work our way through these first four qualities with care. We'll look at the next four in chapter 8. We shall be able to understand both the subtle shading and the rich color of the portrait painted by Jesus for all to appreciate and apply if we take our time and think through each servant characteristic.

"The Poor in Spirit"

At first glance, this seems to refer to those who have little or no money— people of poverty with zero financial security. Wrong. You'll note He speaks of being ". . . poor *in spirit* . . ." (italics mine). One helpful authority, William Barclay, clarifies the meaning:

> These words in Hebrew underwent a four-stage development of meaning. (i) They began by meaning simply *poor*. (ii) They went on to mean, *because poor, therefore having no influence or power, or help, or prestige.* (iii) They went on to mean, *because having no influence, therefore down-trodden and oppressed by men.* (iv) Finally, they came to describe *the man who, because he has no earthly resources whatever, puts his whole trust in God.* So in Hebrew the word *poor* was used to describe the humble and the helpless man who put his whole trust in God.[2]

This is an attitude of absolute, unvarnished humility. What an excellent way to begin the servant's portrait! It is the portrait of one who sees himself/herself as spiritually bankrupt, deserving of nothing . . . who turns to Almighty God in total trust. Augustus M. Toplady caught a glimpse of this attitude when he wrote these words that became a part of the church's hymnody:

> Nothing in my hand I bring,
> Simply to Thy cross I cling;
> Naked, come to Thee for dress,
> Helpless, look to Thee for grace;
> Foul, I to the fountain fly,
> Wash me, Saviour, or I die![3]

This spirit of humility is very rare in our day of strong-willed, proud-as-a-peacock attitudes. The clinched fist has replaced the bowed head. The big mouth and the surly stare now dominate the scene once occupied by the quiet godliness of the "poor in spirit." How self-righteous we have become! How confident in and of ourselves! And with that attitude, how desperately unhappy we are! Christ Jesus offers genuine, lasting happiness to those whose hearts willingly declare:

Oh, Lord
I am a shell full of dust,
    but animated with an invisible rational soul
    and made anew by an unseen power of grace;
Yet I am no rare object of valuable price,
    but one that has nothing and is nothing,
    although chosen of thee from eternity,
        given to Christ, and born again;
I am deeply convinced of the evil and misery of a
    sinful state,
    of the vanity of creatures,
    but also of the sufficiency of Christ.
When thou wouldst guide me I control myself,
When thou wouldst be sovereign I rule myself.
When thou wouldst take care of me I suffice myself.
When I should depend on thy providings I supply
    myself,
When I should submit to thy providence I follow
    my will,
When I should study, love, honour, trust thee, I
    serve myself
I fault and correct thy laws to suit myself,
Instead of thee I look to man's approbation,
    and am by nature an idolater.
Lord, it is my chief design to bring my heart
    back to thee.
Convince me that I cannot be my own god, or make
    myself happy,
    nor my own Christ to restore my joy,
    nor my own Spirit to teach, guide, rule me.
Help me to see that grace does this by providential
    affliction,
    for when my credit is god thou dost cast me
        lower,
    when riches are my idol thou dost wing them
        away,
    when pleasure is my all thou dost turn it
        into bitterness.
Take away my roving eye, curious ear, greedy appetite,
    lustful heart;
Show me that none of these things
    can heal a wounded conscience,
    or support a tottering frame,
    or uphold a departing spirit.
Then take me to the cross and leave me there.[4]

A special promise follows the trait of spiritual helplessness: ". . . for theirs is the kingdom of heaven," says Jesus. The indispensable condition of receiving a part in the kingdom of heaven is acknowledging our spiritual poverty. The person with a servant's heart—not unlike a child trusting completely in his parent's provision—is promised a place in Christ's kingdom. The *opposite* attitude is clearly revealed in that Laodicean congregation, where Christ rebuked them with severe words. They were so proud, they were blind to their own selfishness:

> I know your deeds, that you are neither cold nor hot; I would that you were cold or hot.
>
> So because you are lukewarm, and neither hot nor cold, I will spit you out of My mouth.
>
> Because you say, "I am rich, and have become wealthy, and have need of nothing," and you do not know that you are wretched and miserable and poor and blind and naked (Rev. 3:15–17).

Chances are good that there wasn't a servant in the whole lot at Laodicea.

First and foremost in the life of an authentic servant is a deep, abiding dependency on the living Lord. On the basis of that attitude, the kingdom of heaven is promised.

"Those Who Mourn"

Matthew, in recording Christ's teaching, chose the strongest Greek term in all his vocabulary when he wrote *mourn*. It is a heavy word—a passionate lament for one who was loved with profound devotion. It conveys the sorrow of a broken heart, the ache of soul, the anguished mind. It could include several scenes:

- Mourning over wrong in the world
- Mourning over personal loss
- Mourning over one's own wrong and sinfulness
- Mourning over the death of someone close.

Interestingly, this particular term also includes compassion, a sincere caring for others. Perhaps a satisfactory paraphrase would read: "How happy are those who care intensely for the hurts and sorrows and losses of others. . . ." At the heart of this character trait is COMPASSION, another servant attitude so desperately needed today.

Several years ago one of the men in our church fell while taking an early morning shower. As he slipped on the slick floor he fell against a sheet of glass with all his weight. The splintering glass stabbed deeply into his arm at and around his bicep. Blood spurted all over the bathroom. Paramedics arrived quickly with lights flashing, sirens screaming, and the "squawk box" blaring from within the cab. The man was placed on a stretcher as the family hurriedly raced against time to get him to the emergency ward nearby. Thankfully, his life was saved and he has fully recovered.

As I spoke with his wife about the ordeal, she told me not one neighbor even looked out his door, not to mention stopping by to see if they needed help. Not one . . . then or later. They showed no compassion by their lack of "mutual mourning." How unlike our Savior! We are told that:

> . . . we do not have a high priest who cannot sympathize with our weaknesses, but one who has been tempted in all things as we are, yet without sin (Heb. 4:15).

True servants are like their Lord, compassionate.

And the promise for those who "mourn"? The Saviour promises ". . . they shall be comforted." In return, comfort will be theirs to claim. I find it significant that no mention is made of the source or the channel. Simply, it *will* come. Perhaps from the same one the servant cared for back when there was a need. It is axiomatic—there can be little comfort where there has been no grief.

Thus far we've found two attitudes in true servants—extreme dependence and strong compassion. There is more, much more.

"The Gentle"

The third character trait Jesus includes in His portrait of a servant is gentleness. *"Blessed are the gentle, for they shall inherit the earth"* (v. 5).

Immediately, we may get a false impression. We think "Blessed are the weak for they shall become doormats." In our rough-and-rugged individualism, we think of gentleness as weakness, being soft, and virtually spineless. Not so! The Greek term is extremely colorful, helping us grasp a correct understanding of why the Lord sees the need for servants to be gentle.

It is used several ways in extrabiblical literature:

- A wild stallion that has been tamed, brought under control, is described as being "gentle."
- Carefully chosen words that soothe strong emotions are referred to as "gentle" words.
- Ointment that takes the fever and sting out of a wound is called "gentle."
- In one of Plato's works, a child asks the physician to be tender as he treats him. The child uses this term "gentle."
- Those who are polite, who have tact and are courteous, and who treat others with dignity and respect are called "gentle" people.

So then, gentleness includes such enviable qualities as having strength under control, being calm and peaceful when surrounded by a heated atmosphere, emitting a soothing effect on those who may be angry or otherwise beside themselves, and possessing tact and gracious courtesy that causes others to retain their self-esteem and dignity. Clearly, it includes a Christlikeness, since the same word is used to describe His own makeup:

Come to Me, all who are weary and heavy laden, and I will give you rest.
Take My yoke upon you, and learn from Me, for I am gentle and humble in
heart; and YOU SHALL FIND REST FOR YOUR SOULS (Matt. 11:28–29).

And what does the promise mean ". . . *for they shall inherit the earth*"? It can
be understood as one of two ways—now or later. Either "they will ultimately
win out in this life" or "they will be given vast territories in the kingdom, to
judge and to rule." Instead of losing, the gentle *gain*. Instead of being ripped off
and taken advantage of, they come out ahead! David mentions this in one of his
greatest psalms (37:7–11):

> Rest in the Lord and wait patiently for Him;
> Fret not yourself because of him who prospers in his way,
> Because of the man who carries out wicked schemes.
> Cease from anger, and forsake wrath;
> Fret not yourself, it leads only to evildoing.
> For evildoers will be cut off,
> But those who wait for the Lord, they will inherit the land.
> Yet a little while and the wicked man will be no more;
> And you will look carefully for his place, and he will not be there.
> But the humble will inherit the land,
> And will delight themselves in abundant prosperity.

See the contrast?
From all outward appearance it seems as though the wicked win out. They
prosper in their way, their schemes work, their cheating and lying and unfair
treatment of others appear to pay off. They just seem to get richer and become
more and more powerful. As James Russell Lowell once put it:

> Truth forever on the scaffold
> Wrong forever on the throne.

But God says it won't be "forever." The ultimate victory will *not* be won
by the wicked. "The gentle" will win. Believe that, servant-in-the-making!
Be different from the system! Stay on the scaffold . . . trust your heavenly
Father to keep His promise regarding your inheritance. It is you who will be
blessed.
Before closing this chapter, I want us to consider another character trait of a
servant—the fourth in the list of eight.

"Those Who Hunger and Thirst for Righteousness"

The true servant possesses an insatiable appetite for what is right, a passionate drive for justice. Spiritually speaking, the servant is engaged in a pursuit of
God . . . a hot, restless, eager longing to walk with Him, to please Him.

Eleventh-century Bernard of Clairveaux expressed it in this way in his hymn, *Jesus, Thou Joy of Loving Hearts:*

> We taste Thee, O Thou living Bread,
> And long to feast upon Thee still;
> We drink of Thee, the Fountain-
>   head,
> And thirst our souls from Thee to
>   fill.⁵

Bernard's pen dripped with that insatiable appetite for God.

But there is a practical side of this fourth beatitude as well. It includes not just looking upward, pursuing a vertical holiness, but also looking around and being grieved over the corruption, the inequities, the gross lack of integrity, the moral compromises that abound. The servant "hungers and thirsts" for right on earth. Unwilling simply to sigh and shrug off the lack of justice and purity as inevitable, servants press on for righteousness. Some would call them idealists or dreamers.

One such person was Dag Hammarskjöld, former Secretary General of the United Nations, who died in a tragic airplane crash while flying over northern Rhodesia on a mission to negotiate a cease fire. In his fine book, *Markings*, the late statesman wrote:

> Hunger is my native place in the land of the passions. Hunger for fellowship, hunger for righteousness—for a fellowship founded on righteousness, and a righteousness attained in fellowship.
>
> Only life can satisfy the demands of life. And this hunger of mine can be satisfied for the simple reason that the nature of life is such that I can realize my individuality by becoming a bridge for others, a stone in the temple of righteousness.
>
> Don't be afraid of yourself, live your individuality to the full—but for the good of others. Don't copy others in order to buy fellowship, or make convention your law instead of living the righteousness.
>
> To become free and responsible. For this alone was man created. . . .⁶

And what will happen when this passionate appetite is a part of one's life? What does Jesus promise?

. . . they shall be satisfied.

A. T. Robertson, a Greek scholar of yesteryear, suggests the term *satisfied* is commonly used for feeding and fattening cattle, since it is derived from the term for fodder or grass.⁷ What a picture of contentment! Like well-fed, hefty livestock . . . contented in soul and satisfied within, the servant with an appetite for righteousness will be filled. It's comforting to hear that promise. Normally, one would think such an insatiable pursuit would make one so intense there would be only fretfulness and agitation. But, no, Jesus promises to bring a satisfaction to such hungry and thirsty souls . . . a "rest" of spirit that conveys quiet contentment.

Preliminary Summary and Questions

We are only halfway through the list, but it's a good place to stop and summarize what we have seen in this inspired portrait thus far. Jesus is describing how to be different, how to be His unique servant in a hostile, wicked world. He honors particular character traits and offers special rewards for each.

1. Those who are genuinely humble before God, who turn to Him in absolute dependence, will be assured of a place in His kingdom.

2. Those who show compassion on behalf of the needy, the hurting, will receive (in return) much comfort in their own lives.

3. Those who are gentle—strong within yet controlled without, who bring a soothing graciousness into irritating situations—will win out.

4. Those who have a passionate appetite for righteousness, both heavenly and earthly, will receive from the Lord an unusual measure of personal contentment and satisfaction.

Before examining the final four character traits of a servant in the next chapter, let's ask ourselves these questions (try to answer each one directly and honestly):

• Am I really different!
• Do I take all this seriously . . . so much so that I am willing to change?
• Is it coming through to me that serving others is one of the most Christlike attitudes I can have?
• What significant difference will the ideas expressed in this chapter have on my life?

The bottom-line question is not "What do you want to be when you grow up?" but "What are you becoming, now that you're grown?"

8

Portrait of a Servant, Part Two

You don't run through an art gallery; you walk very slowly. You often stop, study the treasured works of art, taking the time to appreciate what has been painted. You examine the texture, the technique, the choice and mixture of colors, the subtle as well as the bold strokes of the brush, the shadings. And the more valuable the canvas, the more time and thought it deserves. You may even return to it later for a further and deeper look, especially if you are a student of that particular artist.

In the gallery of His priceless work, the Lord God has included a portrait of vast value. It is the portrait of a servant carefully painted in words that take time to understand and appreciate. The frame in which the portrait has been placed is Jesus Christ's immortal Sermon on the Mount. We have examined a portion of the portrait already, but we are returning for another look, hoping to see more that will help us become the kind of persons the Artist has portrayed.

ANALYSIS OF FOUR MORE QUALITIES

In His word-portrait of a servant, Christ emphasizes eight characteristics or qualities. We have studied the first four in the previous chapter. We now return to the picture for an analysis of the final four.

> Blessed are the merciful, for they shall receive mercy.
> Blessed are the pure in heart, for they shall see God.
> Blessed are the peacemakers, for they shall be called sons of God.

Blessed are those who have been persecuted for the sake of righteousness, for theirs is the kingdom of heaven.

Blessed are you when men revile you, and persecute you, and say all kinds of evil against you falsely, on account of Me.

Rejoice, and be glad, for your reward in heaven is great, for so they persecuted the prophets who were before you (Matt. 5:7-12).

"The Merciful"

Mercy is concern for people in need. It is ministry to the miserable. Offering help for those who hurt . . . who suffer under the distressing blows of adversity and hardship. The term itself has an interesting background.

> It does not mean only to sympathise with a person in the popular sense of the term; it does not mean simply to feel sorry for someone in trouble. *Chesedh, mercy,* means the ability to get right inside the other person's skin. . . . Clearly this is much more than an emotional wave of pity; clearly this demands a quite deliberate effort of the mind and of the will. It denotes a sympathy which is not given, as it were, from outside, but which comes from a deliberate identification with the other person, until we see things as he sees them, and feel things as he feels them.[1]

Those special servants of God who extend mercy to the miserable often do so with much encouragement because they identify with the sorrowing—they "get inside their skin." Rather than watching from a distance or keeping the need safely at arm's length, they get in touch, involved, and offer assistance that alleviates some of the pain.

A large group of the collegians in our church in Fullerton, California, pile into our bus one weekend a month and travel together—not to a mountain resort or the beach for fun-n-games, but to a garbage dump in Tijuana, Mexico, where hundreds of poverty-stricken Mexican families live. Our young adults, under the encouraging leadership of Kenneth Kemp (one of our pastoral staff team members), bring apples and other foodstuff plus money they have collected to share with those in that miserable existence. There are times when the students can hardly believe what they see and hear *and smell* as they witness raw, unmasked poverty in the garbage dump at Tijuana.

What are they doing? They are showing mercy . . . a ministry to others that is born out of the womb of identification. In our isolated, cold society, mercy is rarely demonstrated. Shocking stories make headlines today with remarkable regularity.

A young woman was brutally attacked as she returned to her apartment late one night. She screamed and shrieked as she fought for her life . . . yelling until she was hoarse . . . for thirty minutes . . . as she was beaten and abused. Thirty-eight people watched the half-hour episode in rapt fascination from their windows. Not one so much as walked over to the telephone and called the police. She died that night as thirty-eight witnesses stared in silence.

Another's experience was similar. Riding on a subway, a seventeen-year-old youth was quietly minding his own business when he was stabbed repeatedly in the stomach by attackers. Eleven riders watched the stabbing, but none came to assist the young man. Even after the thugs had fled and the train had pulled out of the station and he lay there in a pool of his own blood, not one of the eleven came to his side.

Less dramatic, but equally shocking, was the ordeal of a lady in New York City. While shopping on Fifth Avenue in busy Manhattan, this lady tripped and broke her leg. Dazed, anguished, and in shock, she called out for help. Not for two minutes. Not for twenty minutes. But for *forty* minutes, as shoppers and business executives, students and merchants walked around her and stepped over her, completely ignoring her cries. After literally hundreds had passed by, a cab driver finally pulled over, hauled her into his taxi, and took her to a local hospital.

> If you had a friend who is in need . . . and you say to him, "Well, good-bye and God bless you; stay warm and eat hearty," and then don't give him clothes or food, what good does that do? (James 2:15–16, TLB).

The apostle John probes even deeper when he asks:

> . . . if someone who is supposed to be a Christian . . . sees a brother in need, and won't help him—how can God's love be within him? (1 John 3:17, TLB).

True servants are merciful. They care. They get involved. They get dirty, if necessary. They offer more than pious words.

And what do they get in return? What does Christ promise? ". . . *they shall receive mercy.*" Those who remain detached, distant, and disinterested in others will receive like treatment. But God promises that those who reach out and demonstrate mercy will, in turn, receive it. Both from other people as well as from God Himself. We could paraphrase this beatitude: "O the bliss of one who identifies with and assists others in need—who gets inside their skin so completely he sees with their eyes and thinks with their thoughts and feels with their feelings. The one who does that will find others do the same for him when he is in need."

That is exactly what Jesus, our Savior, did for us when He came to earth. By becoming human. He got right inside our skin, literally. That made it possible for Him to see life through our eyes, feel the sting of our pain, and identify with the anguish of human need. He understands. Remember those great words:

> But Jesus the Son of God is our great High Priest who has gone to heaven itself to help us; therefore let us never stop trusting him. This High Priest of ours understands our weaknesses, since he had the same temptations we do, though he never once gave way to them and sinned (Heb. 4:14–15, TLB).

"The Pure in Heart"

Like the first characteristic—"poor in spirit" (v. 3)—this quality emphasizes the inner man . . . the motive . . . the "heart." It does not refer simply to doing the right things, but doing the right things *for the right reason.* Being free from duplicity, hypocrisy, and/or sham. God desires His servants to be "real" people—authentic to the core. The portrait He paints is realistic.

In Jesus' day many of the religious authorities who claimed to serve the people were not "pure in heart." Far from it! Hypocritical and phony, they played a role that lacked internal integrity. In Matthew 23—one of the most severe rebukes against hypocrisy in all the Bible—we find words in strong contrast with the beatitudes. Instead of eight "Blessed are yous," there are eight "Woe unto yous." Count them—Matthew 23:13, 14, 15, 16, 23, 25, 27, and 29!

Woe unto whom? Well, read verses 25–28.

> Woe to you, scribes and Pharisees, hypocrites! For you clean the outside of the cup and of the dish, but inside they are full of robbery and self-indulgence.
>
> You blind Pharisee, first clean the inside of the cup and of the dish, so that the outside of it may become clean also.
>
> Woe to you, scribes and Pharisees, hypocrites! For you are like whitewashed tombs which on the outside appear beautiful, but inside they are full of dead men's bones and all uncleanness.
>
> Even so you too outwardly appear righteous to men, but inwardly you are full of hypocrisy and lawlessness.

Wow, *Jesus* said that! It is doubtful He despised anything among those who claimed to serve God more than hypocrisy—a lack of purity of heart. Did you notice what characterized the phony Pharisees?

- They were big on rules and little on godliness.
- They were big on externals and little on internals.
- They were big on public commands and little on personal obedience.
- They were big on appearance and little on reality.

On the outside they "appeared righteous to men," but inwardly they were "full of dead men's bones . . . full of hypocrisy." Why did He hate that so much? Because it represented the antithesis of servanthood. Time after time, therefore, He announced, "Woe to you . . . !"

Back to Matthew 5:8—the "pure in heart." Jesus extols this virtue. The term *pure* literally means "clean." It's the idea of being uncontaminated, without corruption or alloy. Without guile . . . sincere and honest in motive.

I love the story of the well-respected British pastor who, many years ago, took the trolley early Monday morning from his home in the suburbs to his church in the downtown section of London. He paid the driver as he got on, preoccupied with his busy schedule and the needs of his large congregation. It wasn't until he was seated that he realized the driver had given him too much change. Fingering the coins, his first thought was an alien one, "My, how wonderfully God provides!" But the longer he sat there, the less comfortable he became. His conscience telegraphed a strong signal of conviction within him. As he walked to the door to get off near his parish, he looked at the driver and quietly said, "When I got on, you accidentally gave me too much change."

The driver, with a wry smile, replied, "It was no accident at all. You see, I was in your congregation yesterday and heard your sermon on honesty. I just thought I'd put you to the test, Reverend."

Christ promises that consistent servants who are pure in heart "shall see God." There is no doubt about the destiny of these individuals. For sure, some glorious day in the future, these servants will see the Lord and hear the most significant words that will ever enter human ears: ". . . Well done, good and faithful slave; you were faithful . . . enter into the joy of your master" (Matt. 25:21).

Before we move on to the next servant quality, let me challenge you to become "pure in heart." Think about what it would mean, what changes you would have to make, what habits you'd have to break . . . most of all, what masks you'd have to peel off.

As I write these words, my family and I are spending Thanksgiving week high up in the Rockies at a ski resort in Keystone, Colorado. I was invited to speak to about five hundred single career people. Many of them are on the Campus Crusade for Christ staff. What a great bunch! All week I have been talking about servanthood (sound familiar?) and emphasizing being real, authentic, pure-in-heart people. We've discussed our tendency to cover up, to say one thing and mean another, to be downright hypocritical—yet in such a clever way that nobody knows it.

Last night I decided to try something I had never done before to drive the point home. At my last birthday my sister gave me a full-face rubber mask . . . one of those crazy things that slip over your entire head. She told me she'd give me ten dollars if I'd wear it into the pulpit one Sunday (my kids raised it to fifteen dollars), but I just couldn't do it! Well, last night I wore that ugly beast when I got up to speak. I figured if anybody could handle it, this gang could. *It was wild!*

I didn't call attention to it. Without any explanation, I just stood up and began to speak on being authentic. There I stood pressing on, making one statement after another as the place came apart at the seams. Why? Anybody knows why! My mask canceled out everything I had to say, especially on *that* subject. It's impossible to be very convincing while you wear a mask.

I finally pulled the thing off and the place settled down almost immediately. As soon as it did, everybody got the point. It's a funny thing, when we wear *literal* masks, nobody is fooled. But how easy it is to wear invisible ones and fake people out by the hundreds week after week. Did you know that the word *hypocrite* comes from the ancient Greek plays? An actor would place a large, grinning mask in front of his face and quote his comedy lines as the audience would roar with laughter. He would then slip backstage and grab a frowning, sad, oversized mask and come back quoting tragic lines as the audience would moan and weep. Guess what he was called. A *hupocritos*, one who wears a mask.

Servants who are "pure in heart" have peeled off their masks. And God places special blessing on their lives.

"The Peacemakers"

Interestingly, this is the only time in all the New Testament that the Greek term translated "peacemakers" appears. Maybe it will help us understand the meaning by pointing out first what it does *not* mean.

• It does not mean, "Blessed are those who avoid all conflict and confrontations."

• Neither does it mean, "Blessed are those who are laid back, easygoing, and relaxed."

• Nor, "Blessed are those who defend a 'peace at any price' philosophy."

• It doesn't mean, "Blessed are the passive, those who compromise their convictions when surrounded by those who would disagree."

No, none of those ideas are characteristics of the "peacemaker" in this verse.

The overall thrust of Scripture is the imperative, "Make peace!" Just listen:

> If possible, so far as it depends on you, be at peace with all men (Rom. 12:18).

> So then let us pursue the things which make for peace and the building up of one another (Rom. 14:19).

> For where jealousy and selfish ambition exist, there is disorder and every evil thing.

> But the wisdom from above is first pure, then peaceable, gentle, reasonable, full of mercy and good fruits, unwavering, without hypocrisy.

> And the seed whose fruit is righteousness is sown in peace by those who make peace.

> What is the source of quarrels and conflicts among you? Is not the source your pleasures that wage war in your members?

> You lust and do not have; so you commit murder. And you are envious and cannot obtain; so you fight and quarrel (James 3:16–4:2).

Get the picture? A "peacemaker" is the servant who . . . First, is at peace with himself—internally, at ease . . . not agitated, ill-tempered, in turmoil . . . and therefore not abrasive. Second, he/she works hard to settle quarrels, not start them . . . is accepting, tolerant, finds no pleasure in being negative.

In the words of Ephesians 4:3, peacemakers ". . . preserve the unity of the Spirit in the bond of peace."

Ever been around Christians who are *not* peacemakers? Of course. Was it pleasant? Did you sense a servant's heart? Were you built up and encouraged . . . was the body of Christ strengthened and supported? You know the answers.

In Leslie Flynn's potent book *Great Church Fights* (I like that title), he does a masterful job of describing just how petty and abrasive we can become. He includes an anonymous poem that bites deeply into our rigid intolerance. Our tendency toward exclusiveness is exposed for all to see:

> Believe as I believe, no more, no less;
> That I am right, and no one else, confess;
> Feel as I feel, think only as I think;
> Eat what I eat, and drink what I drink;
> Look as I look, do always as I do;
> And then, and only then, I'll fellowship with you.[2]
> —Source Unknown

Whoever lives by that philosophy does not qualify as a peacemaker, I can assure you.

But enough of the negative! Solomon gives us wise counsel on some of the things peacemakers do:

• **They build up**. "The wise woman builds her house . . ." (Prov. 14:1).

• **They watch their tongues and heal rather than hurt**. "A gentle answer turns away wrath . . ." (Prov. 15:1). "Pleasant words are a honeycomb, sweet to the soul and healing to the bones" (Prov. 16:24).

• **They are slow to anger**. "A hot-tempered man stirs up strife, but the slow to anger pacifies contention" (Prov. 15:18). "He who is slow to anger is better than the mighty, and he who rules his spirit, than he who captures a city" (Prov. 16:32).

• **They are humble and trusting**. "An arrogant man stirs up strife, but he who trusts in the lord will prosper" (Prov. 28:25).

The Lord Jesus states a marvelous promise that peacemakers can claim: ". . . they shall be called sons of God." God's children. Few things are more godlike than *peace*. When we promote it, pursue it, model it, we are linked directly with Him.

A man I have admired for two decades, the man who taught me Hebrew in seminary many years ago, is Dr. Bruce Waltke. He is not only a Semitic scholar *par excellence*, he is a gracious servant of our Lord. In my opinion, he is one of the finest examples of a peacemaker in the family of God. Too brilliant for words, yet the epitome of grace and love. What a magnificent balance!

A number of years ago, Dr. Waltke, another pastor, a graduate student at Brandeis University (also a seminary graduate), and I toured the mother church of the First Church of Christ Scientist in downtown Boston. The four of us were completely anonymous to the elderly lady who smiled as we entered.

She had no idea she was meeting four evangelical ministers—and we chose not to identify ourselves, at least at first.

She showed us several interesting things on the main floor. When we got to the multiple-manual pipe organ, she began to talk about their doctrine and especially their belief about no judgment in the life beyond. Dr. Waltke waited for just the right moment and very casually asked:

"But, Ma'am, doesn't it say somewhere in the Bible 'It is appointed unto man once to die and after that, the judgment'?" He could have quoted Hebrews 9:27 in Greek! But he was so gracious, so tactful with the little lady. I must confess, I stood back thinking, "Go for it, Bruce. Now we've got her where we want her!"

The lady, without a pause, said simply, "Would you like to see the second floor?"

You know what Dr. Waltke said? "We surely would, thank you."

She smiled, somewhat relieved, and started to lead us up a flight of stairs.

I couldn't believe it! All I could think was, "No, don't let her get away. Make her answer your question!" As I was wrestling within, I pulled on the scholar's arm and said in a low voice, "Hey, why didn't you nail the lady? Why didn't you press the point and not let her get away until she answered?"

Quietly and calmly he put his hand on my shoulder and whispered, "But, Chuck, that wouldn't have been fair. That wouldn't have been very loving, either—now would it?"

Wham! The quiet rebuke left me reeling. I shall *never* forget that moment. And to complete the story, you'll be interested to know that in less than twenty minutes he was sitting with the woman alone, tenderly and carefully speaking with her about the Lord Jesus Christ. She sat in rapt attention. He, the gracious peacemaker, had won a hearing. And I, the scalp-snatcher, had learned an unforgettable lesson.

Do you know what she saw in my friend? A living representation of one of God's sons . . . exactly as God promised in his beatitude . . . *"they shall be called sons of God."*

In this chapter we have been examining a portrait. We have seen the servant as merciful, authentic, and one who actively pursues peace. There remains one final part of the picture we need to linger over and appreciate.

"Those Who Have Been Persecuted"

I don't know how this strikes you, but it seems misplaced at first glance. Especially on the heels of what we just learned about being peacemakers. But it is not misplaced. Realistically, wrong treatment often comes upon those who do what is *right*. I deal with this at length in chapter 12. We who genuinely desire to serve others soon discover that being mistreated isn't the exception. It's the rule! Christ knew that was so. Read the verses carefully.

Blessed are those who have been persecuted for the sake of righteousness, for theirs is the kingdom of heaven.

Blessed are you when men revile you, and persecute you, and say all kinds of evil against you falsely, on account of Me.

Rejoice, and be glad, for your reward in heaven is great, for so they persecuted the prophets who were before you (Matt. 5:10–12).

Did you notice something? Not "if" men revile you . . . but "when" they revile you. And not only will they revile you, they will persecute you and say all kinds of evil against you—lies and slanderous accusations. Clearly, Jesus is speaking of being viciously mistreated. It's tough to bear! But the Savior says you will be "blessed" when you endure it—promising a great reward for your patient, mature endurance. There are times when the only way servants can make it through such severe times without becoming bitter is by focusing on the ultimate rewards that are promised. Jesus even says we are to "rejoice and be glad" as we think on the great rewards He will give to us in Heaven.

Charles Haddon Spurgeon remains one of the most colorful and gifted preachers in the history of the church. Any man who loves to preach and desires to cultivate the art and skill of communication must study Spurgeon. Before the man was thirty, he was the most popular preacher in England. The new Tabernacle was filled to overflowing every Lord's Day as people came miles by horse and buggy to hear the gifted man handle the Word of God. They were challenged, encouraged, exhorted, fed, and built up in the Christian faith. He was truly a phenomenon. As a result, he became the object of great criticism by the press, by other pastors, by influential people in London, and by petty parishioners. The man, not always a model of quiet piety (to say the least), had numerous enemies. Normally, he handled the criticism fairly well . . . but finally it began to get to him. He began to slump beneath the attacks. The persecution started to take a severe toll on his otherwise resilient spirit.

I am told that his wife, seeing the results of those verbal blows on her husband, decided to assist him in getting back on his feet and regaining his powerful stature in the pulpit. She found in her Bible Matthew 5:10–12—the beatitude we have been studying—and she printed in beautiful old English the words of this passage on a large sheet of paper. Then she tacked that sheet to the ceiling of their bedroom, directly above Charles' side of the bed! Every morning, every evening, when he would rest his enormous frame in his bed, the words were there to meet and to encourage him.

Blessed are those who have been persecuted for the sake of righteousness, for theirs is the kingdom of heaven.

Blessed are you when men revile you, and persecute you, and say all kinds of evil against you falsely, on account of Me.

Rejoice, and be glad, for your reward in heaven is great, for so they persecuted the prophets who were before you.

The large sheet of paper remained fixed to the ceiling for an extended period of time until it had done the job. May Mrs. Spurgeon's tribe increase! It is refreshing to think how a marriage partner can be such a vital channel of encouragement.

And it is also encouraging to see that we have no corner on the problem of persecution. Did you observe what Christ said? ". . . so they persecuted the prophets who were before you." Servants, that statement will help us call a halt to the next pity party we are tempted to throw for ourselves. We are not alone. It has been going on for centuries.

A LAST LOOK AT THE PORTRAIT

Shortly before her death in February of 1971, my mother did an oil painting for me. It has become a silent "friend" of mine, a mute yet eloquent expression of my calling. It is a picture of a shepherd with his sheep. The man is standing all alone with his crook in his hand, facing the hillside with sheep here and there. You cannot see the shepherd's face, but the little woolies surrounding him have personalities all their own. Some have the appearance of being devoted and loving, one looks independent and stubborn, another is starting to wander in the distance. But the shepherd is there with his flock, faithfully and diligently tending them.

The rather large piece of art hangs in my study with a light above it. There are occasions when I am bone weary after a huge day of people demands, preaching, and close contact with the Fullerton flock. Occasionally on days like this, I will turn off my desk lamp and my light overhead and leave on only the light on that unique painting. It helps me keep my perspective. It is a reminder . . . a simple, silent affirmation that I am right where God wants me, doing the very things He wants me to do. There is something very encouraging about taking a final look at the shepherd with his sheep at the end of my day.

We have done that in these two chapters. With a close eye on details, we have studied a portrait Jesus painted of a servant. And we have found it to be both enlightening and encouraging. We have found His promises to be assuring and His repeated reminders ("Blessed are . . .") to be affirming. He has described our calling by explaining our role as:
• Poor in spirit
• Mourning
• Gentle
• Hungering and thirsting for righteousness
• Merciful
• Pure in heart
• Peacemakers
• Persecuted.

As we have turned out all the other lights that distract us, it has helped to concentrate our full attention on these eight specifics. The question we now must face is: Can such a person as this really influence a stubborn, competitive, strong-willed world? Is it possible for servants to make an impact?

The next chapter offers a resounding "Yes!" In our tasteless, dark world, servants actually become the only source of salt and light.

9

The Influence
of a Servant

Ours is a tough, rugged, wicked world. Aggression, rebellion, violence, cut-throat competition, and retaliation abound. Not just internationally, but personally. What is true in the secret council chambers of nations is also true behind closed doors of homes. We are stubborn, warring people. "The American home," according to a study completed at the University of Rhode Island, is described as "the most dangerous place to be, outside of riots and a war!"[1] No less than 30 percent of all American couples experience some form of domestic violence in their lifetimes. This helps explain why 20 percent of all police officers killed in the line of duty are killed while answering calls involving family fights, and why it is estimated that anywhere from six to fifteen *million* women are battered in our nation each year.[2] And the figures are on the increase. The heart of mankind is totally and unashamedly depraved!

What possible influence could the servants described in Matthew 5:1–12 have on a hard, hostile society like ours? What impact—how much clout—do the "poor in spirit," the "gentle," the "merciful," the "pure in heart," or the "peacemakers" actually have? Such feeble-sounding virtues seem about as influential as pillow fighting in a nuclear war. Especially with the odds stacked against us. Servants of Jesus Christ will always be in the minority . . . a small remnant surrounded by a strong-minded majority with their fists clenched. Can our presence do much good? Isn't it pretty much a wasted effort?

Jesus—the One who first painted the servant's portrait—did not share this skepticism. But neither did He deny the battle. Don't forget the final touches He put on that inspired canvas which we just examined and admired. Remember these words. They make it clear that society is a combat zone not a vacation spot.

Blessed are those who have been persecuted for the sake of righteousness, for theirs is the kingdom of heaven.

Blessed are you when men revile you, and persecute you, and say all kinds of evil against you falsely, on account of Me.

Rejoice, and be glad, for your reward in heaven is great, for so they persecuted the prophets who were before you (Matt. 5:10-12).

No, He never promised us a rose garden. He came up front with us and admitted that the arena of this world is not a friend of grace to help us on to God. Nevertheless, strange as it may seem, He went on to tell that handful of Palestinian peasants (and *all* godly servants in every generation) that their influence would be nothing short of remarkable. They would be "the salt of the earth" and they would be "the light of the world." And so shall we! So far-reaching would be the influence of servants in society, their presence would be as significant as salt on food and as light on darkness. Neither is loud or externally impressive, but both are essential. Without our influence this old world would soon begin to realize our absence. Even though it may not admit it, society needs both salt and light.

Keeper of the Spring

The late Peter Marshall, an eloquent speaker and for several years the chaplain of the United States Senate, used to love to tell the story of "The Keeper of the Spring,"[3] a quiet forest dweller who lived high above an Austrian village along the eastern slopes of the Alps. The old gentleman had been hired many years ago by a young town council to clear away the debris from the pools of water up in the mountain crevices that fed the lovely spring flowing through their town. With faithful, silent regularity, he patrolled the hills, removed the leaves and branches, and wiped away the silt that would otherwise choke and contaminate the fresh flow of water. By and by, the village became a popular attraction for vacationers. Graceful swans floated along the crystal clear spring, the millwheels of various businesses located near the water turned day and night, farmlands were naturally irrigated, and the view from restaurants was picturesque beyond description.

Years passed. One evening the town council met for its semiannual meeting. As they reviewed the budget, one man's eye caught the salary figure being paid the obscure keeper of the spring. Said the keeper of the purse, "Who is the old man? Why do we keep him on year after year? No one ever sees him. For all we know the strange ranger of the hills is doing us no good. He isn't necessary any longer!" By a unanimous vote, they dispensed with the old man's services.

For several weeks nothing changed. By early autumn the trees began to shed their leaves. Small branches snapped off and fell into the pools, hindering the rushing flow of sparkling water. One afternoon someone noticed a slight yellowish-brown tint in the spring. A couple days later the water was much darker. Within another week, a slimy film covered sections of the water along the banks and a foul odor was soon detected. The millwheels moved slower, some finally ground to a halt. Swans left as did the tourists. Clammy fingers of disease and sickness reached deeply into the village.

Quickly, the embarrassed council called a special meeting. Realizing their gross error in judgment, they hired back the old keeper of the spring . . . and within a few weeks the veritable river of life began to clear up. The wheels started to turn, and new life returned to the hamlet in the Alps once again.

Fanciful though it may be, the story is more than an idle tale. It carries with it a vivid, relevant analogy directly related to the times in which we live. What the keeper of the springs meant to the village, Christian servants mean to our world. The preserving, taste-giving bite of salt mixed with the illuminating, hope-giving ray of light may seem feeble and needless . . . but God help any society that attempts to exist without them! You see, the village without the Keeper of the Spring is a perfect representation of the world system without salt and light.

CRITICAL ESTIMATION OF OUR TIMES

To help describe just how hopeless and empty society really is, let's glance over 2 Timothy 3. Within the first thirteen verses, I find three undeniable descriptions of our world—difficult, depraved, and deceived.

Difficult

Read verses 1 through 7 very carefully.

> But realize this, that in the last days difficult times will come.
> For men will be lovers of self, lovers of money, boastful, arrogant, revilers, disobedient to parents, ungrateful, unholy, unloving, irreconcilable, malicious gossips, without self-control, brutal, haters of good, treacherous, reckless, conceited, lovers of pleasure rather than lovers of God; holding to a form of godliness, although they have denied its power; and avoid such men as these.
> For among them are those who enter into households and captivate weak women weighed down with sins, led on by various impulses, always learning and never able to come to the knowledge of the truth (2 Tim. 3:1-7).

Now, with your pen, go back up to the first verse and circle the term *difficult*. One version renders the word *perilous* (KJV). Another translates it *terrible* (NIV). The Greek root word meant "grievous, harsh, fierce, savage." It is used only one other time in the New Testament. In Matthew 8:28 it appears when the writer describes two men with demons as being "exceedingly violent." What an apt description of our world! Savage, harsh, violent. If you question that, if you need proof that that is not exaggeration, check this morning's newspaper or listen to the evening news. Both will convince you our "village" is in desperate straits.

Depraved

Now, look at the next two verses:

> And just as Jannes and Jambres opposed Moses, so these men also oppose the truth, men of depraved mind, rejected as regards the faith.
> But they will not make further progress; for their folly will be obvious to all, as also that of those two came to be (vv. 8-9).

Paul mentions two men from the days of Moses as representatives of people in these "difficult" times. *Depraved* is the word to describe them. Circle it in verse 8. It means mankind is as bad off spiritually as it can possibly be. Dead toward God. Unmoved by anything spiritual. Hard-hearted and dark within. Two sections out of Isaiah come to my mind as illustrations of human depravity.

> All of us like sheep have gone astray,
> Each of us has turned to his own way;
> But the Lord has caused the iniquity of us all
> To fall on Him (Isa. 53:6).

> For all of us have become like one who is unclean,
> And all our righteous deeds are like a filthy garment;
> And all of us wither like a leaf,
> And our iniquities, like the wind, take us away.

> And there is no one who calls on Thy name,
> Who arouses himself to take hold of Thee;
> For Thou hast hidden Thy face from us,
> And hast delivered us into the power of our iniquities (Isa. 64:6-7).

"All . . . all . . . all . . . all . . . all." Depravity is a universal disease in society. And we are reaping what we have sowed. Our world is on a collision course destined for a Christless eternity. Now let's look at the third descriptive term.

Deceived

It will not surprise you to read these words:

> But evil men and impostors will proceed from bad to worse, deceiving and being deceived (2 Tim. 3:13).

Circle that last word. The "village" is a place where impostors flourish. Rip-off experts flood every profession. Religious charlatans are here as well. Many politicians speak smoothly from both sides of their mouths. No one can deny the phony-baloney façade of ads and fads. And Scripture is right, it proceeds "from bad to worse." Remove "the spring" of life from the village—take away the salt and the light—and within a brief time "the village" becomes a diseased cesspool of contamination. Enter: the Keeper of the spring! He may seem removed and uninfluential, but without the salt and light He quietly provides, there is only hopeless despair.

Technically, there can be only one "Keeper of the Spring": Jesus Christ, the Lord. But we, His servants, His representative-ambassadors, have been commissioned to carry on in His absence. We, His servants, are assigned to the task not unlike the old gentleman in the Alps. But how can the job be done?

INDISPENSABLE INFLUENCES FOR GOOD

Let's turn again to Matthew 5. For the first twelve verses, you'll recall that Christ speaks of the character qualities of the servant. Interestingly, He uses *they, their,* and *those* throughout the verses. But when He applies the influence of servanthood on society, He says *you. "You* are the salt . . . *you* are the light." It is personal. Equally significant is the obvious lack of the words *like* or *as.* Salt and light are things we *are*, not things we represent, not what we provide or attempt to compare with ourselves. Here's the point: A society characterized by savage violence and the darkness of depravity and deception will, without salt and light, deteriorate and ultimately self-destruct. Because servants of Christ are both salt and light, our influence is essential for survival.

John R. W. Stott expresses the value of our influence this way:

> The world is evidently a dark place, with little or no light of its own, since an external source of light is needed to illumine it. True, it is "always talking about its enlightenment," but much of its boasted light is in reality darkness. The world also manifests a constant tendency to deteriorate. The notion is not that the world is tasteless and that Christians can make it less insipid ("The thought of making the world palatable to God is quite impossible"), but that it is putrifying. It cannot stop itself from going bad. Only salt introduced from outside can do this. The church, on the other hand, is set in the world with a double role, as salt to arrest—or at least to hinder—the process of social decay, and as light to dispel the darkness.
>
> When we look at the two metaphors more closely, we see that they are deliberately phrased in order to be parallel to each other. In each case Jesus first makes an affirmation ("You are the salt of the earth," "You are the light of the world"). Then he adds a rider, the condition on which the affirmation depends (the salt must retain its saltness, the light must be allowed to shine). Salt is good for nothing if its saltness is lost; light is good for nothing if it is concealed.[4]

As the servant's salt influences a putrifying society, a measure of preservation is provided. As the servant's light influences a depraved, dying society, a measure of darkness is dispelled. Let's probe a bit into these two metaphors.

The Salt of the Earth

Ever smelled old, rotten meat? Remember forgetting for several weeks something you put in the refrigerator? There is an odor that accompanies decay that's like nothing else. Down in Houston where I was raised, we were only fifty miles from the seaport city of Galveston. Delicious, fresh seafood was available in numerous restaurants in that area—and still is. But there were other ways we used to use seafood, especially shrimp. When a friend would get married, one of our favorite tricks was to secretly pull off the hubcaps of his getaway car and stuff them full of shrimp. It was great! Those shrimp wouldn't make any noise as they sloshed around hour after hour in the heat of South Texas. But the result was unreal. After two or three days of driving, parking in the sun, stop-and-go traffic, the bride (bless her shy heart) would slowly start sliding over closer to the door. She would begin to wonder if maybe her beloved groom had forgotten his Right Guard. As the day wore on, he would begin to wonder the same about her! All the while those little shrimp were doing their thing in each wheel. Finally (and sometimes they wouldn't discover the trick for over a week!), young Don Juan would pop off a hubcap—and I don't need to tell you the result. Old shrimp inside a hot hubcap for a week would make a skunk's spray seem like a shot of Chanel No. 5. *It is gross!* To keep shrimp, you must preserve them. If you don't, they perish. Years ago salt was used. Today we use ice more often.

Think of this earth as shrimp when you read these words:

> You are the salt of the earth; but if the salt has become tasteless, how will it be made salty again? It is good for nothing any more, except to be thrown out and trampled under foot by men (Matt. 5:13).

The earth and all its inhabitants are in a continual state of perishing. We are "salt to the world" (NEB). R. V. G. Tasker, professor emeritus of New Testament exegesis at the University of London, is correct: "The disciples, accordingly, are called to be a moral disinfectant in a world where moral standards are low, constantly changing, or non-existent."[5] Our very presence halts corruption. Salt is also a healing agent. And it creates a thirst. It adds flavor, increasing the delectable taste of most foods. Salt is amazingly beneficial—*but.* Did you miss that little word in verse 13? ". . . but if the salt has become tasteless. . . ." (meaning "if the salt has lost its bite, its uniqueness"). Jesus introduces not an imaginary warning, but a real one. Take away the Christian's distinctive contribution and nothing of worthwhile value remains. We become "good for nothing," exactly as the Lord put it.

I want to be quite direct with you. Secular thought has taken a tragic toll on the servant of God's distinctiveness. This has begun to influence the church of

Jesus Christ. Many a believer has surrendered his mind to the world system. The uniquely Christian mind, therefore, is a rare find. Humanism, secularism, intellectualism, and materialism have invaded our thinking to such a marked degree our salt has become diluted—in some cases, nonexistent. Francis Schaeffer, with prophetlike zeal and determination, has attempted to awaken us to this malady. One who could be called his British counterpart, Harry Blamires (a man C. S. Lewis tutored at Oxford), comes right out and dogmatically declares, "There is no longer a Christian mind."[6] Influenced and impressed by the press, our secularized system of education, shallow social expectations, and the quasi-omnipotent forces of conformity to peer pressure (not to mention the impact of television and movies), Christian servants can be easily caught in the trap. We can literally stop thinking biblically and stop shaking salt.

This is why Jesus states His concern so forcefully—"It is good for nothing any more, except to be thrown out and trampled under foot by men" (Matt. 5:13). We must do a work of preservation . . . or we lose our influence and become as insignificant as a layer of dust on city streets. Servant, take heed!

But before moving on to our other contribution to society—light—I want us to think about some practical, positive aspects of salt.

• **Salt is shaken and and sprinkled . . . not poured.** It must be spread out. Too much salt *ruins* food. A good reminder for Christians to spread out rather than stay huddled all together.

• **Salt adds flavor . . . but it's obscure.** No one every comments, "My, this is good salt." We frequently say, however. "The food is really tasty." Servants add zest to life, a flavor impossible to achieve without them.

• **Salt is unlike any other seasoning.** It's difference, however, is its strength. It can't be duplicated, and it must be applied before it is useful. Salt in the salt shaker does nobody any good. To help you develop this salt quality in your life, I heartily recommend a book by Rebecca Manley Pippert, *Out of the Saltshaker & Into the World,* an InterVarsity Press publication.[7] It is virtually impossible to read and apply her words and remain in the shaker!

The Light of the World

Does it seem important to you that Christ calls us what He called Himself?

> Again therefore Jesus spoke to them, saying, "I am the light of the world; he who follows Me shall not walk in the darkness, but shall have the light of life" (John 8:12).

Servants of Christ shine with His light in a society that is hopelessly lost, left to itself. Now, answer two questions:
1. What is the basic function of light?
2. How can that best occur?

The answer to the first question is obvious—to dispel darkness. Darkness cannot remain when a light is turned on. I don't care how thick the darkness may be. And the answer to the second question is found in Jesus' own words:

> You are the light of the world. A city set on a hill cannot be hidden.
> Nor do men light a lamp, and put it under the peck-measure, but on the lampstand; and it gives light to all who are in the house (Matt. 5:14–16).

How can darkness be dispelled? First, by not hiding the light—"*set on a hill.*" And second, by not limiting the light—"*on the lampstand . . . it gives light to all who are in the house.*" What stars are to the night sky, servants are in a darkened world. It was this analogy that caused one writer to say:

> I sometimes think how splendid it would be if non-Christians, curious to discover the secret and source of our light, were to come up to us and enquire: "Twinkle, twinkle, little star, / How I wonder what you are!"⁸

We pose a weird phenomenon to those in darkness. They cannot figure us out! And that is exactly as Jesus planned it. Think of some distinctive characteristics of light:

• **Light is silent.** No noise, no big splash, no banners—light simply shines. It's like a single lighthouse along a rugged shoreline. All it does is shine as it turns.

• **Light gives direction.** No words, no sermon. Jesus says that others "see" our actions—but nothing is said of their hearing.

• **Light attracts attention.** You don't have to ask people to look at you when you turn a light on in a dark room. It happens automatically. If you are a Christian on an athletic team filled with non-Christians, you are the light in darkness. If you are a Christian family in a non-Christian neighborhood, you are the light in that darkness. The same is true if you are the only Christian nurse on your floor, or student in your school, or professional in your firm or group, or salesman in your district. You are a light in darkness—a servant of God who is being watched, who gives off a very distinct message . . . often with hardly a word being said. At first they may hate the light—but don't worry, they are still attracted to it. Let it shine! Don't attempt to show off how bright and sparkling you are, just shine!

Dr. Martyn Lloyd-Jones emphasizes this:

> As we produce and reveal it in our daily lives, we must remember that the Christian does not call attention to himself. Self has been forgotten in this poverty of spirit, in the meekness and all the other things. In other words, we are to do everything for God's sake, and for His glory. Self is to be absent, and must be utterly crushed in all its subtlety, for His sake, for His glory.
> It follows from this that we are to do these things in such a way as to lead other men to glorify Him, and glory in Him, and give themselves to Him. "Let your light

so shine before men, that they may see your good works." Yes; and so see them that they will themselves glorify your Father; you are to do so in order that these other people may glorify Him also.[9]

What a great reminder.

The "village" is in sad shape. Difficult, depraved, and deceived, those who live in it are living tasteless, hopeless lives. They need *salt* and they need *light* . . . the two ingredients a servant of God models.

PERSONAL RESPONSE TO OUR ROLE

Since God has called us to be His salt-and-light servants in a bland, dark society, it will be necessary for us to commit ourselves to the task before us. Remember, salt must not lose its taste and light must not be hidden. In order to keep us on target, let me suggest three statements that declare and describe how to fulfill this role.

1. **"I am different."** Probably the greatest tragedy of Christianity through its changing and checkered history has been our tendency to become like the world rather than completely different from it. The prevailing culture has sucked us in like a huge vacuum cleaner, and we have done an amazing job of conforming.

But servants are to be different. As one man put it, "as different as chalk is from cheese." As different as salt is from decayed meat . . . as light is from the depths of Carlsbad Caverns. No veneer, remember. We are authentically different.

2. **"I am responsible."** If I read Jesus' words correctly, I see more than being salt and light. I am responsible for my salt not losing its bite and my light not becoming obscure or hidden. Every once in a while it is helpful to ask some very hard questions of myself. True servants do more than *talk*. We refuse to become the "rabbit-hold Christians" John Stott speaks of, popping out of our holes and racing from our insulated caves to all-Christian gatherings only to rush back again. For salt to be tasted and for light to be seen, we must make contact. We are personally responsible.

3. **"I am influential."** Let's not kid ourselves. The very fact that we belong to Christ—that we don't adopt the system, that we march to a different drumbeat—gives us an influence in this society of ours. Maybe the quaint old "keeper of the springs" was not seen very much, but his role meant survival to that village in the Alps. We *are* influencing others—even when we aren't trying to act "religious" or preach from a soapbox.

I mentioned earlier a book by Rebecca Pippert. She tells a story in it that perfectly illustrates how we impact others without even trying. It is a classic example of the world's strange reaction to the presence of a Christian.

Sometimes non-Christians will act oddly around us because they are genuinely convicted by the Holy Spirit in us, and that's good. But all too often they are behaving "differently" because they feel that is the way they are supposed to act around religious types.

I am often put in a religious box when people discover what my profession is. Because I travel a great deal, I have a clergy card which sometimes enables me to travel at reduced rates. The only problem is that occasionally ticket agents won't believe I am authorized to use it! A young female just isn't what they have in mind when they see a clergy card. More than once I've been asked, "Okay, honey, now where did you rip this off?"

Once when I was flying from San Francisco to Portland I arrived at the counter and was greeted by an exceedingly friendly male ticket agent.

"Well, hel-lo-o-o there!" he said.

"Ah . . . I'd like to pick up my ticket to Portland, please."

"Gee, I'm sorry. You won't be able to fly there tonight."

"Why? Is the flight canceled?"

"No, it's because you're going out with me tonight."

"What?"

"Listen, I know this great restaurant with a hot band. You'll never regret it."

"Oh, I'm sorry, I really must get to Portland. Do you have my ticket?"

"Aw, what's the rush? I'll pick you up at eight. . . ."

"Look, I really must go to Portland," I said.

"Well, okay. Too bad though. Hey, I can't find your ticket." He paused, then said, "Looks like it's a date then!"

"Oh, I forgot to tell you, it's a . . . special ticket," I said.

"Oh, is it youth fare?"

"No, um, well, it's . . . ah, *clergy*," I whispered, leaning over the counter.

He froze. "What did you say?"

"It's clergy."

"CLERGY!?!" he shouted, as the entire airport looked our way. His face went absolutely pale, as he was horrified by only one thought. "Oh, no. I flirted with a nun!"

When he disappeared behind the counter, I could hear him whisper to the other ticket agent a few feet away, "Hey, George, get a load of that girl up there. She's *clergy*." Suddenly another man rose from behind the counter, smiled and nodded and disappeared again. I never felt so religious in my entire life.[10]

That's the price we pay, I suppose, for being authentic servants of the Master. Even when we aren't trying, out comes the salt and on comes the light!

10

The Perils
of a Servant

Nobody in this generation will ever forget Jonestown. At least, I hope not. That tragedy stands as a mute reminder of the awful results of a leader gone wild.

I shall never be able to erase from my mind the scene that appeared on one television newscast after another. It was not just death, but a mass suicide—over nine hundred bloated corpses in the steamy jungle of Guyana. People in rows, "looking like full-grown rag dolls," was how one reporter described them. Except for a few defectors who managed to slip away at the last minute, every soul in that cult compound gave up his or her life as the leader demanded. Whoever takes the time to investigate the evidence that led to such a bizarre atrocity soon discovers that the man at the top (who claimed to be a servant of God) fell into the trap that has ruined many a strong, natural leader.

Beneath every horrible picture of that unforgettably sick scene could be written the same five-word caption: THE PERIL OF LIMITLESS CONTROL. Rather than remaining a servant of God and of the people, instead of modeling humility, teachability, and unselfishness, Jim Jones eroded into an empty shell of authoritarianism, sensuality, and unaccountability . . . an untouchable prima donna who fell into the clutches of his own lust and pride.

Most every calling and occupation carries with it peculiar hazards—some subtle, some obvious and overt. It's not just the steeplejack or submarine crew or high-rise window washers or S.W.A.T. teams who face perils in their work. We all do. No exceptions.

Including servants.

That may surprise you. Being a servant seems as safe and harmless as a poached egg on a plate. What could possibly be perilous about serving others?

Some Common Misconceptions

As we return to a section of Scripture we looked at earlier, 2 Corinthians 4, I'd like to suggest three familiar misconceptions regarding servanthood. Read verses 4 through 7 rather carefully:

> . . . in whose case the god of his world has blinded the minds of the unbelieving, that they might see the light of the gospel of the glory of Christ, who is the image of God.
> For we do not preach ourselves but Christ Jesus as Lord, and ourselves as your bond-servants for Jesus' sake.
> For God, who said, "Light shall shine out of darkness," is the One who has shone in our hearts to give the light of the knowledge of the glory of God in the face of Christ.
> But we have this treasure in earthen vessels, that the surpassing greatness of the power may be of God and not from ourselves.

Sounds like servants comprise an elite body of people, doesn't it? They possess a treasure. The "surpassing greatness" of God's power pours out of their lives. But when you look closely, you detect that all of that is of God, not themselves. This introduces misconception number one:

Servants Have Special Powers in Themselves

How very easy it is to look at God's servants through rose-colored glasses!— almost as if they possess a mystical, divine unction or some angelic "mantle" that causes them to ooze with supernatural, heaven-sent power. But this is wrong! Listen to an earlier verse:

> Not that we are adequate in ourselves to consider anything as coming from ourselves, but our adequacy is from God (2 Cor. 3:5).

Mark it well, servants are absolutely human, filled with all the weaknesses and potential for failure that characterize every other human being.

Another common misconception is this:

Servants Don't Struggle with Everyday Problems

Consider 2 Corinthians 4:8-9:

> . . . we are afflicted in every way, but not crushed; perplexed, but not despairing; persecuted, but not forsaken; struck down, but not destroyed.

Afflicted. Perplexed. Persecuted. Struck down. We'll look deeper into these terms in Chapter 12, but suffice it to say that they reflect the struggles common to all of us. Under stress, confused, pursued, rejected—Paul (and every servant since his day) understands what it means to endure the constant blast of problems. In fact, it is in the crucible that the servant learns to release his way for God's way.

Servants do indeed struggle with daily difficulties.

A third misconception:

Servants Are Protected against Subtle Dangers

Read verses 10–11:

. . . always carrying about in the body the dying of Jesus, that the life of Jesus also may be manifested in our body.

For we who live are constantly being delivered over to death for Jesus' sake, that the life of Jesus also may be manifested in our mortal flesh (2 Cor. 4:10–11).

People who serve God and others "carry about in the body" signs of death—dangers and perils that are undeniable.Subtle and silent, these dangers lurk in the most unexpected places, pleading for satisfaction. The true servant, as we have already discovered, is vulnerable. When the servant stumbles into these traps, it isn't long before he is completely ensnared. And it seldom happens fast or boldly. Usually, it comes on the scene in another garb entirely, appearing to be anything but dangerous.

Speaking of this, one man admits about the godly leader:

Although he is by no means immune to the temptations of the flesh, the dangers most to be guarded against lie in the realm of the spirit. He must remember that "sabbathless Satan," his relentless enemy, will take advantage of every inch of ground he concedes in any area of his life.[1]

So let's not be misled. Servants, no matter how useful, godly, unselfish, and admirable, are every bit as human and subject to the perils of life as any other person on earth. Without special powers in themselves, as we have noted, they struggle with everyday problems . . . especially vulnerable to the subtle dangers that can easily trip them up, as we have already realized from the reminder of Jonestown.

A CLASSIC EXAMPLE

To illustrate the truth of this in Scripture, let's turn back to the Old Testament for a change and lift out of obscurity a man who became the helper of one of the greatest prophets God ever raised up. The prophet's name was *Elisha* and his servant's name was *Gehazi*. The story we want to examine starts in 2 Kings, chapter 2.

Background and Role

Times were hard. The nation of Israel was rapidly deteriorating as one wicked ruler following another led the people into increasing depths of depravity. The citizens became wasted, confused, empty shells of humanity. Morally, spiritually, politically, even physically their lives were *zilch*! The few prophets who did appear on the scene stood absolutely alone like cattle in a blizzard, but nevertheless, they *stood*.

Elijah (not to be confused with Elisha), a remarkably courageous prophet of God, had lived out his life by this time. As he departed "by a whirlwind to heaven" (2:1, 11), Elisha (his successor) is standing by and receives from God the same dynamic power that had rested on Elijah. With a whoosh, Elisha was off and running! God had a number of remarkable, even miraculous things for His prophet to do. And on top of all that, he soon comes to be known as a "man of God," a title he well deserved.

The prophet emerges in 2 Kings 4 with a servant named Gehazi. We pick up the story at verse 8:

> Now there came a day when Elisha passed over to Shunem, where there was a prominent woman, and she persuaded him to eat food. And so it was, as often as he passed by, he turned in there to eat food.
>
> And she said to her husband, "Behold now, I perceive that this is a holy man of God passing by us continually.
>
> "Please, let us make a little walled upper chamber and let us set a bed for him there, and a table and a chair and a lampstand; and it shall be, when he comes to us, that he can turn in there."
>
> One day he came there and turned in to the upper chamber and rested.
>
> Then he said to Gehazi his servant, "All this Shunammite." And when he had called her, she stood before him.
>
> And he said to him, "Say now to her, 'Behold, you have been careful for us with all this care; what can I do for you? Would you be spoken for to the king or to the captain of the army?'" And she answered, "I live among my own people."
>
> So he said, "What then is to be done for her?" And Gehazi answered, "Truly she has no son and her husband is old."
>
> And he said, "Call her." When he had called her, she stood in the doorway.
>
> Then he said, "At this season next year you shall embrace a son." And she said, "No, my lord, O man of God, do not lie to your maidservant."
>
> And the woman conceived and bore a son at that season the next year, as Elisha had said to her (vv. 8-17).

This is only the beginning of a series of events Elisha is involved in. But our attention falls upon the one whose job it was to assist the prophet. We want to discover through his experiences some of the common perils that await all who determine to serve others.

Temptations and Reactions

Working alongside a high-profile, greatly respected prophet like Elisha was a privilege. But at the same time it was a particular position that brought about unique temptations, as we shall see. We'll call these temptations, and Gehazi's reactions to them, "perils." I find four of them in Elisha's servant's life. The first is set forth in 2 Kings 4:18–26:

> When the child was grown, the day came that he went out to his father to the reapers.
>
> And he said to his father, "My head, my head." And he said to his servant, "Carry him to his mother."
>
> When he had taken him and brought him to his mother, he sat on her lap until noon, and then died.
>
> And she went up and laid him on the bed of the man of God, and shut the door behind him, and went out.
>
> Then she called to her husband and said, "Please send me one of the servants and one of the donkeys, that I may run to the man of God and return."
>
> And he said, "Why will you go to him today? Is it neither new moon nor Sabbath." And she said, "It will be well."
>
> Then she saddled a donkey and said to her servant, "Drive and go forward; do not slow down the pace for me unless I tell you."
>
> So she went and came to the man of God to Mount Carmel. And it came about when the man of God saw her at a distance, that he said to Gehazi his servant, "Behold, yonder is the Shunammite.
>
> "Please run now to meet her and say to her, 'Is it well with you? Is it well with your husband? Is it well with the child?" And she answered, "It is well."

The "miracle child" God gave the Shunammite woman grows up and is old enough to work in the fields. While doing so he either receives a severe blow on his forehead or suffers a sunstroke or some serious internal problem, causing the young lad to cry out, "My head, my head!" Naturally, the mother thinks immediately of Elisha—if anybody can help, *he* can. When the prophet saw her coming at a distance, he recognized her. It is at this point we see the servant's tendency to react incorrectly. Read verses 26 through 28:

> "Please run now to meet her and say to her, 'Is it well with you? Is it well with your husband? Is it well with the child? '" And she answered, "It is well."
>
> When she came to the man of God to the hill, she caught of his feet. And Gehazi came near to push her away; but the man of God said, "Let her alone, for her soul is troubled within her; and the Lord has hid it from me and has not told me."
>
> Then she said, "Did I ask for a son from my lord? Did I not say, 'Do not deceive me' ?"

The Peril of Overprotection and Possessiveness

Do you see how this reveals itself? Gehazi is obviously committed to Elisha. He wants to be a protective shield around him—so we shouldn't be surprised that when the anxious mother arrived, Gehazi "came near to push her away." It's so easy for those with a servant's heart to get tunnel vision and miss the needs of others. A similar situation occurred in the account in Numbers 11:24–30 when Joshua attempted to restrain two men from prophesying in the camp. He was jealous that nobody took anything away from the special role of Moses, whom he served. Prophesying was Moses' job, not theirs! Greathearted Moses told Joshua to back off. Joshua attempted to overprotect Moses much like Gehazi did with Elisha.

Servants, watch out for the peril of possessiveness.

Let's read on through the 2 Kings 4 passage:

> Then he said to Gehazi, "Gird up your loins and take my staff in your hand, and go your way; if you meet any man, do not salute him, and if anyone salutes you, do not answer him; and lay my staff on the lad's face."
>
> And the mother of the lad said, "As the Lord lives and as you yourself live, I will not leave you." And he arose and followed her (vv. 29–30).

Elisha laid out a plan whereby the young man would be raised up . . . and that plan included Gehazi. The servant is dispatched to the bedside of the mother's son. We can be sure Gehazi's heart was beating fast. He must have anticipated an exciting response, as God would surely raise the lad from death. He would be involved in a miracle! But nothing happened. Not a thing changed.

> Then Gehazi passed on before them and laid the staff on the lad's face, but there was neither sound nor response. So he returned to meet him and told him, "The lad has not awakened" (v. 31).

Suddenly, Elisha burst on the scene—and phenomenal results occurred. A miracle transpired.

> When Elisha came into the house, behold the lad was dead and laid on his bed.
>
> So he entered and shut the door behind them both, and prayed to the Lord.
>
> And he went up and lay on the child, and put his mouth on his mouth and his eyes on his eyes and his hands on his hands, and he stretched himself on him; and the flesh of the child became warm.
>
> Then he returned and walked in the house once back and forth, and went up and stretched himself on him; and the lad sneezed seven times and the lad opened his eyes.
>
> And he called Gehazi and said, "Call this Shunammite." So he called her. And when she came in to him, he said, "Take up your son."

Then she went in and fell at his feet and bowed herself to the ground, and she took up her son and went out.

Try to identify with the servant rather than with the ecstatic mother if you can. As you do so, you'll feel some of the very human feelings Gehazi must have had.

The Peril of Feeling Used and Unappreciated

Serve others long enough and you'll periodically dip into this valley. Gehazi had done exactly what he was told to do. Yet he had witnessed no change, no miracle. In came Elisha who suddenly did it all. And guess who is given the assignment to tell the mother—Gehazi! And if that isn't sufficient, read on— same song, second verse:

When Elisha returned to Gilgal, there was a famine in the land. As the sons of the prophets were sitting before him, he said to his servant. "Put on the large pot and boil stew for the sons of the prophet."
Then one went out into the field to gather herbs, and found a wild vine and gathered from it his lap full of wild gourds, and came and sliced them into the pot of stew, for they did not know what they were.
So they poured it out for the men to eat. And it came about as they were eating of the stew, that they cried out and said, "O man of God, there is death in the pot." And they were unable to eat (vv. 38–40).

Famine has struck the area. Our friend, Gehazi, is told to whip up a pot of stew. Inadvertently, poisonous plants are dropped into the crockpot and everybody screams! But then notice what happened:

But he said, "Now bring meal." And he threw it into the pot, and he said, "Pour it out for the people that they may eat." Then there was no harm in the pot (v. 41).

Gehazi had done the work . . . but Elisha got all the credit. I mean, the servant can't even make stew! How frustrated can one get? Unless I miss my guess, a little embarrassement was added to the frustration . . . and Gehazi probably felt the sting of not being appreciated. You know, always being preempted by the prophet. Even though he had done everything he had been told to do.

So it is with servants today. It is so easy to feel used and unappreciated.

Do I write to you who serve behind the scenes in a ministry or a business? You work faithfully and diligently, yet the glory goes to another. Your efforts make someone else successful. How easy to feel resentful! Assistant directors, associate and assistant pastors, secretaries, administrators, "internal personnel," all members of the I-work-hard-but-because-I'm-not-up-front-I-never-get-the-credit club, *take heart*! Our God who rewards in secret will never overlook your commitment.

> For God is not unjust so as to forget your work and the love which you have shown toward His name, in having ministered and in still ministering to the saints (Heb. 6:10).

A great verse for those of you who feel used and unappreciated.

But a warning is also in order. Keep a close eye on your pride. God's true servant is like the Lord Jesus, who came not "to be served, but to serve, and to give His life a ransom for many" (Mark 10:45) . . . to serve and to give. Pride wants strokes—lots of them. It loves to get the credit, to be mentioned, to receive glory, to have people—ooh and ahhh. Ideally, your superiors will be thoughtful people who give you the credit you deserve, but, unfortunately, that will not always occur. And your pride will need to be held in check. At those tough times when you make the stew and someone else gets the strokes, remember your role: to serve and to give.

J. Oswald Sanders is correct when he writes this of pride:

> Nothing is more distasteful to God than self-conceit. This first and fundamental sin in essence aims at enthroning self at the expense of God. . . .
>
> Pride is a sin of whose presence its victim is least conscious. . . .
>
> If we are honest, when we measure ourselves by the life of our Lord who humbled Himself even to death on a cross, we cannot but be overwhelmed with the tawdriness and shabbiness, and even the vileness, of our hearts.[2]

True love flowing from authentic servants does not keep a record of who did what, and it does not look to others for the credit. In other words, real servants stay conscious of the blindness pride can create.

As we turn to chapter 5 in 2 Kings, an entirely different experience awaits Gehazi, the servant of Elisha. Not one but *two* more perils lurk in the shadows to ensnare the man. As we shall see, the second of the two proved too great a temptation for him and he finally succumbed. But first, let's set the stage.

A man named Naaman was a high-ranking Syrian soldier. He was influential, wealthy, proud, a man of dignity, courage, patriotism, and military clout. There was only one problem, the man had leprosy. Through a chain of interesting events, Naaman was led to Elisha for cleansing from his dread disease. We pick up the biblical narrative at verse 9:

> So Naaman came with his horses and his chariots, and stood at the doorway of the house of Elisha.
>
> And Elisha sent a messenger to him, saying, "Go and wash in the Jordan seven times, and your flesh shall be restored to you and you shall be clean."

But Naaman was furious and went away and said, "Behold, I thought, 'He will surely come out to me, and stand and call on the name of the Lord his God, and wave his hand over the place, and cure the leper.'

"Are not Abanah and Pharpar, the rivers of Damascus, better than all the waters of Israel? Could I not wash in them and be clean?" So he turned and went away in a rage.

I take it that the "messenger" Elisha sent to answer the door was Gehazi, his trusted servant. It fell his lot to be the bearer of news the Syrian officer did not want to hear. As we read in the account, the high-ranking soldier was offended. He became *enraged*. And look who was caught in the crossfire—the servant. The dear guy didn't generate the news, he just communicated it . . . and boom! This introduces us to another peril common to those who faithfully serve others.

The Peril of Disrespect and Resentment

Gehazi has neither rank nor authority, yet his responsibility puts him in a most unpopular dilemma. He has the task of facing a person with the truth that the person does not want to hear. The result? Feeling and hearing the verbal blows of disrespect and resentment. Let me stretch this out and apply it.

There are times when God's servant is called upon to confront or in some way tell another the truth that the individual does not want to hear. The information may be painful to accept, but it is what God wants said. So the faithful servant says it. Graciously yet accurately. And all of a sudden the lid blows sky high. He is caught in the crossfire. What do you do in such precarious moments? Fight back? Yell and scream and threaten in return?

Listen to God's counsel to servants whose job it is to say hard things:

And the Lord's bond-servant must not be quarrelsome, but be kind to all, able to teach, patient when wronged, with gentleness correcting those who are in opposition, if perhaps God may grant them repentance leading to the knowledge of the truth, and they may come to their senses and escape from the snare of the devil, having been held captive by him to do his will (2 Tim. 2:24–26).

What wise counsel! Not quarrelsome, but kind. Not irritated, but patient . . . even when wronged. Not angry, but gentle. God may be using your words to help the hearers "come to their senses," which may sound very noble; but, believe me, there are times it's not a lot to write home about.

As a pastor and a counselor, I frequently find myself in this unpopular spot. An individual who has come to me pours out his soul, not unlike the leper, Naaman. And God very clearly leads me to confront or point out a few specifics that the person finds rather painful to hear, not to mention accept. Suddenly, *I* become the verbal punching bag. Now understand, I didn't write the Book and

I in no way view myself as the individual's judge—even though he may think I do. But I have had counselees scream at me, curse, stomp out of the room, and share with me a piece of their mind they couldn't afford to lose. Some wait until later and write me one of those flaming missiles that burn your eyes when you read them. And what did I do to deserve that treatment? I told the truth. I simply carried a message as tactfully and well-timed as possible, but it was rejected—at least for awhile. But the payoff comes later on when the person realizes the truth was told and I really had his good at heart.

Sometimes it falls the lot of an attorney or a medical doctor to be the bearer of such news. One of the best (and most hilarious) examples I ever heard along this line happened to a dentist, who stood his ground and refused to budge. My good friend, Dr. James Dobson, tells the story better than I could ever describe it:

> In the absence of parental leadership, some children become extremely obnoxious and defiant, especially in public places. Perhaps the best example was a ten-year-old boy named Robert, who was a patient of my good friend Dr. William Slonecker. Dr. Slonecker said his pediatric staff dreaded the days when Robert was scheduled for an office visit. He literally attacked the clinic, grabbing instruments and files and telephones. His passive mother could do little more than shake her head in bewilderment.
>
> During one physical examination, Dr. Slonecker observed severe cavities in Robert's teeth and knew that the boy must be referred to a local dentist. But who would be given the honor? A referral like Robert could mean the end of a professional friendship. Dr. Slonecker eventually decided to send him to an older dentist who reportedly understood children. The confrontation that followed now stands as one of the classic moments in the history of human conflict.
>
> Robert arrived in the dental office, prepared for battle.
>
> "Get in the chair, young man," said the doctor.
>
> "No chance!" replied the boy.
>
> "Son, I told you to climb onto the chair, and that's what I intend for you to do," said the dentist.
>
> Robert stared at his opponent for a moment and then replied. "If you make me get in that chair, I will take off all my clothes."
>
> The dentist calmly said, "Son, take 'em off."
>
> The boy forthwith removed his shirt, undershirt, shoes and socks, and then looked up in defiance.
>
> "All right, son," said the dentist. "Now get on the chair."
>
> "You didn't hear me," sputtered Robert. "I said if you make me get on that chair, I will take off all my clothes."
>
> "Son, take 'em off," replied the man.
>
> Robert proceeded to remove his pants and shorts, finally standing totally naked before the dentist and his assistant.
>
> "Now, son, get in the chair," said the doctor.

Robert did as he was told, and sat cooperatively through the entire procedure. When the cavities were drilled and filled, he was instructed to step down from the chair.

"Give me my clothes now," said the boy.

"I'm sorry," replied the dentist. "Tell your mother that we're going to keep your clothes tonight. She can pick them up tomorrow."

Can you comprehend the shock Robert's mother received when the door to the waiting room opened, and there stood her pink son, as naked as the day he was born? The room was filled with patients, but Robert and his mom walked past them and into the hall. They went down a public elevator and into the parking lot ignoring the snickers of onlookers.

The next day, Robert's mother returned to retrieve his clothes, and asked to have a word with the dentist. However, she did not come to protest. These were her sentiments: "You don't know how much I appreciate what happened here yesterday. You see, Robert has been blackmailing me about his clothes for years. Whenever we are in a public place, such as a grocery store, he makes unreasonable demands of me. If I don't immediately buy him what he wants, he threatens to take off all his clothes. You are the first person who had called his bluff, doctor, and the impact on Robert has been incredible."[3]

I suppose the moral of the story is this: Being a servant may not be very pleasant, but when you do and say what is right—unpopular though it may be— good will come. Or better, in the words of Solomon:

When a man's ways are pleasing to the Lord, He makes even his enemies to be at peace with him (Prov. 16:7).

Gehazi needed that verse to claim back when Naaman threw his fit. And do you know what later happened to Naaman? He finally did precisely what he was told to do, and he received the miraculous result he had been promised.

So he went down and dipped himself seven times in the Jordan, according to the word of the man of God; and his flesh was restored like the flesh of a little child, and he was clean (2 Kings 5:14).

Tremendous!

Unlike many you and I may help, this man returned to thank Elisha and Gehazi. He was so overwhelmed he offered a sizable gift of gratitude. Elisha refused any tangible thank you.

When he returned to the man of God with all his company, and came and stood before him, he said, "Behold now, I know that there is no God in all the earth, but in Israel; so please take a present from your servant now."

But he said, "As the Lord lives, before whom I stand, I will take nothing." And he urged him to take it, but he refused.

And Naaman said, "If not, please let your servant at least be given two mules' load of earth; for your servant will no more offer burnt offering nor will he sacrifice to other gods, but to the Lord.

"In this matter may the Lord pardon your servant: when my master goes into the house of Rimmon to worship there, and he leans on my hand and I bow myself in the house of Rimmon, when I bow myself in the house of Rimmon the Lord pardon your servant in this matter."

And he said to him, "Go in peace." So he departed from him some distance (vv. 15-19).

But that's not the end of the account. You'll notice Naaman offered *Gehazi* a gift as well. And the prophet had refused it. But deep within the heart of the servant crouched a silent beast of the soul, greed—not uncommon among some servants. Lest you think I am being too harsh, read on:

But Gehazi, the servant of Elisha the man of God, thought, "Behold, my master has spared this Naaman the Syrian, by not receiving from his hands what he brought. As the Lord lives, I will run after him and take something from him."

So Gehazi pursued Naaman. When Naaman saw one running after him, he came down from the chariot to meet him and said, "Is all well?"

And he said, "All is well. My master has sent me, saying, 'Behold, just now two young men of the sons of the prophets have come to me from the hill country of Ephraim. Please give them a talent of silver and two changes of clothes.'"

And Naaman said, "Be pleased to take two talents." And he urged him, and bound two talents of silver in two bags with two changes of clothes, and gave them to two of his servants; and they carried them before him.

When he came to the hill, he took them from their hand and deposited them in the house, and he sent the men away, and they departed (2 Kings 5:20–24).

Got the picture? You have just read of the fourth and perhaps the most subtle peril every servant must endure: hidden greed.

The Peril of Hidden Greed

This is the secret, smoldering desire to be rewarded, applauded, and exalted. Elisha said, "No." No way did he want the soldier ever to say, "He did it for what he would get out of it," which prompted the prophet to respond as he did—"I will take nothing" (v. 16). But Gehazi was cut from another piece of cloth. Maybe he was weary of feeling used and unappreciated or perhaps he had had enough of just getting by on a shoestring. Whatever, he possessed some pretty strong feelings, since he second-guessed Elisha's decision (v. 20), falsified the story when he met up with Naaman (v. 22), and attempted to cover his tracks when he later stood before his master (v. 25). Listen to the tragic ending.

But he went in and stood before his master. And Elisha said to him, "Where have you been, Gehazi?" And he said, "Your servant went nowhere."

Then he said to him, "Did not my heart go with you, when the man turned from his chariot to meet you? Is it a time to receive money and to receive clothes and oliveyards and vineyards and sheep and oxen and male and female servants?

"Therefore, the leprosy of Naaman shall cleave to you and to your descendants forever." So he went out from his presence a leper as white as snow (vv. 25–27).

Exposed and sternly judged, Gehazi experienced a horrible punishment. He had not only gone against the decision of the prophet, he had lied to him when confronted with his deeds. The servant was accountable! I repeat this same theme you have already read several times in this book. Accountability is essential in order for any servant to remain pure and pliable clay in the Master's hand. Would to God Jim Jones had applied that same truth before he began his downward spiral, taking hundreds with him.

Jim Jones is so unlike the man Rudyard Kipling had in mind when he wrote *If*. This poem is an undying challenge to every one of us who desires to serve:

> If you can keep your head when all about you
>   Are losing theirs and blaming it on you;
> If you can trust yourself when all men doubt you,
>   But make allowance for their doubting too;
> If you can wait and not be tired by waiting,
>   Or being lied about, don't deal in lies,
> Or being hated, don't give way to hating,
>   And yet don't look too good, nor talk too wise:
>
> If you can dream—and not make dreams your
>   master;
>   If you can think—and not make thoughts your
>   aim;
> If you can meet with Triumph and Disaster
>   And treat those two imposters just the same;
>
> . . . .
>
> If you can talk with crowds and keep your virtue,
>   Or walk with kings—nor lose the common touch;
> If neither foes nor loving friends can hurt you;
>   If all men count with you, but none too much;
> If you can fill the unforgiving minute
>   With sixty seconds' worth of distance run—
> Yours is the Earth and everything that's in it,
>   And—what is more—you'll be a Man, my son!

SOME LINGERING LESSONS

We have attempted to maintain an objective stance as we have investigated the life of a servant in the Old Testament. We have discovered four common perils he faced, identical to those we wrestle with:
- Being overprotective and possessive of the one he served.
- Feeling used and unappreciated.
- Experiencing undeserved disrespect and resentment.
- Having hidden greed—desiring to be rewarded.

From these very real and common perils there emerges at least three timely lessons for all of us to remember.

1. **No servant is completely safe.** A tough truth to accept! We who give and give become increasingly more vulnerable as time passes. As I shall point out in my chapter on the consequences of serving others, there are times we'll get ripped off. We *will* be used. We *will* feel unappreciated. But realizing ahead of time this will happen, we are better equipped to handle it when it comes. The proper perspective will guard us against stumbling into one of these perils.

A statement from one of C. S. Lewis's books often comes to mind:

> To love at all is to be vulnerable. Love anything, and your heart will certainly be wrung and possibly be broken. If you want to make sure of keeping it intact, you must give your heart to no one, not even to an animal. Wrap it carefully round with hobbies and little luxuries; avoid all entanglements; lock it up safe in the casket or coffin of your selfishness. But in that casket—safe, dark, motionless, airless—it will change. It will not be broken; it will become unbreakable, impenetrable, irredeemable. . . . The only place outside Heaven where you can be perfectly safe from all the dangers . . . of love is Hell.[4]

No servant is completely safe. Lean hard on the Master when you serve others.

2. **Most deeds will be initially unrewarded.** Again, this is helpful to know before we plunge in head first. If you are the type who needs a lot of strokes from people, who has to be appreciated before you can continue very long, you'd better forget about being a servant. More often than not, you will be overlooked, passed up, behind the scenes, and virtually unknown. Your reward will not come from without, but from within. Not from people, but from the satisfaction God gives you down inside.

Much of the ministry requires this mentality. A pastor may stand at the door of the church following his sermon and shake hands with the flock as everybody says nice things about him (my friend Howard Hendricks calls this "the glorification of the worm," a description I certainly agree with), but in reality, if that man preaches for those few moments of flattery—*and most don't*—he's in the wrong business. True servants readily accept the truth of this familiar piece:

So send I you to labor unrewarded.
To serve unpaid, unloved, unsought, unknown,
To bear rebuke, to suffer scorn and scoffing,
So send I you to toil for Me alone. . . .

So send I you to leave your life's ambition,
To die to dear desire, self-will resign,
To labor long and love where men revile you,
So send I you to lose your life in Mine.

"As the Father hath sent me, So send I you."[5]

Most of the servant's deeds will be initially unrewarded. That's a basic axiom we must accept.

3. **All motives must be honestly searched.** Learn a lesson from Gehazi. Before jumping, think to ask why. Before accepting any of Naaman's tangible gifts of gratitude (and there are occasions when such is perfectly acceptable), probe into your reason for doing so. Check your motive, fellow servant.

During my days in seminary, I formed a habit that helped me immensely throughout life. I had my artistic sister Luci print a simple, three-word question on a small rectangular card I placed on the wall above the desk where I spent so much of my time. Just black letters on a white card, with a bold question mark at the end:

WHAT'S YOUR MOTIVE?

I no longer have the card, but the question is now indelibly etched on my mind. I ask it almost every day of my life. It has proven to be an essential checkpoint I now apply on a regular basis:
"Why are you planning this?"
"What's the reason behind your doing that?"
"Why did you say yes (or no)?"
"What is the motive for writing that letter?"
"Why are you excited over this opportunity?"
"What causes you to bring up that subject?"
"Why did you mention his/her name?"
"What's your motive, Swindoll?"

Searching, probing, penetrating questions. If Gehazi had only done that, the man would never have died as tragic a death as he did. Frankly, I'm grateful such extreme consequences don't happen to us today when our motives are wrong. If they did, churches would be full of people with leprosy.

Because the path of servanthood is so perilous, we need to cultivate a sensitive walk with God marked by *obedience*. This is so important, I have decided to dedicate the next chapter to it.

11

The
Obedience
of a Servant

A familiar essay anonymously written many years ago says this about Jesus Christ:

> Nineteen long centuries have come and gone and today he is the centerpiece of the human race and the leader of the column of progress. I am far within the mark when I say that all the armies that ever marched, all the navies that ever were built; all the parliaments that ever sat and all the kings that ever reigned, put together, have not affected the life of man upon this earth as powerfully as has that one solitary life.

The late Wilbur Smith, respected Bible scholar of the last generation, wrote:

> The latest edition of the *Encyclopaedia Britannica* gives twenty thousand words to this person, Jesus, and does not even hint that He did not exist—more words, by the way, than are given to Aristotle, Alexander, Cicero, Julius Caesar, or Napoleon Bonaparte.[1]

George Buttrick, in a *Life* magazine article, adds:

> Jesus gave history a new beginning. In every land he is at home. . . . His birthday is kept across the world. His death-day has set a gallows against every city skyline.[2]

Even Napoleon admitted:

> I know men and I tell you that Jesus Christ was no mere man: Between Him and whoever else in the world there is no possible term of comparison.[3]

Impressive words.

So goes the testimony of influential people—and they could be multiplied by the hundreds—regarding the most phenomenal Person who ever cast a shadow across earth's landscape. Without question, He is unique. He is awesome in the truest sense of the term.

But what was He like *personally* down inside His skin? Is there any place, for example, where He describes *Himself*? The answer is yes. Does that description fit the common idea of human greatness? The answer is no. Unlike most influential, celebrity types, Jesus' description of Himself doesn't sound like the popular hype we've grown accustomed to hearing.

For example, recently I received in my daily stack of mail a multicolored brochure advertising and announcing a series of lectures to be delivered in Los Angeles by a man (a Christian "superstar") who has traveled widely, whose name is familiar to most folks in the family of God. I must confess I lifted my eyebrows with surprise when I read these words written in that brochure describing the man:

> *A phenomenal individual . . .*
> *In great demand around the world . . .*
> *Today's most sought-after speaker!*

That's a far cry from the way Jesus Christ described Himself.

A Self-Description of Jesus

I've been involved in a serious study of Scripture for well over twenty years, and in all that time I have found only one place where Jesus Christ—in His own words—describes his own "inner man." In doing so, He uses only two words. Unlike a Los Angeles celebrity, those words are not *phenomenal* and *great*. He doesn't even mention that He was *sought after* as a speaker. Although it is true, He doesn't say: "I am wise and powerful," "I am holy and eternal," or "I am all-knowing and absolute deity." Do you know what He said? Hold on, it may surprise you.

> Come to Me, all who are weary and heavy-laden, and I will give you rest.
> Take my yoke upon you, and learn from Me, for I am gentle and humble in heart; and YOU SHALL FIND REST FOR YOUR SOUL (Matt. 11:28–29).

I am *gentle*. I am *humble*. These are servant terms. *Gentle* is the same word we examined rather carefully in chapter 7 when we analyzed that particular characteristic of a servant. The word means strength under control. You may recall, it is used of a wild stallion that has been tamed. "Humble in heart" means lowly—the word picture of a helper. Unselfishness and thoughtfulness are in the description. It doesn't mean weak and insignificant, however.

Frankly, I find it extremely significant that when Jesus lifts the veil of silence and once for all gives us a glimpse of Himself, the real stuff of His inner person, He uses *gentle* and *humble*. As we came to realize early in this book, when we read that God the Father is committed to forming us to the image of His Son, qualities such as these are what He wants to see emerge. We are never more like Christ than when we fit into His description of Himself.

And how do those things reveal themselves? In what way do we reveal them the best? In our *obedience*. Servanthood and obedience go together like Siamese twins. And the finest illustration of this is the Son Himself who openly confessed, ". . . I do nothing of My own initiative . . . I always do the things that are pleasing to Him . . . (John 8:28–29). In other words, Jesus' self-description was verified by His obedience. Like no one else who has ever lived, He practiced what He preached.

ILLUSTRATION OF JESUS' SELF-DESCRIPTION

The gentle and humble lifestyle of the Savior is nowhere more evident than in the account of John 13 where He washed the feet of His friends, the disciples. In that event, He left us some timeless principles regarding servanthood we dare not ignore. If we are serious about "improving our serve," we must take time to learn and apply the facts as well as the implications of John 13:4–17.

Background Information

The scene before us in this chapter occurred in first-century Jerusalem. Paved roads were few. In fact, within most cities they were unheard of. The roads and alleys in Jerusalem were more like winding dirt trails, all covered with a thick layer of dust. When the rains came, those paths were liquid slush, several inches of thick mud. It was the custom, therefore, for the host to provide a slave at the door of his home to wash the feet of the dinner guests as they arrived. The servant knelt with a pitcher of water, a pan, and a towel and washed the dirt or mud off the feet as each guest prepared to enter the home. Shoes, boots, and sandals were left at the door, a custom still prevalent in the Far East. If a home could not afford a slave, one of the early arriving guests would graciously take upon himself the role of the house servant and wash the feet of those who came. What is interesting is that *none* of the disciples had volunteered for that lowly task . . . so the room was filled with proud hearts and dirty feet. Interestingly, those disciples were willing to fight for a throne, but not a towel. Things haven't changed a lot since then, by the way.

Personal Demonstration

Read rather carefully the account of what transpired:

Jesus . . . rose from supper . . . and taking a towel, girded Himself about.

Then He poured water into the basin, and began to wash the disciples' feet, and to wipe them with the towel with which He was girded.

And so He came to Simon Peter. He said to Him, "Lord, do You wash my feet?"

Jesus answered and said to him, "What I do you do not realize now; but you shall understand hereafter."

Peter said to Him, "Never shall You wash my feet!" Jesus answered him, "If I do not wash you, you have no part with Me."

Simon Peter said to Him, "Lord, not my feet only, but also my hands and my head."

Jesus said to him, "He who has bathed needs only to wash his feet, but is completely clean; and you are clean, but not all of you."

For He knew the one who was betraying Him; for this reason He said, "Not all of you are clean" (John 13:3–11).

As I meditate on the scene John describes for us, a couple or three observations about serving others emerge.

Being a Servant Is Unannounced

Jesus never said, "Men, I am now going to demonstrate servanthood—watch my humility." No way. That kind of obvious pride was the trademark of the Pharisees. If you wondered whether they were humble, all you had to do was hang around them awhile. Sooner or later they would announce it . . . which explains why Jesus came down so hard on them in Matthew 23.

Unlike those pious frauds, the Messiah slipped away from the table, quietly pulled off His outer tunic, and with towel, pitcher, and pan in hand, He moved quietly from man to man. Now understand, please, that they weren't sitting as they are portrayed in Leonardo da Vinci's work *The Last Supper*. All due respect for that genius, but he missed it when he portrayed the biblical scene through Renaissance eyes. They were not sitting in ladderback, dining-room chairs all on one side of a long table! In those days, people reclined at a meal, actually leaning on one elbow as they lay on their side on a small thin pad or a larger rug covering the floor. The table was a low, rectangular block of wood upon which the food was placed. And they ate with their hands, not utensils. This position meant that if your feet were not clean, your neighbor was very much aware of it. It would be hard to ignore a face full of dirty feet.

As Jesus reached Peter, I am sure most of the small talk had dwindled. By now, the men realized their wrong. Guilt had begun to push its way into their hearts. Peter must have drawn his feet up close to him when he said, in effect, "No! Not *my* feet. Never, ever, ever will you wash my feet, from now 'til eternity!" This reveals a second observation about having a gentle and humble heart.

Being a Servant Includes Receiving Graciously as Well as Giving Graciously

Peter wasn't about to be that vulnerable. After all, Jesus was the Master. No way was He going to wash the dirt off Peter's feet! I ask you, is that humility? You know it's not. Being willing to *receive* sometimes takes more grace than giving to others. And our reluctance to do so really exposes our pride, doesn't it?

James "Frog" Sullivan, constantly on the move, heavily involved in one Christian meeting after another (with little regard for his own family's needs), faced a situation not unlike the one Peter experienced. His wife Carolyn broke emotionally. Frog had to admit her into a local psychiatric hospital for an extended period of time. With a mixture of intense feelings ranging from strong resentment and anger to confusion and guilt, he drove home a broken man and sat down to explain everything to his children, Cathy and Scott, that dark night. For the first time in their presence, this hard-charging, always-on-top, fast-moving leader and father began to cry. Listen to his honest admission:

> Not knowing how long it was going to be, or whether she was ever going to come out cured, I took the children for a hamburger and talked with them endlessly. I got them ready for bed and continued to talk. I knew that night that I was facing a crisis in my own life that would either make me or ruin me. That afternoon I had gone to a friend's house and had taken a fifth of whiskey of theirs home with me. After I put those kids to bed and prayed with them, my little Cathy saw me cry for the first time in her life. She said: "Dad, I've never seen you cry before." I think that night she learned some things about her dad. That I was a man, that I was human, that I was hurt, alone and lonely.
>
> I bathed, put on some pajamas, and headed for the icebox to mix a drink. At that very moment I think I acknowledged I was through with God for good, through with the Christian life I'd known because I had given everything to him and had now ended up with nothing but a hurt, lonely, confused wife and nest of problems. I was really angry, knowing once again that I had hurt Carolyn deeply. As I went to the refrigerator, the doorbell rang, and an unbelievably wonderful man, Jack Johnston, was standing in the doorway.
>
> I had already prayed earlier that night, and in the middle of my prayer I told God that I didn't understand. I had kept my end of the bargain, but he had done this dastardly thing to me. I didn't even know where he was or what he wanted from me any longer. I had given him my life blood and my family, and now he was

trying to destroy me. As Jack walked into the room, he grabbed me and hugged me tight for maybe ten or fifteen minutes, I don't remember. He hugged me so tight and with such strength of caring, that my anger, bitterness, and disappointment seemed transferred from my fragile soul to his very being. He never quoted verses, he never said everything was going to be all right; he just blessed me with a short prayer and walked out the door, carrying my hostilities into the night.

I didn't understand it then, and I don't pretend to understand it now. I still don't understand what happened to Carolyn. But because of Jack, I was able to accept the situation. The love we received from Christians in the next few months was astounding, overwhelmingly beautiful. Meals were brought into our home for one solid month. People came to make up our beds, clean our house. I received money in envelopes through the mail from unknown sources to help with medical expenses that soared out of sight . . .

The thing that destroys a good many of us as Christians is our inability to relate to each other in a warm, honest, compassionate sort of way. Even with those to whom I was close, I failed in this endeavor. I was so busy being a "doing" Christian (Boy, that certainly was me!) that I'd forgotten what God called me to be. For so long I didn't know that a Christian was supposed to let someone love him; I thought that he was always supposed to be loving somebody else. I didn't think it was necessary to let anyone love me, including Carolyn. It seems that in the context of my Christian faith, you were adequate if you could love people; but you were considered inadequate if you let them love you.[4]

I cannot criticize the man. I find those same self-sufficient tendencies in myself, I must confess. Being a super high-achiever, I find it difficult to receive from others. *Really* difficult. I'm usually on the giving end, not the receiving. My pride fights hard to stay intact.

This was brought home to me rather forcefully one Christmas season several years ago. A man in our church congregation drove over to our home with his Christmas gift to our family. Not something wrapped up in bright paper with a big ribbon, but a thoughtful gift of love demonstrated by washing all the windows of our home. I was studying that Saturday morning at my office at the church as my wife and our children welcomed him in. He quietly began doing the job. I drove up later that morning and immediately noticed his car out front. I wondered if there was perhaps some need (there I was again, thinking like I usually do).

The kids met me at the door with the news that Phil (not his real name) was there and was washing our windows. My immediate response, of course, was surprise. I knew he was a busy husband and father with many more things to do than clean *my* windows. I went to the patio and saw his smiling face.

"Phil, what's going on? Man, I can't believe this."

Still smiling, he responded, "Chuck, I just wanted to do this for you and your family. Merry Christmas!"

"Hey, Phil," (I'm now a little embarrassed) "what do you say you just finish up the patio doors, and we'll get the rest, okay?"

"Nope, I'd like to go all the way around."

"Gee, thanks, man . . . but you've got lots of other things more important to do. Tell you what, you get all the downstairs and the kids and I will get the upstairs."

"No, I'd really like to get up there too."

"Well, uh—why don't you get the outside all the way around and we'll get the inside?"

Phil paused, looked directly at me and said, "Chuck! I want to wash all the windows, upstairs and downstairs, inside and outside—every one of them. You are always giving. For a change, I'd like you to *receive*."

Suddenly, I realized what a battle I have graciously receiving others' gifts. I understand Peter's reluctance. Servanthood was hard for him, especially when it called for receiving from someone else.

Jesus said a strong thing to Peter when He spoke these words ". . . If I do not wash you, you have no part with me" (John 13:8). Our Lord's rebuke introduces a third observation.

Being a Servant Is Not a Sign of Inner Weakness, but Incredible Strength

There is no way to remove the jab and the twist from Christ's words to Peter. He said, in effect, "If you do not allow Me to do this, that is it. Get out!" Anybody who lives under the delusion that Christ was rather weak and spineless has overlooked such statements as this one. Being a servant in no way implies there will never be a confrontation or strong words shared with others. The Lord may choose to use the reproof of a servant who has earned the right to be heard even more often than that of an aggressive leader type.

It certainly worked with Peter. We know he got the message when he blurted out, in so many words, "Give me a bath!" No, that wasn't necessary, only his feet.

After Jesus brought back into balance Peter's overreaction, He sat down for a time of reflection and instruction among the men. John tells us what followed:

> And so when He had washed their feet, and taken His garments, and reclined at table again, He said to them, "Do you know what I have done to you?"

What a strange question. Obviously, they knew what He had done. He had washed their feet! But He had much more in mind than the obvious—Jesus always does. He wanted them to think deeply, to learn something very insightful and valuable as an obedient servant. Look at what He told them.

> "You call Me Teacher, and Lord; and you are right; for so I am.
> "If I then, the Lord and the Teacher, washed your feet, you also ought to wash one another's feet.
> "For I gave you an example that you also should do as I did to you.

"Truly, truly, I say to you, a slave is not greater than his master; neither one who is sent greater than the one who sent him.

"If you know these things, you are blessed if you do them" (John 13:13–17).

Direct Admonition

He threw them a curve. He began by stating His role of authority among them: the "Teacher," the "Lord." Now what would you expect they thought He would say next? The obvious: "I washed your feet—so—now you should wash My feet." I believe that's what they expected to hear, like our I-scratched-your-back-now-you-scratch-mine reaction.

But with Jesus, that would have been a privilege. Who *wouldn't* want to do that? We'd stand in line to wash our Savior's feet. But that is not what He said. That would not be anything near the epitome of servanthood.

He told them (and us) to wash *one another's* feet. What an admonition! "As I have done to you, you do to one another." Our obedience is put to the maximum test at that level.

Now here's the clincher, verse 15: "For I gave you an example that you should do as I did to you."

Let's read it in a much more popular way:

"I gave you an example that you should study about it on Sundays." No. Or . . .

"I gave you an example that you should form discussion groups and meditate on it." No.

Or how about . . .

"I gave you an example that you should memorize My words and repeat them often." No.

Jesus said it plainly. He was looking for action, not theory.

"I gave you an example that you should *do* as I did to you."

To make the value of obedience just as practical as possible, let's play "Let's pretend." Let's pretend that you work for me. In fact, you are my executive assistant in a company that is growing rapidly. I'm the owner and I'm interested in expanding overseas. To pull this off, I make plans to travel abroad and stay there until the new branch office gets established. I make all the arrangments to take my family in the move to Europe for six to eight months, and I leave you in charge of the busy stateside organization. I tell you that I will write you regularly and give you direction and instructions.

I leave and you stay. Months pass. A flow of letters are mailed from Europe and received by you at the national headquarters. I spell out all my expectations. Finally, I return. Soon after my arrival I drive down to the office. I am stunned! Grass and weeds have grown up high. A few windows along the street are broken. I walk into the receptionist's room and she is doing her nails, chewing gum, and listening to her favorite disco station. I look around and notice the waste baskets are overflowing, the carpet hasn't been vacuumed for weeks, and nobody seems concerned that the owner has returned. I ask about your whereabouts and someone in the crowded lounge area points down the hall and yells, "I think he's down there." Disturbed, I move in that direction and bump into you as you are finishing a chess game with our sales manager. I ask you to step into my office (which has been temporarily turned into a television room for watching afternoon soap operas).

"What in the word is going on, man?"

"What do ya' mean, Chuck?"

"Well, look at this place! Didn't you get any of my letters?"

"Letters? Oh, yeah—sure, got every one of them. As a matter of fact, Chuck, we have had *letter study* every Friday night since you left. We have even divided all the personnel into small groups and discussed many of the things you wrote. Some of those things were really interesting. You'll be pleased to know that a few of us have actually committed to memory some of your sentences and paragraphs. One or two memorized an entire letter or two! Great stuff in those letters!"

"Okay, okay—you got my letters, you studied them and meditated on them, discussed and even memorized them. BUT WHAT DID YOU DO ABOUT THEM?"

"Do? Uh—we didn't *do* anything about them."

Sound a little familiar?

Jesus, the Lord, goes to the bottom line here in John 13. "I left you an example of what you should *do*—carry out my directions, fulfill my commands, follow my instructions." That's obedience—doing what we are told to do. He washed dirty feet, then He said, "You do that too," meaning that we are to serve others. Let's understand, however, that the right attitude must accompany the right actions. Be careful with the temperature of the water you use! It's easy to use boiling water when you "wash feet" . . . or ice cold water. I know some who have come pretty close to dry cleaning a few feet. Ah, that's bad. The goal is to remove dirt, not skin, from the feet.

APPROPRIATION OF CHRIST'S INSTRUCTION

As we think about these things and attempt to read them as our Savior meant them, we realize the tremendous emphasis He put on obedience. As we have seen before, this was a major difference between Him and the Pharisees. They loved to dwell in the realm of theory. Hypocrisy marked their steps. They talked a good fight when it came to servanthood . . . but they lacked the one ingredient that could make everything authentic: *obedience*. Perhaps that explains why He came down so strong on it.

As I think about appropriating Christ's model and command, three specifics seem important enough to mention.

1. **Obedience means personal involvement**.

If I then, the Lord and the Teacher, washed your feet, you also ought to wash one another's feet (John 13:14).

We cannot serve one another in absentia or at arm's length. It means if someone is drowning in a troubled sea, we get wet, we get in touch. It means if someone drifts away, we don't ignore that person, we reach out to help and restore. Nobody ever learned how to water ski in the living room through a correspondence course. You have to get into the water and get personally involved. Think about this. Honestly now, are you willing to get involved and help at least one person in need? Willingness must precede involvement.

2. **Obedience requires Christlike unselfishness**.

For I gave you an example that you also should do as I did to you (John 13:15).

Let your eyes dig into those words. To pull off this concept, we'll need to see others as Christ sees them. We'll need to risk reaching out, giving up the luxury of staying safe . . . giving up *our* preferences for His. Unselfishness never comes easy.

3. **Obedience results in ultimate happiness**.

If you know these things, you are blessed if you do them (John 13:17).

Notice, in the final analysis happiness comes from *doing* these things. Meaning what? Namely this, we have to carry it out before we can enter into the joy of serving. Just studying about it or discussing it produces no lasting happiness. The fun comes when we roll up our sleeves, wrap the towel around our waist, and wash a few feet . . . quietly . . . graciously . . . cheerfully . . . like Christ who was "gentle" and "humble in heart."

Does that mean it will never backfire on us? Am I saying those with servant hearts will not get ripped off or hurt in the process? Does this promise of happiness mean we'll be protected from suffering? No, *a thousand times no*! To keep everything realistic, we must face the very painful consequences. Even when we have been "gentle" and "humble in heart." What else can we expect? The perfect Model of obedience finished His earthly life as a corpse on a cross.

The next chapter will help keep all of this in proper perspective. There are often consequences connected with serving, even when we have been obedient. And those consequences are neither pleasant nor expected, as we shall see. Brace yourself, fellow servant. This may hurt a little.

12

The Consequences of Serving

We Americans like things to be logical and fair. We not only like that, we operate our lives on that basis. Logic and fairness are big guns in our society.

Meaning this: If I do what is right, good will come to me, and if I do what is wrong, bad things will happen to me. Right brings rewards and wrong brings consequences. That's a very logical and fair axiom of life, but there's only one problem with it. *It isn't always true.* Life doesn't work out quite that well. There isn't a person reading these words who hasn't had the tables turned. All of us have had the unhappy and unfortunate experience of doing what is right, yet we suffered for it. And we have also done what is wrong on a few occasions without being punished. The latter, we can handle rather easily . . . but the former is a tough pill to swallow.

I don't find it a nagging problem, for example, to drive 65 miles an hour on the highway and get away with it. Normally, I don't lie awake through the night feeling bad because an officer failed to give me a ticket—even though, in all fairness, I deserved one. But you let one of those guys ticket me when I have done nothing wrong, and I'm fit to be tied! And so are you. We *hate* being ripped off. Consequences belong to wrong actions. When they attach themselves to right actions, we struggle with resentment and anger.

A Realistic Appraisal of Serving

I wish I could say that the only place such things happen is in our driving, but I cannot. They also happen in our serving. You will give, forgive, forget, release your own will, obey God to the maximum, and wash dirty feet with an attitude of gentleness and humility. And after all those beautiful things, you will get ripped off occasionally. I want all of us to enter into this ministry of servanthood with our eyes wide open. If we serve others long enough, we will suffer wrong treatment for doing right things. Knowing all this ahead of time will help "improve your serve," believe me.

Suffering for Doing What Is Right

The Bible doesn't hide this painful reality from us. In 1 Peter 2:20-24 (addressed to servants, by the way—see verse 18), we read:

> For what credit is there if, when you sin and are harshly treated, you endure it with patience? But if when you do what is right and suffer for it you patiently endure it, this finds favor with God.
>
> For you have been called for this purpose, since Christ also suffered for you, leaving you an example for you to follow in His steps, WHO COMMITTED NO SIN, NOR WAS ANY DECEIT FOUND IN HIS MOUTH; and while being reviled, He did not revile in return; while suffering, He uttered no threats, but kept entrusting Himself to Him who judges righteously; and He Himself bore our sins in His body on the cross, that we might die to sin and live to righteousness; for by His wounds you were healed.

Part of this "makes sense," according to our logical and fair standard. Part of it doesn't. If a person does wrong and then suffers the consequences, even though he or she patiently endures the punishment, nobody applauds. Who is really impressed, for example, if Charles Manson quietly spends his years behind bars without complaining? It's no great virtue.

But—now get this clearly fixed in your mind—when you do what is *right* and *suffer* for it with grace and patience, God applauds! Illustration: Jesus Christ's suffering and death on the cross. He, the perfect God-man, was mistreated, hated, maligned, beaten, and finally nailed to a cruel cross. He suffered awful consequences even though He spent His life giving and serving. Listen to 1 Peter 3:17-18.

> For it is better, if God should will it so, that you *suffer* for doing what is right rather than for doing what is wrong.
>
> For Christ also died for sins once for all, the just for the unjust, in order that He might bring us to God, having been put to death in the flesh, but made alive in the spirit.

One thing is certain: If people treated a perfect individual that way, then imperfect people cannot expect to escape mistreatment. If it hasn't happened to you yet, it will. In light of that fact, I would like to dedicate this chapter to those of you who have been mistreated in the past, and to those who are now being mistreated . . . as well as to those who will be mistreated in the future!

Responding to Treatment that Is Wrong

The consequence of serving is no new phenomenon. It goes a long way back in time. Greathearted, loving, caring, sacrificial servants of the living God have known ill-treatment down through the centuries. I'm not aware of a more moving section of Scripture than these verses out of Hebrews 11, which declare the reality of the consequences of serving:

> And some women, through faith, received their loved ones back again from death. But others trusted God and were beaten to death, preferring to die rather than turn from God and be free—trusting that they would rise to a better life afterwards.
> Some were laughed at and their backs cut open with whips, and others were chained in dungeons. Some died by stoning and some by being sawed in two; others were promised freedom if they would renounce their faith, then were killed with the sword. Some went about in skins of sheep and goats, wandering over deserts and mountains, hiding in dens and caves. They were hungry and sick and ill-treated—too good for this world. And these men of faith, though they trusted God and won his approval, none of them received all that God had promised them (Heb. 11:35–39, TLB).

Tortured. Rejected. Threatened. Hungry. Sick. Martyred. People who were "too good for this world" were kicked around like big rag dolls . . . even though they gave and they served. If it happened to them—need I say more? Yes, maybe I should.

My major goal in this chapter is to help prepare you for the inevitable. Bitterness is often bred in a context of disillusionment. Many a Christian, unfortunately, is sidelined today, eaten up by the acid of resentment and bitterness, because he or she was mistreated after doing what was right. If this chapter will preserve you from the paralyzing sting of bitterness and disillusionment, it will have served its purpose.

THE DARK SIDE OF SERVING

Let's go back to 2 Corinthians, chapter 4, a section of Scripture we've looked at several times already. Perhaps, then, you remember these words:

> For we do not preach ourselves but Christ Jesus as Lord, and ourselves as your bond-servants for Jesus' sake.
> For God, who said, "Light shall shine out of darkness," is the One who has shone in our hearts to give the light of the knowledge of the glory of God in the face of Christ.
> But we have this treasure in earthen vessels, that the surpassing greatness of the power may be of God and not from ourselves (2 Cor. 4:5–7).

Words of an honest, humble, transparent servant. We Christians have received a priceless treasure (the glorious gospel) in a very frail and perishable container (our weak bodies). There is a reason. So nobody will have any question about the source of power, it must be of God and not of any human origin. And so—to verify just how frail our humanity is, Paul lists four common struggles servants live with. I'm calling them consequences. Let's see all four in the two verses that follow before we analyze each one and then expand on them in 2 Corinthians 11. If you have a pencil handy, you might circle the four terms in your Bible: afflicted, perplexed, persecuted, struck down.

> . . . we are afflicted in every way, but not crushed; perplexed, but not despairing; persecuted, but not forsaken; struck down, but not destroyed (2 Cor. 4:8–9).

Affliction

This word comes from a Greek term that suggests the idea of pressure. This is stress brought on by difficult circumstances or antagonistic people.[1] In other words, when servants are "afflicted," they feel under pressure, harassed, and oppressed. The Greek verb, *thlibo*, is a strong one, meaning at times "to treat with hostility."

Confusion

Paul goes on to say there are times when servants of God become "perplexed." Interestingly, the combination of Greek terms that comprise the original word means "without a way." It is a picture of confusion—not knowing where or to whom to turn for help. Included in the meaning of this word would be such perplexing predicaments as being without necessary resources, feeling embarrassed, and in doubt so far as procedure is concerned. We have the phrase, "at a loss" which adequately describes that uncertain feeling. There is more.

Persecution

Originally, the term persecution meant "to run after, pursue."[2] It's the idea of being chased, having others "on our case," we would say. It is an active, aggressive word conveying everything from being intimidated to being assaulted, actually attacked. Servants *will* suffer persecution. You may recall our discussing this in chapter 8, when we analyzed and applied the last beatitude. Paul comes right out and predicts it *will* happen. "And indeed, all who desire to live godly in Christ Jesus will be persecuted." Persecution is one of those painful consequences, along with affliction and confusion. Finally, he names one more.

Rejection

"Struck down"—this is the idea of being thrown down, shoved aside, or cast off. This explains why J. B. Phillips paraphrases it,". . . we may be knocked down. . . ." Amazing thing! Even though we may faithfully and consistently do our job, help and serve and give to others, we can expect, on occasion, to be thrown aside and rejected.

A crazy illustration of this occurred to me recently. If you enjoy watching and playing the game of football (I certainly do), you have observed a curious addition in the last several years. It is called a "spike." It's rather unusual. A team fights its way toward the goal line yard by yard. Runs and play-action fakes and passes are mixed in the game plan to catch the defense by surprise. Minutes seem like hours as the offensive team plods along. Suddenly, it happens. A play works beautifully—the defense is out of position—and streaking to the long-awaited touchdown is a muscular running back or some fleet-footed split end. Six points! But as soon as he crosses the line, this athlete takes the ball and *slams* the little thing to the ground. With *all* his might. I mean, that ball bounces like mad as it is mercilessly thrown down. The guy doesn't so much as say, "Thanks, ball."

I've thought, "What if that ball had feeling? What if it could talk?" Can you imagine how it would react after being spiked? It had done its job well. Stayed inflated. Didn't jump out of the player's arms—no fumble. *It* is the reason the team got six points. And after all that, all the thanks it gets is a vicious spike. *Talk about rejection!* So it is with God's servants. We do what is right . . . and we get tossed aside. Sometimes, viciously. It hurts.

Servants, listen up! These four words form an inspired "outline" of the treatment we can expect. These are the consequences—the dark side—of serving. Let's keep our eyes wide open when we grab the towel to do a little one-on-one foot washing. Every once in a while we are going to get kicked. Now, this doesn't mean God has abandoned us or that we are out of His will. It just means people are people, sheep are sheep. It's all part of the humbling process God uses in shaping our lives "to bear the family likeness of His Son" (Rom. 8:29, PHILLIPS).

SPELLING OUT THE CONSEQUENCES

Now—so much for the theory. Let's see how these things impact us in everyday living. Turn to 2 Corinthians 11. The same one who wrote about affliction, confusion, persecution, and rejection in chapter 4 now amplifies each in chapter 11. The fourth chapter tells us what will happen, the eleventh spells out how. But before we see how these chapters fit together, let me show you something interesting. In verse 23 of 2 Corinthians 11, Paul asks: "Are they servants of Christ? . . . I more so." And immediately what does he mention to show that he has a better claim on servanthood than others? The things he *suffered!* Isn't that significant? In the next several verses, Paul lists one painful consequence after another to prove to his readers just how authentic a servant he was. It is an inescapable fact. If you get serious about being shaped into Christ's image, you'll have to learn to cope with the consequences. Those who serve *will* suffer.

Let's read these verses slowly:

> Are they servants of Christ? (I speak as if insane) I more so; in far more labors, in far more imprisonments, beaten times without number, often in danger of death.
> Five times I received from the Jews thirty-nine lashes.
> Three times I was beaten with rods, once I was stoned, three times I was shipwrecked, a night and a day I have spent in the deep.
> I have been on frequent journeys, in dangers from rivers, dangers from robbers, dangers from my countrymen, dangers from the Gentiles, dangers in the city, dangers in the wilderness, dangers on the sea, dangers among false brethren; I have been in labor and hardship, through many sleepless nights, in hunger and thirst, often without food, in cold and exposure.
> Apart from such external things, there is the daily pressure upon me of concern for all the churches (2 Cor. 11:23-28).

What stories Paul could tell!

Now, remember the four words from 2 Corinthians 4? Chapter 11, verses 23-28, amplifies each. The comparison looks like this:

Chapter 4	*Chapter 11*
• Affliction	". . . in far more labors"
• Confusion	". . . in far more imprisonments"
• Persecution	". . . beaten times without number"
• Rejection	". . . often in danger of death"

The two are obviously tied together. Each of the four categories of consequences in chapter 4 is spelled out in chapter 11 where a few of the actual events are given.

In Labors

Answering to the pressure-and-stress (affliction) category are the "labors" Paul mentions when he shares:

> I have been in labor and hardship, through many sleepless nights, in hunger and thirst, often without food, in cold and exposure.
> Apart from such external things, there is the daily pressure upon me of concern for all the churches (2 Cor. 11:27-28).

Now *that's* being under pressure. Funny, we seldom think that a great apostle like Paul ever suffered from insomnia, but he did . . . sometimes because of acute deprivations, like hunger, cold and exposure . . . and sometimes because of his concern for the many ministries to which he had given himself. "Daily pressure" he calls it.

Pressure and stress are cripplers, sometimes killers. I was made aware of this rather forcefully when I read a book (*Executive's Survival Manual*) dealing with the stress executives must endure. In a chapter on "Executive Stress," the authors gauge the impact of pressure on people by measuring the stress factor in "life-change units."[3] The greater the number of units, the greater the risk of emotional or physical illness in the ensuing months. For example, they state if you have to endure 200 to 299 life-change units in a given year, the probability of your suffering some kind of illness within the next two years is 50 percent. If it is 300 or more units, it jumps to 80 percent. I was interested to discover the following list of pressure situations and their corresponding life-change units:[4]

1. Death of spouse	100
2. Divorce	73
3. Marital separation from mate	65
4. Detention in jail or other institution	63
5. Death of a close family member	63
6. Major personal injury or illness	53
7. Marriage	50
8. Being fired at work	47
9. Marital reconciliation with mate	45
10. Retirement from work	45
11. Major change in the health or behavior of a family member	44
12. Pregnancy	40
13. Sexual difficulties	39
14. Gaining a new family member (e.g., through birth, adoption, oldster moving in, etc.)	39
. . . .	
16. Major change in financial state (e.g., a lot worse off or, a lot better off than usual)	38
17. Death of a close friend	37
. . . .	
23. Son or daughter leaving home (e.g., marriage, attending college, etc.)	29
24. In-law troubles	29
. . . .	
30. Troubles with the boss	23
31. Major change in working hours or conditions	20
32. Change in residence	20
33. Changing to a new school	20
. . . .	

Reading what we do of Paul's pressures, we could assume his life-change units must have been 400 or more!

In Imprisonments

Answering to the "confusion" category of consequences, Paul next mentions the disillusioning times of mistreatment and imprisonment. There certainly must have been times he did not know where to turn—or to whom. Doubt and questions might well have haunted him with maddening regularity. Hear again verse 26:

> I have been on frequent journeys, in dangers from rivers, dangers from robbers, dangers from my countrymen, dangers from the Gentiles, dangers in the city, dangers in the wilderness, dangers on the sea, dangers among false brethren.

Here was one of those great men, "too good for this world," being pushed around, threatened, and living on the raw edge of constant danger. Eight times in this single verse Paul uses *kindunos*, a term translated "danger." If you imagine yourself in those many situations—and toss in several imprisonments to boot—you get the feeling of being "strung out," as we say today. Your mind plays tricks on you. You wonder where God is, and you occasionally even doubt God. You get disoriented, "mixed up" inside. And on top of all that is the one most common experience all who have been in prison admit—*profound loneliness*. Mix all that together . . . and you've got the picture.

Those who have read the remarkable story of Corrie ten Boom in *The Hiding Place*[5] have come to love that strong woman of God who emerged from the horrors of World War II with faith as solid as granite. But another story of similar tragedy by Elie Wiesel gives readers a different perspective on the horror of the holocaust. Wiesel's *Night* will grab you and not let you go. In terse, tightly packed sentences, he describes those scenes and his own confusion as he witnessed (in his teenage years) a chapter of life we would prefer to erase.

This young Jew saw it all. Fellow Jews from his village were stripped of their possessions and loaded into cattle cars, where a third of them died before they reached their destination. He saw babies pitchforked, little children hanged, weak and emaciated men killed by fellow prisoners for a single piece of molded bread. He even saw his mother, his lovely little sister, and all his family disappear into an oven fueled with human flesh.[6]

Wiesel's God was murdered at Birkenbau. Something dear and precious within his soul also died as all his dreams turned to dust.

Francois Mauriac, the Nobel Prize-winning French author, in writing the foreword to Wiesel's book, describes the time he first met Wiesel:

It was then that I understood what had first drawn me to the young Israeli: that look, as of a Lazarus risen from the dead, yet still a prisoner within the grim confines where he had strayed, stumbling among the shameful corpses. For him, Nietzche's cry expressed an almost physical reality: God is dead, the God of love, of gentleness, of comfort, the God of Abraham, of Isaac, of Jacob, has vanished forevermore, beneath the gaze of this child, in the smoke of a human holocaust exacted by Race, the most voracious of all idols. And how many pious Jews have experienced this death. On that day, horrible even among those days of horror, when the child watched the hanging (yes) of another child, who, he tells us, had the face of a sad angel, he heard someone behind him groan: "Where is God? Where is He? Where can He be now?"[7]

Confusion. Tragic, horrible confusion. Experiences like those we've just read will do that to you. But the vast difference between Corrie ten Boom and Elie Weisel cannot be ignored. Servants like Corrie ten Boom, who endure the consequences victoriously, testify of God's precious faithfulness even through days of confusion.

In Beatings

Answering to the "persecution" category, Paul mentions several specific examples:

Fives times I received from the Jews thirty-nine lashes.
Three times I was beaten with rods, once I was stoned, three times I was shipwrecked, a night and a day I have spent in the deep (2 Cor. 1:24–25).

Can you imagine being beaten "times without number" (v. 23)? I cannot. Here is the awful reality of physical abuse. Few people will ever know such pain to such an extreme. But if you think the man was pretty much alone in it all, get hold of a copy of *Fox's Book of Martyrs.*[8] You will find one account after another of raw, unashamed persecution. There is no way to get around it, God's servants often become scapegoats.

This is true emotionally more frequently than physically. Man's twisted depravity, for some reason, likes to express itself in this way. Take the prophet Daniel, for example. Faithful, efficient, honest, dedicated to the maximum, the man served others with a pure heart. But it backfired on him. According to the sixth chapter of the book that bears his name in the Old Testament, the very people he worked with turned on him. They set out to prove he lacked integrity. Determined to expose the real truth (which they assumed he was hiding), they left no stone unturned. Can you imagine how that hurt? Just listen:

Then this Daniel began distinguishing himself among the commissioners and satraps because he possessed an extraordinary spirit, and the king planned to appoint him over the entire kingdom.

Then the commissioners and satraps began trying to find a ground of accusation against Daniel in regard to government affairs; but they could find no ground of accusation or evidence of corruption, inasmuch as he was faithful, and no negligence or corruption was to be found in him (Dan. 7:3–4).

They found nothing. Bible students often emphasize that fact . . . and we should. But for a moment, picture yourself in Daniel's sandals. You are the object of investigation. You hear whisperings about your character. Stories swirl around calling into question your words, your actions. Every move you make is viewed with suspicion. And yet there is not a shred of truth to it. You have been a model of authenticity, you have devoted yourself to the dual role of helping others and honoring the Lord . . . and this is the thanks you get. I'll tell you, it takes the grace of Almighty God to press on under those circumstances *and* to accept His plan over our own.

It's like the poet's words:

In Acceptance Lieth Peace

He said, "I will forget the dying faces;
The empty places,
They shall be filled again.
O voices moaning deep within me, cease."
But vain the word; vain, vain:
Not in forgetting lieth peace.

He said, "I will crowd action upon action,
The strife of faction
Shall stir me and sustain;
O tears that drown the fire of manhood
cease."
But vain the word; vain, vain:
Not in endeavour lieth peace.

He said, "I will withdraw me and be quiet,
Why meddle in life's riot?
Shut be my door to pain.
Desire, thou dost befool me, thou shalt cease."
Bur vain the word; vain, vain:
Not in aloofness lieth peace.

He said, "I will submit; I am defeated.
God hath depleted
My life of its rich gain.
O futile murmurings, why will ye not cease?"
But vain the word; vain, vain:
Not in submission lieth peace.

He said, "I will accept the breaking sorrow
Which God to-morrow
Will to His son explain."
Then did the turmoil deep within him cease.
Not vain the word, not vain;
For in Acceptance lieth peace.[9]

In Danger of Death

There is one more comparison of consequences between chapters 4 and 11 of 2 Corinthians: "In danger of death" answers to the category of rejection. In 2 Corinthians 4:9, Paul states we are "struck down." And then to illustrate just how close he came to death itself, he mentions the following experiences in chapter eleven of this letter:

- Shipwrecked three times (11:25)
- A day and a night spent in the ocean (11:25)
- Surrounded by constant dangers (11:26)
- Without sufficient food (11:27)
- Being exposed to the elements (11:27)
- Escaping death by being let down a wall in a large basket (11:33).

This was no criminal. The man was innocent of wrong . . . yet he was misunderstood, mistreated, hunted like a wounded deer, and hated by those who once respected him. What happened? How could so much unfair, near-fatal treatment happen to a man like Paul? An even deeper question is this. How could and why would God permit it?

Without sounding glib . . . it was par for the servanthood course. Still is. Paul even admitted that we are:

. . . always carrying about in the body the dying of Jesus, that the life of Jesus also may be manifested in our body.

For we who live are constantly being delivered over to death for Jesus' sake, that the life of Jesus also may be manifested in our mortal flesh. . . .

Therefore we do not lose heart, but though our outer man is decaying, yet our inner man is being renewed day by day.

For momentary, light affliction is producing for us an eternal weight of glory far beyond all comparison, while we look not at the things which are seen, but at the things which are not seen, for the things which are seen are temporal, but the things which are not seen are eternal (2 Cor. 4:10–11, 16–18).

That sounds beautiful, almost poetic. However, it is one thing to read it as black print on a white page, but it's another thing entirely to embrace that mind-set when all hell breaks loose against us.

How does the servant of God cope when the bottom drops out?

SUGGESTIONS FOR COPING WITH CONSEQUENCES

I have found great help from two truths God gave me at a time in my life when I was bombarded with a series of unexpected and unfair blows (from my perspective). In my darkest hours these principles become my anchor of stability, my only means of survival. Afflicted, confused, persecuted, and rejected in that situation, I claimed these two truths and held onto them like one beaten by wild waves, strong winds, and pounding rain would grab hold of the mast on a ship at sea. God took me through the consequences and kept me from becoming a bitter man.

Because they worked for me, I pass them on to you. At the risk of sounding simplistic, I would suggest that you not only write them down where you can read them often, but also that you might commit them to memory. The day will come when you will be thankful you did, I assure you. They have scriptural support, but I'll not list all those verses for the sake of brevity and clarity.

Here is the first truth to claim when enduring the consequences of suffering: **Nothing touches me that has not passed through the hands of my heavenly Father. Nothing.** Whatever occurs, God has sovereignly surveyed and approved. We may not know why (we may *never* know why), but we do know our pain is no accident to Him who guides our lives. He is, in no way, surprised by it all. Before it ever touches us, it passes through Him.

The second truth to claim is this: **Everything I endure is designed to prepare me for serving others more effectively. Everything.**

Since my heavenly Father is committed to shaping me into the image of His Son, He knows the ultimate value of this painful experience. It is a necessary part of the preparation process. It is being used to empty our hands of our own resources, our own sufficiency, and turn us back to Him—the faithful Provider. And God knows what will get through to us.

When our older daughter Charissa underwent two eye surgeries, an ordeal I mentioned in my book *Three Steps Forward, Two Steps Back*,[10] I thought the test was over. It wasn't. Late in the summer of 1979, she suffered a severe fall, resulting in a fracture of two vertabrae in her back. During the early part of that episode, her mother and I were forced to wait on the physical outcome. The most difficult discipline in the Christian life, in my opinion, is waiting. But God used that to force us to lean on him . . . to trust Him . . . to believe in Him . . .

to release our will and accept His. Words fail to describe the pain of that transfer of wills. Finally, when we made the transfer, empty-handed and totally dependent, Cynthia and I leaned hard on our God. It was a time of *great* stress.

Today, Charissa's broken back has healed. Our daughter is neither paralyzed nor handicapped in any way. She is whole, healthy, energetic, and a very grateful young woman. And—I might add—*all* the Swindolls have learned again the value of being cast upon our God. Admittedly, in the pain of it all, I wrestled with Him. But, looking back, I can clearly see that the process required being emptied of our own strength. God designed the process to equip my family— and especially their dad—to be better servants.

> One by one He took them from me
>   All the things I valued most;
> 'Til I was empty-handed,
>   Every glittering toy was lost.
> And I walked earth's highways, grieving,
>   In my rags and poverty.
> Until I heard His voice inviting,
>   "Lift those empty hands to Me!"
>
> Then I turned my hands toward heaven,
>   And He filled them with a store
> Of His own transcendent riches,
>   'Til they could contain no more.
>
> And at last I comprehended
>   With my stupid mind, and dull,
> That God cannot pour His riches
>   Into hands already full.
>   —Source Unknown

Things may not be logical and fair, but when God is directing the events of our lives, they are right. Even when we suffer the painful consequences of serving others.

13

The Rewards
of Serving

So much for the dark side of serving. Let's end on a positive note. Serving *definitely* has rewards, and they are numerous. They far outweigh the consequences. When we think about them, they motivate us to keep going.

One of the great doctrines of Christianity is our firm belief in a heavenly home. Ultimately, we shall spend eternity with God in the place He has prepared for us. And part of that exciting anticipation is His promise to reward His servants for a job well done. I don't know many believers in Jesus Christ who never think of being with their Lord in heaven, receiving His smile of acceptance, and hearing His "well done, good and faithful servant." We even refer to one who died in this way: "He has gone home to his reward." A lot of strange opinions (some weird and wild ideas) surround this subject. But the Bible is fairly clear regarding the rewards of serving. First and foremost, we need to hear what it says.

I remember, as a little boy in a south Texas Baptist church, singing the words:

> I am thinking today of that beautiful land
>   I shall reach when the sun goeth down;
> When through wonderful grace by my Saviour I stand,
>   Will there be any stars in my crown?
>
> Will there be any stars, any stars in my crown
>   When at evening the sun goeth down?
> When I wake with the blest in the mansions of rest,
>   Will there be any stars in my crown?
>   —Eliza E. Hewitt, "Will There Be Any Stars?"

137

I wondered about that. It seemed spooky, almost unreal. How could stars be in a crown I wore?

Many years later I learned and loved another piece of church music. It came from an old volume of devotional verse bearing the title *Immanuel's Land and Other Pieces* by A. R. C., the initials modestly representing the name of Anne R. Cousin. When she was only thirty-two, the author composed her best-known hymn, "The Sands of Time Are Sinking." The original poem contains nineteen verses,[1] but most Christians are familiar with only four or five. The concluding stanza will always be one of my favorites:

> The bride eyes not her garment,
> But her dear bridegroom's face;
> I will not gaze at glory,
> But on my King of grace:
> Not at the crown He giveth,
> But on His piercéd hand;
> The Lamb is all the glory
> Of Emmanuel's land.

Both those old songs speak of heavenly crowns. They sound interesting, but what does *the Bible* say? Does Scripture support the idea of tangible rewards?

BIBLICAL FACTS ABOUT REWARDS

In 1 Corinthians 3:10–14 we read:

> According to the grace of God which was given to me, as a wise masterbuilder I laid a foundation, and another is building upon it. But let each man be careful how he builds upon it.
> For no-man can lay a foundation other than the one which is laid, which is Jesus Christ.
> Now if any man builds upon the foundation with gold, silver, precious stones, wood, hay, straw, each man's work will become evident; for the day will show it, because it is to be revealed with fire; and the fire itself will test the quality of each man's work.
> If any man's work which he has built upon it remains, he shall receive a reward.

Scripture not only supports the idea of eternal rewards, it spells out the specifics. I find three primary facts about rewards in this section of Scripture:

1. **Most rewards are received in heaven, not on earth.**

Now don't misunderstand. There are earthly rewards. Even the world provides certain people with special honors: the Pulitzer Prize, Nobel Peace Prize, Academy Awards, Emmy, Tony, Grammy . . . and we all know that athletes win

All-American honors or All-Pro and the Heisman Trophy. The military also offers medals of bravery, like the Navy Cross, the Purple Heart, the Bronze Star, and the Medal of Honor. But when it comes to servanthood, God reserves special honor for that day when "each man's work will become evident" and "he shall receive a reward" (3:13–14). Most of the rewards servants will receive will be given after death, not before.

2. **All rewards are based on quality, not quantity.**

Did you notice this in those verses from 1 Corinthians'. ". . . the fire itself will test the *quality* of each man's work" (emphasis mine).

We humans are impressed with size and volume and noise and numbers. It is easy to forget that God's eye is always on motive, authenticity, the real truth *beneath* the surface, never the external splash. When He rewards servants, it will be based on *quality*—which means everybody has an equal opportunity to receive a reward. The dear older lady who prays will be rewarded as much as the evangelist who preaches to thousands. The quiet, faithful friend who assists another in need will be rewarded as much as the strong natural leader whose gifts are more visible. A cool cup of water given to a hurting soul, bruised with adversity, will be rewarded as much as an act of sacrifice on the mission field. God, our faithful Lord, promises to reward the quality of our work. The glory may be postponed until eternity, but it will come, which leads me into the third fact about rewards.

3. **No reward that is postponed will be forgotten**.

Make no mistake about it, the Bible clearly teaches ". . . he shall receive a reward." God doesn't settle His accounts at the end of every day. Nor does He close out His books toward the end of everyone's life. No, not then. But be assured, fellow servant, when that day in eternity dawns, when time shall be no more on this earth, no act of serving others—be it well-known or unknown by others—will be forgotten.

A nineteenth-century senator, Benjamin Hill, spoke with eloquence when he made this fitting tribute to Confederate General Robert E. Lee (a great man with a servant's spirit):

> He was a foe without hate, a friend without treachery, a soldier without cruelty, and a victim without murmuring. He was a public officer without vices, a private citizen without wrong, a neighbor without reproach, a Christian without hypocrisy, and a man without guilt. He was Caesar without his ambition. Frederick without his tyranny. Napoleon without his selfishness, and Washington without his reward.[2]

And the marvelous part of it all is that you don't have to be a Robert E. Lee to be remembered. You don't have to be a courageous soldier in battle or a statesman who graciously accepts defeat. You can be a "nobody" in the eyes of this world and your faithful God will, someday, reward your every act of servanthood. Rewards may be postponed, but they will not be forgotten forever. Unlike many people today, God keeps His promises.

Someone once counted all the promises in the Bible and came up with an amazing figure of almost 7500. Among that large number are some specific promises servants can claim today. Believe me, there are times the only hope to keep you going will be in something God has declared in His Word, promising that your work is not in vain. Let's divide these promises into two groups—those that have to do with *His* faithfulness and those that have to do with *our* faithfulness.

Regarding His Faithfulness

I want to mention several helpful promises that assure us of God's sticking by us before I pinpoint one in particular that deserves special attention.
Isaiah 41:10 has often encouraged me:

Do not fear, for I am with you;
Do not anxiously look about you, for I am your God.
I will strengthen you, surely I will help you,
Surely I will uphold you with my righteous right hand.

And a little further on, Isaiah writes:

But Zion said, "The Lord has forsaken me,
And the Lord has forgotten me."
"Can a woman forget her nursing child,
And have no compassion on the son of her womb?
Even these may forget, but I will not forget you.
"Behold, I have inscribed you on the palms of My hands;
Your walls are continually before Me . . ." (Isa. 49:14–16).

Isn't that fantastic! More faithful than a nursing mother, our God watches over and cares about us.
We have frequently received counsel from Paul the apostle. Let's look now at a few of the promises God led Him to write. In 2 Corinthians 4:16–18 we read:

Therefore we do not lose heart, but though our outer man is decaying, yet our inner man is being renewed day by day.
For momentary, light affliction is producing for us an eternal weight of glory far beyond all comparison.

And who can forget Philippians 4:19?

And my God shall supply all your needs according to His riches in glory in Christ Jesus.

Or his words of hope regarding a choice servant named Onesiphorus?

> The Lord grant mercy to the house of Onesiphorus, for he often refreshed me, and was not ashamed of my chains; but when he was in Rome, he eagerly searched for me, and found me—the Lord grant to him to find mercy from the Lord on that day—and you know very well what services he rendered at Ephesus (2 Tim. 1:16-18).

No, our faithful God will never forget His own. Perhaps the most well-known promises Christians have as their ultimate hope are in Revelation 21:1-4:

> And I saw a new heaven and a new earth; for the first heaven and the first earth passed away, and there is no longer any sea.
> And I saw the holy city, new Jerusalem, coming down out of heaven from God, made ready as a bride adorned for her husband.
> And I heard a loud voice from the throne, saying, "Behold, the tabernacle of God is among men, and He shall dwell among them, and they shall be His people, and God Himself shall be among them, and He shall wipe away every tear from their eyes; and there shall no longer be any death; there shall no longer be any mourning, or crying, or pain; the first things have passed away."

And Revelation 22:3-5:

> And there shall no longer be any curse; and the throne of God and of the Lamb shall be in it, and His bond-servants shall serve Him; and they shall see His face, and His name shall be on their foreheads.
> And there shall no longer be any night; and they shall not have need of the light of a lamp nor the light of the sun, because the Lord God shall illumine them; and they shall reign forever and ever.

Magnificent, incredible, unchanging hope drips from those immortal words. I encourage you to mark them well. There will be thankless days and long nights when these promises will get you through.

But of all the promises of God's faithfulness in taking special note of His servants, one stands out as my favorite—Hebrews 6:10, which reads:

> For God is not unjust so as to forget your work and the love which you have shown toward His name, in having ministered and in still ministering to the saints.

I like the way *The Living Bible* reads:

> For God is not unfair. How can he forget your hard work for him, or forget the way you used to show your love for him—and still do—by helping his children?

The writer is talking to Christians. The word *beloved* in the previous verse assures us of that. And he is writing out of concern for a few of the first-century believers who had begun to cool off and drift from a close walk with God. He wants to encourage them to stay at it, to keep going, to count on the Lord their God to take notice of them and reward them accordingly. In other words, he reminds them of that great truth all of us tend to forget when days turn into a slow grind, *God is faithful*! He uses eight words to convey this fact: ". . . *God is not unjust so as to forget* . . ."

What does it mean to say that God is faithful? It means He is steadfast in His allegiance to His people. He will not leave us in the lurch. It also means He is firm in His adherence to His promises. He keeps His word. Faithfulness suggests the idea of loyalty; dependability; constancy; being resolute, steady, and consistent. God isn't fickle, no hot-and-cold temperamental moods with Him!

And then the verse goes on to tell us what God faithfully remembers about His servants:

1. He remembers our work—each individual act.
2. He also takes note of the love within us that prompted the deed.

No one on earth can do those special things. We forget, but God remembers. We see the action. God sees the motive. This qualifies Him as the best record keeper and judge. He alone is perfectly and consistently just. Servants, you're in good hands with the Almighty!

Even the best of servants get weary. The Lord's desire is to encourage us to be diligent and to trust Him in spite of the demands. That is why this same writer, before the ink is dry on verse 10, adds:

> And we are anxious that you keep right on loving others as long as life lasts, so that you will get your full reward.
>
> Then, knowing what lies ahead for you, you won't become bored with being a Christian, nor become spiritually dull and indifferent, but you will be anxious to follow the example of those who receive all that God has promised them because of their strong faith and patience (Heb. 6:11–12 TLB).

Regarding Our Faithfulness

In several places through the New Testament, there are statements of promise from God to faithful servants. Three stand out in my mind:

> So, my dear brothers, since future victory is sure, be strong and steady, always abounding in the Lord's work, for you know that nothing you do for the Lord is ever wasted as it would be if there were no resurrection (1 Cor. 15:58, TLB).

Underscore "wasted." It's another way of saying, "Your work is not in vain."

> And let us not lose heart in doing good, for in due time we shall reap if we do not grow weary.

So then, while we have opportunity, let us do good to all men, and especially to those who are of the household of the faith (Gal. 6:9-10).

Underscore "we shall reap."

With good will render service, as to the Lord, and not to men, knowing that whatever good thing each one does, this he will receive back from the Lord, whether slave or free (Eph. 6:7-8).

Underscore "he will receive back."

When we have done what was needed, but were ignored, misunderstood, or forgotten . . . we can be sure it was NOT IN VAIN. When we did what was right, with the right motive, but received no credit, no acknowledgment, not even a "thank you" . . . we have God's promise WE SHALL REAP. When any servant has served and given and sacrificed and then willingly stepped aside for God to receive the glory, our heavenly Father promises HE WILL RECEIVE BACK.

To be even more specific, God has organized His "reward system" into a unique arrangement. He offers His servants both temporal and eternal rewards.

Temporal Rewards

Back into the familiar territory of 2 Corinthians 4, read again verses 7 through 11:

But we have this treasure in earthen vessels, that the surpassing greatness of the power may be of God and not from ourselves; we are afflicted in every way, but not crushed; perplexed, but not despairing; persecuted, but not forsaken; struck down, but not destroyed; always carrying about in the body the dying of Jesus, that the life of Jesus also may be manifested in our body.
For we who live are constantly being delivered over to death for Jesus' sake, that the life of Jesus also may be manifested in our mortal flesh.

I'll be candid with you, I have never read anywhere else what God recently revealed to me in the latter half of this Scripture (vv. 10-11), which follows on the heels of what we might call the "painful side" of serving (vv. 7-9). Let me emphasize verses 10 and 11 by recording the way another version renders them:

We always carry around in our body the death of Jesus, so that the life of Jesus may also be revealed in our body. For we who are alive are always being given over to death for Jesus' sake, so that his life may be revealed in our mortal body (NIV).

Do you observe the temporal reward woven into the lines of those verses? It is this: *The quiet awareness that the life of Christ is being modeled.* That is part of what Paul means when he writes, ". . . that the life of Jesus may also be revealed in our body." Frankly, I know of few more satisfying and encouraging rewards than the deep realization that our actions (and the motives behind them) are visible expressions of Christ to others.

There is one more temporal reward mentioned in this same section of 2 Corinthians:

> All this is for your benefit, so that the grace that is reaching more and more people may cause thinksgiving to overflow to the glory of God (v. 15, NIV).

It's not hidden. The Lord comes up front and says that when you and I take the role of a servant, there is *the joyful realization that a thankful spirit is being stimulated.* And, please notice in verse 15, God gets the glory. It overflows!

I mentioned in chapter 11 the man in our church who quietly and graciously washed our windows. Do you know what pervaded our home throughout that entire Christmas season? A thankful spirit. It washed over all of us in the family. Every glance at another clean window created within us a grateful heart.

Consider also the exhausting efforts of mothers with babies and toddlers. I cannot think of a more thankless task than caring for the young week in, week out . . . month after tiring month. But mothers, hear me well! Your servant's spirit has an effect on all your family. And there are those special times when you go far beyond the expected call of duty.

I was reminded of a perfect example of this while reading Joyce Landorf's splendid work, *Mourning Song.* Joyce is a close, personal friend of mine. She has written many fine books, but nothing better, in my opinion, than this courageous and eloquent account of the death of her mother. In dealing with the subject of pain and suffering in the hospital, Joyce tells of another mother whose significance cannot be exaggerated—a woman whose story illustrates how one who serves can change the entire atmosphere of a room. Take the time to read and feel the emotion in Joyce's own words:

> Nurses carry out their various duties with callous indifference. They listen as little as possible and touch only when necessary. How sad, but such is the force of denial.
>
> It's as if they do indeed hear the mourning song, but they run blindly from the sound, holding their ears as they run and hoping none of the message will get through their carefully structured blockades.
>
> I have seen the terminally ill children in several hospitals and I can fully appreciate how soul-tearing it is to try and work around them. However, it still is tragic to let denial rob us of feeling, caring, and loving the dying child.
>
> My co-worker, Dr. James Dobson, told me of a mother who was willing to put down her denial, pick up her own acceptance, and then beautifully prepare her little son for his death.
>
> She was a large, black woman, as picturesque as the plantation mammies of years ago. She came every day to the hospital to visit her little five-year-old son who was dying of the painful disease lung cancer.

One morning, before the mother got there, a nurse heard the little boy saying, "I hear the bells! I hear the bells! They're ringing!" Over and over that morning nurses and staff heard him.

When the mother arrived she asked one of the nurses how her son had been that day, and the nurse replied, "Oh, he's hallucinating today—it's probably the medication, but He's not making any sense. He keeps on saying he hears bells."

Then that beautiful mother's face came alive with understanding, and she shook her finger at the nurse and said, "You listen to me. He is not hallucinating and he's not out of his head because of any medicine. I told him weeks ago that when the pain in his chest got bad and it was hard to breathe, it meant he was going to leave us. It meant he was going to go to heaven—and that when the pain got really bad he was to look up into the corner of his room—towards heaven—and listen for the bells of heaven—because they'd be ringing for him!" With that, she marched down that hall, swept into her little son's room, swooped him out of his bed, and rocked him in her arms until the sounds of ringing bells were only quiet echoes, and he was gone.[3]

You'll never convince me that that great woman in her gallant act of mothering did not leave the hospital a different place from what she found it! The role of serving may seem insignificant . . . but, in reality, it is *dynamite*.

Eternal Rewards

On top of these temporal benefits connected to serving, there are eternal rewards as well. Christ Himself, while preparing the Twelve for a lifetime of serving others, promised an eternal reward even for holding out a cup of cool water. Listen:

> "He who receives a prophet in the name of a prophet shall receive a prophet's reward; and he who receives a righteous man in the name of a righteous man shall receive a righteous man's reward.
> "And whoever in the name of a disciple gives to one of these little ones even a cup of cold water to drink, truly I say to you he shall not lose his reward" (Matt. 10:41–42).

Those words tell us that "improving our serve" begins with little things. It begins with thoughtful things—an understanding embrace of one who is hurting, a brief note to one who is lonely and feeling unappreciated and forgotten, a cup of cool water for one whose lips are parched from the hot blast of a barren desert when all seems futile and worthless. God takes special notice of all these efforts.

These words take on a new shade of significance when we read that familiar account in Matthew 25. The scene is after this life. The Judge is offering His rewards. The servants receiving them were so unselfish, they had long since forgotten the deeds. But not our Lord!

"But when the Son of Man comes in His glory, and all the angels with Him, then He will sit on His glorious throne.

"And all the nations will be gathered before Him; and He will separate them from one another, as the shepherd separates the sheep from the goats;

and He will put the sheep on His right, and the goats on the left.

"Then the King will say to those on His right, 'Come you who are blessed of My Father, inherit the kingdom prepared for you from the foundation of the world.

'For I was hungry, and you gave Me something to eat; I was thirsty, and you gave Me drink; I was a stranger, and you invited Me in; naked, and you clothed Me; I was sick, and you visited Me; I was in prison, and you came to Me.'

"Then the righteous will answer Him, saying 'Lord, when did we see You hungry, and feed You, or thirsty, and give You drink?

'And when did we see You a stranger, and invite You in, or naked, and clothe You?

'And when did we see You sick, or in prison, and come to You?'

"And the King will answer and say to them, 'Truly I say to you, to the extent that you did it to one of these brothers of Mine, even the least of them, you did it to Me'' (Matt. 25:31-40).

Crowns

This chapter would be incomplete if I failed to mention the eternal "crowns" being set aside for God's servants. What an intriguing study! But for our purpose here, I will simply list the eternal crowns mentioned in the New Testament and offer a brief explanation of each. There are at least five crowns promised in the Bible:

1. **The Imperishable Crown** (1 Cor. 9:24-27).
This reward is promised to those who victoriously run the race of life. Taking into consideration verses 26 and 27, that is, the "buffeting" of the body, it is clear that this reward will be awarded those believers who consistently bring the flesh under the Holy Spirit's control, refusing to be enslaved by their sinful nature. In other words, those who carry out the truths of Romans 6:6-14.

2. **The Crown of Exultation** (Phil. 4:1, 1 Thess. 2:19-20).
This crown will be one over which its recipients will glory and rejoice! This is the "soul-winners crown." It is claimed by Paul regarding two bodies of believers whom he had led to and discipled in Christ Jesus . . . the Philippians and the Thessalonians. Our Lord will distribute this crown to those servants who are faithful to declare the gospel, lead souls to Christ, and build them up in Him. And remember—the rewards at this judgment will be based on the *quality* not *quantity* of our earthly works (1 Cor. 3:13).

3. **The Crown of Righteousness** (2 Tim. 4:7-8).
The crown of righteousness will be awarded those who live each day, loving and anticipating Christ's imminent return . . . those who conduct their earthly lives with eternity's value in view. Kenneth Wuest captures the complete meaning of verse 8 with these words:

To those who have considered precious His appearing and therefore have loved it, and as a result at the present time are still holding that attitude in their hearts, to those the Lord Jesus will also give the victor's garland of righteousness.[4]

Those who qualify for this crown anxiously look for His return daily.

4. **The Crown of Life** (James 1:12).

This wonderful reward awaits those saints who suffered in a noble manner during their earthly life. The significance of this reward is not only related to the words *perseveres under trial* but also the words *those who love Him*. This crown is not promised simply to those who endure suffering and trials . . . but to those who endure their trials, loving the Savior all the way! Therefore, loving the Lord and having the desire that He be glorified in and through the trials become the dual motive for the believer's endurance. Those saints who qualify (and the Lord is the Judge!) will receive the crown of life.

5. **The Crown of Glory** (1 Pet. 5:1–4).

This reward is promised to those who faithfully "shepherd the flock" in keeping with the requirements spelled out in verses 2 and 3. Those under-shepherds who fulfill these qualifications (willingness, sacrificial dedication, humility, an exemplary life) will receive this crown of glory.

After receiving these crowns, what then? Listen to Revelation 4:9–11:

> And when the living creatures give glory and honor and thanks to Him who sits on the throne, to Him who lives forever and ever, the twenty-four elders will fall down before Him who sits on the throne, and will worship Him who lives forever and ever, and will cast their crowns before the throne, saying, "Worthy art Thou, our Lord and our God, to receive glory and honor and power; for Thou didst create all things, and because of Thy will they existed, and were created."

What a scene! All God's servants are before His throne. What are they doing? Strutting around heaven displaying their crowns? No. Separated from one another, like peacocks, proudly displaying their tangible trophies? No. The servants are bowing in worship, having cast all crowns before their Lord in adoration and praise, ascribing worth and honor to the only One deserving of praise—the Lord God!

ENCOURAGEMENT TO SERVANTS

We have covered a lot of scriptural territory in this chapter. What began as a simple promise that God will reward us became a rather involved analysis of what, how, when, and why. Perhaps three or four thoughts will help put all of this in proper perspective.

First, every act of servanthood—no matter how small or large—will be remembered by God.

Second, He takes special note of the heart—He knows the love behind our actions.

Third, as servants reach out to others, Christ's life is modeled and a spirit of thankfulness is stimulated.

Fourth, special and specific rewards are reserved in heaven for those who practice the art of unselfish living.

It was well-known author and pastor Charles Allen who first told the story of a little lad named John Todd, born in Rutland, Vermont, in the autumn of 1800. Shortly after the boy's birth, the Todd family moved to the little village of Killingsworth. It was there, when John was only six, that both his parents died. All the children had to be parceled out among relatives—and a kind-hearted aunt who lived ten miles away agreed to take John, to love him, to care for him, and to give him a home.

The boy lived there for some fifteen years and finally left as he went on to school to study for the ministry. Time passed gently as he began and later excelled in his work as a pastor. While he was in middle life, his elderly aunt fell desperately ill. Realizing death was not far off, in great distress she wrote her nephew. The pitiful letter included some of the same questions all of us must one day ask: "What will death be like? Will it mean the end of everything?" Fear and uncertainty were easily traced in the quivering lines of her letter.

Moved with compassion and swamped with the memories of yesteryear, he wrote her these words of reassurance:

It is now thirty-five years since I, a little boy of six, was left quite alone in the world. You sent me word you would give me a home and be a kind mother to me. I have never forgotten the day when I made the long journey of ten miles to your house in North Killingsworth. I can still recall my disappointment when, instead of coming for me yourself, you sent your colored man, Caesar, to fetch me. I well remember my tears and my anxiety as, perched high on your horse and clinging tight to Caesar, I rode off to my new home. Night fell before we finished the journey and as it grew dark, I became lonely and afraid.

"Do you think she'll go to bed before I get there?" I asked Caesar anxiously. "O no," he said reassuringly. "She'll sure stay up FOR YOU. When we get out of these here woods you'll see her candle shining in the window." Presently we did ride out in the clearing and there, sure enough, was your candle. I remember you were waiting at the door, that you put your arms close about me and that you lifted me—a tired and bewildered little boy—down from the horse. You had a big fire burning on the hearth, a hot supper waiting for me on the stove. After supper, you took me to my new room, you heard me say my prayers and then you sat beside me until I fell asleep.

You probably realize why I am recalling all this to your memory. Some day soon, God will send for you, to take you to a new home. Don't fear the summons— the strange journey—or the dark messenger of death. God can be trusted to do as much for you as you were kind enough to do for me so many years ago. At the end of the road you will find love and a welcome waiting, and you will be safe in God's care. I shall watch you and pray for you until you are out of sight, and then wait for the day when I shall make the journey myself and find you waiting at the end of the road to greet me.[5]

I can hardly read those words without choking back the tears. Not only is it a beautiful, true story, it is the hope of all who serve. It is the way it will be. It is the "Well done, good and faithful servant" we shall hear. As the letter indicates, we are expected. He is waiting to welcome us. To those who serve, to those who stand where Jesus Christ once stood many, many years ago, He promises a reward. And we can be sure He will keep his promise.

Conclusion

The art of unselfish living is practiced by few and mastered by even fewer. In the fast-paced world of the 1980s, we shouldn't be surprised. It is difficult to cultivate a servant's heart when you are trying to survive in a chaotic society dominated by selfish pursuits. And the greatest tragedy of such an existence is what it spawns: an independent, self-sufficient, survival-of-the-fittest mentality. As I view the future, I see nothing on the horizon that offers any hope for a change. Nothing external, that is. Grim as it may sound, we are on a collision course, and the travelers are both lonely and confused. Some are downright angry.

They offer cynical advice: "Look, you can't change the world. Just look out for number one, hold on, and keep your mouth shut." We are surrounded by those who embrace this philosophy. I admit there are times in my more hurried and hassled moments when I tend to listen to that counsel. And often those who do listen become successful—adding weight to their words.

But this philosophy doesn't satisfy. Surely man was not designed to live and treat others like that. There *has* to be a better way to enter eternity than being cold-hearted, empty-handed, and out of breath!

There is. I have been writing about it for thirteen chapters.

As you have discovered, however, the principles I have discussed must be implemented from within. They are unlike anything you'll hear from self-made superstars and celebrities whose lifestyles are not compatible with the concept of being a servant. That's to be expected. But you are different. You wouldn't have read this far if you weren't. Unless I miss my guess, you are tired of the superficial. You want to be a force for good in a world of evil— a person of authenticity in a world of hypocrisy. You are tired of just criticizing what you see happening around you—you want to be part of the answer, not part of the problem. You appreciate, as I do, these words of a wise old professor:

150

There is a new problem in our country. We are becoming a nation that is dominated by large institutions—churches, businesses, governments, labor unions, universities—and these big institutions are not serving us well. I hope that all of you will be concerned about this. Now you can do as I do, stand outside and criticize, bring pressure if you can, write and argue about it. All of this may do some good. But nothing of substance will happen unless there are people inside these institutions who are able to (and want to) lead them into better performance for the public good. Some of you ought to make careers inside these big institutions and become a force for good—from the inside.[1]

All the way through this book, I have stated and reaffirmed the same, essential point: Since Jesus Christ, the Son of God, took upon Himself the role of a servant, so must we. The One who could have been or done anything, consciously and voluntarily, chose to be one who served, one who gave. So then, if we are to become increasingly more like Christ (that is still our goal, isn't it?) then we, too, are to give and to serve.

Enough has been written about it. It is time to put these words and principles to use . . . to hammer them out on the anvil of where we live and work and play. If they work there, the truth of this book will have no trouble withstanding those who say, "It won't work, so don't waste your time." But if they fail to produce the kind of men and women who model the life of Jesus Christ, I have been sadly and grossly misled.

Time will prove the value of these truths on servanthood. May God honor His name as you and I commit ourselves anew to improving our serve, to cultivating the art of unselfish living, serving and giving to others.

Like Jesus Christ.

Notes

Chapter One

1. See Frank Sartwell, "The Small Satanic Worlds of John Calhoun," *Smithsonian Magazine*, April 1970, p. 68 ff. Also see John B. Calhoun, "The Lemmings' Periodic Journeys Are Not Unique," *Smithsonian Magazine*, January 1971, especially p. 11.
2. Margery Williams, *The Velveteen Rabbit* (New York: Doubleday and Company, Inc., 1958), pp. 16–17.

Chapter Two

1. Visual Products Division/3M, St. Paul, MN 55101.
2. Wilbur Rees, "$3.00 Worth of God," *When I Relax I Feel Guilty* by Tim Hansel (Elgin, IL: David C. Cook Publishing Co., 1979), p. 49.
3. Paul Zimmerman, "He's a Man, Not a Myth," *Sports Illustrated*, 53, no. 4 (July 21, 1980): 61.
4. J. Grant Howard, *The Trauma of Transparency* (Portland: Multnomah Press, 1979), p. 30.
5. J. B. Phillips, *When God Was Man* (Nashville: Abingdon Press, 1955), pp. 26–27.
6. Juan Carlos Ortiz, *Disciple* (Wheaton, IL: Creation House, 1975), pp. 34–35.

Chapter Three

1. S. Lewis Johnson, Jr., "Beware of Philosophy," *Bibliotheca Sacra*, 119, no. 476 (October-December, 1962): 302–303.
2. Reprinted from *Tell Me Again, Lord, I Forget* by Ruth Harms Calkin © 1974 David C. Cook Publishing Co., Elgin, IL 60120. Used by permission.

3. Alexander Whyte, D. D., *Bible Characters*, vol. 2., *The New Testament* (London: Oliphants Ltd., 1952), p. 190.
4. Marion Leach Jacobsen, *Crowded Pews and Lonely People* (Wheaton, IL: Tyndale House Publishers, 1972), p. 110.

Chapter Four

1. Horatio G. Spafford, "It Is Well with My Soul," copyright 1918 The John Church Co. Used by permission of the publisher.
2. G. Abbott-Smith, *A Manual Greek Lexicon of the New Testament* (Edinburgh: T. & T. Clark, 1921), p. 109.
3. G. Kittle, ed., *Theological Dictionary of the New Testament*, vol. 1 (Grand Rapids: Wm. B. Eerdmans Publishing Co., 1964), p. 253.
4. C. M. Battersby, "An Evening Prayer," copyright 1911 by Charles H. Gabriel. © renewed 1939, The Rodeheaver Co. (a div. of Word, Inc.). Used by permission.
5. Charles Caldwell Ryrie, *The Ryrie Study Bible: The New Testament* (Chicago: Moody Press, 1977), p. 56.
6. Ray C. Stedman, "Breaking the Resentment Barrier" (sermon delivered the Peninsula Bible Church, Palo Alto, CA, *Treasures of the Parable* Series, Message 11, July 13, 1969), p. 6.
7. Amy Carmichael, taken from *If*, copyrighted material, p. 48. Used by permission of the Christian Literature Crusade, Fort Washington, PA. 19034.

Chapter Five

1. Leslie B. Flynn, *Great Church Fights* (Wheaton, IL: Victor Books, a division of SP Publications, Inc., 1976), p. 91.
2. Ibid., p. 85.
3. Earl D. Radmacher, *You and Your Thoughts, The Power of Right Thinking* (Wheaton, IL: Tyndale House Publishers, Inc., 1977), pp. 15, 19.
4. A Merriam-Webster, *Webster's New Collegiate Dictionary* (Springfield, MA: G. & C. Merriam Company, 1974), p. 451.
5. Howard Butt, *The Velvet Covered Brick* (San Francisco: Harper & Row, Publishers, 1973), pp. 41–43.
6. John Edmund Haggai, *How to Win Over Worry* (Grand Rapids: Zondervan Publishing House, 1976), pp. 95–96.

Chapter Six

1. Jack Sparks, *The Mind Benders* (Nashville: Thomas Nelson, Inc., Publishers, 1977), pp. 16, 17.
2. Christopher Edwards, *Crazy for God* (Englewood Cliffs, NJ: Prentice-Hall, Inc., 1979).

3. Ronald M. Enroth, "The Power Abusers," *Eternity* October 1979, p. 25.
4. W. E. Vine, *An Expository Dictionary of New Testament Words* (London: Oliphants Ltd., 1940), p. 113.
5. Larry Christenson, *The Renewed Mind* (Minneapolis: Bethany Fellowship, Inc., 1974), p. 41.
6. Dale E. Galloway, *Dream a New Dream* (Wheaton, IL: Tyndale House Publishers, Inc., 1975), pp. 77–78.
7. Reprinted with permission of Macmillan Publishing Co., Inc. from *Creative Brooding* by Robert A. Raines. Copyright © 1966 by Robert A. Raines.

Chapter Seven

1. Jerry White, *Honesty, Morality, & Conscience* (Colorado Springs, CO: NavPress, 1979), pp. 81, 82.
2. William Barclay, *The Gospel of Matthew*, (Edinburgh: The Saint Andrew Press, 1956), 1:86.
3. Augustus M. Toplady, "Rock of Ages, Cleft for Me," (1776).
4. "Man a Nothing," taken from *The Valley of Vision: A Collection of Puritan Prayers and Devotions*, Arthur Bennett, ed., (London: The Banner of Truth Trust, 1975), p. 91.
5. Bernard of Clairvaux, "Jesus, Thou Joy of Loving Hearts," trans. by Ray Palmer.
6. Dag Hammarskjöld, *Markings* (New York: Alfred A. Knopf, 1978), p. 53.
7. Archibald Thomas Robertson, *Word Pictures in the New Testament*, vol. 1 (Nashville: Broadman Press, 1930), p. 41.

Chapter Eight

1. William Barclay, *The Gospel of Matthew*, (Edinburgh: The Saint Andrew Press, 1956) 1:98.
2. Leslie Flynn, *Great Church Fights* (Wheaton, IL: Victor Books, a division of SP Publications, Inc., 1976), p. 44.

Chapter Nine

1. Tim Timmons, *Maximum Living in a Pressure-Cooker World* (Waco: Word Books Publisher, 1979), p. 163.
2. "The Battered Wife: What's Being Done?" Los Angeles *Times*, April 27, 1978.
3. Catherine Marshall, *Mr. Jones, Meet the Master* (New York: Fleming H. Revell Company, 1951), pp. 147, 148.
4. John R. W. Stott, *Christian Counter-Culture* (Downers Grove, IL: InterVarsity Press, 1978), pp. 58–59.
5. R. V. G. Tasker, ed., *The Tyndale New Testament Commentaries, The Gospel According to St. Matthew* (Grand Rapids: Wm. B. Eerdmans Publishing Company, 1978), p. 63.

6. Harry Blamires, *The Christian Mind* (Ann Arbor: Servant Books, 1963), p. 3.
7. Rebecca Manley Pippert, *Out of the Salt-Shaker & into the World* (Downers Grove, IL: InterVarsity Press, 1979).
8. John R. W. Stott, *Christian Counter-Culture*, p. 61.
9. D. Martyn Lloyd-Jones, *Studies in the Sermon on the Mount*, vol. 1 (Grand Rapids: Wm. B. Eerdmans Publishing Company, 1959), p. 178.
10. Rebecca Manley Pippert, pp. 125–126.

Chapter Ten

1. J. Oswald Sanders, *Spiritual Leadership* (Chicago: Moody Press, 1967), p. 142.
2. Ibid., pp. 142, 143.
3. Dr. James C. Dobson, *Straight Talk to Men and Their Wives* (Waco: Word Books Publisher, 1980). pp. 58–60.
4. C. S. Lewis, *The Four Loves* (New York: Harcourt, Brace & World, Inc., 1960), p. 169.
5. E. Margaret Clarkson, "So Send I You," copyright © 1954 by Singspiration, Inc. All rights reserved. Used by permission of Singspiration, Inc., Grand Rapids.

Chapter Eleven

1. Wilbur Smith, *Have You Considered Him?* (Downers Grove, IL: InterVarsity Press, 1970), p. 5.
2. Taken from *The Encyclopedia of Religious Quotations*, Frank Mead, ed., (Old Tappen, NJ: Fleming H. Revell, n.d.), p. 51.
3. Ibid., p. 56.
4. James "Frog" Sullivan, *The Frog Who Never Became a Prince* (Santa Ana, CA: Vision House Publishers, 1975), pp. 127–131.

Chapter Twelve

1. W. E. Vine, *Expository Dictionary of New Testament Words*, vol. 1 (London: Oliphants Ltd., 1970), p. 38.
2. Op. cit., vol. 3, pp. 177–178.
3. Thomas V. Bonoma and Dennis P. Slevin, ed., *Executive Survival Manual* (Boston: CBI Publishing Company, Inc., 1978), pp. 58–59.
4. Reprinted with permission from *Journal of Psychosomatic Research*, vol. 11, T. H. Homes and R. H. Rahe, "The Social Readjustment Rating Scale," Copyright 1967, Pergamon Press, Ltd.
5. Corrie ten Boom, *The Hiding Place* (Minneapolis: A Chosen Book published for World Wide Pictures, 1971).
6. Elie Wiesel, *Night* (New York: Avon Books, 1969), p. 9.

7. Ibid.
8. Wm. Byron Forbush, ed., *Fox's Book of Martyrs* (Philadelphia: Universal Book and Bible House, 1926).
9. Amy Carmichael, "In Acceptance Lieth Peace" taken from *Toward Jerusalem* (copyright 1936), pp. 40–41. Used by permission of the Christian Literature Crusade, Fort Washington, PA 19034.
10. Charles R. Swindoll, *Three Steps Forward, Two Steps Back* (Nashville: Thomas Nelson Publishers, 1980).

Chapter Thirteen

1. Richard H. Seume, comp. and ed., *Hymns of Jubilee*, (Dallas: Dallas Theological Seminary, n.d.), p. 49.
2. John Bartlett, ed., *Familiar Quotations* (Boston: Little, Brown and Company, 1955), p. 660.
3. Joyce Landorf, *Mourning Song* (Old Tappan, NJ: Fleming H. Revell Company, 1974), pp. 52–53.
4. Kenneth S. Wuest, *The Pastoral Epistles in the Greek New Testament* (Grand Rapids: Wm. B. Eerdmans Publishing Co., 1956), p. 163.
5. Charles L. Allen, *You Are Never Alone* (Old Tappan, NJ: Fleming H. Revell Company, 1978), pp. 77–79.

Conclusion

1. Robert K. Greenleaf, *Servant Leadership* (New York: Paulist Press, 1977), pp. 1–2.

Strengthening Your Grip

With much gratitude this volume
is dedicated to four men, each of whom
helped strengthen my grip
more than he ever realized

In the 1950s .... Bob Newkirk
Who gave the encouragement I needed

In the 1960s .... Howie Hendricks
Who modeled the skills I admired

In the 1970s .... Ray Stedman
Who had the wisdom I appreciated

In the 1980s .... Al Sanders
Who provided the vision I lacked

I count it a privilege today
to call each man my friend

Contents

Acknowledgments

Unless otherwise indicated, Scripture quotations are from *The New American Standard Bible*, (NASB) copyright © The Lockman Foundation 1960, 1962, 1963, 1968, 1971, 1972, 1973, 1975.

Other Scripture quotations in this publication are from the following sources:
The Living Bible, Paraphrased (TLB), copyright © 1971 by Tyndale House Publishers, Wheaton, Illinois.
The Amplified New Testament (AMPLIFIED), copyright © 1958 by The Lockman Foundation.
The New International Version of the Bible (NIV), published by The Zondervan Corporation, copyright © 1978 by the New York International Bible Society.
The New Berkeley Version in Modern English, Revised Edition: copyright 1945, 1959, © 1969 by Zondervan Publishing House. Old Testament © 1959 by Zondervan Publishing House. New Testament © 1945 by Gerrit Verkuyl; assigned 1958 to Zondervan Publishing House.
The Revised Standard Version of the Bible (RSV), copyright © 1946, 1952, © 1971 and 1973 by the Division of Christian Education of the National Council of the Churches of Christ in the U.S.A.
The King James Version of the Bible (KJV).

Introduction

Every decade possesses a particular characteristic. It comes into focus without announcement or awareness as the years unfold. Not suddenly, but quietly. Almost imperceptibly. Like random pieces of a puzzle—each a different shape and size—the events and people and ideas of a decade begin to come together in a meaningful form. First a corner, then a side, finally the entire border falls into place. But the scene is not immediately clear.

Years must pass. As they do, more sections fit together, and meaningfulness starts to emerge. By the end of the decade, the seasoned picture is obvious, including the shading, harmony of colors, and even our feelings about the finished product. Every decade puts a frame around its own particular scene.

I was born in 1934. As I reflect on the decade of the 1930s through the lens of history (and discussion with those who were adults during that era), I get the distinct impression that it was a decade of *idealism*. Renewed hope clawed its way from beneath the devastation of the Great Depression. Optimism and diligence joined hands with determination, giving our country a needed boost out of the ominous shadows of the late 1920s.

I was a growing youngster in the 1940s—a decade of *patriotism*. Nationalistic zeal reached its zenith as "our boys" slugged it out in Europe and the Far East. Simultaneous gasoline and food rationing, plus an unconditional commitment to win, gave us a feeling of pride and partnership as we rallied around the flag. Nobody, it seemed, questioned authority or tolerated the slightest action that smacked of insubordination. Babies born in the forties learned the pledge of allegiance as early in life as they learned the alphabet. Patriotism characterized the 1940s.

By the 1950s, I was a young man. My high school years in East Houston could have been the perfect place to film "Happy Days." My education continued, and a hitch in the Marine Corps, a new bride, and a change in careers marked those days in my life. Looking back, I have little trouble identifying that era. It was a decade of *materialism*, a time of dreaming, learning, earning, and succeeding. "The good life" became attainable to all who would work longer hours and push for the top. War was behind us, new frontiers were open to us, if only we would pay the price—advanced education and additional hours on the job. What we overlooked was the growing number of children and adolescents who got caught in the backwash of our materialistic greed. They would sit down and be quiet only so long. The fuse burned shorter each year that decade. It was only a matter of time before the powder keg would blow.

Then came the 1960s. Who could ever forget the anger, the riots, the frenzy of the sixties? A decade of *rebellion*. A new music with a heavy beat made parents frown in disapproval and kids scream with excitement. The foundations of our new frontiers came unglued. Campus riots, civil rights marches, political assassinations, the growing addiction to television, domestic runaways, sit-ins, drug abuse, unemployment, the threat of nuclear attack, and burning cities and draft cards made the President's job a hell-on-earth nightmare. Snarling defiance replaced submissive allegiance. On top of it all was that weird war in Southeast Asia—the black eye on Uncle Sam's face—the no-win wound that refused to heal. Nothing was quiet on the Western Front in the 1960s.

The overt rebellion of that stormy era led us, limping and licking our wounds, into the 1970s. Depressing folk songs and the strumming of a guitar had now become our national emblem. Increased passivity characterized much of the leadership in the 1970s as more of our youth began to rethink the work-hard-so-you-can-get-rich materialism mentality. Confusion began to replace confidence, ushering us into a decade of *disillusionment*. You name it, a question mark could be attached to it. The integrity of our Oval Office? The "proper" role of women? The need for national defense? Capital punishment? The media? The home? The school? The church? The prisons? The establishment? Nuclear energy? Ecology? Marriage? Education? Rights? And I may as well add: Purpose? Direction? Hope? We lost our grip on absolutes in the 1970s.

All of which brought us into the "aimless 1980s" with a table full of pieces that initially defied reason. The grim-faced, tight-lipped, double-fisted fight of the sixties had turned into a lazy yawn twenty years later. The slogan of the 1940s, "Remember Pearl Harbor!" and the 1960s' "We shall overcome!" were now slowly eroding into the new slogan of the 1980s, "Who really cares?" The muscular patriot who once rolled up his sleeves and dared any enemy to step foot on our shores was now listening to the clicks of a computer, preoccupied in his silent, isolated world of code language all day and the glare of color television half the night. The tide of apathy has risen, and we are seeing the sand castles that once housed our hopes washed out to sea.

Face it, ours is simply not the same world as it was a few short decades ago. The full picture hidden in the puzzle is still unclear, but the border is in place. The scene has changed drastically.

For some reason the truth of all this began to impact me shortly after we entered the decade of the 1980s. I felt jolted as the changes seized my attention. I guess such thoughts occur when one approaches a half century in age. But, more important, as a communicator of God's timeless truth, I found myself having to face the frightening facts of reality. We cannot drift on the ship of aimless indifference very long without encountering diaster. God's eternal and essential principles must be firmly grasped and communicated afresh if we hope to survive. None of them are new. But for too long, too many of them have been buried under the debris of tired clichés and predictable talk of yesteryear. Most people I know who are coping with the complexities and stress of this decade are not at all interested in religious bromides that come across in a dated and dull fashion. We can no longer speak to the issues of the 1980s in the terms of the 1940s or the 1960s or even the 1970s, for that matter. Much of that is now awash.

We need biblical fixed points to hang onto—firm, solid handles that will help us steer our lives in a meaningful manner. What we really want is something to grab—believable, reliable truth that makes sense for today's generation, essential principles for our aimless world.

I have only that to offer in this volume. Within these pages are ancient truths presented in today's terms for today's person, facing today's demands. Each chapter deals with a different essential that will, if applied in a personal manner, increase your confidence and your ability to cope with current crises, because it rests on the bedrock of inspired revelation, the Holy Bible. When these insights are lived out in your life, you will soon discover that they will strengthen your grip on the Life Preserver that won't submerge when the tide rises. And best of all, these principles won't change on you at the dawning of a new decade in the next few years. We have our Lord to thank for that! He is "the same yesterday and today, yes, and forever" (Heb. 13:8).

The puzzle of every new decade rests firmly in His hands. He is still in charge. In spite of how things may appear, our times are still in His hands.

If the aimlessness of the eighties is starting to loosen your confidence in God's sovereign control, this book will help strengthen your grip.

CHARLES R. SWINDOLL
Fullerton, California

1

Strengthening
Your Grip
on Priorities

The Tyranny of the Urgent is a small booklet with a bit fist. Its message is uncomplicated and direct. Actually, it's a warning to all of us. There are times when its penetrating blow punches my lights out! Like a guided missile, it assaults and destroys all excuses I may use.

Here, in one sentence, is the warning: Don't let the urgent take the place of the important in your life.[1] Oh, the urgent will really fight, claw, and scream for attention. It will plead for our time and even make us think we've done the right thing by calming its nerves. But the tragedy of it all is this: While you and I were putting out the fires of the urgent (an everyday affair), the important was again left in a holding pattern. And interestingly, the important is neither noisy nor demanding. Unlike the urgent, it patiently and quietly waits for us to realize its significance.

WHAT IS IMPORTANT TO YOU?

Forgetting the urgent for a few minutes, ask yourself what is really important to you. What do you consider "top priority" in your life? That is a big question, maybe one you need some time to think about. I began to think about it over a year and a half ago. Because I am a minister in a sizable church where I face a busy schedule week after week, I decided to think seriously about my priorities *and* the priorities of our growing ministry. It helped. What I discovered is worth passing on to others. Who knows? It may be just what you need to hear today.

Let me give you a little background. In some ways, people and organizations are alike. Both tend to lose vitality rather than gain it as time passes. Both also tend to give greater attention to what they *were* rather than what they are *becoming*. It's easier to look back into the past and smile on yesterday's accomplishments than it is to look ahead into the future and think about tomorrow's possibilities.

I realized my own tendency to do that when our congregation moved into brand new facilities in March 1980. Almost twelve acres of choice land in a suburb of Los Angeles. Five new, lovely, spacious, efficient structures to house our church family. The answer to years of praying and sacrificial giving. A dream come true. God had again done wonders among us.

It soon became apparent, however, that if we weren't alert and careful, we would slump into a continuous focus on where we had been rather than on where we were going . . . what we were in the process of becoming. God's people are not museum pieces, placed and anchored on a shelf to collect dust. We are alive, moving, and active people called by Him to make an impact on a world that isn't quite sure which end is up. But to do that, we need to determine our priorities.

As I opened my Bible and began to search for direction, I came across the second chapter of 1 Thessalonians, a letter Paul wrote centuries ago to a growing group of Christians. He began this chapter by saying: "For you yourselves know, brethren, that our coming to you was not in vain . . ." (v. 1).

Although he certainly had not stayed there among them very long, his coming was no wasted effort. It may have been brief and, on occasion, discouraging, but it wasn't in vain.

FOUR PRIORITIES FOR LIVING

After declaring this fact, Paul then pinpoints the characteristics of his life and ministry in Thessalonica. In doing so he sets forth four essential priorities for every church in any era—or, for that matter, any life.

Be Biblical

Looking back over the weeks they were together, he recalls his initial impressions.

> But after we had already suffered and been mistreated in Philippi, as you know, we had the boldness in our God to speak to you the gospel of God amid much opposition. For our exhortation does not come from error or impurity or by way of deceit; but just as we have been approved by God to be entrusted with the gospel, so we speak, not as pleasing men but God, who examines our hearts (vv. 2–4).

I'm confident that there was a constant barrage of urgent needs pounding away on Paul's mind, but he made sure that his life and ministry were firmly fixed on the important—the Scriptures.

Did you catch these thoughts as you read those verses?

• When he spoke amidst the strong current of public opposition, it was "the gospel of God" he shared (v. 2).

• The very foundation of his being was not "error" or "impurity" or "deceit," but rather the truth of the Scriptures (v. 3).

• Furthermore, he considerd the Word of God as something "entrusted" to him. And it gave him such security and confidence that he didn't feel the need to compromise and become a "people pleaser" (v. 4).

Even though it may sound old-fashioned, the first and most significant priority we can cultivate is to make the Scriptures a part of our lives. A biblical mentality is the secret to surviving the aimlessness of our day.

> . . . We must daily soak ourselves in the Scriptures. We must not just study, as through a microscope, the linguistic minutiae of a few verses, but take our telescope and scan the wide expanses of God's Word, assimilating its grand theme of divine sovereignty in the redemption of mankind. 'It is blessed,' wrote C. H. Spurgeon, 'to eat into the very soul of the Bible until, at last, you come to talk in scriptural language, and your spirit is flavoured with the words of the Lord, so that your blood is Bibline and the very essence of the Bible flows from you.'[2]

I find it interesting that being committed to a biblical mentality and lifestyle is so old it's new! For sure, it's rare. It also leads to a good deal of self-examination. Did you observe this at the end of verse 4? As we begin to soak up the truths of God's Book, He goes to work on us!

> The word of God is living and active. Sharper than any double-edged sword, it penetrates even to dividing soul and spirit, joints and marrow; it judges the thoughts and attitudes of the heart. Nothing in all creation is hidden from God's sight. Everything is uncovered and laid bare before the eyes of Him to whom we must give account (Heb. 4:12-13, NIV).

Descriptive, isn't it? The principles and precepts of Scripture touch what no surgeon's scalpel can touch—the soul, the spirit, thoughts, attitudes, the very essence of our being. And God uses His truths to help shape us and clean us up and mature us in our walk with Him.

Let's take this to heart. Let's determine that we are not going to allow the tyranny of the urgent to steal from us those all-important moments with our God in His Word. First and foremost, let's become people who are thoroughly committed to biblical thinking and action.

I find a second priority in this same part of 1 Thessalonians.

Be Authentic

Listen to the way Paul talks about himself. For a moment he shifts the emphasis from the message to the messenger.

For we never came with flattering speech, as you know, nor with a pretext for greed—God is witness—nor did we seek glory from men, either from you or from others, even though as apostles of Christ we might have asserted our authority (1 Thess. 2:5-6).

The man was real. He was so secure he peeled off all masks, all cover-ups, and stood vulnerably before God and others. It's beautiful! Even though he was an apostle—a genuine first-century bigwig—he did not push for the limelight. He consciously resisted being a power abuser.

Ronald Enroth, author and professor of sociology at Westmont College, is correct in his analysis of a leader's use of power.

> . . . Bible scholars point out that the New Testament concept of authority as expressed in the Greek word *exousia* does not have the connotation of jurisdiction over the lives of others. Rather, it is the authority of truth, the authority of wisdom and experience which can be evidenced in a leader who is held up as a special example, who can commend himself "to every man's conscience in the sight of God" (2 Cor. 4:2).[3]

Paul was that kind of leader. He did not take unfair advantage of his role as an apostle. Of top priority to him, right alongside being a strong believer in the Scriptures, was being authentic.

Webster's dictionary defines the term *authentic* by suggesting three things "authentic" is *not*: It is *not* imaginary, it is *not* false, it is *not* an imitation. Today we would say that being authentic means not being phony . . . free of the standard hype that often accompanies public gatherings.

Let's make this a priority in the 1980s! Surrounded by numerous religious types to whom everything is "fantastic," "super," and "incredible," let's work hard at being real. This means we are free to question, to admit failure, or weakness, to confess wrong, to declare the truth. When a person is authentic, he or she does not have to win or always be in the top ten or make a big impression or look super-duper pious.

A man I deeply appreciate—a fine student and teacher of the Bible— admitted in a public meeting that the more he studied prophecy the *less* he knew about it! I smiled with understanding and admiration.

Robert Wise, pastor of Our Lord's Community Church in Oklahoma City, helped take some of the tension out of my own tendency to compete and continually achieve, always fearing failure. In his intriguing book *Your Churning Place*, he mentions an experience that encouraged him to be real.

> I had a friend who used to call me on the phone on Monday mornings. I'd pick up the phone and this minister would say, "Hello, this is God. I have a gift for you today. I want to give you the gift of failing. Today you do not have to succeed. I grant that to you." Then he would hang up. I would sit there for 10 minutes, staring at the wall.

The first time I couldn't believe it. It was really the gospel. God's love means it's even OK to fail. You don't have to be the greatest thing in the world. You can just be you.[4]

Authentic people usually enjoy life more than most. They don't take themselves so seriously. They actually laugh and cry and think more freely because they have nothing to prove—no big image to protect, no role to play. They have no fear of being found out, because they're not hiding anything. Let's make the Bible our foundation in the '80s. And as we apply its insights and guidelines, let's also cultivate a style that is authentic.

In doing so we'll need to watch our attitude—our next priority.

Be Gracious

Paul deals with this third priority in 1 Thessalonians 2:7-11 where he writes of the value of being gracious.

> But we proved to be gentle among you, as a nursing mother tenderly cares for her own children.
>
> Having thus a fond affection for you, we were well pleased to impart to you not only the gospel but also our own lives, because you had become very dear to us.
>
> For you recall, brethren, our labor and hardship, how working night and day so as not to be a burden to any of you, we proclaimed to you the gospel of God.
>
> You are witnesses, and so is God, how devoutly and uprightly and blamelessly we behaved toward you believers; just as you know how we were exhorting and encouraging and imploring each one of you as a father would his own children (vv. 7-11).

What a gracious, tolerant spirit! The man was both approachable and tender. Did you notice the word pictures? He cared for others "as a nursing mother" (v. 7) and dealt with them in their needs "as a father" (v. 11). He had compassion. Of high priority to this capable, brilliant man of God was a gracious, compassionate attitude.

He admits that he was interested in doing more than dumping a truckload of theological and doctrinal data on them . . . he wanted to share not only the gospel, but his life.

If there is one specific criticism we hear against our evangelical "camp" more than any other, it is this: We lack compassion. We are more abrasive and judgmental than thoughtful, tactful, compassionate, and tolerant. If we're not careful, we tend to use people rather than love them, don't we? We try to change them and later help them, rather than accept them as they are.

A greatly needed priority for this decade is an attitude or disposition that is characterized by *grace*. Do you recall Peter's final bit of counsel?

> But grow in the grace and knowledge of our Lord and Savior Jesus Christ. To Him be the glory, both now and to the day of eternity. Amen (2 Pet. 3:18).

Am I saying there is no place for conviction or a firm commitment to truth? Of course not. All I plead for are threads of grace woven through the garment of truth. If I live to be one hundred fifty, I will never buy the idea that it is an either-or matter. Our world of hungry, hurting humanity longs for and deserves the message of truth presented in attractive, gentle, gracious wrappings. Don't forget: "As a mother . . . as a father." There is positive affirmation implied rather than negative nitpicking.

Charlie Shedd illustrates this so perfectly as he tells of an experience he had with Philip, one of his sons. The story revolved around a bale of binder twine.

> . . . When we moved from Nebraska to Oklahoma, we brought [the binder twine] along. I had used it there to tie sacks of feed and miscellaneous items. It cost something like $1.15. So I said, "Now, Philip, you see this binder twine? I want you to leave it alone." But it held a strange fascination for him and he began to use it any time he wanted. I would say, "Don't," "No," and "You can't!" But all to no avail.
>
> That went on for six or eight months. Then one day I came home tired. There was the garage, looking like a no-man's land with binder twine across, back and forth, up and down. I had to cut my way through to get the car in. And was I provoked! I ground my teeth as I slashed at that binder twine. Suddenly, when I was halfway through the maze, a light dawned. I asked myself, "Why do you want this binder twine? What if Philip does use it?"
>
> So when I went in to supper that night, Philip was there and I began, "Say, about that binder twine!" He hung his head and mumbled, "Yes, Daddy." Then I said, "Philip, I've changed my mind. You can use that old binder twine any time you want. What's more, all those tools out in the garage I've labeled 'No'—you go ahead and use them. I can buy new tools, but I can't buy new boys." There never was a sunrise like that smile. "Thanks, Daddy," he beamed. And guess what, Peter. He hasn't touched that binder twine since![5]

That's the way it works in a gracious, accepting climate. People become far more important than rigid rules and demanding expectations.

Thus far we've deposited into our memory banks three vital priorities: those of being biblical, authentic, and gracious. In 1 Thessalonians 2:12–13 Paul deals with yet another priority.

> So that you may walk in a manner worthy of the God who calls you into His own kingdom and glory.
>
> And for this reason we also constantly thank God that when you received from us the word of God's message, you accepted it not as the word of men, but for what it really is, the word of God, which also performs its work in you who believe.

Be Relevant

There is a direct link here between talk and walk. Paul's message always has a relevant ring to it. Even though the truth of the Scriptures is ancient, when it is received, it goes to work today; . . . it is up to date and continually at "work in you who believe" (v. 13).

If we are hoping to reach our generation in the '80s, we must make relevance a high priority. That is exactly what Jesus Christ did. He met people as they *were*, not as they "ought to have been." Angry young men, blind beggars, proud politicians, loose-living streetwalkers, dirty and naked victims of demonism, and grieving parents got equal time. They all hung on His every word. Even though He could have blown them away with his knowledge and authority, He purposely stayed on their level. Jesus was the epitome of relevance. And still is.

It is *we* who have hauled His cross out of sight. It is *we* who have left the impression that it belongs only in the sophisticated, cloistered halls of a seminary or beautified beneath the soft shadows of stained glass and cold marble statues. I applaud the one who put it this way:

> I simply argue that the cross be raised again
> at the center of the market place
> as well as on the steeple of the church,
>
> I am recovering the claim that
> Jesus was not crucified in a cathedral
> between two candles:
>
> But on a cross between two thieves;
> on a town garbage heap;
> At a crossroad of politics so cosmopolitan
> that they had to write His title
> in Hebrew and in Latin and in Greek . . .
>
> And at the kind of place where cynics talk smut,
> and thieves curse and soldiers gamble.
>
> Because that is where He died,
> and that is what He died about.
> And that is where Christ's men ought to be,
> and what church people ought to be about.[6]
> George MacLeod

REVIEW AND WRAP-UP

The tyranny of the urgent will always outshout the essential nature of the important . . . if we let it. We have determined not to let that happen. The secret is establishing personal priorities. I have suggested four:

- Set a firm foundation—be *biblical*.
- Apply the truth of the Scriptures—be *authentic*.
- Develop a compassionate attitude—be *gracious*.
- Stay current, always up to date—be *relevant*.

As we begin to do this, Christianity becomes something that is absorbed, not just worn. It is more than believed; it is incarnated.

And if there is anything that will catch the attention of preoccupied people fighting the fires of the urgent, it is God's truth incarnated. It happened in the first century and it can happen in the twentieth. Even in an aimless world like ours.

DISCUSSION QUESTIONS AND IDEAS TO HELP YOU STRENGTHEN YOUR GRIP ON PRIORITIES

Before going on to the next chapter, pause and reflect. Take time to review and apply.

- All of us face the tyranny of the urgent. It has a way of casting an eclipse over the important. Think about the urgent demands on your life. Name a few to yourself. Now consider this: What important things are being ignored because of the urgent?
- In this chapter we thought about four top priority items, according to 1 Thessalonians 2:1–13. Can you name each one as you read this section of Scripture?
- Why are these so important? What happens if they are missing from a person's life? Or from one's church?
- Now consider seriously what you could change in your schedule or your way of living to make room for these priorities. Be specific.
- Spend a minute or two in prayer. Thank God for speaking to you about these essentials. Ask Him to help you give less attention to the urgent and more to the important.

2

Strengthening
Your Grip
on Involvement

"I know of no more potent killer than isolation. There is no more destructive influence on physical and mental health than the isolation of you from me and us from them. It has been shown to be a central agent in the etiology of depression, paranoia, schizophrenia, rape, suicide, mass murder, and a wide variety of disease states."[1]

Those are the words of Professor Philip Zimbardo, a respected authority on psychology from Stanford University, a man who faces the blunt blows of reality in daily doses. His words are not only true, they are downright frightening. No longer are we a share-and-share-alike people. We are independent cogs in complex corporate structures. We wear headsets as we jog or do our lawns or walk to class or eat in cafeterias. Our watchword is "privacy;" our commitments are short-term. Our world is fast adopting the unwritten regulation so often observed in elevators, "Absolutely no eye contact, talking, smiling, or relating without written permission from the management." The Lone Ranger, once a fantasy hero, is now our model, mask and all.

How times have changed! John Donne, a seventeenth-century sage from the Old Country, would never have thought it possible. He wrote these once-familiar, but soon-to-be-forgotten thoughts:

No man is an island, entire of itself; every man is a piece of the continent, a part of the main; if a clod be washed away by the sea, Europe is the less . . . any man's death diminishes me, because I am involved in mankind; and therefore never send to know for whom the bell tolls; it tolls for thee.[2]

176

Our aimless, lonely generation has great difficulty understanding such concepts as the interrelatedness of mankind. Thanks to the now-accepted policy of many businesses to transfer a man and his family across the nation with each promotion, even the extended family bonds are now being loosened. Involvement with our roots is reduced to snapshots and phone calls at Christmas. Family reunions and season rituals are nearly extinct as relatives become curious aliens to our children. All this and much, much more, plus the inevitable, irritating hassles connected with cultivating close relationships, causes us to move away from each other into our own separate houses where we isolate ourselves still further in our own separate bedrooms. We pursue self-sufficient lifestyles that make sharing unnecessary.

As one man observes, "The well-tended front lawn is the modern moat that keeps the barbarians at bay."[3] Anonymity, cynicism, and indifference are fast replacing mutual support and genuine interest. It may seem on the surface to be more efficient, but remember the counsel of Dr. Zimbardo: isolation is actually a "potent killer."

WHAT IS "INVOLVEMENT"?

In the Webster's dictionary, we find that *being involved* means "to draw in as a participant, to relate closely, to connect, to include." When you and I involve ourselves with someone, we "connect" with them. We think of them as we make our plans. We actually operate our lives with others in clear focus. We draw them in as participants in our activities. We include them.

To break this down into manageable terms, Christians have at least four areas of involvement to maintain:

• **Our involvement with God**. In the past, this involvement resulted in our salvation—our new birth through faith in Jesus Christ. Currently it is our everyday walk with Christ through life. To maintain a close connection with our Lord, we think of Him as we make our plans, we pray, we explore the rich treasures of His Word. This is the single most significant involvement in all of life, but it is not automatic.

• **Our involvement with members of our family**. Parents, children, relatives, mates . . . Christian or not—all of these people comprise our circle of close contact. We include them in our thinking, some, of course, more closely than others.

• **Our involvement with other Christians**. Usually, these people are selected from the church we attend. The number grows as we "connect" with others through areas of mutual interest. Some of us could list literally *hundreds* of Christian friends with whom we have a relationship. This becomes a major factor in our ability to cope with life on this planet, an otherwise lonely and discouraging pilgrimage.

• **Our involvement with non-Christians**. We work alongside them, do business with them, live near them, go to school next to them, and are usually entertained by them. Unfortunately, most Christians cut off *all* close ties with non-Christians within a few months after salvation. Small wonder we find it difficult to share our faith with others. I'll talk more about that in chapter 14.

BEING INVOLVED WITH OTHER CHRISTIANS

For the balance of this chapter, let's center our attention on the third area of involvement—our relationship with others in God's family. If you are not a Christian *or* if you are a new believer, you might think that the Christian-with-Christian relationship is one step short of heavenly bliss. On the contrary. Although there are some beautiful exceptions, it has been my observation that we Christians are often at odds with each other.

Someone once suggested that we are like a pack of porcupines on a frigid wintry night. The cold drives us closer together into a tight huddle to keep warm. As we begin to snuggle really close, our sharp quills cause us to jab and prick each other—a condition which forces us apart. But before long we start getting cold, so we move back to get warm again, only to stab and puncture each other once more. And so we participate in this strange, rhythmic "tribal dance." We cannot deny it, we need each other, yet we needle each other!

> To dwell above with saints we love,
>   That will be grace and glory.
> To live below with saints we know;
>   That's another story![4]

How can we break ye olde porcupine syndrome? The answer in one word is involvement. Or, to use the biblical term, it is *fellowship*.

> And they were continually devoting themselves to the apostles' teaching and to fellowship, to the breaking of bread and to prayer (Acts 2:42).

This verse of Scripture is a statement of immense significance. Historically, the church has just come into existence. About three thousand new Christians are huddled together in the streets of Jerusalem. They have nothing tangible to lean on—no building, no organization, no church constitution and bylaws, no "pastor," not even a completed copy of the Scriptures. What did they do? This verse says they devoted themselves to the instruction of the apostles, to the ordinances, to prayer, *and* to fellowship.

The Greek term for fellowship is *koinonia*. The root meaning is "common." The next three verses from Acts 2 reveal just how closely they were bound together.

And everyone kept feeling a sense of awe; and many wonders and signs were taking place through the apostles.

And all those who had believed were together, and had all things in common; and they began selling their property and possessions, and were sharing them with all, as anyone might have need (vv. 43–45).

To borrow from the familiar words of John Fawcett's hymn, "Blest Be the Tie," these first-century Christians shared their mutual woes, their mutual burdens they bore, and often for each other flowed a sympathizing tear.

OBSERVATIONS OF FIRST-CENTURY INVOLVEMENT

I observe that their mutual involvement had four characteristics:
1. It was entered into by everyone (three times we read "all").
2. It helped hold them together in times of great need.
3. It was genuine, spontaneous, never forced. Sincerity was there.
4. It added to their sense of unity and harmony.
In Acts 4 we read more about the early days of the church:

And the congregation of those who believed were of one heart and soul; and not one of them claimed that anything belonging to him was his own; but all things were common property to them.

For there was not a needy person among them, for all who were owners of lands or houses would sell them and bring the proceeds of the sales, and lay them at the apostles' feet; and they would be distributed to each, as any had need (Acts 4:32, 34–35).

Amazing!

Ancient *koinonia* must have been something to behold. As I try to form a mental picture of it, I come up with this description: *Koinonia* is expressions of authentic Christianity freely shared among members of God's family. It is mentioned about twenty times in the New Testament. Without exception it is invariably expressed in one of two directions.

First, it is used in the sense of sharing something *with* someone such as food, money, supplies, encouragement, time, and concern. And second, it is used in the sense of sharing *in* something with someone, like a project, a success, a failure, a need, a hurt.

The significance of all this is that biblical *koinonia* is *never something done alone.* In other words, God's desire for His children is that we be personally and deeply involved in each other's lives. It is not His will that we start looking like touch-me-not automatons covered over with a thin layer of shiny chrome. Our superficial "How ya' doin'" and "Have a nice day" won't cut it. There was none of this lack of involvement in that group of first-century Christians. There wasn't a porcupine among them!

WHY GET INVOLVED?

As I search God's Word for reasons to break with the isolationism of this age, I find two inescapable facts: God commands it and the Church needs it.

God Commands It

We read in Romans 12:9–16 a series of commands:

> Let love be without hypocrisy. Abhor what is evil; cleave to what is good.
> Be devoted to one another in brotherly love; give preference to one another in honor; not lagging behind in diligence, fervent in spirit, serving the Lord; rejoicing in hope, persevering in tribulation, devoted to prayer, contributing to the needs of the saints, practicing hospitality.
> Bless those who persecute you; bless and curse not.
> Rejoice with those who rejoice, and weep with those who weep.
> Be of the same mind toward one another; do not be haughty in mind, but associate with the lowly. Do not be wise in your own estimation.

All those verses are actually an outgrowth of the first command, "Let love be without hypocrisy." Look at the way *The Living Bible* presents verses 9 and 10:

> Don't just pretend that you love others: really love them. Hate what is wrong. Stand on the side of the good. Love each other with brotherly affection and take delight in honoring each other.

Away with hypocrisy! Farewell to indifference! God commands that we reach out, accept, and affirm one another. This means that we consciously resist the strong current of the stream we are in . . . the one that dictates all those excuses:
"I'm just too busy."
"It's not worth the risk."
"I don't really need anyone."
"I'll get burned if I get too close."
"If I reach out, I'll look foolish."
The devil's strategy for our times is working. He has deluded us into believing that we really shouldn't concern ourselves with being our brother's keeper. After all, we have time pressures and work demands (that relentless, fierce determination to be number one), not to mention, anxieties prompted by economic uncertainty. And who really needs our help anyway? I'll tell you

who—just about every person we meet, that's who. Don't be fooled by the secure-looking, self-reliant veneer most of us wear. Deep down inside there's usually a scared little kid who is waiting for someone to care, to hold his or her hand, to affirm and love with authentic affection.

God commands us to be involved because He has made us dependent beings. Remember what He said to Adam just before He gave him Eve? "It is not good for the man to be alone" (Gen. 2:18).

This brings up the second reason we are to be involved.

The Body Needs It

Read again these familiar words:

As it is, there are many parts, but one body.

The eye cannot say to the hand, "I don't need you!" And the head cannot say to the feet, "I don't need you!"

On the contrary, those parts of the body that seem to be weaker are indispensable, and the parts that we think are less honorable we treat with special honor. And the parts that are unpresentable are treated with special modesty, while our presentable parts need no special treatment. But God has combined the members of the body and has given greater honor to the parts that lacked it, so that there should be no division in the body, but that its parts should have equal concern for each other.

If one part suffers, every part suffers with it; if one part is honored, every part rejoices with it.

Now you are the body of Christ, and each one of you is a part of it (1 Cor. 12:20–27, NIV).

In order for Christ's body, the Church, to do its thing, we must be working together as a team. To dispel division, we are to be involved with one another. To keep down disease, to mend fractures, to accelerate healing, we must be interdependent. Furthermore, we need to assist each other as servants and friends—just like a human body comes to the aid of its injured parts.

During an adolescent period in my own spiritual growth, I went through a stage where I felt I really didn't need anyone. I "used" a few people during that time, and I occasionally acted out a role that looked like I was willing to be involved, but deep down inside I kept my distance. Hidden pride played games within me, I am ashamed to admit, as I mouthed the right stuff, but I had no interest whatever in reaching out or allowing anyone else to reach in.

It was at that time God went to work on my attitude. He used every possible means, it seemed, to get my attention and reveal to me my need for others. Looking back, I can now see why He didn't let up. With relentless regularity He stayed on my case, punching, pushing, pulling, pressing, penetrating. The best part of all was the beautiful way others ministered to me—I was forced to face the fact that *I needed them* just like Paul writes in 1 Corinthians 12. I learned by experience: "The eye cannot say to the hand, 'I have no need of you'" (v. 21, RSV).

In the family of God, there is no such thing as a completely independent member of the body. We may act like it for a while, but ultimately He shows us how much we need one another.

WHAT DOES INVOLVEMENT INCLUDE?

As I read verses 25 through 27 of 1 Corinthians 12, I find at least three particular ingredients in meaningful involvement: Spontaneity, vulnerability, and accountability.

Spontaneity

Read again verse 25.

> So that there should be no division in the body, but that its parts have equal concern for each other (NIV).

I'm glad God expresses Himself here like He does. "Should." Not "must." Not "You better, or else!" Spontaneous willingness is implied in "should."

When God prompts involvement, it is not contrived. It's never forced. It flows. There is no legislation, no galling obligation. It's done because the person wants to, not because he *has* to.

Vulnerability

Look at verse 26:

> If one part suffers, every part suffers with it; if one part is honored, every part rejoices with it (NIV).

There is a lot of personal feeling in these words. The one who gets involved doesn't play the role of prim-and-proper Mr. Clean. No, he is human, vulnerable—capable of being wounded, open to attack, misunderstanding, or damage. He is unguarded.

When wounds ooze, vulnerable people get soiled. There is genuine sharing in the hurt. Vulnerable people are fearless, however, when it comes to being broken. In her own, inimitable style, Anne Ortlund writes of this as she reflects on a sermon her husband Ray preached on Mark 14:3.

> . . . "Here came Mary," he said, "with her alabaster vase of nard to the dinner where Jesus was. She broke the bottle and poured it on Him."

An alabaster vase—milky white, veined, smooth, precious.

And pure nard inside! Gone forever. According to John 12:3, the whole house became filled with the fragrance.

Some story.

———

Christians file into church on a Sunday morning. One by one by one they march in—like separate alabaster vases.

Contained.

Self-sufficient.

Encased.

Individually complete.

Contents undisclosed.

No perfume emitting at all.

Their vases aren't bad looking. In fact, some of them are the Beautiful People, and they become Vase-Conscious: conscious of their own vase and of one another's. They're aware of clothes, personalities, of position in this world—of exteriors.

So before and after church (maybe during) they're apt to talk Vase Talk. *Your ring is darling; what stone is that? Did you hear if Harry got that job? What is Lisa's boy doing for the summer? Is that all your own hair? I may take tennis lessons if George wants to.*

———

Mary broke her vase.

Broke it! How shocking. How controversial. Was everybody doing it? Was it a vase-breaking party? No, she just did it all by herself. What happened then? The obvious: all the contents were forever released. She could never hug her precious nard to herself again.[5]

That's the way it is with vulnerability. It's risky, but it's so essential.

There is one final ingredient in meaningful involvement found in this 1 Corinthians passage.

Accountability

Now you are the body of Christ, and each one of you is a part of it (v. 27, NIV).

We are not only one massive body, we are *individuals*, single units who carry out vital functions. This means we are accountable to one another. As I quoted earlier, "No man is an island . . . every man is a piece of the continent."

In our indifferent, preoccupied world of isolation and anonymity, it's a comfort to know we are linked together. Someone cares about us. Someone is interested. Someone notices. That's another benefit of being involved.

I am the senior pastor of a rather large congregation in Southern California. It is easy for a person to get completely lost in the shuffle . . . to be a nameless face in a crowd. To feel no sense of identity. To accept no responsibility. To drift dangerously near perilous extremes without anyone even knowing it. That's why those of us in leadership are constantly thinking of ways to cultivate an identity, to bring people out of anonymity, to assure them that involvement includes accountability. It is easy to think that all who come for worship are involved—are being noticed and encouraged. But such is not the case.

The grim reality of all this struck home to my heart some time ago as I read the true account of an experience my friend, Dr. James Dobson, had at a seminary. Jim had spoken on the subject of the need for self-esteem among men in the ministry. Strangely, many people have the mistaken idea that those preparing for ministry seldom struggle with inferiority. One young man was brave enough to admit that he found himself paralyzed with fear, even though he sincerely desired to help others as he served God. Dr. Dobson spoke openly of this common predicament that gnaws on one's soul.

> Sitting in the audience that same day was another student with the same kind of problems. However, he did not write me a letter. He never identified himself in any way. But three weeks after I left, he hanged himself in the basement of his apartment. One of the four men with whom he lived called long distance to inform me of the tragedy. He stated, deeply shaken, that the dead student's roommates were so unaware of his problems that he hanged there five days before he was missed![6]

Difficult though it may be to believe it, there are Christian people who are *that* out of touch and *that* uninvolved in the town or city where you live. And also in the church where you worship. They need you. What's more, *you need them*. And unless something is done to establish and maintain meaningful involvement, tragedies will continue to occur.

Never forget, isolation is a potent killer. Strengthening our grip on involvement is not simply an enjoyable luxury for those who have time on their hands. It's essential for survival.

Discussion Questions and Ideas to Help You Strengthen Your Grip on Involvement

• In your own words, define *involvement*. Think and talk about how it provides the needed answer to isolation. On a scale of 1 (lowest) to 10 (highest), how high would you rate your level of involvement?

• Remember the "porcupine syndrome"? Be honest with yourself as you reflect on your own tendency to push back when people start getting too close. Is this true? Ever analyzed why?

• We looked into numerous helpful Scripture passages in this chapter. See if you can recall several that took on a deeper meaning. Turn to them and discuss this.

• As we thought about the reasons involvement is important, we considered two: (1) because God commands it, and (2) because the Body needs it. Think this over—especially the *second* reason. What specifically do you gain from someone else, which you yourself cannot provide?

• Spontaneity, vulnerability, and accountability are three vital ingredients in meaningful involvement. Choose one and think about its value. Can you recall an experience when you witnessed this in someone else?

3

Strengthening Your Grip on Encouragement

Keystone, Colorado, is a ski resort area about an hour and a half west of Denver. My family and I were invited to spend Thanksgiving week at that picturesque spot in 1980 with about five hundred single young adults, most of whom were staff personnel with Campus Crusade, an international Christian organization. I cannot recall a time when there was a greater spirit of teachability and enthusiasm among a group of people. The atmosphere was electric!

I spoke all week on the subject of servanthood, emphasizing the importance of today's leader being one who helps, encourages, affirms, and cares for others rather than one who pulls rank and takes advantage of them. Many of the things I presented have now found their way into a book.[1] God *really* changed some lives that week. I continue to hear from various men and women who were a part of that memorable experience.

By Friday of that week I decided to take a break and hit the slopes (emphasis on *hit*, since it was my first time in all my life to attempt to ski). It had snowed all day Thanksgiving. The ski areas were absolutely beautiful and in perfect condition. I struck out on my virgin voyage with a positive mental attitude, thinking, "I'm going to be the first person who learned to ski without falling down. *Guinness Book of World Records* will hear of this and write me up!"

Don't bother to check. I'm not in the book.

It was unbelievable! You have heard of the elephant man? On skis, I'm the rhinoceros man. It is doubtful that anyone else on planet earth has ever come down any ski slope more ways than I did. Or landed in more positions. Or did more creative things in the air *before* landing. I can still hear the words of a ski instructor as she stood before her class of children, staring at me as I zipped past them. I was by then on one leg, leaning dangerously to the starboard side, traveling about thirty-five miles an hour—completely out of control. "Now class, that is what I DON'T want you to do!" As I recall, I ended that slide a few miles from Denver in a field of buffalo. Even they looked surprised.

Working with me that humiliating day was the world's most encouraging ski instructor (yes, I had an instructor!) who set the new record in patience. She is the one whom Guinness needs to interview.

Never once did she lose her cool.

Never once did she laugh at me.

Never once did she yell, scream, threaten, or swear.

Never once did she call me "dummy."

Never once did she say, "You are absolutely impossible. I quit!"

That dear, gracious lady helped me up more times than I can number. She repeated the same basics time and again—like she had never said them before. Even though I was colder than an explorer in the Antarctic, irritable, impatient, and under the snow more than I was on it, she kept on offering words of reassurance. On top of all that, she didn't even charge me for those hours on the baby slope when she could have been enjoying the day with all her friends on the fabulous, long slope up above. That day God gave me a living, never-to-be-forgotten illustration of the value of encouragement. Had it not been for her spirit and her words, believe me, I would have hung 'em up and been back in the condo, warming my feet by the fire in less than an hour.

What is true for a novice on the snow once a year is all the more true for the people we meet every day. Harassed by demands and deadlines; bruised by worry, adversity, and failure; broken by disillusionment; and defeated by sin, they live somewhere between dull discouragement and sheer panic. Even Christians are not immune! We may give off this "I've got it all together" air of confidence, much like I did when I first snapped on the skis at Keystone. But realistically, we also struggle, lose our balance, slip and slide, tumble, and fall flat on our faces.

All of us need encouragement—somebody to believe in us. To reassure and reinforce us. To help us pick up the pieces and go on. To provide us with increased determination in spite of the odds.

THE MEANING OF ENCOURAGEMENT

When you stop to analyze the concept, "encourage" takes on new meaning. It's the act of inspiring others with renewed courage, spirit, or hope. When we encourage others we spur them on, we stimulate and affirm them. It is helpful to remember the distinction between appreciation and affirmation. We appreciate what a person does, but we affirm who a person is. Appreciation comes and goes because it is usually related to something someone accomplishes. Affirmation goes deeper. It is directed to the person himself or herself. While encouragement would encompass both, the rarer of the two is affirmation. To be appreciated, we get the distinct impression that we must earn it by some accomplishment. But affirmation requires no such prerequisite. This means that even when we don't earn the right to be appreciated (because we failed to succeed or because we lacked the accomplishment of some goal), we can still be affirmed—indeed, we need it then more than ever.

I do not care how influential or secure or mature a person may appear to be, genuine encouragement never fails to help. Most of us need massive doses of it as we slug it out in the trenches. But we are usually too proud to admit it. Unfortunately, this pride is as prevalent among members of God's family as it is on the streets of the world. Let's dig deeper into this issue of encouragement.

THERE'S MORE TO WORSHIP THAN PRAYING

Most people who go to church believe that a worship service consists only of a few hymns, a prayer or two, dropping some bucks in a plate, hearing a solo, and finally listening to a sermon. If you gave that answer to my one-question quiz "Why do Christians gather for worship?" I'd have to grade you "incomplete." Let me show you why.

Many centuries ago when Christians began meeting together, persecution was standard operating procedure. Martyrdom was as common to them as traffic jams are to us—an everyday occurrence. As a result, fear gripped congregations. Some believers defected, others sort of drifted to play it safe.

A letter, therefore, began to circulate among the converted Jews, addressed to those who were enduring the blast of persecution. We know the letter today as *Hebrews*. Nobody knows for sure who wrote the letter, but whoever it was understood the value of corporate worship. After warning them against compromising their walk of faith, he informed them of the importance of those special times they spent together.

Spend a few moments thinking through his words that were written, no doubt, with a great deal of emotion.

Since therefore, brethren, we have confidence to enter the holy place by the blood of Jesus, by a new and living way which He inaugurated for us through the veil, that is, His flesh, and since we have a great priest over the house of God, let us draw near with a sincere heart in full assurance of faith, having our hearts sprinkled clean from an evil conscience and our body washed with pure water.

Let us hold fast the confession of our hope without wavering, for He who promised is faithful; and let us consider how to stimulate one another to love and good deeds, not forsaking our own assembling together, as is the habit of some but encouraging one another; and all the more, as you see the day drawing near (Heb. 10:19–25).

He begins this section by describing what we *have*:
1. We have confidence to approach God (v. 19).
2. We have a priest who gives us access to God—referring to Christ (v. 21).

We Christians today tend to forget what magnificent benefits these are. The reason we forget is simple—we've never known it any other way! But back then, during the threatening era of the first century, worshipers *lacked* confidence. They approached God with a spirit of fear and trepidation. Their fathers and forefathers knew nothing of such familiarity with the Father. But now that Christ has opened the way to God (by His death on the cross), we come boldly, confidently. Why? Because Jesus Christ is our go-between. We have confidence because He has given us this immediate access to the throne room of God the Father.

Next, the writer of Hebrews describes what we are *to do*. Did you catch the cues? Three times he prefaces his remarks with "let us."

"Let us draw near . . ." (v. 22).

In other words, come up close. It's an invitation to become intimately acquainted with our God. There's no need for children of God to feel as if they are walking on eggs when they come before Him.

"Let us hold fast . . ." (v. 23).

This verse conveys the importance of standing firm in the reliable truth of God. Today we'd say, "Let's hang tough!"

"Let us consider how to stimulate one another . . ." (v. 24).

This verse seems to focus in on the point the writer has been trying to make. Ultimately, we are to think about ways to stir up each other so that the result is a deeper love for one another and a greater involvement in doing good things for one another. In a word, he is talking about encouragement. How can we know that for sure? Check out the very next verse:

> Not forsaking our own assembling together, as is the habit of some but encouraging one another; and all the more, as you see the day drawing near (v. 25).

You see, there's much more to worship than sitting and listening to a sermon or bowing in prayer. A major objective is that we give attention to what we might do to encourage each other.

One further thought on that passage of Scripture—did you notice that we are not told specifically what to do? We are simply exhorted, "Let us consider how to stimulate one another. . . ." The details are left up to each new generation of people who face new and different challenges.

THE SIGNIFICANCE OF ENCOURAGEMENT

Certainly there is more to encouragement than a smile and a quick pat on the back. We need to realize just how valuable it really is.

A good place to start is with the word itself. *Encouragement*, as used in Hebrews 10:25, is from the same Greek root used for the Holy Spirit in John 14:26 and 16:7. In both those verses He is called "the Helper." The actual term, *parakaleo*, is from a combination of two smaller words, *kaleo*, "to call," and *para*, "alongside." Just as the Holy Spirit is called alongside to help us, so it is with us when you and I encourage someone else. In fact, when we encourage others, we come as close to the work of the Holy Spirit as anything we can do in God's family. Believe me, when Christians begin to realize the value of mutual encouragement, there is no limit to what we can be stimulated to accomplish. It is thrilling to realize that God has "called *us* alongside to help" others who are in need. How much better to be engaged in actions that lift others up rather than actions that tear them down! Realizing this, one man writes:

> One of the highest of human duties is the duty of encouragement. . . . It is easy to pour cold water on their enthusiasm; it is easy to discourage others. The world is full of discouragers. We have a Christian duty to encourage one another. Many a time a word of praise or thanks or appreciation or cheer has kept a man on his feet.[2]

The beautiful part about encouragement is this: *Anybody* can do it. You don't need a lot of money to carry it out. You don't even need to be a certain age. In fact, some of the most encouraging actions or words I've received have come from my own children at a time when my heart was heavy. They saw the need and moved right in . . . they "came alongside and helped."

Local churches are beginning to catch on, too. I read of a congregation in Salem, Oregon, who decided to get serious about this. "Encouragement cards" are placed in the hymn racks on each pew. At the top of the card, the words "Encouraging One Another" appear in bold print. Those who use them place the name of the recipient on one side and their message of encouragement on the other. All cards must be signed—no unsigned cards are mailed. All cards are collected, and early that same week office personnel address, stamp, and mail the cards. Multiple cards to the same person are bunched together and mailed in a single envelope.

Since many are too busy to sit down during the week and write a word of encouragement, this congregation takes time as the worship service begins. Some bow in prayer while others grab a pencil and start encouraging. What a grand idea!

"Aw, it'll get old—lose its punch," you might think. "Not so," says the pastor. For nine years they have been involved in this process of putting encouragement into action, and it is more effective and meaningful today than ever before.[3]

I am absolutely convinced that there are many thousands of people who are drying up on the vine simply because of the lack of encouragement. Lonely, forgotten missionaries, military service men and women away from home, collegians and seminarians, the sick and the dying, the divorced and the grieving, those who serve faithfully behind the scenes with scarcely a glance or comment from anyone.

While I was studying at Dallas Theological Seminary, my wife and I became close friends with a graduate student working toward his doctor of theology degree. He was a winsome, brilliant young man whose future looked promising. He was single at the time, and Cynthia and I often spoke of how fortunate some young lady would be to claim him as her own! As time passed he not only earned the coveted degree, he met and married a young woman. Several years and two children later, our friend was well on his way toward an extremely successful career when suddenly his world collapsed. His wife left him, taking the children and the joys of a home with her.

I shall never forget his description of walking into the house and finding it cold and empty. A dozen emotions swept through him as the grim reality of loss bit deeply into his soul, spreading the paralyzing venom of despair. Time dragged on . . . no change, only memories. Reconciliation became a misty, distant dream, finally an absolute impossibility. The horror of endless hours of loneliness caused our friend to question many things. To say he was low is to understate the obvious—he was at rock bottom. While there, he wrote this piece which I repeat with his permission, but I shall leave it anonymous to protect his privacy.

> The days are long, but the nights longer—and lonelier.
> I wait for the daylight—
>   but darkness holds me in her grip.
> I struggle alone.
>
> Sleep escapes me as memories of the good times—
>   and the bad—
> Crowd out the vestiges of euphoria and leave me restless—
>   hurting—
> Filling my mind with thoughts of love—
>   and hostility,
> Of thoughtlessness—
>   and remorse,
> Of guilt—
>   and despair.
>
> O God, I cry, is there no end to the hurt?
> Must shame plague my steps forever?
> Is there not another who will walk with me—
>   accepting
>   loving
>   caring
>   forgiving—
> Willing to build with me a new life on foundations more sure—
> To whom I will pledge, as will she, faithfulness forever?

Others have cried with me in the darkness—
   they have cared—
But in the confinements of our own humanness.
The demands of their lives must take precedence.
And in the end I stand alone—
   apart from Thee.

I have attempted to build again—
   on my own—
Too soon, unwise and unstable.
New hurts have come to tear open the wounds not yet healed.
The struggle is not ended.

And so I crawl—
   uneasy, yet unyielding to defeat and sure despair—
Toward better days,
   Toward light that is unending,
     Toward God who keeps me in His care.

Encouragement became this man's single oasis in the desert of defeat. A few people graciously and consistently reached out to him, giving him hope and the will to go on as many more turned away, rejecting him and questioning his character. The man has since remarried and is happily engaged in a fulfilling, challenging role as an executive in a Christian organization. Thanks to encouragement, he survived. His case is one in thousands—another example of the strategic significance encouragement plays in the lives of those who hurt.

IMPLEMENTING ENCOURAGEMENT

Going back to the statement found in Hebrews 10:25, we are to "consider how to stimulate one another to love and good deeds." In other words, we are to give thought to specific ways we can lift up, affirm, and help others. God's commands are not theoretical—especially those that relate to people in need. A couple of scriptures come to my mind:

If you have a friend who is in need of food and clothing, and you say to him, "Well, good-bye and God bless you; stay warm and eat hearty," and then don't give him clothes or food, what good does that do? (James 2:15–16, TLB).

But if someone who is supposed to be a Christian has money enough to live well, and sees a brother in need, and won't help him—how can God's love be within him? (1 John 3:17, TLB).

Maybe a few ideas will help spark an interest in putting our encouragement into action.

• Observe and mention admirable character qualities you see in others, such as:

Punctuality	Thoroughness
Tactfulness	Diligence
Faithfulness	Honesty
Good attitude	Compassion
Loyalty	Good Sense of Humor
Tolerance	Vision and Faith

• Correspondence, thank-you notes, small gifts with a note attached. Preferably not so much at birthdays or Christmas, but at unexpected times.

• Phone calls. Be brief and to the point. Express appreciation for something specific that you genuinely appreciate.

• Notice a job well done and say so. I know a few important people who are successful largely because they have splendid assistance from secretaries and support personnel within the ranks . . . but seldom are those people told what a fine job they are doing.

• Cultivate a positive, reassuring attitude. Think and respond along this line. Encouragement cannot thrive in a negative, squint-eyed atmosphere.

• Pick up the tab in a restaurant . . . provide free tickets to some event you know the person (or family) would enjoy . . . send flowers . . . give a gift of money when it seems appropriate.

• Be supportive to someone you know is hurting. Reach out without fear of what others may think or say.

A few final words of clarification are in order. Encouragement should take the sting out of life. But be careful not to create other burdens for those you want to encourage. Do what you do with no interest whatever in being paid back. Reciprocal expectations are guilt-giving trips, not encouraging actions! Also, try to be sensitive to the timing of your actions. A well-time expression of encouragement is never forgotten. Never!

I often think of those who once did their job faithfully for an extended period of time and then were replaced—only to be forgotten. People like former teachers, former officers in a church, former board members, previous pastors, and those who discipled us become lost in the sea of distant memories. Spend some time recalling the important people who had part in building your life . . . and look for ways to encourage them. You and I may be surprised to know how much it means to them just to know they are not forgotten. If you need a tangible reminder of the encouragement this brings, call to mind our P.O.W.'s in Viet Nam and our hostages in Iran. Just the knowledge that they were not out of sight, out of mind, kept most of them going.

The ability to encourage is developed first in one's home. It is here that this vital virtue is cultivated. Children pick it up from their parents as they become the recipients of their mother's and dad's words of delight and approval. Numerous tests document the sad fact, however, that homes tend to be far more negative than positive, much less affirming than critical.

Allow me to challenge you to have a family that is different. Start taking whatever steps that need to be taken to develop in your home a spirit of positive, reinforcing, consistent encouragement. Your family will be forever grateful, believe me. And *you* will be a lot happier person.

I know a young man whose spinal cord was severed in an accident when he was four years old. He has absolutely no use of his legs today. They are like excess baggage stuck to his body. But thanks to a father who believed in him and a wife who absolutely adores him, Rick Leavenworth accomplishes feats today that you and I would call unbelievable. One of his more recent ones is backpacking and mountain climbing. In fact, a film[4] has been made (you *must* see it!) that shows him reaching the top of a mountain over 13,000 feet elevation . . . all alone, just Rick, his wheelchair, and determination cultivated over years of encouragement.

I'm giving serious thought to giving up skiing and taking up backpacking. Maybe Rick will be willing to train me.

DISCUSSION QUESTIONS AND IDEAS
TO HELP YOU STRENGTHEN YOUR GRIP ON ENCOURAGEMENT

• Encouragement plays a vital part in our relationship with one another. Talk about why. Be specific as you describe the things encouragement does for a person.

• Go back over the passage in Hebrews 10 that we referred to in this chapter. Read it aloud and slowly. Talk about the one part that seems most significant to you. Explain why.

• Now then, in your mind list three or four ways we *discourage* others. Be painfully honest with yourself as you answer the questions: Do you do this? If so, *why*? Next, mentally list some ways we *encourage* others. Talk about how you can start doing this more often.

• Can you think of a person who often lifts the spirits of others? Name the individual and describe how you have personally benefited from him or her. Have you ever told the person "Thanks"? Why not write a letter or make a phone call soon and communicate your gratitude?

• Strengthening your grip on encouragement is a slow process. Like the formation of any habit, it takes time. But in order for you to join the ranks of "encouragers," you need to start doing one or two things *daily* to encourage others. Think for a few moments, then share what you plan to start doing to form the habit of encouraging others.

4

Strengthening
Your Grip
on Purity

"Christianity is supremely the champion of purity. . . ."[1]
The words seemed to jump off the page. I grabbed the dictionary on my desk and looked up "champion." It means "a militant advocate or defender." A champion is one who fights for another's rights. As I went back to the original statement, I paraphrased it:

"Christianity is supremely the militant advocate, the defender of purity."

I then fantasized the sparkling image of a muscular man dressed in white with his brightly shining sword drawn. I named him Christianity and envisioned him as he stood in front of Purity, ready to slash to ribbons any enemy who attempted to attack her. She felt safe in his shadow, protected in his presence, like a little sister standing behind her big brother.

And then I thought, "Is that still true?" I checked the date on the book I was reading: 1959. With a sigh, I was forced to face reality, "We've come a long way since '59." Maybe a a better word is *drifted*. Does Purity still have her champion?

Theoretically, she does. There has never been a more valiant defender of Purity than Christianity. Nothing can compare to the power of Christ when it comes to cleaning up a life. His liberating strength has broken the yoke of slavery to sin. His death and resurrection have come to our rescue, offering us dignity in place of moral misery and hope instead of degenerating despair. Unlike the helpless victims without the Savior who try and try to get their act together in their own strength—only to fail again and again—the person who knows Jesus Christ personally, having received Him by faith, has available to himself or herself all the power needed to walk in purity. But let's understand, that walk is not automatic. Ah, there's the rub.

195

It's not that Christianity has begun to lose its punch over the past twenty to twenty-five years; it's that more and more Christians (it seems to me) now opt for a lower standard when confronted with the choice of living in moral purity as set forth in the Scriptures or compromising (then rationalizing away the guilt). Well, just look around. You decide.

The battle of choices is certainly not new. Two sections of the New Testament, written in the first century(!), describe the internal warfare quite vividly:

> Your old evil desires were nailed to the cross with him; that part of you that loves to sin was crushed and fatally wounded, so that your sin-loving body is no longer under sin's control, no longer needs to be a slave to sin. . . .

> Do not let sin control your puny body any longer; do not give in to its sinful desires. Do not let any part of your bodies become tools of wickedness, to be used for sinning; but give yourselves completely to God—every part of you—for you are back from death and you want to be tools in the hands of God, to be used for his good purposes (Rom. 6:6, 12–13, TLB).

> For we naturally love to do evil things that are just the opposite from the things that the Holy Spirit tells us to do; and the good things we want to do when the Spirit has his way with us are just the opposite of our natural desires. These two forces within us are constantly fighting each other to win control over us, and our wishes are never free from their pressures (Gal. 5:17, TLB).

How balanced the Bible is! Without denying the struggle or decreasing the strong appeal of our flesh, it announces that we need not yield as though we Christians are pathetic lumps of putty in the hands of temptation. In Christ, through Christ, because of Christ, we have all the internal equipment necessary to maintain moral purity. Yes, Christianity is *still* the champion of purity . . . but the challenges and attacks against purity have never been greater, and this complicates the problem.

MORAL EROSION: AN INESCAPABLE FACT

In case you are not ready to accept the idea that morals are on a downward trend, think back to 1939. That was the year *Gone With the Wind* was released, including in its script a scandal-making, four-letter word that raised the eyebrows of movie goers around the world. Has there been much change since '39? Do four-letter words still create scandals? What a joke!

Russian-born Pitirim Sorokin, the first professor and chairman of the Sociology Department at Harvard, is an astute observer of our times. His book, *The American Sex Revolution*, pulls no punches as he develops the theme: "Our civilization has become so preoccupied with sex that it now oozes from all pores of American life."[2] Grieved over our ever-increasing appetite for the sensual, Dr. Sorokin does a masterful job of describing the moral erosion of a nation once pure and proud:

> . . . in the last century, much literature has centered on the personalities and adventures of subnormal and abnormal people,—prostitutes and mistresses, street urchins and criminals, the mentally and emotionally deranged, and other social derelicts. There has been a growing preoccupation with the subsocial sewers,— the broken home of disloyal parents and unloved children, the bedroom of a prostitute, a "Canary Row" brothel, a den of criminals, a ward of the insane, a club of dishonest politicians, a street-corner gang of teen-age delinquents, the office of a huckster, the ostentatious mansion of a cynical business Mogul, a hate-laden prison, a "street car named desire," a crime-ridden waterfront, the court-room of a dishonest judge, the jungle of cattle-murdering and meat-packing yards. These and hundreds of similar scenes are exemplary of a large part of modern Western literature, which has become increasingly a veritable museum of human pathology.
>
> There has been a parallel transmutation of the experience of love. From the pure and noble or the tragic, it has progressively devolved. The common and prosaic, but usually licit sexual love that is portrayed in the literature of the eighteenth and nineteenth centuries has in the last fifty years been increasingly displaced by various forms of abnormal, perverse, vulgar, picaresque, exotic, and even monstrous forms,—the sex adventures of urbanized cavemen and rapists, the loves of adulterers and fornicators, of masochists and sadists, of prostitutes, mistresses, playboys, and entertainment personalities. Juicy "loves," "its," "ids," "orgasms," and "libidos" are seductively prepared and skillfully served with all the trimmings.
>
> Designed to excite the fading lust of readers, and thereby increase the sales of these literary sex-tonics, much of contemporary Western literature has become Freudian through and through. It is preoccupied with "dirt-painting" of genital, anal, oral, cutaneous, homosexual, and incestuous "loves." It is absorbed in literary psychoanalysis of various complexes,—the castration, the Oedipus, the Tetanus, the Narcissus, and other pathological forms. It has degraded and denied the great, noble, and joyfully beautiful values of normal married love.[3]

Since Sorokin's book was written, we have degenerated beyond what even *he* would have imagined. Porno shops are now in every major American city. Hard-core X-rated films are now available on pay cable television as well as in some of the larger hotels. We have reached an all-time low with "kiddie porn" and "love" murders (yes, the actual crime) now captured on film. Even prime-time TV isn't exempt from intimate bedroom scenes, verbal explosions of profanity, and a rather frequent diet of so-called humor regarding sexual intercourse, homosexuality, nudity, and various parts of the human anatomy. One wonders when we shall reach the saturation level.

For sure, we've drifted a long way since '39! But this is not to suggest that up until then our land was as pure as the driven snow. No, it's just that there is a boldness, an unblushing, uninhibited brashness in today's immorality that none can deny. And all of this assaults the senses with such relentless regularity that we need the power of God to walk in purity. The good news is this: *We have it!* But I remind you, putting His power into action is not automatic . . . which brings us to one of the more potent biblical passages in the New Testament.

Moral Purity: An Attainable Goal

During Paul's second missionary journey, he traveled into Europe, a region of the world that had not heard of Christianity. In metropolitan cities like Philippi, Thessalonica, Athens, and Corinth he proclaimed the message of salvation, holding out hope and forgiveness to all who would listen. Later, after having had time to think about his ministry among them, he wrote letters to most of those places, desiring to clarify as well as intensify what he had taught them.

An example of this is found in 1 Thessalonians 4. Listen to the first five verses.

> Let me add this, dear brothers: You already know how to please God in your daily living, for you know the commands we gave you from the Lord Jesus himself. Now we beg you—yes, we demand of you in the name of the Lord Jesus—that you live more and more closely to that ideal.
>
> For God wants you to be holy and pure, and to keep clear of all sexual sin so that each of you will marry in holiness and honor—not in lustful passion as the heathen do, in their ignorance of God and his ways (1 Thess. 4:1-5, TLB).

Like a pastor concerned about the flock among whom he ministers, Paul encourages them to do more than give a casual nod to sexual purity. Rather, he exhorts them to "excel still more" (NASB). He comes right out and commands them to "abstain from sexual immorality . . ." (NASB).

The Roman world of that day was a climate much like ours today. Impurity was viewed either with passive indifference or open favor. Christians back then (and now) were like tiny islands of morality surrounded by vast oceans of illicit sex and promiscuity. Knowing the current of temptation that swirled around them, he counseled them to "abstain"—an open and shut case for total abstention from sexual immorality. For Christianity to retain its role as "the champion of purity," the Christian is expected to be above reproach. The same is as true today as it was in the first century.

> Christian holiness, says Paul, requires total abstinence from *porneias* ("sexual immorality," "fornication"). The word requires broad definition here as including all types of sexual sins between male and female.[4]

In our gray, hang-loose, swampy world of theological accommodation that adjusts to the mood of the moment, this passage of Scripture stands out like a lonely lighthouse on a stark, rugged hill. Interestingly, the verses go on to talk about the process of maintaining a pure lifestyle . . . that is to say, how to strengthen our grip on purity.

> For this is the will of God, your sanctification; that is, that you abstain from sexual immorality; that each of you know how to possess his own vessel in sanctification and honor, not in lustful passion, like the Gentiles who do not know God; and that no man transgress and defraud his brother in the matter because the Lord is the avenger in all these things, just as he also told you before and solemnly warned you.
>
> For God has not called us for the purpose of impurity, but in sanctification (vv. 3-7).

Taking Control of the Body

It is impossible to come to terms with moral purity without dealing with some practical facts related to the body—our flesh-and-blood appetites that crave satisfaction. Volumes are written about the mind, our emotional makeup, our "inner man," the soul, the spirit, and the spiritual dimension. But by comparison, very little is being said by evangelicals today about the physical body.

• We are to present our bodies as living sacrifices to God (Rom. 12:1).

• We are instructed *not* to yield any part of our bodies as instruments of unrighteousness to sin (Rom. 6:12–13).

• Our bodies are actually "members of Christ"; they belong to Him (1 Cor. 6:15).

• Our bodies are "temples" literally inhabited by the Holy Spirit (1 Cor. 6:19).

• We are therefore expected to "glorify God" in our bodies (1 Cor. 6:20).

• We are to become students of our bodies, knowing how to control them in honor (1 Thess. 4:4).

You see, these bodies of ours can easily lead us off course. It isn't that the body itself is evil; it's just that it possesses any number of appetites that are ready to respond to the surrounding stimuli . . . all of which are terribly appealing and temporarily satisfying.

Let me ask you: Do you know your body? Are you aware of the things that weaken your control of it? Have you stopped to consider the danger zones and how to stay clear of them—or at least hurriedly pass through them?

When I was in the Marines, I spent nearly a year and a half in the Orient. Some of the time I was stationed in Japan, most of the time on the island of Okinawa. Eight thousand lonely miles away from my wife and family. Lots of free time . . . and plenty of opportunities to drift into sexual escapades. Most of the men in my outfit regularly shacked up in the village. For those who didn't want the hassle of a "commitment" to one woman, there was an island full of available one-nighters. Brightly lit bars, with absolutely gorgeous (externally, that is) females of any nationality you pleased, were open seven nights a week, 365 days a year. And there wasn't anything they wouldn't do to satisfy their customers who were mostly Marines. The sensual temptation was fierce, to say the least.

I was in my midtwenties. I was a Christian. I was also one hundred percent human. It didn't take me long to realize that unless I learned how to force my body to behave, I'd be no different from any other Marine on liberty. Without getting into all the details, I developed ways to stay busy. I occupied my time with creative involvements. When walking along the streets, I walked fast. I refused to linger and allow my body to respond to the glaring come-on signals. My eyes looked straight ahead . . . and sometimes I literally *ran* to my destination. I consciously forced myself to tune out the sensual music. I disciplined my mind through intensive reading, plus a scripture memory program. And I began most days praying for God's strength to get me through. The battle was terribly difficult, but the commitment to sexual purity paid rich dividends, believe me.

It worked, and it will work for you too. Now, before you think I'm the monk type, let me declare to you *nothing could be further from the truth.* I simply refused to let my body dictate my convictions. Just as 1 Thessalonians 4:3-7 implies, moral purity paid off. And by the way, when the Lord began to open doors for me to talk about Christ with others, it is remarkable how willing they were to listen. Down deep inside, behind all that macho mask, the men longed to be rid of that awful, nagging guilt . . . the other side of sexual impurity that the merchants of hedonism never bother to mention. Purity won a hearing.

My whole point in sharing this with you is to underscore the fact that personal purity is an attainable goal. In our day of moral decline, it is easy to begin thinking that purity is some unachievable, outdated standard from the misty past of yesteryear. *Not so.* Hear again the timeless counsel of God's Word:

> For God has not called us for the purpose of impurity, but in sanctification. Consequently, he who rejects this is not rejecting man but the God who gives His Holy Spirit to you (1 Thess. 4:7-8),

and

> But examine everything carefully; hold fast to that which is good; abstain from every form of evil (1 Thess. 5:21-22).

and

> For the grace of God has appeared, bringing salvation to all men, instructing us to deny ungodliness and worldly desires and to live sensibly, righteously and godly in the present age, looking for the blessed hope and the appearing of the glory of

our great God and Savior, Christ Jesus; who gave Himself for us, that HE MIGHT
REDEEM US FROM EVERY LAWLESS DEED AND PURIFY FOR HIMSELF A PEOPLE FOR HIS
OWN POSSESSION, zealous for good deeds (Titus 2:11–14),

and finally,

> Beloved, I urge you as aliens and strangers to abstain from fleshly lusts, which
> wage war against the soul.
> Keep your behavior excellent among the Gentiles, so that in the thing in which
> they slander you as evildoers, they may on account of your good deeds, as they
> observe them, glorify God . . . (1 Pet. 2:11–12).

There is no question about it, God wants us, His people, to strengthen our
grip on purity. His Spirit stands ready to assist us.

Being Accountable to the Body

Before leaving this vital subject, it's necessary that we think about *another*
body that is affected by moral impurity—the larger Body of believers called in
the scriptures "the church." When a Christian willfully and deliberately
chooses to walk in impurity, he or she is not the only one who suffers the
consequences. That decision brings reproach to the whole Body to which he or
she belongs. Since we are members of one another, we are accountable to one
another. Even when one of us may not *want* that accountability, it is still an
undeniable fact.

New Testament passages like 1 Corinthians 12:14–27 (please stop and read
for yourself) paint a vivid picture of mutual concern, mutual interest, and
mutual accountability. We are not isolated islands separate and without identity. Nor are we to respond with casual indifference when one of our brothers or
sisters slides into immorality. Just listen:

> Dear brothers, if a Christian is overcome by some sin, you who are godly should
> gently and humbly help him back onto the right path, remembering that next time
> it might be one of you who is in the wrong. Share each other's troubles and
> problems, and so obey our Lord's command (Gal. 6:1–2, TLB).

> Dear brothers, if anyone has slipped away from God and no longer trusts the
> Lord, and someone helps him understand the Truth again, that person who brings
> him back to God will have saved a wandering soul from death, bringing about the
> forgiveness of his many sins (James 5:19–20, TLB).

The Savior Himself saw the need for this when He instructed His followers to
pursue those who stray.

"And if your brother sins, go and reprove him in private; if he listens to you, you have won your brother.

"But if he does not listen to you, take one or two more with you, so that BY THE MOUTH OF TWO OR THREE WITNESSES EVERY FACT MAY BE CONFIRMED.

"And if he refuses to listen to them, tell it to the church; and if he refuses to listen even to the church, let him be to you as a Gentile and a tax-gatherer" (Matt. 18:15–17).

Very clear. Nothing that complicated. But how many congregations can you name who follow that plan to rescue those who have strayed? Or, for that matter, how many fellow Christians do you know who conscientiously follow Jesus' directions and confront the wayward? Now, I'm not suggesting a harsh, uncompassionate assault on all who temporarily lapse into sin and soon thereafter acknowledge and repent of the wrong. No, this involves much more than that. This is an open-and-shut case of sinful activity that is taking its toll on the person as well as others in the Body.

Who really cares anymore? Where is the Christian friend who is willing to risk being misunderstood to help another believer come to repentance and full restoration?

I'm not the only one concerned about this problem of indifference. On numerous occasions in my ministry I have received phone calls and letters from others who are deeply troubled over the lack of accountability within the Body. Here are a few excerpts from one such letter:

Dear Chuck:

During the past several years the Lord has been putting me into a number of situations involving accountability between Christians. I have and continue to struggle. And I want to share what I am learning.

Two couples in my Sunday school class began living with other partners before their eventual divorces. We didn't know how to respond, especially to the one woman who brought her boyfriend to class. So we ignored them. Just great, huh?

Some time later two . . . classmates started living with fellows. And that stirred up lots of things for me. There were a lot of Corinthian attitudes among my peers which I decided to assess methodically. About the same time a friend . . . dropped by on a business trip and discussed a current case with a rather well-known pastor in his locale who was sleeping around. At (a certain Christian school) coeds came for help with sexual involvements with married employees.

Talk about a thickening plot! In response I have been grappling with biblical and psychological concepts of relationship, confrontation, accountability, etc. Here are some of my observations to date:

. . . in a total of nineteen years . . . I have neither experienced nor heard of any community-level confrontation. It is as though the progressive confrontation of Matthew 18:15 and Paul's injunctions to Timothy on church leaders in 1 Timothy 5:19ff were not in Scripture. . . . I cannot help but conclude that the trend among Christians to divorce, to sin sexually, etc., will increase unless Scripture is taken seriously in the church in this area of confrontation. . . .

I believe that if our relationships in the church are not sufficiently developed such that others can see and respond to trouble brewing in our marriages, then we are in big trouble. Who will help us . . .

Although the letter was addressed to me, think of it as addressed to you. Will *you* help? You see, purity is not only a personal matter; it is a group project. And when we strive for it, it isn't for the purpose of man's glory, but God's. It is *His* name that is at stake, in the final analysis.

Before anyone jumps to the conclusion that accountability is nothing more than a legalistic and systematic way to make an individual squirm, let me repeat that the ultimate objective is to *restore* fellow believers. It is to help them get back on their feet, free of the anchors of guilt and shame that once crippled their walk.

Quite frankly, I can think of few more powerful proofs that Christianity is the champion of purity than the compassionate efforts of one family member helping another brother or sister get out of the ditch. Even if it takes an initial jolt of upfront confrontation . . . or the full process of church discipline. Handled correctly, in a spirit of gentle, loving humility, it can result in the most beautiful, authentic display of repentance and grace one can imagine.

I greatly admire a particular congregation of believers who decided not to ignore the impure lifestyle of one of its members. The man, a Christian, was engaged in a series of illicit sexual relationships that began to bring shame to the name of Christ, not to mention the negative impact it was having on the local church to which he belonged. The leaders followed Christ's guidelines in Matthew 18 as they attempted to rescue the man out of his sensual syndrome . . . all to no avail. He refused their counsel. Finally, the inevitable. With grieving hearts and in obvious humility, they bit the bullet as they brought the case before the church and placed the man under discipline, refusing to fellowship with him until he repented. It was incredibly heart-wrenching, an agonizing episode in the lives of those in leadership. They loved the man too much to let him continue in immorality. The fact that they were acting in obedience to God and the hope that it would someday result in the man's repentance and restoration were the *only* reasons they could carry out such a difficult assignment. They were determined to preserve the purity of the church, no matter the sacrifice or cost.

Years passed before the awful silence was broken. God ultimately honored their obedience. He used their words and actions to bring that man to his knees, broken and repentant before the Lord of absolute holiness. As a result, he wrote an open letter of confession to the church, affirming their efforts, acknowledging his wrong, and declaring his need for forgiveness. With a few deletions, this is what he wrote:

My fellow Christians,

Several years ago the congregation . . . took public action against me in accordance with Matthew 18:15–20. The charges against me were true.

I cannot reverse history and relive the events that led up to my downfall. I have harmed many people and brought ruin to myself. Because I was an outspoken, prominent member of the Christian community, my sins have been all the more deplorable and horrendous.

After I became a Christian some eighteen years ago I failed to deal thoroughly with lust, covetousness and immorality. In time I became self-deceived, proud and arrogant. Moreover, eventually God shouted upon the housetops that which I had tried desperately to keep hidden. . . . Twice I went through the horror and hell of manic-depressive psychoses (as Nebuchadnezzar did) that I might learn that God resists the proud, but gives grace to the humble.

I am very fortunate to be alive. I came very close to suicide and should have died in ignominy and disgrace. . . .

I am in need of your forgiveness, for I have wronged you all. I earnestly desire your prayers for wholeness and complete deliverance. . . .

It is impossible for me to retrace my footsteps and right every wrong. However, I welcome the opportunity to meet and pray with any individuals who have something against me that needs resolution. I am looking and waiting for the further grace and mercy of God in this matter. What you have bound on earth has been bound in heaven, and I now know your actions were done in love for my own good and that of the Body of Christ.

Sincerely,

What a classic example of the truth: "Christianity is supremely the champion of purity" . . . its militant advocate, its defender. Sin was crushed beneath the blows of the sword of the Spirit.

I cannot end this chapter without asking you a few direct questions:

- Are you a Christian who has started to slip morally?
- Will you be man or woman enough to deal with it? I mean *completely*.
- Realizing that you are truly accountable to others in the Body, would you

be willing to get close to another Christian and openly admit your weakness . . . asking for his or her help in overcoming the problem?

• Perhaps you are currently holding a position of leadership in the Christian community and at the same time living an impure life. Will you be honest enough either to turn from your sin or resign your post?

• If you are close to a brother or sister in God's family who is compromising his or her testimony, would you pray about being God's instrument of reproof in confronting the person in a spirit of humility?

Since Christianity and purity belong together, some of us need to champion the cause. Let's get on the same team, I plead with you. Strengthening our grip on purity is a whole lot easier if we do it together.

DISCUSSION QUESTIONS AND IDEAS TO HELP YOU STRENGTHEN YOUR GRIP ON PURITY

• Go back through chapter 4 and read again each scriptural reference, preferably *aloud*. Following each reading, close your eyes and sit quietly for sixty to ninety seconds and let the truth speak for itself.

• In your own words, define *purity*. Try hard not to rely on clichés or traditional terms that aren't specific.

• What happens to a life when it becomes scarred by a lengthy period of sin? Can purity be recovered once a Christian has backslidden? Can you think of any scripture that supports your answer?

• Look deeply into two passages from the New Testament: Galatians 6:1-2 and James 5:19-20. Think and talk about their implications on a church fellowship. In light of 1 Corinthians 6:9-13 (please stop and read), discuss when and how this counsel should be applied.

• It is easy for our sincere interest in each other's walk in purity to degenerate into a judgmental legalism. How can there be cultivated a healthy and necessary sense of accountability without this happening?

• Openly admit your struggle with moral impurity. Ask for prayer in one or two particular areas of weakness. Pray for one another.

5

Strengthening
Your Grip
on Money

Now there's a fitting title! Especially in a day when our checking accounts need month-to-month resuscitation to survive spiraling inflation and off-the-graph interest rates. Unlike those who receive incredible salaries for playing games, making movies, singing songs, and pumping oil, most of us are forced to face the fact that the only way we'll ever see daylight is to moonlight. Even then we feel like nothing more than members of the debt set. So when somebody mentions that there is a way to strengthen our grip on money, we're listening.

Don't misunderstand. I'm in no way interested in promoting greed. We get enough of that in the mercenary jungle-fighting on the job every day. And the flame of materialism is fanned anew each evening, thanks to the commercials that relentlessly pound their way into our heads. But even though we may get weary of that drumbeat, none can deny that money plays an enormous role in all our lives . . . even when we keep our perspective and steer clear of greed. As is often said, money cannot bring happiness—but it certainly puts our creditors in a better frame of mind.

I agree with the late heavyweight champ, Joe Louis: "I don't like money actually, but it quiets my nerves."

THE BIBLE TALKS ABOUT MONEY

To the surprise of many people, the Bible says a great deal about money. It talks about earning and spending, saving and giving, investing and even wasting

206

our money. But in none of this does it ever come near to suggesting that money brings ultimate security. I love the proverb that paints this so vividly:

> Do not wear yourself out to get rich;
>   have the wisdom to show restraint.
> Cast but a glance at riches, and they are gone,
>   for they will surely sprout wings
>   and fly off to the sky like an eagle.
>   (Prov. 23:4–5, NIV)

Can't you just picture the scene? WHOOSH . . . and the whole thing is gone for good.

This is not to say that money is evil. Or that those who have it are wicked. Let's once for all put to bed the old cliche: "God loves the poor and hates the rich." Nowhere does God condemn the rich for being rich. For sure, He hates false gain, wrong motives for getting rich, and lack of compassionate generosity among the wealthy. But some of the godliest biblical characters, even in today's terms, were exceedingly prosperous: Job, Abraham, Joseph, David, Solomon, Josiah, Barnabas, Philemon, and Lydia, to name a few.

It has been my observation that both the prosperous and those without an abundance must fight similar battles: envy of others and greed for more. The Scriptures clearly and frequently condemn both attitudes. This brings to mind a particular section of the Bible that addresses several of the attitudes that frequently accompany money.

ANCIENT COUNSEL THAT IS STILL RELIABLE

In 1 Timothy, a letter written to a young man who was a pastor, the writer (Paul) deals with the subject of money as he draws his thoughts to a close. While encouraging Timothy to carry on in spite of the odds against him, Paul exposes some of the characteristics of religious frauds in chapter 6, verses 4 and 5:

> He is conceited and understands nothing; but he has a morbid interest in controversial questions and disputes about words, out of which arise envy, strife, abusive language, evil suspicions, and constant friction between men of depraved mind and deprived of the truth, who suppose that godliness is a means of gain.

The *Good News Bible* renders the latter part of verse 5: ". . . they think that religion is a way to become rich."

Red flag! Keen-thinking Paul uses this as a launching pad into one of the most helpful discussions of money in all the Bible. Read carefully these words that follow:

But godliness actually is a means of great gain, when accompanied by content-ment.

For we have brought nothing into the world, so we cannot take anything out of it either.

And if we have food and covering, with these we shall be content.

But those who want to get rich fall into temptation and a snare and many foolish and harmful desires which plunge men into ruin and destruction.

For the love of money is a root of all sorts of evil, and some by longing for it have wandered away from the faith, and pierced themselves with many a pang. . . .

Instruct those who are rich in this present world not to be conceited or to fix their hope on the uncertainty of riches, but on God, who richly supplies us with all things to enjoy.

Instruct them to do good, to be rich in good works, to be generous and ready to share,

storing up for themselves the treasure of a good foundation for the future, so that they may take hold of that which is life indeed (vv. 6–10, 17–19).

Go back and check that out. The first series of thoughts is a *reminder* to those without much money. The second section is a *warning*. The third is simply *instruction*. Let's dig deeper.

Reminder to Those Who Are Not Rich (1 Tim. 6:6–8)

Picking up the term "godliness" from verse 5, Paul mentions it again in the next verse, linking it with contentment and offering a primary formula . . . a basic premise for happiness:

Godliness   +   Contentment   =   Great Gain

Meaning:

A consistent, authentic walk with God	+	An attitude of satisfaction and peace within (regardless of finances)	=	That which constitutes great wealth

If there were one great message I could deliver to those who struggle with not having an abundance of this world's goods, it would be this simple yet pro-found premise for happiness. For a moment, let's go at it backwards, from right to left.

That which constitutes great wealth is not related to money. It is an attitude of satisfaction ("enough is enough") coupled with inner-peace (an absence of churning) plus a day-by-day, moment-by-moment walk with God. Sounds so simple, so right, so good, doesn't it? In our world of more, more, more . . .

push, push, push . . . grab, grab, grab, this counsel is long overdue. In a word, the secret is *contentment*.

Consider Philippians 4:11–12:

> Not that I speak from want; for I have learned to be content in whatever circumstances I am.
>
> I know how to get along with humble means, and I also know how to live in prosperity; in any and every circumstance I have learned the secret of being filled and going hungry, both of having abundance and suffering need.

Contentment is something we must learn. It isn't a trait we're born with. But the question is *how*? Back in the 1 Timothy 6 passage, we find a couple of very practical answers to that question:

1. A current perspective on eternity: "For we have brought nothing into the world, so we cannot take anything out of it either" (v. 7).
2. A simple acceptance of essentials: "And if we have food and covering, with these we shall be content" (v. 8).

Both attitudes work beautifully.

First, it really helps us to quit striving for more if we read the eternal dimension into today's situation. We entered life empty-handed; we leave it the same way. I never saw a hearse pulling a U-Haul trailer!

The truth of all this was brought home forcefully to me when a minister friend of mine told of an experience he had several years ago. He was in need of a dark suit to wear at a funeral he had been asked to conduct. He had very little money, so he went to a local pawn shop in search of a good buy. To his surprise, they had just the right size, solid black, and very inexpensive. It was too good to be true. As he forked over the money, he inquired as to how they could afford to sell the suit so cheap. With a wry grin the pawnbroker admitted that all their suits had once been owned by a local mortuary, which they used on the deceased . . . then removed before burial.

He felt a little unusual wearing a suit that had once been on a dead man, but since no one else would know, why not? Everything was fine until he was in the middle of his sermon and casually started to stick his hand into the pocket of the pants . . . only to find *there were no pockets*! Talk about an unforgettable object lesson! There he stood preaching to all those people about the importance of living in light of eternity today, as he himself wore a pair of trousers without pockets that had been on a corpse.

Second, it also helps us model contentment if we'll boil life down to its essentials and try to simplify our lifestyle. Verse 8 spells out those essentials: something to eat, something to wear, and a roof over our heads. Everything beyond that we'd do well to consider as extra.

You see, society's plan of attack is to create dissatisfaction, to convince us that we must be in a constant pursuit for something "out there" that is sure to bring us happiness. When you reduce that lie to its lowest level, it is saying that contentment is impossible without striving for more. God's Word offers the exact opposite advice: Contentment is possible when we *stop* striving for more. Contentment never comes from externals. Never!

As a Greek sage once put it: "To whom little is not enough, nothing is enough."

In the *Third Part of King Henry the Sixth*, Shakespeare draws a picture of the king wandering alone in the country. He meets two men who recognize him as the king. One of them asks, "But, if thou be a king, where is thy crown?" The king gives a splendid answer:

> My crown is in my heart, not on my head;
> Not deck'd with diamonds and Indian stones,
> Nor to be seen; my crown is call'd content;
> A crown it is that seldom kings enjoy.[1]

Great story, but I'll be frank with you. My bottom-line interest is not the words of some Greek sage or the eloquent answer of a king borne in the mind of an English poet. It's *you*. It's helping you see the true values in life, the exceedingly significant importance of being contented with what you have rather than perpetually dissatisfied, always striving for more and more. I am certainly not alone in this desire to help people see through the mask of our world system:

PROMISES, PROMISES. Perhaps the most devastating and most demonic part of advertising is that it attempts to persuade us that material possessions will bring joy and fulfillment. "That happiness is to be attained through limitless material acquisition is denied by every religion and philosophy known to man, but is preached incessantly by every American television set." Advertisers promise that their products will satisfy our deepest needs and inner longings for love, acceptance, security and sexual fulfillment. The right deodorant, they promise, will bring acceptance and friendship. The newest toothpaste or shampoo will make one irresistible. A house or bank account will guarantee security and love.

Examples are everywhere. A bank in Washington, D.C., recently advertised for new savings accounts with the question: "Who's gonna love you when you're old and grey?" Our savings bank sponsors a particularly enticing ad: "Put a little love away. Everybody needs a penny for a rainy day. Put a little love away." Those words are unbiblical, heretical, demonic. They teach the big lie of our secular, materialistic society. But the words and music are so seductive that they dance through my head hundreds of times.

If no one paid any attention to these lies, they would be harmless. But that is impossible. Advertising has a powerful effect on all of us. It shapes the values of our children. Many people in our society truly believe that more possessions will

bring acceptance and happiness. In its "Life-Style" section, *Newsweek* recently
described the craze for $150 belt buckles, $695 rattlesnake belts and exceedingly
expensive jewelry. A concluding comment by New York jewelry designer Barry
Kieselstein shows how people search for meaning and friendship in things: "A
nice piece of jewelry you can relate to is like having a friend who's always there."[2]

And speaking of the power of advertising, I recall hearing some pretty good
counsel on how to overrule those television commercials that attempt to
convince us we need this product or that new appliance to be happy. The guy
suggested that every time we begin to feel that persuasive tug, we ought to
shout back at the tube at the top of our voices: "WHO ARE YOU KIDDING!"

It really works. My whole family and I tried it one afternoon during a
televised football game. Not once did I feel dissatisfied with my present lot or
sense the urge to jump up and go buy something. Our dog almost had a canine
coronary; but other than that, the results were great.

Warning to Those Who Want to Get Rich (1 Tim. 6:9–10)

As we read on, the Scriptures turn our attention from those who are not rich
to those who want to get rich. The warning is bold:

> But those who want to get rich fall into temptation and a snare and many
> foolish and harmful desires which plunge men into ruin and destruction.
> For the love of money is a root of all sorts of evil, and some by longing for it
> have wandered away from the faith, and pierced themselves with many a pang (1
> Tim. 6:9–10).

This person is different from the first one we considered. This individual is
one who cannot rest, cannot really relax until he or she has become affluent.
The word *want* in verse 9, rather than meaning "like" or "desire" (like a
passing fancy), suggests a firm resolve, a strong determination. It isn't an
exaggeration to suggest that it would even include the idea of being possessed
with the thought of getting rich . . . which helps us understand why such a
severe warning follows: Those who *want* to get rich fall into temptation (unexpected traps) and many foolish or harmful desires leading ultimately to destruction.

Interestingly, contrary to popular opinion, the pursuit of wealth—even the
acquiring of it—does not cause the bluebird of happiness to sing its way into
our lives. Rather, the grim, diseased vulture of torment and misery circles over
our carcass.

You need a 'fer instance?

Look at the faces of the super wealthy. Choose the group. The entertainers,
offstage. How about the rock stars? Or even the comedians away from the

camera? Let's name a few specifics: Elvis Presley, Howard Hughes, John Lennon. Those faces, captured in untold numbers of photographs, reflect strain and pain. And let's not forget the stress-ridden physician or executive pushing toward the top. No much peace and calm, in my opinion.

Let's look at what Solomon said:

> A faithful man will be richly blessed,
> but one eager to get rich will not go unpunished. . . .
> A stingy man is eager to get rich
> and is unaware that poverty awaits him.
>   (Prov. 28:20, 22, NIV)

Why? Why is the path of the greedy materialist so strewn with blind spots and traps that lead to ruin? Read again 1 Timothy 6:10, but don't *misread* it.

> For the love of money is a root of all sorts of evil, and some by longing for it have wandered away from the faith, and pierced themselves with many a pang (1 Tim. 6:10).

The verse does not say that money per se is the root of all evil, nor that the love of money is *the* root of all evil. This has reference to the LOVE of money (literally, "fondness of silver") being *a* (not "the") root—a basis of all kinds of evil. The verse also describes the kind of person who pursues money as being one who is "longing for it." The original Greek term means "to stretch oneself out in order to grasp something." And those on this pursuit experience two categories of perils:

• Spiritually, they wander away from the faith.
• Personally, they encounter many griefs.

It's worth remembering that most people with this kind of drive for more and more money really aren't generous; they are selfish. One writer put it all in perspective:

> Money in itself is neither good nor bad; it is simply dangerous in that the love of it may become bad. With money a man can do much good; and with money he can do much evil. With money a man can selfishly serve his own desires; and with money he can generously answer to the cry of his neighbor's need. With money a man can buy his way to the forbidden things and facilitate the path of wrongdoing; and with money he can make it easier for someone else to live as God meant him to live. Money brings power, and power is always a double-edged thing, for it is powerful to good and powerful to evil.[3]

The Bible offers two kinds of counsel: preventive and corrective . . . assistance before the fact and assistance after the fact. This verse is the former—a preventive warning. It stands like a yellow highway sign in a driving rainstorm.

DANGER, CURVE AHEAD
DRIVE SLOWLY

- Up-and-coming young executive, listen!
- Entertainer in the making, pay attention!
- Capable, youthful athlete, watch out!
- Recording artist, be careful!
- Visionary leader and entrepreneur, proceed with caution!
- Rapidly advancing salesperson, be on guard!
- Gifted minister with a lot of charisma, stop and think!

If you are not careful, you'll find yourself caught in the vortex of greed that will inevitably lead to your destruction. Materialism is a killer; at best, a crippler. Fight against it as you would a hungry pack of wolves.

Instruction to Those Who Are Rich (1 Tim. 6:17–19)

Before leaving this timely topic of money, consider one more classification deserving of our attention—those who have been blessed with prosperity. If you are in this category, you have your own unique battles. As I mentioned earlier in the chapter, you are neither suspect nor guilty in God's eyes simply because you are rich. You know if you acquired your wealth legally or illegally. If it has come from hard work, honest dealings, and wise planning, you have absolutely nothing of which to be ashamed. Only the Lord Himself knows how many ministries could not continue (humanly speaking) if it were not for people like you who are able to contribute large sums of money in support of these faith ventures. You are greatly blessed, and that carries with it great responsibility. As the object of innumerable attacks from the adversary (not to mention the envy of many people) you must be a wise servant of what God has entrusted into your care. I know of few paths filled with more dangerous traps and subtle temptations than the one you must walk every day. Hopefully, these things will help you as you attempt to live for Christ on that precarious tightrope.

To begin with, let's hear what the Scriptures say to you:

> Instruct those who are rich in this present world not to be conceited or to fix their hope on the uncertainty of riches, but on God, who richly supplies us with all things to enjoy.
> Instruct them to do good, to be rich in good works, to be generous and ready to share, storing up for themselves the treasure of a good foundation for the future, so that they may take hold of that which is life indeed (vv. 17–19).

If you look closely, you'll find three rather direct pieces of advice; the first two being negative and the third ending on a positive tone.

First, Don't Be Conceited

This is a tough assignment, but it's essential. The term *conceited* means "high-minded." Proud, snobbish arrogance has no place in the life of the wealthy Christian. Because this is mentioned first, it is perhaps wise that we look upon it as the most frequent temptation the rich must guard against. One of the best ways to do that is to remember that everything you have has come from your heavenly Father. If it weren't for Him, think of where you'd be today. It's healthy for all of us to remember the hole of the pit from which He rescued us. That will do a lot to keep conceit conquered.

Marian Anderson, the black American contralto who deserved and won worldwide acclaim as a concert soloist, didn't simply grow great; she grew great simply. In spite of her fame, she has remained the same gracious, approachable lady . . . never one to "put on airs"—a beautiful model of humility.

A reporter, while interviewing Miss Anderson, asked her to name the greatest moment in her life. The choice seemed difficult to others who were in the room that day, because she had had many big moments. For example:

• There was the night Conductor Arturo Toscanini announced, "A voice like hers comes once in a century."
• In 1955 she became the first Negro to sing with the Metropolitan Opera Company of New York.
• The following year her autobiography, *My Lord, What a Morning*, was published . . . a bestseller.
• In 1958 she became a United States delegate to the United Nations.
• On several occasions during her illustrious career, she received medals from various countries around the world.
• There was that memorable time she gave a private concert at the White House for the Roosevelts and the King and Queen of England.
• Her hometown, Philadelphia, had, on one occasion, awarded her the $10,000 Bok Award as the person who had done the most for that city.
• In 1963 she was awarded the coveted Presidential Medal of Freedom.
• There was that Easter Sunday in Washington, D.C. when she stood beneath the Lincoln statue and sang for a crowd of 75,000, which included Cabinet members, Supreme Court justices, and most members of Congress.

Which of those big moments did she choose? None of them. Miss Anderson quietly told the reporter that the greatest moment of her life was the day she went home and told her mother she wouldn't have to take in washing anymore.[4]

The princely prophet Isaiah reminds us to do this very thing when he says: ". . . Look to the rock from which you were hewn, And to the quarry from which you were dug" (Isa. 51:1).

That sounds much more noble and respectable than its literal meaning. In the Hebrew text, the word *quarry* actually refers to "a hole." The old King James

Version doesn't miss it far: "the hole of the pit whence ye are digged." Never forget "the hole of the pit."

What excellent advice! Before we get all enamored with our high-and-mighty importance, it's a good idea to take a backward glance at the "the hole of the pit" from which Christ lifted us. And let's not just *think* about it; let's admit it. Our "hole of the pit" has a way of keeping us all on the same level—recipients of grace. And don't kid yourself, even those who are extolled and admired have "holes" from which they were dug.

With Moses, it was murder.

With Elijah, it was deep depression.

With Peter, it was public denial.

With Samson, it was recurring lust.

With Thomas, it was cynical doubting.

With Jacob, it was deception.

With Rahab, it was prostitution.

With Jephthah, it was his illegitimate birth.

Marian Anderson has never forgotten that her roots reach back into poverty. No amount of public acclaim will ever cause her to forget that her mama took in washing to put food in little Marian's tummy. I have the feeling that every time she starts to get exaggerated ideas of her own importance, a quick backward glance at her humble beginnings is all it takes to conquer conceit. And the best part of all is that she doesn't hide her humble roots.

The next time we're tempted to become puffed up by our own importance, let's just look back to the pit from which we were dug. It has a way of deflating our pride.

Second, Don't Trust in Your Wealth for Security

Earlier in the chapter, we looked at the proverb that talks about riches sprouting wings and flying away. How true! Foolish indeed is the person who considers himself safe and sound because he has money. Part of the reason it is foolish is because the value of our money is decreasing at a frightening rate of speed. As the verse states, money is "uncertain."

In an article that was released at the end of 1980 dealing with the changes ahead of us for the next twenty years, the accelerating prices of new homes were mentioned. Today's average was quoted to be $77,600. By 1985, the same basic dwelling will cost $121,000 if 10 percent inflation continues. I gulped when I read that the same place by 1995 would sell for $314,000.[5]

And another reason it's foolish to trust in riches for security is that money, in the final analysis, brings no lasting satisfaction, certainly not in the area of things that really matter. There are many things that no amount of money can buy. Think of it this way:

Money can buy medicine, but not health.

Money can buy a house, but not a home.
Money can buy companionship, but not friends.
Money can buy entertainment, but not happiness.
Money can buy food, but not an appetite.
Money can buy a bed, but not sleep.
Money can buy a crucifix, but not a Savior.
Money can buy the good life, but not eternal life.

That explains why we are told in this section of the Scriptures that it is God (alone) who is able to supply us "with all things to enjoy." As Seneca, the Roman statesman once said: "Money has never yet made anyone rich."

Third, Become a Generous Person

Look at 1 Timothy 6:18–19 one more time:

Command them to do good, to be rich in good deeds, and to be generous and willing to share. In this way they will lay up treasures for themselves as a firm foundation for the coming age, so that they may take hold of the life that is truly life (NIV).

It is so clear it hardly needs an explanation. Woven through the fabric of these words is the same term: give, give, give, give, give.

You have money? Release it, don't hoard it. Be a great-hearted person of wealth. Let generosity become your trademark. Be generous with your time, your efforts, your energy, your encouragement, and, yes, your money.

Do you know what will happen? Along with being enriched, knowing that you are investing in eternity, you will "take hold of the life that is truly life." You will go beyond "the good life" and enter into "the *true* life." There is a vast difference between the two.

REVIEW AND REMINDER

We haven't exhausted the subject of money, but we have addressed several critical issues. To those who struggle to make ends meet, guard against being envious of the wealthy and work on being contented with life as it is.

To those who would have to admit that the pursuit of money is now a passionate drive, hear the warning again: If you don't come to terms with yourself, it's only a matter of time before you'll find yourself ensnared and miserable. In the process, you'll lose the very things you think money will buy—peace, happiness, love, and satisfaction.

And to those who are rich? Put away conceit, forget about finding ultimate security in your money, and cultivate generosity . . . tap into "the true life."

During His life on earth, Jesus frequently talked about those things that kept people from a meaningful relationship with God. One of the barriers, according to His teaching, is money. It need not be, but it often is.

• He taught that "the deceitfulness of riches" has a way of choking the truth of Scripture, making it unfruitful in a life (Mark 4:19).

• He also taught that we need to "be on guard against every form of greed," since life really doesn't consist of the things we possess (Luke 12:15).

• He even went so far as to say "for where your treasure is, there will your heart be also" (Luke 12:34).

• But the punch line in all His teaching on this subject says it all: "You cannot serve both God and Money" (Matt. 6:24, NIV).

Straight talk, but that's what it takes to strengthen our grip on money. Tell me, are you gripping it or is it gripping you?

DISCUSSION QUESTIONS AND IDEAS
TO HELP YOU STRENGTHEN YOUR GRIP ON MONEY

• What one idea stands out in your mind as the single most helpful thought in this chapter? See if you can state it in your own sentence.

• Turning back to the 1 Timothy 6 passage, review the three categories of people. Any trouble spots?

• Heavy artillery from our world pounds away on our eyes and ears. The media pulsates with a constant message. What is it? Be specific. The next few times you watch television, pay close attention to the commercials. Behind the beautiful camera shots and clever script is a powerful pitch. Discuss it out loud as it happens. Talk about what that pitch does to you as you enter into the commercial.

• Be extremely honest with your answers. Are you caught up in the syndrome of living beyond your means? Are you taking steps to change those habits? Name a few. Are you any further along toward financial stability than you were, say, one year ago? Two years ago? Define your number one weakness in handling your money.

• Finally, is your giving what it ought to be? Is it proportionate to the size of your income, for example? Would you be viewed by others (if they knew your giving habits) as a generous, cheerful giver? Talk briefly about generosity. Pray specifically that the Lord Jesus Christ might be the Master of your money . . . the Master of how you earn it, where you spend it, when and to what you give it, why you save and invest it. End these moments in prayer by making Christ the Lord of your treasure.

6

Strengthening
Your Grip
on Integrity

Dr. Evan O'Neill Kane, the sixty-two-year-old chief surgeon of Kane Summit Hospital in New York City, was convinced that most major operations could be performed while patients were under local anesthesia and thereby avoid the risks of general anesthesia. To prove his point, on February 15, 1921, Dr. Kane *operated on himself* and removed his appendix while under local anesthesia. The operation was a success, and his recovery progressed faster than that usually expected of patients who were given general anesthesia. . . . Another medical breakthrough!

I would like you to operate on yourelf as you read this chapter. Not physically, of course, but spiritually. Let's call it "self-exploratory surgery of the soul." While you are fully conscious, fully aware, I invite you to allow the Spirit of God to assist you, handing you the only instrument you need to do soul surgery—the germ-free scalpel of Scripture. Hebrews 4:12 tells us that God's Word is . . .

> . . . living and active and sharper than any two-edged sword, and piercing as far as the division of soul and spirit, of both joints and marrow, and able to judge the thoughts and intentions of the heart.

With this reliable instrument in your hand, take a hard, honest look deeper into your inner man and see if you can determine and evaluate the condition of your integrity. For some, it will be your first-ever glance; for others, not the first, but one long overdue. Whatever, I can assure you that it is a necessary (though rare) procedure.

Two Tests, Each Revealing and Effective

As is true in the physical realm, so it is in the spiritual that certain preliminary tests must precede surgery. To determine the inner condition of our souls, we must analyze our response to these tests.

The Test of Adversity

When we encounter trouble, calamity, loss, all kinds of adversity, we quickly learn the depth of our stability. Solomon of old tells us this. "If you falter in times of trouble, how small is your strength!" (Prov. 24:10, NIV).

There is nothing like adversity to show us how strong (or weak) we really are. People in Balvano, Italy, who endured that massive earthquake in November of 1980 had a test of strength far more revealing than those of us in Los Angeles who get nervous with a tremor every now and then. And how about those overnight guests at the MGM Hotel in Las Vegas when it became a towering inferno? Or the law-abiding citizens of Afghanistan who watched as their country was swallowed up by Soviet rule? Or Mary Enterline, the mother of a two-year-old son in Middletown, Pennsylvania, who lives within blocks of a nuclear reactor? Talk about a test of strength! Mrs. Enterline admits:

> I am scared to death . . . every night when I pull his shade down at bedtime and look out the window and see the cooling towers, I nearly cry. I am in a panic. I have never considered myself a violent person, but I am beginning to think I am going crazy—I do believe I am.[1]

What's happening? The test of adversity is at work . . . the ultimate limits of our stability. Add double-digit inflation, cancer scares, unemployment, smog, wayward kids, and racial flare-ups, and lots of things come to the surface. I agree with the wag who shrugged: "Anybody who isn't schizophrenic these days just isn't thinking clearly."

Take time to look inside. How are you holding up? Did you think you were stronger than you actually are? Has adversity surprised you with unexpected test results? It has a way of doing that!

But there is a second pre-op test that is equally revealing, perhaps even tougher, yet much more subtle.

The Test of Prosperity

Adversity is a test of our stability—our ability to endure, to survive. But prosperity is a test of our *integrity*. Like nothing else, it reveals the honest-to-goodness truth regarding our most basic value system. Difficult though it may be to grasp this fact, integrity is hammered out on the anvil of prosperity . . . *or* it fails the test completely. Again, let's look at what Solomon says: "The crucible for silver and the furnace for gold, but man is tested by the praise he receives" (Prov. 27:21, NIV).

The path of prosperity is strewn with the litter of its victims. But on a more positive note, those who have integrity possess one of the most respected virtues in all of life. Furthermore, they stand out in any office or school or community. If you can be trusted, whether alone or in a crowd . . . if you are truly a person of your word and convictions, you are fast becoming an extinct species. And the test of prosperity will help reveal the truth.

DANIEL: A BIBLICAL EXAMPLE

Because the Bible contains such a wealth of information on this subject and because all of us have an easier time getting a hold on abstract truth when it is fleshed out in a person's life, I'd like us to strengthen our grip on integrity by seeing it in the life of a man in the Old Testament. He is one of those people we usually associate with just one event (the lions' den) instead of knowing the bottom-line message of his life. For Daniel, it was integrity. He overflowed with it. It was his middle name. In fact, it was the reason he was thrown into the lion's den in the first place.

But enough preliminaries. Let's get into the story.[2] I'll begin by going back to the familiar account of the events leading up to the lions' den and then move into the man's character. Because the background is significant, please take the time to read each line of Scripture.

It seemed good to Darius to appoint 120 satraps over the kingdom, that they should be in charge of the whole kingdom, and over them three commissioners (of whom Daniel was one), that these satraps might be accountable to them, and that the king might not suffer loss.

Then this Daniel began distinguishing himself among the commissioners and satraps because he possessed an extraordinary spirit, and the king planned to appoint him over the entire kingdom.

Then the commissioners and satraps began trying to find a ground of accusation against Daniel in regard to government affairs; but they could find no ground of accusation or evidence of corruption, inasmuch as he was faithful, and no negligence or corruption was to be found in him.

Then these men said, "We shall not find any ground of accusation against this Daniel unless we find it against him with regard to the law of his God."

Then these commissioners and satraps came by agreement to the king and spoke to him as follows: "King Darius, live forever!

"All the commissioners of the kingdom, the prefects and the satraps, the high officials and the governors have consulted together that the king should establish a statute and enforce an injunction that anyone who makes a petition to any god or man besides, you, O king, for thirty days, shall be cast into the lions' den.

"Now, O king, establish the injunction and sign the document so that it may not be changed, according to the law of the Medes and Persians, which may not be revoked."

Therefore King Darius signed the document, that is, the injunction.

Now when Daniel knew that the document was signed, he entered his house (now in his roof chamber he had windows open toward Jerusalem); and he continued kneeling on his knees three times a day, praying and giving thanks before his God, as he had been doing previously.

Then these men came by agreement and found Daniel making petition and supplication before his God.

Then they approached and spoke before the king about the king's injunction, "Did you not sign an injunction that any man who makes a petition to any god or man besides you, O king, for thirty days, is to be cast into the lions' den?" The king answered and said, "The statement is true, according to the law of the Medes and Persians, which may not be revoked."

Then they answered and spoke before the king, "Daniel who is one of the exiles from Judah, pays no attention to you, O king, or to the injunction which you signed, but keeps making his petition three times a day."

Then, as soon as the king heard this statement, he was deeply distressed and set his mind on delivering Daniel; and even until sunset he kept exerting himself to rescue him.

Then these men came by agreement to the king and said to the king, "Recognize, O king, that it is a law of Medes and Persians that no injunction or statute which the king establishes may be changed."

Then the king gave orders, and Daniel was brought in and cast into the lions' den. the king spoke and said to Daniel, "Your God whom you constantly serve will Himself deliver you" (Dan. 6:1–16).

The book of Daniel has twelve good-size chapters filled with events, stories, and vast prophetic scenes. But, to the public, the most familiar topic in all the book is "Daniel and the Lions' Den."

Doing Right, Suffering Wrong

I remember, as a little boy in Sunday school (when they kept me quiet enough to listen), hearing the story of "Daniel and the Lions' Den." Two things always bothered me. First, who threw old Daniel in a dangerous place like that, and second, what had he done that was so bad that they put him in a dungeon where the king of the jungle lived? One of the reasons I was curious about all that was because I did not want to wind up there myself!

As I got older and began to study the story for myself, I was surprised. I found out that Daniel was not in the lions' den because he had done something *wrong*, but because he had done something *right*. That confused me all the more! As a matter of fact, it still confuses many Christians today. We are under the impression that when we do what is wrong, we will be punished for it; but, when we do what is *right*, we will be rewarded for it soon afterwards. Now that makes good, logical, common sense . . . but, it *isn't always true*. Sometimes, when you do things wrong, you are rewarded for it (as far as this world is concerned); and occasionally, when you do what is *right*, you pay a terrible price for it. Invariably, that throws us a curve.

I had a man come to me following a morning worship service in our church in Fullerton, California, and share with me how he had done what was right on his job. He had diligently done his work. As a man of strong conviction, he stood by his guns, believing what he was doing was right. He had been both careful and consistent to do all this with wisdom. But, the very next Monday morning, he faced the threat of losing his job because of doing what was right. As a matter of fact, the following day he *did* lose his job.

That was his "lions' den," so to speak. Daniel was certainly not the last man to suffer for doing what was right.

Promotion and Prosperity

Let's turn to Daniel 6 . . . the lions'-den chapter. But our interest will be on what happened *before* Daniel was dumped into the dungeon.

This chapter revolves around the decision of an exceedingly powerful man named Darius, the sixty-two-year-old king, the man to whom Daniel answered. Notice the first verse of Daniel 6: "It seemed good to Darius to appoint 120 satraps. . . ."

We don't know what *satraps* means, because we do not use the term today. Some translations have rendered it "overseers." These were 120 men who shared Darius' delegation of authority over his kingdom. They were governmental officials serving under the king who were in charge of large sections of the kingdom. Darius set up 120 "overseers" to whom he delegated some of the authority of his responsibility. However, as soon as authority is delegated, a king runs the risk of corruption, and that's exactly what Darius feared, so he placed over those "satraps" an upper echelon. They were called "commissioners." Look at the verses with me.

> It seemed good to Darius to appoint 120 satraps over the kingdom, that they should be in charge of the whole kingdom, and over them three commissioners (of whom Daniel was one), that these satraps might be accountable to them, and that the king might not suffer loss (Dan. 6:1–2).

The commissioners were responsible for the activity of the overseers. Daniel was one of the three commissioners (v. 2). This accountability arrangement was set up so the king would not suffer loss. The second verse clearly states that fact. It was to guard against financial rip-offs, quite frankly. Those 120 overseers or governors could otherwise make off with a lot of illegal revenue and get away with all sorts of illegal acts if they were not kept accountable.

And so these three men, who were apparently the most trusted in the kingdom, were given authority over the whole kingdom. What a responsible position Daniel held! He was, by this time, in his eighties. Even though in his eighties, Daniel wasn't shelved. He wasn't a useless, retired, dust-collecting, rocking-chair type. He was involved. (Was he ever!) He not only had seniority, he had superiority over many others. Look at verse 3.

> Then this Daniel began distinguishing himself among the commissioners and satraps because he possessed an extraordinary spirit, and the king planned to appoint him over the entire kingdom (Dan. 6:3).

INTEGRITY ON DISPLAY

Now, I want you to study verse 3 very carefully. In our world, it's not what you know, it's who you know that usually brings about a promotion. But in God's world, it's what you *are*, not who you know. It's what you are in your character. God saw fit, because of the integrity in Daniel's life, to move in the heart of King Darius to plan a promotion. Notice his extraordinary spirit. The Berkeley Version of the Bible calls it a "surpassing spirit."

Our tendency is to think in terms of the spiritual life—that he was a spirit-filled man. That's true, but I don't take it to mean just that here in verse 3. I take it to refer to his attitude.

An Excellent Attitude

The first sign of integrity in the life of Daniel was his excellent attitude. Now, if we want to be a person of integrity, we must begin down deep within. We must begin with our attitude. It's so easy to mask our lives and look as though our attitude is good when in reality it isn't. One of the first places it shows up is in the realm of our employment.

It's significant that there was no jealousy in Daniel's heart against those other two men who were appointed as commissioners. He could have been threatened, he could have been competitive, he could have been rather nasty and ugly in his responsibilities, because he had the longest time in the kingdom. Long before those men had even come upon the scene, he had been in authority under previous monarchs. But, because he possessed that "extraordinary spirit," the king planned to appoint him over the entire kingdom.

Let me pause right here and ask you about your attitude. How is it? Perhaps it's good right now, but what about tomorrow morning when you punch in on the time clock? Or what about by the end of the day tomorrow evening? How will your eight to ten hours have been? As you work shoulder to shoulder with people in your shop, in your office, or among the sales force where you are employed, or in the secretarial pool, what kind of attitude will you have? An excellent attitude means much! It is so important that I have written an entire chapter on attitudes later in this book.

You might wonder, "Will my boss notice if I have a good attitude?" Don't worry about that. He'll stumble all over it! He'll be amazed by it. In fact he'll be terribly impressed. Maybe I should warn you ahead of time—your problem won't be with your employer. Your main troubles will come from your fellow workers, who are often lazy and dishonest and bothered that you're not like them. And because you won't be like they are, you will discover they will become envious and jealous and so petty that you might even begin to endure what Daniel experienced.

Read on and you'll see that's exactly what happened. Look at the plot that took place against our eighty-year-old friend. First, there were attempted accusations:

> Then the commissioners [that is, the other two—Daniel's peers] and satraps began trying to find a ground of accusation against Daniel in regard to government affairs. . . (Dan. 6:4).

Now, isn't that significant? Here's a man who was doing a splendid job, who had an excellent attitude, and who was working diligently for his superior and among his peers. And yet those who were working around him and under him set up a spying program against him. They began to search for some things they could use as accusations against him. It says they searched in the realm of "government affairs." And what did they find? Well, verse 4 continues: ". . . they could find no ground of accusation or evidence of corruption. . . ."

Wow! How would you like *your* work to come under that kind of close scrutiny? I mean, out there where you make a living—not the way you are on Sunday, but the way you are where you earn your living. How would you make out if for some reason a group of secret investigators began to examine your work? What would they find? Would it make you nervous? Would you have to destroy some evidence? Or hide some of the skeletons you have tucked away in the closet? Daniel was investigated to see if they could find anything amiss with regard to his work—the governmental affairs—his occupational realm. And the remarkable thing is that they could not find one ground of accusation. They could not find one shred of damaging evidence . . . no corruption! That's not only remarkable, today it seems impossible.

Some of us are going through a time of real re-thinking about our total trust in government. We who love this country and love it dearly (and would fight to the last day to preserve it) are becoming increasingly more concerned about integrity at the higher levels of our government. I think it speaks with imme-diate relevance when it says that Daniel was not found guilty of any accusation or corruption.

Faithful in His Work

Here is the second mark of integrity: Daniel was faithful on the job. Now, be careful here. We often use the word "faithful" only as it relates to the spiritual life, the religious life. But it's not talking about faithfulness at church or in the temple, as if referring to worship. They are investigating his occupation. They are looking for something they could criticize in his faithfulness at work. This passage says that when Daniel was investigated, he was found to be faithful in his work. There was an absence of negligence. The Berkeley Version of the Bible says he was faithful "in the discharge of his official duties" (Dan. 6:40). The New International Version says he was ". . . neither corrupt nor negligent."

Look at Proverbs 20:6-7. Verse 6 reads: "Many a man proclaims his own loyalty, but who can find a trustworthy man?"

Superb question! Trustworthy people are rare, I remind you. Only on very few occasions will you find an individual who is completely trustworthy. I had a man tell me recently that in his business it isn't the public that gives him trouble; it's his employees. It isn't just the public that steals his goods, it's more often those who work for him. It has come to the place where many an employer will no longer hire a Christian! As a matter of fact, when we were living in Texas, we were close friends with the president of a bank, and the highest risk for bank loans were preachers! Isn't that significant? Those who gave him the most grief were those who were engaged continually in the ministry of God's Word.

It's time again to appraise our personal lives. Are we trustworthy? Can others count on us to get the job done when the boss isn't around? Are we faithful employees? Can we be trusted with money? An expense account? The privilege of a company car?

Verse 7 goes on to say: "A righteous man who walks in his integrity—How blessed are his sons after him."

A righteous man walks where? He walks in his *integrity*. Now, that's what Daniel 6 is talking about. Daniel was faithful in his work. There was no negligence, no corruption found in him. What a man! Faithful in his work.

Personal Purity

I find in the last part of verse 4 yet another mark of integrity: personal purity. A life of purity that can stand up under the most intense scrutiny. Today, we would say that they "tailed" him. They followed him, spied on him, searched through his personal effects, and they discovered after the examination that there was nothing lacking. No hanky-panky. No hidden dirt. Zero! He was a man of personal purity. They could dig all they wished and Daniel came out smelling like a rose.

Wouldn't you love to hire a person like that? Wouldn't that be great? I am continually hearing from employers that their number one problem is personnel; that is, finding trustworthy personnel. I mean through and through.

Some time ago, I heard about a fellow in Long Beach who went into a fried chicken franchise to get some chicken for himself and the young lady with him. She waited in the car while he went in to pick up the chicken. Inadvertently, the manager of the store handed the guy the box in which he had placed the financial proceeds of the day instead of the box of chicken. You see, he was going to make a deposit and had camouflaged it by putting the money in a fried chicken box.

The fellow took his box, went back to the car, and the two of them drove away. When they got to the park and opened the box, they discovered they had a box full of money. Now that's a very vulnerable moment for the average individual. He realized there must have been a mistake, so he got back in his car and returned to the place and gave the money back to the manager. Well, the manager was elated! He was so pleased that he told the young man, "Stick around, I want to call the newspaper and have them take your picture. You're the most honest guy in town."

"Oh, no, don't do that!" said the fellow.

"Why not?" asked the manager.

"Well," he said, "you see, I'm married, and the woman I'm with is not my wife!"

Now, I think that is a perfect illustration of how on the surface we may look like people of honesty and great integrity—people so thoroughly honest they'd give the dime back at the phone booth. . . but underneath, it isn't unusual to find a lot of corruption there. Look far enough, search deep enough, and we can usually find some dirt.

Not in Daniel! They found him to be incredible—a man with an excellent attitude, faithfully doing his job at work, an honest man who was personally pure. No hypocrisy. Nothing to hide.

Now, that so frustrated those who were investigating him that, as verse 5 tells us, they set up a devastating plan. After their earlier plot began to run its course and they couldn't find an accusation, they then determined to do something worse. They would have an injunction written against him. Maybe Daniel wasn't corrupt, but it was obvious those men were.

> Then these men said, "We shall not find any ground of accusation against this Daniel unless we find it against him with regard to the law of his God" (Dan. 6:5).

One thing they had discovered about Daniel when they investigated him was that he was a man of God. They said, "Look, this man is so consistent in his walk that the only place we're going to trip him up is to use his faith in God against him." Go on to the next verse: "Then these commissioners and satraps came by agreement to the king. . ." (Dan. 6:6).

Interesting, "by agreement." It was all a conspiracy. It was a well-planned program to sell Daniel down the river. Then they appealed to the vanity of the king. "'King Darius, live forever! All the commissioners of the kingdom . . . have consulted together. . . .'"

Wait a minute! That's a lie! All the commissioners had not participated in that decision. Daniel didn't know anything about it, but they acted as though Daniel was part of this plan. Here's the way it reads:

> All the commissioners of the kingdom, the prefects and the satraps, the high officials and the governors have consulted together that the king should establish a statute and enforce an injunction that anyone who makes a petition to any god or man besides you, O king, for thirty days, shall be cast into the lions' den (Dan. 6:7).

Now *that* is the reason for the lions' den. By the way, they didn't want to throw Daniel in a fiery furnace because they were Zoroastrians by faith. That religion believed fire to be sacred, and to have cremated him would have been to make a god out of him. So many who dedicated themselves to fire did it as a worship to the gods. They didn't want to put him into a fire, because that would be worshiping their god through a sacrifice. So they said, "Let's put into a den of lions anyone who doesn't worship Darius for thirty days." How interesting.

Many years ago, there was a program on television entitled, "Queen for a Day." You may remember that the lady who won got top treatment for that entire day. Well, in this case, they were suggesting that Darius be made "God of the Month"! That's exactly what they said, "For these thirty days, if anybody worships anyone else but you, O king, they will be thrown into the lions' den." How flatteringly cruel! How deceitful!

> "Now, O king, establish the injunction and sign the document so that it may not be changed, according to the law of the Medes and Persians. . ." (Dan. 6:8).

Some people use that same phrase today: "the law of the Medes and Persians"—it will never be changed. But let's look again at verses 8 and 9:

> ". . . which may not be revoked." Therefore King Darius signed the document, that is, the injunction.

Darius thought it was a great idea. Naturally, he would. Now what happens? Don't forget that our man Daniel isn't deserving of *any* of this. This sneaky conspiracy against him was because he had done what was right, remember? Verse 10: "Now when Daniel knew that the document was signed. . . ."

That's significant. He knew nothing of it until the document was signed. Dirty deal! Not only had they tried raking through his life to find some slip-up in his service record, but they concocted a law that Daniel's honest and pure lifestyle would automatically violate. And they did it behind his back. Some reward for having nothing to hide!

Consistent Walk with God

But then we learn what Daniel did when he heard that the document was signed.

> Now when Daniel knew that the document was signed, he entered his house (now in his roof chamber he had windows open toward Jerusalem); and he continued kneeling on his knees three times a day, praying and giving thanks before his God, as he had been doing previously (Dan. 6:10).

I submit to you, that's an incredible response to one's own death warrant. I find here his fourth mark of integrity—his consistent walk with God.

I think the last part of that verse is the most remarkable. He came before his God ". . . as he had been doing previously."

Daniel did not turn to prayer in panic. He had been consistently on his knees three times a day before his God, day in, day out, year after year. By the way, remember, he was one of the top officials in the land, yet he had time with God regularly. The psalmist writes: "Evening, and morning, and at noon, will I pray, and cry aloud: and he shall hear my voice" (Ps. 55:17, KJV).

Isn't that a great verse? Evening, morning, noon, I will pray. Daniel was no stranger to prayer. But still he didn't flaunt the fact that he was a man of prayer. Notice his windows were *already* open. He didn't suddenly bang them open so that everyone would know he was praying and be impressed with his piety.

There was an advertisement some time ago from one of the airlines. It said, "When you've got it, flaunt it." That may work for an airline, but it doesn't work for an authentic man or woman of God. When you've got it, you *don't* flaunt it. Why? Because when you flaunt it, you really don't have it.

Daniel just quietly walked to a room in his home and poured out his fear, his concern, his future, his life. Daniel is phenomenal. Just very nearly unreal. We Christians have a low threshold of pain, don't we? When things run along pretty well, we can stay fairly consistent; but a little ripple comes in the water, and we plunge! We pray at those times, but they are usually panic prayers, "Help-me-out-of-this-mess" prayers. Not Daniel! The remarkable thing about him is that he simply went back to God as before. I think if he had had the opportunity to take regular electrocardiograms, the one on this day would read just the same as always, as has been the case with our modern astronauts just before blast off. Scientists and medical specialists doing this test on them found that the results were just like the morning before when they were having breakfast. "What else is new? Going around the earth, ho hum." And off they went.

And Daniel? When he heard the news of the document, he just went right back to God and told God about it. He had a place to meet. By the way, will you observe that he got on his knees. I want to suggest that kneeling is a good way to pray, because it's *uncomfortable*. Our problem is that we pray in such a comfortable position that we just sort of drift off after a few sentences. Try that. Jim Elliot, a missionary slain by the Auca Indians in the 1950s, once said:

God is still on His throne and man is still on his footstool. There's only a knee's distance in between.

How is *your* time in prayer? What does it take to get you on your knees? A tragedy? A real emergency? This man had been doing this as a habit of his life. He had a place to meet with God and he met. He consistently kept his life and his burdens at the throne. Please don't excuse yourself because you're too busy. Not a person reading this page is busier than Daniel could have been as one of the three top men in the country. You can't get busier than that. But somehow, his consistent walk with God was so important, he simply stayed before His presence. I don't think he spent hours there, but I think he spent significant periods of time, week in and week out, just communicating his needs of the day.

If the truth were known, this is not a priority in many of our lives. And I freely confess that it has not been on a number of occasions in my own life. At one of those "low tide" experiences in my life, I saw this quotation hanging on a wall:

When you're faced with a busy day, save precious time by skipping your devotions.

Signed, Satan

The public arrest came as a direct result of Daniel's godly life. "Then these men came by agreement and found Daniel making petition and supplication before his God" (Dan. 6:11).

Isn't that significant? They interrupted him in prayer. That's where they found him "doing wrong." And the final result? The lions' den.

Then the king gave orders, and Daniel was brought in and cast into the lions' den (Dan. 6:16).

How about that? A more godly influence could not be found in the entire kingdom of Persia, and yet he was the man who was thrown into the lions' den. The only man with real, unvarnished integrity was dumped into the dungeon.

INTEGRITY: PASS IN REVIEW

Thanks to the reliable Book of God's Truth, this episode out of the life of Daniel has been preserved for all to read and admire *and appropriate*. Remember those marks of integrity?

- An excellent attitude
- Faithfulness and diligence at work
- Personal purity of the highest caliber
- Consistency in his walk with God.

You have the scalpel in your hand. Self-examination is now up to you. It is not only a good idea, it's a biblical imperative, "But let a man examine himself . . . if we judged ourselves rightly, we should not be judged" (1 Cor. 11:28, 31). One final reminder: Only *you* can do the surgery on your soul, only you. No one else can know the truth. You can cover up, twist the facts in your mind, rationalize, and ignore . . . and no one will know the difference—no one except you. But if you really want to strengthen your grip on integrity, you will come to terms with the *whole* truth, regardless of the consequences.

Chuck Colson, ex-Marine captain and former confidant of the President of the United States, was once described as "tough, wily, nasty, and tenaciously loyal to Richard Nixon" by *Time* magazine. Colson's conversion and subsequent announcement of his faith in Christ jarred Washington. There was laughter from some, bewilderment from a few, and a suspicion on the part of many. But it proved to be real. The middle-aged "hatchet man" was genuinely born again, and as a result, the Spirit of God enabled him to do soul surgery on himself. Before long, he was forced to face the truth. Was he innocent of *all* the charges brought against him . . . or *many* of those charges? As he spoke to a group of people at a prayer breakfast, he concluded his talk with:

No one else seemed to have noticed my slip. There was nothing about it in the press. But the words *many of the charges* throbbed with the pulse of the jet engines flying me back to Washington. Was it a Freudian slip? Or was it God using my voice? "Many, *but not all* the charges, Chuck."

My own words had clinched it. My conversion would remain incomplete so long as I was a criminal defendant, tangled in the Watergate quagmire. I had to put the past behind me completely. If it meant going to prison, so be it!

In his book *The Cost of Discipleship* Dietrich Bonhoeffer wrote of what he called the Great Divide: "The first step which follows Christ's call cuts the disciple off from his previous existence. The call to follow at once produces a new situation. To stay in the old situation makes discipleship impossible."

It had all looked so simple once, just getting in tune with God, finding out who Christ was and believing in Him. But whether I was ready for discipleship or not, here I was and there was no turning back.[3]

The ultimate result is now history. Because Chuck Colson told the truth, he went to prison. He was finally released a free man. Free within. Clean. Able to live without guilt. True to his word. Christ gave him the courage to face the truth, the whole truth. To become a disciple with integrity.

Does it pay? Is it worth it? Ask Chuck Colson.

DISCUSSION QUESTIONS AND IDEAS
TO HELP YOU STRENGTHEN YOUR GRIP ON INTEGRITY

• In your own words, define integrity. See if you can remember the two tests that reveal our character. Why, in your opinion, is the test of our integrity more complicated than the test of our stability?

• Turn in your Bible to Psalm 75:4–7. Compare those verses with Proverbs 27:21. Any significant observations?

• We thought a lot about Daniel's integrity. Of the four marks that characterized his life, which one seems most important to you? Why?

• A couple or three questions need to be answered if we plan to get serious and strengthen our grip on integrity:

1. What things do I allow to occur that hinder me from becoming a person with integrity?

2. Why do I allow them to persist if I know they hinder me from becoming all God wants me to be?

3. How and when shall I face this squarely and begin the process of change?

• Pray. Pray specifically about your own integrity. Ask the Lord to show you ways to implement your desires. Become accountable to at least one other person. Make plans to meet again, soon.

7

Strengthening
Your Grip
on Discipleship

A buzz word in Christian circles during the 1970s was discipleship. Everybody, it seemed, got on the bandwagon. I didn't keep a written record, but during that decade I doubt that I read a dozen books or magazine articles on the church or some specific area of ministry that did *not* mention discipleship.

In a way, one might think that is unfortunate, since overexposure tends to take the punch out of any subject. What else can be said about discipleship that hasn't already been said? But in another sense, it was a refreshing change from years past when much of the emphasis was on big, impersonal, mass gatherings. The shift from simply attending church meetings and evangelistic crusades to "body life" (another buzz word) and discipleship involvements was long overdue. I'll always cast my vote for anything that helps personalize one's faith, moving people out of the spectator realm and onto the playing field. Discipleship certainly does that . . . therefore, it deserves some space in a book that claims to address many of the essentials in today's Christianity. Overused or not, discipleship is indeed an essential. One thing is for sure, everybody may be talking about it, but everybody is certainly *not* doing it.

ORIGIN: WHO THOUGHT UP THE IDEA?

Was discipleship a Dawson Trotman original? Were The Navigators, an organization he founded, the ones who blazed the first trail through the ecclesiastical wilderness? No, not hardly. Well, how about Bill Bright? Since his international organization, Campus Crusade for Christ, claims to place as much emphasis (some say *more*) on follow-up as on evangelism, was it he who got the concept going? Again, the answer is no. How about Inter-Varsity? Or Campus Life? Or some missionary organization? Or what about one of the theological seminaries that trains its students to disciple those with whom they minister?

Obviously, none of these fine parachurch ministries originated the idea. God has used many organizations to fine tune the mechanics of discipleship, but He alone holds the original patent. That's important to remember. If it had been conceived in a human heart, we would have reason to question its validity. We could opt for a better way. We might even call it a fad. But since Christ Himself cut the first record, the concept deserves our full attention and calls for our involvement.

Think back to Jesus' earthly life and ministry. Unlike the "professional clergy" of His generation, He did not fall into the mold of formal religion. His ministry didn't fit the standard scene of first-century rabbis. It started so differently—He simply called a few men to follow Him. No high-powered programs to reach multitudes, no big-time campaigns, not even a strategy to start a school to teach people how to preach. No, He just got close to a handful of men and made them the focal point of his teaching, of His philosophy of life, and of His entire ministry.

And what about later? Did things change by the time He concluded His earthly life and went back to the Father? Hardly. Listen to the words that describe that last scene before His ascension:

> But the eleven disciples proceeded to Galilee, to the mountain which Jesus had designated.
> And when they saw Him, they worshiped Him; but some were doubtful.
> And Jesus came up and spoke to them, saying, "All authority has been given to Me in heaven and on earth.
> "Go therefore and make disciples of all the nations, baptizing them in the name of the Father and the Son and the Holy Spirit, teaching them to observe all that I commanded you; and lo, I am with you always, even to the end of the age" (Matt. 28:16–20).

Those are the closing words in Matthew's Gospel. The last part is familiar to many Christians. We call it "the Great Commission." Look back at those final verses. To what great goal did Christ commission us? To win converts? He doesn't say that. To hold city-wide rallies . . . to give out tracts . . . to study theology so we can defend our faith? Well, as important as those things may be, they do not appear in this commission. One thing stands out—only one: "Make disciples" . . . the heart and center of His command. Three other action words surround this main directive ("go," "baptize," "teach"), but the core assignment is clearly disciple making.

TECHNIQUE: HOW DOES IT WORK?

To understand what discipleship is all about, one needs merely to examine the technique Jesus employed with the training of His disciples. Since it originated with Him and since He modeled the method, it makes good sense to study His style and reproduce it. Space does not allow me to present this in sufficient detail, but perhaps a brief survey will help. If you wish to get serious about disciple making, I'd suggest you purchase a copy of *The Master Plan of Evangelism* and thoroughly digest it. It is a concise yet reliable volume that describes the process without a lot of double-talk. I am indebted to its author, Robert Coleman, for some of the insights I want to share with you.

Mark 3:13–14 reads:

> And he went up to the mountain and summoned those whom He Himself wanted, and they came to Him.
> And He appointed twelve, that they might be with Him, and that He might send them out to preach.

Although brief, these two verses bulge with significance. Jesus is beginning His ministry, He's laying the groundwork for His strategy. Interestingly, He starts quietly and carefully. He gets alone, thinks through His plan, and determines whom He would choose to train, and then He makes His *announcement*. This is followed by an *appointment*. The selection was definite and sure. Apparently, there were many available, but He limited the group to twelve. Afterwards there was *involvement*. The verse not only gives us the facts, it also includes the order. Those men were to be "with Him"—association was the curriculum. Nothing flashy or catchy or clever. Just time spent *with* Him. Finally, there was the *assignment* as He sent them "out to preach."

Selection *then* association. Long before they got involved in the activities of ministering to others, they spent time with the Master. They watched Him, asked Him questions, listened as He taught, caught His vision, absorbed His ideas and philosophy. That's what Mark means when he says they were "with Him." We never read in the New Testament that the twelve were instructed to write something down or to memorize a series of lines He gave them to repeat back to Him or to rehearse with each other some method they would later employ. No, none of that . . . but those men *did* spend time with Him. And finally they did succeed in turning the world upside down.

"Well," you may be thinking, "they were exceptionally bright men . . . sensitive, well-educated, and creative enough to make it work." No, quite the contrary. One authority writes:

> What is more revealing about these men is that at first they do not impress us as being key men. None of them occupied prominent places in the Synagogue, nor

did any of them belong to the Levitical priesthood. For the most part they were common laboring men, probably having no professional training beyond the rudiments of knowledge necessary for their vocation. Perhaps a few of them came from families of some considerable means, such as the sons of Zebedee, but none of them could have been considered wealthy. They had no academic degrees in the arts and philosophies of their day. Like their Master, their formal education likely consisted only of the Synagogue schools. Most of them were raised in the poor section of the country around Galilee. Apparently the only one of the twelve who came from the more refined region of Judea was Judas Iscariot. By any standard of sophisticated culture then and now they would surely be considered as a rather ragged aggregation of souls. One might wonder how Jesus could ever use them. They were impulsive, temperamental, easily offended, and had all the prejudices of their environment. In short, these men selected by the Lord to be His assistants represented an average cross section of the lot of society in their day. Not the kind of group one would expect to win the world for Christ.[1]

I'd suggest that neither you nor I would have chosen any one of those men as a partner in a business venture . . . with the possible exception of Judas Iscariot, no doubt the brightest of the bunch. Do you think that is too strong a statement? Let me remind you that this was the opinion of their contemporaries. That's what made Jesus' ministry so amazing—He pulled it off with that "ragged aggregation of souls."

On one occasion several years later Peter and John were arrested and stood trial for actions that the religious officials resented. According to the biblical account, these two disciples impressed their critics.

"And there is salvation in no one else; for there is no other name under heaven that has been given among men, by which we must be saved."
Now as they observed the confidence of Peter and John, and understood that they were uneducated and untrained men, they were marveling, and began to recognize them as having been with Jesus (Acts 4:12–13).

Even though they were without notable pedigree, lacking in higher education, and unpolished men, one thing was undeniable. They had been "with Jesus." Not shallow converts. Not spiritual babies. They were distinctly "Jesus men." They were different. The time they had spent with the Savior paid off. They were disciples . . . and they were now in the business of making disciples, just as Jesus had done with them. During those years they had spent with Him truth had been carefully transferred, deep convictions replaced superficial belief, and a growing consecration and commitment to the eternal dimension of life emerged slowly yet firmly. Ultimately, they personified Christ's teachings and they qualified as men who could carry on His work without His needing to be present. They had been made into true disciples.

COMMITMENT: WHAT DOES IT MEAN?

Maybe this isn't clear in your mind. You understand that Jesus said we are to "make disciples," but all that that means is still confusing. You are a Christian, but you may not be a disciple—and that bothers you. I mentioned earlier that the original disciples grew in their commitment and consecration and therefore they became "disciples" (in the true sense of the term) not merely casual followers. That needs to be explained, lest it sound spooky and unattainable. After all, how much commitment is enough commitment? And who tells whom, "Ah, you are *now* a disciple"?

To solve that dilemma, we need to look at another section of Scripture, this time from Luke's Gospel.

> Now great multitudes were going along with Him; and He turned and said to them, "If anyone comes to Me, and does not hate his own father and mother and wife and children and brothers and sisters, yes, and even his own life, he cannot be My disciple.
>
> "Whoever does not carry his own cross and come after Me cannot be My disciple.
>
> "For which one of you, when he wants to build a tower, does not first sit down and calculate the cost, to see if he has enough to complete it?
>
> "Otherwise, when he had laid a foundation, and is not able to finish, all who observe it begin to ridicule him, saying, 'This man began to build and was not able to finish.'
>
> "Or what king, when he sets out to meet another king in battle, will not first sit down and take counsel whether he is strong enough with ten thousand men to encounter the one coming against him with twenty thousand?
>
> "Or else, while the other is still far away, he sends a delegation and asks terms of peace.
>
> "So therefore, no one of you can be My disciple who does not give up all his own possessions" (Luke 14:25–33).

Go back to the beginning of the account and read again that opening line. It is strategic to an understanding of Jesus' reaction. Big crowd. Lots of skin-deep attraction. The "Miracle-Maker" was being followed by folks who wanted to see His show. As Dr. Luke put it, they were merely "going along with Him." No depth of commitment, just "going along." Seeing this and no doubt feeling some tension because of the apparent ho-hum attitude of the crowd, Jesus abruptly turned around and said some extremely potent words.

If you study His remarks with an eye for detail, you will observe that no less than three times He told them they could not be His disciples (vv. 26, 27, 33). Why would He say such strong things? Obviously, to thin the ranks. Keep in mind that Jesus was never interested in attracting big crowds. Numbers never turned Him on. I told you He was different! As a matter of fact, He was turned *off* by the large number of those who casually hung around, waiting for the show to start. He was interested in making disciples, not increasing last year's attendance. The best way to get the message across would be to tell the people the level of commitment He was looking for. And so, without hedging a bit, He picked three sensitive areas and announced the nonnegotiable terms of in-depth discipleship. Hold on to your hat.

Personal Relationships

"If anyone comes to Me, and does not hate his own father and mother and wife and children and brothers and sisters, yes, and even his own life, he cannot be My disciple" (Luke 14:26).

How's that for starters? Talk about a statement to thin the ranks! Now, let's be careful how we interpret Jesus' words. He would be contradicting other statements made in the Scriptures if He were telling us to treat our parents and family members hatefully. Obviously, that is not what He meant.

I believe He is talking about the very real possibility of competition in loyalty between the Lord and other close personal relationships. At such times those who are truly His disciples will choose Him rather than them. At those times we follow our Lord, it may appear that we "hate" those whom we seemingly turn away from, out of a greater loyalty to the Lord God. Here's the point: Disciples have no higher priority in their lives than Christ—not even their love for their own family members.

Jim Hutchens, a friend of mine in seminary, comes to my mind. Jim was a chaplain among the paratroopers in the Viet Nam War. His ministry was exceedingly effective as he served his Lord during those dark days of combat in Southeast Asia. When his tour of duty came to an end, he was free to leave and return to his loving wife Patty and their children back in the United States. Because he believed the Lord was not through with him among the troops, he chose *not* to return, but rather to stay in the combat zone and continue to minister to those battleweary fighting men. Chaplain Hutchens dearly loved his wife and family . . . but because he was, in every sense of the word, a disciple, he placed a higher priority on God's will than his own feelings. To use the words of Jesus, he "hated . . . wife and children."

Stop a moment and take an honest look at your priorities as they relate to *your* personal relationships. Can you say that, first and foremost, Jesus Christ is number one in your life? If so, you pass the first of three tests of discipleship. You are well on your way.

Personal Goals and Desires

"Whoever does not carry his own cross and come after Me cannot be My disciple" (v. 27).

The crowd that surrounded Jesus understood exactly what he meant. They were familiar with the scene he referred to. They had often seen criminals carrying their crosses to the place of their execution. In those days carrying one's own cross meant the same as a person in our day walking to the gas chamber or the electric chair. It meant death—sure, absolute death.

But again, to take Jesus' words literally is to confuse His point. He is not saying that *all* His true disciples take their own lives. Notice the sentence includes the fact that those same disciples ". . . come after Me," which removes the idea of literal death.

The subject is commitment, a high level of consecration on the part of those who wish to become disciples. He seems to have in mind our goals in life, our ultimate desires. Those who wish to be His disciples replace their selfish goals and desires with God's desire for them. They sacrifice their way for His way. The New Testament frequently refers to this issue:

> I urge you therefore, brethren, by the mercies of God, to present your bodies a living and holy sacrifice, acceptable to God, which is your spiritual service of worship.
> And do not be conformed to this world, but be transformed by the renewing of your mind, that you may prove what the will of God is, that which is good and acceptable and perfect (Rom. 12:1-2).

> Do nothing from selfishness or empty conceit, but with humility of mind let each of you regard one another as more important than himself; do not merely look out for your own personal interests, but also for the interests of others (Phil. 2:3-4).

Jesus himself modeled his truth the night He was arrested in the Garden of Gethsemane. Luke tells us that prior to his arrest, Jesus "withdrew from them about a stone's throw, and He knelt down and began to pray, saying, 'Father, if Thou art willing, remove this cup from Me; yet not My will, but Thine be done'" (Luke 22:41-42).

On another occasion Jesus openly admitted that He did not come to earth to do His will, but rather the will of the Father. He even said He did nothing on His own initiative (John 8:28) nor did He seek glory for Himself (John 8:50). He openly declared:

> "For I have come down from heaven, not to do My own will, but the will of Him who sent Me" (John 6:38).

The point is clear. A genuine disciple embraces that philosophy of life. He or she comes to that place where no major decision is made without a serious consideration of the question, "What would the Lord want me to do?" as opposed to, "How will this benefit me?" That kind of thinking is rare these days. Driven by our pride and stroked by the endless flow of books (not to mention the media blitz) urging us on to find ourselves and please ourselves and satisfy ourselves and "be our own persons," we tend to recoil when we run upon advice like "Take up your cross and follow Me" or "Present your body a living sacrifice" or "Do nothing from selfishness or empty conceit."

That helps explain why discipleship never fails to thin the ranks. Christians all around the globe will line up to listen to somebody talk on prophecy. Our curiosity knows no bounds when it comes to future events. But instruction on discipleship—on giving up *my* goals and desires if God so leads—well, that will empty the room fast! I have the distinct impression that a few of my readers are also beginning to squirm right now. This teaching has a way of peeling off the veneer and getting down to the nerve endings, doesn't it? If it is any help, that same reaction occurred among people in Christ's day.

> Many therefore of His disciples, when they heard this said, "This is a difficult statement; who can listen to it?"
> As a result of this many of His disciples withdrew, and were not walking with Him any more (John 6:60, 66).

You see, even back then many (yes, the verse says "many") withdrew when the Master pressed the issue of commitment. At the risk of overkill, I want to ask three questions before we turn to the third test of discipleship:

1. As you think through the major decisions you have recently made (during the past six to eight months), have they pleased the Lord or fed your ego?
2. Have you begun to take your personal goals and desires before the Lord for His final approval?
3. Are you willing to change those goals if, while praying about them, the Lord should lead you to do so?

Discipleship refuses to let us skate through life tossing around a few religious comments while we live as we please. It says, "There can be no more important relationship to you than the one you have with Jesus Christ." And it also says, "When you set forth your goals and desires in life, say no to the things that will only stroke your ego, and yes to the things that will deepen your commitment to Christ."

There is one more test of discipleship.

Personal Possessions

> "So therefore, no one of you can be My disciple who does not give up all his own possessions" (Luke 14:33).

Here is another of those extreme statements designed to get us off the fence and into the action. It deals with something that occupies a big chunk of our time and energy—*things*. Jesus' words are neither complicated nor vague. He simply says, "If you are going to call yourself one of My disciples, you must release your grip on materialism." To keep all this in proper perspective, think of it this way. He is not saying that we cannot possess anything, but things must not be allowed to possess us. To use His words, we must "give up" our possessions.

Corrie ten Boom, that saintly lady who endured such brutality from the Nazis in Ravensbruck during World War II, once said that she had learned to hold everything loosely in her hand. She said she discovered, in her years of walking with Him, that when she grasped things tightly, it would hurt when the Lord would have to pry her fingers loose. Disciples hold all "things" loosely.

Do you? Can you think of *anything* that has a tap root to your heart? Let go! Give it up to Him! Yes, it may be painful . . . but how essential! Listen to the wise, tough counsel of the late A. W. Tozer, author of *The Pursuit of God*:

> There can be no doubt that this possessive clinging to things is one of the most harmful habits in the life. Because it is so natural it is rarely recognized for the evil that it is; but its outworkings are tragic.
>
> We are often hindered from giving up our treasures to the Lord out of fear for their safety; this is especially true when those treasures are loved relatives and friends. But we need have no such fears. Our Lord came not to destroy but to save. Everything is safe which we commit to Him, and nothing is really safe which is not so committed. . . .
>
> Let us never forget that such a truth as this cannot be learned by rote as one would learn the facts of physical science. They must be *experienced* before we can really know them. . . .
>
> The ancient curse will not go out painlessly; the tough old miser within us will not lie down and die obedient to our command. He must be torn out of our heart like a plant from the soil; he must be extracted in agony and blood like a tooth from the jaw. He must be expelled from our soul by violence as Christ expelled the money changers from the temple. And we shall need to steel ourselves against his piteous begging, and to recognize it as springing out of self-pity, one of the most reprehensible sins of the human heart. . . .
>
> Father, I want to know Thee, but my coward heart fears to give up its toys. I cannot part with them without inward bleeding, and I do not try to hide from Thee the terror of the parting. I come trembling, but I do come. Please root from my heart all those things which I have cherished so long and which have become a very part of my living self, so that Thou mayest enter and dwell there without a rival. Then shalt Thou make the place of Thy feet glorious. Then shall my heart have no need of the sun to shine in it, for Thyself wilt be the light of it, and there shall be no night there. In Jesus' Name, Amen.[2]

I haven't the slightest idea what you need to release, but *you* know. As difficult as it may be for you to turn it loose, it will be worth it. You will then (and only then) be free, truly free to serve your Lord.

Go back for a moment to that time when Jesus walked the shores of Galilee.

He came upon two brothers, Simon and Andrew, casting nets into the sea. As He called to them and invited them to follow Him, do you remember what they did? They—" . . . immediately left the nets, and followed Him" (Matt. 4:20). Shortly thereafter He saw two other brothers, James and John, mending their nets. Do you recall their response when He called them? They—" . . . immediately left the boat and their father . . ." (Matt. 4:22).

Those four men did more than walk away; they abandoned themselves to Him. They got their first taste of consecration to His cause. Unlike the shallow, "whatever you like is fine" kind of accommodating Christianity being marketed today by smooth-talking pushers of religious mediocrity, Jesus was ever firm and strong on the cost of discipleship. And so must we be as well.

There can be no dilly-dallying around with the commands of Christ. We are engaged in a warfare, the issues of which are life and death, and every day that we are indifferent to our responsibilities is a day lost to the cause of Christ. If we have learned even the most elemental truth of discipleship, we must know that we are called to be servants of our Lord and to obey His Word. It is not our duty to reason why He speaks as He does, but only to carry out His orders. Unless there is this dedication to all that we know He wants us to do now, however immature our understanding may be, it is doubtful if we will ever progress further in His life and mission. . . .

One must ask, why are so many professed Christians today stunted in their growth and ineffectual in their witness? Or to put the question in its larger context, why is the contemporary church so frustrated in its witness to the world? Is it not because among the clergy and laity alike there is a general indifference to the commands of God, or at least, a kind of contented complacency with mediocrity? Where is the obedience of the cross? Indeed, it would appear that the teachings of Christ upon self-denial and dedication have been replaced by a sort of respectable "do-as-you-please" philosophy of expediency.

The great tragedy is that little is being done to correct the situation, even by those who realize what is happening. Certainly the need of the hour is not for despair, but for action. It is high time that the requirements for membership in the church be interpreted and enforced in terms of true Christian discipleship. But this action alone will not be enough. Followers must have leaders, and this means that before much can be done with the church membership, something will have to be done with the church officials. If this task seems to be too great, then we will have to start like Jesus did by getting with a few chosen ones and instilling into them the meaning of obedience.[3]

EVALUATION: WHY SO COSTLY?

I must confess that I misunderstood the teaching of Jesus in Luke 14 for many years. Within the context of declaring the extreme terms of discipleship, He slips in two stories that explain why the terms are so costly.

"For which one of you, when he wants to build a tower, does not first sit down and calculate the cost, to see if he has enough to complete it?

"Otherwise, when he had laid a foundation, and is not able to finish, all who observe it begin to ridicule him, saying, 'This man began to build and was not able to finish.'

"Or what king, when he sets out to meet another king in battle, will not first sit down and take counsel whether he is strong enough with ten thousand men to encounter the one coming against him with twenty thousand?

"Or else, while the other is still far away, he sends a delegation and asks terms of peace.

"So therefore, no one of you can be My disciple who does not give up all his own possessions" (Luke 14:28–33).

The first study has to do with building and the second has to do with fighting. Both emphasize the high cost of doing each correctly . . . the importance of counting the cost. But be careful how you read these words. *We* are not told to count the cost. Look again at the verses and see it for yourself. Who, in the two stories, counts the cost? Well, the one in charge of the building project does that. And the king, who is responsible for the outcome of the battle, does that. Not the construction crews, not the fighting men. No, it's the one in charge.

Obviously it is the Lord Himself whom Jesus has in mind. He has designed the kind of "spiritual building" that will best display His glory . . . He is also fully aware of the battle that must be fought to get the job done. Having that perspective, He *Himself* has counted the cost and determined the quality of workmanship His "building" requires. And He *Himself* has counted the cost and determined the characteristics His soldiers must have to win the battle which will inevitably be waged against His plan. He (not *we*) has counted the cost.

Doesn't that make better sense? I recall, many years ago, preaching strong sermons on counting the cost. I even sang songs with the same idea in mind. But after looking deeply into the whole scene, I really believe it is not the Christian who determines the cost; it's our Lord. After all, the whole arrangement is His entirely.

Why are the qualifications so high? Why are the terms so costly? Stop and think about that. The "building" He has designed cannot be erected correctly without skilled, committed laborers. To lower His standards would lessen the quality of His ultimate product. He isn't willing to do that. And the kind of battle that must be fought cannot be handled by weary, ill-trained, noncommitted, half-hearted troops. That explains why the terms of discipleship must remain top-level . . . and why the ranks will always be thinned when the general, run-of-the-mill crowd of Christians is faced with Christ's no-nonsense call for committed disciples.

I want to close this chapter by sharing with you a slice out of my life you probably don't know about. It will help you understand why I now take these things so seriously.

For a number of years after I became a Christian, I messed around with spiritual things. Just messed around. I ran around with church folks, I learned the God-talk, I sang the hymns, I even memorized the verses. I prayed pretty good prayers, I carried my Bible to church Sunday after Sunday, I sang in the choir, and I added to my schedule a Bible class or two every now and then. But my life was *my* life. I did not let all that religious stuff interfere with things like my career, my home, my strong will, my pursuit of things, my determination to go my own way, or my own personal plans. I wasn't a wife-beater, or a criminal, or an alcoholic, or some awful, notorious sinner. No, I was just a selfish man. I knew how to get what I wanted and nothing was going to stand in my way. Stubborn and opinionated, I rolled up my sleeves and was ready to slug it out with whoever stood in my way . . . including God. I was a Christian, but certainly *not* a disciple.

And then shortly after joining the Marines (another evidence of my determination to be tough and self-assured), I was transferred overseas, as I mentioned in the chapter on purity. For once I was faced with a major decision I could not change. Alone and lonely, I was forced to entrust my wife to the Lord, since she couldn't go to the Orient with me, and to lean on Him for numerous things I had always been able to handle myself.

While overseas I met a man who saw behind my tough mask and was determined to help me come to terms with the Christ I claimed as my Savior. In the words of this chapter, he "discipled" me. Month after month, we met together, talked together, played ball together, laughed together, wept and prayed together, studied the Scriptures and witnessed for Christ together. Like Jesus with His men, this man took the time to help me peel off my mask of religion and absorb the authentic message of Christ. I found myself slowly changing down deep inside. I got to the place where I hated the hypocrisy of my former religious lifestyle. I got into the Scriptures *on my own* and they became my bread and meat. I even addressed the priorities, the goals, and the objectives of my life. I opened each door of my inner house to let Christ in, room after room after room. Not suddenly, but slowly. Quietly. "Things" became less and less important to me. My stubborn will came under the scrutinizing eye of the Spirit of God. And I began to meet each day with my Lord, asking Him to deal with my ugly selfishness . . . and did He ever!

Looking back, I realize now I was in the process of becoming a disciple. Does that mean I have now arrived? Am I suggesting I have a handle on the whole thing? Absolutely not. But in spite of all my humanity (and there is tons of it still with me!), God has really gotten my attention. He has taken me to task about my stubborn will. I humbly praise Him for His patience and mercy as He faithfully stayed on the job and wouldn't let me go until I surrendered. He replaced a "me-only" mentality with a much broader view of the importance of others. He has tempered my opinionated dogmatism and given me a tolerance that is altogether unlike the me of yesteryear.

It is a little difficult sharing this in such detail lest I come off as some superpious saint with wings starting to sprout. Nothing could be further from

the truth! I still blow it. I still fight the urge to have my own way. I still have
those desires to please only myself. But the big difference between now and
years ago is that I no longer defend those urges. I really don't want them to
control me, whereas before I rationalized around it. I want my Lord in control,
and I find myself increasingly more embarrassed when those fleshly drives
express themselves. The difference occurred in my life when I turned the
corner in my spiritual growth and decided I had had enough of the game playing
with God.

I have a feeling that many of you who read these words identify with my
pilgrimage. The details may be different, but the overall scene is similar, right?
For some of you, this represents a risk you want to take, but you're afraid of the
cost. Take it from me, it's worth it! The Lord God will see you through. All you
need to do is get alone with the Master, pour out your fears and your failures,
then tell Him you are ready to take that first step away from a world that centers
on you and into a new life that focuses on Him. That's when you'll begin to
strengthen your grip on discipleship and loosen your grip on mere religion.

> I had walked life's path with an easy tread,
> Had followed where comfort and pleasure led;
> And then by chance in a quiet place—
> I met my Master face to face.
>
> With station and rank and wealth for goal,
> Much thought for body but none for soul,
> I had entered to win this life's mad race—
> When I met my Master face to face.
>
> I had built my castles, reared them high,
> Till their towers had pierced the blue of the sky;
> I had sworn to rule with an iron mace—
> When I met my Master face to face.
>
> I met Him and knew Him, and blushed to see
> That His eyes full of sorrow were fixed on me;
> And I faltered, and fell at His feet that day
> While my castles vanished and melted away.
>
> Melted and vanished; and in their place
> I saw naught else but my Master's face;
> And I cried aloud: "Oh, make me meet
> To follow the marks of Thy wounded feet."
>
> My thought is now for the souls of men;
> I have lost my life to find it again

Ever since alone in that holy place
My Master and I stood face to face.[4]

Author Unknown

DISCUSSION QUESTIONS AND IDEAS TO HELP YOU STRENGTHEN YOUR GRIP ON DISCIPLESHIP

• The "in word" for the seventies was discipleship. We tossed it around the church, mission organizations used it often, and books included long chapters on the subject. But what does it mean? Can you *describe* discipleship? Try to do so in two or three sentences.

• In this chapter we probed into Luke 14:25–33. We first learned that Jesus spoke these words to "thin the ranks" of His followers. Why would He want to do that? How does that relate to discipleship? And while discussing that subject, answer this: Are all believers automatically *disciples*? Explain your answer.

• While developing the whole idea of becoming His disciple, Jesus addressed three particular areas that often give us trouble. Looking back over verses 26 through 33 of Luke 14, see if you can name those three areas. Talk about each briefly. Does one give you more problems than another? Discuss why.

• In Luke 14:28–33 (please take the time to read), Jesus gave a couple of illustrations that were designed to clarify the issue of becoming His disciple. As you look over these verses, see if you can explain how they relate to the subject. In both cases, someone sits down and thinks through the involvement (verses 28, 31). Talk about the importance of what this implies.

• Finally, think seriously about being a part of someone else's spiritual growth. In our age of distance and isolation, the most natural thing is to operate at arm's length . . . to maintain an "aloofness" from one another. Talk about the value of coming in closer. Name two or three specific benefits connected with small-group ministries and even one-on-one relationships. Ask God to lead you into this type of ministry during this year.

8

Strengthening Your Grip on Aging

Numerous possibilities, few inevitabilities—that's life. The sky's the limit, but in that journey there are a few inescapable realities. Growing older is one of them. Aging not only happens, it happens *fast*.

I turned forty-seven this week. Three years shy of half a century! That's enough to make a guy want to lie down and take a nap . . . especially after I looked at myself in our double-width mirror this morning. While I studied my reflection, I immediately remembered a little sign I'd seen in a local gift shop:

> When you get too old for pimples
> you go right into wrinkles.

You know you're getting older when . . .

  . . . most of your dreams are reruns,

  . . . the airline attendant offers you "coffee, tea,
  or Milk of Magnesia,"

  . . . you sit down in a rocking chair and you can't
  get it started,

  . . . your mind makes commitments your body can't keep,

  . . . the little grey-haired lady you help across the
  street is your wife!

  . . . reading *The Total Woman* makes you sleepy,

. . . everything hurts, and what doesn't hurt doesn't work,

. . . you sink your teeth into a juicy steak
and they stay there.

. . . you watch a pretty girl go by and your pacemaker
makes the garage door open.

Those who are retired begin to get the message. They find themselves falling into the rut of inactivity if they're not careful. Like the gentleman who admitted:

> I get up each morning, dust off my wits,
> Pick up the paper and read the obits.
> If my name is missing, I know I'm not dead
> So I eat a good breakfast—and go back to bed.

Although I'm a long way from retirement, I must confess that sounds like a marvelous schedule these days!

But not everyone is smiling. For many, growing older represents a grim reality, a lonely and frightening journey that seems overwhelming . . . at times unbearable.

HUMAN ATTITUDES ON AGING

The more I talk with and listen to older people, the more I sense a growing discontentment rather than acceptance. I witnessed it in my own father during the last decade of his life. My mother died in 1971, but he (although fifteen years older than she) lived on into 1980. He lived a number of those years in our home with us, allowing us a never-to-be-forgotten occasion to observe first-hand the agony of aging alone, even though he was surrounded by our family of six who wanted to relate to him, express our love, and include him in the mainstream of our world. We detected that "Pee-Po" had adopted a series of attitudes that made a close relationship extremely difficult, if not impossible.

Because they are not unique to him, I share them openly. Without wanting to sound critical, I believe it is correct to say that these attitudes come from our humanity . . . not from the Lord. They are therefore terribly demoralizing.

Uselessness

This feeling says, "I'm over the hill" . . . "I get in the way" . . . "I really don't have much to contribute anymore, so I'll just back off from life." This frequently emerges from those who were once resourceful, competent persons. In fact, it isn't uncommon to find that those who once played an extremely significant role in life feel the most useless as the sands of time cover their past achievements.

Guilt

What an awful companion to journey with during our later years! And yet guilt has a way of hijacking our minds as age slows our steps and sensitizes our memories. "I blew it" . . . "If only I had a second chance, I'd rear my family differently" . . . "I'd handle my money more wisely" . . . "I was too this—not enough that." On and on. With more time on our hands, we yield to guilt's finger of blame and to the frowns of "Shame on you!" Inevitably, feelings of dissatisfaction growl and churn within. Like the anonymous verse I learned years ago:

> Across the fields of yesterday he sometimes comes to me,
> A little lad just back from play, the boy I used to be.
> He smiles at me so wistfully when once he's crept within,
> It is as though he'd hoped to see the man I might have been.

Such imaginary visits never fail to grab hold and slam us to the mat. Guilt is a coward and bully, forever picking fights we can't seem to win.

Self-Pity

There's yet another attitude that plagues the aging, that old nemesis, self-pity . . . the woe-is-me syndrome convincing us that no man's land is our own island. "Nobody cares, so why should I? Nobody cares if I live or die!" Self-pity spans the extremes of blame and bitterness. And it often takes us under the proverbial juniper tree with the prophet Elijah as we join in the familiar chorus, "It is enough; now, O Lord, take my life . . ." (1 Kings 19:4).

Fear

Perhaps more than any other attitude, the feelings of fear are most common among those who are getting on in years . . . economic fears, fear of losing health or mind, mate or friends. "The world is spinning by me at a terribly fast clip—I'm afraid I can't stay up with it." Couple this with the impatience of youth, the rising crime rate where senior citizens are victimized by violence and fraud, add hearing loss and crippling disease . . . and it isn't difficult to understand why fear attaches itself to the aged.

I do not want to seem without compassion when I write this next sentence, but it needs to be said right up front. As natural and understandable as feelings of uselessness, guilt, self-pity, and fear may be, *they do not come from God*. The Lord does not prompt those feelings—we do. They are strictly and completely human in their source, leaving us caught in their undertow. To strengthen our grip on aging, these feelings must somehow be counteracted. For the rest of the chapter, let's consider how we might do that.

A PSALM WITH A PRINCIPLE

God's Word never fails to guide us into the right perspective on life. Psalm 90 is no exception. Written by an older gentleman (Moses) in his eighties—perhaps even older than that—the psalm takes a brief, but accurate look at life. It begins by reminding us that God is ageless:

> Lord, you have been our dwelling place
> > throughout all generations.
> Before the mountains were born
> > or you brought forth the earth and the world,
> > from everlasting to everlasting you are God.
> > > (Ps. 90:1-2, NIV)

Once that is settled, the writer then turns his attention to humanity, choosing several different word pictures to paint the brevity and pain of life in vivid color. See if you can locate three or four of those illustrations:

> You turn men back to dust,
> > saying, "Return to dust, O sons of men."
> For a thousand years in your sight
> > are like a day that has just gone by,
> > or like a watch in the night.
> You sweep men away in the sleep of death;
> > they are like the new grass of the morning—
> though in the morning it springs up new,
> > by evening it is dry and withered.
> We are consumed by your anger
> > and terrified by your indignation
> You have set our iniquities before you,
> > our secret sins in the light of your presence.
> All our days pass away under your wrath;
> > we finish our years with a moan.
> The length of our days is seventy years—
> > or eighty, if we have the strength;
> Yet their span is but trouble and sorrow,
> > for they quickly pass, and we fly away.
> > > (Ps. 90:3-10, NIV)

Life? It is "like a day gone by."
Like "a watch in the night."
Like "new grass."
We finish our years with "a moan," sometimes living seventy years, sometimes eighty. No matter, "they quickly pass, and we fly away."

So? So how do we make heads or tails of it? Is there some guideline, some piece of advice, some divine principle to follow that will help us strengthen our grip on aging? Yes!

> Teach us to number our days aright, that we may gain a heart of wisdom (Ps. 90:12, NIV).

The Hebrew text suggests that we correctly "account" for our days. I find it interesting that we are to view life by the days, not *the years*. We are to live those days in such a way that when they draw to a close, we have gained "a heart of wisdom." With the Lord God occupying first place in our lives (we're back to *priorities*, chapter 1) we accept and live each day enthusiastically for Him. The result will be that "heart of wisdom" the psalmist mentions.

I'm forty-seven this week. Forty-seven years, when multiplied by 365 days each year, tallies up to be 17,155 days. I cannot identify with a huge chunk of days that equal one year, but I can certainly bite off a nibble that represents one day. When I live it God's way, as prescribed here in Psalm 90:12, I take that day as His gift to me, which I live under His control and for His glory.

Here, then is the principle:

> SINCE EACH DAY IS A GIFT FROM GOD,
> I LIVE EACH ONE ENTHUSIASTICALLY FOR HIM.

"Aw, come on, Chuck, how idealistic can you get?" I can hear those words bouncing from your mind to mine right now. "If you only knew my situation, you'd have to rework that principle!"

No, I seriously doubt that I would back down, even though you may be in a situation right now that seems somewhere between terrible and impossible.

What might help is seeing this abstract, theoretical principle fleshed out in the life of a person in his eighties. If we can see the truth incarnated, I'm convinced it will help all of us get a tighter grip on aging. The person I have in mind lived a rugged life, experienced his share of disappointments, approached his twilight years with no easy chair in sight—and *loved* the challenge of it all. He's a character in the Bible named Caleb.

A MAN WHO STAYED OUT OF MOTH BALLS

I really do not know of a Bible character in the Old Testament I admire more than Caleb, whose life is beautifully summed up in several verses of Joshua 14.

Everything about the man is concentrated into a nutshell, but the tentacles of his biography stretch back forty-five years earlier. You'll see why I say this as you read his story.

> Then the sons of Judah drew near to Joshua in Gilgal, and Caleb the son of Jephunneh the Kenizzite said to him, "You know the word which the Lord spoke to Moses the man of God concerning you and me in Kadesh-barnea.
> "I was forty years old when Moses the servant of the Lord sent me from Kadesh-barnea to spy out the land, and I brought word back to him as it was in my heart.
> "Nevertheless my brethren who went up with me made the heart of the people melt with fear; but I followed the Lord my God fully.
> "So Moses swore on that day, saying, 'Surely the land on which your foot has trodden shall be an inheritance to you and to your children forever, because you have followed the Lord my God fully.'
> "And now behold, the Lord has let me live, just as He spoke, these forty-five years, from the time that the Lord spoke this word to Moses, when Israel walked in the wilderness; and now behold, I am eighty-five years old today.
> "I am still as strong today as I was in the day Moses sent me; as my strength was then, so my strength is now, for war and for going out and coming in.
> "Now then, give me this hill country about which the Lord spoke on that day, for you heard on that day that Anakim were there, with great fortified cities; perhaps the Lord will be with me, and I shall drive them out as the Lord has spoken."
> So Joshua blessed him, and gave Hebron to Caleb the son of Jephunneh for an inheritance.
> Therefore, Hebron became the inheritance of Caleb the son of Jephunneh the Kenizzite until this day, because he followed the Lord God of Israel fully (Josh. 14:6–14).

Before we get neck deep into Caleb's life, I want to mention two very obvious truths that emerge from his example. They perfectly apply to all who are aging and are beginning to feel the hot breath of that old dragon, Time, on the back of their neck:

1. It is possible for life's greatest achievements to occur in old age.
2. There is no retirement from the Christian life.

Before going any further, we need to understand those two facts. And we also need to realize they apply to you and me just as much as they apply to a man named Caleb. His story is not to be viewed as unique.

Earlier Years

Caleb begins by reflecting on those days forty-five years earlier when he, Joshua, and ten other Israeli spies slipped into Canaan before the Jews invaded and conquered the land. Caleb says he was forty years old at the time. He also remembers that the report he gave back then was a minority report. Ten of the twelve spies were afraid, absolutely convinced there was no way they could occupy the territory.

Numbers 13:25–33 gives us the account Caleb refers to in his words to Joshua.

> When they returned from spying out the land, at the end of forty days, they proceeded to come to Moses and Aaron and to all the congregation of the sons of Israel in the wilderness of Paran, at Kadesh; and they brought back word to them and to all the congregation and showed them the fruit of the land.
>
> Thus they told him, and said, "We went in to the land where you sent us; and it certainly does flow with milk and honey, and this is its fruit.
>
> "Nevertheless, the people who live in the land are strong, and the cities are fortified and very large; and moreover, we saw the descendants of Anak there.
>
> "Amalek is living in the land of the Negev and the Hittites and the Jebusites and the Amorites are living in the hill country, and the Canaanites are living by the sea and by the side of the Jordan."
>
> Then Caleb quieted the people before Moses, and said, "We should by all means go up and take possession of it, for we shall surely overcome it."
>
> But the men who had gone up with him said, "We are not able to go up against the people, for they are too strong for us."
>
> So they gave out to the sons of Israel a bad report of the land which they had spied out, saying, "The land through which we have gone, in spying it out, is a land that devours its inhabitants; and all the people whom we say in it are men of great size.
>
> "There also we saw the Nephilim (the sons of Anak are part of the Nephilim); and we became like grasshoppers in our own sight, and so we were in their sight."

Caleb recalls that neither he nor Joshua ever doubted. Forty-five years ago he stood alone, he trusted God, he publicly announced his confident opinion that they could overcome those "giants" of Canaan. But because the people chose not to believe God, they wandered forty long years in the wilderness. Only he and Joshua—now the oldest in the camp—survived that death march. With younger men and women all around them, they continued to fight, to work, and finally to conquer the land of Canaan. Look again at Caleb's words:

> "I was forty years old when Moses the servant of the Lord sent me from Kadesh-barnea to spy out the land, and I brought word back to him as it was in my heart.
>
> "Nevertheless my brethren who went up with me made the heart of the people melt with fear; but I followed the Lord my God fully.
>
> "So Moses swore on that day, saying, 'Surely the land on which your foot has trodden shall be an inheritance to you and to your children forever, because you have followed the Lord my God fully." (Josh. 14:7–9).

Caleb is getting excited again. Don't forget, he's eighty-five years young. Maybe it was actually his birthday. Whatever, the man has lost none of his enthusiastic zest for life.

Middle Years

I love these next two verses!

> "And now behold, the Lord has let me live, just as He spoke, these forty-five years, from the time that the Lord spoke this word to Moses, when Israel walked in the wilderness; and now behold, I am eighty-five years old today.
> "I am still as strong today as I was in the day Moses sent me; as my strength was then, so my strength is now, for war and for going out and coming in" (Josh. 14:10–11).

Notice, please, I'm referring to this eighty-five year-old man as being in his "middle years." That way we don't offend anybody!

What does this man say of himself? How does he view the person inside his own skin? Struggling with fear or self-pity or uselessness or guilt? Hardly. He sees himself strong as ever. Capable and qualified to fight or give counsel, use a weapon or use his mind. It is so encouraging to read this man's opinion of himself. Although up in years, he was anything but over the hill! And speaking of the hill, read on:

> "Now then, give me this hill country about which the Lord spoke on that day, for you heard on that day that Anakim were there, with great fortified cities; perhaps the Lord will be with me, and I shall drive them out as the Lord has spoken."
> So Joshua blessed him, and gave Hebron to Caleb the son of Jephunneh for an inheritance (Josh. 14:12–13).

Later Years

As Caleb peered into the future, his eyes sparkled with enthusiasm, optimism, hope, and faith.

Not: "Leave me alone, I'm tired."
"I deserve a comfortable, shady spot."
"You owe me some benefits for all those years I've worked and fought."
"I've done my part, now it's *their* turn!"
But: "See that range of mountains—gimme that to conquer."
"Bring on those ugly giants."
"Lemme at those fortified cities."
"Here, you take these bedroom slippers, Joshua. I'm puttin' on the waffle stompers!"

I suggest we start a new club. How about "The Caleb Climbers" or "Sons of Caleb." We could call it "SOC" for short. And you'd have to be sixty-five or older to join! I firmly believe we would have thousands in that club in a matter of hours, once they read these words of Caleb.

You see, age isn't our problem. A traditional attitude is. We suffer from an invisible media fallout. We've been programmed to believe that at sixty-five we turn into an occupational pumpkin. Some kind of black magic has put a hex on our motivation, making us think we need to shuffle, stoop, sneer, and snore our way through the rest of life.

Nonsense!

The real giants are those kinds of thoughts. They growl and roar like a forest full of Big Feet . . . but who says, "SOC" needs to listen? Caleb didn't. He rolled up his sleeves and dared those giants to put up a fight. He *refused* to be intimidated or discouraged. Larry Olsen, author of *Outdoor Survival Skills*, illustrates beautifully the importance of a positive attitude as he describes a man lost in the desert. His attitude is the only thing that enabled him to survive:

> "He has been out of food and water for days. His lips are swollen, his tongue is swollen, he's all beat up and bloody. Some of his bones are almost peeking through. He has been just scraped and beat up by the cactus and sand and sun. He's blistered. As he is crawling over this little hill he comes across this little plant and he props himself up on one bloody elbow and looks down at this plant and he says, 'You know, if things keep going like this I might get discouraged!'" [1]

Sounds a lot like something old Caleb might have said. And the good news is this: He doesn't have a corner on the market.

RESPONDING CORRECTLY TO AGING

Can you recall the principle from Psalm 90? I'll repeat it once again.

SINCE EVERY DAY IS A GIFT FROM GOD
I LIVE EACH ONE ENTHUSIASTICALLY FOR HIM.

Because we cannot alter the inevitable, we adjust to it. And we do that not a year at a time, but a day at a time. Instead of eating our heart out because a few more aches and pains have attached themselves to our bodies, we determine to celebrate life rather than endure it. Aging isn't a choice. But our response to it is. In so many ways we ourselves determine how we shall grow old.

I'd like to talk about that before drawing this chapter to a close. I want you to give serious thought to staying out of moth balls. Really, the choice is yours. The late General Douglas MacArthur realized this on his seventy-fifth birthday.

> In the central place of every heart there is a recording chamber; so long as it receives messages of beauty, hope, cheer, and courage, so long are you young.

When the wires are all down and your heart is covered with the snows of pessimism and the ice of cynicism, then, and then only are you grown old.[2]

Realizing the truth of all that, let's consider a couple of alternate responses to aging.

First, *view life as a challenge not a threat.* You've been around long enough to know that nobody can predict our tomorrows. So, obviously the answer is that we adopt Caleb's mentality and refuse all temptations to hibernate, to worry, to curl up, fold up, and dry up. Grap each day (remember, the secret is handling each *day*) and accept each hour as a challenge. Here's how one man suggests that we do it:

How To Live

Don't be bashful.
> Bite in.
Pick it up with your fingers and
> let the juice that may
> run down your chin.

Life is ready and ripe
> NOW
> > whenever you are.

You don't need a knife or fork
or spoon or napkin or tablecloth

For there is no core
> or stem
> or rind
> or pit
> or seed
> or skin
> > to throw away.[3]

If viewing life as a challenge were an unachievable goal, it would be mockery for me to hold it out as a carrot. But it is definitely attainable. I see older men and women all the time refusing to sink into the swamp of depression. We have recently begun an exciting program in our church here in Fullerton, California, for our older adults. They call themselves the *Forever Young* group, and they mean business! They enjoy a meal together once or twice a week, they travel to various places of interest together, they do projects together, but most of all they are *together*. It's thrilling to see some who once were alone, discouraged, and failing mentally coming out of their shell and enjoying life.

Every once in a while certain American athletes emerge as models of this contagious lifestyle. Ball players like Pete Rose and George Blanda and Alan Page and John Havlicek are only a few of those we could name. Even some coaches seem to be timeless models of enthusiasm—like John Wooden with UCLA for so many years and George Halas with the Chicago Bears and Paul "Bear" Bryant with the Crimson Tide of Alabama. Have you gotten a close look at the old Bear lately? He has more than a wrinkle or two! But don't you think for a minute that he's backing away from the challenge. This tough-minded, continually creative coach has just become the winningest college football coach in the land, passing up Amos Alonzo Stagg (314 wins) and even Pop Warner (313).

And he's definitely still alert. I love the story Frank Broyles, the athletic director at the University of Arkansas tells on Bear. He says that whenever you see Bear standing around the sidelines, he's always so grave and dignified, almost like he's about to say, "Let us pray." But he doesn't. He's thinking. Planning. Always several plays ahead of the game. Broyles testifies there's another side of Bryant many people don't know. When he learns of a good prospect at a little town, no matter what it takes, he pursues!

Like that kid named Gene Donaldson, an offensive guard from a tiny town in Texas. The kid was great, naturally the object of many college coaches' attention. But Broyles says Bear was the only one who found out the boy was Catholic. So what was his strategy? Well, Bryant dressed up one of his assistant coaches as a priest—black suit, white collar, beads, the works—and dispatched him to Donaldson's home town. The youngster had just about decided to go to Notre Dame, but Bear wanted him at Kentucky, where he was coaching at the time. He told his assistant exactly what to say to the wide-eyed kid:

"*Young man, the Pope wants you to go to Kentucky.*"

That did it. A few weeks later he enrolled and became one of Bear's first All-Americans!

Although the Bear's approach here seems rather extreme, it does illustrate how this wrinkled old coach refuses to put his head in neutral. It's the challenge of it all that keeps him interested. He may look old, but age is only skin deep, you know.

The second alternate response to aging is to *follow the Lord fully, not halfheartedly*. That's exactly what Caleb did.

> Therefore, Hebron became the inheritance of Caleb the son of Jephunneh the Kenizzite until this day, because he followed the Lord God of Israel fully (Josh. 14:14).

I'm certain that was a major factor in his youthful response to life. In fact, a close look at this biography will reveal that on two other occasions the same thing is said of Caleb, he ". . . followed the Lord God fully" (vv. 8–9). In other words, Caleb's walk of faith was constant, a regular part of his day. The man determined that the Lord his God would be his life's Partner, regardless.

I want to encourage you to make that same commitment, starting today. Yes, you can! The only thing standing in your way is that decision to turn your life over to Him. When (and *only* when) you do that will you begin to realize that no amount of clouds will dim the Son from your life. Become a part of the Sons of Caleb. Join the club. As soon as you do, you will be amazed at the difference in your outlook on life.

Several years ago an older couple attended a Bible conference in Colorado. Their children were raised and they were facing the sunset years of their lives. Both were Christians, but neither had ever come out of the closet spiritually. The conference theme was "Looking Unto Jesus" and that became the emphasis of the week. While attending the conference and coming to grips with the message of wholesale commitment to Christ, each one decided to place Him on the throne of his or her life. No matter what, they would follow the Lord fully, not halfheartedly. They prayed before starting that long drive back to their home:

"Lord, we give you first place. We have lived too many years for ourselves. No longer. We have decided to spend the balance of our lives for You. No matter what happens, the rest of our days are in Your hands."

En route to their destination late that evening a car swerved over onto their side of the highway, heading straight toward them. The man jerked the steering wheel to the right, slammed on his brakes, and skidded down into a ditch, finally coming to a stop in the middle of a shallow ravine. As water began to pour into their car, she pulled herself out of the window on her side and he did the same on his. They stood on top of their car as the water passed by beneath them. They were stunned, but so grateful to be alive that they embraced tightly then began to sing, spontaneously and softly:

"Praise God from whom all blessings flow;
Praise Him, all creatures here below;
Praise Him above, ye heavenly host;
Praise Father, Son, and Holy Ghost, Amen."[4]

As their voices trailed off, they looked up on the narrow bridge above them and saw a large number of people staring down in silent disbelief. A highway patrolman was there, they said later, who had placed his hat over his heart. Nobody knew what to say.

Suddenly the elderly husband was seized with the realization that even *this* could be used as a testimony to the glory of God. With a twinkle in his eye, a smile on his lips, and with a trembling voice he began, "You might have wondered why we called this meeting here today. . . ." And he then proceeded to tell the onlookers about their decision to "look unto Jesus" no matter what. And instead of complaining and succumbing to fear, the two of them spoke openly of the Lord their God, whom they now followed fully, not halfheartedly.

Are you getting older? Yes, we all are. Are you interested in strengthening your grip on that inevitable aging process? I'm sure you are. Don't postpone it any longer. Regardless of your age, your circumstance, your past, or your feelings, be a modern-day Caleb. Give in no longer to feelings of uselessness, guilt, self-pity, or fear.

> View life as a challenge, not a threat.
> Follow the Lord fully, not halfheartedly.
> And one more thing, start today, not later

Discussion Questions and Suggestions to Help You Strengthen Your Grip on Aging

• See if you can recall some of the common attitudes found among those who are aging. In your opinion, why would these feelings be so strong? Can you think of an example of someone you know who is currently caught in the grip of one or more of these attitudes?

• As we looked at Psalm 90 in this chapter, we observed several word pictures that describe the brevity of life. Then we suggested a principle that grew out of Psalm 90:12. Can you state that principle? Talk about what helps you the most. Try to be specific.

• Caleb, the eighty-five-year-old warrier, determined not to be covered over with moth balls. Call to mind one of two reasons he stayed young at heart. How does that apply to you?

• Toward the end of this chapter, we thought about a couple of ways to respond correctly to aging. Name them, then discuss their significance in your own, personal situation.

• Perhaps it's a good time to pray about your major struggle with aging. In an honest, simple manner, express yourself to God and ask for His assistance. Is there something you need to do to help relieve that struggle?

9

Strengthening Your Grip on Prayer

I should tell you up front that this is not going to be your basic religious-sounding chapter on prayer. Sorry, I just don't have it in me.

No, I'm not sorry.

To be painfully honest with you, most of the stuff I have ever read or heard said about prayer has either left me under a ton-and-a-half truckload of guilt or wearied me with pious-sounding cliches and meaningless God-talk. Without trying to sound ultra cynical, I frequently have walked away thinking, "Who needs it?" Because I didn't spend two or three grueling hours a day on my knees as dear Dr. So-and-So did . . . or because I failed to say it just the "right way" (whatever that means) . . . or because I wasn't able to weave several Scripture verses through my prayer . . . or because I had not been successful in moving mountains, I picked up the distinct impression that I was out to lunch when it came to this part of the Christian life. If seemed almost spooky, mystical, and (dare I say it) even a little superstitious. A lot of verbal mumbo-jumbo laced with a secret jargon some people had and others didn't. And I definitely *didn't*.

If you had asked me twenty or more years ago if prayer was one of the essentials in an aimless world like ours, I would surely have said, "No." At least, not the brand of prayer I had been exposed to. It wasn't that I was unaware of the high-profile prayer plays in the Bible. I was simply turned off by the exposure I had had. So I pretty well tuned it out.

Maybe you have too. It is quite possible, therefore, that you have put off reading this chapter for a while. I fully understand it. And I do not blame you. On the contrary, I admire you for plunging in! Let's see if there is something I can say that will help put prayer in a better light for you. Hopefully, you will see rather soon that it isn't *authentic* prayer you've been struggling with, but rather a caricature, a distortion, a pitiful imitation of the genuine item.

PERSPECTIVE FROM PAUL

In the fourth chapter of Philippians, a small first-century letter Paul wrote that found its way into the New Testament, he mentions a series of things all of us want:

- We all *want* to stand firm in our faith (v. 1).
- We all *want* to have a joyful attitude through the day (v. 4).
- We all *want* to have minds that dwell on beneficial things (v. 8).
- We all *want* to apply God's principles so completely that we are flooded with His peace (v. 9).
- For sure, we all *want* contentment and satisfaction (vv. 10–12).

Yes, we all *want* these things, but few of us experience them on a regular basis. So? Our anxiety level rises higher and higher. Worries multiply. Cares increase. Irritation often invades, making us feel resentful and confused. We can't even crank it out. We struggle with thoughts like, "I'm a hypocrite, I'm a poor Christian example." What's most interesting is this: THE FIRST AND ONLY THING THAT WILL WORK IS THE LAST THING WE TRY . . . PRAYER. Take a look at this:

Be anxious for nothing, but in everything by prayer and supplication with thanksgiving let your requests be made known to God.

And the peace of God, which surpasses all comprehension, shall guard your hearts and your minds in Christ Jesus (Phil. 4:6–7).

Most Christians are so familiar with those words, I fear they may have lost their punch. To guard against that, let's read them from another translation— The Amplified Bible:

Do not fret or have any anxiety about anything, but in every circumstance and in everything by prayer and petition [definite requests] with thanksgiving continue to make your wants known to God.

And God's peace [be yours, that tranquil state of soul assured of its salvation through Christ, and so fearing nothing from God and content with its earthly lot of whatever sort that is, that peace] which transcends all understanding, shall garrison and mount guard over your hearts and minds in Christ Jesus (Phil. 4:6–7, AMPLIFIED).

Now *that's* a mouthful! If I understand this correctly, the anxiety that mounts up inside me, the growing irritation and the struggles that make me churn, will be dissipated—and, in fact, replaced with inner peace plus all those other qualities I want so much—if I will simply talk to my God. Prayer is the single most significant thing that will help turn inner turmoil into peace. Prayer is the answer.

But wait! Why, then, is it such a struggle? What is it about prayer that makes even the great and the godly (those we admire so much) so guilty? So dissatisfied? So unhappy with their own prayer life?

In no way do I wish to be disrespectful by saying the following things, but I believe it's time somebody declared them to help clarify the barrier that keeps us from entering into authentic prayer. That barrier is the traditional wrappings that have been placed around prayer. Not even the grand models of church history admitted to much joy or peace or satisfaction in their prayer life!

Dietrich Bonhoeffer, for example, once admitted that his prayer experience was something to be ashamed of. The German reformer, Martin Luther, anguished in prayer, saving three of the best hours of the day to pray . . . yet he seldom seemed satisfied. Go down through the list and we find one after another working hard at prayer, but frequently we'll find they're disatisfied, some of them even *woefully* unhappy about their prayer life.

E. M. Bounds, Alexander Maclaren, Samuel Rutherford, Hudson Taylor, John Henry Jowett, G. Campbell Morgan, Joseph Parker, Charles Haddon Spurgeon, F. B. Meyer, A. W. Tozer, H. A. Ironside, V. Raymond Edman, William Culbertson, and on and on. Great men, strong Christian examples, magnificent models, yet you can hardly find one of that number who was satisfied with his prayer life. Oh, they labored in prayer, they believed in prayer, they taught and preached prayer . . . but why the dissatisfaction? Why the guilt? Or disappointment? Or, for some, embarrassment? I ask you—why?

At the risk of sounding downright heretical, I'm convinced that for centuries Christians have forced prayer into a role it was never designed to play. I would suggest we have *made* it difficult, hard, even painful. The caricature that has emerged through years of traditional (not biblical) modeling is now a guilt-giving discipline, not an anxiety-relieving practice. It is self-imposed. It doesn't come from God.

Remember Philippians 4:6–7? Paul's perspective on prayer was this: It *results* in peace, it doesn't take it away. It *alleviates* anxiety, it isn't designed to create it! But, you see, we have been led to believe that in order for prayer to be effective, it must be arduous, lengthy, even painful. And we must stay at it for hours on end . . . pleading, longing, waiting, hurting.

Are you ready for a shocker? You don't find any of that in the Scriptures. Except in very few and extreme cases, prayer is neither long nor hard to bear. And I cannot find any biblical characters who struggled with guilt because they didn't pray long enough or because they weren't in enough pain or because they failed to plead and beg sufficiently. Check it for yourself. It isn't there.

During my years in seminary, there was an upperclassman who believed God was calling him to the mission field. He was a sincere, careful student who read numerous biographies of great men and women who served Christ throughout their lives. The more he read, the more convinced he became that commitment required an infliction of bodily pain, sleepless nights spent in prayer. He even slept on the floor instead of his bed. He became increasingly more masochistic in his pietism, firmly dedicated to his self-imposed lifestyle of rigorous denial. A marked fanaticism characterized the man's attitude. He became more distant and defensive, less tolerant and balanced in his whole view of life. He was a driven man who, by the way, often spoke of his lack of enough time spent in prayer and his need for greater devotion to Christ. I recall, on one occasion, asking him to show me the biblical basis of his enough-is-never-enough mentality. I'm still waiting for his answer.

A warning: Let's be careful about making the extreme our standard. When it comes to prayer, let's get rid of all the traditional garbage and come back to the original model our Savior gave to us when He walked and talked among us.

INSTRUCTION FROM JESUS

Religious people in Jesus' day took their cues from the leaders of the synagogue—the Pharisees, the Sadducees, and the scribes. Didn't *they* believe in prayer? Yes, indeed. They had a saying, "He who prays within his house surrounds it with a wall that is stronger than iron." They only regretted they couldn't pray all day long. And it was this intensity that caused prayer to degenerate from a flowing spontaneity to a rigid, packaged plan, dispensed routinely by the religious leaders. Prayer changed from a privilege to an obligation. From pleasure in God's presence to man-made requirements. To help us understand what Jesus had to face, let's examine for a few minutes the impact of tradition on first-century Judaism.

How Prayer Had Degenerated

Anyone who makes a serious study of the life of Christ in the first four books of the New Testament (Matthew, Mark, Luke, John) quickly picks up the idea that Jesus' teachings were different from the official leaders of Judaism. He was, in every sense of the term, a radical revolutionary in their eyes, ultimately a threat to their system. In other words, He blew them away! That is evident when we read His now-famous "Sermon on the Mount" which is punctuated with a repeating of the same statement: "You have heard . . . but I say to you . . ." Time after time He addressed the teaching they had received from the Pharisees and then offered a fresh and much-needed alternative. Take, for example, prayer.

In those days prayer had degenerated in five specific areas.

1. Prayer became a formal exercise rather than free expression. There were stated prayers for all occasions. Prayer was liturgical, standardized, a cut-and-dried routine.

. . . certain faults had crept into the Jewish habits of prayer. It is to be noted that these faults are by no means peculiar to Jewish ideas of prayer; they can and do occur anywhere. And it is to be noted that they could only occur in a community where prayer was taken with the greatest seriousness. They are not the faults of neglect; they are the faults of misguided devotion. . . .

. . . Jewish liturgy supplied stated prayers for all occasions. There was hardly an event or a sight in life which had not its stated formula of prayer. There was prayer before and after each meal; there were prayers in connection with the light, the fire, the lightning, on seeing the new moon, comets, rain, tempest, at the sight of the sea, lakes, rivers, on receiving good news, on using new furniture, on entering or leaving a city. Everything had its prayer. Clearly there is something infinitely lovely here. It was the intention that every happening in life should be brought into the presence of God. But just because the prayers were so meticulously prescribed and stated, the whole system lent itself to formalism, and the tendency was for the prayers to slip off the tongue with very little meaning.[1]

2. Prayer was ritualistic, not spontaneous. There were set times to pray, much like the Muslims of today who bow toward Mecca at specific times daily. In Jesus' day the "required" hours were 9:00 A.M., 12 noon, and 3:00 P.M.. There were certain places to pray as well; the most preferred were the synagogues.

3. Prayers were long, filled with verbiage. It was actually believed that whoever was long in prayer was heard more readily by God. And the more flowery, the better. One well-known prayer had no less than sixteen adjectives preceding the name of God! There was this strange subconscious idea that whoever banged long and hard enough on the doors of heaven was granted God's attention.

4. There were repetitious words and phrases. We remember reading about this among Gentile idol-worshipers ("O Baal, hear us! O Baal, hear us!" in 1 Kings 18, for example), but by the first century the same tendency crept into the synagogue. Prayer led to an almost intoxication with words as those engaged in the practice, fell under the spell of meaningless repetition.

5. Praying became a cause for pride rather than the humble expressions of one in need. It was a legalistic "status symbol" to pray well. The religious system, when followed to the letter, led to an ostentatious public display with hands outstretched, palms up, head bowed, three times a day . . . out on a public street corner!

Is it any wonder prayer had lost its value? As it degenerated into an insignificant routine marked by overt hypocrisy and meaningless terms, coupled with a judgmental spirit, prayer hit the skids. Such high expectations that became impossible for the common person to achieve resulted in the entire act become a fleshly display proudly performed by the religious hot shots. This explains why our Lord took them to task in His immortal sermon. It also helps us understand why He says what He does about prayer and other religious attitudes in Matthew 6.

How Prayer Can Be Effective

Jesus makes three strong statements (all of them negative) as He suggests a plan to follow if we want a satisfying and God-honoring prayer life.

1. Don't be hypocritical.

"Beware of practicing your righteousness before men to be noticed by them; otherwise you have no reward with your Father who is in heaven.

"When therefore you give alms, do not sound a trumpet before you, as the hypocrites do in the synagogues and in the streets, that they may be honored by men. Truly I say to you, they have their reward in full.

"And when you pray, you are not to be as the hypocrites; for they love to stand and pray in the synagogues and on the street corners, in order to be seen by men. Truly I say to you, they have their reward in full.

"And whenever you fast, do not put on a gloomy face as the hypocrites do; for they neglect their appearance in order to be seen fasting by men. Truly I say to you, they have their reward in full' (Matt. 6:1-2, 5, 16).

Jesus reserved some of His strongest comments for hypocrisy. It is safe to say He *depised* it. The comment He repeats (for the sake of emphasis) is that those who do their thing to be seen get all the reward they will ever get *now*. He makes it clear there will be nothing gained later. Rather than making a cheap show of it, Jesus says:

"But you, when you pray, GO INTO YOUR INNER ROOM, AND WHEN YOU HAVE SHUT YOUR DOOR, pray to your Father who is in secret, and your Father who sees in secret will repay you" (Matt. 6:6).

Prayer is never something we do to be seen. It loses its whole purpose if it becomes a platform to impress others. It is a private act of devotion, not a public demonstration of piety. According to Jesus, it belongs in the closet of our lives, an act done in secret.

We looked previously at Daniel in the chapter on integrity. Remember the decision of the king and how Daniel continued to pray three times a day? Do you recall where he went to pray?

Now when Daniel knew that the document was signed, he entered his house (now in his roof chamber he had windows open toward Jerusalem); and he continued kneeling on his knees three times a day, praying and giving thanks before His God, as he had been doing previously (Dan. 6:10).

No big public demonstration, just a quiet retreat to his room where he met, in secret, with his Lord. And you'll note he had done it many times before. This was a regular habit with Daniel. The absence of hypocrisy impresses us.

2. Don't use a lot of repetition.

"And when you are praying, do not use meaningless repetition, as the Gentiles do, for they suppose that they will be heard for their many words.

"Therefore do not be like them; for your Father knows what you need, before you ask Him" (Matt. 6:7–8).

Even a casual reading of these words will lead us to realize that Christ never saw prayer as pleading or begging or hammering away at the throne of God. No, the Father knows His children, He knows what we need. Therefore, there is no reason to think that connecting with Him requires special words excessively repeated.

Now, let me be even more specific. Today, just as in that day, there is no part of the Christian life more in need of freshness and spontaneity than prayer. Whether it is prayer from a pulpit or a church group meeting for prayer or prayer before meals or before a meeting gets started, meaningless repetition abounds! Tired, overworked words and phrases keep returning. Break loose from those old bromides! For starters, I dare you to pray without using *"bless"* or *"lead, guide, and direct"* or *"help so-and-so"* or *"Thy will"* or *"each and every"* or any number of those institutionalized, galvanized terms. I dare you!

On one occasion, evangelist Dwight L. Moody had been the recipient of numerous benefits from the Lord. In his abundance, he was suddenly seized with the realization that his heavenly Father was showering on him almost more than he could take. Encouraged and overwhelmed, he paused to pray. With great volume he simply stated, "Stop, God!" Now *that's* spontaneous. It is also a beautiful change from, "Eternal, almighty, gracious Father of all good things, Thy hand hath abundantly and gloriously supplied our deepest needs. How blessed and thankful we are to come to Thee and declare unto Thee . . .," and on and on and on, grinding into snore city. Can you imagine one of your kids approaching you like that? I'll tell you, if one of mine did, I would stare directly at him and wonder, "What in the world is wrong?"

Listen to brand new Christians pray. You know, those who are fresh from birth who haven't learned "how to do it" yet, thank goodness. They talk to God like He's their friend, they use street terms anybody can understand, and they occasionally laugh or cry. It's just beautiful. Another tip that may add a new dimension to your prayer is the use of music. Sing to your God. We've started doing more and more of that in our church family . . . even the pastoral prayer often includes a chorus of worship. Or when you have prayer before your meals, have each person pray for one thing or pray for the specific food, naming the vegetables or the meat dish. Occasionally, our family will spend a few minutes before supper telling one thing that happened that day, then the one who prays mentions two or three of those matters before God. The point is clear: Guard against meaningless verbiage.

3. Don't harbor anything against another.

"For if you forgive men for their transgressions, your heavenly Father will also forgive you.

"But if you do not forgive men, then your Father will not forgive your transgressions" (Matt. 6:14–15).

Before God will forgive us, we must be certain that our conscience is clear. A familiar verse from the Psalms frequently pops into my mind when I begin to pray: "If I regard wickedness in my heart, The Lord will not hear" (Ps. 66:18). If I want cleansing, I must be certain things are right between myself and others.

Prayer includes praise and thanksgiving, intercession and petition, meditation, and confession. In prayer we focus fully on our God, we capture renewed zeal to continue, a wider view of life, increased determination to endure. As we strengthen our grip on prayer, it is amazing how it alters our whole perspective.

The late Dr. Donald Barnhouse, greatly admired American pastor and author of the last generation, once came to the pulpit and made a statement that stunned his congregation: "*Prayer changes nothing!*" You could've heard a pin drop in that packed Sunday worship service in Philadelphia. His comment, of course, was designed to make Christians realize that God is sovereignly in charge of everything. Our times are literally in His hands. No puny human being by uttering a few words in prayer takes charge of events and changes them. God does the shaping, the changing, it is He who is in control. Barnhouse was correct . . . except in one minor detail. Prayer changes *me*. When you and I pray, *we* change, and that is one of the major reasons prayer is such a therapy that counteracts anxiety.

A FINAL ENCOURAGEMENT

Prayer was never intended to make us feel guilty. It was never intended to be a verbal marathon for only the initiated . . . no secret-code talk for the clergy or a public display of piety. None of that. Real prayer—the kind of prayer Jesus mentioned and modeled—is realistic, spontaneous, down-to-earth communication with the living Lord that results in a relief of personal anxiety and a calm assurance that our God is in full control of our circumstances.

I encourage you to start over. Form some brand new habits as you fight off the old tendency to slump back into meaningless jargon. Get a fresh, new grip on prayer. It is essential for survival.

Many years ago I decided to do that very thing. I was fed up with empty words and pharisaical phrases. In my search for new meaning, I came across this brief description of prayer, which I set on my desk and carried in the front of my Bible for years. I cannot locate the book from which it was taken, but I do know the author, a seventeenth-century Roman Catholic Frenchman named François Fenelon. Although written centuries ago, it has an undeniable ring of relevance:

Tell God all that is in your heart, as one unloads one's heart, its pleasures and its pains, to a dear friend. Tell Him your troubles, that He may comfort you; tell Him your joys, that He may sober them; tell Him your longings, that he may purify them; tell Him your dislikes, that He may help you to conquer them; talk to Him of your temptations, that He may shield you from them; show Him the wounds of your heart, that He may heal them; lay bare your indifference to good, your depraved tastes for evil, your instability. Tell Him how self-love makes you unjust to others, how vanity tempts you to be insincere, how pride disguises you to yourself and to others.

If you thus pour out all your weaknesses, needs, troubles, there will be no lack of what to say. You will never exhaust the subject. It is continually being renewed. People who have no secrets from each other never want for subjects of conversation. They do not weigh their words, for there is nothing to be held back; neither do they seek for something to say. They talk out of the abundance of the heart, without consideration they say just what they think. Blessed are they who attain to such familiar, unreserved intercourse with God.

DISCUSSION QUESTIONS AND SUGGESTIONS TO HELP YOU STRENGTHEN YOUR GRIP ON PRAYER

• Give your own definition of prayer . . . without the aid of a dictionary. Describe the things that come to your mind as you think of the struggles *you* have with prayer. Try to be very candid and open.

• We looked into several scriptures in this chapter. Can you recall one or two passages that "came alive" for you? What stands out as one of the most helpful insights you received in dealing with prayer? Explain why it was important to you.

• This may take some time, so before you bite into it, make sure you have more than a few minutes. Does prayer itself actually change anything? Try to be biblical in your answer. If "yes" is your answer, describe how you arrived at that response. If "no" then *why pray?* Think hard.

• How can a person break the habit of using meaningless words and phrases in prayer? Why do we cling to these so tightly?

• Let's do some honest evaluation of our own prayer lives. Share a few of the things that have helped you overcome the tendency to put off prayer. Talk also about a recent difficulty you were facing in which prayer helped you through. Take the time to describe how the burden was shifted from your shoulders to the Lord's. Describe the difference in your emotions once the anxiety was shifted from your shoulders to the Lord's.

• Finally, give some thought and time to the value of praise and thanksgiving. How can these two expressions become a part of your day on a regular basis? Before ending this discussion, spend some time in prayer. Make it more meaningful by speaking in conversational tones and by talking with God as with a close, personal friend . . . something like Fenelon mentions in his piece on prayer.

10

Strengthening Your Grip on Leisure

This chapter builds upon the principles I have dealt with in the booklet *Leisure*[1] and has one major objective: to help you enjoy yourself, your life, and your Lord more than ever without feeling guilty or unspiritual. Yes, you read correctly . . . *enjoy* is the word I used.

In our work-worshiping world, learning to enjoy life is no small task. Many have cultivated such an unrealistic standard of high-level achievement that a neurotic compulsion to perform, to compete, to produce, to accomplish the maximum has taken control of their lives. Getting with it twelve to fifteen hours a day is now the rule rather than the exception. Enough is no longer enough.

And I'll be honest with you, those who need to strengthen their grip on leisure as much as anyone I come into contact with are Christians—especially vocational Christian workers. I often think of this segment of society when I see the familiar Datsun commercials that shout, "We are driven!"

How many Christian leaders can you name who really take sufficient time to relax? More often than not, we hear them boast about not having vacationed for several years. Or being too busy to take time to get away to rest and repair, even for a day or two.

The Christian's primary source of identity is fast becoming his or her work. Soon after giving someone our name, we describe what we "do for a living." And to add the ultimate pressure, we operate under the old banner, "You aren't really serving the Lord unless you consistently push yourself to the point of fatigue." It's the tired yet proud-sounding *burn-out-rather-than-rust-out* line. Either way we're "out," which never has made much sense to me.

Let's face it, as essential as leisure is to our physical, emotional, and mental health, we are strangers to it. We would rather hear our family members and other people tell us we shouldn't work so hard than face the possibility of someone thinking we lacked diligence. For many of us raised under the work ethic of our parents, fatigue and burn-out are proofs of the deepest level of commitment, to which I say—*hogwash!*

This chapter offers a different rationale. It says not only, "It's okay to relax," but also, "It's absolutely essential." Without encouraging laziness or irresponsibility, I want to open your eyes to the fact that you can enjoy times of leisure and still be efficient. In fact, you'll be *more* efficient.

And so to all workaholics and churchaholics . . . overcommitted, hassled, grim-faced, tight-lipped believers . . . plowing through responsibilities like an overloaded freight train under a full head of steam, I invite you to slow down, find a siding, and take a break. Pour yourself a refreshing glass of iced tea or a cup of coffee, kick off your shoes, prop your feet up, and take time to digest these pages slowly, quietly. If you are in a hurry to get somewhere, close the book and come back to it later. The counsel you're about to receive is too important to glance over on the run.

IS FATIGUE NEXT TO GODLINESS?

Strangely, the one thing we need is often the last thing we consider. We've been programmed to think that fatigue is next to godliness. That the more exhausted we are (and look!), the more committed we are to spiritual things and the more we earn God's smile of approval. We bury all thoughts of enjoying life . . . for those who are genuinely dedicated Christians are those who work, work, work. And preferably, with great intensity. As a result, we have become a generation of people who worship our work . . . who work at our play . . . and who play at our worship.

Hold it! Who wrote that rule! Why have we bought that philosophy? Whatever possessed someone to make such a statement? How did we ever get caught in that maddening undertow?

I challenge you to support it from the Scriptures. Start with the life (and *lifestyle*) of Jesus Christ and try to find a trace of corroborating evidence that He embraced that theory. Some will be surprised to know that there is not one reference in the entire New Testament saying (or even implying) that Jesus intensely worked and labored in an occupation to the point of emotional exhaustion. No, but there are several times when we are told he deliberately took a break. He got away from the demands of the public and enjoyed periods of relaxation with His disciples. I'm not saying He rambled through His ministry in an aimless, halfhearted fashion. Not at all! But neither did He come anywhere near an ulcer. Never once do we find Him in a frenzy.

According to Mark 6:30–34, Jesus purposely sought relief from the hurried pace of ministering to others and advised his apostles to do the same.

> The apostles gathered around Jesus and reported to him all they had done and taught. Then, because so many people were coming and going that they did not even have a chance to eat, he said to them, "Come with me by yourselves to a quiet place and get some rest."
> So they went away by themselves in a boat to a solitary place (Mark 6:30–32, NIV).

His was a life of beautiful balance. He accomplished everything the Father sent Him to do. Everything. And He did it without ignoring those essential times of restful leisure. If that is the way *He* lived, then it makes good sense that that is the way we, too, must learn to live. If you have formed the habit of overwork and you haven't cultivated the ability to take a break and relax, these things may appear difficult to you, but they are not impossible.

THE PLACE TO START: GOD

Since most humans suffer from a lack of balance in their lives, our best counsel on this subject comes from God's Word, the Bible. In that Book, there appears a most unusual command: "Be imitators of God, therefore, as dearly loved children . . ." (Eph. 5:1, NIV). Maybe you never realized such a statement was in the Bible. What a strange command: "Be imitators of God"!

The Greek term translated "be imitators" is *mimeomai*, from which we get the English word *mimic*. One reliable scholar, W. E. Vine, says that this verb "is always used in exhortations, and always in the continuous tense, suggesting a constant habit or practice."[2]

In other words, this is neither a passing thought nor a once-in-a-blue-moon experience. The practice of our being people who "mimic God" is to become our daily habit. We are to do what He does. Respond to life as He responds. Emulate similar traits. Model His style.

But to do that, to be an imitator of God, requires that we come to terms with the value of quietness, slowing down, coming apart from the noise and speed of today's pace and broadening our lives with a view of the eternal reach of time. It means saying no to more and more activities that increase the speed of our squirrel cage. Knowing God *requires* that we "be still" (Ps. 46:10).

It means if I'm a pastor, I do more than tend the sheep. I must, or I ultimately begin to walk dangerously near the ragged edge of emotional disintegration. The same applies if I'm a businessman or a homemaker. It means I refuse to be driven by guilt and unrealistic demands (mine or others). To be God-mimics, we must begin to realize that leisure is not a take-it-or-leave-it luxury. It is necessary for survival.

Please understand that leisure is more than idle free time not devoted to paid occupation. Some of the most valuable work done in the world has been done at leisure . . . and never paid for in cash. Leisure is free activity. Labor is compulsory activity. In leisure, we do what we like, but in labor we do what we must. In our labor we meet the objective needs and demands of others—our employer, the public, people who are impacted by and through our work. But in leisure we scratch the subjective itches within ourselves. In leisure our minds are liberated from the immediate, the necessary. As we incorporate leisure into the mainstream of our world, we gain perspective. We lift ourselves above the grit and grind of mere existence.

Interestingly, *leisure* comes from the Latin word *licere*, which means "to be permitted." If we are ever going to inculcate leisure into our otherwise utilitarian routine, we must give ourselves permission to do so. God did (as we shall see) and so must we if we intend to mimic Him.

But this calls for a closer look. We need some specific guidelines on which to focus that will help us imitate God and at the same time "permit" us to cultivate leisure in our lives.

FOUR GUIDELINES FROM GENESIS

If we are to imitate God as a daily habit of life, we need to nail down some specific guidelines. It occurred to me recently that an excellent place to locate those specifics in the Scriptures would be the first place He reveals Himself to us—the book of Genesis, especially the first two chapters.

I want to encourage you to read this familiar section. You will discover that God is involved in four activities:

- He creates
- He communicates
- He rests
- He relates

Let's limit our thoughts to those four specifics. Each one fits perfectly into the cultivation of leisure. They form some excellent guidelines to follow as we begin to develop an accurate concept of leisure.

Creativity

First and foremost, God is engaged in the act of creation, according to Genesis 1 and 2. He begins with that which is "formless and void" (1:2), lacking meaning, beauty, and purpose.

He takes time to create with His own hands. In His mind are thoughts of a universe, indescribably beautiful. He mentally pictures vast expanses of land masses, deep oceans, colorful vegetation, an almost endless variety of living creatures . . . not to mention the stars, the planets, and the perfect motion and rhythm of all those celestial bodies. Finally, He creates mankind with a body and mind that still amazes students of physiology and psychology.

As He created He added the music, harmony, and coordination of movement—the miracle of birth and growth, the full spectrum of colors, sights, and sounds. He cared about details—from snowflakes to butterfly wings, from pansy petals to the bones of bodies, from the microscopic world of biology to the telescopic world of astronomy.

In doing all this, He set the pace. He, the first to create, announced its significance.

If I may suddenly jump forward to today, let me ask a penetrating question: *Are you taking time to create?* Obviously, you cannot create a solar system or bring forth an ocean from nothing, but you *can* make things with your hands. You can write things with your pen . . . or paint things with your brush . . . or compose things, using your piano or guitar or harmonica. You can dream things with your mind and then try to invent them or draw them or, in other ways, bring them to reality through some creative process.

You hold in your hand a book. In the book are numerous chapters filled with thousands of words. There was a time when none of these things existed. It all began as a dream, an idea that was mine which, by the way, occurred in one of my leisure moments. I gave myself permission to relax for several days on vacation, and the idea of this book emerged and began to take shape. There was no required or forced structure. It has been almost entirely a creative experience. One of my most enjoyable leisure activities is writing . . . something I would never have thought possible twenty years ago. But now I realize I've had this itch inside me most of my life. It wasn't until I began to let it out freely and fully that a whole new dimension of my life was added. And it is *such* fun!

All children have built-in creativity. Just look at the things they make and do (and say!) on their own. There is an enormous wealth of creative powers in the mind of a child. Walt Disney believed that and often spoke of it. But if we aren't careful, we adults will squelch it. We'll fail to encourage it or cultivate it or even let it out of its cage. Why? Well, it takes a little extra time and it often costs some money. I should add that it tends to be messy. Not many really creative people—in the process of creating—keep everything neat, picked up, and in its place.

There's a good motto to remember if you're determined to encourage and cultivate creativity:

A CREATIVE MESS
   . . . IS BETTER THAN TIDY IDLENESS.

If we are going to imitate God, we will need to find creative outlets in times of leisure. Yours may be music or one of the arts. It may be in the area of interior design. My wife enjoys house plants and quilting. Yours may be gardening or landscaping projects, woodworking or brick and stone work around the house. We had our patio enclosed during the remodeling of our house. Both the bricklayer and the carpenter who did the work employed a great deal of creativity in their skills. It's an added plus when we can create and even get paid for it! But regardless, our creativity needs expression.

If you intend to strengthen your grip on leisure, give some thought to how you might utilize your creativity in the process. God did and so can we.

Communication

If you read the Genesis account of creation rather carefully, you'll see that interspersed within the creative week were times of communication. He made things, then said, "That's good." After the sixth day, His evaluation increased to, "That's *very* good."

The Godhead communicated prior to the creation of man, you may recall:

> Then God said, "Let us make man in our image, according to our likeness; and let them rule over the fish of the sea and over the birds of the sky and over the cattle and over all the earth, and over every creeping thing that creeps on the earth" (Gen. 1:26).

And after God created man, the highest form of life on earth, He communicated with him.

> And God blessed them; and God said to them, "Be fruitful and multiply, and fill the earth, and subdue it; and rule over the fish of the sea and over the birds of the sky, and over every living thing that moves on the earth."
> Then God said, "Behold, I have given you every plant yielding seed that is on the surface of all the earth, and every tree which has fruit yielding seed; it shall be food for you;
> and to every beast of the earth and to every bird of the sky and to every thing that moves on the earth which has life, I have given green plant for food"; and it was so (Gen. 1:28–30).

Again, I'd like to apply this to our times. Initially, in leisure, we take time to communicate with ourselves (as God did) and affirm ourselves, "That's good . . . that's *very* good." Do you do that? Most of us are good at criticizing ourselves and finding fault with what we have done or failed to do. I'd like to suggest an alternate plan—spend some of your leisure time finding pleasure and satisfaction in what you have done as well as in who and what you are. Sound too liberal? Why? Since when is a good self-esteem liberal?

There are times we need to tell ourselves, "Good job!" when we know that is true. I smile as I write this to you, but I must confess that occasionally I even say to myself, "That's *very* good, Swindoll," when I am pleased with something I've done. That isn't conceited pride, my friend. It's acknowledging in words the feelings of the heart. The Lord knows that we hear more than enough internal put-downs! Communicating in times of leisure includes self-affirmation, acknowledging, of course, that God ultimately gets the glory. After all, He's the One who makes the whole experience possible.

Alan McGinnis, in his fine book *The Friendship Factor*, views affirmation so significant he devotes an entire chapter to the subject. Appropriately, he entitles it "The Art of Affirmation,"[3] for it is indeed an art practiced by few and mastered by even fewer.

Leisure also includes times of communicating with others who are important to us, just as God the Creator did with man the creature. Unless we are careful, the speed of our lives will reduce our communication to gutteral grunts, frowns, stares, and unspoken assumptions. Be honest. Has that begun to happen? Sometimes our children mirror the truth of our pace.

I vividly remember several years ago being caught in the backwash of too many commitments in too few days. It wasn't long before I was snapping at my wife and our children, choking down my food at mealtimes, and feeling irritated at those unexpected interruptions through the day. Before long, things around our home started reflecting the pattern of my hurry-up style. It was becoming unbearable. I distinctly recall after supper one evening the words of our younger daughter Colleen. She wanted to tell me about something important that had happened to her at school that day. She hurriedly began, "Daddy, I wanna tell you somethin' andIwilltellyoureallyfast."

Suddenly realizing her frustration, I answered in a rather deliberate manner, "Honey, you can tell me . . . and you don't have to tell me *really fast*. Say it slowly."

I'll never forget her answer: "Then *listen* slowly."

I had taken no time for leisure. Not even at meals with my family. Everything was up tight. I hit the floor running at breakneck speed. And guess what began to break down? You're right, those all-important communication lines.

God not only made man, He talked with him, He listened to him. He considered His creature valuable enough to spend time with, to respond to. It took time, but He believed it was justified. As we mimic Him, we must do the same.

There are entire books written on communication, so I'll not be so foolish as to think I can develop the subject adequately here. I only want to emphasize its importance. It is *imperative* that we understand that without adding sufficient leisure time to our schedule for meaningful communication, a relationship with those who are important to us will disintegrate faster than we can keep it in repair.

Take time to listen, to feel, to respond. In doing so, we "imitate God" in our leisure. And the rewards are far reaching, so very satisfying.

Rest

Following the sixth day of creation, the Lord God deliberately stopped working. Do you remember the Genesis account?

> Thus the heavens and the earth were completed, and all their hosts.
> And by the seventh day God completed His work which He had done; and He rested on the seventh day from all His work which He had done.
> Then God blessed the seventh day and sanctified it, because in it He rested from all His work which God had created and made (Gen. 2:1–3).

He rested. Take special note of that. It wasn't that there was nothing else He could have done. It certainly wasn't because He was exhausted—omnipotence never gets tired! He hadn't run out of ideas, for omniscience knows no mental limitations. He could easily have made many more worlds, created an infinite number of other forms of life, and provided multiple millions of galaxies beyond what He did.

But He didn't. He stopped.

He spent an entire day resting. In fact, He "blessed the seventh day and sanctified it," something He did not do on the other six days. He marked this one day off as extremely special. It was like no other. Sounds to me like He made the day on which He rested a "priority" period of time.

If we intend to imitate God, we, too, will need to make rest a priority.

- A good night's rest on a regular basis;
- A full day's rest at least once a week;
- Moments of rest snatched here and there during the week;
- Vacation times of rest for the refreshment and repair of both body and soul;
- A release from the fierce grip of intense stress brought on by daily hassles.

I feel so strongly about declaring war on personal anxiety that I have written an entire booklet dealing specifically with stress[4] and the toll it can take on our lives. Several things contribute to our lack of inner rest:

- A poorly developed sense of humor;
- Focusing more on what we don't have rather than on what we *do* have;
- Failure to give play, fun, rest, and leisure a proper place of dignity;
- Our strong tendency to compete and compare, leading to a wholesale dissatisfaction with things as they are;
- Our continual preoccupation with getting more;
- Self-imposed guilt . . . unrealistic expectations;
- An "all-work-and-no-play-will-make-me-happy" philosophy of life.

And the result? Look around. Stretched across most faces of Americans driving to and from work is boredom. Not fulfillment. Not a deep sense of satisfaction. Not even a smile of quiet contentment.

Even though our work-week is decreasing and our weekend time is increasing, our country lacks inner peace. External leisure does not guarantee internal rest, does it?

For sure, our nation believes in the *theory* of leisure. I heard over a television documentary that we spend more on recreation each year than we do on education, construction of new homes or national defense. The latest figures I've read show that Americans will spend more than $300 billion on leisure products and activities by 1985. But I question the chewing gum ads that tell us that if we double our pleasure, we'll automatically double our fun. Mental hospitals remain overcrowded . . . and most of the patients are not what we would call senior citizens.

Time on our hands, we have. But we don't have meaningful "rest" in a biblical sense of the term.

I suggest that you and I do more than cluck our tongues and wag our heads at the problem. That helps nobody! Our greatest contribution to the answer is a radical break with the rut of normal living. My good friend, Tim Hansel of Summit Expedition, suggests taking different kinds of vacations: midget vacations or mini-vacations (two minutes or more!) or, if you're able, maxi-vacations . . . or even, if possible, *super*-maxi-vacations where you take time to enjoy extended leisure. He calls it the "Year of Adventure" where we try our hand at sailing or rock climbing, skydiving, or learning karate. Or whatever.

Change your routine, my friend. Blow the dust of boredom off your schedule. Shake yourself loose and get a taste of fresh life. Here are several suggestions for adding "zip" to your leisure.

• Begin jogging and/or an exercise program.

• Buy a bicycle and start pedaling two to three miles each day.

• Get an album or two of your favorite music and drink in the sounds as you lie flat on your back.

• Enroll in a local art class and try your hand at painting.

• If you have the money, travel abroad.

• Build a small sailboat with a friend.

• Take up a new hobby, like photography or ceramics or making artificial floral arrangements.

• Start writing letters of encouragement to people you appreciate.

• Make something out of wood with your own hands.

• Dig around in the soil, plant a small garden, and watch God cooperate with your efforts.

• Take a gourmet cooking class.

• Spend some time at the library and pick up several good books on subjects or people of interest to you . . . then sit back, munch on an apple, and read, read, read.

• Plan a camping or backpacking trip soon with one of your children, your mate, or your friend and spend a night or two out under the stars.

• Pull out all those old snapshots, sort them, and put them into albums.

- Write some poetry.
- Visit a museum or zoo in your area.
- By the way, don't forget the simple pleasures of life. Take time to enjoy the beauty of a sunrise or sunset . . . smell the roses along the way.

Broaden your world. Kick away the thick, brick walls of tradition. Silence the old enemy Guilt, who will sing his same old tune in your ears. And work on that deep crease between your eyes. Look for things to laugh at . . . and *laugh out loud.* It's biblical! "A joyful heart is good medicine, But a broken spirit dries up the bones" (Prov. 17:22).

Comedian Bill Cosby is right. There's a smile down inside of you that is just dying to come out! It won't until you give yourself permission. Take time to smile. Rest releases humor.

One more glance at the Genesis passage will be worth our effort. Remember where we've been?

- God created . . . in leisure; so do *we.*
- God communicated . . . in leisure; so must *we.*
- God rested . . . in leisure; so will *we.*

But He also *related* with the man and woman He made.

Relating

The passage in Genesis 2 is so familiar. After God made man, He observed a need inside that life, a nagging loneliness that Adam couldn't shake. "Then the Lord God said, 'It is not good for man to be alone; I will make him a helper suitable for him'" (Gen. 2:18). As a fulfillment to the promise to help Adam with his need for companionship, God got involved.

> So the Lord God caused a deep sleep to fall upon the man, and he slept; then He took one of his ribs, and closed up the flesh at that place.
> And the Lord God fashioned into a woman the rib which He had taken from the man, and brought her to the man (Gen. 2:21–22).

Later we read that the Lord came to relate to His creatures "in the cool of the day" (Gen. 3:8). I take it that such a time must have been a common practice between the Lord God and His friends, Adam and Eve.

He considered them valuable, so the infinite Creator-God took time to relate to the couple in the Garden of Eden. He got personally involved. He observed their needs. He carved out time and went to the trouble to do *whatever* was necessary to help them. He cultivated that friendship. He saw it as a worthwhile activity.

I was amused at a cartoon that appeared in a magazine. It was a picture of a thief wearing one of those "Lone Ranger" masks. His gun was pointed toward his frightened victim as he yelled: "Okay, gimme all your valuables!"

The victim began stuffing into the sack all his *friends.*

How valuable to *you* are relationships? If you have trouble answering that, I'll help you decide. Stop and think back over the past month or two. How much of your leisure have you spent developing and enjoying relationships?

Jesus, God's Son, certainly considered the relationship He had with His disciples worth His time. They spent literally *hours* together. They ate together and wept together, and I'm sure they must have laughed together as well. Being God, He really didn't "need" those men. He certainly did not need the hassle they created on occasion. But He loved those twelve men. He believed in them. They had a special relationship—a lot like Paul, Silas, and Timothy; David and Jonathan; Barnabas and John Mark; Elijah and Elisha.

As the poet Samuel Taylor Coleridge once put it, "Friendship is a sheltering tree."[5] How very true! Whatever leisure time we are able to invest in relationships is time well spent. And when we do, let's keep in mind we are "imitating God," for His Son certainly did.

HOW TO IMPLEMENT LEISURE

The bottom line of all this, of course, is actually *doing* it. We can nod in agreement until we get a whiplash, but our greatest need is not inclination; it's demonstration.

Here are two suggestions that will help.

1. *Deliberately stop being absorbed with the endless details of life.* Our Savior said it straight when He declared that we cannot, at the same time, serve both God *and* man. But we try so hard! If Jesus' words from Matthew 6 are saying anything, they are saying, "Don't sweat the things only God can handle." Each morning, deliberately decide not to allow worry to steal your time and block your leisure.

2. *Consciously start taking time for leisure.* After God put the world together, He rested. We are commanded to imitate Him.

For rest to occur in *our* lives, Christ Jesus must be in proper focus. He must be in His rightful place before we can ever expect to get *our* world to fall in place.

A bone-weary father dragged into his home dog tired late one evening. It had been one of those unbelievable days of pressure, deadlines, and demands. He looked forward to a time of relaxation and quietness. Exhausted, he picked up the evening paper and headed for his favorite easy chair by the fireplace. About the time he got his shoes untied, *plop!* into his lap dropped his five-year-old son with an excited grin on his face.

"Hi, Dad, . . . let's play!"

He loved his boy dearly, but his need for a little time all alone to repair and think was, for the moment, a greater need than time with Junior. But how could he maneuver it?

There had been a recent moon probe and the newspaper carried a huge picture of earth. With a flash of much-needed insight, the dad asked his boy to bring a pair of scissors and some transparent tape. Quickly, he cut the picture of earth into various shapes and sizes, then handed the pile of homemade jigsaw puzzle pieces to him.

"You tape it all back together, Danny, then come on back and we'll play, okay?"

Off scampered the child to his room as dad breathed a sigh of relief. But in less than ten minutes the boy bounded back with everything taped perfectly in place. Stunned, the father asked: "How'd you do it so fast, Son?"

"Aw, it was easy, Daddy. You see, there is this picture of a man on the back of the sheet . . . and when you put the man together, the world comes together."

And so it is in life. When we put the Man in His rightful place, it's amazing what happens to our world. And, more importantly, what happens to *us*. I can assure you that in the final analysis of your life—when you stop some day and look back on the way you spent your time—your use of leisure will be far more important than those hours you spent with your nose to the grindstone. Don't wait until it's too late to enjoy life.

Live it up *now*. Throw yourself into it with abandonment. Get up out of the rut of work long enough to see that there is more to life than a job and a paycheck. You'll never be the same!

Maybe it would help to pray right now. Allow me to express the feelings of my heart, which may reflect many of your own thoughts.

Lord, our God:

It is true that we are spending our entire life preparing to live indefinitely. Habits and fears, guilt and discontentment have teamed up against us and pinned us to the mat of monotony.

We find ourselves running in a tight radius, like a rat in a sewer pipe. Our world has become too small, too routine, too grim. Although busy, we have to confess that a nagging sense of boredom has now boarded our ship in this journey of life. We are enduring the scenery instead of enjoying it. We have really begun to take ourselves too seriously.

We desire change . . . a cure from this terminal illness of dullness and routine.

We are sheep, not rats. You have made us whole people who are free to think and relax in leisure, not slaves chained to a schedule. Enable us to break loose! Show us ways to do that. Give us the courage to start today and the hope we need to stay fresh tomorrow . . . and the next day and the next.

Bring the child out from within us. Introduce us again to the sounds and smells and sights of this beautiful world you wrapped around us. Convince us of the importance of friendships and laughter and wonder. Put our world back together.

May we become people like Your Son, committed to the highest standard of excellence and devotion to Your will, yet easy to live with, at peace within, taking time for leisure.

In His strong name we pray,

Amen.

DISCUSSION QUESTIONS AND SUGGESTIONS TO HELP YOU
STRENGTHEN YOUR GRIP ON LEISURE

• Without the aid of a dictionary, define *leisure*. Afterwards, discuss what there is about our culture that makes us view leisure as either an enemy of the diligent or a luxury reserved especially for the rich. Why is that false?

• Do a little scriptural survey. Locate three or four verses or passages that lend support to the need for leisure. After reading each one, personalize it by relating it to something occurring today—preferably either in your own life or in your home situation.

• Think deeply about this before answering. What is the reason for leisure? Is it true that its basic purpose, its most primary function, is to provide relief from work? Is the point of leisure restoration . . . a pick-me-up time of relaxation?

• Do you agree with this statement?

Most middle-class Americans tend to worship their work, to work at their play, and to play at their worship. As a result, their meanings and values are distorted. Their relationships disintegrate faster than they can keep them in repair and their lifestyles resemble a cast of characters in search of a plot" (Gordon Dahl).

If you do agree, express your reaction. If not, why not?

• Leisure, stillness, silence, and rest go together. They belong to one another. They fit. In light of this, substitute the words *Have leisure* for *Be still* in Psalm 46:10. And in place of the repeated term *rest* in Hebrews 4:1–11, try using the word *leisure*. Talk about how this broadens the concept of leisure.

• Finally, sit quietly and evaluate the normal level of your intensity. Are you "always on the go"? Does it give you strokes to have people say you're a workaholic? Is it hard for you to be quiet, to be alone and still? Pray about this.

11

Strengthening Your Grip on Missions

My first serious encounter with God's world program occurred a few miles from Alcatraz.

No, I wasn't at church or in a seminary chapel surrounded by moving, melodic strains of Bach on an enormous pipe organ. I did not feel lifted up to glory by huge heavenly arms, giving me a panoramic view of this planet, nor was there a strange cloud formation, like divine skywriting, spelling out "Go overseas. Be a missionary!" I never saw an angel pointing at me like the old patriotic image of Uncle Sam, saying, "I want you." No, none of that. From start to finish, there was absolutely *nothing* religious about the entire episode. To be candid with you, I didn't like God very much at the time. I felt He had let me down after I had counted on Him to help me out.

This needs a little explanation. It was back in the latter half of the 1950s— 1957 to be exact. I had been married for less than two years. I had been deferred from military service while I finished my schooling, but time was up. The hot breath of the United States Defense Department was hitting the back of my neck, and it wasn't going to be long before my exemption card would be replaced with a 1-A draft card. The question was not would I go, but which branch would I choose. In those days, one's military service was not an option.

All those Navy posters "Join the Navy and See the World" had no appeal. Being married, I had no interest in seeing the world. I just wanted to do my duty, have my wife with me throughout the time, and get it over with. Because the Marine Corps recruiting officer promised me that I would have nothing to worry about ("No chance you'll go abroad, young man") and because he assured me when it was all behind me I'd have something to look back on with pride, I enlisted in the Corps. Some of you veterans are smiling right now.

Throughout boot camp, before I knew where my wife and I would be stationed, I prayed that God would fulfill my desire that I'd be in a stateside area. By the way, I also prayed that I would survive boot camp. Both seemed pretty shaky at the time. Well, less than six months later both prayers were granted . . . initially, that is.

We set up housekeeping in a quaint little apartment in Daly City, California. My first (I hoped my *only*) military assignment was 100 Harrison Street, downtown San Francisco. Great duty! I had been the envy of my entire company in our Advanced Infantry Regiment at Camp Pendleton a few weeks earlier when all of us received our orders. Some guys were sent to Barstow, others to Twenty-Nine Palms—both lovely, picturesque spots in the middle of the Mohave Desert. A few were shipped immediately overseas to an infantry or tank outfit (ugh!) in some jungle or wilderness region. Not me, pal. "Open up those golden gates, San Francisco, here I come." And there we stayed. It was just delightful . . . for a few months.

And then one foggy afternoon as I was checking out for the day, a letter was pressed into my hand. Because it looked like another governmental form letter, I never bothered to open it until I parked my car on a hill across the street from the place where my wife was employed. I slit open the envelope, unfolded the letter, *and had my first serious encounter with world missions.* It was from Washington, D.C., alerting me to the fact that I was being transferred to Okinawa . . . and that it would not be possible for me to bring my wife—"Against Marine Corps policy." I sat there, stunned. An enormous knot in my throat made me gag.

One word burned itself into the pit of my stomach—Okinawa—"The Rock." Ironically, I looked up through tears and in the distance I saw Alcatraz. It was a grim yet timely reminder that I might think twice before going AWOL! There was no escape. That's why I felt let down by God. Ripped off might be a better way to put it. I was confused, resentful, disillusioned about the whole thing.

Within weeks I was back at Camp Pendleton, this time terribly despondent. I was alone in a staging regiment, being made ready for overseas duty. There were dozens of innoculations, classes, and briefing sessions, mixed with long, lonely hours of time on my hands. I visited my older brother Orville and his wife in Pasadena one weekend. As I got on the bus to return to the base one grey Sunday evening, he handed me a book that was destined to change my attitude, my future, my perspective, my career . . . my entire life—*Through Gates of Splendor.*[1] It was the true story of the martyrdom of five young missionaries who were attempting to reach and win the tribe of Auca Indians in the interior of Ecuador. A lady I had never heard of back then was the author, Elisabeth Elliot, one of the five widows.

As that old Greyhound bus rumbled along Highway 5 toward Oceanside and the rain blew across my window, I devoured the book, page after page. I must say, for the first time I (1) began to tolerate the possibility that my transfer overseas might have been arranged by God, and (2) that God's world program might somehow include me. *Me, of all people!* You really cannot imagine what foreign thoughts those were. Looking back, however, it is so obvious, so clear.

In my broken, desperate, lonely, inescapable situation, God showed me a world much bigger than my own. Through each one of those 256 pages, He got more and more of my attention. Chapter by chapter I released more and more of my selfish territory. He scaled the walls I had built and sealed off with the words "Private Property." As I mentioned in chapter 7 on discipleship, I was a Christian, but I had made certain that none of that would get out of hand! Little did I realize what a wedge this book would drive into my self-serving, well-sealed, do-not-disturb lifestyle. I realize now that God timed everything perfectly. Without His forceful plan to get me overseas, I would never have caught His vision of an entire world without Christ. Never!

A Visit with a Prophet in the Time Tunnel

Maybe it was a similar situation with young Isaiah. Twenty-seven centuries ago this young aristocrat was born into the home of a man named Amoz in the city of Zion. As he grew up, he was somewhat aware of his world and its troubles. The lengthening shadow of Assyria was a growing threat. Names like Tiglath-pileser III, Shalmanezer, Sargon, and Sennacherib were as familiar to the Jews as names like Fidel Castro, Mao Tse-tung, and Breshnev are to Americans today. Isaiah knew his nation was weak. He probably sighed a little over the superstition, idolatry, immorality; and heathen customs from the East that ate like bone cancer on the structure of his society. The people were drifting, eroding. Even the priests were lacking in moral and spiritual purity. Most of the prophets—those once-courageous men who served as a conscience to their nation—were equally weak. Women were coarse, sensual, shallow. The needs were acute.

But Isaiah probably had no plans to get mixed up in all that. He had his life mapped out, and he was off and running in the direction he was comfortable with . . . until . . . until a part of his world caved in . . . until God got his attention and turned him around one hundred eighty degrees!

Not on a bus. Not through a book. Not because a small band of men had been killed while attempting to reach a tribe of nameless Indians. Not while he was separated from his home, serving in the Israeli Marines, but through the death of a friend, whose name was Uzziah—a king, a good man, and one of the few people in that day who modeled a righteous life.

Isaiah, still in his twenties, was grieving the loss of Uzziah, whose death was as untimely to the nation Judah as Lincoln's death was to our nation back in 1865.

Relevant Principles from an Ancient Prophet

Isaiah 6 includes a remarkable story some twenty-seven centuries old. I find woven through this ancient account several principles that help strengthen our grip on God's world program. But before getting into a discussion of these principles, let's take a look at what the prophet wrote:

> In the year of King Uzziah's death, I saw the Lord sitting on a throne, lofty and exalted, with the train of His robe filling the temple.
> Seraphim stood before Him, each having six wings; with two he covered his face, and with two he covered his feet, and with two he flew.
> And one called out to another and said, "Holy, Holy, Holy, is the Lord of hosts, the whole earth is full of His glory."
> And the foundations of the thresholds trembled at the voice of Him who called out, while the temple was filling with smoke.
> Then I said, "Woe is me, for I am ruined! Because I am a man of unclean lips, And I live among a people of unclean lips; For my eyes have seen the King, the Lord of hosts."
> Then one of the seraphim flew to me, with a burning coal in his hand which he had taken from the altar with tongs.
> And he touched my mouth with it and said, "Behold, this has touched your lips; and your iniquity is taken away, and your sin is forgiven."
> Then I heard the voice of the Lord, saying, "Whom shall I send, and who will go for us?" Then I said, "Here am I. Send me!" (Isa. 6:1–8).

In reading these verses it is easy to become so impressed with the vision that we pass over the circumstance that brought it about. If I understand this correctly, it was a time of loss, an experience of grief for Isaiah. His friend had died. Perhaps the prophet had slipped into the house of God for some quietness and prayer. Maybe he was feeling lonely or abandoned. *The Living Bible* links the vision with the grief: "The year King Uzziah died I saw the Lord!"

Principle 1: God Uses Circumstances to Make Us
Aware of His Presence

Isaiah says, "I saw the Lord!" His earthly situation turned this eyes upward. That's what happened to me back in the late 1950s. My disappointment, my loneliness and confusion, rather than hardening the soil of my soul, plowed deeply. Those things cut away at me, made me sensitive to my Lord . . . in a way I would otherwise *never* have been.

For you it may be a lingering illness or an unexpected move to a new location, a job change, or perhaps a sudden loss of employment entirely. I know an individual who claims that it took a divorce to bring him to his knees and (for the first time in his life) to become aware of God's presence. A couple my wife had known for fifteen years lost their eighteen-month-old baby girl. Their grief could hardly be relieved—some wondered if they would *ever* be the same. As time passed, it became obvious that her death was the turning point in their spiritual pilgrimage. That couple got off the fence and into the action. God became more real, more significant to that couple as a result of the loss of their child than He had ever been before.

It was the year his friend died that Isaiah "saw the Lord. . . ." And what was He doing? Was He frowning or pacing back and forth? No. Was He anxious or puzzled or angry? No. He was sitting down. The Lord was calmly seated on His throne. I think of majestic sovereignty when I read of Jehovah's position. He was totally in charge. He was not wringing His hands, wondering what in the world He was going to do. He was "lofty and exalted." With height comes *perspective*. And His exalted role speaks of *authority*. Isaiah saw no confused or anxious deity, but One who sat in sovereign, calm control with full perspective and in absolute authority. Interestingly, the death of Uzziah is not mentioned again. From now on it's the prophet and His God—His presence "filling the temple."

A group of multiple-winged creatures called "seraphim" (one Old Testament scholar refers to them as "flaming angels") were also present in Isaiah's vision. They formed an antiphonal choir, chanting and repeating in alternating voice: "Holy, Holy, Holy is the Lord of hosts, the whole earth is full of His glory." It must have been some kind of sight! In *Unger's Bible Dictionary* we read, "From their antiphonal chant . . . we may conceive them to have been ranged in opposite rows on each side of the throne."[2] One group would cry out and the other would answer. And again, as the dumbfounded Isaiah stared in silence, it would happen again. Over and over. Small wonder the foundations of the earthly temple trembled. Those voices sounded like deafening thunderclaps roaring over the hillside. *It was awesome!*

Several years ago, our large chancel choir at the church I pastor in Fullerton, California, sang one of the most worshipful and beautiful musicals I have ever heard. It was entitled "Greater Is He." There is a particular part of the composition that is woven through the piece—a haunting melody with accompanying lyrics that stay with you for months afterward:

Surely, the presence of the Lord is in this place.
I can feel His mighty power and His grace.
I can hear the brush of angel's wings,
I see glory on each face,
Surely the presence of the Lord is in this place.[3]

That's what Isaiah felt. The "brush of angels' wings" coupled with their antiphonal words of adoring praise caused the prophet to say (the NIV reads "I cried"):

Woe is me, for I am ruined!

The Berkeley Version renders his response:

> Alas for me, I feel beaten!

The Living Bible says:

> My doom is sealed, for I am a foul-mouthed sinner, a member of a sinful, foul-mouthed race. . . .

Isaiah is frightened, beaten, and broken. Not only does he see the Lord sovereign, high and exalted, not only does he witness the antiphonal choir of angels swarming the heavenly throne, he also hears that God is infinitely holy. And in contrast to his own sinfulness and depravity, he feels doomed . . . beaten.

Principle 2: God Reveals His Character to Make Us See Our Need.

This is a major part of the process as the Lord opens our eyes to His world program we call "missions." He shows us Himself first, not the starving millions, not the heathen in gross darkness. No, He begins with a one-on-one. He uses certain painful circumstances to make us look up, then He reveals some things about His character (theologians refer to these as God's "attributes") to make us see our need for Him. Did you catch the sharp contrast?

| "Holy, Holy, Holy is the Lord of hosts. . . ." | "I am ruined! . . . I am a man of unclean lips. . . ." |

Suddenly, Isaiah is no longer viewing a vision from a safe distance, removed and out of touch. The whole scene literally comes to life as one of those seraphs steps out of the vision and flies toward our frightened friend. Without announcement, the winged creature sweeps into the prophet's presence and does something most unusual.

> Then one of the seraphim flew to me, with a burning coal in his hand which he had taken from the altar with tongs.
> And he touched my mouth with it and said, "Behold, this has touched your lips; and your iniquity is taken away, and your sin is forgiven" (Isa. 6:6–7).

The flaming angel touches Isaiah with a hot coal. Did you notice *where* he touched the prophet? On his lips. I suggest there is significance in that act. Isaiah had just admitted he was "a foul-mouthed sinner" (TLB). It shouldn't shock us, therefore, to take his confession literally. He no doubt struggled with profanity. And that is probably what the young man was using as an excuse to disqualify himself from God's service.

We all have such excuses:

I'm not physically well. I'm sickly—not strong enough."

"I've got this temper problem."

"I can't speak very well in public."

"I don't have a lot of education."

"My past is too raunchy. If you only knew!"

"I have a prison record."

"I once had an abortion."

"I've been on drugs."

"You see, I'm a divorcee."

"I was once in a mental hospital."

And on and on and on. It's the old bird-with-the-broken-pinion routine. But God is bigger than *any* of those reasons. He specializes in taking bruised, soiled, broken, guilty, and miserable vessels and making them whole, forgiven, and useful again. Remember what the angel said to Isaiah when he touched his lips?

" . . . your guilt is taken away and your sin atoned for" (NIV).

What affirmation! Where sin abounded, grace *super* abounded. The one thing Isaiah had been hiding behind, ashamed to admit but unable to conquer, God dealt with.

Principle 3: God Gives Us Hope to Make Us Know We Are Useful.

You won't grasp the full impact of this principle until you read the dialogue that followed.

Then I heard the voice of the Lord, saying, "Whom shall I send, and who will go for us?" Then I said, "Here am I. Send me!" (v. 8).

Don't miss that first word, "Then. . . ." When? After the grief that brought Isaiah to his knees. After God revealed Himself as all the things the prophet wasn't. After the seraph had touched his lips (the specific area of struggle) and assured him he was useful. After all that, God asked, "Whom shall I send?" You see, God's perspective is much broader than ours. In those days, He saw villages by the thousands, people by the millions. His heart was on a world in need. Up to that moment, Isaiah was swimming in his own tight radius, preoccupied with a limited view of his world.

Every summer I enjoy taking my family to see the Dodgers and the Angels play some of their games. Occasionally, there will be a time during each game when it gets a little slow and boring. The crowd gets unusually quiet and even the players lack spark. That happened at an Angel game last summer, and I rolled up the printed game program and looked all over the stadium through the hole at the end of the tube. We've all done this as kids. As I looked out on the field I could see only the batter and the catcher, no one else. Or I could spot only the first baseman and right fielder from where I sat. When I looked up in the stands, I could see thirty-five to forty people inside the hole, but that was all. As soon as I pulled the program away from my eye, I could immediately see thousands of heads among the baseball fans or the entire field of players.

My world back in the late 1950s was a very tight, limited radius composed of my wife, my future, my career, my desires, my perspective—almost as if I were viewing the world through a rolled-up game program. God stepped in and pushed the limitation away, exposing me to a world I had never, never considered important before. He did the very same thing with Isaiah. Anyone who makes a determined effort to strengthen his or her grip on missions will sooner or later have to toss aside the rolled-up game program and get a glimpse of God's world program, which brings us to the next principle.

Principle 4: God Expands Our Vision to Make Us Evaluate Our Availability.

I haven't words to describe the jolt I received by being exposed to that seventeen-day journey across the Pacific and then the vast numbers, cultures, and needs of people in Japan, Okinawa, Formosa, and the Philippines. An entire world literally opened up to me. Up until then I was restricted in my vision and limited in my awareness. Being from Texas, I viewed God as an American God with a Texas accent. He smiled on fried okra, sliced tomatoes, chili, red beans, cornbread, banjo pluckin' and barbeque. He liked big spreads (ranches), folk songs, family reunions, salt-water fishing. But let me tell you, when this "good ole boy" walked wide-eyed through the quaint and unusual paths of the Orient, heard the strange music from the samisen, saw those idol altars that stood several stories high, and witnessed mile after mile of rice paddies and hundreds of other foreign sights, God and His world program took on a whole new meaning. Things like personal prejudices began to fade along with my own selfish pride of my race. The determination to get my own way became increasingly less desirable. I didn't work hard to be pious or a super-spiritually minded "missionary type." No, it all just began to fall into place so naturally. I honestly found myself saying, like Isaiah, "Here am I. Send me!" I became strangely motivated to break loose from that tight little radius of *my* career, *my* future, and *my* plans. Without realizing it, my attention slowly shifted from my world to God's world. But before all this starts sounding like one of those cloud-nine, dreamy testimonies, let me add that the Lord kept me in constant touch with reality. Keep in mind that I was living in a Marine barracks, one of the toughest places on earth to practice authentic Christianity. This helps introduce the fifth and final principle we find interwoven in the Isaiah 6 passage.

Principle 5: God Tells Us the Truth to Make Us Focus On Reality.

A decision like the one Isaiah was considering was far too significant for it to be based on emotion alone. Lest he assume it would be a downhill slide, God hit him with the truth.

And He said, "Go, and tell this people: 'Keep on listening, but do not perceive; Keep on looking, but do not understand.'

"Render the hearts of this people insensitive, Their ears dull, and their eyes dim, Lest they see with their eyes, Hear with their ears, Understand with their hearts, And repent and be healed."

Then I said, "Lord, how long?" And He answered "Until cities are devastated and without inhabitant, House are without people, And the land is utterly desolate" (vv. 9–11).

Now that's straight talk! None of this, "If you go and serve me, I'll bring untold millions into the kingdom!" business. No heavenly hype. Not even a lot of encouraging promises like, "You'll really feel good!" or "People will admire you, Isaiah." None of that. Instead, He told His man that the challenge would be gigantic, the response to his efforts would be less than exciting, and in the final analysis there wouldn't be a lot to write home about! That explains why Isaiah answered, "Lord, how long?" Strengthening one's grip on missions requires a firm handle on reality. The greatest confirmation that one needs is not the tangible results of one's labors, but the inner assurance he or she is in the nucleus of God's will.

AND WHAT ABOUT YOU AND ME . . . TODAY?

So much for that ancient scene. As valuable and important as it was, we cannot afford to stay there and live in those memories. What about all this today? Is God saying anything specific about His world program to you and me? Each one of us must answer that alone. Go back over those five principles very slowly, very carefully. Personalize them by imagining *yourself* in each one.

You may be thinking, "Hey, not me!" That's exactly what I said back in 1957 . . . until . . . until I had every crutch yanked away. Until I sat on a Greyhound bus that rainy night. Until I read about a group of men who could have been quite successful as businessmen in the States, but settled on reaching a tribe of Indians in South America. Until I was literally shipped overseas and introduced to a vast vision for the world I would never have otherwise cared to know existed. You may *think* this chapter has not been talking to you or about you, but not until you personalize these things will you know for sure.

> In some unlikely quarter, in a shepherd's hut, or in an artisan's cottage, God has his prepared and appointed instrument. As yet the shaft is hidden in his quiver, in the shadow of his hand; but at the precise moment at which it will tell with the greatest effect, it will be produced and launched on the air.[4]

Five bodies floated face down in the Curary River in the Ecuadorian interior: Jim Elliot, Nate Saint, Pete Fleming, Ed McCully, and Roger Yoderian. Five widows sat in stunned silence as the news of their husbands' heroic yet tragic deaths was announced to them. The American press either stated or implied the same verdict as the story of their martyrdom reached the States, "In vain. In vain . . . all in vain!" No! Tragic loss, but not "in vain."

Since that time the Auca tribe has been reached and evangelized. The dream of those five was ultimately realized. And who will ever know how many hundreds, perhaps thousands, of young men and women took up the torch of world missions?

It was not in vain. I know. I was one of them.

Discussion Questions and Suggestions to Help You Strengthen Your Grip on Missions

• Someone has said, "You can't take the 'go' out of the gospel." Jesus specifically commissions His followers to "Go . . . make disciples of all the nations. . . ." Talk about this issue of being *personally* involved in God's world-wide program. Obviously, everybody isn't called to travel abroad and minister in another culture. How can Christians "go" yet stay here in the States?

• In this chapter, we looked closely at Isaiah's experience when the Lord revealed Himself to the prophet. Did you put yourself in the man's sandals and think, "What if that happened today?" Do so now. See if you can recall the major principles we uncovered. Are there any analogies with your life today?

• Forcing yourself to be painfully honest, try to think of some of the reasons missions turns you off. If you feel free to say so, verbalize your feelings. Remember such things as manipulation by guilt, playing on emotions, and mass exploitation.

• What stands out in your mind when you consider that God told the prophet Isaiah, in effect, that his mission would be met by insensitive people, dull ears, dim eyes, and hard hearts (Isa. 6:10)? Talk about the whole issue of success in ministry today. Don't dodge the truth that God doesn't plan for everybody to enjoy vast blessings. Discuss obedience.

• How can a Christian know *for sure* that his or her place of ministry is *not* outside the United States? How can one know it *is*? And another question: How can the person who is called to serve Christ abroad be restrained from feeling resentment toward those who stay here at home?

• Pray. If you aren't sure where God would have you serve Him, be sure to ask the Lord exactly what you can do to know His will regarding your future. Are you thoroughly willing to say, "Here am I, send me"? If so, freely say so as you pray.

12

Strengthening Your Grip On Godliness

Fast-lane living in the 1980s does not lend itself to the traits we have traditionally attached to godliness. Remember the words to the old hymn we sang in church years ago?

> Take time to be holy, speak oft with Thy Lord;
> Abide in Him always and feed on His Word.
>
> ....
>
> Take time to be holy, the world rushes on;
> Spend much time in secret with Jesus alone.[1]

Chances are good that we who read those words believe them and would even defend them, but we sigh as we confess that more often than not we are strangers to them. There was once a time when a stroll through the park or a quiet afternoon spent in solitude was not that uncommon. But no more. The days of sitting on the porch swing, watching the evening pass in review are relics of the past, unfortunately. We may still squeeze in an hour or so around the fireplace every now and then, but the idea of taking the kind of time "to be holy" that our grandparents once did is rather dated.

Does this mean, then, that we cannot be holy? Does an urban lifestyle force us to forfeit godliness? Must we return to the "Little House on the Prairie" in order to be godly? Obviously, the answer is "No." If godliness were linked to a certain culture or a horse-and-buggy era, then most of us are out of luck! As much as we might enjoy a slower and less pressured lifestyle, God has not called everyone to such a role, certainly not those of us who live in the Greater Los

Angeles area. Yet, some of the godliest people I have ever known live in Southern California (though some of you may find that hard to believe!).

WHAT IS GODLINESS, ANYWAY?

This brings us to a bottom-line question I seldom hear addressed these days: What exactly does it mean to be godly? Now be careful. Try hard not to link your answer with a certain geography or culture or traditional mentality. It is easy to let our prejudices seep through and erroneously define the concept on the basis of our bias.

• Does being godly mean living high up in the mountains, cutting wood to heat a log cabin, and reading the Bible under the flickering flame of a kerosene lamp?
• Or how about this? The godly person must be old, deliberate, one who prays for hours everyday, and doesn't watch much television. Is that godliness?
• Can a person be godly and yet competitive in business, keen thinking, and financially successful?
• Is it possible to be godly and drive a Porsche . . . and never get married and . . . (hold on!) not go to church every Sunday evening?
• Does being holy require that I squat on a hillside, strum a guitar with my eyes closed, eat a bagful of birdseed, and write religious music from the book of Psalms?
• Are people disqualified if they are good athletes or if they are famous entertainers (with agents!) or if they are rich or if they have champagne tastes or if they wear diamonds and furs? Can anybody in that category be a godly Christian?
• One more . . . and this may hurt. How about believers who still struggle, who don't have some of the theological issues settled, who don't understand many of the hymns sung in church, who don't read a lot of missionary biographies . . . and who don't necessarily go along with the whole Moral Majority package?

Oh, oh . . . now I've done it. So far you have been willing to hang in there with me, but now you really aren't sure. Before you categorize me, tar and feather me, and toss everything out—baby and bathwater alike—please understand that I'm just asking a few questions. I'm probing, honestly trying to discover the answer to a simple question: What *is* godliness?

You'll have to agree that it can't be confused with how a person looks (hard as it is for us to get beyond that) or what a person drives or owns. As tough as it is for us to be free of envy and critical thoughts, it is imperative that we remind our selves that "God looks on the heart" (1 Sam. 16:7); therefore, whatever we may say godliness is, it is *not* skin deep. It is something below the surface of a life, deep down in the realm of an attitude . . . an attitude toward God Himself.

The longer I think about this, the more I believe that a person who is godly is one whose heart is sensitive toward God, one who takes God seriously. This evidences itself in one very obvious mannerism: the godly individual hungers and thirsts after God. In the words of the psalmist, the godly person has a soul that "pants" for the living God.

> As the deer pants for streams of water,
> so my soul pants for you, O God.
> My soul thirsts for God, for the living
> God.
> (Ps. 42:1–2a, NIV)

The one who sustains this pursuit may be young or old, rich or poor, urban or rural, leader or follower, of any race of color or culture or any temperament, active or quiet, married or single; none of these things really matter. But what *does* matter is the individual's inner craving to know God, listen to Him, and walk humbly with Him. As I mentioned, the godly take Him seriously.

Don't misread this, I'm not suggesting that all godly people are themselves serious-minded folk. I *am* saying, however, that they possess an attitude of willing submission to God's will and ways. Whatever He says goes. And whatever it takes to carry it out is the very thing the godly desire to do. Remember, the soul "pants" and "thirsts" for God. There is an authentic pursuit of and delight in the Lord. Let's think about strengthening our grip on godliness. Maybe a negative example will help.

THE ANCIENT HEBREWS: RELIGIOUS, BUT NOT GODLY

I've been poring over the first thirteen verses of 1 Corinthians 10 in recent days, trying to get a handle on this matter of godliness. I was attracted to this section of Scripture because it revolves around a group of people who had every reason to be godly, but they were not. That intrigues me. Why in the world wouldn't those ancient Hebrews, who were supernaturally delivered from Egyptian bondage under Moses' leadership, model true godliness?

Paul is writing these words under the inspiration of the Holy Spirit. His thoughts in 1 Corinthians 10 are a spin-off from his closing remarks in chapter 9, where he writes:

> Do you not know that in a race all the runners run, but only one gets the prize? Run in such a way as to get the prize. Everyone who competes in the games goes into strict training. They do it to get a crown that will not last; but we do it to get a crown that will last forever. Therefore I do not run like a man running aimlessly; I do not fight like a man beating the air. No, I beat my body and make it my slave so that after I have preached to others, I myself will not be disqualified for the prize (1 Cor. 9:24–27, NIV).

Those are the words of a godly man. He wasn't playing games with his life. Therefore, he refused to let his body dictate his objectives. He "beat it black and blue" (literal rendering of the last verse) and determined to make it his slave rather than the other way around. Why? Look again at what he says. He didn't want to finish his life as a washout. Paul dreaded the thought of being disqualified. A strong preacher of righteousness who ultimately shriveled into a weak victim of his own fleshly drives. I get the distinct impression that he feared the age-old problem of trafficking in unlived truth . . . of not taking God seriously.

That can happen so easily in this generation of superficiality. We can run with religious people, pick up the language, learn the ropes, and never miss a lick—publicly, that is. We can even defend our lifestyle by a rather slick system of theological accommodation. The better we get at it, the easier it is to convince ourselves we are on target. All it takes is a little Scripture twisting and a fairly well-oiled system of rationalization and we are off and running. Two results begin to transpire: (1) all our desires (no matter how wrong) are fulfilled, and (2) all our guilt (no matter how justified) is erased. And if anybody attempts to call us into account, label them a legalist and plow right on! It also helps to talk a lot about grace, forgiveness, mercy, and the old nobody's-perfect song.

Paul rejected that stuff entirely. He refused to be sucked into such a system or rationalization. He panted after God. He thirsted deep within his soul for the truth of God so he might live it. He longed to take God seriously.

Suddenly Paul was seized with a classic example—the Hebrews who left Egypt at the Exodus. It's like he thought. "Now, if you need an illustration of people who had everything and yet blew it, who disqualified themselves, think about this: . . ."

> For I do not want you to be unaware, brethren, that our fathers were all under the cloud, and all passed through the sea and all were baptized into Moses in the cloud and in the sea; and all ate the same spiritual food; and all drank the same spiritual drink, for they were drinking from a spiritual rock which followed them; and the rock was Christ (1 Cor. 10:1–4).

Take a pencil and circle the frequent repetition of the little word *all*, and you'll begin to understand. They all had everything!
• Supernatural guidance: a cloud by day and a pillar of fire by night
• Supernatural deliverance: the Red Sea escape
• Supernatural leadership: God's man, Moses
• Supernatural diet: manna from heaven and water from the rock.
Get the picture? They were surrounded by unparalleled privileges. Miracles were everyday occurrences. God's presence was constant and His workings were evident. Talk about overexposure! Everywhere there was God-talk. It was like a high-level Bible conference atmosphere day in and day out, week in and week out. Surely they flourished in such a hot house, right?

Wrong!

What happens when photographic film is overexposed? Sometimes the image is lost entirely. What about a dishtowel that never dries out but rather stays wet, wadded up in a pile? It gets sour. How about a clay pot that stays only in the sun—no rain, no cool breeze, no shade? It gets hard, brittle, easily cracked.

So it was with most of the Exodus crowd. An exaggeration? No, read the facts for yourself: "Nevertheless, with most of them God was not well pleased; for they were laid low in the wilderness" (v. 5).

That ominous word, "nevertheless . . ." says it all. They had it . . . nevertheless. They witnessed God's abundant provisions in daily doses . . . nevertheless. In the process of time, miracles lost their significance. Their incessant God-talk became sour in their mouths. They turned dark in all that overexposure.

AN ANALYSIS OF CARNALITY

What exactly happened? How could that have occurred? Why wouldn't they have flourished in such a marvelous and protective bubble of blessing? In short, they failed to take God seriously. To them, the divine became commonplace. Their respect for Jehovah which caused their mouths to open in silent awe had now degenerated into a jaded yawn of disrespect.

Paul describes the sordid scene of carnal litter for all of us to read with a sigh.

> Now these things happened as examples for us, that we should not crave evil things, as they also craved. And do not be idolaters, as some of them were; as it is written, "THE PEOPLE SAT DOWN TO EAT AND DRINK, AND STOOD UP TO PLAY." Nor let us act immorally, as some of them did, and twenty-three thousand fell in one day. Nor let us try the Lord, as some of them did, and were destroyed by the serpents. Nor grumble, as some of them did, and were destroyed by the destroyer. Now these things happened to them as an example, and they were written for our instruction, upon whom the ends of the ages have come (vv. 6–11).

The grim record is punctuated with a warning on both ends: "These things happened as examples . . . they were written for our instruction. . . ." God takes no sadistic pleasure in recording failure just to make people of the past squirm. No, he tells us that these stand as timeless warnings—warnings for all to heed—like those huge pictures of the atrocities of World War II, exhibited outside the Dachau prison camp in West Germany.

- They craved evil things. "Don't do that!"
- They were idolatrous. "Watch out!"
- They started practicing immorality. "Stop it!"
- They became guilty of presumption. "No!"
- They were cynical and negative. "Guard against this!"

Amazing as it may seem the people with the most ultimately appropriated the least. In the warmth of God's best blessings, they became cool, distant, indifferent. Not suddenly, but slowly, the keen edge of enthusiasm became dull. And like a snail's shell, one perilous attitude rolled into another, each increasingly more brash, until the people stood up against their God with snarling lips and tightened fists.

Wait! Who are we talking about? A body of brutal ignorant savages who never knew the name of Jehovah? No, these were those who had been relieved of the taskmaster's whip in Egypt . . . once for all delivered from bondage and promised a new land to inhabit. But their smile of delight became a sneer of defiance because they allowed a "business as usual" mentality to replace the fresh walk of faith. They no longer took God seriously.

APPLICATION AND WARNING

Does this still occur? Yes, the peril is always a potential . . . in a Christian home where discussion of the things of God is easily taken for granted . . . in a Christian school or seminary where God-talk can become sterile and academic . . . in a Christian church where a strong pulpit becomes commonplace, where saints easily get spoiled and occasionally become sour. Even in a missionary enterprise or a Christian conference ministry, it can occur. We can slump into a tired routine if we don't stay alert to the danger of erosion.

Two reactions usually emerge as we hear such warnings from God's Word.
1. "This will never happen to me!"

If that is your response, listen to verse 12: "Therefore let him who thinks he stands take heed lest he fall."

Paul feared the age-old problem of trafficking in unlived truth . . . of not taking God seriously.

I never will forget the letter I received some time ago that addressed this very subject of not taking God seriously. It read:

Dear Pastor Chuck,

This past week I had a tragic illustration of the price of failure to take God seriously. Only the names have been changed. . . .

Some years ago three fresh-faced young girls came to work where I am employed.

They were quick to tell all who would listen that they were Christians, out to turn the place upside down for Christ.

Within a few months all three had decided to get a "little taste" of the world. One is now raising an out-of-wedlock child alone.

The second came back to the Lord and has since married a keen Christian fellow who is a converted heroin addict. They have some problems from their former lifestyle, but it looks as though they might make it.

And then there was Gerry. Raised in a moral, religious home of a different faith, she rebelled in her teen years, left her faith, and was a little wild.

When she professed Christ in her late teens, her parents looked on it as part of her rebellion. It was easy to slide back into the old life. After about a year of out-of-fellowship living, Gerry began actively pursuing a married man at work. Unhappily married, he put up little resistance.

Several fellow workers, including at least one Christian, approached her about her folly. She was sure she couldn't give him up. He left his wife and moved in with her.

Gerry was disciplined at work. Her lover intervened, threatening the life of her foreman over the matter, and as a result was fired. (The discipline was unrelated to their relationship.)

When his divorce was final, they married. She dismissed his violent threats toward the foreman as "all talk," and his having beaten his former wife as the result of extreme provocation. The husband's two children came to live with them. The elder was only eight years younger than 22-year-old Gerry.

The children lacked training and discipline. They asked hard questions about their father and Gerry's relationship.

At this point Gerry confided to me that she knew she had done wrong, and had now repented. She was surprised that the repercussions of her sin continued, even after repentance.

Within a few months the marriage disintegrated into a bitter feud, each returning hurt for hurt.

Gerry filed for divorce and moved back home. Last Tuesday morning . . . as she was leaving for home after her graveyard shift, she told a fellow worker, "I've got it together now. When my divorce is final, I'm going to marry this really neat guy."

That was yesterday. Yesterday Gerry was happy. Today Gerry is dead. Shot by her estranged husband who then turned the gun on himself.

Today two broken-hearted families grieve. Two children are fatherless. All because of failure to take God seriously.

For Gerry the wages of sin was literal, physical death.[2]

Yes, I warn you, it *could* happen to you. Stay alert! Tell the Lord you *do* take Him seriously . . . you desire true godliness.

2. "I'm into the syndrome you have described. I am already too far gone to recover!"

No temptation has overtaken you but such as is common to man; and God is faithful, who will not allow you to be tempted beyond what you are able; but with the temptation will provide the way of escape also, that you may be able to endure it (v. 13).

Nothing is to hard for the Lord. No one is beyond hope. *It is never too late to start doing what is right.*

I offer a series of questions for you to answer:

- Have you begun to lose the fresh delight of your walk with the Lord?
- Is it becoming perfunctory and boring?
- Can you name a turning point or two when things began to change for the worse?
- Do you realize the extreme danger of your future if nothing changes?
- Are you willing to confess the lack of vitality in your spiritual life?
- Will you do that NOW?

I promise you this: If you will come to terms with these things and come clean before the Lord your God, the power you once knew will return. You can count on this, He will take you seriously.

DISCUSSION QUESTIONS AND SUGGESTIONS TO HELP YOU STRENGTHEN YOUR GRIP ON GODLINESS

- Define *godliness*. Using your own words, explain the difference between external religion and an internal attitude of spirituality.
- Can people who are active, on the move, living in an urban community maintain an authentic godliness? Talk about some of the perils and how they can be counteracted.
- Returning to the 1 Corinthians 10 passage of Scripture, see if you can recall several of the traps the ancient Hebrews fell into. What keep us from blaming them?
- Share one or two techniques or habits you have begun to use that help you take God more seriously. What are two or three things that make godliness seem so far removed? Pray for one another.
- During this week, commit to memory 1 Corinthians 10:12–13. Repeat them several times a day until you can do so without looking at your Bible. See if that helps you in the weeks to come.

13

Strengthening Your Grip on Attitudes

The colorful, nineteenth-century showman and gifted violinist Nicolo Paganini was standing before a packed house, playing through a difficult piece of music. A full orchestra surrounded him with magnificent support. Suddenly one string on his violin snapped and hung gloriously down from his instrument. Beads of perspiration popped out on his forehead. He frowned but continued to play, improvising beautifully.

To the conductor's surprise, a second string broke. And shortly thereafter, a third. Now there were three limp strings dangling from Paganini's violin as the master performer completed the difficult composition on the one remaining string. The audience jumped to its feet and in good Italian fashion, filled the hall with shouts and screams, "Bravo! Bravo!" As the applause died down, the violinist asked the people to sit back down. Even though they knew there was no way they could expect an encore, they quietly sank back into their seats.

He held the violin high for everyone to see. He nodded at the conductor to begin the encore and then he turned back to the crowd, and with a twinkle in his eye, he smiled and shouted, "Paganini . . . and one string!" After that he placed the single-stringed Stradivarius beneath his chin and played the final piece on *one* string as the audience (and the conductor) shook their heads in silent amazement. "Paganini . . . and one string!" *And*, I might add, an attitude of fortitude.

Dr. Victor Frankl, the bold, courageous Jew who became a prisoner during the Holocaust, endured years of indignity and humiliation by the Nazis before he was finally liberated. At the beginning of his ordeal, he was marched into a gestapo courtroom. His captors had taken away his home and family, his cherished freedom, his possessions, even his watch and wedding ring. They had shaved his head and stripped his clothing off his body. There he stood before the German high command, under the glaring lights being interrogated and falsely accused. He was destitute, a helpless pawn in the hands of brutal, prejudiced, sadistic men. He had nothing. No, that isn't true. He suddenly realized there was one thing no one could ever take from him—just one. Do you know what it was?

Dr. Frankl realized he still had the power to choose his own attitude. No matter what anyone would ever do to him, regardless of what the future held for him, the attitude choice was his to make. Bitterness or forgiveness. To give up to go on. Hatred or hope. Determination to endure or the paralysis of self-pity. It boiled down to "Frankl . . . and one string!"[1]

Words can never adequately convey the incredible impact of our attitude toward life. The longer I live the more convinced I become that life is 10 percent what happens to us and 90 percent how we respond to it.

How else can anyone explain the unbelievable feats of hurting, beat-up athletes? Take Joe Namath for instance; at age thirty he was a quarterback with sixty-five-year-old legs. Although he might have difficulty making one flight of stairs by the time he's fifty years of age, maybe before, it was attitude that kept the man in the game.

Or take Merlin Olsen and his knees. In an interview with a sports reporter, the former Los Angeles Ram all-pro defensive lineman admitted:

> That year after surgery on my knee, I had to have the fluid drained weekly. Finally, the membrane got so thick they almost had to drive the needle in it with a hammer. I got to the point where I just said, ". . . get the needle in there, and get that stuff out."[2]

Joe Namath . . . Merlin Olsen . . . *and one string!*

ATTITUDES ARE ALL-IMPORTANT

This may shock you, but I believe the single most significant decision I can make on a day-to-day basis is my choice of attitude. It is more important than my past, my education, my bankroll, my successes or failures, fame or pain, what other people think of me or say about me, my circumstances, or my position. Attitude is that "single string" that keeps me going or cripples my progress. It alone fuels my fire or assaults my hope. When my attitudes are right, there's no barrier too high, no valley too deep, no dream too extreme, no challenge too great for me.

Yet, we must admit that we spend more of our time concentrating and fretting over the strings that snap, dangle, and pop—the things that can't be changed—than we do giving attention to the one that remains, our choice of attitude. Stop and think about some of the things that suck up our attention and energy, all of them inescapable (and occasionally demoralizing).

- The tick of the clock
- The weather . . . the temperature . . . the wind!
- People's actions and reactions, *especially* the criticisms
- Who won or lost the ball game
- Delays at airports, waiting rooms, in traffic
- Results of an X-ray
- Cost of groceries, gasoline, clothes, cars—everything!
- On-the-job irritations, disappointments, workload.

The greatest waste of energy in our ecologically minded world of the 1980s is not electricity or natural gas or any other "product," it's the energy we waste fighting the inevitables! And to make matters worse, *we* are the ones who suffer, who grow sour, who get ulcers, who become twisted, negative and tight-fisted fighters. Some actually die because of this.

Dozens of comprehensive studies have established this fact. One famous study, called "Broken Heart," researched the mortality rate of 4,500 widowers within six months of their wives' deaths. Compared with other men the same age, the widowers had a mortality rate 40 percent higher.[3]

Major F. J. Harold Kushner, an army medical officer held by the Viet Cong for over five years, cites an example of death because of an attitudinal failure. In a fascinating article in *New York* magazine, this tragic yet true account is included:

Among the prisoners in Kushner's POW camp was a tough young marine, 24 years old, who had already survived two years of prison-camp life in relatively good health. Part of the reason for this was that the camp commander had promised to release the man if he cooperated. Since this had been done before with others, the marine turned into a model POW and the leader of the camp's thought-reform group. As time passed he gradually realized that his captors had lied to him. When the full realization of this took hold, he became a zombie. He refused to do all work, rejected all offers of food and encouragement, and simply lay on his cot sucking his thumb. In a matter of weeks he was dead.[4]

Caught in the vice grip of lost hope, life became too much for the once-tough marine to handle. When that last string snapped, there was nothing left.

THE VALUE OF ATTITUDES: SCRIPTURE SPEAKS

In the little letter Paul wrote the Christians in Philippi, he didn't mince words when it came to attitudes. Although a fairly peaceful and happy flock, the Philippians had a few personality skirmishes that could have derailed them and hindered their momentum. Knowing how counterproductive that would be, he came right to the point: their attitudes.

If therefore there is any encouragement in Christ, if there is any consolation of love, if there is any fellowship of the Spirit, if any affection and compassion, make my joy complete by being of the same mind, maintaining the same love, united in spirit, intent on one purpose (Phil. 2:1–2).

What does all this mean? Well, let's go back and take a look. There *is* encouragement in the Person of Christ. There *is* love. There is also plenty of "fellowship of the Spirit" for the Christian to enjoy. Likewise, affection and compassion. Heaven is full and running over with these things even though earth is pretty barren at times. So Paul pleads for us to tap into that positive, encouraging storehouse. How? By "being of the same mind." He's telling us to take charge of our own minds; clearly a command. We Christians have the God-given ability to put minds on those things that build up, strengthen, encourage, and help ourselves and others. "Do that!" commands the Lord.

Attitude of Unselfish Humility

Paul gets specific at verses 3 and 4 of Philippians 2:

Do nothing from selfishness or empty conceit, but with humility of mind let each of you regard one another as more important than himself; do not merely look out for your own personal interests, but also for the interests of others.

This is a mental choice we make, a decision not to focus on self . . . me . . . my . . . mine, but on the other person. It's a servant mentality the Scriptures are encouraging. I have written an entire book[5] on this subject, so I'll not elaborate here except to say that few virtues are more needed today. When we strengthen our grip on attitudes, a great place to begin is with humility—authentic and gracious unselfishness.

Our example? Read on:

Have this attitude in yourselves which was also in Christ Jesus, who, although He existed in the form of God, did not regard equality with God a thing to be grasped, but emptied Himself, taking the form of a bond-servant, and being made in the likeness of men.

And being found in appearance as a man, He humbled Himself by becoming obedient to the point of death, even death on a cross (Phil. 2:5–8).

Maybe you have never stopped to think about it, but behind the scenes, it was an attitude that brought the Savior down to us. He deliberately chose to come among us because He realized and valued our need. He placed a higher significance on it than His own comfort and prestigious position. In humility, He set aside the glory of heaven and came to be among us. He refused to let His position keep us at arm's length.

Attitude of Positive Encouragement

Listen to another verse in the same chapter: "Do all things without grumbling or disputing" (v. 14).

Ouch! If ever a generation needed that counsel, *ours* does! It is virtually impossible to complete a day without falling into the trap of "grumbling or disputing." It is so easy to pick up the habit of negative thinking. Why? Because there are so many things around us that prompt us to be irritable. Let's not kid ourselves, life is *not* a bed of roses!

On my last birthday my sister Luci gave me a large scroll-like poster. Since our humor is somewhat similar, she knew I'd get a kick out of the stuff printed on it. She suggested I tack it up on the back of my bathroom door so I could review it regularly. It's a long list of some of the inescapable "laws" of life that can make us irritable "grumblers and disputers" if we let them. They are commonly called "Murphy's Laws." Here's a sample:

- Nothing is as easy as it looks; everything takes longer than you think; if anything can go wrong it will.
- Murphy was an optimist.
- A day without a crisis is a total loss.
- The other line always moves faster.
- The chance of the bread falling with the peanut butter-and-jelly side down is directly proportional to the cost of the carpet.
- Inside every large problem is a series of small problems struggling to get out.
- 90% of everything is crud.
- Whatever hits the fan will not be evenly distributed.
- No matter how long or hard you shop for an item, after you've bought it, it will be on sale somewhere cheaper.
- Any tool dropped while repairing a car will roll underneath to the exact center.
- The repairman will never have seen a model quite like yours before.
- You will remember that you forgot to take out the trash when the garbage truck is two doors away.

- Friends come and go, but enemies accumulate.
- The light at the end of the tunnel is the headlamp of an oncoming train.
- Beauty is only skin deep, but ugly goes clear to the bone.[6]

Every item on the list is an attitude assailant! And the simple fact is they are so true, we don't even have to imagine their possibility—*they happen*. I have a sneaking suspicion they happened in Paul's day too. So when he writes about grumbling and disputing, he wasn't coming from an ivory tower. A positive, encouraging attitude is essential for survival in a world saturated with Murphy's Laws.

Attitude of Genuine Joy

Joy is really the underlying theme of Philippians—joy that isn't fickle, needing a lot of "things" to keep it smiling. . . . joy that is deep and consistent—the oil that reduces the friction of life.

Finally, my brethren, rejoice in the Lord (Phil. 3:1a).

Therefore, my beloved brethren whom I long to see, my joy and crown, so stand firm in the Lord, my beloved. . . . Rejoice in the Lord always; again I will say, rejoice! Let your forbearing spirit be known to all men. The Lord is near. Be anxious for nothing, but in everything by prayer and supplication with thanksgiving let your request be made known to God. And the peace of God, which surpasses all comprehension, shall guard your hearts and your minds in Christ Jesus (Phil. 4:1, 4–7).

There it is again—*the mind*. Our minds can be kept free of anxiety (those strings that snap) as we dump the load of our cares on the Lord in prayer. By getting rid of the stuff that drags us down, we create space for the joy to take its place.

Think of it like this: Circumstances occur that could easily crush us. They may originate on the job or at home or even during the weekend when we are relaxing. Unexpectedly, they come. Immediately we have a choice to make . . . an attitude choice. We can hand the circumstance to God and ask Him to take control or we can roll up our mental sleeves and slug it out. Joy awaits our decision. If we do as Philippians 4:6–7 suggests, peace replaces panic and joy moves into action. It is ready, but it is not pushy.

AGGRESSIVE-PASSIVE ALTERNATIVES

Let's not kid ourselves. When we deliberately choose not to stay positive and deny joy a place in our lives, we'll usually gravitate in one of two directions, sometimes both—the direction of blame or self-pity.

Blame

The aggressive attitude reacts to circumstances with blame. We blame ourselves or someone else, or God, or if we can't find a tangible scapegoat, we blame "fate." What an absolute waste! When we blame ourselves, we multiply our guilt, we rivet ourselves to the past (another "dangling" unchangeable), and we decrease our already low self-esteem. If we choose to blame God, we cut off our single source of power. Doubt replaces trust, and we put down roots of bitterness that can make us cynical. If we blame others, we enlarge the distance between us and them. We alienate. We poison a relationship. We settle for something much less than God ever intended. And on top of all that, we do not find relief!

Blame never affirms, it assaults.
Blame never restores, it wounds.
Blame never solves, it complicates.
Blame never unites, it separates.
Blame never smiles, it frowns.
Blame never forgives, it rejects.
Blame never forgets, it remembers.
Blame never builds, it destroys.

Let's admit it—not until we stop blaming will we start enjoying health and happiness again! This was underscored as I read the following words recently:

> . . . one of the most innovative psychologists in this half of the twentieth century . . . said recently that he considers only one kind of counselee relatively hopeless: that person who blames other people for his or her problems. If you can own the mess you're in, he says, there is hope for you and help available. As long as you blame others, you will be a victim for the rest of your life.[7]

Blame backfires, hurting us more than the object of our resentment.

Self-pity

The passive attitude responds to circumstances in an opposite manner, feeling sorry for oneself. I find this just as damaging as blaming, sometimes more so. In fact, I'm ready to believe that self-pity is "Private Enemy No. 1." Things turn against us, making us recipients of unfair treatment, like innocent victims of a nuclear mishap. We neither expect it nor deserve it, and to make matters worse, it happens at the worst possible time. We're too hurt to blame.

Our natural tendency is to curl up in the fetal position and sing the silly little children's song:

> Nobody loves me, everybody hates me,
> I think I'll eat some worms.

Which helps nobody. But what else can we do when the bottom drops out? Forgive me if this sounds too simplistic, but the only thing worth doing is usually the last thing we try doing—turning it over to our God, the Specialist, who has never yet been handed an impossibility He couldn't handle. Grab that problem by the throat and thrust it skyward!

There is a familiar story in the New Testament that always makes me smile. Paul and his traveling companion Silas had been beaten and dumped in a dungeon. It was *so* unfair! But this mistreatment did not steal their joy or dampen their confidence in God. Their circumstance, however, could not have been more bleak. They were there to stay.

> But about midnight Paul and Silas were praying and singing hymns of praise to God, and the prisoners were listening to them (Acts 16:25).

I would imagine! The sounds of confident praying and joyful singing are not usually heard from a stone prison. But Paul and Silas had determined they would not be paralyzed by self-pity. And as they prayed and sang, the unbelievable transpired.

> And suddenly there came a great earthquake, so that the foundations of the prison-house were shaken; and immediately all the doors were opened, and everyone's chains were unfastened.
>
> And when the jailer had been roused out of sleep and had seen the prison doors opened, he drew his sword and was about to kill himself, supposing that the prisoners had escaped.
>
> But Paul cried out with a loud voice, saying, "Do yourself no harm, for we are all here" (vv. 26–28).

With calm reassurance, Paul spoke words of encouragement to the jailer. He even promised there would be no attempt to escape. And if you take the time to read the full account (vv. 29–40) you will find how beautifully God used their attitude to change the entire face of their situation. I love such stories! They stand as monumental reminders that the right attitude choice can literally transform our circumstance, no matter how black and hopeless it may appear. And best of all, the right attitude becomes contagious!

I was sharing some of these thoughts at a large gathering in Chicago not long ago. It was Founders' Week at Moody Bible Institute, the annual time of celebration when Christians from all over the United States come to the school for a week of Bible teaching, singing, and interaction together. Following one of my talks, a lady I never met wrote me this letter.

> Dear Chuck:
> I want you to know I've been here all week and I've enjoyed every one of your talks. I know they will help me in my remaining years. . . .

I love your sense of humor. Humor has done a lot to help me in my spiritual life. How could I have raised 12 children starting at age 32 and not have had a sense of humor! I married at age 31. I didn't worry about getting married, I just left my future to God's will. But every night I hung a pair of men's pants on the bed and knelt down and prayed:

> "Father in heaven, hear my prayer
> And grant it if you can,
> I've hung a pair of trousers here,
> Please fill them with a man!"

I had a good laugh. In fact, I thought it was such a classic illustration of the right mental attitude toward life that I read it to my congregation in Fullerton, California, when I returned. In the congregation that day was half of one of our families. Mom and a sick daughter were home, but dad and an older son in his twenties were present and heard me read the letter. The mother (who knew nothing of the letter) wrote me a note a couple weeks later. She was brief and to the point. She was concerned about her older son. She said that for the last week or so he had been sleeping in his bed with a bikini draped over the footboard. She wanted to know if I might know why . . . or if this was something she needed to worry about.

FOOD FOR THE RIGHT ATTITUDE

Since our choice of attitude is so important, our minds need fuel to feed on. Philippians 4:8 gives us a good place to start.

> Finally, brethren, whatever is true, whatever is honorable, whatever is right, whatever is pure, whatever is lovely, whatever is of good repute, if there is any excellence and if anything worthy of praise, let your mind dwell on these things.

Good advice. "Let your mind *dwell* on these things." Fix your attention on these six specifics in life. Not unreal far-fetched dreams, but things that are *true*, real, valid. Not cheap, flippant, superficial stuff, but things that are *honorable*; i.e., worthy of respect. Not things that are wrong and unjust, critical and negative, but that which is *right*. Not thoughts that are carnal, smutty, and obscene, but that which is *pure* and wholesome. Not things that prompt arguments and defense in others, but those that are *lovely*, agreeable, attractive, winsome. Finally, not slander, gossip, and put-downs, but information of *good report*, the kind that builds up and causes grace to flow.

Do you do this? Is this the food you serve your mind? We are back where we started, aren't we? The choice is yours. The other discouraging strings on your instrument may snap and hang loosely—no longer available or useful, but nobody can *make* you a certain way. That is strictly up to you.

And may I take the liberty to say something very directly? Some of you who read these words are causing tremendous problems because of your attitude. You are capable. You are intelligent. You are qualified and maybe even respected for your competence. But your attitude is taking a toll on those who are near you—those you live with, those you work with, those you touch in life. For some of you, your home is a battleground, a mixture of negativism, sarcasm, pressure, cutting comments, and blame. For others, you have allowed self-pity to move in under your roof and you have foolishly surrendered mental territory that once was healthy and happy. You are laughing less and complaining more. You have to admit that the "one string" on which you can play—if you choose to do so—is out of tune.

As your friend, let me urge you to take charge of your mind and emotions today. Let your mind feast on nutritious food for a change. Refuse to grumble and criticize! Reject those alien thoughts that make you a petty, bitter person. Play that single string once again! Let it yield a sweet, winsome melody that this old world needs so desperately. Yes, you *can* if you *will*.

I was sitting at the Christian Bookseller's Association final banquet the last evening of the convention in 1981. My mind was buzzing as I was arranging my thoughts for the speech. I was a bit nervous and my attitude was somewhere between blame ("Why in the world did you say 'yes,' Swindoll?") and self-pity ("There are a dozen or more people sitting among those thousands out there who could do a lot better job than you, dummy!") when the spotlight turned from the head table to a young woman sitting in a wheelchair off to the side. She was to sing that evening.

I was greatly encouraged to see her. I was strengthened in my spirit as I thought back over Joni Eareckson's pilgrimage since 1967—broken neck; loss of feeling from her shoulders down; numerous operations; broken romance; the death of dreams; no more swimming, horseback riding, skating, running, dancing; not even an evening stroll, ever again. All those strings now dangled from her life. But there sat a radiant, remarkable, rare woman who had chosen not to quit.

I shall never forget the song she sang that quieted my nerves and put things in persepctive:

> When peace, like a river, attendeth my way.
> When sorrows like sea billows roll;
> Whatever my lot, Thou hast taught me to say,
> "It is well, it is well with my soul."
>
> Though Satan should buffet, tho' trials should come,
> Let this blest assurance control,
> That Christ has regarded my helpless estate,
> And hath shed His own blood for my soul.[8]

Do you know what all of us witnessed that evening? More than a melody. More than grand and glorious lyrics. Much, much more. In a very real sense, we witnessed the surpassing value of an attitude in a life that literally had nothing else to cling to. Joni Eareckson . . . and one string.

DISCUSSION QUESTIONS AND SUGGESTIONS TO HELP YOU STRENGTHEN YOUR GRIP ON ATTITUDES

• Let's begin by describing or defining *attitude*. What is it? How does it differ from things like conduct and competence? Since it *is* different from both, does one's attitude affect either one? Explain your answer.

• Biblically, we found that God says a lot about our attitudes in His Book. Can you recall one or two passages in particular that took on new meaning as a result of this chapter? Try to be specific as you state the practical significance of the scriptural references.

• Because Philippians 4:8 was a scriptural climax to the chapter, let's zero in on the six areas the verse instructs us to "let your mind dwell on." Taking each, one at a time, work your way along. Stop, think, meditate, and then talk about how each fits into some category of your life that has begun to trouble you or perhaps challenge you.

• Now let's talk about some of the darker sides of our attitudes. Risk being deeply honest as you open up and admit the battleground within. In which area(s) do you face your greatest struggles? For example, are you more often negative than positive? Or are you stubborn and closed rather than open and willing to hear? How's your attitude toward people very different from you? Are you prejudiced? Look over James 2:1-4.

• Compare a few verses from the book of Proverbs. Like Proverbs 4:20-23; 12:25; 15:13, 15, 30. Choose one and explain how it applies to your own personal life.

• And now—let's pray. For a change, don't pray for yourself, but for the person sitting on your left. Call his or her name before the Lord and ask for one or two specifics on that person's behalf. Give Him thanks for the changes He will bring in your attitude and the attitudes of others. As they happen this week in your life, note the changes and give God praise in your heart.

14

Strengthening
Your Grip
on Evangelism

"The evangelistic harvest is always urgent. The destiny of men and of nations is always being decided. Every generation is strategic. We are not responsible for the past generation, and we cannot bear the full responsibility for the next one; but we do have our generation. God will hold us responsible as to how well we fulfill our responsibilities to this age and take advantage of our opportunities."[1]

Those are the words of Billy Graham. And the man ought to know. He has spoken publicly about Christ to more people in our generation than anyone else. His evangelistic crusades have had an impact on more cities around the world and invaded more homes (thanks to television) than any other evangelistic outreach in the history of time. We cannot think of the name *Billy Graham* without attaching the word *evangelism* to it. He has a strong grip on the subject, but the question is, do we?

Probably not.

Most of us want to. We *wish* we did. We are certainly aware of the need and, if the whole truth could be told, some of us have even taken courses to help us become better at witnessing, but we still stumble. Our grip on evangelism is weak—embarrassingly weak.

A fellow pastor was honest enough to admit this in an article he wrote for a Christian magazine. Because it illustrates so well the problem all of us wrestle with, I want to share it with you. The pastor, dressed in a comfortable pair of old blue jeans, boarded a plane to return home. He settled into the last unoccupied seat next to a well-dressed businessman with the *Wall Street Journal* tucked under his arm. The minister, a little embarrassed over his casual attire,

311

decided he'd look straight ahead and, for sure, stay out of any in-depth conversation. But the plan didn't work. The man greeted him, so, to be polite, the pastor asked about the man's work. Here's what happened:

"I'm in the figure salon business. We can change a woman's self-concept by changing her body. It's really a very profound, powerful thing."

His pride spoke between the lines.

"You look my age," I said. "Have you been at this long?"

"I just graduated from the University of Michigan's School of Business Administration. They've given me so much responsibility already, and I feel very honored. In fact, I hope to eventually manage the western part of the operation."

"So, you are a national organization?" I asked, becoming impressed despite myself.

"Oh, yes. We are the fastest growing company of our kind in the nation. It's really good to be a part of an organization like that, don't you think?"

I nodded approvingly and thought, "Impressive. Proud of his work and accomplishments. . . . Why can't Christians be proud like that? Why are we so often apologetic about our faith and our church?"

Looking askance at my clothing, he asked the inevitable question, "And what do you do?" . . .

"It's interesting that we have similar business interests," I said. "You are in the body-changing business; I'm in the personality-changing business. We apply 'basic theocratic principles to accomplish indigenous personality modification.'"

He was hooked, but I knew he would never admit it. (Pride is powerful.)

"You know, I've heard about that," he replied, hesitantly. "But do you have an office here in the city?"

"Oh, we have many offices. We have offices here and down the state. In fact, we're national: we have at least one office in every state of the union, including Alaska and Hawaii."

He had this puzzled look on his face. He was searching his mind to identify this huge company he *must* have read or heard about, perhaps in his *Wall Street Journal.*

"As a matter of fact, we've gone international. And Management has a plan to put at least one office in every country of the world by the end of this business era."

I paused.

"Do you have that in your business?" I asked.

"Well, no. Not yet." he answered. "But you mentioned management. How do they make it work?"

"It's a family concern. There's a Father and a Son. . . . And they run everything."

"It must take a lot of capital," he asked, skeptically.

"You mean money?" I asked. "Yes, I suppose so. No one knows just how much it takes, but we never worry because there's never a shortage. The Boss always seems to have enough. He's a very creative guy. . . . And the money is, well, just there. In fact those of us in the Organization have a saying about our Boss, 'He owns the cattle on a thousands hills.'"

"Oh, he's into ranching too?" asked my captive friend.

"No, it's just a saying we use to indicate his wealth."

My friend sat back in his seat, musing over our conversation. "What about with you?" he asked.

"The employees? They are something to see," I said. "They have a 'Spirit' that pervades the organization. It works like this: the Father and Son love each other so much that their love filters down through the organization so that we all find ourselves loving one another too. I know this sounds old-fashioned in a world like ours, but I know people in the organization who are willing to die for me. Do you have that in your business?" I was almost shouting now. People were starting to shift noticeably in their seats.

"Not yet," he said. Quickly changing strategies, he asked, "But do you have good benefits?"

"They're substantial," I countered, with a gleam. "I have complete life insurance, fire insurance—all the basics. You might not believe this, but it's true: I have holdings in a mansion that's being built for me right now for my retirement. Do you have that in your business?"

"Not yet," he answered, wistfully. The light was dawning.

"You know, one thing bothers me about all you're saying. I've read the journals, and if your business is all you say it is, why haven't I heard about it before now?"

"That's a good question," I said. "After all, we have a 2000-year-old tradition."

"Wait a minute!" he said.

"You're right," I interrupted. "I'm talking about the church."

"I knew it. You know, I'm Jewish."

"Want to sign up?" I asked.[2]

We've all been there, haven't we? Most of us are not as creative as the minister, however. We just stumble through a few words and hope the person soon changes the subject. We feel awkward.

FOUR HINDRANCES TO EVANGELISM

When you analyze our lack of evangelistic success and skill, it boils down to four primary reasons.

1. *Ignorance*

We just don't know how to do it. We have no method or proven "technique" that allows us to feel comfortable talking to others about Christ. We don't like a canned approach so we wind up with no approach.

2. *Fear*

Most of us are just plain scared. We're afraid the person will ask us a question we can't answer. Or he or she may become angry and tell us off.

3. *Indifference*
Hard as it is to admit it, many Christians just don't care. We think, "If that's the way the person wants to believe, that's fine. To each his own."
4. *Bad Experience*
More and more I meet believers who were turned off during their non-Christian years by some wild-eyed fanatic who pushed and embarrassed them, trying to force a decision. The result? A reluctance to say *anything* at all.

ONE MAJOR PRINCIPLE TO REMEMBER

If it's possible, let's set aside all those excuses and start from scratch. In fact, let's start *below* scratch. There is one principle that has helped me more than any other. It never fails to rescue me from dumb mistakes, and when I forget to employ it, I suffer the consequences. Here it is:

PUT YOURSELF IN THE OTHER PERSON'S PLACE.

If we can keep in mind that the person is not coming from where we are, nor does he or she understand where we are going, it will help greatly. Not infrequently will we encounter people who have an entirely different mindset or cultural background from ours, thus adding immeasurably to the complication. Jim Petersen, with The Navigators in Brazil, tells of witnessing to a well-educated industrial chemist named Osvaldo. Jim had been studying the Bible with the man's brother and Osvaldo was curious about why his brother became so interested. Jim attempted to answer the chemist's questions by explaining the gospel to him.

> I got a piece of chalk and a Bible and used the wooden floor as a chalkboard. I spent the next two hours showing him a favorite diagram I often used to explain the message. I was quite satisfied with my performance, and when I finally finished, I leaned back to observe his reaction, certain he would be on the verge of repentance.
> Instead, he gazed at my illustration, then at me. He was puzzled. "Do you mean to tell me that this is why you came all the way to Brazil, to tell people that?" he said.
> To Osvaldo, what I had said seemed insignificant and irrelevant. I recognized at that moment that I was facing a communication problem I had never been aware of before.[3]

Jim was wise not to argue or push. He was honest enough to realize the man wasn't being argumentative . . . he was just coming from another frame of reference. Those who cultivate the skill of evangelism do their best to put themselves inside the other person's skin. They do this by thinking thoughts like:

"Please think about what I'm saying. Don't just expect me to listen, you listen, too."

"If you want me to hear you, scratch my itches."

"Talk with me—don't talk down to me."

"Make sense. No riddles or secret religious code words, okay?"

SIX GUIDELINES WORTH REMEMBERING

All of this leads us to an account in the New Testament where one man witnessed to another with remarkable success—because he did so with wisdom and skill. I never cease to marvel at the beautiful way God used him to reach out to a person (a total stranger!) from another culture and graciously guide the man to faith in Jesus Christ.

The story is found in Acts 8, a story that begins in the midst of an exciting revival, much like one that sweeps across a city during a Billy Graham Crusade. In Acts 8 the territory where revival fires are spreading is Samaria.

> And so, when they had solemnly testified and spoken the word of the Lord, they started back to Jerusalem, and were preaching the gospel to many villages of the Samaritans (Acts 8:25).

There was renewed enthusiasm. Those bold Christians were proclaiming Christ from village to village. The Spirit of God was working. The atmosphere was electric. If you've ever been a part of a scene like this, you need no further explanation. If you haven't, you cannot imagine the excitement. A contagious, authentic enthusiasm ignites the souls of men and women with such spiritual fire it's almost frightening.

Suddenly God steps in and does something strange. Without prior announcement—out of the clear blue—He dispatches an angel from heaven and redirects a man named Philip.

> But an angel of the Lord spoke to Philip saying, "Arise and go south to the road that descends from Jerusalem to Gaza." (This is a desert road.)
> And he arose and went . . . (Acts 8:26–27a).

I'd like us to remember several guidelines that relate to personal evangelism. Each one will help us hurdle the barriers and become skilled in sharing our faith. The first of six is found here at the beginning of this account.

Sensitivity

How easy it would have been for Philip to be so caught up in the excitement and electricity of that Samaritan revival—where God was obviously at work— that he wasn't sensitive to a new direction. Not this man! He was alert and ready. Each day marked a new beginning. He had walked with God long enough to know that He has the right to throw a surprise curve—*and often does*!

Without stating His reason, without revealing the ultimate plan, God led Philip away from Samaria and out onto a desert road. The man was so sensitive to God's leading there was no struggle. People who become skilled in sharing their faith possess this sensitivity to God.

Availability

With sensitivity comes availability. There's no use having a sensitive spirit if we are not available and willing to go . . . wherever. Take a look at the next episode in Philip's life:

> . . . and behold, there was an Ethiopian enuch, a court official of Candace, queen of the Ethiopians, who was in charge of all her treasure and he had come to Jerusalem to worship.
> And he was returning and sitting in his chariot, and was reading the prophet Isaiah.
> And the Spirit said to Philip, "Go up and join this chariot" (Acts 8:27b–29).

Like our pastor friend on the plane, Philip encountered a choice opportunity. Who was riding along that desert road? A political leader from the third world. The Secretary of the Treasury of the Candace Dynasty, no less! And where had he been? To church! But the Ethiopian official had not met the Lord—he had only had his curiosity aroused. But out there in the middle of the desert is this guy in a chariot reading the Scriptures. Don't tell me God can't pull it off! And of all places to be reading, the man is reading Isaiah 53, the seed plot of the gospel in the Old Testament. God says to His servant Philip, "Go for it . . . join up with that chariot!"

Those who are available experience exciting moments like this. It's thrilling to be a part of the irresistible momentum, caught in the current of the Spirit's working. Philip's obedience pays off. His heart must have begun to beat faster.

Initiative

Look at the next move Philip made:

> And when Philip had run up, he heard him reading Isaiah the prophet, and said, "Do you understand what you are reading?" (Acts 8:30).

He took the initiative. But there is not a hint of offense or put down in his approach. Just simply, "Do you know what you are reading?" He genuinely wanted to know if the stranger in the chariot understood those words.

Initiative is so important. It is the first plank in the bridge-building process. But like the cornerstone, it must be placed very carefully. And the use of questions is an excellent approach. Here are a few I have used with a good deal of success:

"Say, I've been reading a lot about our world lately. Do you have any idea what's gone wrong?"

"I'm interested in the lives of great men and women. Who, in your opinion, was the greatest person who ever lived?"

"What do you think of our President? I mean, with that former football player as his minister in California, do you think he's really a Christian?"

"With all these earthquakes and other calamities that happen so quickly, what keeps you from being afraid? Do you pray or something?"

Authoress Ann Kiemel asks, "Can I sing to you?" Now *that's* a creative starter! The late Paul Little was a master at taking the initiative. He mentions a few suggestions that I have found helpful.

After even a vague reference to "religion" in a conversation, many Christians have used this practical series of questions to draw out latent spiritual interest: First, "By the way, are you interested in spiritual things?" Many will say, "Yes." But even if the person says, "No," we can ask a second question, "What do you think a real Christian is?" Wanting to hear his opinion invariably pleases a person. From his response we'll also gain a more accurate, first-hand—if perhaps shocking—understanding of his thinking as a non-Christian; and because we have listened to him he'll be much more ready to listen to us. Answers to this question usually revolve around some external action—going to church, reading the Bible, praying, tithing, being baptized. After such an answer we can agree that a real Christian usually *does* these things, but then point out that that's not what a real Christian *is*. A real Christian is one who is personally related to Jesus Christ as a living Person . . .

The bait can also be thrown out succinctly if we are prepared for questions we are asked frequently. Often we recognize after it is too late that we have had a wonderful opportunity to speak up but we missed it because we didn't know what to say at the moment. Sometimes we are asked questions like: "Why are you so happy?" "What makes you tick?" "You seem to have a different motivation. You're not like me and most people. Why?" "Why is it you seem to have purpose in life?" Again, we can say, "An experience I had changed my outlook on life." And then, as we are asked, we can share that experience of Christ with them.[4]

Above all, take it easy. Proceed with caution. It's like fishing. Patience, intelligence, and skill are not optional. They're *essential*. No one ever caught fish by slapping the water with an oar or by hurriedly racing through the process. Taking the initiative requires that we do so with a lot of wisdom, which brings us to the fourth guideline.

Tactfulness

There is one very obvious observation regarding Philip's method I find extremely appealing. He was completely unoffensive. It is important for Christians to remember that it is the *cross* that will be offensive, *not the one who witnesses*. Philip used tact as he became involved in a discussion with the Ethiopian official.

> And when Philip had run up, he heard him reading Isaiah the prophet, and said, "Do you understand what you are reading?"
> And he said, "Well, how could I, unless someone guides me?" And he invited Philip to come up and sit with him.
> Now the passage of Scripture which he was reading was this:
>
> "HE WAS LED AS A SHEEP TO SLAUGHTER;
> AND AS A LAMB BEFORE ITS SHEARER IS SILENT,
> SO HE DOES NOT OPEN HIS MOUTH,
> IN HUMILIATION HIS JUDGMENT WAS TAKEN AWAY;
> WHO SHALL RELATE HIS GENERATION?
> FOR HIS LIFE IS REMOVED FROM THE EARTH."
>
> And the eunuch answered Philip and said, "Please tell me, of whom does the prophet say this? Of himself, or of someone else?" (Acts 8:30–34).

He listened without responding as the man confessed his ignorance. He graciously awaited an invitation to climb up into the chariot before doing so. He started where the man was, rather than cranking out a canned sermon. Not once did Philip put the man down. Or pull rank. Or attempt to impress. He gave the stranger space to think it through without feeling foolish.

Rebecca Pippert, in her fine book on evangelism, *Out of the Salt Shaker and Into the World*, mentions the need for this approach:

> . . . I remember a skeptical student who said, "I could never be a Christian. My commitment to scholarship makes any consideration of Christianity impossible. It's irrational and the evidence supporting it is totally insufficient."
> I answered, "I'm so glad you care so much about truth and that you really want evidence to support your beliefs. You say the evidence for Christianity is terribly insufficient. What was your conclusion after carefully investigating the primary biblical documents?"
> "Ahhh, well, you mean the Bible?" he asked.
> "Of course," I said. "The New Testament accounts of Jesus, for example. Where did you find them lacking?"
> "Oh, well, look, I remember mother reading me those stories when I was ten," he replied.
> "Hmm, but what was your conclusion?" I continued and as a result discovered he had never investigated the Scriptures critically as an adult. This is all too often

the case. But we can arouse curiosity in others to investigate the claims of the gospel when we help them see that their information and understanding about Christianity is lacking.

Another person who was quite hostile to what she perceived as Christianity told me in anger, "I can't stand those hypocrites who go to church every Sunday. They make me sick."

"Yes," I responded, "isn't it amazing how far they are from true Christianity? When you think of how vast the difference is between the real thing and what they do, it's like worlds apart. Ever since I've discovered what Christianity is really about, the more mystified I am."

"Ah, the real thing? Well, what do you mean by that?" she asked. We talked for an hour about faith because her hostility had been changed into curiosity.[5]

Rather than arguing, try to find a way to agree. Rather than attacking, show genuine concern. Uphold the dignity of the individual. He or she may not be a Christian, but that is no reason to think the person lacks our respect. As questions are asked (like the Ethiopian asked in verse 34), kindly offer an answer. That man was a Gentile. He had no idea of whom Isaiah, the Jewish prophet was speaking. Philip stayed calm and tactful. But when the moment was right, he came to the point.

Preciseness

In answer to the man's question, Philip spoke precisely and clearly of Jesus Christ, the Messiah:

And the eunuch answered Philip and said, "Please tell me, of whom does the prophet say this? Of himself, or of someone else?"
And Philip opened his mouth, and beginning from this Scripture he preached Jesus to him (Acts 8:34–35).

He started at square one—no mumbo-jumbo, no jargon, no double-talk, no scary charts of pyramids of multiheaded beasts or superaggressive "believe now or you'll go to hell" threats. Just *Jesus*—Jesus' person and work, Jesus' love for sinners, Jesus' perfect life and sacrificial death, Jesus' resurrection and offer of forgiveness, security, purpose, and hope. "He preached Jesus. . . ."

Stay on the issue of Christ when witnessing. Not the church or denominations or religion or theological differences or doctrinal questions. Speak precisely of Jesus, the Savior. Refuse to dart down rabbit trails. Satellite subjects are often tantalizingly tempting, but *refrain*! When self-control is applied, the other person will realize that the gospel revolves strictly around Christ and nothing else. See what happened?

And Philip said, "If you believe with all your heart, you may." And he answered and said, "I believe that Jesus Christ is the Son of God."

And he ordered the chariot to stop; and they both went down into the water, Philip as well as the eunuch; and he baptized him.

And when they came up out of the water, the Spirit of the Lord snatched Philip away; and the eunuch saw him no more, but went on his way rejoicing (Act 8:37–39).

Decisiveness

The African gentleman suggested that he be baptized. Wisely, Philip put first things first. With decisive discernment, Philip explained that faith in Jesus *precedes* baptism. That did it! The man believed and was *then* baptized. No ifs, ands, or buts. *First* there was an acceptance of the message and *after that* there was a public acknowledgment of his faith as he submitted to baptism.

SUMMARY AND CONCLUSION

Do you genuinely desire to strengthen your grip on evangelism? Are you honestly interested in sharing your faith with this generation of lost and confused people? Begin to cultivate these six guidelines:

- *Sensitivity*. Listen carefully. Be ready to follow God's leading.
- *Availability*. Stay flexible. If the Lord is directing you to move here or there, go.
- *Initiative*. Use an appropriate approach to break the ice.
- *Tactfulness*. With care and courtesy, with thoughtfulness, with a desire to uphold dignity, speak graciously.
- *Preciseness*. Remember the issue is Christ. Stay on that subject.
- *Decisiveness*. As the Spirit of God is evidently at work, speak of receiving Christ. Make it clear that Jesus Christ is ready to receive whoever may come to Him by faith.

I began this chapter with a statement evangelist Billy Graham once made. I close with the same question for emphasis.

The evangelistic harvest is always urgent. The destiny of men and of nations is always being decided.

Every generation is strategic. We are not responsible for the past generation, and we cannot bear the full responsibility for the next one; but we do have our generation. God will hold us responsible as to how well we fulfill our responsibilities to this age and take advantage of our opportunities.[6]

Because today's harvest is urgent, because we are held responsible to make Christ known to our generation, let's not allow our laid-back, who-really-cares society to weaken our enthusiasm or slacken our zeal.

Let's strengthen our grip on evangelism.

DISCUSSION QUESTIONS AND SUGGESTIONS TO HELP YOU STRENGTHEN YOUR GRIP ON EVANGELISM

• What do you think of when *evangelism* is mentioned? Talk about how you heard of Christ—the very first time you can remember being told of the gospel. What was the method used? Did it turn you on or off? Why? What stands out most in your mind when you recall the person who witnessed to you?

• We worked our way fairly carefully through a section of Acts 8 in this chapter. Turn to those verses (vv. 26–40) and see if you can remember a few of the guidelines. Ideally, see if all those in your group can reconstruct all six of them, in order.

• Pick one from the list and talk it over. Why is this so significant that you chose it over all the others?

• If you have a copy of *The Living Bible*, try this for a change. One of you read the part of Philip and another the part of the Ethiopian official. In this role-playing episode, imagine yourself in that person's skin. Afterwards, discuss what it was, humanly speaking, that caused the official to stay interested.

• Now then discuss ways that open the door to a meaningful witnessing experience. State (and write down) some of the verbal wedges that help you win a hearing.

• Complete the following:

Things to Guard Against   Things to Remember
(The Negative Turn-offs)   (The Positive Approaches)

• Here's a project for each one of you to try. During the coming week *pray* that you might be sensitive to at least one opportunity to witness. *Think* about what you want to communicate ahead of time. As the occasion occurs, *speak* graciously and carefully. Finally, be ready to *ask* the person if he or she would wish to receive the gift of eternal life. Report back and tell of your encounter.

15

Strengthening
Your Grip
on Authority

Question authority!—These words are not simply a bumper sticker slogan on vans in Southern California, they're fast becoming the unwritten motto of the 1980s. Let's face it, this generation is tough, not tender.

No longer . . .

. . . is the voice of the parent respected in the home.

. . . is the sight of the policeman on the corner a model of courage and control.

. . . is the warning of the teacher in the classroom feared and obeyed.

. . . is the reprimand of the boss sufficient to bring about change.

. . . is the older person treated with dignity and honor.

. . . is the husband considered "the head of the home" (God help him if he even *thinks* such a thing!).

THE PROBLEM IS OBVIOUS

Not even the President of our nation carries the clout he once did. Ours is a talk-back, fight-back, get-even society that is ready to resist—and sue—at the slightest provocation. Instead of the obedient Minute Man representing our national image, a new statue with a curled upper lip, an open mouth screaming obscenities, and both fists in the air could better describe our times. Defiance, resistance, violence, and retaliation are now our "style." If you can believe it,

323

there is even a Children's Rights Movement now established. This organization has declared its objectives in a "Child's Bill of Rights,"[1] that doesn't simply weaken parental authority, it *demolishes* it. As you would expect, it shifts the final controls from the home to the courtroom . . . making the judge the authority (what a joke!), not the parent.

Dr. James Dobson, a personal friend of mine and a man I respect for his unbending commitment to marriage and the family, addresses this whole issue quite forcefully in one of his books. He then cites a case in point:

> Only last month I received a letter from an attorney who sought my help in defending a father who was threatened with the loss of his child. The details are difficult to believe. It appears that the Department of Social Service in his community is attempting to remove a six-year-old girl from her home because her father will not permit her to attend movies, listen to rock music or watch certain television programs. This child is well adjusted emotionally and is popular with her friends in school. Her teacher reports that she ranks in the top five students in her class, academically. Nevertheless, the courts are being asked to remove her from her home because of the intolerable "abuse" she is experiencing there.[2]

We have a large number of educators in our church in Fullerton. One is a gentleman who teaches high school math in a Los Angeles public school. The man could keep all of us occupied for three hours or more relating one story after another about discipline problems in his classroom. He once told me he spends about ten minutes each class period actually teaching math and about forty minutes dealing with rebellion and related disciplinary issues.

Another teacher in her fifties informed me at a dinner party one evening that she was retiring from the classroom. Knowing her love for the profession, I asked why she was opting for an early retirement.

"I can't take the abuse another year!" she answered. Stating further, "We teachers once had the authority and (when challenged) the backing of the principal. No more." Almost with a sigh, she added, "The teachers are now afraid of the principals, the principals are afraid of the superintendents, the superintendents are afraid of the school boards, the boards are afraid of the parents, and the parents are afraid of the children . . . but the *children*? They're not afraid of anybody!"

I'll save you the dirty details, but I should mention the whole growing concern of crime, another evidence of a society in rebellion. *Newsweek* magazine dedicated an issue to this subject, calling it "The Plague of Violent Crime."[3] I thought I was ready for the facts. I wasn't. On top of that, add child and wife batterings, street demonstrations, the ever-present plague of vandalism, employer-employee squabbles, endless lawsuits of unprecedented proportions, prison riots, political blackmail kidnappings, religious in-fighting, and the abuse of many who enforce their authority without wisdom or compassion . . . and you have the making of madness.

I fully realize there are times when resistance is needed. We would not be a free nation had we not fought for our liberty. Furthermore, the lawless would rule over the righteous if we allowed ourselves to be walked on, stolen from, and otherwise taken advantage of. There *are* times when there must be resistance and a strong determination to defend one's rights. That is not the issue I'm referring to in this chapter. My concern is the obvious erosion of respect for needed and fair authority . . . the lack of submission toward those who *should* be over us, who earn and deserve our cooperation. Instead, there is a growing independence, a stubborn defiance against *any* authority that attempts to criticize, correct, or even caution. No one can deny that this self-centered rebellion is on the rise. My desire is that we see the difference, then respond correctly to God-given authority with an attitude of true humility, the mentality mentioned in the New Testament modeled so beautifully by Jesus Christ.

> Humble yourselves in the presence of the Lord, and He will exalt you (James 4:10).

> Servants, be submissive to your masters with all respect, not only to those who are good and gentle, but also to those who are unreasonable.
> For this finds favor, if for the sake of conscience toward God a man bears up under sorrows when suffering unjustly.
> For what credit is there if, when you sin and are harshly treated, you endure it with patience? But if when you do what is right and suffer for it you patiently endure it, this finds favor with God.
> For you have been called for this purpose, since Christ also suffered for you, leaving you an example for you to follow in His steps, WHO COMMITTED NO SIN, NOR WAS ANY DECEIT FOUND IN HIS MOUTH; and while being reviled, He did not revile in return; while suffering, He uttered no threats, but kept entrusting Himself to Him who judges righteously; and He Himself bore our sins in His body on the cross, that we might die to sin and live to righteousness; for by His wounds you were healed (1 Pet. 2:18–24).

> You younger men, likewise, be subject to your elders; and all of you, clothe yourselves with humility toward one another, for GOD IS OPPOSED TO THE PROUD, BUT GIVES GRACE TO THE HUMBLE.
> Humble yourselves, therefore, under the mighty hand of God, that He may exalt you at the proper time, casting all your anxiety upon Him, because He cares for you (1 Pet. 5:5–7).

It is easy to discount such counsel in an angry age that considers rebellion a way of life and sees resistance as a virtue. To strengthen our grip on authority, it may be helpful to expose the dark, ugly side of rebellion that never gets much press.

King Saul: Personification of Rebellion

Back in the Old Testament we find a man who had a choice opportunity to lead the Hebrew people into victory. He was tall, strong, and capable. He had the charisma of a popular public figure and the vote of the nation. Saul had what it took to be the king. But the man had one major problem—himself. He could rule the people, but he couldn't rule himself. Deep down inside his soul was a carnal caldron that stayed on a low boil, belching up pride, selfishness, jealousy, and a stubborn streak of rebellion.

This is never more obvious than in 1 Samuel 15, the chapter that records the turning point in his reign. The chapter begins with a conversation the prophet Samuel had with King Saul.

> Then Samuel said to Saul, "The Lord sent me to anoint you as king over His people, over Israel; now therefore listen to the words of the Lord.
>
> "Thus says the Lord of hosts, 'I will punish Amalek for what he did to Israel, how he set himself against him on the way while he was coming up from Egypt.
>
> 'Now go and strike Amalek and utterly destroy all that he has, and do not spare him; but put to death both man and woman, child and infant, ox and sheep, camel and donkey" (1 Sam. 15:1–3).

The directive was neither complicated nor vague. God had spoken through Samuel and there was to be one response: *Obedience*. Saul was to go into battle, assault the Amalekites, and completely annihilate the enemy, including all living creatures in the enemy camp. Reading 1 Samuel 15:7, you'd think that is what occurred:

> So Saul defeated the Amalekites, from Havilah as you go to Shur, which is east of Egypt.

But no, read on.

> And he captured Agag the king of the Amalekites alive, and utterly destroyed all the people with the edge of the sword.
>
> But Saul and the people spared Agag and the best of the sheep, the oxen, the fatlings, the lambs, and all that was good, and were not willing to destroy them utterly; but everything despised and worthless, that they utterly destroyed (vv. 8–9).

I find in this biblical account four characteristics of rebellion. The first emerges from the verses we just read.

Defiance Against Authority to Accomplish One's Own Desire

The authority in this case is Almighty God. God had said, ". . . utterly destroy all." Saul had not misunderstood. He had willfully disobeyed. He wasn't confused, he was insubordinate. He did not want to follow those directions because he had his own desires. He thought of an alternate plan.

Recently my wife and I had the pleasure of spending an evening with former astronaut, General Charles M. Duke. All of us in the room sat in rapt fascination as the man told of the *Apollo 16* mission to the moon, including some interesting tidbits related to driving "Rover," the lunar vehicle, and actually walking on the surface of the planet. We were full of questions which General Duke patiently and carefully answered one after another.

I asked, "Once you were there, weren't you free to make your own decisions and carry out some of your own experiments . . . you know, sort of do as you pleased—maybe stay a little longer if you liked?" He smiled back, "Sure, Chuck, if we didn't want to return to earth!"

He then described the intricate plan, the exact and precise instructions, the essential discipline, the instant obedience that was needed right down to the split second. By the way, he said they had landed somewhat "heavy" when they touched down on the moon. He was referring to their fuel supply. They had plenty left. Guess how much. *One minute.* They landed with sixty seconds of fuel remaining. Talk about being exact! I got the distinct impression that a rebel spirit doesn't fit inside a space suit. Whoever represents the United States in the space program must have an unconditional respect for authority.

That's what King Saul lacked. He knew the game plan. He had been briefed by Samuel. But he chose to defy authority and go with Plan "B," namely his own desire. Read on.

Then the word of the Lord came to Samuel, saying, "I regret that I have made Saul king, for he has turned back from following Me, and has not carried out My commands." And Samuel was distressed and cried out to the Lord all night.

And Samuel rose early in the morning to meet Saul; and it was told Samuel, saying, "Saul came to Carmel, and behold, he set up a monument for himself, then turned and proceeded on down to Gilgal."

And Samuel came to Saul, and Saul said to him, "Blessed are you of the Lord! I have carried out the command of the Lord" (1 Sam. 15:10–13).

God saw what had happened. He also knew why. So did Samuel. But Saul? The man was so blinded, so capable at rationalization, so quick to rewrite the rules to fit his own setup, he didn't even feel guilty. With open arms and a big smile, he welcomes Samuel to the site.

. . . Saul greeted him cheerfully. "Hello there," he said. "Well, I have carried out the Lord's command" (v. 13, TLB).

328 / STRENGTHENING YOUR GRIP

This brings us to the second characteristic of a rebellious spirit.

Rationalization and Coverup to Excuse Sinful Actions

Those who resist authority become masters at this. They develop an amazing disregard for the truth. They also redefine sin. And these people, who are often Christians, are so convinced that they are right, that they are shocked when they discover otherwise. I came across an interesting statement in my reading some time ago, "Excuses are often lies packed into the skin of reason."

To highlight the contrast, compare God's statement in 1 Samuel 15:11 with Saul's remark in verse 13.

God	Saul
". . . he has turned back . . . and . . . and has not carried out My commands."	"I have carried out the command of the Lord."

The people who perfect resisting authority (especially God's) will not run out of ideas or ways to excuse wrong. They will search for reasons—often found in books!—that make wrong appear right. They will be ready to show how their actions make better sense. They will even explain how it is better for their health or welfare or future plans. And they will have no guilt whatever!

Webster's dictionary defines the act of rationalization, "to provide plausible but untrue reasons for conduct . . . to attribute one's actions to rational motives without analysis of true motives." I've heard them by the dozens every year. It makes no difference whether it's rationalizing oneself out of a marriage or into another job, away from a geographical area, or back to a friendship that isn't wholesome, rationalization works.

Saul employed it, but Samuel didn't fall for it, not for a minute. In unvarnished integrity, the prophet saw through the whole mess and asked a basic empirical question: ". . . 'What then is this bleating of the sheep in my ears, and the lowing of the oxen which I hear?'" (v. 14).

There's nothing quite like being sawed off the limb by a set of hard facts! Samuel wanted to know how there could be the sounds of life if indeed Saul had silenced all life. The king looked like the cat with canary feathers all over his mouth. Whether he was willing to admit it or not, he was guilty. He had deliberately ignored God's authoritative instruction, which reveals a third characteristic that is common to a person in his rebellious condition.

Defensiveness When Confronted with the Truth

After hearing Samuel's question, the king reacted defensively. There was no vulnerability, no repentance, no admission of wrong, no humble willingness to come clean and repent. Proud, stubborn, and maybe a bit embarrassed, he said:

. . . "They have brought them from the Amalekites for the people spared the best of the sheep and oxen, to sacrifice to the Lord your God; but the rest we have utterly destroyed" (v. 15).

Saul is scratching around for answers. Cornered, his eyes dart in the direction of those who stood near—"They did it! It was all these people." Then to soften the blow, "We saved only a few to sacrifice to Jehovah." Now he's *really* backpedaling. No matter how obvious it is that he failed to obey, Saul is not giving in.

I had a two-and-a-half hour layover at the Denver Airport last winter that proved to be an experience I'll never forget. I aged about ten years. It wasn't because of the delay, even though I usually hate to wait. It wasn't because of incompetent airline personnel. They were great. It was a small child—simply a preschooler—who also had to wait with her mother. But this child was not your basic little girl. She was uncontrollable. Her mother? You guessed it. Your typical, preoccupied, can't-be-bothered type . . . who bargains, threatens, gives in, wrings her hands, looks away, sighs, *everything but disciplines* her monster . . . er, *daughter*.

This child did it all. Dumped over ashtrays (I counted four), crawled over every seat (unoccupied or occupied) at least twice, screamed for something to drink or eat until she finally got both several times. The creature grabbed newspapers out of men's hands as they were reading, and finally she did the unpardonable. *She walked all over my shoes.* Now, dear hearts and gentle people, I don't have many untouchables. Having raised four busy children, having been engaged in public service for twenty years, and having been married almost twenty-seven years, I don't have many things left to call strictly my own. But my shoes have withstood the test of time. They are very carefully spit-shined (don't ask why, just accept it), placed in shoe trees each night, protected in the closet when I'm home, and covered with socks when I put them in luggage for travel. As each of my kids (and wife) will tell you, when I'm wearing my shoes, only one person walks on them, and that's me. If someone else steps on them, I have an immediate reaction. And it is not to pray for them. Or smile and say, "That's okay." Or brush the shoe across the back of my other leg and think, "I'll touch it up later." No—my instant reaction is to punch their lights out. I'm just being honest.

Well, I had a slight problem in the Denver Airport, you see. The one who stepped onto the holy of holies was a little child. Just a little girl. I rather doubt that she will do that again. I am happy to report she has fully recovered. (Just kidding.) No, I never placed a hand on her. Or a foot! With incredible and rare restraint I bit my tongue and tried to stay out of her path. Finally, when none of us could stand it any longer, the mother was given some loud and directive counsel. And guess what. She was offended. Why, the very idea that someone would even *think* of her child as being out of control! She was defensive when confronted with the truth. Even though surrounded by sand and ashes from dumped-over ashtrays, litter from several junk food-and-drink containers, irritated businessmen and women, plus one enraged minister with scuffed shoes, that mother could not imagine how rude we could be when one of us (!) finally and firmly stated, "Get control of your child!"

Samuel had heard enough. With a stern look and penetrating eyes, the exasperated prophet held up his hand and exclaimed: "Wait . . ."

In today's terms, "Be quiet!" or "Shut up!"

> ". . . let me tell you what the Lord said to me last night." And he said to him, "Speak!"
>
> And Samuel said, "Is it not true, though you were little in your own eyes, you were made the head of the tribes of Israel? And the Lord anointed you king over Israel, and the Lord sent you on a mission, and said, 'Go and utterly destroy the sinners, the Amalekites, and fight against them until they are exterminated.'
>
> "Why then did you not obey the voice of the Lord, but rushed upon the spoil and did what was evil in the sight of the Lord?" (vv. 16b–21).

Old Saul stubbornly stood his ground. He refused to give in, illustrating the fourth characteristic of a rebel heart.

Resistance to Authority When Wrong Has been Committed

Still passing the buck, unwilling to confess the wrong of his actions, Saul again dodges Samuel's counsel. The man *refuses* to see the error of his way. He continues to talk of offering sacrifices and using the animals they preserved for holy purposes. He mixes in a little religion to convince Samuel that a burnt offering and a sacrificial altar will make everything right.

Sound familiar?

• "I've prayed about it and I believe God led me to do it" (superpious rationalization).

• "I'm forgiven. Grace has covered it all. The Lord will use me in a greater way. He understands" (accommodating theology).

• "Even though I may have altered His plan, in the end He will be pleased" (end justifies the means).

• "Nobody's perfect" (universal generalization).

• "God wants me to be happy" (guilt-relieving excuse).

Let's take a close look at God's counsel through Samuel. Read it as though the man were saying it to us:

> And Samuel said, "Has the Lord as much delight in burnt offerings and sacrifices as in obeying the voice of the Lord? Behold, to obey is better than sacrifice, and to heed than the fat of rams (vv. 22–23).

This is one of the strongest warnings in all of Scripture. It strips away all our excuses, all our attempts at lowering His standard. It brings us back to the one thing that pleases and glorifies Him (whether or not it satisfies us!) . . . *obedience.*

Take the time to reread that last verse. God says that rebellion is not a slight misdemeanor, something we needn't fuss over. No, it is in the same category as demonic involvement. And what about insubordination? Is it just a little difficulty all of us have to get used to? No way. It is "as iniquity and idolatry." Strong, strong, strong! *The Living Bible* says:

> . . . rebellion is as bad as the sin of witchcraft, and stubbornness is as bad as worshipping idols (1 Sam. 15:23).

Stunned, Saul finally submits, "I have sinned" (v. 24).

YOU AND ME: A PERSONAL APPLICATION

In a world hell-bent on having its own way, it is terribly difficult to cultivate the right attitude toward authority. The "QUESTION AUTHORITY!" mentality is so interwoven into the fabric of our society, it seems impossible to counteract it. Realistically, about the only place we can come to terms with it is in our homes. Are you doing this? Be honest, now. Within the walls of your dwelling are you maintaining the controls? Maybe these three warnings will encourage you to stay at it . . . or start today.

1. *Childhood.* A rebellious nature is conceived in a home where parents relinquish control.

2. *Adolescence.* A rebellious spirit will be cultivated among peers who resist control. And if it isn't curbed there, it culminates at—

3. *Adulthood.* A rebellious life must be crushed by God when He regains control.

And take it from one who experienced it and deals with it week after week, nothing is more painful to endure. Some must discover the need for a submissive spirit behind bars. Others, following a divorce. Still others, through a crippling disease or a horrible automobile accident or a series of blows in life that drive us to our knees and force us to learn how to walk humbly with our God.

When Cain curled his lip and stood tight-fisted in rebellion before his Maker, he was given a sobering warning that has been preserved in Scripture for all to read and heed:

> . . . if you do not do well, sin is crouching at the door; and its desire is for you, but you must master it (Gen. 4:7b).

Nothing has changed. The mark of Cain has been branded on this generation. Resisting authority still crouches like a beast at the door, ready to spring and pounce on its prey, be it parent or policeman or teacher or employer or minister or President—whomever. Some never learn to "master it" and therefore spend their lives "under the smarting rod of God," as the old Puritans used to say. Those who question authority face a hard future.

My friend, are you in that category? Do you have a loose grip on authority? Do you think you can continue to endure God's attempts to humble you? I heard a statement many years ago that provides an appropriate ending to this chapter. If it applies to you, let its message go deep within:

> When God wants to do an impossible task,
> He takes an impossible person and crushes him.

With one word, I close—
Surrender.

Discussion Questions and Suggestions to Help You Strengthen Your Grip on Authority

• Rebellion, according to one of the scriptures we looked at toward the end of this chapter, "is as the sin of divination" (1 Sam 15:23). What does that say to you—what does it mean? Discuss the implications of comparing rebellion with such a horrible sin. Why do you think God takes that strong a stand against it?

• No sin with the magnitude of rebellion "just happens." It is not an overnight occurrence. What prompts it? Are there hints that it is brewing before it actually comes to the surface?

• Obviously, ours is a rebellious world. Talk about this. Try to be specific as you think through the reasons for this rebellion. Can you name a few examples from recent events that illustrate rebellion? Need a few hints? How about the American home, the school, riots, Iran, and the increase in crime?

• Using Romans 1:28-32 as your guide, talk about the direct link between refusing to "acknowledge God any longer" and the scene that follows. In verse 32, there is mentioned those who "give hearty approval to those who practice" rebellious deeds. Can we be "passive rebels"?

• Discuss the difference between honest (and even humble) disagreement and overt rebellion. Can't there be a genuine, necessary resistance without the presence of sinful insubordination and rebellion? Look at Acts 5:40-42 for a scriptural case in point. Compare that with Genesis 4:6-7.

• Okay, how do we resist or disagree *without* rebelling, in the wrong sense of the term. Think of a few examples and describe both right and wrong responses. Any scriptures come to mind?

• Finally, spend some time in prayer. Before doing so, honestly admit an area of your own life where you struggle with rebellion. Your superior at work? Your mate or parents at home? The policeman in the squad car? Some "authority figure" who represents a source of irritation? Pray for one another, asking the Lord to assist your friend in that dilemma.

16

Strengthening
Your Grip
on the Family

In 1975 Edith Schaeffer, wife of Dr. Francis Schaeffer, asked a question that deserves an answer every year. That question became the title of her book, *What Is a Family?*[1] It's a good question. Every twelve to fifteen months, each one of us would do well to analyze and evaluate our family, facing up to the truth of our answer. Certainly every generation would be wise to do so. It may surprise us.

Edith Schaeffer suggests several answers, each one forming a separate chapter in her book. For example:

A Changing Life Mobile
The Birthplace of Creativity
A Formation Center for Human Relationships
A Shelter in a Time of Storm
A Perpetual Relay of Truth
A Door That Has Hinges and a Lock
A Museum of Memories.

Good answers. Insightful answers. Beautiful . . . almost *too* beautiful. But we cannot deny that these are the ideal, the ones most of us would embrace. *But are they real?* To help us determine that answer, let's just change one word, "What is *your* family?" What terms would best describe the things that go on under the roof where *you* live, among the members of *your* family?

Today's Family: The Picture Is Grim

It comes as a surprise to nobody that the family is under fire these days. When one national periodical did a special report on the American domestic scene, the issue was not entitled "Strengthening the Family" or "Examining the Family" or "Depending on the Family." It was *"Saving* the Family."[2] Like the prairie bison and the sperm whale and the crane, the family is fast becoming an endangered species. For sure, it is a different scene from the quiet, heart-warming scenes of yesteryear when mom was always home, dad was the sole breadwinner, children lived predictable lives of ease and relaxation, and the lifestyle was laid back and simple.

From a combination of several television documentaries plus the popular program "60 Minutes," a couple of seminars I have attended in recent months, magazine and newspaper articles, conversations with authorities on the family, and a few books I have read on the subject, I have compiled the following list of facts. Without attempting to document each one, allow me a few moments to outline a general profile of today's family. I warn you, the picture is grim.

- 38 percent of all first marriages fail (conservative figure).
- 79 percent of those people will remarry and 44 percent of the *second* marriages will fail.
- During the 1970s, four out of ten babies born in that decade will spend part or all of their childhood in single-parent homes.
- 15 percent of all births today are illegitimate (also conservative) and 50 percent of the out-of-wedlock babies are born to teenagers.
- Approximately two million American children who do live with both parents are "latch key kids" . . . they come home from school to an empty house. Both parents work.
- Two hundred thousand American children are physically abused each year. Of those, between sixty and one hundred thousand are *sexually* abused.
- 15 percent to 20 percent of American families abuse their children.
- The No. 1 killer of children under five years of age is child abuse.
- Child abusers are in every category of our society. No social, racial, economic, or religious group is excluded.
- Only 10 percent of reported child abusers are classified "mentally disturbed." The rest are people who appear to be very normal but "cannot cope."
- 30 percent of all American couples experience some form of domestic violence during their lifetime. Two million (again a conservative estimate) have used a lethal weapon on each other during their marriage.
- 20 percent of all police officers who die in the line of duty are killed while answering calls involving family conflicts.
- An average of thirteen teenagers kill themselves each day in the United States—an out-of-date statistic . . . much higher now. Suicide is now the No. 2 killer among Americans aged fifteen to twenty-four.
- Wife battering is now reaching an epidemic level in our nation. In the

opinion of one Los Angeles police official, "This is probably the highest unreported crime in the country. Approximately twelve to fifteen million women are battered each year."

A study completed at the University of Rhode Island described the American home as the most dangerous place to be outside of riots and a war. The scene is desperate. And I haven't even mentioned the impact of alcoholism, drug abuse, mental and emotional breakdowns, and the ever-present tension caused by runaway teens, runaway wives, walk-out husbands, and gross neglect of the aged by their family members. If ever there is a need for a nation to strengthen her grip on any one area of need, it is obviously *the family*.

HOPE FOR THE FAMILY UNDER FIRE

Enough of statistics and doomsday predictions! Let's spend the balance of our time thinking through some answers, getting help from the ancient, time-tested wisdom of the Scriptures. Here (and *only* here) will we find counsel that is inspired of God, workable, realistic, and full of promise. And best of all, the Bible is constantly relevant, never anchored to the lifestyle of a particular era. The things we are about to discover are for us today just as much as they were for the people to whom they were originally written.

To help us come back to some basics about the family and strengthen our grip on this vital area of life, we'll dig into a couple of the ancient psalms that appear back-to-back in the Bible, Psalm 127 and Psalm 128.

The Family in Four Stages

When we read through the eleven verses that comprise these two psalms, we have little difficulty seeing how they flow together. Actually, they cover four major stages through which a family passes . . . sort of a panoramic, time-sequence scenario of the family as it progresses from one stage to the next. We could call these psalms a domestic mural.

Stage 1: The family in its early years, from marriage to the birth of the first child (Ps. 127:1-2).

Stage 2: The family expands to include the birth of children (Ps. 127:3-5).

Stage 3: The family goes through the years of training, loving, discipling, and ultimately releasing the children (Ps. 128:1-3).

Stage 4: The family is reduced to its original condition—a husband and wife in their twilight years together (Ps. 128:4-6).

The Family from God's Perspective

Before going into each stage and drawing insight from God's Word for today's family, let's understand that we are interested in *God's* perspective, not man's.

Bookshelves in stores are running over with volumes on every conceivable subject about family living. In a local bookstore I counted twenty-three titles on books for helping parents with their babies—just for parents with babies. I found another seventeen books promising help in raising teenagers. And, by the way, several of them suggest methods that contradict the counsel of other authors, so whom do we believe? Which philosophy should I adopt? And if I adopt *this* one, how do I ignore *that* one (since it is written by an authority of equal significance)? The scene gets increasingly more complicated the more we seek divided human opinions as opposed to divine counsel from God's Book.

In my more exasperated moments as a parent, I'm tempted to believe that Mark Twain's philosophy is the one to follow: When a kid turns thirteen, stick him in a barrel, nail the lid on top, and feed him through the knot hole. When he turns sixteen . . . *plug up the knot hole.* But not even that plan will work. Neither you nor I have ever seen a teenager who could get enough food to survive through the knot hole of a barrel!

No, what we need most is God's perspective on family life.

STAGE 1: THE INCEPTION OF THE FAMILY

These are the foundational years, the time when a man and woman join their lives together in marriage and learn to adjust to the new experience of living intimately with another person. God says this about that important and often difficult period of time.

Unless the Lord builds the house,
They labor in vain who build it;
Unless the Lord guards the city,
The watchman keeps awake in vain.

It is vain for you to rise up early,
To retire late,
To eat the bread of painful labors;
For He gives to His beloved even in his sleep.
(Ps. 127:1-2)

Using word pictures from a Jewish mentality, Solomon, himself a Jew, compares the home to a city. In those days it was not uncommon for an ancient city to be built by having its walls finished first to keep out the enemy. After its completion and dedication to Jehovah, the wall would be walked upon by guards continually on the lookout for attack.

What is Solomon saying in this analogy? "Unless the city officials and the military guards depend completely on Jehovah, and not just the city wall, no enemy will be kept out."

Twice the writer uses the same words, "Unless the Lord . . . in vain . . . unless the Lord . . . it is vain. . . ." Here's the idea. During those all-important early months and years of marriage, make sure that the Lord your God is the heart and center of your family! If He is not, the whole experience is a study in futility—a wasted, empty, counterproductive effort. It will all be in vain. He doesn't have in mind a home that hangs a lot of religious mottos on the walls or a couple that simply goes to church regularly or offers up a quick prayer before meals or places a big Bible on the living room coffee table. No, the essential ingredient is "the Lord." A family gets started on the right foot when Jesus Christ is in each life (husband and wife are both born again), and when the lengthening shadow of His Lordship pervades that relationship. When a couple makes Christ a vital part of their life, in the terms of the psalm, that's when "the Lord builds the house," that's when He "guards the city."

But you know how we are, especially those caught in the grip and grind of materialism. We are so busy—anxious to get ahead, pushing and pulling for more, always more—that we begin to tell ourselves lies. Like, "What we need is more things, a nicer car, bigger-and-better stuff." The psalmist warns us that rising up early and dropping in bed late (hoping to find satisfaction in things) is vain. We "eat the bread of painful labors" when we worship the god of materialism. Interestingly, if that philosophy is adopted by a couple, it is often during their first few years together.

If you want a family that is different, distinctly set apart for God's glory—a family that enjoys life and reaps the rewards of His best gifts, then *start right*. And if you failed to start right back then, *start today*. As I mentioned earlier in this book, it is never too late to start doing what is right. Put your Lord back in top priority. As a husband-wife team, acknowledge the fact that you have sowed the wind and reaped the whirlwind. It will be a slow and tedious process putting first things first, but you can do it! And don't forget the closing statement of verse 2: "He gives to His beloved even in his sleep." God will work overtime helping you and giving to you the things that will make your renewed commitment stick.

STAGE 2: THE EXPANSION OF THE FAMILY

Behold, children are a gift of the Lord;
The fruit of the womb is a reward.
Like arrows in the hand of a warrior,
So are the children of one's youth.
How blessed is the man whose quiver is full of them;
They shall not be ashamed,
When they speak with their enemies in the gate.
                    (Ps. 127:3–5)

By now, the child-bearing years have come. Good years, but physically and financially exhausting. And I might add *surprising*. God often enlarges our quiver beyond what we expected (or planned!) and yet He calls each one of our offspring "a gift," "fruit," a "reward." Since I have already analyzed each of these terms in my book, *You and Your Child*,[3] I'll not repeat myself here. But it is worth noting that the birth of a child is not taken lightly by the Lord. Each one is significant. Each one is viewed by God as a transfer of love from His heart to the couple receiving the gift.

God never wastes parents. He doesn't inadvertently "dump" kids haphazardly into homes. Nor does He deliver "accidents" into our lives. It is exceedingly important that families place the same significance on children that God does. Again, this is contrary to the mentality of many people in our society today. We are considered as somewhere between weird and ignorant if we have this kind of attitude toward children, especially if we have a large number of them.

But the psalm says we are "blessed" if our "quiver is full of them." We'll also be busy and tired! And a minister's home is no different than yours, pal. It's amazing to me how many people have the idea that a divine aura hovers over the pastor's home, making it unlike the "average dwelling." Now *that's* weird and ignorant! Our home is no different from any other busy neighborhood dwelling. The scene is just like yours. Mounds of laundry—and a dryer that eats two or three socks per load. Dog messes on the carpet. Kids that sleep with their clothes on—shoes too. A garbage disposal that gets clogged on rubber bands and paper clips. Stopped-up toilets. Expensive orthodontist's headgears forgotten and left at restaurants sixty miles back while on vacation. I have kissed hamsters goodnight, rocked sick rabbits to sleep, helped raise new puppies, delivered newspapers in the rain, mopped up vomit, and often wondered, "Will we ever make it?" You see, just like you.

But in the meantime, my wife and I have a treasure of memories that will keep us warm through many years in the future, exactly as God promised. What a difference when the attitude is right. I love the story Gordon MacDonald tells.

Among the legends is the tale of a medieval sidewalk superintendent who asked three stone masons on a construction project what they were doing. The first replied that he was *laying bricks*. The second described his work as that of *building a wall*. But it was the third laborer who demonstrated genuine esteem for his work when he said, "I am *raising a great cathedral*."

Pose that same question to any two fathers concerning their role in the family, and you are liable to get the same kind of contrast. The first may say, "I am supporting a family." But the second may see things differently and say, "I am *raising children*." The former looks at his job as *putting bread on the table*. But the latter sees things in God's perspective: he is *participating in the shaping of lives*.[4]

The "arrows" God delivers into our quiver come ready-made, needing to be shaped and pointed toward the right target, which brings us to the next three verses in our scriptural mural.

STAGE 3: CHILD-REARING YEARS

Perhaps the most taxing of all, are the years a family finds itself in and out of crisis situations. Little babies that cooed and gurgled grow up into challenging, independent-thinking adolescents. The protective, sheltered environment of the home is broken into by the school, new friends, alien philosophies, financial strain, illness, accidents, hard questions, constant decisions, and busy schedules. Throw in a husband's mid-life crisis (I've earned one, but I haven't had time to enjoy it) and a wife's awareness that there's a bigger world than carpooling and making lunches . . . and it isn't difficult to feel the pressure mounting—especially when you add dating, new drivers in the family, leaving for college, talk of marriage, and moving out. Whew! And what does God say about these years?

> How blessed is everyone who fears the Lord,
> Who walks in His ways.
> When you shall eat of the fruit of your hands,
> You will be happy and it will be well with you.
> Your wife shall be like a fruitful vine,
> Within your house,
> Your children like olive plants
> Around your table.
>
> (Ps. 128:1–3)

He says we'll be "blessed." We'll be "happy." It will "be well" with us during these years. A dream? No. Remember this is a domestic mural, one scene growing out of the former and leading into the next. In the family portrayed on this scriptural canvas, "the Lord" is still central. When children come, they are viewed as "a gift of the Lord," a reward, "fruit" provided by Him.

As they are reared, the process is carried out God's way.* Which means that even in the teen years, it can be fun and enjoyable. Believe me, it can be.

I don't know how many people, some years ago, told Cynthia and me, "Enjoy your children when they're small. When they grow up and become teenagers with a mind of their own—you're gonna hate it. It's dreadful!" I've got news for all those prophets of doom. We don't "hate it," and it has *never* been "dreadful." Challenging, yes. Stretching, always. Humbling, occasionally. Rewarding, often.

Our quiver first began to expand twenty years ago. Now, as the Psalm states it, we have begun to "eat of the fruit of our hands." And our family grows

---

*In my book, *You and Your Child*, I explain in detail a philosophy of rearing children God's way, according to scriptural guidelines. If you are struggling with this process and want to read some child-rearing insights based on the Bible, I suggest you read this book.

closer together with each passing year. This does not mean it has been easy. Or simple. Raising "olive plants" and providing the necessary stability and wisdom so that each of our four could grow and become the people God would have them be has been no pushover. The father and mother in this family have had to flex and change. We have also had to stand firm on occasion and uphold the standard we established as a Christian couple. But we have had to be honest—painfully honest—with our children, admitting when we were wrong and apologizing for it; declaring how we felt, yet leaving room for each child to discover on his or her own; being vulnerable and open regarding our fears, our uncertainties, our disagreements, our weaknesses; loving and supporting one another through failure, mistakes, and sinful behavior.

The real bills come due at home, don't they? It is here that life ultimately makes up its mind. And it is during the child-rearing/adolescent years that a parent is called by God to carry out one major mission: the mission *to model authenticity*—authentic Christianity, authentic humanity, authentic vulnerability and approachability. Teens can handle almost anything except hypocrisy. Cynthia and I determined years ago that we would do everything in our power to resist hypocrisy. Although this meant our children would see and hear painful things, at times harsh reality, we determined they would not have to struggle through double messages and phony-baloney junk as they grew up. Above all, we would be real people . . . touchable, available and approachable.

I was encouraged recently to read of an experiment with monkeys that seemed to affirm our philosophy of rearing children.

Dr. Harry F. Harlow loved to stand by the animal cages in his University of Wisconsin laboratory and watch the baby monkeys. Intrigued, he noticed that the monkeys seemed emotionally attached to cloth pads lying in their cages.

They caressed the cloths, cuddled next to them, and treated them much as children treat a teddy bear. In fact, monkeys raised in cages with cloths on the floors grew huskier and healthier than monkeys in cages with wire-mesh floors. Was the softness and touchability of the cloth an important factor?

Harlow constructed an ingenious surrogate mother out of terry cloth, with a light bulb behind her to radiate heat. The cloth mother featured a rubber nipple attached to a milk supply from which the babies could feed. They adopted her with great enthusiasm. Why not? She was always comfortingly available, and, unlike real mothers, never roughed them up or bit them or pushed them aside.

After proving that babies could be "raised" by inanimate, surrogate mothers, Harlow next sought to measure the importance of the mother's touchable, tactile characteristics. He put eight baby monkeys in a large cage that contained the terry cloth mother plus a new mother, this one made entirely out of wire mesh. Harlow's assistants, controlling the milk flow to each mother, taught four of the babies to nurse from the terry cloth mother and four from the wire mesh mother. Each baby could get milk only from the mother assigned to it.

A startling trend developed almost immediately. All eight babies spent almost all their waking time (sixteen to eighteen hours per day) huddled next to the terry cloth mother. They hugged her, patted her, and perched on her. Monkeys assigned to the wire mesh mother went to her only for feeding, then scooted back to the comfort and protection of the terry cloth mother. When frightened, all eight would seek solace by climbing onto the terry cloth mother.

Harlow concluded, "We were not surprised to discover that contact comfort was an important basic affectional or love variable, but we did not expect it to overshadow so completely the variable of nursing; indeed the disparity is so great as to suggest that the primary function of nursing is that of insuring frequent and intimate body contact of the infant with the mother. Certainly, man cannot live by milk alone."[5]

It might be good for you, my friend, to stop right now and think about the difference between being a "terry cloth" parent and a "wire mesh" parent. Even before you finish the chapter, it may be the right time for you to come to terms with the truth regarding your family. I must be honest with you, in most of the family conflicts I have dealt with involving trouble with teenagers, the problem has been more with parents who were either too liberal and permissive or too inflexible, distant, rigid (and sometimes hypocritical) than with teen-agers who were unwilling to cooperate. When the modeling is as it should be, there is seldom much trouble from those who fall under the shadow of the leader. Strengthening your grip on the family may start with an unguarded appraisal of the leadership your family is expected to follow.

STAGE 4: THE TWILIGHT YEARS

Behold, for thus shall the man be blessed
Who fears the Lord.
The Lord bless you from Zion,
And may you see the prosperity of Jerusalem all the days of your life.
Indeed, may you see your children's children.
Peace be upon Israel!

(Ps. 128:4–6)

What will life be like when the dust settles and quietness returns? What will be the rewards for beginning and cultivating a family according to God's direction? How will it be in the empty nest?

To begin with, we will be "blessed" (v. 4). I take this to mean that we, personally, will be happy. There will be happy memories. There will also be the happiness sustained through good relationships with our adult offspring.

Furthermore, the psalmist states that "Jerusalem" will be a better place. That was the city where he lived. There will be civil blessings that come as a result of releasing into society a happy, healthy, young adult. The cities where our offspring choose to live will be better places if they emerge from a family that has prepared them for life.

Finally, "Peace be upon Israel!"—SHALOM ISRAEL! Ultimately, the nation will be blessed of God. It is axiomatic. Healthy, well-disciplined, loving homes produce people who make a nation peaceful and strong. As the family goes, so goes the nation. When you boil it down to the basics, the pulse of an entire civilization is determined by the heartbeat of its homes.

> When it comes to rearing children, every society is only 20 years away from barbarism. Twenty years is all we have to accomplish the task of civilizing the infants who are born into our midst each year. These savages know nothing of our language, our culture, our religion, our values, our customs of interpersonal relations. The infant is totally ignorant about communism, fascism, democracy, civil liberties, the rights of the minority as contrasted with the prerogatives of the majority, respect, decency, honesty, customs, conventions, and manners. *The barbarian must be tamed if civilization is to survive.*[6]

DISCUSSION QUESTIONS AND SUGGESTIONS TO HELP YOU STRENGTHEN YOUR GRIP ON THE FAMILY

• The family. Can there be anything more essential, more basic to healthy human existence than the family? See if you can name six or eight impressions of life we learn first in the family. Next, talk about how an unhappy, broken family relationship can affect initial impressions of life.

• Discuss some of the major problems families struggle with in this generation. How are they different from ten or fifteen years ago? Is there any scriptural support from the home suffering more as we move closer to the end times?

• Now let's get more specific. Let's talk about *your* home. Use several adjectives to describe family life within the walls where you live—like, "busy" or "peaceful" or "strained" or "accepting." Try to be completely honest as you answer this one: What influence do *you* bring into your family relationships?

• How has this chapter helped you with your particular relationship to others in your family? Which passage or verse of Scripture seemed especially relevant to your situation? Give an example of what you mean.

• If you could reach inside your own life and change one thing that would help with relationships at home, which one would it be? Talk about what it would take to start moving in that direction.

• As you have analyzed what has happened to hurt family relationships, maybe you've begun to wonder if there's anything good at home. Of course, there is! Be just as honest to name the *good* things as you were to admit the weaknesses.

• Finally, turn to the two psalms we examined in this chapter and share an application that encourages you and gives you hope. Thank God for that. Call on Him for assistance in the one major area you need help. Pray for one another.

Conclusion

A funny thing happened after my book, *Improving Your Serve*, was released. A friend of mine up in the Northwest went into a secular bookstore in hopes of finding a copy. She patiently combed through the religious section, but it was not there. She was surprised because a friend of hers had picked up a copy the day before and had mentiond it to her. Puzzled, the lady asked the clerk if they had sold out. "Oh, no," she said quickly, "we just got in a new shipment of *Improving Your Serve* this week." As they walked back together, the clerk turned right as my friend turned left . . . just about the time the clerk was saying, "It's right over here in the sports section, among Connors, McEnroe, and Borg."

Smiling, my friend informed the lady that the book actually had nothing to do with tennis. To which the clerk replied, "Well, they're selling so well in this section, I think we'll just leave 'em here!"

As *Strengthening Your Grip* arrives at bookstores, it may appear on the shelf near Palmer, Nicklaus, and Hogan . . . but as you know by now, it actually has nothing to do with golf. And although the name seems to suggest a sequence volume to *Improving Your Serve*, it is not that either. This book was not intended to be another series of chapters encouraging the reader to serve better, but rather to think deeper. To think about what and how and why in a day when "who really cares" is fast becoming our world's favorite phrase. Hopefully, you have found *Strengthening Your Grip* provocative. But my main concern is that you found it relevant, not just another pile of words wrapped in dated religious garb. I *loathe* that thought!

The penetrating words of the German Reformer Martin Luther frequently flash through my mind:

> If you preach the Gospel in all aspects with the exception of the issues which deal specifically with your time—you are not preaching all the Gospel.

Although he was a sixteenth-century monk, his cry was a plea for relevance. With boldness he addressed the things that mattered. He saw his church diseased and paralyzed by tradition, corruption, and apathy. He brushed aside the dry debris of meaningless formalities, he challenged inaccurate interpretations, he declared the truth at the risk of being branded a heretic. As the Spirit of God gave him refreshing insight and strength to continue unintimidated, he strengthened the grip of a new brand of Christians—"Protestants"—as he led them into a reformation, a movement that was destined to acquaint the world with the essentials of the faith. We admire his efforts to this day.

A "new" Reformation is in order, in my opinion. Christians in the last two decades of the twentieth century need a fresh, vital word for our times. Not further revelation. Not more doctrines. Not even a new system of theology, necessarily. What we need is a message, securely riveted to scriptural foundations, that has a ring of relevance to it—an authentic reality about it. Ancient truth in today's talk. In Luther's day that meant one thing—the need for clarification to dispel ignorance. *Today* it means another—a new style of communication to dispel indifference. *Strengthening Your Grip* has been an effort in that direction.

As I drive home on Sunday evenings after a full day of preaching and involvement with our flock here in Fullerton, I am usually exhausted. I drive slowly, thinking back over those hours I have invested. I ask myself many questions. Invariably, those questions include, "Was I connecting?" and "Did that make sense?" and "Is my communication relevant?" You see, I have this burning passion never to be out of touch with my times. God did not call me to be a prophet out of the time tunnel—one who looks and sounds like he was born two or three millenniums late. But I *would* like to have the commitment of the prophets, though not their style . . . because I need to connect with my day, not theirs. It is my wish that more and more of God's people would become a part of this "new" Reformation—committed to communicating divine revelation so clearly that the public is stunned to realize how eternally relevant God and His Word really are.

As I complete this book, I find myself, again, exhausted. Still asking those haunting questions: "Do these chapters make sense?" and "Can anybody understand them . . . even the uninitiated?" and mainly, "Will it make any difference?" You cannot imagine how much I care about these things.

Was the book worth the effort? If your grip is now stronger in an area of your life that once was weak . . . if Jesus Christ is more real to you than when you started . . . if you are more convinced than before that God's Word "connects" with wisdom and authority, then the answer is "Yes" . . . even for those of you who thought you were buying a book about golf, but discovered that you came home with a book about God.

Notes

Chapter One

1. Charles E. Hummel, *Tyranny of the Urgent* (Downers Grove, IL: InterVarsity Press, 1967), p. 4.
2. John R. W. Stott, *The Preacher's Portrait* (Grand Rapids, MI: Wm. B. Eerdmans Publishing Company, 1961), p. 31.
3. Ronald M. Enroth, "The Power Abusers," *Eternity*, October 1979, pp. 25-26.
4. *Your Churning Place* by Robert L. Wise. © copyright 1977, Regal Books, Ventura, CA 93006. Used by permission.
5. Charlie W. Shedd, *Promises to Peter*, copyright © 1970 by Charlie W. Shedd, pp. 12-13; used by permission of Word Books, Publisher, Waco, TX, 76796.
6. A poem by George MacLeod, taken from *Focal Point*, the Conservative Baptist Theological Seminary Bulletin, Denver, CO, Spring, 1981.

Chapter Two

1. Philip G. Zimbardo, "The Age of Indifference," *Psychology Today*, August 1980, p. 72.
2. From John Donne, *Devotions*, XVII, as quoted in *Familiar Quotations*, ed. John Bartlett (Boston: Little, Brown and Company, 1955), p. 218.
3. Philip G. Zimbardo, p. 76.
4. Leslie B. Flynn, *Great Church Fights* (Wheaton, IL: Victor Books, a division of SP Publications, 1976), p. 14.
5. *Up With Worship* by Anne Ortlund. © copyright 1975, Regal Books, Ventura, CA 93006. Used by permission.
6. James C. Dobson, *Hide or Seek* (Old Tappan, NJ: Fleming H. Revell Company, 1974), p. 134.

Chapter Three

1. Charles R. Swindoll, *Improving Your Serve* (Waco, TX: Word Books, 1981).
2. William Barclay, *The Letter to the Hebrews*, The Daily Study Bible (Edinburgh: The Saint Andrews Press, 1955), pp. 137–38.
3. Donald Bubna with Sue Multanen, "The Encouragement Card," *Leadership* 1, no. 4 (Fall, 1980): 52–53.
4. Lee Stanley, producer, *Mountain Top*, (Agoura, CA: Morning Star Film, Inc., distributed by Pyramid Film & Video Santa Monica, CA).

Chapter Four

1. William Barclay, *The Letters to Philippians, Colossians, Thessalonians*, The Daily Study Bible (Edinburgh: The Saint Andrews Press, 1959), p. 232.
2. Pitirim Sorokin, *The American Sex Revolution* (Boston: Porter Sargent Publisher, 1956), p. 19.
3. Ibid., pp. 21–22.
4. Frank E. Gaebelein, ed., *The Expositor's Bible Commentary*, vol. 11 (Grand Rapids: Zondervan Publishing House, 1978), p. 271.

Chapter Five

1. *The Third Part of King Henry the Sixth*, act 3, sc. 1, lines 62–65.
2. Taken from *Rich Christians in an Age of Hunger* by Ronald J. Sider. © 1977 by Inter-Varsity Christian Fellowship of the USA and used by permission of InterVarsity Press, Downers Grove, IL 60515, USA.
3. William Barclay, *The Letters to Timothy*, The Daily Study Bible (Edinburgh: The Saint Andrews Press, 1955), p. 152.
4. Alan Loy McGinnis, *The Friendship Factor* (Minneapolis: Augsburg Publishing House, 1979), p. 30.
5. Stanley N. Wilburn, "What the Next 20 Years Hold for You," *U.S. News & World Report 89*, no. 22 (December 1, 1980): 51, 54.

Chapter Six

1. "Voices: U.S.A. '80," *Life* 4, no. 1 (January 1981): 21.
2. Charles R. Swindoll, *Integrity: The Mark of Godliness* (Portland, OR: Multnomah Press, 1981), pp. 6–21, 23.
3. *Born Again:* Copyright © 1976 by Charles W. Colson. Published by Chosen Books Lincoln, VA 22078. Used by permission.

Chapter Seven

1. From *The Master Plan of Evangelism* by Robert E. Coleman copyright © 1972 by Fleming H. Revell Company. Used by permission.
2. From *The Pursuit of God* by A. W. Tozer. Copyright Christian Publications, Inc., Harrisburg, PA 17105. Used by permission.
3. *The Master Plan of Evangelism* pp. 59–60.
4. "I Met My Master," taken from *Poems That Preach*, ed. John R. Rice, (Wheaton, IL: Sword of the Lord Publishers, 1952), p. 18. Used by permission of the publisher.

Chapter Eight

1. Larry Dean Olsen, *Outdoor Survival Skills* (Provo, UT: Brigham, 1976), p. 4.
2. Lloyd Cory, ed., *Quote Unquote* (Wheaton, IL: Victor Books, a division of SP Publications, 1977), p. 15.
3. Reprinted with permission. *When I Relax I Feel Guilty* by Tim Hansel. © 1979 David C. Cook Publishing Co. Elgin, IL 60120.
4. Thomas Ken, "Praise God from Whom All Blessings Flow."

Chapter Nine

1. William Barclay, *Gospel of Matthew*, 2 vols., The Daily Study Bible (Edinburgh: The Saint Andrews Press, 1956), 1:191, 193.

Chapter Ten

1. Charles R. Swindoll, *Leisure* (Portland, OR: Multnomah Press, 1981).
2. W. E. Vine, *An Expository Dictionary of New Testament Words*, vol 2 (Westwood, NJ: Fleming H. Revell Company, 1940), p. 248.
3. Alan Loy McGinnis, *The Friendship Factor* (Minneapolis: Augsburg Publishing House, 1979), pp. 93–102.
4. Charles R. Swindoll, *Stress* (Portland, OR: Multnomah Press, 1981).
5. Samuel Taylor Coleridge, "Youth and Age," stanza 2, *Familiar Quotations* (Boston, MA: Little, Brown and Company, 1955), p. 425a.

Chapter Eleven

1. Elisabeth Elliot, *Through Gates of Splendor* (New York: Harper & Brothers, 1957).

2. Merrill F. Unger, *Unger's Bible Dictionary* (Chicago: Moody Press, 1957), p. 997.
3. "Surely the Presence of the Lord Is in This Place" by Lanny Wolfe © (Nashville: The Benson Company, copyright 1977 by Lanny Wolfe Music Co. International copyright secured. All rights reserved. Used by permission of The Benson Company, Inc., Nashville.
4. F. B. Meyer, *David, Shepherd Psalmist—King* (Grand Rapids: Zondervan Publishing House, 1953), p. 11.

Chapter Twelve

1. William D. Longstaff, "Take Time To Be Holy," 1882.
2. Letter from an anonymous person to Dr. Charles R. Swindoll, April 21, 1981.

Chapter Thirteen

1. Dale E. Galloway, *Dream a New Dream* (Wheaton, IL: Tyndale House Publishers, 1975), p. 59.
2. Mark Kram, "The Face of Pain," *Sports Illustrated*, 44, no. 10 (March 8, 1976): 60.
3. Philip Yancey, *Where Is God When It Hurts* (Grand Rapids: Zondervan Publishing House, 1978), p. 142.
4. Douglas Colligan, "That Helpless Feeling: The Dangers of Stress," *New York*, July 14, 1975, p. 28.
5. Charles R. Swindoll, *Improving Your Serve* (Waco, TX: Word Books Publisher, 1981).
6. "Murphy's Law," (231 Adrian Road, Millbrae, CA: Celestial Arts, 1979).
7. Bruce Larson, *There's a Lot More to Health Than Not Being Sick* (Waco, TX: Word Books Publisher, 1981), p. 46.
8. Horatio G. Spafford, "It Is Well with My Soul," copyright 1918 The John Church Co. Used by permission of the publisher.

Chapter Fourteen

1. Billy Graham, *Quote Unquote*, ed. Lloyd Cory (Wheaton, IL: Victor Books, a division of SP Publications, 1977), p. 102.
2. Jeffrey L. Cotter, "Witness Upmanship," *Eternity* March 1981, pp. 22–23.
3. Jim Petersen, *Evangelism as a Lifestyle* (Colorado Springs, CO: NavPress, 1980), pp. 24–25.
4. Taken from *How to Give Away Your Faith*, by Paul Little. © 1966 by Inter-Varsity Christian Fellowship of the USA and used by permission of Inter-Varsity Press, Downers Grove, IL 60515, USA.

5. Taken from *Out of the Salt-Shaker and Into the World* by Rebecca Manley Pippert. © 1979 by Inter-Varsity Christian Fellowship of the USA and used by permission of InterVarsity Press, Downers Grove, IL 60515, USA.
6. Billy Graham, *Quote Unquote*, p. 102.

Chapter Fifteen

1. Richard Farson, *Birthrights: A Child's Bill of Rights* (New York: Macmillan, 1974).
2. James C. Dobson, *Straight Talk to Men and Their Wives* (Waco, TX: Word Books Publisher, 1980), p. 63.
3. Aric Press with Jeff B. Copeland, et al., "The Plague of Violent Crime," *Newsweek*, March 23, 1981, pp. 46–50, 52–54.

Chapter Sixteen

1. Edith Schaeffer, *What Is a Family?* (Old Tappan, NJ: Fleming H. Revell Company, 1975), p. 7.
2. David Gelman et al., "Saving the Family," *Newsweek* 91, no. 20 (May 15, 1978).
3. Charles R. Swindoll, *You and Your Child* (Nashville, TN: Thomas Nelson Publishers, 1977), pp. 52–54.
4. Gordon MacDonald, *The Effective Father* (Wheaton, IL: Tyndale House Publishers, 1977), pp. 183–84.
5. Taken from *Fearfully and Wonderfully Made* by Paul Brand, M.D. with Philip Yancey. Copyright © 1980 by Dr. Paul Brand and Philip Yancey. Used by permission of Zondervan Publishing House.
6. Albert Siegel, *Stanford Observer*, as quoted in *The Wittenburg Door* (San Diego: Youth Specialties).

Dropping Your Guard

Several years ago I made an extremely important decision.

Finding myself pushed and pressured from a dozen different sources, I realized the need to pull up close to a small group of men—objective men, trustworthy men—tough-minded and insightful enough to see things I could not see, yet honest enough to tell me the truth and caring enough to encourage me. Integrity, confidentiality, availability, humility, and a consistent, sensitive walk with the Lord were essential traits each man needed to model.

Now that God has led us together and some stability has returned to my life (as well as my sanity), I realize the value of being surrounded by and accountable to such a wholesome body of counselors. They have become my closest friends. I am grateful for the hours they have willingly invested on my behalf. The nature of our relationship requires that they remain anonymous . . . but God, who will reward openly all efforts expended for Him in secret, will one day unload the truck of His heavenly riches and crown them with many crowns.

To these faithful friends, who have taught me so much about dropping my guard and who have given me the freedom to be completely myself, I dedicate the pages and the principles of this book.

Contents

Introduction

"Okay, everybody, *masks off!*"

There are times I want to stand up and make that announcement. I've never done it, you understand, but I sure have been tempted. Can you imagine the reaction?

It would be a scary thing for most folks, especially those who have learned that survival comes a lot easier behind a mask. There's a mask for whatever the occasion—have you noticed? No matter how you really feel, regardless of the truth, if you become skilled at hiding behind your guard, you don't have to hassle all the things that come with full disclosure. You feel safe. What you lack in honesty, you make up for in pseudosecurity.

If you wear an "I'm tough" mask, you don't have to worry about admitting how weak and frightened you actually are. If you keep your "I'm holy" mask in place, you never need to bother with people wondering if you struggle with spirituality. Furthermore, the "I'm-cool-because-I've-got-it-all-together" mask comes in handy if you resist stuff like hard questions, vulnerable admissions, straight talk. Another familiar front is the "I'm-able-to-handle-all-this-pain-and-pressure" mask. No tears, not even a frown or hint of bewilderment is revealed. That one helps when you're surrounded by superpious folks who are impressed with answers like, "Oh, I'm fine" and "I'm just claiming the victory," accompanied by eyelids at half mast and a nice, appropriate smile. There are even "intellectual-and-scholarly" masks that protect you from having to face the practical nitty-gritty.

There is just one major difficulty in this mask-wearing game—*it isn't real.* It therefore forces us to skate rather than relate. It promotes a phony-baloney, make-a-good-impression attitude instead of an honest realism that relieves and frees. What's worse, as we hide the truth behind a veneer polished to a high gloss, we become lonely instead of understood and loved for who we are. And the most tragic part of all is that the longer we do it, the better we get at it . . .

357

and the more alone we remain in our hidden world of fear, pain, anger, insecurity, and grief—all those normal and natural emotions we hesitate to admit but that prove we are only human.

The result? Distance. Distance that makes you out of focus with me—removed from me by closed-off compartments that stay locked, keeping us from being able to know each other and, when and where necessary, to help each other. But the fact remains that distance must be removed if we hope to cope in this generation of excessive individualism. We need each other! All the uncertainty notwithstanding, the rewards of dropping your guard will far outweigh the risks involved. But the problem is how to convince you that it is worth the effort, especially if you have become adept at using masks . . . and who hasn't?

This, in a single statement, is my objective in writing this book: I would like to convince you of the value of open relationships. Perhaps you wonder why I want to do that, since you and I don't know each other. Why would I write a book like this? How could it help you?

I can think of two reasons. First, because I, personally, lived too many of my years with my guard up. I will never forget the consequences, nor would I if I could. Living a closed life, trying to play a part that wasn't me led to nothing but greater fear and higher defenses. I want to identify with where you are and help you know there's a better way to spend the rest of your life. I care too much to let you go on thinking you're stuck with that mask from now on.

Second, because I now know the joy and freedom of having my guard down, I no longer feel any need to fool anybody, to play the mask game, to make verbal sounds with my mouth that my mind knows aren't true. I want you to make the same discovery. And what a great way to live!

"Is it really *that* different?" you ask. It's the difference between a slow fuzzy worm and a lacy butterfly . . . between being bound up in some dark corner questioning your own worth, hoping people won't find out how human you really are, and being free to let the truth be known . . . to hide no longer . . . to be confident and secure while you remain one hundred percent human, without any mask of hypocrisy. I want to help you start your journey down that road.

The purpose of the journey, of course, is not simply to unmask and parade our pain as we expose the truth of who we are. That's merely the means to an end. The *ultimate* objective is to cultivate an atmosphere of such openness that we are free to share our dreams in an unguarded manner, talk about hopes, and hammer out our goals in life. By becoming people who are comfortable to be around, we encourage the same in others. In the process, a grinding existence changes into meaningful living as we replace our isolationism with involvement in the lives of others.

Let me assure you of something lest you assume the wrong thing. This book is not based on some humanistic philosophy or pop psychology or ego-centered mentality. I should tell you up front, I am one who believes completely in the Bible. As a minister by profession, I have been absorbing the teachings of Scripture every year of my adult life since the late 1950s, and I have been communicating those principles every week, often several times a week, since that time. The lens through which I filter my perceptions and my convictions is, therefore, the Bible. Its relevance and its wisdom will be seen as each chapter of this book develops. Hopefully, you will discover that God's Word is both timely and true, able to release you from the thick cocoon of fear and give you wings to fly free of all masks. Contrary to popular opinion, God gave us His Book to release us to reach our full potential . . . not to push us into a corner and watch us squirm!

I am indebted to my secretary, Helen Peters, for her tireless and patient efforts as she has happily typed and retyped the manuscript. All authors should have such superb assistance! My friends at Word Books also deserve a round of applause for their incessant commitment to me and to a quality product: "Doc" Heatherley, Floyd Thatcher, Ernie Owen, Bob Wolgemuth, and my careful editor with an eye for detail, Beverly Phillips. Each one has played a valuable part in seeing this volume reach completion.

I appreciate the artistic skills of my long-time friend, Paul Lewis, who created the cover idea and design . . . and also my thanks to Jim Killion for helping me choose the title.

I also declare my gratitude to the congregation I have had the privilege of serving as senior pastor since 1971, the First Evangelical Free Church of Fullerton, California. With contagious enthusiasm, this faithful flock packs the house Sunday after Sunday to worship and to respond to the truths of God's Word, the Bible. Originally, the thoughts that have now found their way into these chapters were sermons I preached. Because of the positive reaction of so many who first heard those sermons and encouraged me to publish the insights God showed me and allowed me to share, the book is now a reality.

Finally, I wish to thank my wife and family for understanding how much I love to write and how much time and effort such an undertaking demands. Had they not surrounded me with the freedom, affirmation, and encouragement to stay at the task, *Dropping Your Guard* would have been renamed *Losing Your Mind*.

CHARLES R. SWINDOLL
Fullerton, California

1

Loosening the Mask:
How It All Began

Anniversaries are great occasions for evaluation. Once we get beyond the nostalgia and choke back a few tears, it's amazing how objective we can become. Hindsight has a lot of insight.

A couple of years ago I completed ten years of ministry at the church I serve in Fullerton, California. We don't make big deals out of anniversaries (I'm happy to say), but it was a good time to appraise where we had been. We have gone through the common cycle familiar to growing churches: solid beginning, steady growth, expansion on the original site, greater growth, multiple services (ultimately *five* services a Sunday for almost four years!), plans for relocation, purchase of larger site, construction phase, and final move followed by dedication of the new facilities. Whew! Makes me weary just writing all that down. Each part of the cycle carried with it its own set of problems and delights.

As I reflected on the previous decade that Sunday afternoon following the brief anniversary commemoration, I had several flashes of insight. Strong were my feelings of gratitude both to God and to the Fullerton flock. How flexible those people had been . . . how forgiving . . . how supportive and enthusiastic! Through all the changes and cramped conditions and parking problems and crowded hallways and financial crises and personal demands, they hung in there. Even though we looked more like Disneyland than a church (especially to our neighbors on the outside), we maintained our sanity and our unity within, and we finally were able to settle down and get back to the business of ministry. There was only one problem—*we were full again!* We were having to turn people away. And I should add that our parking lot was woefully inadequate. It had all the signs of the old "same-song-second-verse" syndrome.

Rethinking Growth

There are times when a leader is forced to face some very painful facts. That afternoon I began to do that. I realized that growth can be measured in more ways than numerically. There is something significantly more important than growing larger. Even though it is the most popular way to determine "success," more isn't necessarily better. In spite of all the excitement that goes along with rapid growth and crowded conditions, there are some drawbacks. It is easy to be lost and feel lonely in a crowd—even at a place of worship. People begin to look the same. Names start running together and before long seem less important. Needs are by-passed. The main concerns seem to be finding a parking space and getting a seat. If we're not careful, we begin to resemble a school of voracious piranha instead of a tender flock of sheep. Worst of all, the church becomes like the world rather than distinct from it. "Dog eat dog" is simply changed to "sheep eat sheep."

None of this is intended, you understand. No one ever stands up and blows a whistle to make everybody run like rats on a ship. And, believe me, none of this growth was orchestrated in my mind or the minds of my colleagues. I distinctly remember the first time I read that our congregation was referred to as a "super church." I felt uneasy with the label. It smacked of Madison Avenue hype, shallow and slick programming, all the stuff that I've never wanted to be identified with. But I couldn't get around it, our numerical size gave us the label. How could we solve the dilemma? Was it possible to be large in number yet deep in the things that matter? Why couldn't we have greater personal involvement along with a broader base of ministry? Can't size and depth coexist? Isn't it possible to relate to one another even though there are several thousand of us? Those questions haunted me. And even though a large number of "authorities" had attempted to answer them (many of whom said, "It can't happen"), none seemed to satisfy.

Hearing God's Appraisal

I decided to hear what God had to say. While doing a brief survey of the growth of the early church in the book of Acts, I discovered how large a body the first century church actually was. First, three thousand; soon, a couple more thousand; and some time later, several thousand more. It was, nevertheless, a dynamic and caring group. I found myself intrigued and relieved. There was balance between taking in and giving out, between hearing and doing, between receiving instruction and being personally involved in each others' lives. I smiled as I read words like:

> And they were continually devoting themselves to the apostles' teaching and to fellowship, to the breaking of bread and to prayer.
> And everyone kept feeling a sense of awe; and many wonders and signs were taking place through the apostles.

And all those who had believed were together, and had all things in common; and they began selling their property and possessions, and were sharing them with all, as anyone might have need (Acts 2:42–45).

And the congregation of those who believed were of one heart and soul; and not one of them claimed that anything belonging to him was his own; but all things were common property to them.

And with great power the apostles were giving witness to the resurrection of the Lord Jesus, and abundant grace was upon them all.

For there was not a needy person among them, for all who were owners of land or houses would sell them and bring the proceeds of the sales, and lay them at the apostles' feet; and they would be distributed to each, as any had need (Acts 4:32–35).

And at the hand of the apostles many signs and wonders were taking place among the people; and they were all with one accord in Solomon's portico.

But none of the rest dared to associate with them; however, the people held them in high esteem.

And all the more believers in the Lord, multitudes of men and women, were constantly added to their number; to such an extent that they even carried the sick out into the streets, and laid them on cots and pallets, so that when Peter came by, at least his shadow might fall on any one of them.

And also the people from the cities in the vicinity of Jerusalem were coming together, bringing people who were sick or afflicted with unclean spirits; and they were all being healed (Acts 5:12–16).

Therefore, those who had been scattered went about preaching the word.

And Philip went down to the city of Samaria and began proclaiming Christ to them.

And the multitudes with one accord were giving attention to what was said by Philip, as they heard and saw the signs which he was performing.

For in the case of many who had unclean spirits, they were coming out of them shouting with a loud voice; and many who had been paralyzed and lame were healed.

And there was much rejoicing in that city (Acts 8:4–8).

Now that's what I would call dynamic enthusiasm! I mean, those folks (though large in number) were in touch with one another. They were well-instructed yet deeply involved. Even though they were surviving in a day of persecution and martyrdom, they weren't satisfied simply to come together, soak up the scoop, then hide out until the next secret meeting. I didn't find an uninvolved isolationist in the entire bunch.

While pondering that thought, I turned back to Solomon's comment regarding our need for other people:

Two are better than one because they have a good return for their labor.

For if either of them falls, the one will lift up his companion. But woe to the one who falls when there is not another to lift him up.

Furthermore, if two lie down together they keep warm, but how can one be warm alone?

And if one can overpower him who is alone, two can resist him. A cord of three strands is not quickly torn apart (Eccles. 4:9–12).

As I think back, I recall getting a pencil and making a few notes in the margin of my Bible. I thought about our congregation in light of those four verses, and I wrote down "Crucial Factors to Be Convinced of. . . ." There were three:

- Unhealthy Consequences of Isolationism
- Essential Benefits of Relationships
- Absolute Necessity of Assimilation

I closed my eyes and allowed each point to turn over and over in my head until all the sharp edges were worn smooth. I began to realize that if we were going to keep calling ourselves a church, we would have to get serious about each of those three issues. That's how it all began. Little did I realize it would someday be the basis of a book. But now that two more years have passed and we've been infected with these germ thoughts—and a contagious excitement now marks our ministry because of it—I can hardly wait to share with you the benefits we've begun to reap.

Before I get into that, however, let me go back to those three crucial factors I listed. I want to be sure that each one is clearly understood before I build my case in the remaining chapters.

Unhealthy Consequences of Isolationism

Before anyone can ever be convinced of the value of involvement and mutuality, that person must come to terms with the consequences of isolationism. The fact is, *we need each other*. The other side of the coin is also axiomatic. Without each other, unhealthy and unhappy things happen to us. Emperical studies and psychological analyses strongly suggest that individuals cannot function effectively without deep links to others. Continuous, meaningful, and secure bonds are essential or we risk losing our humanity.

As Bernard Berelson and Gary Steiner discovered in their overview of more than one thousand social science studies: "Total isolation is virtually always an intolerable situation for the human adult—even when physical needs are provided for."[1]

We Americans are not so convinced. Independence is our watchword and "Think for Yourself" is our motto. Declaring a need is a sign of weakness, an open admission of failure and lack of character. Furthermore, we are on the move so much, who has time to share and to care? As one wife of an executive (whose corporation moved him and his family three times in a seven-ear period) recently confessed, "To decrease the pain of saying 'good-by' to our neighbors, we no longer bother to say 'hello.'" It has been my observation that we Christians are not immune from this hurry-up, hassle-hustle mentality.

Do we really move that often? I was amazed to find that the average American moves about fourteen times in his lifetime. One authority states:

> Americans move around more than most people, and hence find it more difficult to sustain intensive friendships and bonds among neighbors, even kinship. In an average year, some 40 million Americans move. Put another way, every ten years, between 40 and 60 percent of an average American town's population leaves.[2]

Do you realize the average worker keeps his job only 3.6 years?[3] It is no small wonder that popular sociologist Vance Packard believes:

> . . . rootlessness seems clearly to be associated with a decline in companionship, a decline in satisfying group activities, a decline in mutual trust, and a decline in psychological security. It encourages a shallowness in personal relationships and a relative indifference to community problems.[4]

You and I probably don't need a great deal more literary evidence from professional journals to prove how damaging isolationism can be. Just read the backgrounds of those who climb up into towers and shoot total strangers on the street below. Or do your own investigation of twisted and sadistic murderers. How often we find that they are products of our do-your-own-thing philosophy that holds people at a distance and implies a sneering "who needs you?" This whole ego-centered mentality is being pushed to an extreme and popularized by numerous volumes that make their way to the best-seller list . . . such as *How to Be Your Own Best Friend*, in which psychologists Newman and Berkowitz assert: "We are accountable only to ourselves for what happens to us in our lives."[5]

Even though it is easy to buy into the selfish lifestyle and opt for isolationism instead of involvement, the consequences are bitter and inescapable. That's why the simple, profound counsel of Solomon remains so needed: "Two are better than one. . . ." Swimming with the current of today's me-ism mindset has a way of eclipsing the contrasting light of Scripture.

Essential Benefits of Relationships

If you will return with me to that ancient king's comment, you'll find several reasons behind his statement "Two are better than one. . . ." This is true because:

- they have a good return for their labor (v. 9)
    Mutual effort
- one will lift up his companion (v. 10)
    Mutual support
- they keep [each other] warm (v. 11)
    Mutual encouragement
- they can resist an attack (v. 12)
    Mutual strength

If ever we needed a renewal, a renewal of meaningful relationships is long overdue! I'm not suggesting we must surrender our own individuality and become submerged in the slimy swamp of group-think. Nor do I extol the virtues of mediocrity as our standard. That's not my interest or concern. What does disturb me is the mentality that implies an excessive independence.

Thinking back upon Solomon's words, it is only when I *share* life's experiences with others that I can enjoy them or endure them to the greatest advantage. This is what those early Christians did. They learned quickly that survival would go hand-in-hand with "fellowship." Unfortunately, that term has lost its punch now that it has fallen into the bag of Christian clichés. But originally, the Greek word *koinonia* conveyed the idea of sharing, having something in common with another, entering into another's life and, if needed, assisting the person. You see, having a relationship calls for being in fellowship with others, and that cannot be done very easily at arm's length. It implies getting in touch, feeling the hurts, being an instrument of encouragement and healing. Fences must come down. Masks need to come off. Welcome signs need to be hung outside the door. Keys to the locks in our lives must be duplicated and distributed. Bridges need to be lowered that allow others to cross the moat and then share our joys and our sorrows.

Our pioneer forefathers realized the need for this.

The Europeans who came here to settle North America found it vast and unexplored. "Self-reliant" was the watchword, and the scout, the mountain man or the pioneer, with his axe and rifle over his shoulder, became the national hero.

In those early days the government gave away quarter sections of land to anyone who would homestead, in order to encourage settlement. People flocked west from crowded cities and villages to have their own land at last. Before they could farm the land they had chosen, their first job was to build a sod hut to live in, and we know that most families built them right smack-dab in the middle of their quarter section. The reason was obvious. People who had never owned land before had a new sense of pride and ownership. They wanted to feel that everything they saw belonged to them.

But that custom changed very quickly. This chosen isolation did strange things to people. Occasionally, photographers went out to record life on the frontier and returned with photographs of weird men, wild-eyed women, and haunted-looking children. Before long most of these families learned to move their houses to one corner of their property in order to live in proximity with three other families who also lived on the corners of their property. Four families living together, sharing life and death, joy and sorrow, abundance and want, had a good chance of making it.[6]

In our local church, when this whole idea moved from theory to tangible reality, we decided to stop treating our single parents like second-class citizens. We announced the formation of *Single Parents Fellowship* (notice that last word), and we invited them to come together. Hundreds emerged from our congregation. Some were frightened and hurting. Some were reluctant, insecure, and suspicious. Some were angry, others anxious. But out they came. And what a "fellowship" it has become! Since then we have encouraged those who have struggled with drug abuse and alcoholism to drop their guard, come out of the closet, and meet with others who have similar battles. Although naturally more reluctant than our SPF group to begin with, they now meet each week— over fifty brave, vulnerable men and women—to share their pain and to enter into a meaningful relationship with one another.

As I mentioned in one of my films,[7] the group wanted to have a name (certainly something other than "All Those Who Struggle with Booze and Dope"!), so they carried out an intense search through the Scriptures. When they came upon 1 Peter 5:8, they found their name—*Lion Tamers Anonymous*. Remember the verse? "Be sober, be vigilant; because your adversary the devil walks about like a roaring lion, seeking whom he may devour" (NKJV). What a great group of unmasked souls . . . and what honesty when they meet and relate!

And next, in light of the economic crunch that has struck our country in the early 1980s, we have established a fellowship group for the unemployed— *Breadwinners in Transition*. We have developed ways to encourage these often-depressed individuals, giving serious thought to how we might preserve their dignity and uphold their self-esteem. Along with providing regular meetings, we have several of our laymen and laywomen helping them find employment. Containers for nonperishable foods are filled, distributed, and maintained by others who assist in this ministry.

We have also opened our arms to the parents of the brain-damaged, the mentally retarded in our church and community. We call this once-a-month group meeting PEP—*Parents of Exceptional People*. One of their activities is a Special Olympics program. And on a Saturday afternoon not long ago, many of us gathered to encourage these marvelous people who were participating in this program. It took one youngster in a wheelchair about twenty minutes to finish the fifty-yard dash, but young and old alike were on the sidelines cheering her on.

I could easily fill another page or two describing how we are learning to relate to our many senior citizens with a group called *Forever Young*. We also have a group for those who are left with the responsibility of caring for their dependent parents. This group is called CODA—*Children of Dependent Adults*. The benefits of relating brought about by these groups seems limitless.

ABSOLUTE NECESSITY OF ASSIMILATION

We've considered the consequences of isolationism and the benefits of relationships. You probably agree with both, but your question is "How?" How can a large church that attracts so many people from such varied backgrounds harness the energy and move people from mere spectators to participants? I can assure you it doesn't happen automatically. People don't suddenly get involved, drop their guard, and devote themselves to one another. The secret is a firm commitment to assimilation.

As I realized how easily our church could become a huge body of spectators, strangers to one another and rootless in our commitment to Christ, I began to speak on the value of becoming involved in a small-group ministry—an adult-fellowship group, a choir, an evangelistic team, a prayer group, a weekly home Bible class, one of our women's organizations or men's groups. In any one of these special groups, there could be more in-depth sharing and involvement. I began digging into the Scriptures to find out all I could from God's Word. To my amazement, there was a massive amount of biblical material supporting the concept of assimilation. In fact, the balance of this book is a compilation of my findings. And it is my hope that each one who reads these pages will realize the necessity of being more than a Sunday spectator, rather a consistent participant in the things of God.

Perhaps it would help, as I close this chapter, if I gave you a working definition of *assimilation*. When I use that term I have in mind *becoming absorbed in the function of the Body of Christ as an active participant, relating to, sharing with, and caring for others in the Body*. Until this becomes a part of our lives, until we move out of the stands of formal religion and onto the playing field of authentic Christianity, it is extremely doubtful that our walk with God will ever reach its full potential.

Let me ask you a tough question, my friend. How serious is your interest in your spiritual growth? If you are satisfied to skate along, pushed by this gust of wind and attracted by that shallow fad, then you'll not have much interest in the pages that follow. In fact, if you've decided not to let Christ get much beyond the front door of your heart, you may feel that I'm getting into areas that are none of my business. But if you are sincerely hungry for maturity—if you are sick and tired of being a spectator and you long to let Christ invade every room of your life, rearranging the furniture of your mind and getting control of the appetites of your heart—you are obviously ready to dig deeper.

DISCUSSION IDEAS AND QUESTIONS

- In your own words, state the main idea of chapter 1, using a sentence or two.
- Do you agree or disagree? Discuss why.
- Can you remember the three crucial factors that were developed in the last half of the chapter? Try to name them.

• Choose one of the three and talk about some actual cases you are aware of in your neighborhood, your church, or where you work. In other words, can you think of an individual or group of individuals who fit into one of those three categories?

• Turn back to the references from the book of Acts. Read each passage aloud and slowly. Discuss the thing(s) that stand out most significantly to you as you picture those early Christians in your mind.

• Read Ecclesiastes 4:9–12. Share a particular occasion in your own life where you benefited from having someone alongside as you went through a specific need.

• Pause and pray. Give God thanks for someone who helped you at a hard time in your past.

• Before leaving, find someone in your group to thank for something he/she has done for you. Try to express to that individual what he/she has meant to you.

2

Digging Deeper,
Risking Change

It is the nature of the beast within all of us to resist change. The familiar draws us in and constrains us like a magnet. Most folks would rather stay the same and suffer than risk change and find relief. This is especially true when the future seems threatening. Being creatures of habit, many would much rather frown at today's familiar misery and stay in the mess than smile at tomorrow's unsure adventure.

If I don't miss my guess, you drive to work the same way day after day. Unless you are among the few who fight routine, it probably doesn't interest you to consider a new route. And how about your approach to solving problems? If you're like most, it's doubtful that creativity plays a big role in that process either. The strangest part of all is this: Even when we know ever so clearly that it is God who is leading us away from the familiar and into a new adventure, we break out in a rash.

How often I have seen this in couples who fall in love and make plans for marriage. God brings them together, strengthens their relationship, and convinces them they should leave the single life behind and go for it. Farewell to studio apartments and loneliness; good-by skydiving, no insurance, tiny sports cars, and tables set for one. Long live joint-checking accounts and double beds and bicycles built for two and new babies and station wagons! But something weird happens when ye olde wedding day arrives. We're talking cold, sweaty palms and feelings of doubt, maybe sheer panic. Why? It's the "What in the world am I doing?" syndrome—the familiar versus the unfamiliar wrestling match.

Church congregations can go through the same mental crunch. For a period of time things stay pretty much the same. Everybody knows everybody. All is quiet on the stained-glass front. Things are little and manageable and predict-

369

able. Friends and families remain close, intimacy flows naturally. Then God steps in and shakes things up. New faces; rapid growth; increased staff; adjustments; less than comfortable surroundings; additional services to meet the demand; loss of the laid-back, relaxed style of yesteryear . . . and there it is again—resistance, reluctance to change. As Cervantes says in *Don Quixote*, we long to "return to our flesh pots of Egypt."

That's not an original thought with Cervantes, you know. He lifted it from the biblical account of the ancient Hebrews when they left Egypt under Moses' leadership. What a story! I'd like us to think about it for a while.

The Exodus was not only remarkable, it was the next thing to a miracle. God broke the yoke of over four hundred years of slavery, mistreatment, and all manner of indignity. He promised them a new land—one they could call their own. But, like the ship's crew on Columbus's maiden voyage across the Atlantic, mutiny soon replaced unity.

Get a load of this:

"Why did we ever leave Egypt?" (Num. 11:20).

And a little later:

> Then all the congregation lifted up their voices and cried, and the people wept that night.
>
> And all the sons of Israel grumbled against Moses and Aaron; and the whole congregation said to them, "Would that we had died in the land of Egypt! Or would that we had died in this wilderness!
>
> "And why is the Lord bringing us into this land, to fall by the sword? Our wives and our little ones will become plunder; would it not be better for us to return to Egypt?"
>
> So they said to one another, "Let us appoint a leader and return to Egypt" (Num. 14:1–4).

Who said that? A bunch of ill-treated, forgotten wanderers who had been abandoned and left to die? No way! Those are the words of folks who had been delivered from bondage, miraculously protected, divinely fed, and securely led—the people of the Exodus. And yet they are begging to return, pleading for those "flesh pots of Egypt." Why?

TESTS THAT TEMPT US TO RETREAT

Under Moses' direction the Jews escaped from Pharaoh's rule. Obviously, it was the Lord God who made this possible, as Moses himself declared.

> And Moses said to the people, "Remember this day in which you went out from Egypt, from the house of slavery; for by a powerful hand the Lord brought you out from this place. And nothing leavened shall be eaten.
>
> "On this day in the month of Abib, you are about to go forth.

"And it shall be when the Lord brings you to the land of the Canaanite, the Hittite, the Amorite, the Hivite and the Jebusite, which He swore to your fathers to give you, a land flowing with milk and honey, that you shall observe this rite in this month (Exod. 13:3–5).

Their destination? He called it "a land flowing with milk and honey"—the country of Canaan. God assured them that He would see them through *regardless*. Little did they realize, however, the way He would accomplish that objective. That's where things got sticky. They were going to be challenged and stretched like never before in their lives. The predictable, business-as-usual routine they and their fathers before them had known was about to be disrupted by a series of tests—tests designed by God to force them to drop their defensive and traditional guard and trust Him! I find five such tests: unfamiliar surprises, unwanted fears, unpleasant adversaries, unfair accusations, unexpected resistance.

Unfamiliar Surprises

Read the following rather carefully.

Now it came about when Pharaoh had let the people go, that God did not lead them by the way of the land of the Philistines, even though it was near; for God said, "Lest the people change their minds when they see war, and they return to Egypt."

Hence God led the people around by the way of the wilderness to the Red Sea; and the sons of Israel went up in martial array from the land of Egypt.

And Moses took the bones of Joseph with him, for he had made the sons of Israel solemnly swear, saying "God shall surely take care of you; and you shall carry my bones from here with you."

· Then they set out from Succoth and camped in Etham on the edge of the wilderness.

And the Lord was going before them in a pillar of cloud by day to lead them on the way, and in a pillar of fire by night to give them light, that they might travel by day and by night.

He did not take away the pillar of cloud by day, nor the pillar of fire by night, from before the people (Exod. 13:17–22).

You can't appreciate the full meaning of these words without a map of that ancient region. Suffice it to say, the most logical journey would have been "by the way of the land of the Philistines." It was nearer and less arduous. The other route was farther, less comfortable, more threatening, and included a dead end at the Red Sea. But since when did human logic dictate to divine leading?

By the way, are you going through a few surprises these days? Are you being led away from familiar turf and into a "wilderness" journey? There's nothing to fear so long as you know God is in it. He's good at surprises, you know.

Unwanted Fears

They got as far as the sea. Naturally, they were forced to stop and wait for the next move. The scene was frightening.

> Then the Egyptians chased after them with all the horses and chariots of Pharaoh, his horsemen and his army, and they overtook them camping by the sea, beside Pi-hahiroth, in front of Baalzephon.
> And as Pharaoh drew near, the sons of Israel looked, and behold, the Egyptians were marching after them, and they became very frigthened; so the sons of Israel cried out to the Lord.
> Then they said to Moses, "Is it because there were no graves in Egypt that you have taken us away to die in the wilderness? Why have you dealt with us in this way, bringing us out of Egypt?
> "Is this not the word that we spoke to you in Egypt, saying, 'Leave us alone that we may serve the Egyptians'? For it would have been better for us to serve the Egyptians than to die in the wilderness" (Exod. 14:9–12).

Remember, these people who have above their heads a visible cloud assuring them of God's presence *and* still ringing in their ears is God's promise of protection—Canaan would be theirs to claim. But it's astounding how fear can silence all that. Behind them was an army of Egyptians, south of them was a desert, north of them was a range of mountains, and immediately in front of them was a large, wet, intimidating body of water. Enter: fear. Exit: faith. So Moses spoke to the issue.

> But Moses said to the people, "Do not fear! Stand by and see the salvation of the Lord which He will accomplish for you today; for the Egyptians whom you have seen today, you will never see them again forever.
> "The Lord will fight for you while you keep silent." Then the Lord said to Moses, "Why are you crying out to me? Tell the sons of Israel to go forward.
> "And as for you, lift up your staff and stretch out your hand over the sea and divide it, and the sons of Israel shall go through the midst of the sea on dry land.
> "And as for Me, behold, I will harden the hearts of the Egyptians so that they will go in after them; and I will be honored through Pharaoh and all his army, through his chariots and his horsemen.
> "Then the Egyptians will know that I am the Lord, when I am honored through Pharaoh, through his chariots and his horsemen" (Exod. 14:13–18).

> Then Moses stretched out his hand over the sea; and the Lord swept the sea back by a strong east wind all night, and turned the sea into dry land, so the waters were divided.
> And the sons of Israel went through the midst of the sea on the dry land, and the waters were like a wall to them on their right hand and on their left (Exod. 14:21–22).

And that's *exactly* what occurred. To top it off, once the Hebrews got across the sea, God took care of any further worry they might have concerning the Egyptians.

> Then the Lord said to Moses, "Stretch out your hand over the sea so that the waters may come back over the Egyptians, over their chariots and their horsemen."
>
> So Moses stretched out his hand over the sea, and the sea returned to its normal state at daybreak, while the Egyptians were fleeing right into it; then the Lord overthrew the Egyptians in the midst of the sea.
>
> And the waters returned and covered the chariots and horsemen, even Pharaoh's entire army that had gone into the sea after them; not even one of them remained (Exod. 14:26–28).

I'd call that covering all the bases. Wonder what the Hebrews thought as they watched an unexpected Plan B take place before their eyes. Did they learn a permanent lesson? Hardly.

Unpleasant Adversities

A little later, as they were getting closer to their destination and weary from their long trip, the Hebrews did what came naturally. They started longing for the familiar.

> Now the people became like those who complain of adversity in the hearing of the Lord; and when the Lord heard it, His anger was kindled, and the fire of the Lord burned among them and consumed some of the outskirts of the camp.
>
> The people therefore cried out to Moses, and Moses prayed to the Lord, and the fire died out.
>
> So the name of that place was called Taberah, because the fire of the Lord burned among them.
>
> And the rabble who were among them had greedy desires; and also the sons of Israel wept again, and said, "Who will give us meat to eat?
>
> "We remember the fish which we used to eat free in Egypt, the cucumbers and the melons and the leeks and the onions and the garlic, but now our appetite is gone. There is nothing at all to look at except this manna" (Num. 11:1–6).

You see, it takes a heavenly appetite to enjoy a heavenly food. Back in Egypt they wanted relief—but they wanted it on *their terms*. They desired to break free from slavery, but there wasn't any reason for everything to be taken away! They longed for the familiar and satisfying surroundings of the fertile Nile valley. After all, there was a nice variety of things to eat back in Egypt—fresh, fresh stuff for salads, a few spices. But now? Warm water from a rock and manna. Every day . . . manna. They boiled it, baked it, sliced it, fixed it in pies. You name it, they tried it. I can see it now:

Mrs. Moses' 1001 Ways to Fix Manna was a bestseller. When they heard the dinner bell, nobody asked, "What's for supper?" but rather, "How'd you fix it this time?" And that was getting old. Egypt was looking better to these weary travelers with each step they took and Canaan was fast losing its luster.

Unfair Accusations

Add to all this the burdens of leading a thankless crowd like those Hebrews, and you can understand the following:

> But two men had remained in the camp; the name of the one was Eldad and the name of the other Medad. And the Spirit rested upon them (now they were among those who had been registered, but had not gone out to the tent), and they prophesied in the camp.
> So a young man ran and told Moses and said, "Eldad and Medad are prophesying in the camp."
> Then Joshua the son of Nun, the attendant of Moses from his youth, answered and said, "Moses, my lord, restrain them."
> But Moses said to him, "Are you jealous for my sake? Would that all the Lord's people were prophets, that the Lord would put His Spirit upon them!"
> Then Moses returned to the camp, both he and the elders of Israel (Num. 11:26-30).

> Then Miriam and Aaron spoke against Moses because of the Cushite woman whom he had married (for he had married a Cushite woman); and they said, "Has the Lord indeed spoken only through Moses? Has He not spoken through us as well?" And the Lord heard it (Num. 12:1-2).

How unfair to strike out against the leader at a time like this! But they did. It still happens. Anyone who has been in leadership for even a little while knows the pain of being verbally assaulted. You're either king o' the hill or (more often) the bull's eye on people's dartboard.

I remember the words of Sonny Jurgensen when he was quarterback of the Washington Redskins professional football team. He was being attacked by fan and sportswriter alike as his team was in a slump. Somebody asked him if all the flack was getting to him. He flashed a big toothless grin and replied, "Naw, not me. I've been in this game long enough to know that every week the quarterback is in either the penthouse or the outhouse!" The penthouse is a lot more fun, but a leader isn't in it nearly as much as the outhouse. And when those accusations start penetrating, we're tempted to pull out the map and retreat.

Unexpected Resistance

By the time they got to the edge of the promised land, Canaan, a final shoe hit the floor.

Then the Lord spoke to Moses saying, "Send out for yourself men so that they may spy out the land of Canaan, which I am going to give to the sons of Israel; you shall send a man from each of their fathers' tribes, every one a leader among them."

So Moses set them from the wilderness of Paran at the command of the Lord, all of them men who were heads of the sons of Israel.

So they went up and spied out the land from the wilderness of Zin as far as Rehob, at Lebo-hamath.

When they had gone up into the Negev, they came to Hebron where Ahiman, Sheshai and Talmai, the descendants of Anak were. (Now Hebron was built seven years before Zoan in Egypt.)

Then they came to the valley of Eshcol and from there cut down a branch with a single cluster of grapes; and they carried it on a pole between two men, with some of the pomegranates and the figs. When they returned from spying out the land, at the end of forty days, they proceeded to come to Moses and Aaron and to all the congregation of the sons of Israel in the wilderness of Paran, at Kadesh; and they brought back word to them and to all the congregation and showed them the fruit of the land.

Thus they told him, and said, "We went in to the land where you sent us; and it certainly does flow with milk and honey, and this is its fruit (Num. 13:1–3, 21–23, 25–27).

They not only had made it, they had it made. The spies stood there with undeniable evidence. Beautiful fruit . . . and not one Medfly in the country! Fabulous soil, bumper crops, plenty of water—it must have seemed unreal.

If only the story ended here and "they lived happily ever after." It doesn't. There is a big NEVERTHELESS of unbelief.

"Nevertheless, the people who live in the land are strong, and the cities are fortified and very large; and moreover, we saw the descendants ot Anak there.

"Amalek is living in the land of the Negev and the Hittites and the Jebusites and the Amorites are living in the hill country, and the Canaanites are living by the sea and by the side of the Jordan."

Then Caleb quieted the people before Moses, and said, "We should by all means go up and take possession of it, for we shall surely overcome it."

But the men who had gone up with him said, "We are not able to go up against the people, for they are too strong for us."

So they gave out to the sons of Israel a bad report of the land which they had spied out, saying, "The land through which we have gone, in spying it out, is a land that devours its inhabitants; and all the people whom we saw in it are men of great size.

"There also we saw the Nephilim (the sons of Anak are part of the Nephilim); and we became like grasshoppers in our own sight, and so we were in their sight" (Num. 13:28–33).

"Oh, no! Not giants! Not *another* problem on top of all we've had to face. Not that!" Have you felt like that lately? Have you been hearing the footsteps of giants? Or have you run into the belly of some unexpected giant that has lumbered across the landscape of your life?

I distinctly recall an evening I went to the Los Angeles Forum to watch the Los Angeles Lakers play the Philadelphia '76ers. A friend of mine had season tickets right down on the floor, just behind the Laker bench. Talk about feeling insignificant! Those guys are big even when they are sitting down. Then when they unfolded those legs and stood to full height, it was Operation Grasshopper in our section! I fully expected Abdul-Jabbar or Moses Malone to bring rain. You can't appreciate how massive those giants are until you have them within arm's reach. It's enough to make a grown man run and hide.

While I understand the spies' feeling intimidated, I cannot excuse their forgetting God's unconditional promise. Furthermore, no giant is any match for God. When God stands, everybody is smaller. When God promises, nobody dares to question it.

Barriers That Keep Us from Returning

"How does all this relate to me personally?" you, no doubt, are asking. It's a good question, and I commend you for thinking it.

My hope is to help you feel more and more comfortable being who you really are. Without trying to frighten you, I want to challenge you to risk a new horizon . . . to trust God to free you from your Egypt and to help you discover your Canaan. Now I should warn you, it will not be a quick 'n easy process. That's why I took so much time spelling out some of the tests you can expect to encounter. You'll have an "army" of voices out of your past hot on your trail, bound and determined to bring you back into captivity. You will face a Red Sea (perhaps *several* of them) that will appear uncrossable. And count on this, when you start getting near your objective, so near you can almost touch it, up come the giants of *resistance*, shouting, "Get out of here! You're not welcome . . . go back to where you belong! *Move!*"

How can we keep from running back? Does God say anything about what we can do to sustain the courage to keep risking? Indeed He does. All we need to do is take another look at this same Old Testament story to find those handles to grab hold of.

Let's look again at Exodus 13. That's the scene immediately following the Exodus. Fresh out of Egypt, those Hebrews had every reason to feel insecure. Why didn't they return? What was it that kept them from doing that?

Clear Direction from Above

Exodus 13:21–22 gives us the answer:

And the Lord was going before them in a pillar of cloud by day to lead them on the way, and in a pillar of fire by night to give them light, that they might travel by day and by night.

He did not take away the pillar of cloud by day, nor the pillar of fire by night, from before the people.

If Moses and those people were tempted to return, all they needed to do was look up. There it was, day after day . . . night after night. A distinct cloud covered them and led them during the daylight hours and after sundown . . . a "pillar of fire." It was no guessing game, no multifaceted Rubic's cube they had to figure out. No, God wanted them freed from Egyptian bondage.

I really don't know where you are in your pilgrimage from bondage to freedom. But I am confident of this, God will not leave you or give up on you. He wants you to know the joy of living an unmasked life. His Book, the Bible, is full of verses and principles that promise you His commitment. He won't leave you in the lurch. May I share a few of His promises with you?

Therefore, let everyone who is godly pray to Thee in a time when Thou mayest be found; Surely in a flood of great waters they shall not reach him.

Thou art my hiding place; Thou dost preserve me from trouble; Thou dost surround me with songs of deliverance.

I will instruct you and teach you in the way which you should go; I will counsel you with My eye upon you (Ps. 32:6-8).

Do not fear, for I am with you;
Do not anxiously look about you, for I am your God.
I will strengthen you, surely I will help you.
Surely I will uphold you with My righteous right hand.
Behold, all those who are angered at you will be shamed and dishonored; Those who contend with you will be as nothing, and will perish.

You will seek those who quarrel with you, but will not find them, Those who war with you will be as nothing, and nonexistent.

For I am the Lord your God, who upholds your right hand, Who says to you, "Do not fear, I will help you" (Isa. 41:10-13).

Can a woman forget her nursing child, And have no compassion on the son of her womb? Even these may forget, but I will not forget you.

Behold, I have inscribed you on the palms of My hands; Your walls are continually before Me (Isa. 49:15-16).

"And you shall know the truth, and the truth shall make you free" (John 8:32).

What then shall we say to these things? If God is for us, who is against us?

He who did not spare His own Son, but delivered Him up for us all, how will He not also with Him freely give us all things?

Who will bring a charge against God's elect? God is the one who justifies; who is the one who condemns? Christ Jesus is He who died, yes, rather who was raised, who is at the right hand of God, who also intercedes for us.

Who shall separate us from the love of Christ? Shall tribulation, or distress, or persecution, or famine, or nakedness, or peril, or sword?

Just as it is written,

"For Thy sake we are being put to death all day long;
We were considered as sheep to be slaughtered."

But in all these things we overwhelmingly conquer through Him who loved us (Rom. 8:31–37).

These are scriptural "anchors" you can claim, trusting God to stabilize you in the storm. Consider these words as *your* cloud by day and fire by night. Believe me, you will need them when the journey gets long and the giants are loud. These truths will keep you from returning to the misery of *your* Egypt.

Timely Relief from Discouragement

The Lord therefore said to Moses, "Gather for me seventy men from the elders of Israel, whom you know to be the elders of the people and their officers and bring them to the tent of meeting, and let them take their stand there with you.

"Then I will come down and speak with you there, and I will take of the Spirit who is upon you, and will put Him upon them; and they shall bear the burden of the people with you, so that you shall not bear it all alone (Num. 11:16–17).

Remember how Moses had become the target of their criticism and complaints? Well, he began to crack under the pile. . . . Like any one of us, it got too much for him. But God graciously relieved the pressure. And He still does that today.

In the case of Moses, the Lord brought alongside His servant a group of people to help shoulder the load he was carrying. In fact, *seventy* of them. Strong natural leaders tend not to delegate responsibility as they should. They often adopt the I'm-all-alone-in-this-battle mentality. Add to that the nobody-knows-or-cares exaggeration, and you've got stress personified. Soon discouragement slips in on the blind side and cuts our feet out from under us. At these weak points in our lives there is nothing like a friend—or a group of friends—to pull us out of our rapid descent.

My wife and I have learned that life can get pretty grim without some folks alongside us to add perspective amidst the pressure. On several occasions we have been grateful for a few couples with whom we have had the freedom to share the pain and thereby diffuse the discouragement. I have come to the conclusion that it is not possible to maintain an isolated, untouchable profile and carry out all that is involved in peeling off all the masks that keep us from being fully who we are. Moses, just like everybody else, *needed* others. So do we.

Internal Fortification from Threat

But then there are times when there is very little anyone else can do to assist us. Maybe you recall the occasion when a couple of men in the Israeli camp began to prophesy. Jealous for Moses' singular role of authority, Joshua urged him to "restrain" them. With calm, unthreatened confidence, greathearted Moses refused to do that. His answer reveals how secure he was: "But Moses said to him, 'Are you jealous for my sake? Would that all the Lord's people were prophets, that the Lord would put His Spirit upon them!' Then Moses returned to the camp, both he and the elders of Israel" (Num. 11:29–30).

Only the Lord can give us that kind of internal fortitude. And as you and I ask the Lord to give us that spirit, let's resist every temptation to think of ourselves or our particular style or thrust as exclusive. If someone else is doing it (and maybe doing it better than we), let's reject jealousy and replace it with applause. Competition has no place in the ranks of Christianity.

When I consider this problem of competition and how it affects our churches, I'm reminded of the story a lady mentioned to me several years ago. She and her family were traveling across the country in their recreational vehicle. As they drove through a small town in one of the midwestern states, they passed a little church with a most unusual name. To make sure they had not misread the sign, they drove around the block and read it again:

THE ORIGINAL CHURCH OF GOD, NUMBER TWO

Now there's a church with some history worth looking into. On another occasion Moses was in need of being vindicated. It was when Miriam and Aaron criticized him. If you'll take the time to read the twelfth chapter of Numbers, you'll see that God personally intervened on His servant's behalf. There are still such occasions today when we are at a loss to defend ourselves or vindicate our integrity. At such times we are forced to rely solely on God's intervention. And although His timing is usually different from what we expect, He gets the job done beautifully.

I have a close, personal friend whose father has been a pastor for many, many years. The father was a man of faithfulness and consistency. But a tragic event occurred in the midyears of his ministry. He was falsely accused of adultery by the vicious tongues of several gossips. The man, though completely innocent, became the object of scandalous words which followed him like his own shadow for years. There was nothing he could say or do to vindicate himself. His son, my friend, watched during his young adult years as the unfounded lies took their toll on the lives of his parents. With silent heroism they continued to serve, trusting God to confound the critic and, in His time, vindicate the minister.

Finally, it happened. It had taken ten long years, but early one morning, unannounced, the person responsible for the false accusations appeared on the doorstep of the pastor's home. As he opened the door, he stood face-to-face with the one who had started the rumor. Tears ran down the cheeks of the critic, now broken in spirit. Pleading for forgiveness, the individual openly confessed the transgression, fully admitting guilt and blaming no one else. That person, by the way, had been under such deep conviction and turmoil that there had been no freedom to serve others or find any relief within.

Graciously and tearfully, the pastor expressed his forgiveness and assured the guilty party that there was absolutely no bitterness in his heart. He and his wife had worked their way through all that pain many years earlier. Now that he was finally vindicated, the offense had long since been diffused.

I cannot relate that story without remembering the words of Amy Carmichael:

> If I say, "Yes, I forgive, but I cannot *forget*," as though the God, who *twice* a day washes all the sands on all the shores of all the world, could not wash such memories from my mind, then I know nothing of Calvary love.[1]

How painful some of the days in that decade of silence must have been for my friend's father. How hard it is to wait!

Perhaps that's where you are. The details may differ, but not the pain. In your case, God may not have stepped in yet. Perhaps you're still waiting, still trusting. If so, don't quit. In the meantime, here's a proverb that you might grab onto: "When a man's ways are pleasing to the Lord, He makes even his enemies to be at peace with him" (Prov. 16:7).

Observe that there is an absence of any reference to time in those words. We aren't told when bitter enemies become peaceful friends . . . only that it will occur. Hang onto that and try your best not to be overcome by bitterness. The risk for you is simply continuing on, regardless. It's been my observation that bitterness restrains openness. If you really desire to drop your guard, you must first drop any lingering offense and the bitterness it has produced.

A PENETRATING PRAYER

One final question needs an answer: What will keep us risking? In other words, how can we counteract the old "Egyptian magnet" and continue pressing on into new unfamiliar territory?

If I were to put it in the form of a prayer, it would have three simple lines, then an "Amen."

Since it's God's desire that we demonstrate a message distinct from the insecure, fearful world around us, the first line would be: *"Lord, intensify your distinctiveness in me."*

And since it's the uncertainty of our future that strengthens our faith, the second would be: *"Lord, increase the risk."*

And since it's true that each one of us is to be a unique vessel of power . . . not a faded copy, the third line would be *"Lord, enlarge the difference. Amen."*

DISCUSSION IDEAS AND QUESTIONS

• Why is change so difficult, so threatening? Try to be specific in your answer.

• Can you think of a risk you took that opened a door you never dreamed possible? If you feel comfortable sharing it, please do.

• Look back into the chapter and read the five "tests" that tempt us to retreat to the familiar. Which one(s) represents a major battle in your life? Why?

• Identify with Moses for a few minutes. If you were standing in his sandals, describe how you would have felt when the criticism and grumbling began. How do you handle it when you are the target?

• Remember the passages of Scripture listed under the subheading "Clear Direction from Above"? Which one encourages you the most? Is there something that troubles you about these passages? Openly talk about the struggle.

• Finally, take a glance at the closing three-line prayer. Can you ask those things of God today? Perhaps before leaving this time of meditation, you might want to expand these three lines . . . or choose one and talk with God about it.

3

Getting Closer,
Growing Stronger

Nestled in the hills of western Virginia is a stately old southern resort named "The Homestead"—sixteen thousand Alleghany acres of mountains, valleys, forest, deep blue sky, and clear, rippling streams. The place drips with elegance and is rich in historical significance. Washington and Jefferson strolled along those winding paths. There are few settings more suitable for gaining renewed perspective than places like this.

In the Spring of 1983, I was invited by the Christian Embassy to speak at a retreat in which several Cabinet members, senators, congressmen, and high-ranking Pentagon officers and their wives were present. The Homestead was the site where we met—about fifty or more of us—to be refreshed and encouraged. Those in attendance were Christians, but the lines on their faces revealed the marks of pressure, loneliness, stress, and fatigue. There they were, some of the most decisive and important people in America, setting aside a weekend to meet with the Lord, to unload their burdens, to be together as couples, hopefully to find a little relief from their pressure-cooker world. I considered it a choice privilege to be the speaker at that retreat. God's Word met many needs as these courageous and battle-weary men and women opened their lives to the truths of Scripture. The Homestead became a haven of renewed hope.

The difference between the group at the first session on Friday and the last session on Sunday was amazing. It was the same people, you understand, but those hours they spent together paid rich dividends. At first there was distance and formality. But by the time we left one another, there had emerged a beautiful blend of oneness, mutual understanding, a breakdown of defenses, and great openness. By getting closer, we grew stronger. *It was magnificent!* As beautiful as our natural surroundings were, they could not compare with the harmony, the love, and the closeness our group cultivated in three brief days.

In all my twenty-plus years of ministry, I don't believe I have ever been among a more influential (yet emotionally battered) body of believers, but even *they*, when given the opportunity to draw close to others in a context of unguarded honesty and mutual caring, responded like you can't believe. What was it? How did the magic occur? Why would over fifty high-powered, strong leaders holding some of the most enviable positions in our nation drop their guard and blend their lives together? Believe me, it wasn't the surroundings or the food or the music or the accommodations or the speaker or the weather. It was something only the Spirit of God could have done. I shall never forget that eventful weekend in May of '83. My only regret is that *you* were not present to witness it personally. Had you been, you wouldn't be satisfied simply to read about it. You'd want to *experience* it because there are few things quite as contagious as authentic, spontaneous, unguarded love in action. It cannot be legislated or manipulated. It can only be demonstrated.

Essential Ingredients

There must be certain ingredients, however. Otherwise, every time Christians met together, this same scenario would occur, and you and I know it doesn't. What are those ingredients? At this point I am somewhat reluctant to analyze and scrutinize too specifically. Like a breathtaking sunset or the sound of a pounding surf, some things defy explanation. So let me suggest three big-picture generalizations.

First, *there must be an admission of need for others*. This means that self-sufficiency and isolationism are set aside. That's hard to do in our world of superindependence. And how easily that mindset slips into the Christian ranks: "Look, I don't need others—just gimme a good sermon on Sunday, a few cassette tapes to hold me over during the week, and my privacy." To help you realize how off the wall that philosophy really is, imagine the same idea as I couch it in the terms of a hotshot, independent football player who shows up at practice and yells:

"Hey, coach! Don't bug me with a thick playbook and all this talk about teamwork and pulling together, okay? All I need is a stadium, a big crowd, and the ball. Working with ten other guys is a hassle and learning plays is a drag. Just gimme the ball and have everybody get outa my way. I do better all alone."

Let me ask you, how long would that young athlete be around? You see, in God's sovereign plan, He arranged things so that we would do our best work as team members. To repeat what I've said all along, we need each other. Isolationism won't work.

Second, *there must be the cultivation of deeper relationships*. This takes time, effort, and a spirit of willingness. Yes, and as we saw in chapter 2, even some risk. The larger the group, the more difficult. As we just discovered when Moses attempted to lead the Hebrews to Canaan, it is easy to pick up a blame-the-leader mentality or adopt a cynical view toward God when we fail to cultivate relationships.

The thing that drew our group together so quickly at The Homestead was the similarity of circumstances. Everybody there was being shot at by critics. They were all coming out of the same stormy political scene. There was an affinity that gave everyone immediate understanding. In a context like that, relationships flourish. But it isn't so in most churches. Thus there is a need for small groups where people can begin to build bridges to one another. By the way, the leader will need to be secure and unthreatened. Pastors, for example, who must maintain tight controls and a strongly centralized ministry where events and meetings must revolve around them will not create the climate of freedom in which relationships can flourish.

Third, *there must a firm commitment to assimilation.* This is ground we have already covered, but because it is new terminology to many of you, repetition will help establish it clearly in your mind. It isn't enough simply to admit we need others. Nor is it sufficient to say rather loosely, "Oh, yeah, knowing a few other Christians is nice." No, I'm talking about being committed to getting beneath the surface of superficial talk . . . being interested in and accountable to other believers.

The seventeenth-century John Donne was absolutely right when only seven days before his death he wrote:

> No man is an island, entire of itself; every man is a piece of the continent, a part of the main; if a clod be washed away by the sea, Europe is the less, as well as if a promontory were, as well as if a manor of thy friends or of thine own were; any man's death diminishes me, because I am involved in mankind; and therefore never send to know for whom the bell tolls; it tolls for thee.[1]

Funny thing, folks in God's family are often far more committed to the up-front leader (pastor, director, spokesperson) than to one another. But if I understand the thrust of New Testament Christianity, God never intended our earthly allegiance to be so limited. Remember those insightful words addressed to the Corinthians?

> Now the body is not one member but many. If the foot should say, "Because I am not a hand I don't belong to the body," does that alter the fact that the foot is a part of the body? Or if the ear should say, "Because I am not an eye I don't belong to the body," does that mean that the ear really is not part of the body? After all, if the body were all one eye, for example, where would be the sense of hearing? Or, if it were all one ear, where would be the sense of smell? But God has arranged all the parts in the one body, according to his design. . . . So that the eye cannot say to the hand, "I don't need you!" nor, again, can the head say to the feet, "I don't need you!" (1 Cor. 12:14–21, PHILLIPS).

Somehow, hero-worshiping twentieth-century Christians have great difficulty believing these words. Hopefully, *you* are different. Not until we begin to see the value of *each* member of the Body (rather than just a few of the more prominent people) will we enter into this full dimension of family life. Assimilation won't happen when most in the group are busy pushing one or two up on a pedestal.

DANGERS THAT LURK: BE ON THE ALERT!

These thoughts take me back to our story in the Old Testament as Moses led the Hebrews from Egypt to Canaan. There are many remarkable and relevant analogies to be found in that story. So let's return to that ancient scene and continue our investigation. I find in Deuteronomy, chapter 6, four very real dangers that apply to us today even though they have their roots in an event that transpired many centuries ago.

The Israelites are on the edge of Canaan, you'll recall. They are about to step into a country that will challenge their commitment to Jehovah God. Moses is not only concerned for their welfare, but also for the welfare of their children, once he says good-by and they move into the promised land. He wouldn't be going with them, so his words were quite intense:

> "Now this is the commandment, the statutes and the judgments which the Lord your God has commanded me to teach you, that you might do them in the land where you are going over to possess it, so that you and your son and your grandson might fear the Lord your God, to keep all His statutes and His commandments, which I command you, all the days of your life, and that your days may be prolonged.
>
> "O Israel, you should listen and be careful to do it, that it may be well with you and that you may multiply greatly, just as the Lord, the God of your fathers, has promised you, in a land flowing with milk and honey.
>
> "Hear, O Israel! The Lord is our God, the Lord is one!
>
> "And you shall love the Lord your God with all your heart and with all your soul, and with all your might" (Deut. 6:1-5).

Feel the emotion? The man is pouring out his soul. Realizing that he would not be among them as they invaded and inhabited Canaan, he spoke of their need to passionately love the Lord their God . . . to listen to His voice . . . to obey His commands . . . to serve Him with all their heart, soul, and might. This introduces the first danger.

1. *Falling more in love with the leader than with the Lord.* Will you observe how clearly he turned their attention away from himself and toward the Lord. You see, Moses is dispensable in the Canaan project. Don't misunderstand, he was exceedingly significant in leading them from Point A (Egypt) to Point B

(edge of Canaan), but his role of importance was obviously decreasing. Within a matter of days, he would be gone forever from their sight. But the Lord would be there to sustain them. He would never leave them.

Many years ago I read a statement that has stuck in my head ever since. I can't remember the source, but the words have been permanently etched in my mind: "When a man of God dies, nothing of God dies." There is no question that leaders are used in mighty ways to shape the lives of God's people. Where would some of us be were it not for "the shakers and the movers" who challenged us and motivated us? But no leader, regardless of his or her vision, gifts, or model, is indispensable to God's overall plan. Only God is that. We are fooling ourselves and heading for an abrupt, disillusioning fall if our love for the leader is greater than our love and loyalty to the Lord Himself.

On top of that, God's desire to have the Body get closer and grow stronger together will be hindered if the center of affection and attention is the leader. To go back to my football example, it is teamwork that makes for a winning season and healthy intrasquad morale. Even teams that have superstar athletes frequently mention that while they appreciate and admire the star's ability, they are a team of varied talent, not a one-man operation. A difficult struggle though it may be, Christians who hope to cultivate meaningful, lasting, and deep relationships with each other must maintain the right perspective at this point. Had the Hebrews lost their focus, Joshua would have been unable to carry on when Moses stepped aside. The servant-leader Moses made Joshua's task easier by continually turning the people's allegiance away from himself and back on the Lord.

This danger of exalting the leader above the Lord is a hindrance to closeness occuring in a group because it tends to emphasize rank and positions of earthly authority above the oneness we all have in the Savior, Jesus Christ. It's His lordship that cements us together in one unified whole, placing everyone in the same role—sheep belonging to their Shepherd. But when the leader occupies a conspicuous place of prominence, the group becomes divided rather than unified and up go the defenses, on go the masks.

With rare, masterful strokes of humility, Moses instructed the people to devote themselves to the Lord their God. That brings us to danger number two.

2. *Fixing our eyes on our immediate convenience instead of our ultimate objective.* Take a look at Moses' wise counsel:

"And these words, which I am commanding you today, shall be on your heart; and you shall teach them diligently to your sons and shall talk of them when you sit in your house and when you walk by the way and when you lie down and when you rise up.

"And you shall bind them as a sign on your hand and they shall be as frontals on your forehead.

"And you shall write them on the doorposts of your house and on your gates" (Deut. 6:6–9).

It is obvious they were not to sit back, relax, and "let whatever happens, happen" in the future. Not on your life. These familiar words may have become too familiar to us. Between the lines are written diligence, hard work, a solid family life, open and very natural communication. Without these things becoming a high priority, those folks would not survive. They were to give themselves to a lifestyle of mutual sharing and caring, reminding one another of the things that had held them together and kept them strong down through the years. A careful look will help you see that this wouldn't happen automatically once they got into Canaan. They were to teach, to talk, to bind, and to write this information as they got established in the promised land.

How much easier it would have been to give their attention to getting comfortable and focusing on immediate convenience instead of this ultimate objective . . . especially since they must have been weary of the wilderness. But God knew best. If they didn't *start* right, it's doubtful they would be able to sustain their distinctiveness—ever. Objectives are easily lost. They slowly erode rather than suddenly explode, have you noticed? To illustrate how this can happen, consider this actual experience one man had in the Deep South.

When I lived in Atlanta, several years ago, I noticed in the Yellow Pages, in the listing of restaurants, an entry for a place called Church of God Grill. The peculiar name aroused my curiosity and I dialed the number. A man answered with a cheery, "Hello! Church of God Grill!" I asked how his restaurant had been given such an unusual name, and he told me: "Well, we had a little mission down here, and we started selling chicken dinners after church on Sunday to help pay the bills. Well, people liked the chicken, and we did such a good business, that eventually we cut back on the church service. After a while we just closed down the church altogether and kept on serving the chicken dinners. We kept the name we started with, and that's Church of God Grill."[2]

While we're smiling at that true story, allow me to ask you a question. What are *your* personal objectives? How about your family's objectives? Are you still on target? Maybe in the race and pace of these days you've begun to compromise and shift for the sake of convenience. It is so easy and so natural to do. That church, for example, was originally established with one clear objective—to dispense salt and display light in a community. But now it dispenses grilled cheese sandwiches, hamburgers, french fries, and cokes. Its salt is now in a little glass container on the counter. Its light is now a neon sign.

How about your church? Given to be a lighthouse, a place of hope and refuge, is it accomplishing that ultimate objective? Are hurting people really able to be at home there? Can brokenness and pain be admitted? Is there room for those who have failed rather than achieved, those who have lost rather than won, those who *don't* have it all together? Is there still a willingness to reach out and help wounded people find inner healing and the courage to go on? I'll have much more to say about this in chapter 8, but here I wanted to direct your

attention toward the "lurking danger," of focusing our interests on our immediate convenience instead of our ultimate goal.

As we continue through the sixth chapter of Deuteronomy, we read:

> "Then it shall come about when the Lord your God brings you into the land
> which He swore to your fathers, Abraham, Isaac and Jacob, to give you, great and
> splendid cities which you did not build, and houses full of all good things which
> you did not fill, and hewn cisterns which you did not dig, vineyards and olive trees
> which you did not plant, and you shall eat and be satisfied.
>
> Then watch yourself, lest you forget the Lord who brought you from the land of
> Egypt, out of the house of slavery.
>
> "You shall fear only the Lord your God; and you shall worship Him, and swear
> by His name.
>
> "You shall not follow other gods, any of the gods of the peoples who surround
> you" (Deut. 6:10–14).

Before we examine this interesting section of Scripture and this relevant
series of warnings, let's consider the third danger that emerges from these
words.

3. *Assuming that size means strength.*

Here was a massive body of people, somewhere between one and two *million*
individuals. Yet Moses announces to them, "Watch yourself!" Picture the scene.
They have finally arrived at the promised land. Their future home was waiting for
them—fertile fields, sufficient water, fruit trees and vineyards, homes ready to
occupy (once the Canaanites were driven out), even entire cities all set for their
arrival. All those things would be virtually laid in their laps.

Verse 10: ". . . cities . . . you did not build."

Verse 11: ". . . houses full of good things . . . you did not fill, . . . cisterns
. . . you did not dig, vineyards . . . trees . . . you did not plant."

Verse 12: "Then watch yourself, lest you forget the Lord!"

Although they were a huge number of people and they would occupy ready-
made cities and suburbs with all the comforts of home, none of the above
guaranteed their strength. Even when Joshua was given a preinvasion briefing
by the Lord (the account is found in Joshua 1:1–9) on no less than *three*
occasions the commander-in-chief was told to "be strong and courageous" (vv.
6, 7, 9). In other words, their strength was not in their number or possessions,
only the Lord could make them strong. If they got smug and proud, weakness
would eat into their nation like acid. If they adopted the Canaanite culture and
lost their distinctiveness in the morass of Gentile intermarriage, idolatry, and
other forms of spiritual infidelity, they were goners! In a society overly impressed by size, this is a timely word for all of us. We would be foolish to believe
that a family is strong because it has lots of children, that a city is strong simply
because it's big, or a company is strong because its buildings are so extensive or
because its employees are so numerous. That's the point—size and strength are
not synonymous.

What's true of a family or a city or a company is equally true of a church. I'm not saying a large church *cannot* be strong, but only that it isn't automatically strong *because* it is large. Strength comes by being close, in touch, unmasked, and available to one another much more than by being big. Here are two examples of what I mean from Alan Lay McGinnis's book, *The Friendship Factor:*

> He was the world's ultimate mystery—so secretive, so reclusive, so enigmatic, that for more than 15 years no one could say for certain that he was alive, much less how he looked or behaved.
>
> Howard Hughes was one of the richest men in the world, with the destinies of thousands of people—perhaps even of governments—at his disposal, yet he lived a sunless, joyless, half-lunatic life. In his later years he fled from one resort hotel to another—Las Vegas, Nicaragua, Acapulco—and his physical appearance became odder and odder. His straggly beard hung down to his waist and his hair reached to the middle of his back. His fingernails were two inches long, and his toenails hadn't been trimmed for so long they resembled corkscrews.
>
> Hughes was married for 13 years to Jean Peters, one of the most beautiful women in the world. But never in that time were the two seen in public together, and there is no record of their ever having been photographed together. For a while they occupied separate bungalows at the Beverly Hills Hotel (at $175 per day each), and later she lived in an opulent and carefully guarded French Regency house atop a hill in Bel Air, making secretive and increasingly infrequent trips to be with Hughes in Las Vegas. They were divorced in 1970.
>
> "As far as I know," a Hughes confidant once said, "he's never loved any woman. It's sex, or a good secretary, or good box office—that is all a woman means to him." Hughes often said, "Every man has his price or a guy like me couldn't exist," yet no amount of money bought the affection of his associates. Most of his employees who have broken the silence report their disgust for him.
>
> Why was Hughes so isolated and so lonely? Why with almost unlimited money, hundreds of aides, and countless beautiful women available to him, was he so unloved?
>
> Simply because he chose to be.
>
> It is an old axiom that God gave us things to use and people to enjoy. Hughes never learned to enjoy people. He was too busy manipulating them. His interests were machines, gadgets, technology, airplanes, and money—interests so consuming as to exclude relationships.[3]

> In the Spring of 1887, a 20-year-old arrived in Tuscumbia, Alabama, to attempt the tutoring of a deaf-blind creature. The tutor's name was Anne Sullivan and the student's name was Helen Keller. They were to develop one of the most admired friendships of the century.
>
> At seven, Helen Keller was a wild vixen who uttered unintelligible animal sounds. When in a rage, she would snatch dishes from the table and throw them and herself on the floor. More than one person had told Mrs. Keller that her child was an idiot.

For weeks Anne spelled words into Helen's small hand, but she could not break through to her consciousness. Then, on April 5, something wonderful happened. Here are Helen Keller's recollections of that day, written more than 60 years later:

It happened at the well-house, where I was holding a mug under the spout. Annie pumped water into it, and when the water gushed out into my hand she kept spelling w-a-t-e-r into my other hand with her fingers. Suddenly I understood. Caught up in the first joy I had known since my illness, I reached out eagerly to Annie's ever-ready hand, begging for new words to identify whatever objects I touched. Spark after spark of meaning flew from hand to hand, miraculously, affection was born. From the well-house there walked two enraptured beings calling each other "Helen" and "Teacher."

Anne Sullivan recognized that Helen was a prodigy and had unlimited possibilities for thinking and feeling. There was no question as to which of the two had the higher IQ. By the time she was 10, Helen was writing to famous persons in Europe in French. She quickly mastered five languages and displayed gifts which her teacher never pretended to have.

But did that change Anne Sullivan's devotion? Not so far as we know. She was satisfied to be Helen's companion and encourager, allowing her to be applauded by kings and presidents and to be her own unique personage. In short, she gave her friend room to grow.[4]

That brings us to the fourth danger for which we need to be alert.

4. *Living in the glow of yesterday instead of the challenge of tomorrow.* Listen again to God's counsel to Joshua: "'Have I not commanded you? Be strong and courageous! Do not tremble or be dismayed, for the Lord your God is with you wherever you go'" (Josh. 1:9).

There it is again—strength and courage come from the Lord. Then the commander turned and said to the Hebrews:

"Pass through the midst of the camp and command the people, saying, 'Prepare provisions for yourselves, for within three days you are to cross this Jordan, to go in to possess the land which the Lord your God is giving you, to possess it'" (Josh. 1:11).

The command was for them to go on, to pursue new horizons. To face the future with renewed determination, not to live in the warm soft glow of the past. Those Hebrews were not instructed to relax and drift as they recalled the Exodus or their crossing the Red Sea, nor were they to spend their time erecting monuments and building shrines depicting their illustrious history. No, they were to tighten their belts and take on the challenge of conquering Canaan.

Ever been around a group of Christians who had adopted a holding pattern philosophy? You know, the old occupy-and-protect game plan rather than the pursue-new-territory-and-risk strategy. The sports world calls this "sitting on the lead" and coaches I know say that's lethal. It certainly is in a church. I cannot think of one Christian Organization, either here in the United States or abroad, that decided to maintain the status quo yet remained fresh, creative, or vital very long after that decision was implemented. Neither do we as individuals. We advance or we retreat, but we don't remain static . . . not if we hope to stay in touch with our times and not if we are committed to open relationships and close friendships.

LONELINESS—EVEN AT "THE HOMESTEAD"

In this chapter we have considered several essential ingredients that make meaningful relationships take root, grow, and blossom. We have also exposed some of the dangers that lurk in the shadows—dangers that can sound the death knell to coming closer and thereby growing stronger together.

To illustrate just how effective our enemy is at keeping us isolated and distant, please return with me to The Homestead, that beautiful old resort in Virginia. Over fifty responsible, influential, and well-educated individuals are present . . . Christian statesmen embroiled in life-shaping decisions, at the hub of our nation's capital—good folks, solid citizens, family people you can't help but respect. They are folks who believe in our country and are willing to go on record for such basics as decency, integrity, patriotism, and godliness in our land. Most have been in the military or high-ranking political arenas for years. I didn't meet a novice in the whole gathering.

Do you know the single most-often mentioned dilemma they confessed to me? It wasn't public criticism or personality conflicts and pressure among their peers, or some issue they had believed in, fought for, and lost by a narrow margin. It wasn't even the news media, as vicious and insulting as that can be at times.

It was their own personal isolationism. Some came right out and called it loneliness. They may appear to be terribly involved. In fact, they are. Fourteen-to-sixteen-hour days are not that uncommon. There are staff and committee meetings and public speeches and congressional hearings and news conferences by the dozens. No doubt about it, they're busy. Public servants have little time to call their own. But meaningful friendships? Open and deep relationships? Other couples with whom they spend time, letting down their hair, sharing together, and entering each others' lives? No. Without an exception, those who talked with me alone admitted this was woefully absent from their experience.

Time and again I heard words like "superficial," "shallow," "skin deep," and "formal" as they candidly described their horizontal relationships. Wives of these public figures admitted, during our three-day retreat, that they live ultraprivate, guarded lives . . . and in some cases, it has really taken a toll on their children. It's hard for families to flourish in secret caves.

At supper one evening with a popular Cabinet member and his wife, I decided to come up front and ask them a direct question regarding this subject. I leaned toward the statesman and said, "Honestly, how deep are your friendships? Do you have even *one* person or couple with whom you can be yourselves—totally open and unguarded?"

The answer came quickly. After admitting, "No—no close friends, Chuck," he held out his hand, pointed his index finger in my direction, then pulled up his thumb with about an eighth of an inch of daylight showing in between and added, "All our relationships are about *that* deep." I looked at his wife and gave her one of my is-that-the-truth? looks. Without hestitation she nodded, "That's no exaggeration. We're close to no one." I told them that I believed they were not that unusual, certainly not in Washington, D.C. Then I mentioned I was in the process of writing this book. They smiled with approval, as if to say, "Good! Folks like us need all the help we can get." Who would've ever guessed?

As I think back, I find it ironic that all those capable Christian people, servants to the public, admitted their loneliness and isolation at a place named "The Homestead."

DISCUSSION IDEAS AND QUESTIONS

• Spend a few minutes discussing the three "essential ingredients" of developing close relationships with other people:
—Admission of need for others
—Cultivation of deeper relationships
—Firm commitment to assimilation.

• Of the three, which one is the most difficult for *you* personally. Explain why.

• Read 1 Corinthians 12:14–21 aloud. Talk about the importance of these verses.

• One of the dangers connected with getting closer to others relates to the high-profile role of the leader . . . almost to the point of exalting the leader more than the Lord. What can leaders do to encourage assimilation rather than thwart it?

• In working our way through Deuteronomy 5, we discovered that it is easy to lose sight of the ultimate objective. Pause and consider the objective(s) of your small group. Write down two or three (not more than four) that everyone can agree on. Periodically review them to help you stay on target.

• We may be quick to ask "Wonder why public servants live such isolated lives?" when, in reality, we do the same thing. What are you doing to keep that from occurring in your life? If someone looked into your eyes and asked, "Do you have a close meaningful relationship with one or more people?" what would you say?

• Pray for those who serve our country in places of high-level responsibility. Ask God to help them cultivate nonsuperficial friendships. If you know the names of a few such leaders, call their names in prayer.

4

Operation
Assimilation

Close relationships aren't automatic. They are the direct result of time, energy, and cultivation.

The first time it really came clear to me that we naturally relate to one another on a superficial level, I was standing in line in cap and gown, about to graduate from seminary. Here we stood as a class of young men, having completed four tough years of graduate school education and training. Although weary and anxious to get on with our lives, most of us were seized with a touch of nostalgia. We'd never be together again. Within a matter of hours we would be separated by miles, and in some case, by continents and oceans.

Perhaps that is what prompted the man standing behind me to reach around me and tap the fella standing in front of me on the shoulder. He asked rather embarrassingly, "Now what was your full name?"

You need to understand that our graduating class was not that large, less than seventy in all. We had been through four consecutive years of classes (some of them quite small), chapel services every day (we sat alphabetically), out-of-school sports activities, picnics, dinners, and ministry involvements. And most of our contact was on a campus no more than one square block in size . . . many of us living right on campus for at least part, if not all, of that time. Yet one man didn't even know the first and last name of another man who sat only two seats away from him for four long years. Seems incredible, I realize, but it did actually happen.

Popular psychologist and one of my dear personal friends, Dr. James Dobson, tells a similar story, only far more tragic than mine. He was a visiting lecturer at a seminary where he had spoken on the subject of self-esteem. His emphasis was that we cannot assume people have a healthy view of themselves just because they are studying for vocational Christian service. In fact, some struggle with this problem far more intensely than we can possibly imagine.

393

I was recently invited to conduct a lecture series for faculty and students at a seminary. It seemed appropriate that I talk to these future ministers about the subject of inferiority, since they would soon be dealing with many such problems in their own congregations. During the course of my first address, I relayed a story of "Danny." Danny was a distressed high-school student whose grief over his inadequacy became intolerable and eventually turned to anger. After I had spoken that day, I received the following anonymous letter:

Dear Dr. Dobson—

I am one of the "Dannys" you spoke of in chapel today. Believe me, for I have experienced this for as long as I can remember. It is a miserable way to live.

Yes, I'm a student at the seminary, but that doesn't make the problem any less acute. Through the years, particularly the last five, I have periodically gained a revived hope that somehow(?) this problem can be overcome—go away or something. Then to my great disappointment, I find it is still very much a part of me. That's when I lose hope of ever conquering it. I want to be a minister of the gospel and feel that this is God's will. *At the same time I am aware of the paralyzing effect this deep problem has upon me.* I want so badly to be adequate so that I could better serve God and others.

I wish I could talk with you, even for a short time. However, I realize your busy schedule. At any rate, thank you for coming to the seminary.

Sincerely,
A troubled seminarian

Since this broken young man had not identified himself publicly, I read and discussed his letter with the student body the following morning. Many of the three hundred young men who were present seemed moved by his words; for some, it undoubtedly reflected their own predicament as well. Following my lecture that morning, the "troubled seminarian" came and introduced himself to me. He stood with tears streaming down his cheeks as he spoke of the great sense of inadequacy he had experienced since early childhood. Later, an administrator of the seminary told me that this young man was the last member of the student body whom he would have expected to feel this way. As I have observed so many times, this sense of inferiority is the best-kept secret of the year. It is harbored deep inside, where it can gnaw on the soul.

Sitting in the audience that same day was another student with the same kind of problems. However, he did not write me a letter. He never identified himself in any way. But three weeks after I left, he hanged himself in the basement of his apartment. One of the four men with whom he lived called long distance to inform me of the tragedy. He stated, deeply shaken, that the dead student's roommates were so unaware of his problems that he hung there five days before he was missed?[1]

The first time I read those words my mouth dropped open and I almost gasped out loud. The suicide was, of course, tragic beyond description, but to think that the student's *roommates* didn't miss him for five days seems absolutely unbelievable. If that can happen in a school where dedicated Christians are supposedly in close contact with one another, it can certainly happen in your neighborhood . . . on your job . . . in your church . . . yes, and even in your home. That's a major reason I was prompted to write this book. Somehow, in our hurry-up, high-tech times, people can drop through the cracks and nobody even notices.

ASSIMILATION DEFINED

Close, open relationships are therefore vital. A glib "Hi, how are ya" must be replaced with genuine concern. The key term is *assimilation*. You won't get much help from Webster if you're searching for a definition. I know, I checked. Are you ready?

> . . . the incorporation or conversion of nutrients into protoplasm that in animals follows digestion and absorption and in higher plants involves both photosynthesis and root absorption.[2]

Uh, nope . . . that's not exactly what I have in mind. We're talking about people in society, not animals in the field or plants in a garden. When I use the word in this book, I'm referring to people reaching out to one another.

Being absorbed in the function of the family of God
  as a participant (rather than a spectator)
    . . . relating to
     . . . working with
      . . . caring for others
       whom I know and love.

That would be my definition of assimilation. As I read it over, I see written between the lines the reminder:

This
  is
    not
      automatic.
        I am personally responsible.
        So are you!

Somehow we have picked up the erroneous idea that open relationships and consistent assimilation will just start happening. If you like to fantasize, you could entertain the thought that some technically gifted inventor will one day devise an electronic gizmo that will solve our tendency toward isolation. It won't happen. Don't wait for a new video game or home computer or hand-held calculator that will tear down our relational barriers. On the contrary, those things seem to accomplish quite the opposite. If you question that, stroll through the local video arcade. Nobody relates to anybody!

In his mind-stretching work, *Megatrends*, John Naisbitt addresses and assaults what he calls "the danger of the technofix mentality."

> When we fall into the trap of believing or, more accurately, hoping that technology will solve all our problems, we are actually abdicating the high touch of personal responsibility. Our technological fantasies illustrate the point. We are always awaiting the new magical pill that will enable us to eat all the fattening food we want, and not gain weight; burn all the gasoline we want, and not pollute the air; live as immoderately as we choose, and not contract either cancer or heart disease.
>
> In our minds, at least, technology is always on the verge of liberating us from personal discipline and responsibility. Only it never does and it never will.
>
> The more high technology around us, the more the need for human touch.[3]

When our congregation got serious about close relationships and assimilation, we decided that they weren't going to happen *to* us, but *among* us. Otherwise, we would erode into an uninvolved body of spectators who come and watch a few folks "up front" do their thing. Being the senior pastor, I felt the need to address these things from the pulpit, which I did in a series of Sunday morning sermons I entitled "Congregational Relationships." Not a very creative title, but the content and the consistency of the series (twelve messages in all) began to have an effect. People realized there was much more to Christianity than sitting, singing, listening, and leaving. Our youth and adult ministries got even more involved in implementing ways to "assimilate" those who desired closer relationships. During-the-week, small-group gatherings proliferated like never before, and a contagious spirit of enthusiasm was reborn.

The old "saved, sanctified, galvanized" mentality was no longer satisfying. Mere pew sitting and sermon sampling by uninvolved isolationists were now being challenged as we allowed God's Word to inform and reprove us. Without in any way suggesting that I spoke out against a strong pulpit, my emphasis was that there should be other things just as strong—strong relationships, strong music and worship. My emphasis was on caring for others, involving ourselves in needs around us, and opening our lives to one another in smaller groups. In other words, we needed to be setting a pace in more areas than the preaching ministry. We were (and still are) committed to biblical exposition—perhaps more than ever in our history—but now we are hoping to follow through in some areas of biblical application. I'm pleased to say that it's working beautifully.

How the Ancient Hebrews Did It

So much for us . . . let's step back into the time tunnel once again and see if all this has biblical roots. Maybe a quick review will help.

• The Hebrews had left the familiar surroundings of Egypt, and God had shown Himself faithful as He led them, protected them, and fed them (even though they grumbled).

• The Jewish nomads remained disjointed and lacking in unity as they worked their way from Egypt to Canaan.

• After spying out the land, they were *again* divided. Some said, "Let's go, we can conquer!" But many more said, "No, let's return."

• For almost forty years they wandered around in the wilderness until the entire older generation died off. With the new generation came a new leader—Joshua.

That's were we take up the story.

> Now it came about after the death of Moses the servant of the Lord that the Lord spoke to Joshua the son of Nun, Moses' servant, saying, "Moses My servant is dead; now therefore arise, cross this Jordan, you and all this people, to the land which I am giving to them, to the sons of Israel.
>
> "Every place on which the sole of your foot treads, I have given it to you, just as I spoke to Moses.
>
> "From the wilderness and this Lebanon, even as far as the great river, the river Euphrates, all the land of the Hittites, and as far as the Great Sea toward the setting of the sun, will be your territory.
>
> "No man will be able to stand before you all the days of your life. Just as I have been with Moses, I will be with you; I will not fail you or forsake you" (Jos. 1:1–5).

That's what I would call reassurance. Such inspiring words would naturally prompt motivation. But they needed more than motivation. They needed to be melted together into a solidly committed unit, ready to invade and conquer Canaan. As I read through this chapter, no less than four principles leap off the page, each one illustrating how "assimilated" they were once they marched securely into Canaan.

1. *They relied on God for their future.* God and Joshua were in close communication (v. 1). The plan was clearly set forth (vv. 2–4), and the people were promised success (v. 5). It was God's voice against the odds. Unintimidated, Joshua and the people believed. Although outnumbered, they pressed on.

This kind of faithfulness reminds me of the Reformation when a relatively small band of men deliberately placed their faith in an infinitely awesome God. What followed didn't simply "happen" . . . it was the direct result of men like Luther, Calvin, Zwingli, Savonarola, Melanchthon, Knox, and a dozen or so more who relied on God for their future. The same could be said of the Great Awakening in England or the Second Awakening in America. Those who became a part of those movements were committed to the living God and to His unfailing promises.

But that's history, some of it centuries old. How about some more relevant examples. Do we have such? Indeed. To list only a few:

- "Uncle Cam" Townsend and the Wycliff Bible Translators
- Dawson Trotman and The Navigators
- M. R. DeHaan and the Radio Bible Class and Day of Discovery.
- Henrietta Mears and Forest Home Christian Conference Center
- Bill Bright and Campus Crusade for Christ, International
- Billy Graham and his Worldwide Evangelistic Crusades and Films.

I'll not take time to mention others equally deserving of our attention and respect. Those names stand out like modern-day Joshuas, people who relied on God and created a following of unified, committed disciples of the Savior. The good news is this: History *continues* to be written. Who knows? Someday your name might appear in such a list as you, too, become a pacesetter.

There is more. Let's look at a second principle which illustrates how assimilated the Hebrews were as they marched into Canaan.

2. *They accepted the challenge without fear of failure.* No less than four times we read that they were to be strong, courageous, confident, fearless (vv. 6, 7, 9, 18). In fact, the ninth verse comes right out and says, "Do not tremble or be dismayed." Today we would say, "Don't get shook up. Don't let intimidation do a number on you."

Anytime (yes, *any* time) there is a new furrow to be plowed, a new path to be cleared, a new idea to be tried, or a new strategy to be implemented, fear of failure stands tall as a giant. And all too often, it pushes its way in and gains a foothold. It has been my observation that the greater the possibility of impact, the greater the fear of failure ahead of time. That is what makes the Canaan invasion so exciting. It was so incredible, so humanly impossible, it had all the makings of a classic, *Guinness Book of World Records* failure.

How often we Christians unknowingly tip our hands. We pray with beseeching hands lifted high, "'Oh, Lord, almighty and omnipotent God, who knows no barrier and who cannot fail, we present this need to you today in prayer . . .'" And then immediately on the heels of that theologically powerful petition, we frown as we look around the table and say, "Gentlemen, the situation we face today is completely hopeless . . . *nothing* can be done." When will we ever learn that there are no hopeless situations, only people who have grown hopeless about them? What appears as an unsolvable problem to us is actually a rather exhilirating challenge. People who inspire others are those who see invisible bridges at the end of dead-end streets.

There was a Cabinet meeting in London during the darkest days of the Second World War. France had just capitulated. Prime Minister Churchill outlined the situation in its starkest colors. Quite literally, the tiny British Isles stood alone. Grim faces stared back at him in stoic silence. Despair and thoughts of surrender were written in their looks. The visionary statesman momentarily remained silent, lit a cigar, showed a hint of a smile, and with a twinkle in his eye, responded to that dispirited company of officials, "Gentlemen, I find it rather inspiring." He was the one who, on another occasion, said, "Nothing in life is so exhilirating as to be shot at without result." What a great line! No wonder people followed the man. Fear of failure never entered his mind.

When we read on in the Joshua account, we discover that the Hebrews took courage and got their stuff together:

Then Joshua commanded the officers of the people, saying, "Pass through the midst of the camp and command the people, saying, 'Prepare provisions for yourselves, for within three days you are to cross this Jordan to go in to possess the land which the Lord your God is giving you, to possess it.'"

And to the Reubenites and to the Gadites and to the half-tribe of Manasseh, Joshua said, "Remember the word which Moses the servant of the Lord commanded you, saying, 'The Lord your God gives you rest, and will give you this land.'

"Your wives, your little ones, and your cattle shall remain in the land which Moses gave you beyond the Jordan but you shall cross before your brothers in battle array, all your valiant warriors, and shall help them, until the Lord gives your brothers rest, as He gives you, and they also possess the land which the Lord your God is giving them. Then you shall return to your own land, and possess that which Moses the servant of the Lord gave you beyond the Jordan toward the sunrise" (Josh. 1:10–15).

As I read these words, I observe a couple or three things they did: They prepared provisions for themselves, they ignored tribal distinctions (no discrimination), and they demonstrated no selfishness—they helped one another. Isn't that exciting? An entire fighting force—a mighty army—moving ahead without fear of failure. By faith, they moved out.

Everyone who starts a new venture—whether a Charles Lindbergh carefully planning to cross the Atlantic, a Henry Ford launching an infant industry into the mainstream of world transportation, or a homemaker deciding to go back to school or start a business—faces certain fears, inner struggles, and temptations to quit. But there are ways of planning and of handling adversity and setbacks which have often made the difference between those who have risked and succeeded and those who have never really begun.[4]

Those are the words of a man who literally turned garbage into a multimillion dollar business mainly because he refused to be intimidated by the fear of failure.

As I think about those ancient Jews and the magnificent way God assimilated and mobilized them into a secure fighting force, I realize a third principle was put into operation.

3. *They ignored their differences and closed ranks in unity.* It's nothing short of remarkable how powerful and how effective a body of people can become when concern for who gets the credit or the emphasis on rank and status or talk about differences is dropped. These Hebrews, once they heard Joshua's game plan and

realized it was actually *God's* strategy for victory, rallied around the plan and promised their allegiance.

> And they answered Joshua, saying, "All that you have commanded us we will do, and wherever you send us we will go.
> "Just as we obeyed Moses in all things, so we will obey you; only may the Lord your God be with you, as He was with Moses.
> "Anyone who rebels against your command and does not obey your words in all that you command him, shall be put to death; only be strong and courageous" (Josh. 1:16–18).

Don't forget, these are words of affirmation declared spontaneously from the lips of those whose history was checkered with failure, unbelief, and defeat. But all that was past. It was now time to close ranks as they forgot their differences. What a refreshing atmosphere is created when God's people march together in unity toward the same objective!

Perhaps you remember one of the verses from the nineteenth-century gospel song, "Onward, Christian Soldiers" bySabine Baring-Gould:

> Like a mighty army
> Moves the church of God;
> Brothers, we are treading
> Where the saints have trod;
>
> We are not divided,
> All one body we,
> One in hope and doctrine,
> One in charity.

How can there be such a spirit today? Such unity? It's neither mysterious nor complicated. The adversary would have us believe there's no way. He will do *anything* to divide us. But you and I know that all that is required to maintain incessant, invincible confidence is a willingness to focus on the many things we have in common rather than the few things that make us different. Assimilation and pettiness cannot coexist. I love (and often quote) the words of the seventeenth-century German theologian Rupertus Meldenius, "In essentials, unity; in nonessentials, liberty; in all things, charity." I suggest you make that your motto of the year. "We are not divided, all one body we!"

John Wesley and George Whitefield were good friends in their earlier years. Wesley having begun his outdoor preaching ministry at Whitefield's encouragement. As time went on the men disagreed, with Whitefield leaning more heavily toward Calvinism than his younger friend's Arminianism. When Whitefield died, Wesley was asked if he expected to see Dr. Whitefield in heaven. In exaggerated but honest respect he answered, "No, he'll be so near the throne of God that men like me will never even get a glimpse of him!" Though differing, they did not lose their sense of oneness in Christ.[5]

It has been my observation that well-meaning but narrow-minded evangelicals in this generation have spent far too much time camping on a few differences—and thereby opening our ranks to disunity and petty infighting—and not enough time accentuating the vast number of things that link us together. And the result has been weakness rather than strength—a divided, splintered, fractured body of Christian cripples instead of that "mighty army" of crack troops.

In the fall of 1981, I was speaking at a banquet in a city where almost two thousand Christian people had gathered. The spirit was electric with excitement as folks realized we were not alone in the battle. We had enjoyed a delicious meal and some superb music. God was using His truth to cement our hearts together in a rare blend of unity and love. Assimilation was happening as relational masks and professional status were being replaced with a renewed commitment to one another. It was wonderful.

Suddenly, the meeting was disrupted by a young man who pushed his way into the room. He began to shout his disapproval and proclaim some particular conviction which he held. He was asked to leave as people stared in disbelief. He refused, continuing his diatribe at top volume. His face was stern and his voice shrill. Finally, after he was forcibly removed from the meeting, we were able to continue and complete the evening, though the spirit of unity and mutual enthusiasm was never fully recovered. I found out later that the same man—a fellow believer—regularly does such things. He believes it is his calling. He is convinced he has "the gift of rebuking" (try to find *that* in Scripture!), so he travels around disrupting meetings and declaring how wrong other Christians are who do not agree with his particular (and in my opinion *insignificant*) doctrinal slant.

By the way, as we left the banquet the man's stern-faced disciples were outside with leaflets and propaganda brochures verbally taking issue with the things that had been done and said at our banquet. As my wife and I drove away, we felt sick at heart. It was a never-to-be-forgotten proof that sincere people can become tools in the hands of the adversary, all the while thinking they are doing the work of God. On more than a few occasions since then I have heard of the same man doing the same thing in similar settings. Until we are big enough to ignore our few differences and close ranks, the strength brought on by unity will not be there. And the enemy will continue dancing for joy. That brings us to the fourth principle illustrated by the Hebrews as they crossed into the promised land.

4. *They abandoned themselves to the plan as they fixed their attention on the Lord.* Take a close, final look at these words once again. See if you don't detect true motivation:

And they answered Joshua, saying, "All that you have commanded us we will do, and wherever you send us we will go.

"Just as we obeyed Moses in all things, so we will obey you; only may the Lord your God be with you, as He was with Moses" (Jos. 1:16–17).

That's abandonment! "All . . . wherever . . ." And talk about willing obedience! ". . . we will do . . . we will go . . . we will obey. . . ." And how do you think Joshua felt when they promised him the same loyalty they had given to Moses? How could they have been so willing? What prompted such wholesale commitment? Aren't these the offspring of that mob of independent, stubborn, and spoiled nomads who struck out against Moses and resisted the Lord in the wilderness? Indeed they are! Then how can we explain the change? What could possibly be powerful enough to turn the hearts of these people? Their eyes were fully on the Lord. He was now in focus. They saw Him at work. As a result, their entire perspective had changed. He was giving the drumbeat, and they were marching in step with the cadence. There was no reluctance; they now wanted Him and His will. With that mindset, phenomenal adjustments and adaptations are possible. But let us all be warned, without it, forget about being drawn closer. Operation assimilation becomes a distant dream, abandonment becomes a joke, and unity, an impossibility. Trite though it may sound, it's true—not until our eyes are on the Lord will we be big enough to overlook differences and open enough to adapt and adjust.

IMPLICATIONS AND RAMIFICATIONS

Let me close this chapter by mentioning three practical areas of our lives that are affected when we get serious about assimilation: our churches, our acquaintances, our one-on-one relationships.

In Our Churches

For us to go on, for us to get the job done, we need to pull together, ignoring our petty differences. Let's not let the enemy do a number on us. If he is successful in dividing our interests and fracturing our fellowship, the world has more evidence that Christianity does not work. And don't think the world isn't ready to pounce on our disunity.

Just this morning on the front page of the *Los Angeles Times* (circulation well over one million), there's a picture and a lead article of a church doing battle with the state over its tax status. And, believe it or not, on the front page of Part II, in the Orange County Edition, the same newspaper has placed in headline print, "300 MEMBERS SPLINTER FROM CHURCH," and three more columns are used to cover the story of a church split that has occurred in a large, highly visible ministry that is now fighting within its own ranks.[6] Tragically, hundreds of thousands of non-Christians will become more convinced than ever that Christianity lacks the very things they are in need of—love, affirmation, and integrity.

Among Our Acquaintances

For us to be involved, we must be willing to reach out and risk relating. This won't "just happen." If my friend in graduate school wasn't aware of a man's name after four years of similar activity in a close geographical context, I seriously doubt that others in a much broader base would be that much different. May I urge you? Risk reaching. Take the initiative. Walk a few feet to your neighbor's yard. Or start with a simple and a warm, sincere wave of the hand. Find some common ground of mutual interest and use that as a basis of conversation. Open up. Be warm and transparent. You may be pleasantly surprised by the results.

One on One

If assimilation is ever to make the journey from theory to reality, we'll have to be willing to adapt and adjust the closer we get. One-on-one sooner or later requires give-and-take. Don't kid yourself, this is where the rubber and the road meet. And sometimes the road is uphill. Reuben Welch so aptly describes the journey in his poem, "We Really Do Need Each Other."

> You know something—
> we're all just people who need each other.
>   We're all learning
>   and we've all got a long journey ahead of us.
>   We've got to go together
>   and if it takes us until Jesus comes
>   we better stay together
>   we better help each other.
>   And I dare say
>   that by the time we get there
>   all the sandwiches will be gone
>   and all the chocolate will be gone
>   and all the water will be gone
>   and all the backpacks will be empty.
>   But no matter how long it takes us
>   we've got to go together.
>   Because that's how it is
>   in the body of Christ.
>   It's all of us
>   in love
>   in care
>   in support
>   in mutuality—
>   we really do need each other.[7]

Remember what is written between the lines:
This
  is
    not
      automatic.
        I am personally responsible.
          So are you.

DISCUSSION IDEAS AND QUESTIONS

• Time and again we were reminded in chapter 4 that close relationships are not automatic. Nor are they necessarily easy to develop. Spend a few minutes discussing some of your own experiences that prove this is true.

• High-tech times seem to result in superficial conversations and unsatisfying relationships. Why? Do you see any tie-in between shallow neighbor relations and families who frequently move? Can you site some examples?

• Let's think now about your church and the matter of assimilation. In light of what you read in this chapter, how could you help draw people closer together? Be specific. Think of realistic ways to break down barriers and convey Christ's love and affirmation.

• The first chapter of Joshua throbs with fresh excitement. We found four principles from the lines of these eighteen verses. Go back and review them. Which one speaks most directly to you? Explain why.

• Toward the end of the chapter we focused in on the subject of unity. Remember the John Wesley–George Whitefield story? Discuss its implications. What impresses you the most about the humility of Wesley?

• How's your A.Q. (Adaptability Quotient)? Share an occasion when you adjusted your life to help someone else—or they did that for you—and the benefits that resulted. Pray for someone who needs to be encouraged and helped. Make yourself available.

5

United and
Invincible

There once lived a king who loved to write music. And, even though he has been dead for centuries, his songs live on. This king's name was David. And today we call his songs psalms. Although ancient, some of his pieces have a relevance about them that make them timeless. Listen to this one. It's one of his best:

> How good and pleasant it is
>   when brothers live together in unity!
> It is like precious oil poured on the head,
>   running down on the beard . . .
>   down upon the collar of his robes (Ps. 133:1–2, NIV).

If there had been a *Hit Parade of Psalms* back then, that's one I would have voted for. The longer I live, the more I realize the value of that imperative, "brothers live together in unity." As David wrote, unity is like oil. It removes the friction in relationships so that brothers and sisters can live closely without fighting. Difficult as it may be for some to believe it, God planned it so that we might relate together even though we are different in taste, preference, style, culture, color, education, and language. It is "good and pleasant" that we live in unity—all our differences notwithstanding.

Some jokesters tell about a group of theologians who were discussing predestination and free will. The longer they talked, the hotter it got. And, as you might expect, the dissidents split into two groups. One poor fella didn't know which he believed, so he slipped into the ranks of the predestination crowd. They challenged him as to why he was there. "I came of my own free will," he answered innocently. Frowning, they responded, "*Free will?* You can't join us.

405

You get over there!" He retreated to the opposite group and faced the same challenging spirit. "Listen, I was *sent* here," he answered honestly. "Leave!" they demanded. "You can't join us unless you come of your own free will!"

Poor guy, he needed some of that oil David wrote about. And so do a lot of other dear souls who have spun into their own isolated orbit, having been kicked around by various narrow-minded, exclusive groups.

BIBLICAL BASIS OF UNITY

According to the Scriptures, all Christians are knit together in an invisible bond. The bond transcends personality and geography . . . or perhaps it's safer to say, it *should*. A believer in mid-America is linked with another believer in the heart of Brazil or Norway and just as closely knitted with a Christian in a dormitory in Oxford University or, for that matter, with a suffering, persecuted Russian believer in a slave camp behind the Iron Curtain.

The Apostles' Creed calls this bond "the communion of the saints." The great apostle Paul refers to it in the first Corinthian letter as the "body," as he declares that we are "members of it" (1 Cor. 12:27). To remind ourselves of this united bond that links believers together, our congregation in Fullerton often blends voice and heart as we sing the lovely chorus of worship:

> We are one in the bond of love;
> We are one in the bond of love;
> We have joined our spirits with the Spirit of God;
> We are one in the bond of love.[1]

What makes that bond possible? How is it that you and I are united in the same body as "members" one with another? That answer is extremely important—it is Jesus Christ. He, alone, brings the body together. As the Head, He is in charge of all the body members. He, therefore, makes the blend of unity possible. "He is also head of the body, the church; and He is the beginning, the first-born from the dead; so that He Himself might come to have first place in everything" (Col. 1:18).

Think in terms of the familiar mathematical axiom, "Things equal to the same thing are equal to each other." An everyday illustration would be a roomful of pianos, all of which are out of tune. What a maddening job it would be if the piano tuner tried to tune each instrument according to the others in the room, or worse, according to his own "inner pitch." He would be tightening this string and loosening that one in such a hit-or-miss manner that he would *never* get the job done. Instead, he begins with a tuning fork. That simple one-tone instrument becomes the standard for each piano in the room. And pianos tuned to the same thing are tuned to each other.

Wouldn't it be wonderful if it were that simple! But in the body, we're not talking about multistringed pianos but rather multifaceted people with different bents, temperaments, levels of maturity, and backgrounds. Jesus, knowing this was true, once prayed concerning our need for unity. That prayer is recorded in the seventeenth chapter of John. In fact, the entire chapter is His prayer. An outline of John 17 would look like this:

- In verses one through five, He prays for Himself.
- In verses six through nineteen, He prays for His disciples.
- In verses twenty through twenty-six, He prays for all those yet to believe on Him—including us.

And what is the theme of that prayer? Obviously, *unity*. Let's look closer:
Verse 21: "That they may all be one."
Verse 22: "That they may be one, just as We are one."
Verse 23: "That they may be perfected in unity."
Literally, the last reference could be rendered "that they may be perfected *into a unit*." How beautifully the New International Version translates verse 23: ". . . May they be brought to complete unity to let the world know that you sent me and have loved them even as you have loved me."

What has happened to our unity? This simple plan, so beautifully articulated by Jesus and so wonderfully begun in the first century, has been woefully complicated and confused by man. Denominations now number into the *hundreds*. Even the restrictive ranks of evangelicalism are divided into more than thirty various groups, all confessing a common faith in the Lord Jesus Christ. Surely the world scratches its head at that. And lest you think denominational lines or religious labels are not drawn that tightly, stop and ask people on the street if they are Christians. Chances are good they will identify themselves not as a Christian or non-Christian, but as a Methodist or Presbyterian or Catholic or Baptist or Charismatic or some such identification.

Have you stopped to think lately what God's opinion of all these categories must be? We have drifted a long way from Jesus' prayer, "that they may be perfected into a unit." And at times when unity *is* present, it's a cold formalism, more of a rigid requirement than a free-flowing spontaneity. As one Christian admitted to me with a smile, "Unity? Yeah, my church has unity. We're *frozen* together!" Behind that smile his teeth were set firm. No, that's not the unity Christ wants in His body. The unity He desires is one that strengthens and encourages us in our pilgrimage. In fact, when that unity is present, we begin to walk in such confidence that there's a definite hint of invincibility in our faith. It's all part of the way God arranged it. We even see it illustrated in the lives of those Hebrews who invaded Canaan under Joshua's leadership.

THE HEBREWS: HORIZONTAL UNITY, VERTICAL VICTORY

As we travel through the pages of ancient history, we find ample evidence that God honors a spirit of unity among His people. Let's return to the book of

Joshua and pick up the story of the Hebrews right where we left off at the end of the previous chapter.

> And they answered Joshua, saying, "All that you have commanded us we will do, and wherever you send us we will go.
>
> "Just as we obeyed Moses in all things, so we will obey you; only may the Lord your God be with you, as He was with Moses.
>
> "Anyone who rebels against your command and does not obey your words in all that you command him, shall be put to death; only be strong and courageous" (Josh. 1:16-18).

These three verses throb with anticipation. They are the words of a motivated body of people. Within their response are promises of cooperation ("we will do"), availability ("we will go"), commitment ("we will obey"), loyalty ("anyone who rebels . . . shall be put to death"), and encouragement ("be strong and courageous"). What an unusual twist! The people are encouraging the leader. That's one of the many by-products of a unified body of people— their eyes are off themselves and on others.

If you don't think that is rare, here are a few questions worth consideration:

• How many congregations have you ever been a part of (or *heard* of) who regularly encouraged their pastor?

• How often have you witnessed students in the classroom who encouraged and affirmed the teacher?

• When was the last time you saw on television or read in the newspaper where the news media spoke unanimously in appreciation of the President?

• Look at your place of occupation. Is it a common thing to hear employees speak favorably of their supervisors?

• I wonder how many who serve on the city council or school board in your community can remember the last time a group of citizens gathered for one reason . . . simply to tell them "thanks, nice job." (I'm sure you're smiling.)

We are all much better at complaining than affirming—much better at criticizing than encouraging. Those folks in Joshua's day were a refreshing exception to the rule. And to make matters even better, when it came time to put action to words, they proved the sincerity of their allegiance. Let me show you what I mean.

An Unusual Strategy Accepted without Resistance

Let's take a close look at the sixth chapter of Joshua. Combat is around the corner. In comparison to the tough resilient forces of Canaan, those Hebrews must have appeared as a rag-tag bunch of unorganized nomads. But there was one giant factor that made the difference. They had Jehovah on their side. And He wasn't about to let his reputation be ruined by a pack of godless pagans.

> Now Jericho was tightly shut because of the sons of Israel; no one went out and no one came in.
> And the Lord said to Joshua, "See, I have given Jericho into your hand, with its king and the valiant warriors (vv. 1-2).

Jericho must have appeared formidable. A massive stone wall no less than three stories high and eighteen feet thick surrounded that city full of "valiant warriors." Yet Joshua was given a promise, "I have given Jericho into your hands." But how? Some secret weapon? Some powerful explosive? No. Just an unusual strategy.

> "And you shall march around the city, all the men of war circling the city once. You shall do so for six days.
> "Also seven priests shall carry seven trumpets of rams' horns before the ark; then on the seventh day you shall march around the city seven times, and the priests shall blow the trumpets.
> "And it shall be that when they make a long blast with the rams' horn, and when you hear the sound of the trumpet, all the people shall shout with a great shout; and the wall of the city will fall down flat, and the people will go up every man straight ahead" (Josh. 6:3-5).

Now *that's* a novel idea. No big deal. Just believe God and do exactly what He says. If He says the wall will fall, count on it. He's awfully good at walls, you know. Nobody laughed. Nobody even snickerd. I mean, those folks were willing and ready! They'd wandered in the wilderness long enough to know better than to question God's plan.

> So Joshua the son of Nun called the priests and said to them, "Take up the ark of the covenant, and let seven priests carry seven trumpets of rams' horns before the ark of the Lord."
> Then he said to the people, "Go forward, and march around the city, and let the armed men go on before the ark of the Lord."
> And it was so, that when Joshua had spoken to the people, the seven priests carrying the seven trumpets of rams' horns before the Lord went forward and blew the trumpets; and the ark of the covenant of the Lord followed them.
> And the armed men went before the priests who blew the trumpets, and the rear guard came after the ark, while they continued to blow the trumpets.
> But Joshua commanded the people, saying, "You shall not shout nor let your voice be heard, nor let a word proceed out of your mouth, until the day I tell you, 'Shout!' Then you shall shout!"
> So he had the ark of the Lord taken around the city, circling it once, then they came into the camp and spent the night in the camp (Josh. 6:6-11).

Then came that final trip.

> Then it came about on the seventh day that they rose early at the dawning of the day and marched around the city in the same manner seven times; only on that day they marched around the city seven times.
> And it came about at the seventh time, when the priests blew the trumpets, Joshua said to the people, "Shout! For the Lord has given you the city" (Josh. 6:15–16).

> So the people shouted, and priests blew the trumpets; and it came about, when the people heard the sound of the trumpet, that the people shouted with a great shout and the wall fell down flat, so that the people went up into the city, every man straight ahead, and they took the city.
> And they utterly destroyed everything in the city, both man and woman, young and old, and ox and sheep and donkey, with the edge of the sword (Josh. 6:20–21).

Talk about invincible! When they began to see and hear the walls of Jericho crumble, those Hebrews must have smiled with indescribable delight. Especially after they had obeyed the Lord's orders so perfectly. What a game plan! March, blow, scream—then stand back. I love the utter ridiculousness of it all . . . from a human point of view, that is. Whoever heard of such a weird strategy? In our day of high-tech sophistication, who would ever consider cooperating? But the good news is that, when we *do* obey, unusual though the plan may seem, only God can get the glory.

When our church congregation decided to relocate and build a new facility from scratch, one formidable piece of the puzzle required massive faith—selling the old facility. It was during a financial slump. Futhermore, who was in the market for the ultimate white elephant of real estate, a used church (and I do mean *used*)? God made it clear that all we should do is put it on the market and trust Him. There was no need for panic, no need to worry about the odds. Just pray and refuse all temptations to manipulate or manufacture a manmade plan. Or, in the words of Psalm 46:10 (a verse I must have repeated to myself fifty or more times during the long months of waiting): "Cease striving and know that I am God."

We came right down to the wire. In fact, it was the final week. Sunday was the ultimate deadline. No breakthrough. On Saturday, the day before, a small unassuming body of believers contacted one of our church officers. They came by and looked things over. They asked if it would be possible to visit again on Sunday afternoon. When they returned and said, "We want it," the walls of our financial Jericho fell down flat.

Those who stand united become an invincible force through whom God does His greatest work. The secret, remember is closed ranks and open relationships. If you forget that, you can forget everything.

A TEAM VICTORY ACCOMPLISHED WITHOUT JEALOUSY

Moving forward a couple of chapters in the Book of Joshua, we come to another scene entirely, and a completely different strategy. This time its not Jericho, it's a place named Ai. The plan is an ambush.

Now the Lord said to Joshua, "Do not fear or be dismayed. Take all the people of war with you and arise, go up to Ai; see, I have given into your hand the king of Ai, his people, his city, and his land.

"And you shall do to Ai and its king just as you did to Jericho and its king; you shall take only its spoil and its cattle as plunder for yourselves. Set an ambush for the city behind it."

So Joshua rose with all the people of war to go up to Ai; and Joshua chose 30,000 men, valiant warriors, and sent them out at night.

And he commanded them, saying, "See, you are going to ambush the city from behind it. Do not go very far from the city, but all of you be ready.

"Then I and all the people who are with me will approach the city. And it will come about when they come out to meet us as at the first, that we will flee before them.

"And they will come out after us until we have drawn them away from the city, for they will say. 'They are fleeing before us as at the first.' So we will flee before them.

"And you shall rise from your ambush and take possession of the city, for the Lord your God will deliver it into your hand.

"Then it will be when you have seized the city, that you shall set the city on fire. You shall do it according to the word of the Lord. See, I have commanded you."

So Joshua sent them away, and they went to the place of ambush and remained between Bethel and Ai, on the west side of Ai; but Joshua spent that night among the people (Josh. 8:1–9).

Get the picture? Again, it's not complicated. Different people were to do different jobs. Some were up front with Joshua, others would be away from the glory. It didn't matter to them because they were committed to a team victory, regardless. Nobody asked, "Now, who gets the credit?" Or "Do I have to be one of those out of the limelight?" No, a unified team spirit has no room for that.

So they stationed the people, all the army that was on the north side of the city, and its rear guard on the west side of the city, and Joshua spent that night in the midst of the valley.

And it came about when the king of Ai saw it, that the men of the city hurried and rose up early and went out to meet Israel in battle, he and all his people at the appointed place before the desert plain. But he did not know that there was ambush against him behind the city.

And Joshua and all Israel pretended to be beaten before them, and fled by the way of the wilderness.

And all the people who were in the city were called together to pursue them, and they pursued Joshua, and were drawn away from the city.

So not a man was left in Ai or Bethel who had not gone out after Israel, and they left the city unguarded and pursued Israel.

And the men in ambush rose quickly from their place, and when he had stretched out his hand, they ran and entered the city and captured it; and they quickly set the city on fire.

When the men of Ai turned back and looked, behold, the smoke of the city ascended to the sky, and they had no place to flee this way or that, for the people who had been fleeing to the wilderness turned against the pursuers.

When Joshua and all Israel saw that the men in ambush had captured the city and that the smoke of the city ascended, they turned back and slew the men of Ai (Josh. 8:13-17, 19-21).

How interesting! There was no argument, no struggle among the troops to be a javelin assistant or the lead man in the rear guard, no competition. True humility prevailed among everyone on the team, including the star players.

I was thumbing through one of the national periodicals recently and happened upon a picture of President Reagan sitting in the Oval Office. He was behind his desk, signing some document as others were standing on either side. I noticed a small sign on his desk that was too small to read. It intrigued me. I found a magnifying glass and looked closer; the print was blurred, but I could read enough of the sign to know it was worth the effort to pursue. The next morning I had my secretary telephone the White House and talk with someone who could give us the information we wanted. It was well worth the effort. The sign on President Reagan's desk says:

THERE IS NO LIMIT TO WHAT A MAN CAN DO OR WHERE HE CAN GO IF HE DOESN'T MIND WHO GETS THE CREDIT.

The ancient Hebrews didn't have such a sign, but they practiced its truth. They won the victory at Ai because each person was willing to be absorbed in the plan, regardless of who got the credit.

This reminds me of something Dietrich Bonhoeffer once wrote. See if you don't find it insightful and penetrating.

"There arose a reasoning among them, which of them should be the greatest" (Luke 9:46). We know who it is that sows this thought in the Christian community. But perhaps we do not bear in mind enough that no Christian community ever comes together without this thought immediately emerging as a seed of discord. Thus at the very beginning of Christian fellowship there is engendered an invisible, often unconscious, life-and-death contest. "There arose a reasoning among them": this is enough to destroy a fellowship.

Hence it is vitally necessary that every Christian community from the very outset face this dangerous enemy squarely, and eradicate it. There is no time to lose here, for from the first moment when a man meets another person he is looking for a strategic position he can assume and hold over against that person. There are strong persons and weak ones. If a man is not strong, he immediately claims the right of the weak as his own and uses it against the strong. There are gifted and ungifted persons, simple people and difficult people, devout and less devout, the sociable and the solitary. Does not the ungifted person have to take up a position just as well as the gifted person, the difficult one as well as the simple? And if I am not gifted, then perhaps I am devout anyhow; or if I am not devout it is only because I do not want to be. May not the sociable individual carry the field before him and put the timid, solitary man to shame? Then may not the solitary person become the undying enemy and ultimate vanquisher of his sociable adversary? Where is there a person who does not with instinctive sureness find the spot where he can stand and defend himself, but which he will never give up to another, for which he will fight with all the drive of his instinct of self-assertion?

All this can occur in the most polite or even pious environment. But the important thing is that a Christian community should know that somewhere in it there will certainly be "a reasoning among them, which of them should be the greatest." It is the struggle of the natural man for self-justification. He finds it only in comparing himself with others, in condemning and judging others. . . .

[When the Christian community eradicates this enemy] strong and weak, wise and foolish, gifted or ungifted, pious or impious, the diverse individuals in the community, are no longer incentives for talking and judging and condemning, and thus excuses for self-justification. They are rather cause for rejoicing in one another and serving one another.[2]

A Trust in God Claimed without Doubt

Faced with battle fatigue, the Hebrews realized that unless the Lord intervened, they would never make it. Exhausted, they needed divine strength to carry on.

Then the men of Gibeon sent word to Joshua to the camp at Gilgal, saying, "Do not abandon your servants; come up to us quickly and save us and help us, for all the kings of the Amorites that live in the hill country have assembled against us."

So Joshua went up from Gilgal, he and all the people of war with him and all the valiant warriors.

And the Lord said to Joshua, "Do not fear them, for I have given them into your hands; not one of them shall stand before you."

So Joshua came upon them suddenly by marching all night from Gilgal (Josh. 10:6-9).

During my days in the Marines, I remember a nonstop march that lasted for about four hours—but *never* all night. I cannot imagine how exhausted Joshua and his fighting men must have been. They really needed God to step in and supplement their weakness with His strength. And did He ever! He did a never-to-be repeated miracle.

> And the Lord confounded them before Israel, and He slew them with a great slaughter at Gibeon, and pursued them by the way of the ascent of Beth-horon, and struck them as far as Azekah and Makkedah.
> And it came about as they fled from before Israel, while they were at the descent of Beth-horon, that the Lord threw large stones from heaven on them as far as Azekah, and they died; there were more who died from the hailstones than those whom the sons of Israel killed with the sword.
> Then Joshua spoke to the Lord in the day when the Lord delivered up the Amorites before the sons of Israel, and he said in the sight of Israel,
>
> "O sun, stand still at Gibeon,
> And O moon in the valley of Aijalon."
> So the sun stood still, and the moon stopped.
> Until the nation avenged themselves of their enemies.
>
> Is it not written in the book of Jashar? And the sun stopped in the middle of the sky, and did not hasten to go down for about a whole day.
> And there was no day like that before it or after it, when the Lord listened to the voice of a man; for the Lord fought for Israel (Josh. 10:10-14).

There's one for *That's Incredible!* Can't you see it? By now, feeling confident in God, General Joshua looks up and shouts, "Sun, stop!" And then, "Moon, you too!" Don't view the man as presumptuous. No, it's not that. It's the realization that God is very much involved in one's motive and totally glorified in one's actions. It's like Theodore Epp has written: "Once a man is satisfied that he is in the center of God's plan and God is working out His will through him, that man is invincible."[3]

You can read the results for yourself in Joshua 10:11-27. The territory was successfully invaded, the kings were captured and killed, and God was glorified. Such was the result of a team of dedicated warriors who were committed to unity, who willingly became examples of humility and determined to believe God, regardless.

SOME SUGGESTIONS FOR APPLICATION

How easy it is to leave all these great accounts riveted to ancient history. And how wrong to do so! Here are a couple of thoughts worth our time and consideration.

1. *The pursuit of unity is hard work, but it's worth it.*

If you are in a Christian leadership role, you are commanded to "preserve the unity of the Spirit in the bond of peace" (Eph. 4:3). There will be every temptation *not* to do that. Others around you will encourage you to choose sides or stand against certain people rather than finding ways to stand with them. You'll be tempted to manipulate or control or in some other way gain mastery over others . . . and for one reason—to get your way, to massage your own pride.

I suggest you be different. Commit yourself to freeing others so they can grow and discover on their own. For a change, as much as is possible, walk away from an argument rather than inviting one. Become more of a peacemaker.

You may have heard the story; nevertheless, I find folks smile every time I tell it. A man and his wife were married for over fifty years. Someone asked the gentleman the secret of their marital bliss. "Well," the old man drawled, "the wife and I had this agreement when we first got married. It went like this: When she was bothered about somethin', she'd jus' tell me an git it off her chest. And if I was mad at her about somethin', I was to take a long walk. I s'ppose you could attribute our happy marriage to the fact that I have largely led an outdoor life."

Now *there's* a guy committed to unity. It will not come easily, but it's worth every effort, believe me. That brings us to my next thought for consideration.

2. *The place of humility is of highest value, but it's rarely seen.*

By now you realize how closely unity and humility are tied together. One breeds the other; neither can exist without the other. They're like Siamese twins, perpetually connected. Personally, I have seen numerous occasions when pride won out (even though it was never called that) and harmony faded away . . . and I mean fast. It's like James says, "What is the source of quarrels and conflicts among you? Is not the source your pleasures that wage war in your members? You lust and do not have; so you commit murder. And you are envious and cannot obtain; so you fight and quarrel" (James 4:1–2).

Contrary to the stuff you might read today, the words, *fight* and *quarrel*, are not apt descriptions of the way to get ahead. They won't ultimately glorify God. Friends are made by *not* fighting and by *refusing* to quarrel.

I've appreciated the wise words of Alan McGinnis so much. In his fine little book, *The Friendship Factor*, he addresses this head on.

Pop psychology has produced a new wave of self-help books that advocate asserting yourself, doing your own thing, taking advantage of the other person before the other person takes advantage of you, and telling anyone who does not give you what you "need" in your relationship to get lost. Actually, the movement is not entirely new. Arrogance has been around for some time.

But there is a pathos to such a philosophy. It is the attempt of unhappy people to find some joy for themselves. Someone has told them that they will find it by ignoring the needs and wants of people around them and elbowing their way to the front of the line. But my experience in counseling such people is that when they push others away, intimidate their competitors, and disregard those to whom they have responsibility, they get to the front of the line and discover that there is no one there to hand them anything. Jesus dismissed such a life-style, saying that those who save their lives will end up losing them.

Christ also said that those who lose their lives will save them, and the Bible is replete with statements to the effect that sacrificing ourselves and denying ourselves for some higher good will in the long run bring happiness. In other words, happiness does not ordinarily come to those who set out to "be happy." Happiness is more often a by-product.

I notice that the happiest people do not have to shove and push. They do not worry about intimidating others; they are confident of their own self-worth, much of which comes from making other people happy. There are rewards for such acts, for the friend who is willing to sacrifice for you is not easily forgotten.[4]

David's song lives on. Although he composed it centuries ago, long before books like *Pulling Your Own Strings* or *Looking Out for #1* made the bestseller list, it is still true. Listen to the lyrics once again:

> How good and pleasant it is
> when brothers live together in unity!
> It is like precious oil poured on the head,
> running down on the beard. . . .

Want some good counsel? Spread a little oil around. Don't be too careful. Pour it out. Let it splash and run down. Start today.

Discussion Ideas and Questions

• Define unity in your own words. Be a little creative. Add some thoughts that embellish your definition.

• Why are we, by nature, rigid rather than free? Why are we more narrow than open?

• Go back to Jesus' prayer in John 17:20–26. Analyze it in light of today's push for independence and intimidation. Name one way you could be more committed to unity.

• Discuss the need for affirmation. Can you recall a time when someone affirmed you and it renewed your spirit? Share it.

• Talk openly about the acid of jealousy. Is this one of your battles? Or have you been the brunt of someone's jealous assault? How can jealousy be conquered?

• Go back and read again the words of Dietrich Bonhoeffer. Discuss his remarks concerning the strong and the weak.

• Finally, take time to think through the two principles on unity and humility. Why are they so closely connected? Read Philippians 2:3–4. Talk about how that applies to you today.

6

When the Fellowship
Breaks Down

It's time for a big dose of reality. So far things seem fairly smooth. You may have thought a little bit about disharmony and periodic conflicts, but for the most part, you could begin to get the impression that open relationships and vulnerability are like a downhill slide. With your rose-colored glasses in place, you might even start believing that fellow members of the body invariably pull together as they get closer. You may be on the verge of thinking that once you unmask and deal honestly with others, an uninterrupted path of peace will be yours to enjoy. It ain't necessarily so! Occasionally, mutiny occurs among the body members, and the results can be devastating.

As I read the following words of a surgeon describing the presence of cancer in a human body, I thought of how vividly his description fit the family of God when there is a breakdown in our fellowship.

A tumor is called benign if its effect is fairly localized and it stays within membrane boundaries. But the most traumatizing condition in the body occurs when disloyal cells defy inhibition. They multiply without any checks on growth, spreading rapidly throughout the body, choking out normal cells. White cells, armed against foreign invaders, will not attack the body's own mutinous cells. Physicians fear no other malfunction more deeply: it is called cancer. For still mysterious reasons, these cells—and they may be tissues—grow wild, out of control. Each is a healthy, functioning cell, but disloyal, no longer acting in regard for the rest of the body.

Even the white cells, the dependable palace guard, can destroy the body through rebellion. Sometimes they recklessly reproduce, clogging the bloodstream, overloading the lymph system, strangling the body's normal functions—such is leukemia.[1]

417

And such is the spiritual disease called relational conflicts. When the fellow-ship breaks down, the fun stops and the body aches. How damaging those times can be!

They are certainly not new. The path of the church is strewn with the litter of conflict, disagreement, friction, in-fighting, and discord. Just think back to the church in the first century as you mentally stroll through the book of Acts.

- Acts 5: Hypocrisy resulting in divine discipline.
- Acts 6: Unfair treatment of minorities and the needy.
- Acts 9: Resistance to allow Paul, a recent convert, to minister.
- Acts 11: Legalism rears its ugly head.
- Acts 15: Doctrinal disagreement so strong that an official council was needed to settle the issue. And toward the end of the same chapter, a personal clash between Paul and Barnabas occurred.

Neither time nor space permit me to trace the scene of conflict from then until now (that would take multiple volumes), but there is sufficient evidence to prove that this mighty army, the Church of God, has never been completely free of conflict or crisis.

It may be as severe and explosive as the time of the Inquisition when Christians were killed by church officials who thought they were doing God a favor. Or it may be as mild and commonplace as a Sunday school teacher unable to control a class of preteens.

Leadership magazine, known for its choice cartoons about the church, made all of us smile with understanding as this particular scene pictured a grim-faced preacher pausing during his sermon delivery and reading a note that said: "We interrupt this sermon to inform you that the fourth-grade boys are now in complete control of their Sunday school class and are holding Miss Moseby hostage."[2]

REASONS FELLOWSHIP BREAKS DOWN

Since conflicts do occur, since the fellowship does break down, it seems only right that we face it head on. Let's begin by looking at the big picture. When are the times people pull away and resist assimilation? When are we especially prone to be isolated and keep our masks securely in place? I can think of at least five times, and each one is illustrated in biblical accounts.

Extreme Suffering and Sickness

Given enough pain, most of us will seek to be alone. Whether it be physical or emotional pain, few are the sufferers who remain in the mainstream of involvement. The reasons are many. We can be embarrased by what we are struggling with. Or we can be so broken and bruised within that depression pulls us aside. Obviously, if we are enduring a physical illness that saps our strength or requires long days of bedrest, we're simply unable to stay up with life's demands.

Job fell victim to a dread bodily disease—boils all over his body. You'll recall that he sat *alone* in his misery (Job 1:20-21; 2:7-13). Even when his alleged "friends" came to comfort him (*confront* is a better description), Job stayed away from his normal responsibilites. Pain does that to us. If it endures long enough and hits us hard enough, we opt for isolation. Like Job, we often prefer to be outside the gaze of the inquisitive.

King Saul did too. Remember, he sat all alone in the darkness of his despair submerged in the swamp of depression (1 Sam. 15-16).

Our Savior also sought to be alone when the agony of the cross began to take its toll on Him (Matt. 26:36-44). We should not be surprised or offended, therefore, when others, today, remove themselves from involvement due to pain. On the contrary, a sensitive understanding heart of compassion is our best response. However, when we reach out to them it must be with utmost tact and sensitivity. I'll address that subject at length in chapter 8.

Burnout and Fatigue

In this day of great pressure, high stress, constant demands, and little leisure, more and more of God's people are dropping through the cracks as victims of burnout and fatigue. It is not uncommon to meet those in the Lord's business who have worked themselves into a frenzy, burning the proverbial candle at both ends until there is neither candle nor wick left to burn. They find themselves weary and dreary souls greatly in need of rest—time to repair and heal—not at all interested in programs or projects that require energy and more time. Those folks need to be respected, not harrassed. They need time to work through and silence "the tyranny of the urgent."

Dear old Elijah would say a resounding "Amen." From the frying pan of intense involvement as God's prophet, who stood alone against King Ahab and his wife Jezebel, into the fire on Mount Carmel as he faced the prophets of Baal, Elijah was in the thick of it for years (if you include the time he endured the lengthy drought). He had prayed, prophesied, fought, preached, suffered, confronted the king, and mocked the false prophets. Suddenly his equilibrium snapped as he stumbled into the wilderness all alone and begged Jehovah to take his life (1 Kings 19:1-5). Burned out and fatigued, the prophet was finished and famished. His vision of the big picture was blurred and his motivation for ministry had vanished. It is beautiful to study how graciously God dealt with His man. No guilt trip. No long sermon. Not even a frown or a threat. With divine compassion He allowed the prophet time to repair, and He gave him space to recover. He even catered a meal for the exhausted prophet to enjoy. All of us could learn much for God's therapy.

Periodically, we'll have folks slip into our church who are in need of inner healing. They are spent. Hungry for a place to repair, they long for the freedom to be still and to gain renewed perspective. Such folks are to be respected and allowed some room to recover. They don't need somebody to corner them and "put 'em to work." In such cases, assimilation and involvement need to be put on hold. Their greater need (as in the case of Elijah) is to be allowed the freedom to relax. In due time, the energy and perspective will return. Burnout isn't a terminal disease in most cases.

Trouble at Home or Personal Turmoil

Shame is often added to pain when trouble at home or inner personal turmoil sends us running for cover. Who can describe the intense anxiety connected with domestic conflicts or financial reversal or moral compromise? Any number of such dilemmas create within us a desire to be isolated even though that may not be the best course of action.

David, while guilty of the affair with Bathsheba, was not engaged in his normal high-level standard of responsibilities. Read 2 Samuel 11 and 12 and Psalm 32:3–5 and Psalm 51:1–17 for yourself. They give us sufficient reason to believe that during those dark days, he wrote no songs, he fought no war, he made no significant decisions. Rather, he was caught in his self-made web, removed and preoccupied. Whipped by guilt, he hurt alone.

The same can occur when a family struggles with a rebellious teenager or young adult. This kind of problem can sap a family's strength and steal their joy. Such folks usually isolate themselves and walk through that dismal valley alone.

As a pastor I often find myself impaled on the horns of a dilemma. Should I step in? Should I "intrude" and offer my assistance, even though uninvited? Or should I stay out of the way and let the individuals involved work through the conflict themselves? There are no hard-and-fast rules. I've done both . . . and had both *backfire!* I have also had both result in a wonderful healing and recovery. In my head I can still hear both extremes:

"What business is this of yours? If you had stayed out of it, we could've worked things out."

And:

"Thank you. Thank you! Had you not stepped in and cared enough to comfort (or confront or listen—whatever), who knows where we'd be today?"

And:

"We appreciate the fact that you gave us room to work through the conflict. Thank you for not pushing your way in and forcing the issue."

And:

"Where were you? Why didn't you make yourself available? Obviously, you didn't care even though you knew we were hurting."

It's enough to make an isolationist out of a preacher. Wouldn't it be helpful to have fail-safe rules to follow on certain supersensitive occasions? But when the fellowship breaks down, black and white rule books need to be tossed into the sea. And people who tend to follow them should take a hike.

Friction between Two or More Individuals

Another barrier to involvement and unguarded relationships is the familiar problem of people-with-people conflicts—personality clashes, disagreement with another's decision, offenses that lack closure and full forgiveness, misunderstandings that get complicated by rumor and gossip. This is *especially* so if the person who is isolated and licking his wounds got hurt because he or she reached out to another in sincerity and got burned in the process.

I often call to mind the words of Solomon: "A brother offended is harder to be won than a strong city, and contentions are like the bars of a castle" (Prov. 18:19).

Can you picture it? Thick, rusty, foreboding bars that say, "Stay away from me! I want to be left alone." But if you track the analogy to its limit, you see that it's the offended one who suffers the most. He is the person who shuts himself off and steps out of circulation. How bitter one can become behind those invisible bars.

> A story is told of two unmarried sisters who had so bitter a ruckus they stopped speaking to each other. Unable or unwilling to leave their small home, they continued to use the same rooms and sleep in the same bedroom. A chalk line divided the sleeping area into two halves, separating doorway and fireplace, so that each could come and go and get her own meals without trespassing on her sister's domain. In the black of night each could hear the breathing of the foe. For years they co-existed in grinding silence. Neither was willing to take the first step to reconciliation.[3]

How much better to follow the model of two other unmarried sisters, Betsy and Corrie ten Boom. In Corrie's book, *The Hiding Place*, she mentions seeing Betsy's face swollen and bruised. Corrie asked her if she had been beaten by the guard. Her sister's answer amazed Corrie. Betsy said, "I felt sorry for that man." Who knows how many of us frequently call to mind the forgiving spirit of Corrie ten Boom, which she learned from her sister?

Paul and Barnabas had a face-off, according to Acts 15:36–40. Two mature, strong, determined men disagreed and parted company. Each was so convinced he was right that he was willing to end a relationship because of an inner conviction. We read nothing more of Barnabas as he slipped away to Cyprus following that sharp disagreement.

How unusual we are! If we have trouble with our car, we don't give up driving. If we have a roof that leaks, we don't abandon the house and move to another place. But the irony of it all is that when a couple of folks have a conflict, only rarely are they big enough to stay at it and work things out. More often, they walk away and live lives of quiet desperation. If antiques are worth the time and energy and expense involved in restoring, so are broken relationships.

Open Disobedience against God

This is a category I'd like to explore in greater depth, since it is illustrated so clearly in the narrative of the ancient Hebrews, which we have been following.

Simply stated, this is a subject that has to do with the isolation that comes as a direct consequence of disobedience. How easy it is to pull away from God's people and live the rest of our days in seclusion because we once blew it royally and suffered because of it. Since we're His children, God disciplines us for our disobedience, not so we'll spend the rest of our lives in isolation, but that we might learn the value of walking in obedience.

For a classic example look at what happened when certain Hebrews were disobedient at Ai.

AI AND THE HEBREWS

The book of Joshua is sort of an *Indianapolis 500* of the Old Testament. Racing from one battle to another, those Hebrews set new records for speed in triumph. With hardly a moment's hesitation, they swept through Jericho, driving a wedge into the central section of Canaan and weakening the enemy's defense. Then they pressed on to other challenges, ready to handle whatever opponent they might encounter . . . until Ai. Joshua 7 is the pit stop. Everything suddenly screeches to a halt. The driver (Joshua) sits there confused, wondering to himself, "What happened? Why the problem? What's wrong?" Not even his crew could figure it out.

You need to understand that, militarily, Ai was a pushover. Compared to formidable Jericho, it was a "hole in the road," a clod of dirt on the road to victory. But the Israeli army was soundly whipped . . . blown away by a bunch of rednecks from a country town in Canaan.

> Now Joshua sent men from Jericho to Ai, which is near Bethaven, east of Bethel, and said to them, "Go up and spy out the land." So the men went up and spied out Ai.
>
> And they returned to Joshua and said to him, "Do not let all the people go up; only about two or three thousand men need go up to Ai; do not make all the people toil up there, for they are few."
>
> So about three thousand men from the people went up there, but they fled from the men of Ai.
>
> And the men of Ai struck down about thirty-six of their men, and pursued them from the gate as far as Shebarium, and struck them down on the descent, so the hearts of people melted and became as water (Josh. 7:2–5).

Let's understand that we're not interested in merely studying ancient history. Our goal is to gain insight and reproof as God teaches us from these Old Testament scriptures. Neither are we concerned about all the details of military strategy. We're thinking about relationships in this book and, particularly in this chapter, why and how those relationships break down. In light of that, the first step in dealing with a broken relationship is an awareness that something is different, something is wrong. Actually, there are four stages we must work through in restoring relationships.

Stage One: "Something Is Wrong"

We'll call this the "symptom stage." As I study the Ai battle, I find a couple of things out of whack. First, there was a breakdown in the normal routine—the Hebrews encountered an opposite reaction from what they expected. Instead of a slight skirmish, there was wholesale resistance. Instead of the enemy's being little more than a corporal's guard, they became an imposing body of warriors. The normal routine was disrupted. Second, there was discouragement and a loss of morale as the Hebrews' "hearts . . . melted and became as water" (v. 5).

In relationships that begin to break down, the "symptom stage" takes on a similar setting. We notice first an alteration in routine. The person no longer comes around. Or when he or she does come, there are strained feelings —awkwardness, lack of eye contact, a rush to leave. There is no longer the free-flowing give-and-take in conversation. The sense of humor is decidedly absent. Things are definitely different. "Something is wrong," we whisper to ourselves.

Also, to use the words from verse 5, your heart "melts" within you. You churn. Deep within your spirit you feel a distance, a space that once was not there. By the way, the more sensitive you are toward people, the quicker you detect such symptoms. You feel "bad vibes" as you encounter one another.

This leads to the "concern stage."

Stage Two: "What Has Happened?"

Go back with me to the battle scene at Ai. Imagine yourself in Joshua's place as you read these words:

> Then Joshua tore his clothes and fell to the earth on his face before the ark of the Lord until the evening, both he and the elders of Israel; and they put dust on their hands.
>
> And Joshua said. "Alas, O Lord God, why didst Thou ever bring this people over the Jordan, only to deliver us into the hand of the Amorites, to destroy us? If only we had been willing to dwell beyond the Jordan!
>
> "Oh Lord, what can I say since Israel has turned their back before their enemies?

"For the Canaanites and all the inhabitants of the land will hear of it, and they will surround us and cut off our name from the earth. And what wilt Thou do for Thy great name?" (Josh. 7:6–9).

There is confusion. The man is naturally concerned about the strange twist of events. He gets together with his most trusted friends (called "elders"— v. 6), and they seek God's mind for wisdom. Those men are serious as they pray and as they enter into this concern together. The confusion drives them to their knees.

We do the same, don't we? Having felt the distance between us and the other person, we talk it over and pray with a few very close—and I should add very *confidential*—friends. Through times in prayer, we gain insight. God gives us the ability to penetrate the surface.

I have a few very close and confidential friends. They are so important to me that you may have noticed I dedicated this book to each one of them. These men hold our relationship in highest regard and great trust. They view our times together (as I do) as exceedingly important occasions. We talk. We think. We evaluate decisions. We share our struggles. We pray. We invest these hours with the realization that God uses us in each other's lives. We are available and we are in touch. Our goal is to strengthen and help one another any way we can. By being accountable and vulnerable in our times together, we are able to get to the heart of the issue without the standard smoke screens and fog that frequently cloud friendships. I rather suspect that Joshua had something like this going with the men who shared his burden.

The Lord honored their pursuit as He broke the silence and unveiled the mystery.

So the Lord said to Joshua, "Rise up! Why is it that you have fallen on your face?

"Israel has sinned, and they have also transgressed My covenant which I commanded them. And they have even taken some of the things under the ban and have both stolen and deceived. Moreover, they have also put them among their own things.

"Therefore the sons of Israel cannot stand before their enemies; they turn their backs before their enemies, for they have become accursed, I will not be with you any more unless you destroy the things under the ban from your midst.

"Rise up! Consecrate the people and say, 'Consecrate yourselves for tomorrow, for thus the Lord, the God of Israel, has said, "There are things under the ban in your midst, O Israel. You cannot stand before your enemies until you have removed the things under the ban from your midst."

'In the morning then you shall come near by your tribes. And it shall be that the tribe which the Lord takes by lot shall come near by families, and the family which the Lord takes shall come near by households, and the household which the Lord takes shall come near man by man.

'And it shall be that the one who is taken with the things under the ban shall be burned with fire, he and all that belongs to him, because he has transgressed the covenant of the Lord, and because he has committed a disgraceful thing in Israel'" (Josh. 7:10–15).

Jehovah didn't reveal *everything*, but He certainly made it clear that disobedience was on the loose among the Israeli army. Someone was guilty of transgression. Names weren't revealed, but the disease was found. Perhaps it would help to go back and read about the "ban" God had placed on His people as they invaded Canaan.

"But as for you, only keep yourselves from the things under the ban lest you covet them and take some of the things under the ban, so you would make the camp of Israel accursed and bring trouble on it.

"But all the silver and gold and articles of bronze and iron are holy to the Lord; they shall go into the treasury of the Lord" (Josh. 6:18–19).

Because someone had willfully and deliberately broken with God's directive, defeat had entered the ranks of that otherwise victorious army. Now it was time to discover that person. The "discovery stage" is next.

Stage Three: "Who Is Involved?"

Through a careful probing process of analysis, Joshua seeks to determine the source.

So Joshua arose early in the morning and brought Israel near by tribes, and the tribe of Judah was taken.

And he brought the family of Judah near, and he took the family of the Zerahites; and he brought the family of the Zerahites near man by man, and Zabdi was taken.

And he brought his household near man by man; and Achan, son of Carmi, son of Zabdi, son of Zerah, from the tribe of Judah, was taken.

Then Joshua said to Achan, "My son, I implore you, give glory to the Lord, the God of Israel, and give praise to Him; and tell me now what you have done. Do not hide it from me."

So Achan answered Joshua and said, "Truly, I have sinned against the Lord, the God of Israel, and this is what I did; when I saw among the spoil a beautiful mantle from Shinar and two hundred shekels of silver and a bar of gold fifty shekels in weight, then I coveted them and took them; and behold, they are concealed in the earth inside my tent with the silver underneath it" (Josh. 7:16–21).

Great effort was expended. Confrontation followed. The commander didn't jump to conclusions or put words in the guilty party's mouth. He listened. He was willing to hear him out, to let the whole thing be confessed. He invited the whole truth, "Do not hide it from me" (v. 19).

This is not at all enjoyable. It doesn't come easily and it is often not by invitation. If the fellowship has broken down because of open disobedience against God (as in this case with Achan), the confrontation is usually painful and tearful. So it is important that things be done in the right spirit. I will go so far as to say if you enjoy such encounters, you have the wrong motive. Paul writes wise words:

> Brothers, if someone is caught in a sin, you who are spiritual should restore him gently. But watch yourself, or you also may be tempted. Carry each other's burdens, and in this way you will fulfill the law of Christ (Gal. 6:1–2, NIV).

James adds:

> My brothers, if any of you should wander away from the truth and another should turn him back on to the right path, then the latter may be sure that in turning a man back from his wandering course he has rescued a soul from death, and his loving action will "cover a multitude of sins" (James 5:19–20, PHILLIPS).

These times of discovery, confrontation, and confession among fellow Christians are not to be carried out in the courtroom of law (1 Cor. 6:4–8), nor are they to be pushed in front of a church congregation unless *every* effort toward reconciliation has been tried and met with resistance (Matt. 18:15–17). I repeat, the spirit in which we go about such painful times is as important as the actions themselves, sometimes more so.

Invariably, this leads to the "assistance stage."

Stage Four: "What Is Needed?"

In the case of Achan, there was no alternative. God had spoken. His law had been broken. Death was the required penalty in that era under the Mosaic Law. Joshua did not hesitate. Maximum punishment was carried out. The people never forgot the scene.

> So Joshua sent messengers, and they ran to the tent; and behold, it was concealed in his tent with the silver underneath it.
>
> And they took them from inside the tent and brought them to Joshua and to all the sons of Israel, and they poured them out before the Lord.
>
> Then Joshua and all Israel with him, took Achan the son of Zerah, the silver, the mantle, the bar of gold, his sons, his daughters, his oxen, his donkeys, his sheep, his tent and all that belonged to him; and they brought them up to the valley of Achor.
>
> And Joshua said, "Why have you troubled us? The Lord will trouble you this day." And all Israel stoned them with stones; and they burned them with fire after they had stoned them with stones.

And they raised over him a great heap of stones that stands to this day, and the Lord turned from the fierceness of His anger. Therefore the name of that place has been called the Valley of Achor to this day (Josh. 7:22–26).

In our day, an era of mercy and grace, we are occasionally the instruments of judgment. This is never a pleasant role to fill, but nevertheless, it is an essential one. The full recovery of a brother or sister in God's family often depends on our willingness to step in and assist the person to face and admit the truth, then, hopefully, reach full repentance.

Nathan was God's instrument of confrontation in David's life. Had he not gone to the adulterous king and looked him squarely in the eye and said, "You are the man!" who knows how much longer David would have lingered in sin? Who can tell how many more people would have suffered in the fallout of his transgression?

On several occasions it has fallen my lot to be the Nathan in someone's life. I have *never* enjoyed that role, I can assure you. More often I have begged the Lord to have someone else do the dirty work. But after the whole episode has ended in confession and repentance, I have been grateful to God for His giving me the courage to step in and help a brother or sister come to terms with the things they were refusing to face. Sometimes, like it or not, it is necessary to blast before we can build.

Let me repeat something to make it so clear that no one will misunderstand. Not all breakdowns in fellowship call for confrontation and direct intervention. In the case of open disobedience against God where the Lord's family and His name are suffering (as was clearly the case with Achan at Ai), those drastic measures must be taken . . . yet even then, the *way* they are done is as important as *that* they are done.

AI AND ME

Three lasting principles linger as we draw this chapter to a close.

- Most fellowship breakdowns that are the result of open disobedience against God will not heal themselves. GET INVOLVED.
- The longer the breakdown, the greater the impact. START TODAY.
- Solutions will be initially but ultimately rewarding. DON'T QUIT.

Let me ask you, if you had a tumor and your doctor, having examined you, had determined that it was malignant, would you want him to ignore telling you the hard truth? Would he be a friend and a competent professional if he acted as though everything were great and that you had nothing to be concerned about? Would you recommend him to others?

If we want the truth from those who keep watch over our physical condition, how much more we should want the truth from those who keep watch over our souls.

Painful, thankless, and grim though it may be, telling our brothers and sisters the truth—in love—is still one of the most important functions we can carry out in the body of Christ. May God give us the courage to keep doing so . . . for the sake of keeping His body healthy . . . and that occasionally calls for a big dose of reality.

DISCUSSION IDEAS AND QUESTIONS

• Think about the family of God as a body made up of many parts. Think of a breakdown in the body as a disease. What are some things we can do to keep the body healthy so that disease doesn't invade?

• Looking back over the various reasons fellowship breaks down, discuss each one briefly. Can you think of someone who might be drifting today because of one of these problems? Without calling their name, consider ways you could reach out and be a healing agent.

• A term we sometimes hear these days is "wounded healer." Someone who has been broken or bruised through previous pain ("wounded") is often the best instrument for helping others recover ("healer"). Talk about why this is true.

• Achan's sin had a tremendous impact on the entire Hebrew army. Are there times when *our* transgressions have a similar impact on the broader body of Christ?

• Read Galatians 6:1–2 and James 5:19–20. As you meditate on these verses, talk about the importance of going with the right spirit to those who have been ensnared by sin. Address the importance of humility.

• Turn to 1 Corinthians 10:12. What does it say to you about this matter of confrontation?

• Are you close to at least one other person, preferably several? Is that relationship open and unguarded so that others have the freedom to say the hard thing to you, if necessary? Describe how you have cultivated this intimacy. Give God thanks for the gift of friendship.

7

Authentic Love

Hal David and Burt Bacharach are familiar names to music lovers all over America. What Rogers and Hammerstein were in the '40s and '50s, David and Bacharach were in the '60s and '70s.

The former did the lyrics and the latter wrote the melodies to such well-known pieces as "I Say a Little Prayer for You." and "Close to You" and "One Less Bell to Answer" . . . and, of course, the Academy Award-winning "Raindrops Keep Fallin' on My Head."

But, of all their music, the single tune that won our country's heart more than any other was the one that sang its way into our loneliness and hunger for love.

> What the world needs now is love, sweet love,
> No—not just for some but for everyone;
> Lord, we don't need another mountain,
>
> There are mountains and hillsides enough to climb,
> There are oceans and rivers enough to cross . . .
> Enough to last 'til the end of time.
>
> What the world needs now is love, sweet love;
> No—not just for some, but for everyone
> It's the only thing that there's just too little of.[1]

Do you believe that? Probably so. But the world doesn't need phony love; or mushy, fickle, wimpy love; or conditional love that says "if you ———, then I'll love you;" or swap-meet love that says "Because you gave me this, I'll swap you love in return." No. What the world needs now is tough love, *authentic* love.

That's the stuff open relationships are all about. It's *that* kind of love that makes me care enough to confront and big enough to forgive. David and Bacharach were exactly right, this rare commodity is "the only thing there's just too little of."

A Case of Authentic Love

Gayle Sayers was the best running back the Chicago Bears ever had. He was black. Brian Piccolo was the other running back, also quite an athlete. He was white. This was nothing new, not even back in 1967. Blacks and whites often played on the same professional teams. But these two were different. They were roommates on the road—a first for race relations in professional football. You need to realize that Sayers had never had a close relationship with *any* white man, with the exception, perhaps, of George Halas, the head coach of the Bears. And Piccolo admitted he had never *known* a black person—not really.

But within the span of two brief years, 1967–1969, their relationship had deepened into one of the most memorable friendships in the history of sports. As the movie *Brian's Song* poignantly depicted, the men truly *loved* each other. Part of the reason they grew so close together was the tragic fact that Brian Piccolo contracted cancer during the 1969 season. Although he fought to play the season out, he was in the hospital more than he was on the playing field. Frequently, Sayers flew to be beside his friend as the disease refused to go away. The smell of death became increasingly more obvious though the two of them, both winners through and through, refused to surrender.

They and their wives had longstanding plans to sit together at the annual Professional Football Writer's Banquet in New York where Gayle Sayers, appropriately, was to receive the George S. Halas award as "the most courageous player in professional football." By the time of the banquet, Piccolo was too sick to attend. He was confined to his bed at home.

As the lean, muscular black athlete stood to his feet to receive the award amid the resounding applause of the audience, tears began to flow which he could not restrain. I'll never forget his words.

> You flatter me by giving me this award, but I tell you here and now that I accept it for Brian Piccolo. Brian Piccolo is the man of courage who should receive the George S. Halas Award. I love Brian Piccolo and I'd like you to love him. Tonight, when you hit your knees, please ask God to love him too.

How often do we hear grown men say such words? "I love Brian Piccolo." What a remarkable yet rare statement! Sayers and Piccolo had cultivated more than a superficial, tough-guy relationship. Although rugged, heterosexual, competitive men to the core, authentic love had developed between these two strong athletes.

David Smith has written a timely and long-overdue book I wish men would take the time to read, *The Friendless American Male*. In it he puts his finger on a basic flaw in masculine relationships.

> Men find it hard to accept that they need the fellowship of other men. The simple request, "Let's have lunch together" is likely to be followed with the response, "Sure, what's up?" The message is clear: the independent man doesn't need the company of another man. In fact, the image of the independent man is that he has few if any emotional needs. Therefore, men must manufacture nonemotional reasons for being together—a business deal must be discussed or a game must be played. Men often use drinking as an excuse to gather together. Rarely do men plan a meeting together simply because they have a need to enjoy each other's company.
>
> Even when men are frequently together their social interaction begins and remains at a superficial level. Just how long can conversations about politics and sports be nourishing to the human spirit? The same male employees can have lunch together for years and years and still limit their conversation to sports, politics, and dirty jokes and comments about the sexual attractiveness of selected female workers in their office or plant. They do not know how to fellowship.[2]

Ours is a weird world in which we can't win. We men stand aloof from one another to somehow prove we are rugged individualists, yet everyone knows most of us aren't. But if we want to get close to other men, people suspect homosexuality. So we hide behind the "real man" macho mask, adhering to a counterfeit law that could easily be called "The Commandments of Masculinity":

> He shall not cry.
> He shall not display weakness.
> He shall not need affection or gentleness or warmth.
> He shall comfort but not desire comforting.
> He shall be needed but not need.
> He shall touch but not be touched.
> He shall be steel not flesh.
> He shall be inviolate in his manhood.
> He shall stand alone.[3]

Those who obey that law will never know authentic love, mark it down. Never. What the world needs now is not that phony-baloney cheap imitation, but love—authentic love.

WHOM DO YOU LOVE?

Enough of others. Let's apply this to ourselves. Whom do *you* love? Of whom could *you* use the words Gayle Sayers used? "I love ——— ———?" You may feel a little cornered right now, maybe a tad defensive. "Hey, I love lots of folks . . . I don't *hate* anybody." No, I'm not talking about that. In fact, I don't believe hate is the opposite of love. Apathy is. If we treat someone with a cool indifference, if we convey to other people "I really couldn't care less," we are sending a signal loud and clear. And it doesn't say, "I love you."

So let me reword the question, "To whom are you indifferent?" You see, authentic love is in the process of building bridges, spanning chasms, reaching, risking, demonstrating, expressing, showing interest. That explains why authentic love belongs right in the middle of this book on open relationships. It is the heartbeat of a healthy body.

WATCH OUT FOR INAUTHENTIC TRAPS!

Now before we get into the positive dimensions of love, let's clear away some of the negative debris. There are pitfalls to avoid in this matter of showing true love. I am indebted to Alan McGinnis once again for those three "traps" we fall into rather easily—the gusher, the pressurizer, the ramrod.[4]

The Gusher

As the name implies, the gusher is the individual who dumps tons of nice-sounding verbiage on others with a sweet, syrupy smile. You know it's mere flattery, completely lacking in depth of feeling. There is an old southern expression that describes the action of "gushers"—they are "blowing smoke on you," nothing more.

Authentic love tells the truth. Unlike guhers, those who demonstrate true love have integrity in their words. They don't indiscriminately dump the truck of artificial emotion into the ears of the public. Let's not get caught in that subtle yet popular trap.

The Pressurizer

The pressurizer is the you-scratch-my-back-since-I-scratched-yours kind of person. The reason he says "I love you" is to hear the same words said back to him. Love is not to be a lever, a manipulative grip which enables us to hold onto others. If it is authentic, it is spontaneous, devoid of hidden agendas. It is freeing not smothering. Remember Jesus' words? "You shall know the truth and the truth shall make you free."

For too many years in my marriage I confused smothering with loving. My "love" was designed to control my wife, to pressure her, to corner her. Although a "pressurizer," I really believed I was loving her.

The Ramrod

Some folks are so determined to push their love on you, they lack a sensitive spirit. They seem more bent on delivering their passionate lines and getting their script read than on finding our green-light signals that say, "I'm listening, I'm ready, I'm responsive to you."

Ramrod people are notoriously determined to travel along their one-way streets, regardless of others' reactions. Love—authentic love—remains sensitive, careful not to force its way in like a savage cutting his way through the jungle with a massive machete.

So much for what love is *not*. Let's spend the rest of this chapter on what it *is*. Instead of returning to our story in the Old Testament, let's take a break and draw our thoughts from the familiar lines of 1 Corinthians 13, the greatest treatise ever written on the subject.

AN ANALYSIS OF AUTHENTIC LOVE

Allow me the freedom to offer a free rendering of the first three verses of 1 Corinthians 13. It's a "duke's mixture" of various paraphrases, my own translation from the original Greek, and several versions:

> If I have the ability to speak in polished and impressive fashion, or
> If I can utter sounds only angels understand, or
> If I have such a pronounced prophetic gift that I know the entire future . . . everything about everything, or
> If I possess such unswerving faith so that I can remove mountains,
> If I am so genuinely sacrificial that all my possessions are given away to the needy, or even
> If I commit the supreme act of unselfishness and go to the gas chamber for the sake of the gospel, and yet lack love, the essential ingredient; then,
> All my speaking has the sound of a hollow basin of brass and
> All my knowledge and faith is of no use and
> All my philanthropy and martyrdom gains *nothing* at all!

I find no less than four facts about the true love as I meditate on these verses. And each one helps me understand just how valuable love is in having open relationships. I think you will agree.

Love Is Essential, Not Optional

First we see that love is not optional, but necessary. On no less than three occasions, Paul writes, ". . . but do not have love . . ." (vv. 1, 2, 3). Then he adds the clincher ". . . a noisy gong . . . nothing . . . nothing." Take away love, that essential ingredient, and it's like a car without wheels, a train without an engine, a plane without wings, a house without a foundation. Take away love and we are left with zero.

Love Is a Demonstration, Not an Inclination

When we describe love as a demonstration, it's because there is action, involvement, movement, expression. "Love is . . . love does. Love is not . . . loves does not." Love doesn't sit back and snooze. It is not apathetic. It is ready and willing. It is neither passive nor indifferent. It refuses to yawn its way through life. Authentic love is demonstrative, not sterile and dull.

I distinctly remember reading about a very interesting case that came before the courts in the state of Massachusetts back in the late 1920s. It concerned a man who had been walking along a pier when suddenly he tripped over a rope and fell into the cold, deep waters of that ocean bay. He came up sputtering, screaming for help, then sank beneath the surface. For some reason he was unable to swim or stay afloat. His friends heard his faint cries in the distance, but they were too far away to rescue him. But within only a few yards was a young man lounging on a deck chair, sunbathing. Not only could the sunbather hear the drowning man plead, "Help, I can't swim," he was also an excellent swimmer.

But the tragedy is that he did nothing. He only turned his head to watch indifferently as the man finally sank and drowned.

The family of the victim was so upset by that display of extreme indifference, they sued the sunbather. The result? They lost the case. With a measure of reluctance, the court ruled that the man on the dock had no *legal* responsibility whatsoever to try to save the drowning man's life.

I suppose we could say the law agrees with Cain: "Am I my brother's keeper?" You and I have our legal right to mind our own business—to turn a deaf ear to anyone in need, to continue sunbathing while someone is drowning. We are not obligated to respond. Indifference may not be illegal, but it certainly is immoral! Which brings us back to my earlier comment: The opposite of love is apathy, not hatred. Love, sweet love, is a demonstration, not merely an inclination.

Love Is a Magnet That Draws Us Together, Not a Wall That Keeps Us Apart

In verse 4 through 7 of 1 Corinthians 13, there are fifteen specific expressions of love, each one magnetic enough to draw people together. Just listen to them:

- Love is patient.
- Love is kind.
- Love is not jealous.
- Love does not brag and is not arrogant.

- Love does not act unbecomingly.
- Love does not seek its own.
- Love is not provoked.
- Love does not take into account a wrong suffered.
- Love does not rejoice in unrighteousness.
- Love rejoices with the truth.
- Love bears all things.
- Love believes all things.
- Love hopes all things.
- Love endures all things.
- Love never fails.

Look at that climax: "Love never fails."
When we summarize these fifteen magnetic characteristics that "never fail,"
I find five statements that say it all.

"I *a*ccept you as you are."
  "I *b*elieve you are valuable."
    "I *c*are when you hurt."
      "I *d*esire only what is best for you."
        "I *e*rase all offenses."

We could call that the ABCs of love. And I don't know of anybody who would
turn his back on such magnetic, encouraging statements.

A number of years ago, back when the street people were all over Southern
California, we had a young man stumble into our church one Sunday evening.
He was wretched looking—dirty, torn shirt, cutoffs, disheveled hair, a scraggly
beard, and dazed eyes. He smelled of beer, the beach, and body odor. But one of
our members saw beyond the surface and lovingly offered the stranger a seat in
the meeting.

We found out later the guy had never been inside a church before in his life.
He had been kicked out of his house by his parents, so he'd taken up residence
in the garage, sleeping on a cot. He existed on a six pack and corn chips during
the day and drugs at night. He was useless to society (but not personally
worthless), and several in our congregation decided not to lose contact with
him. They followed the ABCs of love and Steve could not get over it. He'd never
known such attention, never felt such a magnet. He realized that these people
really cared.

Slowly the walls began to crumble. Steve began to change all on his own—
nothing forced. He changed from within first. His attitude changed. His habits
changed. His language changed. His appearance then began to change. He even
changed his clothes! His hunger for God and for God's Word knew no bounds.
He decided to go back to work . . . then to return to school. He made things
right with his folks. He and I used to talk about his relationship with others and
with the Lord. Love totally won that young man! He entered seminary and

ultimately graduated. He is currently ministering here in Southern California. In fact, my older son and his wife, Curt and Debbie, now fellowship in his church. Steve is their pastor.

Love never fails . . . it draws us like a magnet.

Love Is a Long-Term Investment, Not a Quick-Return Loan

There is nothing shallow about authentic love. Nor is it a magic wand that we whip out and wave over a problem with a whoosh, hoping all the pain will go away. Real love has staying power. Authentic love is tough love. It refuses to look for ways to run away. It always opts for working through. It doesn't cop out because the sea gets stormy and rough. It's fibrous and resilient. Who knows how many of us would've walked away from our commitment many long years ago if it hadn't been for this powerful and essential ingredient deep down inside saying, "Put away that white flag. Do not quit. Don't even *tolerate* the thought." While the world around us gives the opposite counsel, love stands firm.

As an example of this, I want to close this chapter by sharing part of a letter I received. The woman who wrote it is a beautiful and rare illustration of authentic love. She and her husband renewed their marriage vows many years after they originally took them as a result of God's honoring her faithfulness.

Dear Pastor Swindoll,

. . . God has restored a marriage and rekindled a love that was virtually dead. God used your ministry, Chuck, to break, bend, and finally mold me to be more the person God wanted me to be, so I would be ready when God began His work in my husband's life.

You were doing the early part of the Romans series when I first attended Ev. Free five years ago. As I sat in the last row, I thought surely you were talking just to me, as you told of Jesus' love, forgiveness, and hope for the despairing. As my tears quietly fell, I found God's loving forgiveness and a real hope in His strength. I went home that day with my one-year-old son to a husband who worked constantly, drank heavily, and was emotionally hurting; but this time Jesus came too. You will never know the strength God gave me over the months that followed, through your insightful messages, to go on each day. Some days with peace and others by sheer endurance. How many times I wanted to run away and start over, only to walk into church and have you say, "When you are between a rock and a hard place, you stay, 'cause God's going to let you grow, if you let Him." So I stayed and let God begin His work of changing me.

I stopped praying for God to fix my marriage and change my husband, and started to consciously submit to God's will, asking Him to change me. Through the pain, He sheltered me in the shadow of His wings and I sang for joy. He brought me out of the pit of destruction and set my feet upon a rock. God was at work.

Two years ago, God removed my husband's desire for alcohol, and God did it overnight. This past summer, I decided to get off the fence, so I committed my whole life to Christ. I gave Him all those areas that I had stubbornly held on to. I said, "God, whatever it takes to bring me closer to you, you do it. I'm going to stay in this marriage and let you work your will in my life."

Well, three months later, through God's gracious timing and His circumstances, my husband accepted Jesus as his Savior. Talk about an answer to prayer! I am married to a new man, one who now loves God and wants our family to live according to God's will.

Chuck, you have said on occasion, how God can rekindle a dead love. Well, my husband and I are proof of God's caring, His power and ability to change hearts and to bring life to a dead relationship. I love my husband more now than ever before. Our priorities as a family are straight, with God first. God is so faithful, Who restored the years that the locust had eaten, Who dealt wondrously with us.

And, Chuck, our eyes fill with tears of joy when our six-year-old son says, "Thank you, Jesus, for coming into my daddy's heart and making him nice to me, and not so mean. I love my daddy."

Thank you, Pastor, for conveying God's truth and love, and being such an encouragement to me. I know God will continue to use you and the total ministry at Ev. Free to spread the truth of the gospel.

As a family, we now anticipate growing in the Lord, participating in fellowship and, as God wills, being an encouragement to others.

Sincerely,

(signed)

If authentic love can work in that woman's life, guess what. Yes, you're right. It will work for you too.

But you'll never know until you release it. You'll never know as long as it remains mere words on the pages of this book . . . or as long as it remains the lyrics to a song . . . or the lines in someone else's speech . . . or the words of some other person's letter. Yes, authentic love is the only thing there's just too little of.

DISCUSSION IDEAS AND QUESTIONS

• Of all the subjects written about in songs and poetry, love is no doubt the most popular. We've thought about it all through this chapter. What single ingredient do you most appreciate about love? Can you explain why?

• Go back over that list describing the popular idea of what men "should" be—what they "should" and "should not" do. What do you think of those things? How can a man demonstrate love without appearing weak or feminine?

• Finish the sentence, "I love —— ——." Why are those words to hard to say?

• Discuss the "gusher," the "pressurizer," and the "ramrod." Do you have to fight falling into one of those traps? Which one?

• This may be a little painful. Is there someone you have become indifferent toward? Do you feel free to acknowledge that to others so they can pray that your attitude and response might change?

• Work your way through the four observations made about 1 Corinthians 13:1-8. Is there something special about one of them? Why?

• Review the ABCs of love. Talk about each one briefly. How about memorizing these five sentences and reviewing them the next time you meet with the group?

• Do you have children? Do they know you love them? When did you last tell them so? Do that soon. Take your time and make the conversation meaningful.

8

Needed: Shelter
for Storm Victims

Churches need to be less like national shrines and more like local bars . . . less like untouchable cathedrals and more like well-used hospitals, places to bleed in rather than monuments to look at . . . places where you can take your mask off and let your hair down . . . places where you can have your wounds dressed.

It's like my Marine-buddy, recently turned Christian, said, as he lamented the absence of a place of refuge:

> . . . the only thing I miss is that old fellowship all the guys in our outfit used to have down at the slop shoot . . . we'd sit around, laugh, tell stories, drink a few beers, and really let our hair down. It was great!
>
> But now I ain't got nobody to tell my troubles to, to admit my faults to. I can't find anybody in church who will put their arms around me and tell me I'm still okay. Man, it's kinda lonely in there!

He was looking for people who demonstrated authentic love, like that discussed in chapter 7. I found myself churning, wishing it were not so. I was hoping the new Christian was nit-picking, but he wasn't. Stop and think. Where does a guy go when the bottom drops out? To whom do we Christians turn when stuff that's embarrassing or a little scandalous happens? Who cares enough to listen when we cry? Who affirms us when we feel rotten? Who will close their mouths and open their hearts? And, even though we deserve a swift kick in the pants, who will embrace us with understanding and give us time to heal without quoting verses? Without giving us a cassette tape of some sermon to listen to? Without telling a bunch of other Christians so they can "pray more intelligently"? Yeah, we need more shelters for storm victims. It's okay if they look like churches on the outside, just so folks don't act churchy on the inside. Most hurting people I meet are fed up with churchy Christians. What we *really* need is that special something many people find in the local bar. Put on your shock boots and see if you agree with the following comparison between the bar and the church.

> The neighborhood bar is possibly the best counterfeit there is to the fellowship Christ wants to give His church. It's an imitation, dispensing liquor instead of grace, escape rather than reality, but it is a permissive, accepting, and inclusive fellowship. It is unshockable. It is democratic. You can tell people secrets and they usually don't tell others or even want to. The bar flourishes not because most people are alcoholics, but because God has put into the human heart the desire to know and be known, to love and be loved, and so many seek a counterfeit at the price of a few beers.
>
> With all my heart I believe that Christ wants His church to be . . . a fellowship where people can come in and say, "I'm sunk!" "I'm beat!" "I've had it!"[1]

What if your wife is an alcoholic? Or your son recently told you he's a practicing homosexual?

Let's say your husband just walked out . . . or what if he is sexually abusing your two daughters? Or you?

Who can you turn to if you just got fired? . . . Or you just got out of jail? . . . Or your 15-year-old daughter told you last night that she was pregnant? . . . Or you beat your kids and you're scared—and ashamed? . . . Or you can't cope with your drug habit any longer? . . . Or you need professional help because you're near a breakdown?

Do you know what you need? You need a shelter. A place of refuge. A few folks who can help you, listen to you, introduce you, once again, to ". . . the Father of mercies, the God of all comfort; who comforts us in all our affliction (2 Cor. 1:3–4). Christianity may be "like a mighty army," but we often handle our troops in a weird way. We're the only outfit I've ever heard of who shoots their wounded. That's what my Marine buddy was afraid of. He had had enough of getting shot. Frankly, so have I.

SHELTERS: WHY DO WE NEED THEM?

Psalm 31 is one of those ancient hymns with an up-to-date set of lyrics. David is the composer, but he obviously got his inspiration from God. The man has run out of crutches to lean on. He's in trouble. He needs some shelter. Since there's nobody on the horizon to help, David looks up:

> In Thee, O Lord, I have taken refuge;
> Let me never be ashamed;
> In Thy righteousness deliver me.

Incline Thine ear to me, rescue me quickly;
Be Thou to me a rock of strength.
A stronghold to save me (Ps. 31:1-2).

There it is, big as life—*refuge.* The Hebrew word is CHA-SAH, meaning "a safe place, a place of protection and secrecy." Soldiers in David's day would seek a place on the hillside that gave them a place to hide from the enemy. When they were wounded or surrounded by adverse forces or in need of security, they looked for huge boulders to hide behind, often those high up on the mountainside—a CHA-SAH hideout.

But why would David seek a place of shelter? For the same reasons we would! He mentions several of those reasons in Psalm 31. I find at least three: distress, sin, and adversaries.

Because We Are in Distress . . . Sorrow Accompanies Us

Be gracious to me, O Lord, for I am in distress; My eye is wasted away from grief, my soul and my body also.
For my life is spent with sorrow, And my years with sighing (Ps. 31:9-10).

Vivid, honest words—an unguarded admission. He says his eyes are red from weeping—here was a grown man who cried! He admits his life was "spent with sorrow." Things were dark, days were drab, the hope of tomorrow being different was doubtful. Joe Bayly calls such times "gray slush" days.

"A PSALM IN A HOTEL ROOM"

I'm alone, Lord,
alone,
a thousand miles from home.
There's no one here who knows my name
except the clerk,
and he spelled it wrong,
no one to eat dinner with,
laugh at my jokes,
lisen to my gripes,
be happy with me about what happened today
and say that's great.
No one cares.
There's just this lousy bed
and slush in the street outside
between the buildings.
I feel sorry for myself
and I've plenty of reason
to.

> Maybe I ought to say
> I'm on top of it,
> praise the Lord,
> things are great;
> but they're not.
> Tonight
> it's all
> gray slush.[2]

Those are depressing, lonely times. Sorrow won't go away. And CHA-SAH shelters are hard to come by.

Because We Are Sinful . . . Guilt Accuses Us

> My strength has failed because of my iniquity, And my body has wasted away (Ps. 31:10).

There is shame here—embarrassment. David's words drip with guilt. He confesses that he is physically ill as a direct result of his iniquities. It's bad enough that he feels terrible, but knowing that much of it is his own fault, "that the vulture which feeds on the vitals is a nestling of [his] . . . own rearing,"[3] added insult to injury.

Who can't identify with that? Who hasn't done battle with the slimy beast out of the swamp of guilt? Its accusations are debilitating, and its blows are always below the belt.

In addition to distress and guilt, David mentions a third reason for shelter—adversaries.

Because We Are Surrounded by Adversaries . . .
Misunderstanding Assaults Us

> Because of all my adversaries, I have become a reproach,
> Especially to my neighbors,
> And an object of dread to my acquaintances;
> Those who see me in the street flee from me.
> I am forgotten as a dead man, out of mind,
> I am like a broken vessel.
> For I have heard the slander of many,
> Terror is on every side;
> While they took counsel together against me,
> They schemed to take away my life (Ps. 31:11–13).

Did you observe how the hurting are treated?

- "I have become a reproach . . . to my neighbors."
    Ridicule
- ". . . an object of dread to my acquaintances."
    Criticism
- "Those who see me in the street flee from me . . . forgotten
    . . . like a broken vessel. . . ."
    Rejection
- "I have heard the slander of many."
    Gossip
- "They schemed to take away my life."
    Threat

We are talking misery! David was like a tiny, wounded mouse in the paws of a huge, hungry cat. Punched, kicked, tortured by words, and terrified with fear, the man was hanging by his fingernails. Maybe you are, too. It's bad enough to struggle with sorrow and live with guilt. But the final straw is the condemnation of others—the wagging tongues and glaring eyes. And worse yet, the silence— the absence of reassuring phone calls and hugs of affirmation.

How we need places of relief and people of refuge! Especially if we are committed to dropping our guard.

REFUGE: HOW THE HEBREWS HANDLED IT

Believe it or not, the Old Testament story of the Hebrews' pilgrimage from Egypt to Canaan includes some very interesting information about places of refuge they established. After they had sucessfully invaded Canaan, the land was divided among the Hebrews so that each tribe had territory it could call its own. (Joshua 13–19 tells how it happened.) In their new society God did not ignore those in need, however. He instructed the leaders to set apart "cities of refuge," actual territories preserved for protection and relief.

Commanded by God

Joshua 20:1–3 speaks for itself.

Then the Lord spoke to Joshua, saying, "Speak to the sons of Israel, saying, 'Designate the cities of refuge, of which I spoke to you through Moses, that the manslayer who kills any person unintentionally, without premeditation, may flee there, and they shall become your refuge from the avenger of blood," (Josh. 20: 1–3).

One Old Testament scholar adds this helpful clarification:

According to the rabbins, in order to aid the fugitive it was the business of the Sanhedrin to keep the roads leading to the cities of refuge in the best possible repair. No hills were left, every river was bridged, and the road itself was to be at least thirty-two cubits broad [about 48 feet]. At every turn were guide posts bearing the word *Refuge*; and two students of the law were appointed to accompany the fleeing man, to pacify, if possible, the avenger, should he overtake the fugitive.[4]

The point is this, every effort was made to assist, not harrass, the fugitive. People in trouble were to be protected from violent outbursts of avengers. These places of refuge were well-marked and awareness of their availability was known by all. They were not superficial tokens of concern, but well-kept and carefully maintained areas of protection.

Procedure for Entrance

The individual in trouble would run to this haven of refuge. Upon arriving, he was required to state the details of his case. He would then be admitted entrance.

> And he shall flee to one of these cities and shall stand at the entrance of the gate of the city and state his case in the hearing of the elders of that city; and they shall take him into the city to them and give him a place, so that he may dwell among them (Josh. 20:4).

The New International Version captures an even more personal touch in the procedure: ". . . they are to admit him into their city and give him a place to live with them."

Please understand, those who were allowed entrance were not wanton, cold-blooded murderers. Nor were they senseless and sadistic sexual perverts and brutal rapists. They were people who had made tragic mistakes—victims of unintentional, unpremeditated offenses. Without getting carried away here by my imagination, I'd rather suspect that those who raced to these places of refuge would be under intense stress, emotionally broken by the events that had transpired, wishing in vain to erase what had happened . . . strung out, frightened, confused souls.

In recent days a Los Angeles policeman was called to a scene where someone reported trouble. He had no idea who or what was in the house in question. After asking neighbors and others several questions, he entered the dwelling with his pistol drawn. A door leading to a back bedroom was closed. He knocked. No answer. He yelled and gave his identity. Still no answer. He entered the room. Sitting on the bed was a boy with a gun pointed directly at the officer. The policeman shot first. The boy was killed. The tragedy is that the little fella was holding a toy pistol. He had been left alone that day by his mother. Words cannot describe the awful anxiety of that policeman—nor the angry reaction of the neighborhood! As I read the account and as my family and I followed the story from week to week (the officer was subsequently found to be not guilty), I thought to myself, "A classic case for a city of refuge." The man needed protection.

Can you imagine the policeman's need for reassurance? His deeply shaken father stated that he was doubtful his son would ever fully recover from the incident. Without taking away any of the grief of the dead child's mother (another need for someone to comfort and console), the sorrow, the guilt, the misunderstanding of the policeman defies description. By the way, if he were in *your* church, would there be a circle of shelter, a place for the policeman to find refuge and relief? I sincerely hope so. All too often our churches operate as though such people don't even exist. The fact is, the number of folks with this kind of need is often large.

Better than any other analogy I can think of, we are probably describing something like the old Spanish missions of yesteryear. That's perhaps as close as religious America has come to our own brand of "cities of refuge." Places of solitude, where broken people have time to recover a sense of self-worth and dignity. Where there are a few compassionate "priests" who will hear their stories and give wise counsel.

Protection from Avengers

A major purpose of those ancient places of refuge was to protect the person from those who would take it upon themselves to avenge the death of their loved one. "Now if the avenger of blood pursues him, then they shall not deliver the manslayer into his hand, because he struck his neighbor without premeditation and did not hate him beforehand" (Josh. 20:5).

For further clarification, Numbers 35 describes the difference between an intentional murder and one that was unintentional.

> But if he struck him down with an iron object, so that he died, he is a murderer; the murderer shall surely be put to death.
>
> And if he struck him down with a stone in the hand, by which he may die, and as a result he died, he is a murderer; the murderer shall surely be put to death.
>
> Or if he struck him with a wooden object in the hand, by which he may die, and as a result he died, he is a murderer; the murderer shall surely be put to death.
>
> The blood avenger himself shall put the murderer to death; he shall put him to death when he meets him.
>
> And if he pushed him of hatred, or threw something at him lying in wait and as a result he died, or if he struck him down with his hand in enmity, and as a result he died, the one who struck him shall surely be put to death, he is a murderer; the blood avenger shall put the murderer to death when he meets him (Num. 35:16–21).

That person would not be granted asylum according to the Hebrews. But this person would:

But if he pushed him suddenly without enmity, or threw something at him without lying in wait, or with any deadly object of stone, and without seeing it dropped on him so that he died, while he was not his enemy nor seeking his injury, then the congregation shall judge between the slayer and the blood avenger according to these ordinances.

And the congregation shall deliver the manslayer from the hand of the blood avenger, and the congregation shall restore him to his city of refuge to which he fled; and he shall live in it until the death of the high priest who was anointed with the holy oil.

But if the manslayer shall at any time, go beyond the border of his city of refuge to which he may flee, and the blood avenger finds him outside the border of his city of refuge, and the blood avenger kills the manslayer, he shall not be guilty of blood because he should have remained in his city of refuge until the death of the high priest. But after the death of the high priest the manslayer shall return to the land of his possession (Num. 35:22–28).

The person was safe as long as he stayed within the boundaries of the city of refuge. But if he left . . . *zap!* Interestingly, the death of the high priest provided the manslayer with a perpetual pardon. He could then leave without fear.

Involvement of the Assembly

It is quite important that we understand what happened *within* the place of refuge. Let's return to a couple of verses:

Then the congregation shall judge between the slayer and the blood avenger according to these ordinances.

And the congregation shall deliver the manslayer from the hand of the blood avenger, and the congregation shall restore him to his city of refuge to which he fled; and he shall live in it until the death of the high priest who was anointed with the holy oil (Num. 35:24–25).

In these verses, I find three particular involvements of those who formed the assembly or "the congregation" in those ancient havens of relief. You might circle the words in your Bible for the sake of emphasis:

• "The congregation shall *judge*. . . ."
• "The congregation shall *deliver*. . . ."
• "The congregation shall *restore*. . . ."

The original term translated "judge" suggests the idea of deciding cases of controversy. It would include the necessary time and wisdom, objectivity and integrity to reflect on the evidence and to weigh the story carefully. It is the same thing asked of jurors who hear the case of the accused in courtrooms all across our country. In the days of Joshua "the congregation"—an assembly of the Levites (ancient "churchmen")—was called upon to do that.

Next, they were to *deliver* the accused from the avengers. The causative stem of the Hebrew verb translated "deliver" suggests the idea of the assembly "causing to be released," or being the cause for the removal (sometimes translated the "survival") of the accused. In other words, having heard him out and being convinced of the man's innocence, they actively pursued his recovery, his survival. There is a positive and affirming tone in the action they took.

Finally, the assembly worked together to "restore" the man fully. Again the causative stem suggests they were directly involved in the project. They not only saw to it that the man was released from guilt with full pardon, they assisted him in his restoration of personal worth and dignity. At the death of the high priest the man was free to return to his home.

> "'And he shall dwell in that city until he stands before the congregation for judgment, until the death of the one who is high priest in those days. Then the manslayer shall return to his own city and to his own house, to the city from which he fled.'"
>
> So they set apart Kedesh in Galilee in the hill country of Naphtali and Shechem in the hill country of Ephraim, and Kiriatharba (that is, Hebron) in the hill country of Judah.
>
> And beyond the Jordan east of Jericho, they designate Bezer in the wilderness on the plain from the tribe of Reuben, and Ramoth in Gilead from the tribe of Gad, and Golan in Bashan from the tribe of Manasseh.
>
> These were appointed cities for all the sons of Israel and for the stranger who sojourns among them, that whoever kills any person unintentionally may flee there, and not die by the hand of the avenger of blood until he stands before the congregation (Josh. 20:6–9).

PROVIDING SHELTER TODAY: WHAT IS REQUIRED?

Those are unusual and unfamiliar names, the names of those six cities: Kedesh, Shechem, Kirath-arba, Bezer, Ramoth, and Golan. We've never heard of them. But we've all heard of Cincinnati and Dallas and Seattle and Minneapolis and Chicago and Los Angeles. Any places of refuge there? Any assemblies in the city where *you* live who care about the hurting enough to listen objectively, to help folks survive, to bring people full circle back to complete restoration? Is your town a "city of refuge"? How about it? Waco? San Jose? Flagstaff? Portland? Fort Lauderdale? Birmingham? Colorado Springs? Wheaton? No, let's face it, towns are no longer designated places of refuge. Not even good, decent towns. But within towns are some pretty important and strategic havens of hope. They're called churches.

I'm not referring to highly polished silver sanctuaries made mainly to be looked at. I'm talking about people—truly Christian people, caring to the core.

These folks form pockets of hope for the despairing, regardless of the appearance of the buildings where they worship.

We could call such places shelters for storm victims, hospitals for those who hurt, healing centers that specialize in wounded hearts, broken dreams, and shipwrecked souls. What is involved? What does it take to occupy those places? Listen to these words:

> We know and, to some extent realise, the love of God for us because Christ expressed it in laying down His life for us. We must in turn express our love by laying down our lives for those who are our brothers. But as for the well-to-do man who sees his brother in want but shuts his eyes—and his heart—how could anyone believe that the love of God lives in him? My children, let us love not merely in theory or in words—let us love in sincerity and in practice! (1 John 3:16–18, PHILLIPS).

If we take those words seriously, then it's quite clear what is involved:

* A willingness to go the distance for someone in trouble.
* An attitude of loving compassion for the needy.
* Availability to help in practical, tangible ways.
* Helping people feel needed and important in this high-tech, contemporary society of ours that makes us acutely aware of our insignificance.

As one clear-thinking writer put it:

> Our technological age has made us more aware of our smallness. As the world gets more and more sophisticated we increasingly feel insignificant. Our suspicion that we are not loved for who we are is confirmed daily by the impersonal nature of twentieth century living. Someone, reflecting on this observed:

> > To the doctor I'm a patient
> > To the lawyer—a client
> > To the editor—a subscriber
> > To the retailer—a shopper
> > To the educator—a student
> > To the manufacturer—a dealer
> > To the politician—a constituent
> > To the banker—a depositor-borrower
> > To the sports promoter—a fan
> > To the airlines—a passenger
> > To the minister—a parishioner
> > To the military—a number or a soldier

Is it any wonder that we feel dehumanized? We have come to be treated more as things than human beings. We're no longer a person but a number, no longer a human being but merely a statistic.[5]

Long enough have those who need a place of refuge occupied the local bar. It's time we made the church of Jesus Christ—the family of God—a place of refuge. It's time we held high the lamp of forgiveness, the torch of grace. Until we are willing to do that, we can forget about dropping our guards.

Several years ago I was in New York City, indeed a fascinating hub of activity. With a few hours to spare, I took the ferry out into the harbor. We circled Liberty Island (formerly Bedloe's Island), and we lingered near that famous statue, no doubt the most famous in all America.

There she stood, a proud woman, dressed in a loose robe that falls in graceful folds to the top of the pedestal on which she stands. Grasped by her left arm is a tablet bearing the date of our Declaration of Independence. Her right arm, extended high, holds a torch. At her feet is a broken shackle representing the overthrow of tyranny. One hundred tons of compassion and welcome stand as a mute testimony to the message inscribed at its base on a bronze tablet. That message is a sonnet by Emma Lazarus entitled "The New Colossus." Have you read it lately?

> Not like the brazen giant of Greek fame,
>> With conquering limbs astride from land to land;
>> Here at our sea-washed, sunset gates shall stand
> A mighty woman with a torch, whose flame
> Is the imprisoned lightning, and her name
>> Mother of Exiles. From her beacon-hand
>> Glows world-wide welcome; her mild eyes command
> The air-bridged harbor that twin cities frame.
> "Keep ancient lands, your storied pomp!" cries she
>> With silent lips. "Give me your tired, your poor,
> Your huddled masses yearning to breathe free,
>> The wretched refuse of your teeming shore.
> Send these, the homeless, tempest-tost to me,
>> I lift my lamp beside the golden door!"

Would that inscription be appropriate on a sign in front of your church? How about your home? Or your heart? Are you engaged in the refuge business?

People needing refuge look for such statues. Tell me, where would they find one in the city or town where you live?

DISCUSSION IDEAS AND QUESTIONS

• What made the greatest impression on you in chapter 8? Why did that stand out as most important?

• Written between those lines were words like "compassion," "sympathy," "mercy," and "tolerance." Take an honest, straight-ahead look at your life. Evaluate it in light of those qualities. Where did we learn how to treat people like we do?

• David's words in Psalm 31 are to the point. Review the three reasons we need places of refuge according to this psalm. Do any of them fit you today? Explain. How about someone you know and love?

• Is there some way you (and perhaps others in your group) could reach out to your friend and convey this shelter and hope of which the chapter speaks?

• One psychologist, after watching a group of us Christians over an extended period of time, said we reminded him of a pack of procupines on a cold winter's night. The elements push us together, but then when we get really close . . . we tend to jab and pick at one another. Have you found this to be true? Do you find yourself more comfortable around non-Christians, especially when you are struggling?

• Because there are no longer "cities of refuge" where can the hurting people in your own town turn for relief, affirmation, and recovery? Have you ever given thought to starting a ministry that reaches out to people in need . . . like alcoholics, divorcees, innocent victims of abuse, the brain-injured/retarded and their parents, the senior citizens of your community, the single parents in your church? Would you be willing to pray and take that risk?

9

Some Things Have Gotta Go!

Meaningful, healthy relationships need the right kind of environment in which to flourish. Before we can expect to nurture open unmasked honesty, genuine assimilation, and a spirit of tolerance and compassion, *some things have gotta go!*

The same idea applies to plants and flowers. Being tender, fragile things, they need special care and the right kind of soil. Equally important is the need to protect them from enemies that assault growth. Here in Southern California we have numerous varmints that have ways of knowing every time we stick little plants in the ground. Snails, slugs, spiders, and a half dozen other ugly creatures are ready and hungry for those juicy morsels. Funny thing about them—you seldom see them. They don't carry signs that say, "Better watch out, we're dangerous!" They don't even make noise. But give them a few hours, and you can forget about a colorful garden in the spring. If you want your stuff to survive, those pests have *gotta go*. You can't simply hope they will leave. Ignoring them never works.

In God's family, in order for fragile, tender lives to survive, the enemies of growth must be exterminated. We have been saying a lot of positive things and offering affirming suggestions thus far in this book, and we've needed that emphasis. But now it's time to address some of the negatives. In order for true, first-century fellowship to flourish, we'll need to get rid of the things that attack and assault twentieth-century folks in God's family. They won't leave on their own, believe me.

EXISTENCE: ESSENTIALS FOR PHYSICAL SURVIVAL

On several occasions in previous pages, I have mentioned the word *body* as a synonym for the family of God, the universal church. This word picture comes from 1 Corinthians 12 where Paul develops the idea in great detail. Personally, I love word pictures. They give us mental handles with which to grasp truth. Occasionally, we can draw on the analogy to such an extent that we are able to gain fresh insight into the biblical text. This happened to me recently when I came across a paraphrase of a section in 1 Corinthians 12. The author of the paraphrase is a surgeon. And here are his words:

> The body is one unit, though it is made up of many cells, and though all its cells are many, they form one body. . . . If the white cell should say, because I am not a brain cell, I do not belong to the body, it would not for that reason cease to be part of the body. And if the muscle cell should say to the optic nerve cell, because I am not an optic nerve, I do not belong to the body, it would not for that reason cease to be part of the body. If the whole body were an optic nerve cell, where would be the ability to walk? If the whole body were an auditory nerve, where would be the sense of sight? But in fact God has arranged the cells of the body, every one of them, just as He wanted them to be. If all cells are the same, where would the body be? As it is, there are many cells, but one body.[1]

The human body consists of cells. In order for us to exist, those cells must be kept healthy. This means certain things must be present: nutrition, exercise, cleanliness, rest. And other things must be absent: disease . . . alien germs from without and wild growths from within.

No competent physician takes disease lightly. At times the doctor may suggest surgery, occasionally *radical* surgery. Usually, he will prescribe medication and occasionally a specific diet and exercise program. That's all part of the plan for a healthy existence. It's a serious (and expensive) matter.

Obedience: Key to National Preservation

Now let's shift gears from the physical body to a national body. Let's take another look at the ancient Hebrew people. Just as health is essential for our survival, *obedience* was essential for theirs.

Under Joshua, the Israelis invaded and conquered Canaan. The big war finally ended as they possessed the land God had promised them. For the first time in almost five hundred years they had their own identity. No longer were they residents on foreign soil. This was now their land. It was time to reflect and give praise to Jehovah for His faithfulness. Joshua 23 records the events that transpired.

Review of God's Faithfulness

> Now it came about after many days, when the Lord had given rest to Israel from all their enemies on every side, and Joshua was old, advanced in years, that Joshua

called for all Israel, for their elders and their heads and their judges and their officers, and said to them, "I am old, advanced in years.

"And you have seen all that the Lord your God has done to all these nations because of you, for the Lord your God is He who has been fighting for you.

"See, I have apportioned to you these nations which remain as an inheritance for your tribes, with all the nations which I have cut off, from the Jordan even to the Great Sea toward the setting of the sun" (Josh. 23:1-4).

God had seen them through. How good He had been to His people! He gave them rest (v. 1) after the battle ended. He had "apportioned" the land as their inheritance. What a moment! It must have brought tears to their eyes to look out across those vast spaces and realize it was now all theirs to claim. God's grace, nothing more, nothing less, nothing else!

But it was no time to stop and relax. After the brief review, Joshua announces the need to press on and do a complete job of clearing out the remaining Canaanites in the land.

Command to God's People

Lest they get the impression that it was back to "business as usual," the commander-in-chief declared:

"And the Lord your God, He shall thrust them out from before you and drive them from before you; and you shall possess their land, just as the Lord your God promised you.

"Be very firm, then, to keep and do all that is written in the book of the law of Moses, so that you may not turn aside from it to the right hand or to the left, in order that you may not associate with these nations, these which remain among you, or mention the name of their gods, or make anyone swear by them, or serve them, or bow down to them.

"But you are to cling to the Lord your God, as you have done to this day.

"For the Lord has driven out great and strong nations from before you; and as for you, no man has stood before you to this day.

"One of your men puts to flight a thousand, for the Lord your God is He who fights for you, just as He promised you.

"So take diligent heed to yourselves to love the Lord your God" (Josh. 23:5-11).

Get the picture? "Don't mess around! There's more to be done . . . some things have gotta go!" The great concern on Joshua's part is that the Hebrews might drift into a holding pattern, you know, adopt a status quo mentality.

First, he talks about their *attitude*. "Be very firm," (v. 6) he begins. He warns them about slipping to the right or to the left—about wandering from the straight path of absolute obedience to the winding paths of rationalization.

Second, he mentions their *actions*. The whole issue of concern revolved around small pockets of heathen people in Canaan, tribes people not yet driven from the territory. In today's terms, the job of "mopping up" was not complete. These Canaanites formed a threat they did not dare ignore.

Was God that serious? You decide as you read again His words of warning found in Joshua 23:7:

- Do not associate with them.
- Do not mention the names of their gods.
- Do not make anyone swear by them.
- Do not serve them.
- Do not bow down to them.

I'd call that serious, wouldn't you? That helps explain why strong words like "thrust them out" and "drive them out" (v. 5) were used by Joshua. They were to get rid of all Canaanite influence, lest they become ensnared by it.

Third, he mentions their *alternative*. They were to love the Lord their God. They were to remain distinctively His, bearing His mark, declaring His message, being uncompromisingly pure and unique.

Warning from God's Heart

If you think the warning has been serious so far, read the rest:

"For if you ever go back and cling to the rest of these nations, these which remain among you, and intermarry with them, so that you associate with them and they with you, know with certainty that the Lord your God will not continue to drive these nations out from before you; but they shall be a snare and a trap to you, and a whip on your sides and thorns in your eyes, until you perish from off this good land which the Lord your God has given you" (Josh. 23:12–13).

"If you ever go back. . . ." Wow! That's what I call an attention getter. Don't think of this as merely a scare tactic, a manipulative threat. This was a divine warning with consequences attached. He's saying that if they ever lose their distinctiveness by clinging to those heathens, by intermarrying with them, by identifying with them, they could count on two sure and severe consequences:

1. Jehovah would not continue as their shield of protection.
2. They would suffer unmercifully at the hands of the Canaanites.

Let's not skip over those words in verse 13 too quickly:

- "They shall become a *snare and a trap* [for your feet]."
- "They shall become *a whip* [on your sides]."
- "They shall become *thorns* [in your eyes]."

Ouch! Joshua crowds his descriptive terms together to depict the intense misery and oppression that would accompany their failure. We'll be back to those three word pictures before we're through with this chapter, so don't forget them. They are the reasons *some things have gotta go.*

Final Farewell

After delivering that sobering word of warning, the old leader says good-by.

"Now behold, today I am going the way of all the earth, and you know in all your hearts and in all your souls that not one word of all the good words which the Lord your God spoke concerning you has failed; all have been fulfilled for you, not one of them has failed.

"And it shall come about that just as all the good words which the Lord your God spoke to you have come upon you, so the Lord will bring upon you all the threats, until He has destroyed you from off this good land which the Lord your God has given you.

"When you transgress the convenant of the Lord your God, which He commanded you, and go and serve other gods, and bow down to them, then the anger of the Lord will burn against you, and you shall perish quickly from off the good land which He has given you" (Josh. 23:14–16).

Okay, what happened? Let's track the story permanently etched in the record of inspired Hebrew history. Did they do as Joshua commanded? Did they obey?

CONSEQUENCE: ACCOUNT OF PERSONAL FAILURE

We'll need to look ahead into the early part of the book of Judges, the sequel to Joshua. It traces the events that came on the heels of Joshua's death. In brief, here's what transpired:

• Judges 1:19. "They could not drive out the inhabitants of the valley . . . they had iron chariots."
• Judges 1:27. ". . . so the Canaanites persisted in living in that land."
• Judges 1:28. "And it came about when Israel became strong, that they put the Canaanites to forced labor, but they did not drive them out completely."
• Judges 1:29. The same for Ephraim, ". . . they didn't drive out the Canaanites . . . so the Canaanites *lived* . . . among them." (Can you believe it?)
• Judges 1:30. Same for Zubulun.
• Judges 1:31–32. Same for Asher . . . they "lived among the Canaanites." (Note change in wording . . . clearly, a reversal of roles.)
• Judges 1:33. Same for Naphtali, who "lived among the Canaanites."

And, now, are you ready for the ultimate?

• Judges 1:34. "Then the Amorites [a Canaanite tribe] forced the sons of Dan [a Hebrew tribe] into the hill country, for they did not allow them to come down to the valley."

The tables turned! Instead of the Hebrews' keeping the upper hand, they loosened their grip on absolute obedience, they talked themselves out of Joshua's game plan, they opted for compromise with wrong . . . and they became victims instead of victors.

Compromises like that never work. We always get burned. Even though we rationalize around our weak decisions and tell ourselves that wicked associations really won't harm us ("they'll get better, our good will rub off on their *bad!*"), we get soiled in the process.

If you put on a pair of clean white gloves on a rainy day and then go out into the backyard to the flowerbed and pick up a glob of mud, trust me, the mud will never get "glovey." The gloves will definitely get muddy. Every time. In all my forty-nine years on earth, I have never seen glovey mud. Not once. In simple terms, that's what 1 Corinthians 15:33 is saying: "Do not be deceived: 'Bad company corrupts good morals.'"

Read on:

> Then Joshua the son of Nun, the servant of the Lord, died at the age of one hundred and ten.
>
> And they buried him in the territory of his inheritance in Timnath-heres, in the hill country of Ephraim, north of Mount Gaash.
>
> And all that generation also were gathered to their fathers; and there arose another generation after them who did not know the Lord, nor yet the work which He had done for Israel.
>
> Then the Sons of Israel did evil in the sight of the Lord, and served the Baals, and they forsook the Lord, the God of their fathers, who had brought them out of the land of Egypt, and followed other gods from among the gods of the peoples who were around them, and bowed themselves down to them; thus they provoked the Lord to anger.
>
> So they forsook the Lord and served Baal and the Ashtaroth.
>
> And the anger of the Lord burned against Israel, and He gave them into the hands of plunderers who plundered them; and He sold them into the hands of their enemies around them, so that they could no longer stand before their enemies.
>
> Wherever they went, the hand of the Lord was against them for evil, as the Lord had spoken and as the Lord had sworn to them, so that they were severely distressed (Judg. 2:8–15).

Tragic, tragic consequences. If only they had obeyed!

Earlier I asked you to remember the snare and trap, the whip, and the thorns that are mentioned in Joshua 23:13. Here's why. If you return to the account of Judges, chapter 1, you'll find that the Hebrews endured exactly what Joshua predicted.

"*Snare and trap.*" Not only did they allow the Canaanites to stay, they began living among them. This became "a snare and a trap" to them. By living among them, they learned their ways, they tolerated their gods, they soon adopted their lifestyle.

"*Whips in your side.*" These are words of greater intensity. One reputable authority suggests that the Hebrew phrase could also be rendered "scourges in your side." In Judges 1:34 we find that the Amorites *forced* the Israeli Danites into the hill country, and they did not allow them to come back down and live in the valley. A classic example of being whipped in their sides by the scourge of the Amorites!

"*Thorns in your eyes.*" Judges 3:5–6 describes how blinded the Hebrews became when they adopted the lifestyle of the heathen Canaanites and allowed themselves to be intimidated and whipped by them.

> And the sons of Israel lived among the Canaanites, the Hittites, the Amorites, the Perizzites, the Hivites, and the Jebusites; and they took their daughters for themselves as wives,and gave their own daughters to their sons, and served their gods (Judg. 3:5–6).

That spelled inescapable consequences! The rest of the book of Judges is one account after another of compromise, weakness, tyranny, and defeat.

RESISTANCE: HOPE FOR OPEN RELATIONSHIPS

If you've stayed with me thus far, you're to be commended! Ancient history is sometimes tough sledding, but when it is biblical history, it is rewarding, as you'll see. The application of all this is to our study on open relationships will prove helpful, I believe.

Let me review where we've been. Just as the human body cannot grow and survive unless disease is removed . . . and just as the national body of Israel could not remain strong and healthy unless Canaanite lifestyle was removed, so it is in the body of Christ. If our resistance breaks down, alien germs will cause us to lose our health and hinder our ability to function.

Things That Become Snares and Traps Have Gotta Go!

It is often the subtle things that become snares and traps for us—usually unspoken things that we communicate in our body language and our looks . . . attitudes that speak volumes to young, tender, and fragile folks struggling to survive.

Let me list a few such snares and traps:

Judgmental spirit
Intolerance
Suspicion
Prejudice
Pride
Exclusive attitude

Unkind, unfriendly remarks
Sophistication
Cynicism
Unforgiving reaction
Condemning looks
Unapproachability

We may not tell too many people off, but it sure is easy for us to freeze them out! And I do not believe we can expect to encourage and nourish open, unguarded relationships in an atmosphere of snares and traps, so some things have gotta go. What better place to start ridding ourselves of these snares and traps than the list just mentioned!

Things That Become Whips Have Gotta Go!

People come to us personally, or they visit our churches, greatly in need of affirmation, authentic love, compassion, big doses of esteem, hope, and forgiveness—all those things you've been reading about in the first eight chapters. They need release from the strange hold of self-imposed guilt and relief from the I'm-no-good-I'm-only-a-worm syndrome.

They may reach out in one of many ways . . . but if "the whip" routine is there to assault, the results are often disastrous. Here are a few whips which you may have either encountered or used yourself!

• Attempting to pressure people to "straighten up" or "snap out of it" before they're able to get on their feet.
• Forcing people to become more and more like we are—"if you really want to be mature."
• Expecting adherence to highly structured demands, tight-fisted rules, and rigid requirements.
• Placing the painful twist of legalistic demands, that is, tightening the screws on others to give up certain habits and adapt to our set of preferences or convictions, the old "shape up or ship out" stiff-arm.

Whips like these will beat you to death, like scourges in your side. And you'll not be given the freedom to learn, to discover, to fail, or to be your own person.

Things That Become Thorns Have Gotta Go!

"Thorns" are from without. They are things we bring to the body that cause offense and disease to other members—alien germs that enter into weakened, bruised, and broken places. And remember, thorns blind.

Now let's take a look at a few such thorns:

• Persisting in unchecked, willful sin without genuine repentance.
• Deliberately operating under the control of the flesh, walking contrary to the will of God in unashamed carnality.
• Hiding behind blame or self-pity or some other rationalization to justify wrong actions . . . and refusing to face the truth.
• Living a lie, taking unfair advantage of young, tender believers who are impressionable and naive.

• Practicing hypocritical spiritual leadership, ignoring the fact that some day the truth will be known and many will be disillusioned.

Enough said. These things have gotta go!

I close on a positive note with these wise words—not my own—that describe the inestimable value of affirmation. I wish there were some way you and I could be sufficiently convinced to commit them to memory.

Life breaks down not so much because of the terrible things that happen to us. Life breaks down because so few good things have happened to us. Just a few along the way can be like branches we can cling to as we climb up a mountain trail. No matter how steep the ascent, we can make it, if from time to time along the trail someone communicates to us that he or she loves us and therefore we are important.[2]

DISCUSSION IDEAS AND QUESTIONS

• Go back to the first part of chapter 9 and reread the surgeon's paraphrase of those verses out of 1 Corinthians 12. Talk about how it applies to the body of Christ. In what condition are the "cells" you spend your time with—the other Christians in your life? Are you strengthening your walk?

• As we looked through Joshua 23, we found some strong words against compromise and associating too closely with the wrong crowd. What have you found that helps you maintain good and healthy associations? If this is a battle, talk about your struggle. Ask for prayer.

• Remember the snares and traps, whips, and thorns? It might be helpful to go back into the chapter and refresh your memory. In your own words, define each of the three.

• As you think about your home, are there any snares and traps, whips, or thorns that need to be removed? It may take an exceptional amount of courage, but try to name a few.

• On a positive note, can you think of a Christian who might be in need of some affirmation? Maybe there is someone who has suffered from the attack of another's tongue or attitude. How about giving him or her a phone call . . . or writing a brief letter of sincere interest? Make yourself available as a healing agent. It could be exciting!

10

Choose
for Yourself

It is easy to get so hot and bothered about the insignificant, we miss the significant . . . to focus on little petty stuff with such intensity, we lose sight of the big picture.

I was reminded of that when I read of the crash of an Eastern Airlines jumbo jet in the Florida Everglades. The plane was the now-famous flight 401, bound for Miami from New York City, with a heavy load of holiday passengers. As the huge aircraft approached the Miami Airport for its landing, a light that indicates proper deployment of the landing gear failed to come on. The plane flew in a large, looping circle over the swamps of the Everglades while the cockpit crew checked out the light failure. Their question was this: Had the landing gear actually not deployed or was it just the light bulb that was defective?

To begin with, the flight engineer fiddled with the bulb. He tried to remove it, but it wouldn't budge. Another member of the crew became curious and tried to help him out . . . and then another. By and by, if you can believe it, all eyes were on the little light bulb that refused to be dislodged from its socket. No one noticed that the plane was losing altitude. Finally, it flew right into the swamp. Many were killed in that plane crash. While an experienced crew of high-priced and seasoned pilots messed around with a seventy-five-cent light bulb, an entire airplane and many of its passengers were lost. The crew momentarily forgot the most basic of all rules in the air—"Don't forget to fly the airplane."

That same thing can happen in a local church. The pastor can be so busy fighting petty fires and focusing so much of his attention on insignificant issues that he loses sight of what church is all about. It is possible for the church to have so many activities, programs, clubs, projects, committee meetings, banquets, and community involvements—so many wheels spinning without really accomplishing anything of eternal significance—that the congregation forgets its primary objective. Many churches are like that impressive invention which had hundreds of wheels, coils, gears, pulleys, belts, bells, and lights which all went around and rang and flashed at the touch of a button. When the inventor was asked about the function of the weird machine, he replied, "What does it do? Oh, it doesn't *do* anything, but doesn't it run beautifully?"

A PRIMARY OBJECTIVE

Ask around. See if folks in your church know why the ministry exists. Be ready for a surprise. Don't be shocked if most of them shrug and say, "Oh, I don't know—to hear somebody preach, I guess . . . we're here just to be fed." It is not an exaggeration to say that the common opinion in many evangelical churches is just that—"We're here to be informed." As important as preaching may be (and I really believe in good preaching), it is only a part of the greater objective. The church is called a body, remember? We gather for more reasons than simply to take in more and more food.

Think of your family. I doubt that you would say, "Our family is a family because we eat together. That's why we are in existence. We eat often and we eat a lot. The food is so nourishing, so well-prepared, and always served right on time. We love to eat! Because of that, we're a family." No, a family shows itself to be a family in ways other than gathering at a dining-room table loaded with food. For instance:

• By how it responds to those who hurt.
• By the way it listens when family members talk.
• By the extent to which it reaches out and supports those who cannot keep up.
• By how it communicates affirmation . . . how it sticks together through the hard times . . . how it laughs at fun times.
• By the basis on which it establishes accountability, responsibility, and evaluation.
• By allowing room for its members to express true feelings—joy, grief, anger, elation, doubt, disagreement, anticipation, loss, disillusionment, disappointment, pleasure, pain—the full spectrum.

It is easy to see that a family is much more than taking in good food. And so is a church. The church is a training base, and we must never forget it! It is a place where God's family members are encouraged to grow; to learn; to exercise; to find rest, refreshment, and stability for facing life's realities . . . a body of fellow strugglers who meet together and relate openly, honestly, and freely. It is a place of prayer and quiet solitude . . . an anvil where ideas are hammered out and convictions take shape . . . a hospital for those needing time and room to heal . . . a place where compassion and forgiveness and grace are dispensed just as readily and regularly as information. That's the big picture. If we lose sight of that we're headed for a swamp, full throttle.

Let me go back to the example of the Statue of Liberty I used previously, to those moving words of Emma Lazarus: "Give me your tired, your poor, your huddled masses . . . the wretched . . . the homeless, tempest-tost."[1] I honestly wonder if today's church hasn't rewritten those lines to read:

> "Give me your ignorant, and I will instruct
> (but don't expect us to get involved)."

Or:

> "Give me your wealthy, and I will buy and invest
> (but don't ask us to relate)."

Or:

> "Give me your strong and your willing, and I will keep
> them busy
> (but don't expect much compassion)."

In other words, "If you have life pretty much together; if your theology is screwed down tightly; if you're willing to give, but not in need of receiving anything other than some sermons, songs, and superficial talk, let's get together." Somehow, that doesn't seem anywhere near the message Jesus modeled. He touched people, He made room for relationships. He taught, but He never taught just for the sake of filling up heads like gas tanks at a pump. With Him love was linked with truth; compassion was never far behind command. The balance in His life makes a bold statement, doesn't it?

If you pick up nothing else from these pages, don't miss this: Unguarded, open relationships within the body of Christ are just as important as the nourishing, accurate dispensing of scriptural truth. We need both. There must be meaningful fellowship, not just scholarship. To have one without the other results in an unbalanced and unhealthy church. It really is a matter of choice, however. No one can force a congregation to believe this.

DECISIONS THAT ENCOURAGE RELATIONSHIPS

Let's return to the biblical story we've been following throughout this book. We have come through the Exodus and the sea with Moses and the Hebrews. We have arrived at Canaan, invaded and inhabited the country, and heard the warnings about snares and traps, whips, and thorns. We have come to admire Joshua as a courageous leader who told the truth, regardless. The sad news is that he is near death. He knows it. As he looks into the faces of those he's led into the promised land, he has mixed emotions. He is pleased at what they have accomplished, but he is uneasy over their tendency toward passivity. Like a wise parent with an irresponsible child, Joshua knows there are painful consequences awaiting the people if they do not heed God's warnings. He decides to tell it straight. They need to hear it before he passes off the scene.

The Major Factor

Who knows how many times he must have repeated his concern? "Don't forget to finish the task. Those Canaanites must be removed. Keep on loving and obeying Jehovah. Don't lose your distinctiveness now that you are living in homes you didn't build and eating from trees you didn't plant. Stay strong!" Familiar words are these:

"'And you crossed the Jordan and came to Jericho; and the citizens of Jericho fought against you, and the Amorite and the Perizzite and the Canaanite and the Hittite and the Girgashite, the Hivite and the Jebusite. Thus I gave them into your hand.

"'Then I sent the hornet before you and it drove out the two kings of the Amorites from before you, but not by your sword or your bow.

"'And I gave you a land on which you had not labored, and cities which you had not built, and you have lived in them; you are eating of vineyards, and olive groves which you did not plant'" (Josh. 24:11–13).

God had done it all. But there is one major factor He left for them to act upon . . . one thing that could make or break their entire future. Do you know what it was? They had the freedom to choose for themselves. Joshua says so.

"Now, therefore, fear the Lord and serve Him in sincerity and truth; and put away the gods which your fathers served beyond the River and in Egypt, and serve the Lord.

"And if it is disagreeable in your sight to serve the Lord, choose for yourselves today whom you will serve: whether the gods which your fathers served which were beyond the River, or the gods of the Amorites in whose land you are living; but as for me and my house, we will serve the Lord" (Josh. 24:14–15).

Personal righteousness does not happen because somebody requires and commands it of us. Obedience cannot be legislated. Godliness cannot be forced. People don't live pure lives due to warnings and threats. These things must come from the heart as a result of right choices.

Are you a superintense brother or sister—the type who relies on firm, strong commands and a good deal of push and shove? Let me level with you. I'll drop my guard and admit that I spent far too many years in my life marching to that drumbeat . . . lots of frowns and demands, long drawn-out requirements that prompted guilt but never did much for desire. People got the message, but they really didn't change that much. I burned up enormous amounts of internal energy, but in the final analysis most of it was for naught. That method is about as effective as pushing a rope.

People respond much better to personal models than to verbal demands. They are motivated much more by the Joshua method of leadership ("as for me and my house, we will serve the Lord, but you must choose for yourself") than by the rip-snorting, smoke-and-fire screams and threats of the uptight types. It's been my observation in recent years (I learned this *so* late!) that most Christians really don't want to live mediocre lives, but neither do they desire to be driven like cattle. Folks respond more like sheep than steers.

I received this letter recently.

Dear Chuck,

I was deeply moved by your talk on Martin Luther. In fact, I tried to sing with you at the end, but I cried instead. I feel so small. Our heros look so big, so deep, so much better than me. I'm so comfortable. And so mediocre.

I want to know something. When you were 27, were you like you are now? Had you already read all the right books? Did you know all the hymns? More importantly, were you as deep as you are now? Was Christ so real in your life that your words pierced people's hearts? I ask that because I want to know if there is any hope for me. I am not broad, nor very deep. I wasn't raised in the church. I don't know the hymns. I still have to read them in the hymnal. I wasn't raised to be a big reader, either. I want to read the right books, but I get very frustrated when I go to the Christian bookstore. Who needs books like "Pray Your Way to Big Bucks," "If You're Sick—You're a Lousy Christian," "Positive Thinking—Never Say 'Sin'" or a book full of goofy rhymes to replace talking with God.

I've also heard you say that one becomes like those with whom he spends his time. I'm surrounded by mediocre people. The more I mature in the Lord, the fewer people I find worth imitating. I'm not so mature, though, that God is the only model . . . you are a model for me . . . I want to know—are you like my other "models"? Do you rip your wife apart in front of other married people? . . . Do you talk big but turn wimpy when it's time for action? Are you worth imitating?

How can I be excellent? I don't care about impressing anyone. I just don't want to be mediocre.

Do you know what that young man wants? He wants a model. He wants to be sure, however, that the model is authentic. I appreciate his questions. He's looking for ways to move from mediocrity to maturity, but he is not anxious to jump on any bandwagon. He's struggling with some basic choices. He doesn't need a preacher like me screaming at him to shape up or ship out. He needs room to work through some choices so that his life reflects genuine godlikeness. The major factor is this: *He must choose for himself.* No one else can make him godly.

So it was in Joshua's day. The leader had made up his mind. He and his household would serve the Lord, no question about that. But when it came to everyone else, "Choose for yourselves today whom you will serve. . . ." My! I wish I had adopted that method of leading earlier in my ministry. I could have saved myself so much anxiety, and the sheep I led would have been encouraged by my model rather than harrassed by my demands.

Three Essential Parts

With the freedom to choose, the Hebrews declared their intentions. Drawn by Joshua's commitment, they chose to align themselves with his cause. His desires became their desires *by choice*. His dedication became their dedication *by choice*. If you look deeply into this section of the narrative you can find three essential parts in their decision.

1. They chose to "fear the Lord" (v. 14). In other words, they chose to hold Him, not the Canaanite culture, in awesome respect, to revere Him, to let Him be the standard of their lives.

2. They chose to "serve the Lord" (v. 14). It was their voluntary decision to "serve Him in sincerity." On three subsequent occasions they declared their unequivocal commitment to follow Him—"we will serve the Lord" (vv. 18, 21, 24).

3. They chose to "obey His voice" (v. 24). They decided to listen to His counsel and to heed His advice. They deliberately announced their decision to respond in obedience.

Joshua must have beamed from ear to ear. He responded with these words: "You are witnesses against yourselves that you have chosen for yourselves the Lord, to serve Him." And they said, "We are witnesses" (Josh. 24:22).

There it is again, "you have chosen for yourselves." There isn't anything more encouraging to the leader of a congregation than this, when they voluntarily decide to obey the Lord, regardless. Why? Because choices have a direct bearing on behavior.

> . . . we have very little direct control over our emotions, but we have maximum control over our behavior. In other words, we can change our feelings with our will only to a certain degree, whereas our behavior is under the complete and maximum control of our will.[2]

This helps pastors realize that messages which simply arouse a lot of emotion aren't nearly as vital as those directed to the will. Emotions heat up or cool off within a brief span of time, but when truth makes an impact on the will, lives begin to change.

Ultimate Benefit

What ultimately happens when our choices are linked to God's directives? (This is the best part of all!) He offers His true and lasting support. He takes us at our word, and He weaves His power into the fabric of our lives. In place of our turmoil, He brings peace. Instead of our weakness and instability, He provides strength and stability.

Are you beginning to get serious about dropping your guard? Have you come to the place where you're willing to admit that a church is more than a pulpit and pews? Do relationships matter enough to you that it's worth the effort and risk for you to get involved in others' lives? Are those some of the choices you are making? If so, I have some great news for you. God will honor and support such choices. He will supplement your desires with His ability. Even when you don't realize it, He will be working behind the scenes, bringing many of your dreams to reality.

When we act upon scriptural truth, the Lord offers His divine assistance. The secret, however, is that we make the right choices . . . not just consider the options.

One of the most familiar stories Jesus told is recorded in Matthew 7:24-27. As soon as you begin reading it, you'll remember it.

> "Therefore every one who hears these words of Mine, and acts upon them, may be compared to a wise man, who built his house upon the rock.
> "And the rain descended, and the floods came, and the winds blew, and burst against that house; and yet it did not fall, for it had been founded upon the rock.
> "And every one who hears these words of Mine, and does not act upon them, will be like a foolish man, who built his house upon the sand.
> "And the rain descended, and the floods came, and the winds blew, and burst against that house; and it fell and great was its fall" (Matt. 7:24-27).

What an amazing difference! A close look will reveal the reason one house stood and the other house fell. The first was occupied by "one who hears these words of Mine and acts upon them," but the second was occupied by "one who hears . . . and does not act upon them." It boiled down to choice, didn't it? Jesus isn't concerned with literal houses and literal rocks and sand. These are symbols of life and the choices we make that result in whether we stand or fall. If right choices are made, it's like building our lives on rock. They will stand the test of time.

BOTTOM LINE: WHAT DO YOU CHOOSE?

Maybe it's time to ask a couple of hard questions. Are you one who hears and then acts on what God says? Or are you one who simply hears and keeps all the options open? It sure is easy to mess around with insignificant stuff and miss the big picture. Remember flight 401? You and I are surrounded by people who focus on needless incidentals and wind up in the swamp.

Jesus helps clear away the smoke screen. He's a master at bringing us to terms with things that really matter. He not only offers us His insight so we can see the big picture, He offers us Himself. Perhaps you have been so busy doing church work, keeping all those wheels and gears turning, you've missed the most basic point of all . . . we cannot be rightly related to others until we are rightly related to Him. Coming to know Him, by faith, moves our lives from shifting sand to a solid rock. Could it be—could it *possibly* be—that you have lived all your life having never made the most important choice of all? Not one of us is programmed to be righteous. It's a matter of choice. Choosing to let Christ come into your life is not insignificant. He is the only One who can give you the wisdom you need to handle the rains, the floods, and the winds that are sure to assault your life. Give some serious thought to turning your life over to Christ. Believe me, it's no insignificant decision.

In fact, in comparison to choosing Christ, all other decisions fall into the category of seventy-five-cent light bulbs.

DISCUSSION IDEAS AND QUESTIONS

• This has been a chapter about the value of right choices. Time and again we've considered how important they are. Why is that true? Can you think of a particular decision you made that had life-changing ramifications? Talk about it.

• In thinking about the basic purpose of the church, answer this question in your own words: What's the reason for the existence of the body of Christ? Try to be brief and to the point.

• Is your day full of what seems to be seventy-five-cent-light-bulb concerns instead of big-picture essentials? Discuss the frustrations that accompany such struggles.

• Joshua's style of leadership is admirable. He modeled the message he proclaimed. He didn't demand or force the people to adopt his convictions, but he did declare where he stood. Do you find that appealing? Are you more persuaded to follow Joshua's approach or do you prefer a stronger stance? If you are a leader, what is your style?

• As the people voluntarily aligned themselves with Joshua and his household, they chose to fear, to serve, and to obey the Lord. What did that imply? When would it be most difficult to carry out?

• Read again the story Jesus told (Matt. 7:24–27). Talk a little about building a life on sand. What does "sand" represent? Can a life built on sand ever be shifted over to a rock foundation? How? Be very specific.

• Go back to the last page of chapter 10. Read the section under "Bottom Line." Have you ever made that choice? Describe in a few sentences how and when you chose to have Christ come into your life.

11

The Necessity
of Accountability

I drive a spotless, white 1979 Volkswagen Superbeetle convertible. It's a fun little car, and I treat it with the kind of kidglove care and massive doses of T.L.C. that only vintage car lovers can understand. Hopefully, it will be around for many, many years. There are few things to compare with the feeling of zipping along with the top down on a breezy sun-drenched afternoon. It sorta flushes out my nervous system and keeps me from getting too serious about myself. There's only one problem, I'm a marked man! My white and shining little bug (with Porsche wheels and Michelin sneakers!) has a way of attracting a lot of attention, even when I'm not aware of it, which is illustrated by the following letter that I received several months ago.

Dear Pastor Chuck:

Hello! Just a short note to say that we have been enjoying very much your series on relationships. Your message last Sunday on "Choose for Yourself" was especially inspiring as we were motivated to make a definite conscious decision to follow and trust Jesus Christ.

A group of men from our Sunday school class meets each Wednesday morning at seven in Fullerton to discuss and pray over some of the many choices involved in being husbands, friends, employees, etc., from a Christian point of view. As a matter of fact, just today we saw someone make a definite, conscious decision as two of us drove from La Habra to Fullerton for our weekly time together. I'll set the scene . . .

After setting our alarms at what we thought was plenty early to allow time to shower, shave, and take out the trash before leaving, we found ourselves late! Well, after meeting at my friend's house to share a ride, we headed down Harbor Boulevard towards Fullerton, late and probably going a little too fast! Yep, you guessed it, good ol' Murphy caught us. You know, he's the guy that said, "If a traffic light can change when you're late, IT WILL!" So, there we sat, 7:10 A.M. at the intersection of Harbor and Brea Boulevard, late for our 7 A.M. meeting and thinking we'd have to wait through the whole cycle of light changes.

Using the time to tuck in our shirts and comb our hair, we suddenly noticed a small, white, soft-shelled insect of a car headed up Brea Boulevard from west of Harbor, also caught in the same exact predicament—STUCK AT THE LIGHT! The surprisingly familiar face inside looked rushed, yet willing to wait it out. All of a sudden, the driver's head (almost as if powered by an outside force) furtively and daringly glanced right, then left, into the rear-view mirror, and WHOOOSH!!!! Right through the red light!

"Brother, was that who I thought it was running that red light?"

"If you thought it was who I thought it was, then who you thought it was was *exactly* who I thought it was!"

"What shall we do?"

"Let's write up a complete account of this late breaking story and submit it to *Moody Monthly, Christianity Today, Leadership, Wittenburg Door,* and *Dad's Only* ("Come on Junior, it's Saturday morning, so let's go run some red lights together!").

Before mailing off our own "Choose for Yourself" sermon, we were struck from above with an option that, if exercised, would alleviate the whole scene of the TV crews on the front porch, crying wife, and "talk to my lawyer" episodes. It just so happens that the same two of us who observed the crime have breakfast together every Wednesday at 8 A.M. after our small-group at Randy's Coffee Shop in Fullerton. We felt if that certain individual who drives the white, soft-shelled insect would show up for breakfast on either Wednesday, November 25, or on Wednesday, December 2, at 8 A.M. at Randy's Coffee Shop, we could avoid the whole media smear! The article would be mailed at 9:00 A.M. on Wednesday, December 2, if there's a no-show. If you do show, we'll identify ourselves and even treat you to breakfast . . . if we choose . . . CHOOSE FOR YOURSELF!!!!

Naturally, it was *unsigned.* Well, I was caught redhanded by the rascals. So I decided to show up at the coffee shop bright and early on November 25. I stuck a big sign on my shirt that read "Guilty as Charged." I walked up to the startled waitress at 7:45 that morning and asked her to seat me at a table where several could join me. I told her I was meeting with some Pharisees that morning. She put some menus down and walked away shaking her head. At eight o'clock sharp in they walked! When we all had a laugh at my sign, I turned it over. On the back I had written "He who is without sin, let him cast the first stone!" They bought my breakfast.

If I live to the ripe old age of 100, I doubt that I'll ever forget that whole episode. Every time I'm tempted to run a light, the letter comes back to haunt me . . . one of the many benefits of accountability!

Accountability: What It Is and Isn't

I've purposely saved the subject of accountability for the latter part of my book. The major reason for this is that I wanted you to understand the full picture of unguarded, close, loving, meaningful relationships *before* we dealt with this particular subject. Without that backdrop, accountability could carry with it a harsh and abrasive sound.

Just the term sounds pretty legal, doesn't it? And rightly so, for that's the way we use it most often. If we go to the bank and secure a loan, we are legally responsible to pay it back. That's *financial* accountability. If we get a job, we agree to work under certain terms and regulations. That's *occupational* accountability. If we enroll in a university and decide on a curriculum that requires our being a student at the school, studying under various faculty members, we must fulfill the course requirements, including homework and examinations in order to get a degree. That's *academic* accountability.

There's usually no problem with this kind of accountability—we consider it a matter of good business dealings or standard educational expectations. But when someone mentions our being accountable to others outside those "legal" settings, our tendency is to recoil. We resist the idea of mixing something as exacting as accountability with something as loving and encouraging as our spiritual lives, don't we? To be accountable to a boss is not only acceptable, it's essential. In fact, those who resist it and don't cooperate with it wind up unemployed. But why not be accountable to someone who loves me and wants what is best for me? What's so wrong with *friendship* accountability, especially if it has what it takes to improve and enhance our walk with God? Perhaps our secret resistance is yet another proof of what isolationists we really are.

Nontechnical Definition

Rather than scope out some scholarly definition, let's consider this practical one. When I use the term *accountability*, I have several things in mind as it relates to the subject matter of this book. Being accountable includes:

- Being willing to explain one's actions.
- Being open, unguarded, and nondefensive about one's motives.
- Answering for one's life.
- Supplying the reasons why.

Again, if you take away the context of love and affirmation, those aspects of accountability could seem terribly galling. And if we erased the all-important factor of friendship, we could find ourselves saying, "That's none of your business." So let's not do that. Let's understand that when I speak of accountability, I'm referring to one of the involvements, a by-product if you please, of a deep and meaningful relationship with one or a few intimate friends. In that sense, therefore, I'm talking about voluntary accountability.

The more I think about accountability, the more I realize why it is so rare. It requires at least four character traits that are not normally found in folks who are satisfied to live mediocre lives—and that's a whole lot of people! The qualities are:

- *Vulnerability* . . . capable of being wounded, open, and unguarded. Non-defensives.
- *Teachability* . . . anxious to learn. Humble, quick to hear, willing to change, inviting advice.
- *Honesty* . . . committed to the truth. Hating anything phony, counterfeit, or false. Models sincerity.
- *Availability* . . . touchable, accessible. Can be interrupted. Willing to meet on a regular basis.

See why this is so rare? Offhand, how many people can you name who possess such valuable traits?

Accountability on a personal level is not that unusual. Or perhaps I should say *should* not be that unusual. When two people marry and choose to give up their independent single life, they opt for mutual accountability. In most marriages I'm acquainted with (this certainly applies to mine), when one of the mates is gone much, much longer than the other anticipated, an explanation is expected and *willingly* provided. If one goes home and finds a sleek new speedboat in the driveway, more is expected than an exuberant, "Isn't it beautiful!"

Pertinent Scripture

What is true between partners in a marriage is equally true among members in the body of Christ. Take a look at Hebrews 13:16–17:

> And do not neglect doing good and sharing; for with such sacrifices God is pleased.
> Obey your leaders, and submit to them; for they keep watch over your souls, as those who will give an account. Let them do this with joy and not with grief, for this would be unprofitable for you (Heb. 13:16–17).

I'd say that's pretty clear, wouldn't you? Pastors, priests, bishops, and other leaders who God selects for places of great responsibility (even though they themselves are imperfect and human) are those who "keep watch over your souls." And what about the leaders? Are they not also responsible? Indeed they are! They, too, need people around them who have the freedom to ask why and who feel the liberty to talk about any issue.

Solomon offers good counsel: "Faithful are the wounds of a friend, But deceitful are the kisses of an enemy" (Prov. 27:6). We'll come back to this verse later on in the chapter, but let's probe below the surface of the words for a few moments. Some time ago I did a careful investigastion of this proverb, searching out the original meanings of the terms and some of the syntactical significance of the Hebrew language. I came up with a paraphrase:

> Trustworthy are the bruises caused by the wounding of one who loves you, but deceitful are the kisses (of flattery) from those who hate you.

When someone knows us well enough and therefore loves us deeply enough to "wound" us with the truth, the bruises that remain (and they *are* bruises) are trustworthy, reliable. This is true for both the leader and the led. Please note that everybody is not "fair game." Some people who believe they have "the gift of criticism" (every church has a few) think they have the right to take on whomever. But this proverb says that reproofs from *"a friend"* (one who knows you well and loves you intensely) are reliable and beneficial. Strangers or casual acquaintances do not have the wholesale freedom to punch people's lights out. That isn't accountability, that's brutality. Solomon is not advocating a watchdog mentality among casual acquaintances. He's attempting to convince us of the value of having a few folks so near and dear to us that they have the freedom to "bruise" us with the truth. Such friends are worthy of our trust.

Extreme Dangers

It's at this very juncture that some things need to be added, lest I turn a few who read these words into a pack of vultures with a Gestapo mindset. Actually, there are two extremes we need to be aware of and guard against—being too severe and being too loose.

1. *We are not to be too severe.* When I think of this extreme, I think of a man who lived toward the end of the first century. His name was Diotrephes. John mentions him in his third letter:

> I wrote something to the church; but Diotrephes, who loves to be first among them, does not accept what we say.
> For this reason, if I come, I will call attention to his deeds which he does, unjustly accusing us with wicked words; and not satisfied with this, neither does he himself receive the brethren, and he forbids those who desire to do so, and puts them out of the church.
> Beloved, do not imitate what is evil, but what is good. The one who does good is of God; the one who does evil has not seen God (3 John 9–11).

What a savage! I get the distinct impression that Diotrephes would have made a great first-century Hitler . . . or Attila the Hun. I mean, when that guy took over the leadership, he *took over*. John correctly condemns such oppressive measures.

The whole tenor of Scripture stands against such a legalistic, militant, rigid accountability. It is pharisaical and judgmental, sadly lacking in servanthood. This extreme style uses accountability to control and manipulate people, actions never justified in Scripture.

2. *We are not to be too loose.* The Corinthians fell into this trap. They were the classic "live and let live" congregation who had no standard of purity and weren't about to concern themselves with such.

> It is actually reported that there is immorality among you, and immorality of such kind as does not exist even among the Gentiles, that someone has his father's wife.
>
> And you have become arrogant, and have not mourned instead, in order that the one who had done this deed might be removed from your midst.
>
> For I, on my part, though absent in body but present in spirit, have already judged him who has so committed this, as though I were present (1 Cor. 5:1–3).

These folks sound a lot like the Hebrews in the book of Judges where everyone wound up doing what was right in his own eyes. But the sad fact is that in Corinth they not only refused to hold the man accountable and deal with his sinful, shameful, scandalous actions, they justified their actions by claiming *grace* as their reason.

Both extremes are dangerous and damaging. I am not advocating that we become severe and stern saints with a watchdog mentality like Diotrephes. But neither is the answer a casual, "who-really-cares?" approach like the Corinthians employed. Obviously, the world prefers the latter extreme, and this has its own tragic consequences. Not only does secular society "live and let live," it also advocates "die and let die."

I was reminded of that when I read the report of the late actor William Holden's death. It began:

> William Holden was a private man, and he died a very private death. Alone in his apartment in Santa Monica, Calif., he bled to death from a gash in his forehead caused by a drunken fall against his bedside table. It was four or five days later that his body was found. He was 63.[1]

Does this seem as incredible to you as it does to me? There was a famous man over 60 years old whose name was a household word in the film industry and among moviegoers the world over. He'd been making movies for over four decades, yet he was dead for "four or five days" before he was found . . . or even missed. How could it be? There's a hint in the closing paragraph of that same article: "Holden guarded his privacy with increasing vigilance."

Privacy is one thing. We all need it, no one would deny that. But being so out of touch and unaccountable? That's the part no one can justify. There are times when it is essential that someone say *something*. Sometimes it's a matter of life and death that somebody speak up.

Take the case of Martin Niemoller, a Lutheran pastor in Germany in the 1930s. Here is his often-quoted, honest confession:

> In Germany they came first for the communists, and I didn't speak up because I wasn't a communist. Then they came for the Jews, and I didn't speak up because I wasn't a Jew. Then they came for the trade unionists, and I didn't speak up because I wasn't a trade unionist. Then they came for the Catholics, and I didn't speak up because I was a Protestant. Then they came for me, and by that time no one was left to speak up.

Examples from Scripture

There is nothing quite so reassuring as scriptural support. Experience is fine and illustrations from life help bring light on the subject, but when we can find passages and verses from the Bible, we've got an open-and-shut case. Is accountability scriptural? Does God really stand behind the things we are considering in this chapter? Indeed he does.

Vertical and Horizontal Accountability

It is clearly stated in the New Testament that the members of Christ's body are accountable to the Head. Who hasn't thought of the implications of Jesus' words?

> "The good man out of his good treasure brings forth what is good; and the evil man out of his evil treasure brings forth what is evil.
> "And I say to you, that every careless word that men shall speak, they shall render account for it in the day of judgment" (Matt. 12:35–36).

In terse, clear terms Paul adds the fact that "each one of us shall give account of himself to God" (Rom. 14:12).

God doesn't toss His people into a heap and expect them to somehow wind up in glory. He cares about His own. He, in fact, holds us accountable for the way we live. No doubt about it, we'll answer to our Lord. There *will be* vertical accountability. And such accountability will be the basis of our heavenly rewards (2 Cor. 5:10).

But accountability doesn't stop here, it also applies horizontally.

> Let love be without hypocrisy. Abhor what is evil; cling to what is good.
> Be devoted to one another in brotherly love; give preference to one another in honor; not lagging behind in diligence, fervent in spirit, serving the Lord; rejoicing in hope, persevering in tribulation, devoted to prayer, contributing to the needs of the saints, practicing hospitality.
> Bless those who persecute you; bless and curse not. Rejoice with those who rejoice, and weep with those who weep.

Be of the same mind toward one another; do not be haughty in mind, but associate with the lowly. Do not be wise in your own estimation (Rom. 12:9-16).

Now we who are strong ought to bear the weaknesses of those without strength and not just please ourselves.

Let each of us please his neighbor for his good, to his edification.

And concerning you, my brethren, I myself also am convinced that you yourselves are full of goodness, filled with all knowledge, and able also to admonish one another (Rom. 15:1-2, 14).

We are not islands of independence, living lives free of one another. We are made to relate, to blend into one another, to touch one another, to answer to one another.

In her fine little book *Up with Worship*, Anne Orlund uses a splendid word picture to communicate this very point.

Every congregation has a choice to be one of two things. You can choose to be a bag of marbles, single units that don't affect each other except in collision. On Sunday morning you can choose to go to church or to sleep in: who really cares whether there are 192 or 193 marbles in a bag?

Or you can choose to be a bag of grapes. The juices begin to mingle, and there is no way to extricate yourselves if you tried. Each is part of all. Part of the fragrance. Part of the "stuff."[2]

Sometimes we "grapes" really bleed and hurt. At such times it is not God's desire that we tighten our belts and plow right on. Remember 1 Corinthians 12:26-27?

And if one member suffers, all the members suffer with it; if one member is honored, all the members rejoice with it.

Now you are Christ's body, and individually members of it.

And what about those occasions when fellow members fall into a slump and begin to walk in a carnal manner, operating their lives from the realm of the flesh instead of the Spirit? Again, do we ignore them and shrug it off thinking, "Well, that's none of my business." No, we are given some explicit biblical counsel regarding this.

If we live by the Spirit, let us also walk by the Spirit.

Let us not become boastful, challenging one another, envying one another.

Brethren, even if a man is caught in any trespass, you who are spiritual, restore such a one in a spirit of gentleness; each one looking to yourself, lest you too be tempted.

Bear one another's burdens, and thus fulfill the law of Christ (Ga. 5:25-26; 6:1-2).

Unlike the sign on delicate pieces of china in a gift shop, God directs us—
"*Please Touch.*" For sure, we do need to handle with care, but the worst thing
we can do is pass by our brother's or sister's carnality as if it's of no concern
to us.

Who can say how many Christians who have defected could have been
rescued and restored had someone been honest enough to step in and assist
them back to decency and godliness? Ideally, we would hope the person would
want help . . . but not all do. Those who choose to be accountable have the
greatest hope of change.

One experienced author-counselor writes:

> . . . Behavioral sciences in recent years have expounded the simple truth that
> "behavior that is observed changes." People who are accountable by their own
> choice to a group of friends, to a therapy group, to a psychiatrist or a pastoral
> counselor, to a study group or prayer group, are people who are serious about
> changing their behavior, and they are finding that change is possible.
>
> Studies done in factories have proven that both quality and quantity of work
> increase when the employees know that they are being observed. If only God
> knows what I am doing, since I know He won't tell, I tend to make all kinds of
> excuses for myself. But if I must report to another or a group of others, I begin to
> monitor my behavior. If someone is keeping an eye on me, my behavior improves.[3]

When we are in need, people to whom we are closely accountable can come
up close and support us. If we begin to drift and stray off course, those same
people are there to restore us. Congregations that implement such principles
don't have too many in the flock drop out of sight unnoticed or uncared for.

I have never known of one person who has some deep need to ask for some
cassette tape to listen to. They want flesh-and-blood people. Take the case of a
young couple who began attending our church in recent months. Acting on my
counsel from the pulpit that people get involved with each other beyond the
worship service, they decided to visit one of our adult fellowships.

During the first visit to the class, a member pulled the couple aside to
describe in detail the supportive nature of the class—how they minister to each
other in practical ways when needs arise.

That very week the husband suffered a serious accident at his work. He fell
from a scaffolding on an oil rig and crushed his spine. After the initial shock,
his wife wondered who might be able to help. She thought of the group they had
visited on Sunday and found in her purse the name and number of one of the
ladies who had invited her to a women's meeting of the class. She called the
woman.

After being called, the woman in the class immediately contacted a class
officer who got a prayer chain going of about eighty people. Food and baby-
sitting were offered so that the wife could spend time with her husband at the
hospital. A ministry of encouragement was activated within an hour of the
initial phone call.

The husband was hospitalized for an extended period of time. Some feeling has returned to his legs and there is hope that he will eventually walk again. In the meantime, he and his family are surrounded by a group of Christians who are expressing God's love in many practical ways.

By being accountable and in touch, the couple found a whole group of people ready to help.

Positive and Negative

There is another dimension in all this, which we might call the positive-negative experiences connected with accountability. With this in mind, let's take a look at the wisdom of Proverbs.

1. *By being accountable, we are less likely to stumble into a trap.*

> Through presumption comes nothing but strife,
> But with those who receive counsel is wisdom (Prov. 13:10).

> The teaching of the wise is a fountain of life,
> To turn aside from the snares of death (Prov. 13:14).

> Poverty and shame will come to him who neglects discipline,
> But he who regards reproof will be honored (Prov. 13:18).

> He who walks with wise men will be wise,
> But the companion of fools will suffer harm (Prov. 13:20).

> He whose ear listens to the life-giving reproof
> Will dwell among the wise (Prov. 15:31).

> He who neglects discipline despises himself.
> But he who listens to reproof acquires understanding (Prov. 15:32).

> Oil and perfume make the heart glad,
> So a man's counsel is sweet to his friend (Prov. 27:9).

> Iron sharpens iron,
> So one man sharpens another (Prov. 27:17).

> As in water face reflects face,
> So the heart of man reflects man (Prov. 27:19).

There are snares and unseen reefs beneath the surface of our own independent perception. We all have blind spots. That includes you, too. Wise are those who place themselves in the secure and objective sphere of others' care.

2. *By being accountable, we don't get away with unwise and sinful actions.*

> Faithful are the wounds of a friend,
> But deceitful are the kisses of an enemy (Prov. 27:6).

> Stripes that wound scour away evil,
> And strokes reach the innermost parts (Prov. 20:30).

Not even the so-called "superstars" have a corner on life. They, too, are (*especially?*) fallible and subject to blind spots of pride and of failure to carry out their own admonitions to others.

Paul reproved Peter for his hypocrisy.

> But when Cephas came to Antioch, I opposed him to his face, because he stood condemned.
> For prior to the coming of certain men from James, he used to eat with the Gentiles; but when they came, he began to withdraw and hold himself aloof, fearing the party of the circumcision (Ga. 2:11–12).

Samuel had the unhappy task of confronting Saul:

> Then Samuel said to Saul, "Wait, and let me tell you what the Lord said to me last night." And he said to him, "Speak!"
> And Samuel said, "Is it not true, though you were little in your own eyes, you were made the head of the tribes of Israel? And the Lord anointed you king over Israel, and the Lord sent you on a mission, and said, 'Go and utterly destroy the sinners, the Amalekites, and fight against them until they are exterminated.'
> "Why then did you not obey the voice of the Lord, but rushed upon the spoil and did what was evil in the sight of the Lord?"
> The Saul said to Samuel, "I did obey the voice of the Lord, and went on the mission on which the Lord sent me, and have brought back Agag the king of Amalek, and have utterly destroyed the Amalekites.
> "But the people took some of the spoil, sheep and oxen, the choicest of the things devoted to destruction to sacrifice to the Lord your God at Gilgal."
> And Samuel said, "Has the Lord as much delight in burnt offerings and sacrifices as in obeying the voice of the Lord? Behold, to obey is better than sacrifice. And to heed than the fat of rams.
> "For rebellion is as the sin of divination, and insubordination is as iniquity and idolatry. Because you have rejected the word of the Lord, He has also rejected you from being king" (1 Sam. 15:16–23).

David admitted that such times of affliction and internal bruising were beneficial.

Before I was afflicted I went astray, but now I keep Thy word . . .
It is good for me that I was afflicted, that I may learn Thy statutes . . .
I know, O Lord, that Thy judgments are righteous, and that in faithfulness
Thou hast afflicted me (Ps. 119:67, 71, 75).

As I said at the beginning of this chapter, when I'm tempted to fudge at a
traffic signal, there's that letter to haunt me! That is precisely the kind of thing
David had in mind.

Four Practical Suggestions

Now that we have come to an understanding of what accountability is and
isn't . . . and since we have ample support from Scripture that it is not only
valid but, in fact, vital, let's finalize the issue by thinking through several
practical suggestions for implementation.

1. *Stop and consider the value of becoming accountable.* Personalize this suggestion by using "I," "me," "my."

• Like everyone else, I have blind spots. By being accountable, I will gain
insight I don't have in myself.
• Because I lack sufficient strength and wisdom to cope with pressure,
temptation, and pride all on my own, I need others near me.
• The kind of world I live in has too many booby traps and subtle snares for
me to handle on my own (especially when I travel . . . or when I'm all alone). I
need additional strength.

2. *Ask yourself two questions.* Asking is easy, but answering them may hurt.

• Why do I remain isolated and unaccountable?
• What if I stay in this condition?

If you are in the category of a highly visible leader, a much-respected pastor,
a Christian entertainer, a speaker who is often on the road, a media personality,
I *plead* with you. The adversary has you in the cross wires of his scope. His
darts are pointed in your direction. Your hope of survival, your means of
escaping the traps, is largely connected with your willingness to place yourself
within the circle of a few friends *outside* your family. I urge you to do this soon.

3. *Choose at least one other person (preferably two or three) with whom you will
meet regularly.* They need to be *very* carefully chosen. These are some traits to
look for:

• Confidentiality (if married, that person's mate must have the same trait).
• Honesty (someone who is not in awe of you).

- Authenticity (free from hypocrisy, sincere).
- Objectivity (won't always agree with you or tell you what you want to hear).
- Godliness (you respect their walk with God—each is definitely a Christian).
- Availability (accessible, able to meet within a short notice).
- Loyalty (faithful, staying power, consistent).

4. *Develop a relationship that strengthens your grip on spiritual things.*

I'm not talking about a business consultant or a financial counselor, helpful as those may be. Nor am I talking about a professional therapist who may help you work through your emotional struggles. This individual with whom you meet is one who helps "encourage you in God" (1 Sam. 23:16) as Jonathan did with David. It is your spiritual sensitivity that needs monitoring and appraisal.

I'll not linger much longer (this chapter has almost become a book unto itself), but I cannot close without mentioning once again that one of the best decisions I every made several years ago was to seek out several men I respected who would meet with me, pray, talk, evaluate, counsel, weigh decisions, assist me in keeping my head together and make sure my heart was right before God. They are honest with me, open, affirming yet not gullible, tactful yet confronting, good listeners yet wise counselors.

God has used them to show me some of the traps I would have missed and to alter my course when I was moving in the wrong direction. Words fail to describe the benefits I have reaped—actually we have reaped together—as a result of having them near.

If only they could do something about my driving habits; but then, they're only human. Some things can only be dealt with by prayer and fasting!

DISCUSSION IDEAS AND QUESTIONS

- Define accountability in your own words. Give some examples of what you believe it includes.
- Can you remember the two dangerous extremes? Talk about them. Have you ever witnessed or been the recipient of either? Share what you went through at the time.
- Discuss the difference between necessary and healthy privacy and unwise isolationism. How can a person tell if he or she is moving from the former to the latter?
- A great deal of chapter 11 was a presentation of the biblical justification of accountability. Choose a passage or two that clarified an issue or encouraged you and share your thoughts.
- Turn back to Proverbs 27:6. Dig into it with others in the group. Try your hand at your own paraphrase. Name one specific way in which the verse helps you.

• The chapter closes with four practical suggestions. Review them orally. Talk them over. Are you willing to put each suggestion to use in your life?

• Pick a particular individual you really admire, perhaps some high-profile leader whom God has used in your life. Pray for him or her. As you pray, work your way through the four suggestions and ask the Lord to protect your leader-friend from the subtle traps of our adversary, the devil.

12

A Hope Transplant:
The Essential Operation

Churches are like children. They come in different shapes and sizes, personalities and styles. No two are exactly alike.

In the process of well over two decades of preaching and ministering, I have had the opportunity to be in all kinds of churches. The variety has been nothing short of remarkable. While traveling late last summer, I sat down and drew up a list of the different types, sort of a cross-section sampling of churches where I have visited and ministered. Here's what it looked like:

- Extremely conservative and theologically buttoned-up-tight style.
- Fairly liberal, what I'd call theologically loosey-goosey style.
- Highly emotional, informal, answer-back congregations.
- Absolutely silent, stoic, straight, and stern.
- Biblically illiterate . . . not a Bible within gunshot distance.
- Well-taught, in fact, almost a classroom atmosphere.
- Some have been large, a few *huge* with multiple balconies.
- Others were tiny, only a handful meeting in a home.
- Old, I mean hundreds of years old.
- A few less than a month in existence.
- Some were English-speaking . . . others called for translators.

I've preached in black churches where I thought we'd never finish the service! There were three offerings, over an hour of music, lengthy times of prayer, and two full-length sermons (emphasis on length) both from me and the pastor. I left the place dripping wet and hoarse. I don't think I've had so much fun since "the hogs ate my little brother." I mean, when those folks say "Amen" to a preacher, it's like saying "sic 'em" to a bulldog. And then I've

482

preached in other places where a twenty-minute sermon was considered a marathon. Those places usually have weird-looking pulpits, by the way.

Some churches where I've been loved music. They had a full orchestra, over one hundred in the choir, a lovely pipe organ, and employed music as a beautiful enhancement to worship. While others didn't believe in using musical instruments. Everything was a cappella. A few were highly cultured and sophisticated "clubs" where elegance and scholarship were the passwords of entrance, and others were dirt poor. I remember one place that requested that I wear cutoffs and a T-shirt (in California, naturally). Once they saw my knees and legs, they were sorry they had made that request.

I've spoken in churches torn by strife (several splits in their brief history) and others that have hung together for decades, unified and still excited about the Lord. One has had the same pastor for over forty years, and when you consider that the average minister stays only three to five years, then moves on, the man who remains *that* long today is a phenomenon. Some churches were more like entertainment centers than houses of worship; whereas, others were as plain and unimaginative as a weather-beaten clapboard barn. One in particular resembled a cinder block fortress—square corners, no windows, cement floors, hard pews, an upright piano, naked lightbulbs hanging from long wires, and a flat ceiling. I couldn't imagine being sentenced to the place. The echo, however, allowed everyone to hear the sermon twice, so nobody ever left feeling cheated.

I have not exaggerated. Some churches were so winsome and warm that I never wanted to leave. Others were so scary that I'm still trying to believe they actually exist. Whoever doesn't think God has a sense of humor hasn't seen the churches I've been in.

THE MOST TRAGIC CHURCHES ON EARTH

Two churches stand out, however, as the most tragic of all. Both are urban ministries with a rich, illustrious history. One is located in a dangerous section of an angry, volatile neighborhood. There are wrought-iron bars on the windows, double locks on all the doors (the congregation is actually locked in when they gather for worship), and women are escorted to their cars when the meetings end . . . day or night. The other has a completely different external appearance. Those folks aren't frightened, they are proud. Proud of all the wrong things. From the outside you would think they had it all together, but when you get in and listen and observe, you realize something terribly important is missing. It's what's missing in the other church too. And that is what makes both ministries so tragic.

Interestingly, both places talk of their past. "The Way We Were" would be an appropriate offertory in either church. Great men and women once ministered there. There used to be an aggressive, pace-setting outreach program of evangelism in the community, a broad vision for mission in God's world program, attractive youth ministries, grand and stimulating preaching, an educational program for people from the cradle to the grave, exciting, crowded conditions, discipleship, and concerned people in prayer . . . the whole scene. But no longer. . . . All that is left of the past glory of those two great ministries is a row of pictures hanging in the hallway and the memories in the minds of a few.

It's not so much a problem of what is there as it is a problem of what is missing. That's what makes it so tragic. There is an absence of vitality and power. The folks are not dreaming about tomorrow and seeking God's mind for their future. They're thinking only of the past. They are churches that have lost their *hope.* The Spirit of God is no longer free to move among them, it seems. In that "hopeless" atmosphere it's almost as if He has lifted His presence from those places. It is enough to make you weep. Perhaps Samuel Stevenson who wrote these words *was* weeping:

> A city full of churches
> Great preacher, lettered men,
> Grand music, choirs and organs;
> If these all fail, what then?
> Good workers, eager, earnest,
> Who labour hour by hour;
> But where, oh where, my brother,
> Is God's Almighty power?
>
> Refinement: education!
> They want the very best.
> Their plans and schemes are perfect
> They give themselves no rest;
> They get the best of talent,
> They try their uttermost,
> But what they need, brother,
> Is God the Holy Ghost![1]

What the heart is to your physical body, what morale is to a unit of fighting men, what spirit is to a ball team, hope is to a church. Remove it and you have reduced the place of worship to a morgue with a steeple. An empty shell. A building, perhaps even a lovely external structure housing zombie-like creatures going through the motions of religion but lacking vitality. Sunday meetings are like narcotic fixes to deaden the pain of empty lives. Hope, the prince and power of motivation, has vanished.

That may describe the place where you worship. Perhaps not to the same extreme, but you sense something is missing. You have read these chapters, and you've felt the excitement and challenge of the Hebrews as they left Egypt and struck out for Canaan. You've watched the Red Sea open, you've seen the cloud by day and felt the warmth of the pillar of fire by night. You've witnessed

Jericho's walls crumble to the ground. You've marched into Canaan and heard the warnings of Joshua. You've been stirred (as I have) with the realization that drawing closer, being open, dropping your guard, and becoming accountable are all attainable and exciting goals. You want that . . . but when you think about trying it in your church, you lose heart. Maybe you are to the place of thinking, "It may work for others, but it won't at the church I attend." Maybe some of that same hopelessness has colored your thinking and you are about to slam this thing closed with a silent sigh, "It's only a dream." You may be the pastor of a seemingly hopeless church. You are seriously wondering if it is worth the effort. Perhaps the hopelessness has begun to affect your preaching and your leadership.

Before going any further, let me encourage you. It is never too late to start doing what is right! Things may seem without hope, but that's *today*. And that's the *past*. What you have read about open relationships and becoming deeper, closer, and stronger in friendship and love with others can help. It *cannot* hurt. It may be the central catalyst God would use to bring a fresh touch of His Spirit back into your church and its congregation. Take heart, my friend. You could be on the verge of a God-ordained renewal that has the potential of turning your place of ministry right-side up. In light of that, I'd like to transplant hope from the pages of Scripture into your heart and, ultimately, into your place of worship. I spent my first chapter describing how hope was revived in the place where I worship. Now let's spend this final chapter thinking about how it can be implemented where you worship. We've spent enough time talking about individual people; let's think about churches for a while . . . churches of hope. How can we bring the hope back?

A Brief Analysis of Hope

We toss around words like *faith* and *love* all the time. And most of us can describe both with minimal difficulty. But *hope?* What in the world is it? And is it really *that* essential?

Description

Webster defines hope, "to desire with expectation of fulfillment." To hope is to anticipate. It is more than dreaming, however. It is possessing within ourselves an expectation that someday there will be the fulfillment of that desire. It will become a reality. Hope always looks to the future, it's always on tiptoes. It keeps us going. It makes a dismal today bearable because it promises a brighter tomorrow. Without hope, something inside all of us dies.

The Greek term translated "hope" means much the same as our English word—"favorable and confident expectation." We can live several weeks without food, days without water, and only minutes without oxygen, but without hope—forget it.

Take from a man his wealth, and you hinder him; take from him his purpose, and you slow him down. But take from man his hope, and you stop him. He can go on without wealth, and even without purpose, for a while. But he will not go on without hope.[2]

The *Good News Bible* renders Proverbs 13:12: "When hope is crushed, the heart is crushed, But a wish come true fills you with joy."

The New American Standard Bible says: "Hope deferred makes the heart sick, but desire fulfilled is a tree of life." A loss of hope *sickens* the heart. The Hebrew term CHA-LAH (translated "sick") is a word that suggests the idea of being "diseased." When the noun *sickness* is used in reference to a nation, it presents the idea of calamity, grief, or affliction. The term is often used in a severe sense, hence the word picture of the heart being "crushed" is an apt description.

A rather remarkable series of tests and dozens of comprehensive studies have established the fact that hope and survival are inseparably connected.

In an article in *New York* magazine, Douglas Colligan writes of the "Broken Heart" study. This study researched the mortality rate of 4,500 widowers within six months of their wives' deaths. The findings of the study showed that the widowers had a mortality rate 40 percent higher than other men the same age.

In the same article Colligan cites the example of Major F. J. Harold Kushner, who was held by the Viet Cong for five and a half years:

Among the prisoners in Kushner's POW camp was a tough young marine, 24 years old, who had already survived two years of prison-camp life in relatively good health. Part of the reason for this was that the camp commander had promised to release the man if he cooperated. Since this had been done before with others, the marine turned into a model POW and the leader of the camp's thought-reform group. As time passed he gradually realized that his captors had lied to him. When the full realization of this took hold he became a zombie. He refused to do all work, rejected all offers of food and encouragement, and simply lay on his cot sucking his thumb. In a matter of weeks he was dead.[3]

Philip Yancey in his book *Where Is God When It Hurts?* says "Kushner's experience is a tragic, negative example of the need for some hope to live for."[4]

It is a proven fact that hope must be present or disease sets in. I've seen this in marriages, haven't you? The bride-to-be has her "hope chest" in which she places tangible things and intangible dreams. Her heart beats faster as she opens the chest and anticipates her joys of the future. She marries the man of her dreams. Hope keeps them going as he grinds his way through school. Hope takes them to their first home, through the births of their three children, and into a second home, large enough for their full-size family and a few pets. Then midlife seizes the reins, somehow getting a strangle hold on their hope. She loses some interest, he stops bringing her flowers, they begin to spin in separate orbits. Hope fades. They half-heartedly try to work it out . . . but the disease has taken its toll. As one lady said to me with a sigh, "It wasn't until I lost all hope of recovery that I finally gave up. When the hope vanished, so did my energy. It was all over—the fun, the intimacy, the drive, the dreams, all that stuff that made it stick died."

A Question

Can that happen in a church? Yes. Never overnight, you understand. It's often so imperceptible that you aren't even aware it is happening. If you were, you'd stop it. But it's like erosion—silent, never sudden, yet constant. The good news is that this disease isn't always terminal.

The big question is: What does it take to keep a congregation full of hope? Or, to use other words: How can we keep the disease of hopelessness away? Or, perhaps: What will restore our hope?

I have thought about this a lot. If you recall my words in chapter 1, in our case I became concerned that our size and the sameness of routine, once we got settled in our new facilities, would "steal our enthusiasm" . . . which is another way of saying, "take away our hope." Congregational hope and health go hand in hand.

SOME WAYS TO KEEP HOPE STRONG

While thinking about how to fan the flame of hope in a church, I came across the first letter Peter wrote. Since he was the one so intimately involved in the first-century congregation at Jerusalem, he should offer some guidelines or ideas worth duplicating today. When I arrived at the fifth chapter of that letter, things began to fall into place. No less than five realistic suggestions seemed to stand out. Each one is an ingredient found in churches I'm aware of today who are getting the job done . . . each one enhances hope.

The Right Kind of Leadership

> Therefore, I exhort the elders among you, as your fellow elder and witness of the sufferings of Christ, and a partaker also of the glory that is to be revealed, shepherd the flock of God among you, not under compulsion, but voluntarily, according to the will of God; and not for sordid gain, but with eagerness; nor yet as lording it over those allotted to your charge, but proving to be examples of the flock (1 Pet. 5:1–4).

Those dear people were slugging it out in a tough time when persecution, misunderstanding, even martyrdom were grim realities. Therefore, we shouldn't be surprised that Peter speaks first to those in leadership. If hope leaves the heart of the leader, it isn't long before the entire congregation follows suit. Naturally, they need his initial words of counsel.

Take a close look at the verses you just read. See the contrasts? They follow the strong imperative, "shepherd the flock!" But how? What should characterize those who serve as shepherds of God's flock? Let me diagram it for you:

Not . . . (negatively)	But . . . (positively)
. . . under compulsion	. . . voluntarily
. . . for sordid gain	. . . with eagerness
. . . lording it over	. . . being an example

The same old nemesis awaits all who serve local congregations, regardless of the era or geography: silver, sloth, and self! Those who desire to cultivate a close, unguarded, deeply committed congregation must come to terms with each of these three temptations. There are stories—some of them almost too frightening to believe—which have come to my attention, stories of pastors who are "in it for the money" . . . who have long since lost the joy of ministry (and there are hundreds of joys!) . . . who are so insecure they must dominate and browbeat the congregation. These leaders should not be surprised that hope is fading in their congregations.

For flocks to flourish they need acceptance, freedom, love, lots of reinforcement, regular nourishment, room to fail, an atmosphere of expectation, and true enthusiasm. This is true for young and old alike, for singles and marrieds, for women and men, for the cultured and refined as well as those with limited interests, for blue collar and white collar workers, for Democrats and Republicans. Regardless of color and with no concern for financial status, they are all God's flock, not the pastor's people. They belong to Him, not the preacher or the pastoral staff. They want to be challenged to think. They need to know it's okay to disagree, to ask questions, to hold other opinions. Yes, and even to fuss (most already know that). They have to have the freedom to laugh, to respond, to serve, to weep, to be completely who they are . . . and they get their cues from their leader.

Uptight, intense, superdefensive, easily threatened leaders do not spawn congregations of close, caring, relaxed, accepting, completely human, and believable relationships. If the congregation sense that their leader's "example to the flock" is all these things and more of the same, they will have all the green lights they need to proceed. But if they witness that the most important thing to him is biblical instruction (almost to the exclusion of much else) they will begin to be instructors. If he is harsh and rigid, they will be too. If he always has to be right, they put great emphasis on who's right and who's wrong. If he likes to exhort and put down, so will they. The style and "flavor" of a church come from those in leadership. As is always true, right leadership results in maximum benefits.

True Humility toward One Another

Peter goes on to say:

> You younger men, likewise, be subject to your elders; and all of you, clothe yourselves with humility toward one another, for God is opposed to the proud, but gives grace to the humble.
>
> Humble yourselves, therefore, under the mighty hand of God, that He may exalt you at the proper time (1 Pet. 5:5-6).

There's a beautiful balance here, isn't there? Younger men are encouraged to listen to the older gentlemen. There is cross-generational respect and free communication. But does this suggest the older guys have a corner on truth? Is this some kind of king-of-the-hill power play? Hardly. Peter goes on to say that *all* of them (older, mid-adults, teens, young singles, older singles, children, parents, pastors, elders, ushers, you name it) were to wear the same garment. What is it? Is it biblical accuracy? As important and valuable as that is, no, that's not the garment everybody in the congregation is to wear. Nor is it education. Nor wealth. Nor poverty. It is one of those absolutely essential ingredients that assure everyone it is safe to drop your guard—humility. Pride kills openness! With that in mind, there are more murders in churches than any other place in the world.

How does God respond to pride? Verse 6 says He *opposes* it. Peter uses a strong battle term here. Pride calls out God's armies. It brings in His heavy artillery. On more than one place in Scripture we read He flat out *hates* pride. Why? What's the big deal?

- Pride creates an "exclusive club" mentality in churches.
- Pride resists sharing, making room for the stronger, those who may be different than most.
- Pride stops innovation and change.
- Pride always has to have the answers. The definite article is terribly important to pride.
- Pride is dogmatic, unteachable, closed-minded.

That's why God hates it. That's why churches who have hope are comprised of folks who wear the garment of humility. God exalts us "at the proper time" if we wear the right clothing—a teachable spirit, vulnerability, approachability toward one another.

There's a third ingredient we don't want to forget.

Release of Anxiety

For release of anxiety what better advice than 1 Peter 5:7, "casting all your anxiety upon Him, because He cares for you!"

Worry robs us of hope. It immobilizes the body of Christ by reminding us of all the things that are wrong and bad and threatening. Worry suffocates us, pushing our heads under the water of all our troubles and trials.

A worried church doesn't risk. It reacts. It reacts. Instead of staying on the cutting edge, it retreats and adopts a fight-back mentality. It spends less time dreaming and more time defending. An anxious congregation is more aware of what's wrong in the world than what's right with the Lord.

Have you spent much time with worry-warts in the Christian ranks? They look like they been baptized in lemon juice. Anxiety-prone people carry burdens; they don't cast them off. And the longer folks do that the "stranger" they get—the more paranoid, the less joyful. Some become self-styled "prophets" who get a little wide-eyed and fanatical with doomsday declarations, have you noticed? And they seem to feed on congregations that are growing and excited. They're attracted to churches on the move. I agree with the wag who first observed this and shrugged, "Where there's light, there are bugs!"

In every church there are enough problems to make any pastor an emotional basket case. Parking problems. Vandalism. Gossip. Wayward and carnal Christians. Neighborhood complaints. Sickness. Bad marriages. Financial woes. Staff disharmony. Poor location. Loud traffic outside. Lack of forgiveness, "Get rid of the pastor" talk. You name it, some churches have it in spades.

By the way, I just heard of a super way to get rid of your pastor! C'mon, it's time for a laugh. There's this new chain letter going around among churches. No cost is involved. You just send a copy of the letter to six other churches that are tired of their ministers too. Then you bundle up your pastor and ship him to the church at the bottom of the list. In one week you will receive in return 16,436 ministers . . . one of whom should be a dandy! But beware, one church broke the chain and got their old minister back.

You see, there are any number of creative ways to break with the anxiety syndrome. The best is still "casting all your anxiety upon Him."

An Alert and Discerning Awareness of the Adversary

Churches that stay healthy and full of hope, vision, and enthusiasm possess a keen awareness of the enemy. See how Peter deals with this?

> Be of sober spirit, be on the alert. Your adversary, the devil, prowls about like a roaring lion, seeking someone to devour.
> But resist him, firm in your faith, knowing that the same experiences of suffering are being accomplished by your brethren who are in the world (1 Pet. 5:8-9).

To be "sober" is to be strong, stable, self-controlled.
To be "on the alert" is to be watchful, aware.
Those are our commands, fellow Christians. Orders from headquarters. We are in no fun-'n-games, carefree work, you know. There's an enemy on the

loose. And whether or not we are aware of him (we *should* be!), he is certainly aware of us. He knows us thoroughly. He is crafty, brilliant, experienced, and resilient in combat. And he despises whatever represents God and whoever is carrying out God's work. Since he is on the prowl and dedicated to our defeat, we are to be mindful of this and not deceived into thinking he couldn't care less. The truth is that he couldn't care more!

Look again at his objective: to *devour*. I'd call that an aggressive strategy, wouldn't you? He will stop at nothing. If a strategy to attack from without doesn't work, he will use an internal maneuver—other people, alien thoughts, wild imagination, some caustic comment, a season of low-grade depression, an unexplainable series of events, and I might add *apathy*. Yes, plain old indifference, passive unconcern.

And what does a church do under such attacks? Resist! Resist! Resist! Stand firm in faith! I have found it to be helpful if I acknowledge an awareness of his presence to other Christians. If there is one tactic the adversary cannot abide, it's exposure.

We were going through a difficult time in our church a few months ago. Many were not aware of the intensity nor was it appropriate for me to announce it. I was struggling. I could not get on top. For the life of me, I was unable to unravel the whole thing and reach some kind of conclusion. My lack of decisiveness irritated me and there were other noticeable problems created in the fallout of the whole episode. I became preoccupied. My leadership faltered. I began to withdraw, pull in, get quiet, and lie low. Not being the low-lying type, I couldn't continue in that posture. Finally, in a conversation with a man I've admired for years, he made a comment that put everything in proper perspective. After listening for ten or fifteen minutes, he said, "Sounds like a satanic attack to me, Chuck. I mean, if he can get his foot into the door of your life and get you intimidated and full of doubt and waiting for the next shoe to fall, he's won a massive victory. Just think of the lives that are affected if your leadership begins to falter." It clicked. I was amazed to think I had failed to realize I wasn't wrestling against mere flesh and blood. No way! The prowler had found a weak spot and was making his moves. What a difference once we become aware of his insidious and deceptive strategies!

Thus far, we've considered four ways to keep hope revived and alive in our lives and churches. Peter mentions one more:

Respond Well to Adversity

> And after you have suffered for a little while, the God of all grace, who called you to His eternal glory in Christ, will Himself perfect, confirm, strengthen and establish you.
> To Him be dominion forever and ever. Amen (1 Pet. 5:10–11).

How easy to fall prey to self-pity! It is the most natural and acceptable response to suffering. In fact, people will often encourage it in us! Peter takes a different stance. He realizes his readers are in the trenches. It's not a matter of will they suffer, but how much more can they endure?

Interestingly, he refuses to focus on their hardship and affliction. He immediately jumps to the benefits—"After you have suffered—God will. . . ." What *great* perspective! He refuses to get all bogged down in the pain of it all. He turns their (and our) attention to the end results.

Churches that have hope take a hitch in their belts when the going gets rough. They stand instead of shrink. They realize this temporary test will reap permanent benefits. To use a runner's term, they "lean into the wind" rather than give up and surrender to it.

Look at the benefits. God will:

- Perfect: This term carries with it the idea of repairing weak or broken parts.
- Confirm: To make firm, solid as granite, tough as fiber, strong as tempered steel.
- Strengthen: Take away the flab, replace fragility with stability.
- Establish: This is the idea of laying down a foundation. Suffering drives us back to the bedrock of our faith.

It's time for more people to talk straight about how we view pain and problems. I've read and heard enough to know that we are viewing it all wrong! I realize that's a sweeping generalization, but I'm convinced that it's true. We have become masters of explanation in this generation. Everything now has its label and we quickly look for such when something happens, especially something that brings discomfort. Instead of anticipating the positive ramifications of the affliction, we settle into our martyr mentality, we look for pity and are resentful when we don't find it. Rather than adopt a victor's stance (this will be beneficial, this is no unfair accident of fate, "God is in this"), we resort to the pathetic wail of a victim ("Why? Woe is me. If only people knew how bad I've got it. Will it ever end?").

You see, hope dies with that kind of thinking. It is crushed beneath the load of our self-appointed misery. Problems do not go away. They must be worked through or else they remain forever a barrier to the growth and development of our spirit. And we pass much of this kind of thinking on to our children. How much better to teach (and to model) a determination that refuses to quit when we encounter the pain that conflicts and events bring our way. Carl Jung was correct, "Neurosis is always a substitute for legitimate suffering."[5]

In an excellent book that tracks this view in great detail, *The Road Less Traveled*, the author boldly declares:

. . . it is in this whole process of meeting and solving problems that life has its meaning. Problems are the cutting edge that distinguishes between success and failure. Problems call forth our courage and our wisdom; indeed, they create our courage and our wisdom. It is only because of problems that we grow mentally and spiritually. When we desire to encourage the growth of the human spirit, we challenge and encourage the human capacity to solve problems, just as in school we deliberately set problems for our children to solve. It is through the pain of confronting and resolving problems that we learn. As Benjamin Franklin said, "Those things that hurt, instruct." It is for this reason that wise people learn not to dread but actually to welcome problems and actually to welcome the pain of problems.

Most of us are not so wise. Fearing the pain involved, almost all of us, to a greater or lesser degree, attempt to avoid problems. We procrastinate, hoping that they will go away. We ignore them, forget them, pretend they do not exist. We even take drugs to assist us in ignoring them, so that by deadening ourselves to the pain we can forget the problems that cause the pain. We attempt to skirt around problems rather than meet them head on. We attempt to get rid of them rather than suffer through them.

This tendency to avoid problems and the emotional suffering inherent in them is the primary basis of all human mental illness.[6]

A CLOSING COMMENT

I would suggest that you take the time to review each of Peter's five suggestions for keeping hope strong, especially if you are serious about inculcating some workable ideas into your life and into your church. It has been my observation that things don't suddenly or automatically change externally . . . they shift and move around first in our heads, in there where we turn ideas over, where we plant the seeds that later grow into action.

If developing open relationships in your life and in your church is something that you consider worth all the effort, be ready for a challenge. In my opinion it is the best way to survive on this lonely, busy planet, and it is worth whatever risk it requires. The alternative is no longer an option to me.

DISCUSSION IDEAS AND QUESTIONS

• Spend a while talking about your church. Do some evaluating. What is it that you appreciate most? What are the ministries that appeal to your family members? If you brought a visitor next Sunday, what do you think would leave the greatest impression?

• Where are you able to make the greatest contribution in your church? What ministry would interest you the most? Talk about why.

• Is hope lagging or flourishing in your church? Go back and read again the description of hope in chapter 12. Is it possible that you could help strengthen the hope of your church? How?

• Go around the room and each person read a verse from 1 Peter 5:1–11. Now, taking the five suggestions for strengthening the hope of a church, discuss them together. Try to be specific as you honestly imagine *your* church in light of Peter's words.

• Pain is an inescapable reality in life. As we saw at the end of the chapter, affliction and hardship may be tough to bear, but they bring marvelous benefits and depth of character. Share one or two things you have learned in the crucible.

• Before leaving, give God thanks for teaching you these lessons you learned in the furnace of affliction.

Conclusion

It was back in 1981 that I decided to write a book on servanthood. The result was *Improving Your Serve*, a volume dedicated to the art of unselfish living. As time passed and the publisher informed me of its success, I was encouraged to write a second with a similar-sounding title but completely different in content. That was 1982, the year *Strengthening Your Grip* was released. As you who read it will remember, it is a book about some of the essentials we need to get a grip on in this aimless world of ours. I considered those two would surely be sufficient—sort of a one-two punch to help a few folks who are trying to stay on their feet in this wild 'n woolly generation.

Before 1983 had dawned, however, my friends at Word Books were back for round three (no, this isn't a fifteen-round bout), telling me "a trilogy would be appreciated" since the first and second books had been met with such approval by the general public, Christian and non-Christian alike. Hence, *Dropping Your Guard* has found its way into your hands. As you know by now, this has been another kind of book entirely, quite distinct from either of the first two.

The content of the first was primarily directed to those who wish to assist others in the family of God. The second looked more into the world and addressed pertinent issues that are up for grabs in our fast-paced society. But this one looks within. This volume talks about you and me, down deep inside. It explores and exposes our tendency to protect ourselves . . . even though we may not realize we are doing so.

> Most of us can't see how we have become protective. We prefer to see ourselves as open and gentle; it may be shocking to hear that others—especially those closest to us—may see us as hard, critical, and closed. . . .
>
> To paraphrase the poet: "How do I protect myself? Let me count the ways."[1]

This book encourages our dropping all those protective guards. It appeals for the value of open relationships. It says, in effect, be who you are, let the truth be known, come on . . . open up . . . let's not mask the truth any longer.

Of the three, this one is the most personal. Even though you didn't invite me to do so, I have taken the liberty to probe within you, helping you search for and discover some clues that might explain why you have opted for isolation instead of openness.

Now the work begins. With the period at the end of this conclusion, theory stops and reality starts. The gauge of this book's effectiveness will not be measured by how much you've marked in it or by whether you quote from it, but rather by the extent to which you put it to the test.

You see, if you really believe these things are valuable, if you are convinced that being unprotected and open is better than being somebody else behind a mask, you will start living that way. You will take the risk. And I've got great news for you—someday you will discover you are not able to live any other way. Living without masks is addictive. It's also terribly contagious.

It makes me smile when I think of the benefits that you will begin to enjoy as you lift the truth from these printed pages and transfer it into your talk and your walk. Think of the difference in your home, where you work, at your church, with your friends! Think of the relief you will feel from removing all those thick and phony masks that have plagued you for years!

Okay, my friend, toss this thing aside. You've read about it enough. You don't need more theoretical information. What you need is practical exposure . . . a lifetime to do what you say you believe.

So what are you waiting for? Get out there and dare to be authentic, whole, uniquely who you are. You're in for the time of your life!

Notes

Chapter 1. Loosening the Mask: How It All Began

1. Bernard Berelson and Gary A. Steiner, *Human Behavior: An Inventory of Scientific Findings* (New York: Harcourt, Brace & World, 1964), 252.
2. "Mobility," *Society*, 14 (Jan./Feb. 1977): 9. Published by permission of Transaction, Inc. from *Society*, vol. 14, #2. Copyright © 1977 by Transaction, Inc. See also Robert Kanigel, "Stay-Put Americans," *Human Behavior*, May 1979.
3. U.S. Bureau of Labor Statistics, *Monthly Labor Review* (October 1963):1145 and (December 1979):48. This trend, which reversed that for the period 1951-63, reflects at least in part the growing proportion of young workers, whose job tenure is much shorter than that of older Americans.
4. Vance Packard, *A Nation of Strangers* (New York: David McKay, 1972), 270.
5. Mildred Newman and Bernard Berkowitz, *How to Be Your Own Best Friend* (New York: Random House, 1971), 7. Used by permission.
6. From Bruce Larson, *There's a Lot More to Health Than Not Being Sick*, copyright © 1981, pp. 59–60; used by permission of Word Books, Publisher, Waco, Texas 76796.
7. Charles R. Swindoll, *People of Refuge*, a film produced by Word, Inc., Waco, Texas, 1982.

Chapter 2. Digging Deeper, Risking Change

1. Amy Carmichael, *If* (Montreal: Christian Literature Crusade [n.d.]), 48. Take from copyrighted material; used by permission of the Christian Literature Crusade, Fort Washington, PA 19034.

Chapter 3. Getting Closer, Growing Stronger

1. From John Donne, *Devotions*, XVII, as quoted in *Familiar Quotations*, ed. John Bartlett (Boston: Little, Brown and Company, 1955), 218.
2. Charles Paul Conn, *Making It Happen* (Old Tappan, NJ: Fleming H. Revell Co., 1981), 95.
3. Alan Loy McGinnis, *The Friendship Factor* (Minneapolis: Augsburg Publishing House, 1979), 20. Reprinted by permission from *The Friendship Factor* by Alan Loy McGinnis, copyright 1979 Augsburg Publishing House.
4. Ibid., 60–61.

Chapter 4. Operation Assimilation

1. From *Hide or Seek* by James Dobson, copyright © 1974, 1979 by Fleming H. Revell Co., pp. 133, 134. Published by Fleming H. Revell Co. Used by permission.
2. *Webster's New Collegiate Dictionary* (Springfield, MA: G. & C. Merriam Company, 1980), 67.
3. John Naisbitt, *Megatrends* (New York: Warner Books, 1982), 53.
4. From Tom J. Fatjo, Jr., and Keith Miller, *With No Fear of Failure*, copyright © 1981, p. 16; used by permission of Word Books, Publisher, Waco, Texas 76796.
5. Leslie B. Flynn, *Great Church Fights* (Wheaton, IL: Victor Books, A Division of SP Publications, Inc., 1976), 44. Used by permission of the author.
6. *The Los Angeles Times*, 9 May 1983, Orange County Edition, Sec. CC††/ Part II, p. 1.
7. Excerpted from *We Really Do Need Each Other* by Reuben Welch (pp. 110–111). Copyright © 1976 by Impact Books, A Division of John T. Benson Publishing Company. Reassigned to the Zondervan Corporation, 1982. Used by permission.

Chapter 5. United and Invincible

1. "The Bond of Love" by Otis Skillings, © 1971 by Lillenas Publishing Co. All rights reserved. Used by permission.
2. From pp. 90–91, 93 from *Life Together* by Dietrich Bonhoeffer, tr. by John W. Doberstein, copyright © 1954 by Harper & Row Publishers, Inc. and used by permission of the publisher.
3. Theodore H. Epp, *Elijah: A Man of Like Nature* (Lincoln, NB: The Good News Broadcasting Association, Inc., 1965), 63.
4. Alan Loy McGinnis, *The Friendship Factor* (Minneapolis, MN: Augsburg Publishing House, 1979), 179–180. Reprinted by permission from *The Friendship Factor* by Alan Loy McGinnis, copyright 1979 Augsburg Publishing House.

Chapter 6. When the Fellowship Breaks Down

1. Taken from *Fearfully and Wonderfully Made* by Paul Brand, M.D., with Philip Yancey (pp. 59-60). Copyright © 1980 by Dr. Paul Brand and Philip Yancey. Used by permission of Zondervan Publishing House.
2. Mouton Chambers, *Leadership*, A Publication of *Christianity Today*, vol. 2, no. 3 (summer 1981): 80.
3. Leslie B. Flynn, *Great Church Fights* (Wheaton, IL: Victor Books, A Division of SP Publications, 1976), 91. Used by permission of the author.

Chapter 7. Authentic Love

1. Hal David and Burt Bacharach, "What the World Needs Now" (Los Angeles, CA: Blue Seas Music Publishers & Jac Music, Inc., 1965). Lyric by Hal David; music by Burt Bacharach. Copyright © 1965 Blue Seas Music, Inc. and Jac Music Company, Inc. International copyright secured. Made in USA. All rights reserved.
2. *The Friendless American Male* by David W. Smith. © Copyright 1983, Regal Books, Ventura, CA 93006. Used by permission.
3. Reprinted from *Men: A Book for Women* (p. 165), edited by James Wagenvoord. Copyright © 1978 by Product Development International Holding, n.v. Reprinted by permission of Avon Books, New York.
4. Alan Loy McGinnis, *The Friendship Factor* (Minneapolis: Augsburg Publishing House, 1979), 48–49. Reprinted by permission from *The Friendship Factor* by Alan Loy McGinnis, copyright 1979 Augsburg Publishing House.

Chapter 8. Needed: Shelter for Storm Victims

1. From Bruce Larson and Keith Miller, *The Edge of Adventure*, copyright © 1974, p. 156; used by permission of Word Books, Publisher, Waco, Texas 76796.
2. From *Psalms of My Life* by Joseph Bayly (p. 16). Published by Tyndale House Publishers, Inc., © 1969. Used by permission.
3. Taken from *Christ in Isaiah* by F. B. Meyer (p. 9), made and printed in Great Britain by Purnell and Sons, Ltd. Paulton (Somerset) and London. Zondervan Publishing House edition 1950, 1952. Used by permission.
4. From *Unger's Bible Dictionary* by Merrill F. Unger (p. 208). Copyright © 1957, 1961, 1966. Moody Press. Moody Bible Institute of Chicago. Used by permission.
5. Lars Wilhelmsson, *Making Forever Friends* (Torrance, CA: The Martin Press, 1982), 112–113. Used by permission.

Chapter 9. Some Things Have Gotta Go!

1. Taken from *Fearfully and Wonderfully Made* by Paul Brand, M.D., with Philip Yancey (p. 20). Copyright © 1980 by Dr. Paul Brand and Philip Yancey. Used by permission of Zondervan Publishing House.
2. From Bruce Larson, *There's a Lot More to Health Than Not Being Sick*, copyright © 1981, p. 104; used by permission of Word Books, Publisher, Waco, Texas 76796.

Chapter 10. Choose for Yourself

1. Emma Lazarus, "The New Colossus."
2. From *Happiness Is a Choice* by Frank B. Minirth and Paul Meier. Copyright 1978 by Baker Book House and used by permission.

Chapter 11. The Necessity of Accountability

1. David Ansen, "Golden Boy of the Movies," *Newsweek*, 30 Nov. 1981, 106.
2. *Up with Worship* by Anne Ortlund (revised edition 1982, p. 102). © Copyright 1975, Regal Books, Ventura, CA 93006. Used by permission.
3. From Bruce Larson, *There's a Lot More to Health Than Not Being Sick*, copyright © 1981, p. 61; used by permission of Word Books, Publisher, Waco, Texas 76796.

Chapter 12. A Hope Transplant: The Essential Operation

1. Samuel Stevenson, "Where Is God's Power?" from *Poems That Preach*, compiled by John R. Rice (Wheaton, IL: Sword of the Lord Publishers, 1952), 78. Used by permission from The Sword of the Lord.
2. C. Neil Strait, *Quote Unquote*, compiled by Lloyd Cory (Wheaton, IL: Victor Books, A Division of SP Publications, Inc., 1977), 156. Used by permission.
3. Douglas Colligan, "That Helpless Feeling: The Dangers of Stress," *New York*, 14 July 1975, 30, 31.
4. Philip Yancey, *Where Is God When It Hurts?* (Grand Rapids, MI: Zondervan Publishing House, 1977), 142.
5. Carl Jung, quoted in M. Scott Peck, M.D., *The Road Less Traveled* (New York: Touchstone, Simon and Schuster, 1978). From *Collected Works of C. G. Jones*, Bollingen, Ser., No. 20, 2d ed. (Princeton, NJ: Princeton Univ. Press, 1973) trans. R. F. C. Hull, Vol. II, *Psychology and Religion: West and East*, 75.

6. M. Scott Peck, M.D., *The Road Less Traveled* (New York: Touchstone, Simon and Schuster, 1978), 16–17. Copyright © 1978 by M. Scott Peck, M.D. Reprinted by permission of Simon and Schuster, Inc.

Conclusion

1. Jordan Paul, Ph.D., and Margaret Paul, Ph.D., *Do I Have to Give Up Me to Be Loved By You?* (Minneapolis, MN: Comp-Care Publications, 1983), 165. Used by permission.